CONTENTS AT A GLANCE

TABLE OF CONTENTS

ABOUT THE AUTHOR

Warren W. Gay is a supervisor at Mackenzie Financial Corporation in Toronto, Canada. There he supervises a small team of UNIX programmers who manage the Mackenzie Investment Management System (IMS). Warren is also the author of *Sams Teach Yourself Linux Programming in 24 Hours* and Que's *Linux Socket Programming by Example*.

Programming professionally since 1980, he has used a number of assembler languages and PL/1, Lisp, C, and C++. He has been programming UNIX since 1986 and Linux since 1994. Warren has contributed Linux software packages, such as the ftpbackup program and the rewrite of the popular wavplay program. You can find these and his other Linux packages at `sunsite.unc.edu` and its mirror FTP sites.

Warren holds an advanced amateur radio license and is occasionally active on 75 meters with radio call sign VE3WWG. On August 3, 1991, he made contact with Musa Manarov, call sign U2MIR, aboard the Soviet MIR space station using a PC and packet radio gear. The contact was made on the 2-meter band.

Warren lives with his wife Jacqueline and his three children, Erin, Laura, and Scott, in St. Catherines, Ontario, Canada.

DEDICATION

I dedicate this book to my wife Jackie, my daughters Erin and Laura, and my son Scott. Without their willingness to put up with a virtually absent husband and father, this book would not have been possible.

ACKNOWLEDGMENTS

A complete set of acknowledgements would require another book to be written. In it, I would thank my parents, relatives, and the various secular and Sunday school teachers that I have had. I would also thank many friends and acquaintances with whom I have had the pleasure to meet. I must thank them all but briefly here.

I gratefully thank Carol Ackerman, Acquisitions Editor for this project, for her patience as I wrestled with deadlines. I thank Tony Amico as Development Editor for his enthusiasm for this project. I am also thankful for the watchful eye of Hang Lau as the Technical Editor. This book enjoys many improvements from his helpful suggestions. Thanks go to George Nedeff as Project Editor and Gene Redding as Copy Editor for their diligent efforts. To the rest of the publishing team, please accept my thanks for your contributions.

Many others have helped me to progress in my career. To all of you, please accept my humble thanks for your support and patient help.

TELL US WHAT YOU THINK!

As the reader of this book, *you* are our most important critic and commentator. We value your opinion and want to know what we're doing right, what we could do better, what areas you'd like to see us publish in, and any other words of wisdom you're willing to pass our way.

As an Associate Publisher for Sams Publishing, I welcome your comments. You can fax, email, or write me directly to let me know what you did or didn't like about this book—as well as what we can do to make our books stronger.

Please note that I cannot help you with technical problems related to the topic of this book and that, due to the high volume of mail I receive, I might not be able to reply to every message.

When you write, please be sure to include this book's title and author as well as your name and phone or fax number. I will carefully review your comments and share them with the author and editors who worked on the book.

Fax: 317-581-4770

Email: opsys_sams@macmillanusa.com

Mail: Michael Stephens
          Sams Publishing
          201 West 103rd Street
          Indianapolis, IN 46290 USA

INTRODUCTION

This is a book about UNIX programming. It starts with basic concepts and ends with coverage of advanced topics. It is a self-teaching guide, and yet it functions as a UNIX reference book.

The examples provided are written in the C and C++ languages. The examples are short programs, each intended to demonstrate use of a particular programming facility. The C++ programs are written as simple programs and should be well understood by those that do not program in C++.

This book attempts to be UNIX platform neutral. Throughout the book, differences in functionality are noted for your convenience. This will save you time when you must write projects that must be UNIX portable.

FreeBSD 3.4 release is used throughout this book for demonstration purposes. This guarantees that the example programs will compile and run without any additional effort on that platform. This also grants a specific level of functionality, since some functions are lacking or vary on other platforms. You can obtain FreeBSD from the Internet or purchase it on a CD-ROM at a nominal cost. This allows you to work through the book on a platform that is on a par with other professional UNIX platforms.

Who Should Use This Book

This book is written for C and C++ UNIX programmers, but it is not limited to that audience. Even a Java or Perl programmer might have an occasional need to write a small C function to invoke a UNIX system call.

Programmers at both the application and system levels will benefit from this book. There is coverage ranging from basic to advanced functionality that will aid any UNIX application developer. And difficult topics such as semaphores and memory-mapped files are covered for system level programmers.

What You Should Know

To gain the most from this book, the reader should be comfortable with the C programming language. A rudimentary understanding of C++ is helpful but not mandatory. Most C language texts cover the use of the standard I/O stream functions such as `fopen(3)` and `fgets(3)`. Consequently, these file stream functions are not repeated in this book.

It is assumed that the reader has mastered the basics of working with the UNIX shell and has a basic familiarity with the standard commands. Some examples used in this book run the programs in the background using the shell **&** character. Consequently, the reader should be familiar with basic job control within the shell.

What You Will Learn

This book should appeal to both the beginning and the advanced programmer. The first part of the book covers the basics of UNIX file system concepts, file input and output, and directory management. For the advanced reader, this functions as a review and a reference.

The second part of the book covers intermediate basics, such as numeric conversion and date/time facilities. Other application concepts such as command-line processing and embedded database routines are also covered. Consequently, this part tends to be focused somewhat toward UNIX applications.

The third and final part of the book covers advanced topics. It begins with coverage of signals, input and output scheduling, and interval timers. Process control and the use of pipes and forked processes are also covered. Combined with complete coverage of interprocess communication, this part tends to benefit primarily the system programmer. Chapters on pattern matching and regular expressions and an introduction to X Window programming are helpful to the application programmer.

The Structure of This Book

This section outlines the general structure of the book and describes what each chapter explores.

Chapter 1: Compiler Notes and Options

Chapter 1 begins with basic coverage of the `man(1)` command and provides references to Internet resources for manual pages of other UNIX platforms. An introduction to compiling under FreeBSD is included, with a review of standard compile options for all UNIX platforms. The remainder of the chapter provides helpful hints on how to manage compiler warnings effectively.

Chapter 2: UNIX File System Objects

This chapter reviews the various UNIX file system object types. Some discussion of the unique characteristics of each is provided, primarily for the beginner's benefit. The chapter continues with a review of the role that access permissions play with each file object type. The remainder of the chapter introduces file descriptors and illustrates how UNIX files are opened, duplicated, and closed.

Chapter 3: Error Handling and Reporting

This is a foundation builder, primarily for the benefit of the novice, and demonstrates how system and library calls interact with the global variable errno. The reader is shown the various ways that system error codes are translated into text error messages.

Chapter 4: UNIX Input and Output

This chapter provides an overview of the basics of UNIX input and output. It begins with a review of permission bits and discusses the effect of the umask(2) system call. The chapter continues with coverage of the read(2) and write(2) system calls, with examples. The seeking and truncation file operations are also covered. Other topics include sparse files, the sync(2) and fsync(2) system calls, and scatter read and scatter write calls.

Chapter 5: File Locking

Here we cover all aspects of locking files and file regions under UNIX. This includes the use of lock files and the use of advisory and mandatory locks on regions and entire files.

Chapter 6: Managing Files and Their Properties

Chapter 6 concerns itself with the management of files and their UNIX properties. The system calls covered allow a program to remove, link, rename, and inquire of file properties. Functions that manage symbolic links are also covered. The chapter concludes with coverage of the system calls that permit changing permissions and ownership of file system objects.

Chapter 7: Directory Management

This chapter is focused on the UNIX handling of directories. Functions that change, save, and restore the current directory are covered. Additional coverage includes creating, removing, opening, searching, and closing directories. Finally, changing the root directory is explored.

Chapter 8: Temporary Files and Process Cleanup

In Chapter 8, we cover the various library functions that are available for creating and managing temporary files. The chapter also explores ways that applications can clean up temporary files, even when they terminate unexpectedly.

Chapter 9: UNIX Command-Line Processing

Even X Window graphical programs accept command-line arguments. This chapter explores the UNIX standard method of parsing command-line arguments, with a minimum of written user code. Coverage includes the GNU long option support for the GNU-based function getopt_long(3). Suboption processing is also explored using the getsubopt(3) function.

Chapter 10: Conversion Functions

This chapter looks at the challenges that programmers must face when they convert ASCII strings into numeric values. The simplest methods are contrasted with the more effective functions such as `strtol(3)`. Detailed instruction for dealing with conversion errors is included.

Chapter 11: UNIX Date and Time Facilities

Date and time facilities are the focus of this chapter. Functions that obtain date and time components are described in detail. Conversion to and from various date and time formats is covered.

Chapter 12: User ID, Password, and Group Management

Complete descriptions of the UNIX user and group ID functions are provided in this chapter. The effects of real, saved, and effective IDs are documented. Supplementary user and group IDs are discussed, complete with their management functions.

Chapter 13: Static and Shared Libraries

This chapter explores the differences between static and shared libraries, covering the creation and management of each type of library. It concludes with the functions that permit a program to dynamically load shared libraries upon demand.

Chapter 14: Database Library Routines

Chapter 14 explores the embedded database routines known as the NDBM functions. It covers the functions necessary to create, open, and close these databases. Additionally, the text explains and demonstrates how to create, retrieve, and delete records from the database.

Chapter 15: Signals

This chapter explores the UNIX concept of signals. The reliable signal interface is described, complete with all functions that manage aspects of signal handling.

Chapter 16: Efficient I/O Scheduling

The `select(2)` and `poll(2)` system calls are explained with examples in this chapter. These system calls permit applications to perform input and output effectively on several different file descriptors.

Chapter 17: Timers

This chapter focuses its discussion on sleep function calls and interval timers. A possible implementation of the `sleep(3)` system call is demonstrated in an example program.

Chapter 18: Pipes and Processes

In this chapter we introduce the concept of process management by looking at the functions `popen(3)` and `system(3)`. These are described and explored with example programs.

Chapter 19: Forked Processes

This chapter examines the more advanced methods of process management by describing the `fork(2)` and `exec(2)` sets of system calls. The chapter also includes a discussion of zombie processes and the `wait(2)` family of system calls.

Chapter 20: Pattern Matching

Library functions that perform simple file pattern matching, as used by the shell, are examined. The chapter includes a description of the `fnmatch(3)` and `glob(3)` functions, with test programs that permit you to put them through their paces.

Chapter 21: Regular Expressions

Building upon the previous chapter, the more advanced regular expression matching functions are explored. A review of regular expression syntax is provided before presenting the support functions. A demonstration program puts the various optional features to the test.

Chapter 22: Interprocess Communications

This chapter provides an introduction to interprocess communications. The reader is introduced to IPC keys, IPC IDs, and how various IPC resources are created and accessed.

Chapter 23: Message Queues

The message queue is a member of the interprocess communication set of resources. The system calls that manage its creation, use, and destruction are covered with a demonstration program.

Chapter 24: Semaphores

This chapter continues the interprocess communications theme by exploring what a semaphore is, how it helps, and how it is used. An example program allows you to experiment.

Chapter 25: Shared Memory

The last on the topic of interprocess communication, this chapter focuses on the creation, use, and destruction of shared memory. An example program that makes use of the semaphore and shared memory demonstrates its use.

Chapter 26: Memory-Mapped Files

Memory-mapped files are explored, with a description of the different ways they can be applied. A demonstration program shows how a memory-mapped file can be used to select the language of text messages within an application.

Chapter 27: X Window Programming

The emphasis of this chapter is on event-driven programming. The reader is introduced to some of the basic concepts of X Window programming, focusing on the event loop and X Window event processing, which the example program demonstrates.

PART I

FILES AND DIRECTORIES

CHAPTER 1

COMPILER NOTES AND OPTIONS

You are reading this book because you want to write software for UNIX. Perhaps you are interested in developing software to run on several UNIX platforms. Whether you must write for several platforms or a few, writing your software to compile successfully for each UNIX platform is a challenge. This chapter is aimed at reducing that challenge and improving your success rate. Additionally, you will find some valuable Internet resources in this chapter, along with some cross-platform examples and advice.

Online Manual Pages

Throughout this text, you will see references to online documents that exist on most UNIX systems. These online documents save the programmer a great deal of time when he is writing programs. Rather than fetch a book and look in the index for the correct page, you can pull up the information within seconds, instead. This electronic documentation can be brought into an editor, or segments of it can be cut and pasted using the normal X Window facilities. For this reason, this text places some emphasis on online manual page references for your convenience.

A document reference will appear in this text in the form **open(2)**, for example. To view the online document for that reference, you would normally enter

`$ man 2 open`

This causes the manual page for the **open** entry in section **2** to be displayed (the section is specified first). The section number is not always necessary, but it often is (otherwise, a manual entry from an earlier section will be presented instead).

A manual page section is a grouping of related documents. The following sections will be the sections of primary importance throughout this book:

User commands	1
System calls	2
Library calls	3

Most of this book will be focused on facilities documented in sections 2 and 3. Functions that interface to the UNIX kernel are grouped into section 2. Other function calls, which are documented in section 3, are those functions that perform commonly required services. These may or may not involve additional calls to the UNIX kernel. Commands such as the man(1) command are grouped in section 1.

If you don't know the name of the man(1) page you want, you can perform a keyword search. The following shows how you could search for information about changing owners of a file:

```
$ man -k owner
chown(2), fchown(2), lchown(2) - change owner and group of a file
chown(8)                       - change file owner and group
$
```

This produces a number of references that have the keyword owner in them. Another way this can be done on most systems is to use the apropos(1) command:

```
$ apropos owner
chown(2), fchown(2), lchown(2) - change owner and group of a file
chown(8)                       - change file owner and group
$
```

Both of these commands result in the same action being taken. If you have an unusual UNIX system and these don't work, then you might look up man(1) for additional insight.

Most sections are documented on most UNIX systems. For example, to find out what section 8 is all about under FreeBSD, you would enter

```
$ man 8 intro
```

A lookup of the man page intro(x), where x is the section, will usually yield additional documentation about the section specified.

Note

On some systems, you may have to specify the section number differently. For example, Solaris 8 supports the following syntax:

```
$ man -s 2 open
```

In this example, the section number follows the -s option. Some implementations of the man(1) command will work with or without the -s option for section numbers.

Manual References Used in This Book

References to man(1) pages will be used throughout this book when referring to functions and other programming entities. However, as you might expect, different UNIX platforms place the same information in different sections and sometimes under completely different headings.

An example of this problem is the function strftime(3). For many UNIX implementations, including FreeBSD, the reference strftime(3) will provide the correct location of the online document for the `strftime()` function. However, UnixWare 7 uses the manual reference `strftime(3C)` instead. UnixWare has chosen to split some of its functions into a separate section 3C.

Consequently, a choice in convention had to be made for this book. The manual page references used throughout this text are based on the FreeBSD (3.4 release) platform. This should provide a good reference for users of most UNIX systems. In places where it is important, the differences will be noted.

`man(1)` Resources on the Internet

If you must write code that is portable to many UNIX platforms, one valuable resource is the Internet. Table 1.1 lists a few Internet resources that can be used when you want to review manual pages for different UNIX platforms.

TABLE 1.1   Table of Internet `man(1)` Resources

URL	Description
`http://www.FreeBSD.org/cgi/man.cgi`	BSD
`http://docs.hp.com/index.html`	HPUX 10 & 11
`http://docs.sun.com/`	SunOS, Solaris
`http://www.ibm.com/servers/aix/`	IBM's AIX
`http://support.sgi.com/search/`	SGI IRIX/Linux
`http://doc.sco.com/`	UnixWare & SCO

There are probably many more resources available, in addition to those listed in Table 1.1. The `www.FreeBSD.org` reference is worth special mention because its Web site appears to have `man(1)` pages for a wealth of other releases listed next.

- 2.8 BSD, 2.9.1 BSD, 2.10 BSD, and 2.11 BSD
- 386BSD 0.0 and 386BSD 0.1
- 4.3BSD NET/2, 4.3BSD Reno, 4.4BSD Lite2
- FreeBSD 1.0-RELEASE to FreeBSD 4.0-RELEASE
- FreeBSD 5.0-current
- FreeBSD Ports
- Linux Slackware 3.1
- Minix 2.0
- NetBSD 1.2 to NetBSD 1.4

- OpenBSD 2.1 to OpenBSD 2.6

- Plan 9

- RedHat Linux/i386 4.2, 5.0, and 5.2

- SunOS 4.1.3, 5.5.1, 5.6, and 5.7

- ULTRIX 4.2

- UNIX Seventh Edition

There will likely be additions to this list by the time you read this.

Example Code in This Book

Even more challenging than having uniform man page references is the creation of example programs that would compile for all UNIX platforms. While this could be attempted, it has the danger that it would not be universally successful unless the code was tested on every platform. Even then, pitfalls abound, because there exist many different choices in compilers, libraries, and other customizable aspects of the UNIX platform.

The examples in this book have tried to be UNIX platform neutral. Practical considerations, however, made it necessary to pick one development platform for the examples. The major differences are addressed in the text as they come up. Look for additional tips, warnings, and notes for other UNIX differences that may be worth noting.

The challenges of supporting multiple UNIX platform differences include the following:

- Subtle differences in the different make(1) commands

- Differences in the feature set macros required to compile the programs

- Differences in location of the include files

- Differences in function prototype definitions

- Differences in C data types (int vs. size_t)

To deal with all of these problems would end up leaving the reader with a rat's nest of ugly source code to look at. Rather than give you difficult-to-read source code and complicated make(1) procedures, this book will simply use the FreeBSD Release 3.4 platform as the foundation for all program examples. Important differences in compilers and other areas will be noted along the way.

This approach provides the professional the advantage that learning can take place at home. FreeBSD is a stable and secure platform that can be loaded onto just about any reasonable Intel PC. Yet it remains very similar to many commercial UNIX platforms in the workplace.

Note

While FreeBSD can be installed with many useful Linux enhancements, the FreeBSD 3.4 Release used for the examples in this book did not have *any* Linux support installed. This was intentionally done to present a more traditional UNIX experience.

Compiling C Programs

This is an area in which there is considerable variation among the different UNIX platforms. The FreeBSD 3.4 Release of UNIX uses the very capable GNU compiler:

```
$ gcc --version
2.7.2.3
$
```

This is linked to the same command as the more commonly recognized UNIX command name cc, as demonstrated in the next FreeBSD session:

```
$ type cc
cc is a tracked alias for /usr/bin/cc
$ ls -li /usr/bin/cc
7951 -r-xr-xr-x  2 root  wheel  49680 Dec 20 00:46 /usr/bin/cc
$ type gcc
gcc is a tracked alias for /usr/bin/gcc
$ ls -li /usr/bin/gcc
7951 -r-xr-xr-x  2 root  wheel  49680 Dec 20 00:46 /usr/bin/gcc
$
```

Since both /usr/bin/cc and /usr/bin/gcc link to the same i-node 7951 in the example, you know that these two files are linked to the same executable file.

Other UNIX platforms that provide their own proprietary forms of C and C++ compilers differ substantially from the GNU compiler in the options they support, the warning messages they produce, and their optimizing capability. This chapter will look at some of the commonality between them and some of the differences.

The C Compile Command

Most UNIX platforms invoke their C compilers by the name cc. Linux and FreeBSD platforms support the gcc command name in addition to the standard cc name. Sometimes the GNU compiler will be installed as gcc on commercial platforms to distinguish it from the standard offering or in addition to the crippled (non-ANSI) one. For example, HP includes a non-ANSI compiler with the HPUX operating system, which is called the "bundled" compiler (this compiler is sufficient to rebuild a new HPUX kernel). The ANSI-capable compiler must be purchased separately and, when installed, replaces the bundled cc command.

However, within the same platform, there can also be choices. HPUX 10.2 supports

HP-UX C compiler	cc
HP-UX POSIX-conforming C	c89

The IBM AIX 4.3 platform supports:

C language "extended"	cc
ANSI C compiler	xlc or c89

The difference between the **xlc** and **c89** compilers under AIX is the configured defaults. In the following sections, the relatively standardized options will be examined.

The -c Compile Option

This option is probably the most universally standardized. The -c option indicates that the compiler should produce a translated object file (`*.o` file) but not attempt to link the translation into an executable. This option is used when compiling several separate source modules that will be linked together at a later stage by the linker. The following demonstrates a compile and link in one step:

```
$ cc hello.c
```

This all-in-one step command translates the C source file `hello.c` into the final output executable file `a.out`. The filename `a.out` is the default executable name for linker output. This practice dates back to at least 1970 when UNIX was written in assembler language on the PDP-11. Digital Equipment's (DEC) default linker output file name was `a.out`.

Alternatively, the object file can be produced separately and then linked as a separate step, as follows:

```
$ cc -c hello.c
$ cc hello.o
```

In this example, the first **cc** command with the -c option, produces the file `hello.o` as the result of the compile. Then the second **cc** command accepts the object file `hello.o` as input and produces the final executable file name `a.out`, which can then be run.

The -o Compile Option

This option is fairly standard also. The -o option allows the user to specify the name of the output file. For example, it could be explicit, as follows:

```
$ cc -c hello.c -o hello.o
```

The -c option indicates that an object file is being produced, and the -o option names the output object file as `hello.o`. The -o option can also be used to name the executable file, if that is the type of output requested:

```
$ cc hello.o -o my_hello_prog
```

The example shown indicates that the output executable file name will be named my_hello_prog.

The -g Option (Debug)

This standard option indicates to the compiler that debugging information should be generated in the output of the compile. This debugging information makes source code and variable name references possible in the debugger or when analyzing the core file after a program abort. Include this option whenever you need to debug the program interactively or perform a post-mortem on the core file. Be sure to use this option on all object modules that will be inspected by the debugger.

Warning

Most C compilers will not accept both the -g (debug) and -O (optimize) options at the same time. The GNU compiler will tolerate -g and first-level optimization (-O), but this may lead to a few surprises in the debugger.

The -D Option (Define)

This standard compiler option permits you to define a macro symbol from the compiler command line. It is most frequently done from a Makefile but is not limited to this practice. For example

```
$ cc -c -D_POSIX_C_SOURCE=199309L hello.c
```

defines the C macro constant _POSIX_C_SOURCE with a value of 199309L. This macro definition has the effect of choosing a particular POSIX standard from the files included in the compile. Additional macros can be defined on the same command line:

```
$ cc -c -D_POSIX_C_SOURCE=199309L -DNDEBUG hello.c
```

In this example, the additional C macro NDEBUG was defined (with no value), in order to disable the code generation in the assert(3) macro invocations used within the program.

The -I Option (Include)

The standard -I compile option permits you to specify additional places to look for include files. For example, if you have additional include files located in an unusual place such as /usr/local/include for example, you could add the -I option as follows:

```
$ cc -c -I/usr/local/include -I/opt/include hello.c
```

Additional -I options can be added as shown, and the directories will be searched in the order given. Many UNIX compilers (non-GNU) will process the C statement

```
#include "file.h"
```

by looking in the current directory first, and then all of the directories given by the -I options, and then finally in the directory /usr/include.

The same (non-GNU) UNIX compilers will process the C language statement

```
#include <file.h>
```

by the same means, except that the current directory is *not* searched. However, the GNU compiler extends the `-I` option somewhat, as follows:

- `-I` directories preceding a `-I-` option are searched only for statements of the form `#include "file.h"` only.

- Directories provided with `-I` options following a `-I-` option are searched for both forms `#include "file.h"` and `#include <file.h>`.

- If no `-I-` option appears on the command line, then the behavior is the same as the non-GNU C compiler.

An example of this is provided in the following compile command:

```
$ gcc -c -I/usr/informix/include -I- -I/opt/oracle/include convutil.c
```

The example shown would allow the C language statement

```
#include "sqlca.h"
```

to include the file `/usr/informix/include/sqlca.h`. Another C language statement

```
#include <sqlca.h>
```

would include the file `/opt/oracle/include/sqlca.h` instead. This happens because the `<file.h>` form is not searched in the directories preceding the `-I-` separating option.

The -E Option (Expand)

This option is relatively standard among UNIX C compilers. It permits you to modify the command line to cause the compiler to emit the preprocessed C text to standard output without actually compiling the code.

This is useful when attempting to wade through C preprocessing directives and C macros. The output of a would-be compile can be directed to a file and then examined with an editor:

```
$ cc -c -E hello.c >cpp.out
```

In the example shown, the `-E` option causes the `include` files and the program to be preprocessed and redirected to the file `cpp.out`. You can then examine the file `cpp.out` with an editor or paging command and determine what the final C language code looks like. This is especially helpful when trying to debug new C macros that are causing compile errors that are difficult to diagnose.

The -O Option (Optimize)

This option is not standard among compilers. Some compilers require an argument to follow the `-O`, some don't, and some will optionally take an argument. FreeBSD accepts the following:

- `-O` and `-O1` specify level 1 optimization.

- `-O2` specifies level 2 optimization (increased optimization).

- -O3 specifies level 3 optimization (more than -O2).

- -O0 specifies no optimization.

For the GNU compiler, these options can be repeated, with the last appearing option establishing the final optimization level. For example

```
$ gcc -c -O3 -O0 hello.c
```

would compile with no optimization, because -O0 appears last.

Recall that the debug option (-g) is incompatible with optimization with most C compilers.

As a contrast to the GNU compiler, HP's compiler supports the following optimizing options in increasing levels of optimization:

Default optimization	+O0
Level 1 optimization	+O1
Level 2 optimization	+O2 (-O)
Level 3 optimization	+O3
Level 4 optimization	+O4

The -O (with no argument) option is equivalent to the HP option +O2 (note the plus sign).

The IBM AIX 4.3 compiler supports the options -O, -O2, and -O3 in increasing levels of optimization.

All of this emphasizes a need to review the compiler options in the cc(1) man page for the compiler you are using.

Warning Options

Warning messages is one area in which the GNU compiler excels. This compiler is so good at this that there is no need for a lint(1) command under FreeBSD or Linux. However, the warnings options for compilers vary considerably by platform and vendor.

The GNU compiler uses the -W option with an argument to indicate what is to be reported as warnings. In this book, the option -Wall will be used to cause the GNU compiler to report anything that looks suspicious.

It is also possible to specify individual warnings of interest. For example, -Wreturn-type can be specified to cause the compiler to report any return values that are missing or mismatched or a function that is defaulting to returning an int because no return type was declared for the function.

While the -Wreturn-type warning appears to be included with the specification of the -Wall option under FreeBSD, there were versions of the GNU compiler in which -Wreturn-type was not included under Linux. Since this is an important warning that can save you a lot of time, you may want to include it in addition to the -Wall option, just to be certain it is enabled.

ANSI C Compile Options

On some UNIX platforms you must indicate to your compiler that you are compiling ANSI C source code. HPUX UNIX compilers, for example, will assume the older K&R C code is being compiled instead, usually leading to a lot of compile errors. Therefore, for HPUX you will need to supply the option `-Aa` to compile any modern C source code. A few other commercial UNIX compilers have similar requirements.

Managing Compiler Warnings

The C compiler will often report messages. These messages can be divided into *error messages* and *warning messages*. Error messages indicate things that must be corrected in order for the compile to succeed. Warnings alert the programmer to bad practices and problems that might occur later when the program is run.

With the maximum compile warning level set, the compiler reports on the smallest of infractions, but it usually does so intelligently and diligently. Sometimes warnings are issued for valid C programming practices, and some developers disable these warnings with certain compiler options. By doing this, they prevent the C compiler from providing useful advice.

The best advice that can be provided here is to always use the maximum warning level available. This forces the developer to address all source code issues until the warnings disappear from the compilation. The only justifiable reason for going to a lower warning level is when you've inherited someone else's source code and you do not have the luxury of time to fix all the causes of warnings.

Tip
Always compile with the maximum warning level turned on. Time spent eliminating causes of warning messages, can save a lot of time later while debugging your program. With the GNU compiler under FreeBSD and Linux, this is done by adding the `-Wall` option.

The following shows how to use the GNU compiler under FreeBSD with the maximum warning level enabled:

```
bash$ gcc -Wall hello.c
```

The compile examples in this book will all use the `-Wall` option unless the example involves a non-GNU compiler.

Note
Most UNIX command-line options do not require a space to appear between the option letter and the option's argument. For example, the option may be specified as `-Wall` or `-W all`, since these are equivalent.

Working with Compiler Warning Messages

When a high warning level is used by the compiler, every possible warning message is reported. A low warning level will report only the most important messages and suppress the rest.

As noted earlier, there is one drawback to using a high warning level with your C compiler: Sometimes you'll receive warning messages for valid C language constructs. Well-designed compilers will help you cope with these problems, however, since they allow you to use tricks to convey your real intention.

Warnings About Assignments

A programmer often loves the economy of expression available in the C language. This means that the programmer will employ the smallest number of statements or operators to accomplish a task. Sometimes this involves doing an assignment and a test for non-zero all in one step. Consider the `if` statement in Listing 1.1.

LISTING 1.1   `asgn1.c`—Warnings About Value Assignment in the `if` Statement

```
1:    #include <string.h>
2:
3:    char *
4:    Basename(char *pathname) {
5:        char *cp;                    /* Work Pointer */
6:
7:        if ( cp = strrchr(pathname,'/') )
8:            return cp + 1;           /* Return basename pointer */
9:        return pathname;             /* No directory component */
10:   }
```

> **Note**
>
> The program listings in this book include line numbers at the extreme left. Do not type these if you are entering the example programs manually. They are included only for ease of reference.

Here is the compile session for Listing 1.1:

```
$ cc -c -Wall asgn1.c
asgn1.c: In function `Basename':
asgn1.c:7: warning: suggest parentheses around assignment used as truth value
$
```

Notice the statement in line 7. The reason the compiler flags this statement as a possible error is that often the C programmer really intends to use the comparison operator `==` to compare values instead of assigning a value in an `if` statement. The compiler has no way of confirming whether the actual assignment is correct or whether a comparison was intended instead. The developer is left to decide the issue after the compiler has issued the warning.

Note that the statement is not incorrect, but neither is it certain that it reflects the programmer's true intention. Some might be tempted to argue that comparison is normal in an **if** statement and that the assignment in an **if** statement is unusual. The fact remains, however, that the C language is defined such that both are equally valid expressions.

Compiler writers have developed clever tricks for dealing with these thorny issues. This particular case can be resolved this way: If an assignment is coded as shown in Listing 1.1, it is flagged with a warning because it represents a possible error on the programmer's part. If this does represent an error, the programmer replaces the single equals symbol with a double equals symbol and recompiles. If the assignment is the intent, the programmer encloses the assignment with a set of brackets. When this is done, the compiler will assume that the programmer knows what he is doing.

Listings 1.2 and 1.3 show two different ways to resolve the warning issue in favor of the assignment.

LISTING 1.2   `asgn2.c`—Additional Parentheses Quiet an Assignment Warning

```
 1:   #include <string.h>
 2:
 3:   char *
 4:   Basename(char *pathname) {
 5:       char *cp;                    /* Work Pointer */
 6:
 7:       if ( (cp = strrchr(pathname,'/')) )
 8:           return cp + 1;           /* Return basename pointer */
 9:       return pathname;             /* No directory component */
10:   }
```

LISTING 1.3   `asgn3.c`—Parentheses and Comparison Quiet an Assignment Warning

```
 1:   #include <string.h>
 2:
 3:   char *
 4:   Basename(char *pathname) {
 5:       char *cp;                    /* Work Pointer */
 6:
 7:       if ( (cp = strrchr(pathname,'/')) != 0 )
 8:           return cp + 1;           /* Return basename pointer */
 9:       return pathname;             /* No directory component */
10:   }
```

Note the extra pair of parentheses around the assignment in line 7 of both Listings 1.2 and 1.3. The C syntax here did not require the parentheses, but the compiler took this as a cue from the developer that he knows what he is doing. While Listing 1.2 shows a solution acceptable to the GNU compiler, some other UNIX compilers will insist on the construct shown in Listing 1.3. For this reason, the solution in Listing 1.3 is preferred. It is clearer to the reader of the source code.

Tip
There is normally no longer a need to economize in C language expressions for the sake of optimization. Today's optimizing compilers are very effective at producing optimal code without any help from the programmer. For this reason it is better to make an expression easier to read than to reduce it to the fewest number of C operators.

This discussion has been presented using the C language `if` statement, but this issue applies to other statements as well. Warnings about assignments in the `switch` and `while` statements can be quieted in the same manner.

Warnings About Unused Arguments

Some compilers will complain about unused arguments. The thinking appears to be that if the argument is defined, then it was meant to be used. The truth of the matter is that the function arguments define an interface. There is no real requirement to fully use the interface that is defined, since an interface may also be intended for future use.

An example of the unused argument problem is the ubiquitous `main()` program. The main program interface is often defined as follows:

```
int main(int argc,char *argv[]);
```

If the program being written does not use the arguments that are present, it doesn't seem proper to remove the arguments simply because they are unused. This is what often is done by programmers to eliminate the compiler warnings.

Instead, it seems preferable to leave the arguments declared to indicate that the interface supports passing those values in that way. Listing 1.4 shows a simple way to avoid this problem.

LISTING 1.4 `uargs.c`—Quieting Unused Argument Warnings

```
1:    #include <stdio.h>
2:
3:    int
4:    main(int argc,char **argv) {
5:
6:        (void) argc;
7:        (void) argv;
8:
9:        puts("Hello World!");
10:       return 0;
11:   }
```

The C language permits a reference of a value in isolation, within a statement. Normally, this is not a useful construct, since there is no useful side effect in this case. However, it can be used as a useful compiler side effect, and this is exactly what is done with the `(void)` cast in lines 6 and 7 of Listing 1.4.

It should be noted that the GNU compiler in the FreeBSD 3.4 Release does not warn about unused arguments (`gcc` version 2.7.2.3). However, the compiler that you are using might.

Resolving Unused Variable Warnings

Sometimes the compiler will warn you about unused variables that you have declared in your code. These warnings create a strong temptation to remove the variables from your code immediately. You should exercise great care before doing so.

Warning

Be extremely careful about removing unused variables and buffers. Make sure that you fully evaluate the C preprocessing directives of the source code before you assume that these values are never used. Sometimes compiling a program with different macro settings can cause these variable declarations to be needed. This is especially true when source code is compiled on different UNIX platforms.

The problem of unused variables often occurs in code that is designed to be portable to many different UNIX platforms. The specific problem is normally that the original developer never properly allowed for the unused declarations at the right time with the help of the correct C preprocessing directives. What often happens is that the source code is patched and modified by several people, and those changes never get fully retested on the other platforms on which it was meant to compile.

Listing 1.5 illustrates a program that, when compiled a certain way, will have unused variables. But are these variables truly unnecessary?

LISTING 1.5   uvars.c—An Example of Unused Variable Declarations

```
 1:    /* uvars.c */
 2:
 3:    #include <stdio.h>
 4:    #include <unistd.h>
 5:    #include <sys/types.h>
 6:
 7:    int
 8:    main(int argc,char **argv) {
 9:        pid_t PID;               /* Process ID */
10:
11:        (void) argc;
12:        (void) argv;
13:
14:    #ifdef SHOW_PID
15:        PID = getpid();          /* Get Process ID */
16:        printf("Hello World! Process ID is %d\n",(int)PID);
17:    #else
18:        puts("Hello World!");
19:    #endif
20:
21:        return 0;
22:    }
```

When Listing 1.5 is compiled without defining the C macro SHOW_PID, the result looks like this:

```
$ cc -Wall uvars.c
uvars.c: In function `main':
uvars.c:9: warning: unused variable `PID'
$
```

The compiler in this example has complained that the declared variable PID in line 9 is not used. This happens because the macro SHOW_PID is not defined, causing line 18 to be compiled in the place of lines 15 and 16. In this compile, the variable PID is unreferenced.

However, if you take this warning message at face value and remove the declaration of variable PID in line 9, then you will solve the immediate problem but create another, longer-term problem. If you define the macro SHOW_PID in the next compile, you find that it is necessary under different compile conditions:

```
$ cc -Wall -DSHOW_PID uvars.c
$ ./a.out
Hello World! Process ID is 73337
$
```

Adding the option -DSHOW_PID to the cc command line defined the SHOW_PID macro for this particular compile. As shown, you can see that the compile was successful and without any warning messages.

While this concept is obvious in this small example program, this same scenario often occurs in many real-life examples of UNIX code that are much more complex. The message here is to be careful about what you assume should be deleted from the source code when you get unused variable warnings.

Resolving Unreferenced String Warnings

Unreferenced string constants will also cause warnings to be generated. Sometimes programmers leave a string constant in a program so that it will become part of the final executable. A common practice is to define version strings in a program so that the executable file can be dumped and matched up with a particular version of a source module.

Tip
To eliminate compiler warnings about unreferenced string constants, simply declare the string constant as a constant using the C language const keyword.

The solution to these warnings is simply to define the string constant as a constant using the const keyword. The compiler does not complain about unreferenced constants. Listing 1.6 shows an example of an embedded CVS string that causes an unreferenced string warning to be issued by the compiler.

LISTING 1.6   `ustring.c`—Example of an Unreferenced CVS String

```
 1:    /* ustring.c */
 2:
 3:    #include <stdio.h>
 4:
 5:    static char cvsid[] =
 6:     "$Header: /home/cvs/prj/ustring.c,v 1.6 2010/03/30 01:59:34 uid Exp $";
 7:
 8:    int
 9:    main(int argc,char **argv) {
10:
11:            (void) argc;
12:            (void) argv;
13:
14:            puts("Hello World!");
15:            return 0;
16:    }
```

The compile session for Listing 1.6 is as follows:

```
$ cc -Wall ustring.c
ustring.c:5: warning: 'cvsid' defined but not used
$
```

Note lines 5 and 6 of Listing 1.6, where the string array `cvsid[]` is declared. The purpose of this declaration is simply to have the string constant appear in the final executable file. This allows you to identify the version of the source code that went into the executable program. It can be displayed with the `ident` command:

```
$ ident a.out
a.out:
     $Header: /home/cvs/prj/ustring.c,v 1.6 2010/03/30 01:59:34 uid Exp $
$
```

The `ident(1)` command locates the string constants that start with `$Header:` and end with the `$` character. The problem is that the compiler complains about this string constant because the string itself is not used within the code.

Tip
Some prefer to use the CVS/RCS identification string `$Id$` instead of `$Header$`, since the string is shorter (the directory path is not included). However, note that some versions of the `ident(1)` command will not report the `$Id$` string (for example, HPUX 10.2 and 11.0 will not report `$Id$`, but Linux and FreeBSD will). Other UNIX platforms may not have the `ident(1)` command at all (AIX 4.3 and SunOS 5.6, for example). In that case you can use the `strings(1)` command and `grep(1)` for the string `'$Header:'` instead: `$ strings a.out | grep '$Header:'`

The compiler is easily quieted about the unreferenced string by simply defining the string as a constant. The compiler does not require constants to be referenced. See Listing 1.7 for the corrected source code.

LISTING 1.7   `ustring2.c`—Eliminating the Unused String Constant Warning

```
 1:    /* ustring.c */
 2:
 3:    #include <stdio.h>
 4:
 5:    static const char cvsid[] =
 6:     "$Header: /home/cvs/prj/ustring.c,v 1.6 2010/03/30 01:59:34 uid Exp $";
 7:
 8:    int
 9:    main(int argc,char **argv) {
10:
11:            (void) argc;
12:            (void) argv;
13:
14:            puts("Hello World!");
15:            return 0;
16:    }
```

Line 5 of Listing 1.7 shows the added **const** keyword that is necessary to soothe the compiler. The compile session that follows confirms this:

```
$ cc -Wall ustring2.c
$
```

Unlike the other compile, there are no warning messages.

Compiling to Standards

Many UNIX platforms strive to adhere to various C and C++ standards where possible. Additionally, they all tend to support various enhancements that are not included in these standards. Most UNIX development environments will also support multiple C standards. So how does the programmer choose the standard to which he is compiling his source code?

Under UNIX, the choice of compile standard is established by a feature test macro that is defined. Generally, for any given platform, a standard is chosen by default. However, it is wiser to choose one explicitly to avoid difficulties compiling your project on the various UNIX platforms that you might be supporting. This may avoid other compile error surprises that might come about with newer releases of a vendor's UNIX platform.

FreeBSD 3.4-Release describes its standards support in `posix4(9)`. There you will find the following two feature test macros that will be used in this book:

- `_POSIX_SOURCE`
- `_POSIX_C_SOURCE`

The `_POSIX_SOURCE` feature macro is an older C macro that indicates that only POSIX and ANSI functionality should occur in the name space.

The one that will be used in this book is the _POSIX_C_SOURCE macro, because it allows you to choose a specific POSIX standard for compiling. The two FreeBSD documented values are

_POSIX_C_SOURCE=199009L	POSIX.1
_POSIX_C_SOURCE=199309L	POSIX.1B

Since the second selection allows the newer standard features to be compiled, it is preferred for new programs.

Listing 1.8 shows a simple feature macro test program. You can compile it in different ways and have it report information about standards to you.

LISTING 1.8   posix.c—Feature Macro Test Program

```
 1:   /* posix.c */
 2:
 3:   #include <stdio.h>
 4:   #include <unistd.h>
 5:
 6:   int
 7:   main(int argc,char **argv) {
 8:
 9:       (void) argc;
10:       (void) argv;
11:
12:   #ifdef _POSIX_SOURCE
13:       printf("_POSIX_SOURCE = %ld\n",(long)_POSIX_SOURCE);
14:   #endif
15:
16:   #ifdef _POSIX_C_SOURCE
17:       printf("_POSIX_C_SOURCE = %ld\n",(long)_POSIX_C_SOURCE);
18:   #endif
19:
20:   #ifdef _POSIX_VERSION
21:       printf("_POSIX_VERSION = %ld\n",(long)_POSIX_VERSION);
22:   #endif
23:
24:       return 0;
25:   }
```

Note that the include file <unistd.h> is necessary for this program to evaluate the various POSIX C feature macros. You will find that there is a considerable variety of responses to this test on different UNIX platforms.

FreeBSD 3.4-Release Feature Tests

When Listing 1.8 is compiled with various combinations of the _POSIX_SOURCE and
_POSIX_C_SOURCE feature macros, you will see the following program responses:

```
$ cc posix.c && ./a.out
_POSIX_VERSION = 199009
$
```

In these examples, the a.out file is both compiled and invoked on the same command line for
convenience (the shell && operator will invoke the next command if the previous command
was successful). In the above test, it is evident that FreeBSD defines the macro _POSIX_
VERSION to indicate the version of the system for which the system is built. Here, it is reported
that the default is the POSIX.1 standard (199009). It will be seen later, however, that not all
UNIX environments will provide a _POSIX_VERSION value by default.

```
$ cc posix.c -D_POSIX_SOURCE && ./a.out
_POSIX_SOURCE = 1
_POSIX_VERSION = 199009
$
```

In this example, the compile explicitly defines the feature test macro _POSIX_SOURCE. It can be
seen that the same macro is reassigned the value of 1 and that the _POSIX_VERSION macro is
set to the value of 199009.

```
$ cc posix.c -D_POSIX_C_SOURCE=199009L && ./a.out
_POSIX_C_SOURCE = 199009
_POSIX_VERSION = 199009
$
```

Here the standard is chosen by setting the feature macro _POSIX_C_SOURCE and specifically
choosing POSIX.1 (199009). The _POSIX_VERSION macro is set to match in this example.

```
$ cc posix.c -D_POSIX_C_SOURCE=199309L && ./a.out
_POSIX_C_SOURCE = 199309
_POSIX_VERSION = 199009
$
```

This example chooses the POSIX.1B standard, but the feature test macro remains at the
POSIX.1 value of 199009. The FreeBSD posix4(9) documentation indicates that this tells your
program that the operating system features are based on the POSIX.1 standard (even thought
POSIX.1B was requested).

```
$ cc posix.c -D_POSIX_C_SOURCE=199506L && ./a.out
_POSIX_C_SOURCE = 199506
_POSIX_VERSION = 199009
$
```

This example is similar to the preceding one. A more recent standard is requested, but the
_POSIX_VERSION macro suggests that only POSIX.1 (199009) is being supported.

HPUX 10.2 Feature Tests

For comparison, the `posix.c` module was tested under HPUX 10.2. With only the option `-Aa` specified to request a compile of ANSI C code, the following output was obtained from running `posix.c`:

```
$ cc -Aa posix.c && ./a.out
/usr/ccs/bin/ld: (Warning) At least one PA 2.0 object file (posix.o)
➥was detected. The linked output may not run on a PA 1.x system.
$
```

Even though `a.out` was invoked, there was no output. This indicates that none of the feature test macros were defined by default (unlike FreeBSD). The next example defines the macro `_POSIX_SOURCE`:

```
$ cc -Aa -D_POSIX_SOURCE posix.c && ./a.out
/usr/ccs/bin/ld: (Warning) At least one PA 2.0 object file (posix.o)
➥was detected. The linked output may not run on a PA 1.x system.
_POSIX_SOURCE = 1
_POSIX_VERSION = 199009
$
```

This is now identical to the FreeBSD output (with the exception of the pesky HP loader warning, which can be eliminated with several other options). Choosing the POSIX.1B standard yields the following results:

```
$ cc -Aa -D_POSIX_C_SOURCE=199309L posix.c && ./a.out
/usr/ccs/bin/ld: (Warning) At least one PA 2.0 object file (posix.o)
➥was detected. The linked output may not run on a PA 1.x system.
_POSIX_C_SOURCE = 199309
_POSIX_VERSION = 199309
$
```

This differs from the FreeBSD example in that the `_POSIX_VERSION` value shows support for POSIX.1B here (the value is `199309`).

AIX 4.3 Feature Tests

The AIX tests are presented here because of a few other wrinkles that were encountered. The next example shows the results of the default compile case:

```
$ cc posix.c && ./a.out
"posix.c", line 13.55: 1506-046 (S) Syntax error.
"posix.c", line 21.58: 1506-276 (S) Syntax error: possible missing ')'?
$
```

The error messages indicate that no defaults are established here. Defining the macro `_POSIX_SOURCE` helps and yields the following results:

```
$ cc -D_POSIX_SOURCE posix.c && ./a.out
_POSIX_SOURCE = 1
_POSIX_VERSION = 199506
$
```

Notice that _POSIX_SOURCE is redefined with the value 1, and the macro _POSIX_VERSION is given the value 199506, indicating the most recent POSIX standard value of all of the tests that are reported in this chapter. Specifically choosing an older standard is attempted next:

```
$ cc -D_POSIX_C_SOURCE=199309L posix.c && ./a.out
"posix.c", line 13.55: 1506-046 (S) Syntax error.
"posix.c", line 17.60: 1506-276 (S) Syntax error: possible missing ')'?
$
```

This just seems to buy trouble. Another attempt is made to specify the version that is apparently supported using the _POSIX_C_SOURCE feature test macro:

```
$ cc -D_POSIX_C_SOURCE=199506L posix.c && ./a.out
"posix.c", line 13.55: 1506-046 (S) Syntax error.
"posix.c", line 17.60: 1506-276 (S) Syntax error: possible missing ')'?
$
```

This seems to yield more compile errors. For AIX compiles, it would appear that you should only specify the _POSIX_SOURCE macro and avoid defining the _POSIX_C_SOURCE macro for a specific standard release.

SunOS 5.6 Feature Tests

The last example presented involves the reaction of the SunOS 5.6 release to various standards settings. The default case is attempted first:

```
$ cc posix.c && ./a.out
_POSIX_VERSION = 199506
$
```

Isn't this fun? In this case, the _POSIX_VERSION macro is set to the value of 199506, but no _POSIX_SOURCE macro is defined. In the next test, _POSIX_SOURCE is defined:

```
$ cc -D_POSIX_SOURCE posix.c && ./a.out
_POSIX_SOURCE = 1
_POSIX_C_SOURCE = 1
_POSIX_VERSION = 199506
$
```

This gets even more interesting. Now the _POSIX_SOURCE macro is redefined with the value of 1, which is what was expected. Here, the _POSIX_C_SOURCE macro now gets the value 1, which is interesting. Finally, the _POSIX_VERSION macro gives us the value of 199506, which indicates the level of support the C program can expect. The next test explicitly asks for this version of the standard:

```
$ cc -D_POSIX_C_SOURCE=199506 posix.c && ./a.out
_POSIX_C_SOURCE = 199506
_POSIX_VERSION = 199506
$
```

In this output, we lose the _POSIX_SOURCE macro, and the _POSIX_VERSION macro matches what was requested. One more test was conducted, this time requesting an older standard of POSIX.1B (199309):

```
$ cc -D_POSIX_C_SOURCE=199309L posix.c && ./a.out
_POSIX_C_SOURCE = 199309
_POSIX_VERSION = 199506
$
```

The _POSIX_C_SOURCE macro remains at the level that was requested, but the _POSIX_VERSION macro remains at the value 199506. What does this tell you? It would seem that _POSIX_VERSION indicates what you have at your disposal, while _POSIX_C_SOURCE tells you what was requested.

Feature Test Summary

A writer of portable UNIX code must face a number of challenges to support multiple UNIX platforms. From the foregoing sections, it is plain that even just choosing the POSIX standard that you want to compile to is somewhat platform specific.

It would appear that the safest route with the platforms tested here is to specify the compile option. -D_POSIX_SOURCE is the most platform-neutral course to take, from a feature macro point of view. However, this is not a perfect solution, because it is evident that different POSIX standards were chosen on different UNIX platforms. This may cause other compile problems.

It seems that until UNIX vendors reach more agreement on the way that the feature test macros work, each UNIX platform will require its own special tweaking of feature test macros. You must first determine the lowest common denominator of the standard that your code is written for. Then determine how to select that standard on the UNIX platform chosen.

To simplify matters for this book, FreeBSD will be used for the program examples. The POSIX.1B standard will be requested in the example compiles (_POSIX_C_SOURCE=199309L), even though the FreeBSD 3.4-Release's _POSIX_VERSION macro indicates that only the POSIX.1 standard is supported.

Summary

This chapter has been a primer of sorts, to prepare you for all of those nasty compile issues that jump out at you when you begin a new project or port an old project on a new UNIX platform. The relatively standard compile options were covered to give you a quick start. You may find, however, that you still need to visit the vendor-specific options that were not discussed here. For example, HP has options that permit you to choose different instruction sets for the different PA-RISC platforms that are supported by the compiler.

You also learned (or reviewed) some tips on how to eliminate warning messages. This should enable you to keep the highest level of warnings enabled on your compiler and still accomplish tasks that the compiler might otherwise question.

Finally, you had an introduction to compiler feature test macros, which let you choose a standard to compile to. This treatment was by no means complete, since the other possibilities such as `_GNU_SOURCE` for Linux or `_HPUX_SOURCE` for HP were not tested. While these are not standards, they are often chosen to get the best combination of features for the specific platforms in question.

The next chapter will cover the subject of UNIX file system objects. For non-UNIX veterans, this is an essential foundation to build upon. Consequently, you are encouraged to absorb that chapter carefully. After an introduction to the various types of UNIX file system objects, the chapter will cover basic UNIX permissions as they affect the different objects. Then the core set of UNIX system calls as they affect the file system objects will be covered, giving you the core knowledge necessary for the remainder of this book.

## CHAPTER 2

UNIX FILE SYSTEM OBJECTS

T he early aspects of the UNIX file system design were conceived in the summer of 1969, largely by Ken Thompson at Bell Telephone Labs (BTL). An early version of the UNIX file system was loaded onto disk by paper tape. This allowed Ken Thompson and Dennis Ritchie to "drive the file system into the contortions that we wanted to measure," as Ken has been quoted.

Since this humble beginning, the basic ideas of the UNIX file system design have been copied in all other modern operating systems. This chapter will focus mostly on the objects that the UNIX file system presents to the users of the system. You will also examine some of the most basic operating system calls for working with file system objects from within your C program.

File System Objects

Modern UNIX file systems support the following types of file system objects:

- Regular Files (`S_IFREG`)
- Directories (`S_IFDIR`)
- Character Devices (`S_IFCHR`)
- Block Devices (`S_IFBLK`)
- Named Pipes (`S_IFIFO`)
- Sockets (`S_IFSOCK`)
- Symbolic Links (`S_IFLNK`)

The C macro names given within parentheses are provided by the include file `<sys/stat.h>` (see `stat(2)`). You'll see more of these in Chapter 6, "Managing Files and Their Properties."

Regular Files

A regular file is generally what is most important to users of a system. It stores the data that the user wants to retrieve and work with at a later time. The UNIX file system presents this data as a continuous stream of bytes.

A regular file consists of any number of data bytes, from zero to some maximum number. This is an important distinction to note, since many file systems, including CP/M and DOS, will present only multiples of a particular block size. This forces the DOS operating system to adopt the ^Z character as a marker for the end of a text file. Without this marker byte, it is otherwise impossible to have a file logically contain 3 bytes or 300 bytes, for example. However, UNIX has no such restriction, since it is logically able to present a file of any byte length.

Note

Although the UNIX file system is able to logically present a file of any size, it will still physically occupy a multiple of some block size. The precise nature of file allocation is hidden from the user and is determined by the type of file system in use.

Another feature of the UNIX file system is that the programmer can work with the file logically. There is no longer any need for the program to care about the block size in use by the underlying file. This permits the program to seek to any offset within the file and read any number of bytes, which may or may not span multiple disk blocks. For operating systems in 1969, this was a radical concept.

A regular file is identified by ls(1) as follows:

```
$ ls -l /etc/hosts
-rw-r--r--  1 root  wheel  112 Feb 19 11:07 /etc/hosts
$
```

The first character of the ls(1) output is a - (hyphen) to indicate that /etc/hosts is a regular file.

Directories

You cannot have more than one file in a file system without a directory. The first version of DOS created files only under the root directory. However, when a file was opened, this directory was searched to see if the file existed and where it was physically allocated.

The second step is important to the operating system in question.

UNIX supports a hierarchical file system, which allows directories to contain subdirectories. This allows the file system to be subdivided into logical groups of files and other file system objects. Can you imagine how difficult UNIX would be to use if the FreeBSD 3.4-Release contained all of its 60,014 (or more) files under the root directory?

Early releases of UNIX permitted directories to be read and written like regular files. Over time, several problems with this open concept emerged:

- Program errors or accidental writes to a directory could cause the loss of several files.

- New file systems supported different directory structure entries.

- Long filename support made it inconvenient to work directly with directory entries.

The first point illustrates one of the big weaknesses of early directory management. It was possible to lose the contents of an entire directory by accidentally overwriting the directory. The following command used to create havoc:

```
$ echo OOPS >directory
```

If *directory* was the name of a directory, this command would overwrite its contents, causing UNIX to lose track of all the files that it managed. Even worse, it usually meant that the space occupied by the files in that directory was lost, since the file system was not notified of any deletion. The following shows a modern response to this problem:

```
$ mkdir testdir
$ echo STUFF >testdir/file
$ ls -l testdir
total 1
-rw-r--r--  1 myid  megrp  5 Apr 15 15:16 file
$ echo OOPS >testdir
testdir: Is a directory.
$ ls -l testdir
total 1
-rw-r--r--  1 myid  megrp  5 Apr 15 15:16 file
$
```

The example creates a test directory and file and then attempts to overwrite the directory. The response from the UNIX kernel is that `testdir: Is a directory`.

When all file object names were limited to 14 characters, as they were in the earlier days, it was simple to work with the directories using direct file reads and writes. However, as different directory formats emerged and long filename support was introduced, this method proved to be unsafe and inconvenient.

For all of the reasons listed here, modern UNIX provides a set of library routines to search and manage directories. These will be covered in Chapter 7, "Directory Management."

A directory is identified by `ls(1)`, as the following example illustrates:

```
$ ls -dl /etc
drwxr-xr-x  14 root  wheel  2048 Apr  5 01:47 /etc
$
```

The first character shown by `ls(1)` is the letter d, indicating that /etc is a directory. Note especially the use of the -d option in the `ls(1)` command line. Without this option, `ls(1)` will attempt to list the contents of the directory, rather than the directory itself.

Block Devices

A block device is within a class of devices that work with fixed block sizes. A disk drive is a good example of this type of device. While the operating system permits you to logically read and write to your regular files using any transfer size, the operating system must read and write the disk device in terms of disk blocks of a fixed size.

Although disk devices get faster and larger each year, they are still slow when compared to the speed of the CPU. In addition to slow data transfer, disk rotation and head seek latencies add to the overall wait time involved in a disk I/O operation. Consequently, block devices are buffered with a disk cache by the UNIX kernel.

The disk cache will usually retain the most recently used disk blocks, but cache algorithms vary in order to achieve different performance goals. Because disk cache dramatically improves the performance of the file system, all file systems tend to be mounted using the block device.

Block devices can be readily identified by the `ls(1)` command as follows:

```
$ mount
/dev/wd0s2a on / (ufs, local, writes: sync 4505 async 92908)
/dev/wd0s2e on /usr (ufs, local, writes: sync 6924 async 118551)
procfs on /proc (procfs, local)
$ ls -l /dev/wd0s2a
brw-r-----  1 root  operator    0, 0x00030000 Feb 19 11:05 /dev/wd0s2a
$
```

The `mount(8)` (on many systems `mount(1M)`) command is used to find out what block devices have been used. Then the device `/dev/wd0s2a` was chosen in this example. The first character, shown by `ls(1)` in this example, is the letter **b**, indicating that `/dev/wd0s2a` is a block device.

Block devices are not necessarily representative of the entire disk. In most cases, these represent a disk partition so that an error in file system software cannot corrupt another partition. Additionally, each block device within the system usually has a corresponding character device as well. Block and character devices are also referred to as *block raw devices* and *character raw devices*, respectively.

When applied to a device, the word "raw" indicates that the disk space and structure are not managed. The raw device does not maintain a structure of files and directories within it. This is the job of file system software. Similarly, a database manages tables and rows within a raw device.

The cache feature of block devices may seem to suggest that a block device should be a good candidate for a database. This is usually not the case, however, since the database engine has its own custom cache algorithms that are tuned to the way that the database accesses the disk device. For this reason, database engines like Oracle, Sybase, and Informix usually perform better with the corresponding character device. This is one of the reasons that raw (character) device access to disks and partitions is being added to the Linux 2.4 kernel.

Character Devices

Character devices are a class of devices that work with various byte-sized inputs and outputs. These generally work with variable lengths of data, but not necessarily so (disks will insist on fixed block sizes). Your terminal (or pseudo-tty) is a special form of character device. As you type characters at your keyboard on the console, the operating system must read the characters and make them available to the program that is currently reading input from the terminal. This differs from the way that block devices work, in that the amount of data input is often small or variable in length.

QIC (Quarter-Inch Cartridge) tapes are another example of character devices. Tape devices will accept a program's idea of a record (within limits) and write a physical record to tape matching that size.

A character device is easily identified by the `ls(1)` command as shown below:

```
$ ls -l /dev/tty
crw-rw-rw- 1 root  wheel   1,   0 Apr 15 14:56 /dev/tty
$
```

The device `/dev/tty` is always known to the current session as your terminal device (the actual device name is different). The first character shown in the `ls(1)` output is `c`, telling you that this is a character device.

The mouse attached to the console is another example (FreeBSD):

```
$ ls -l /dev/sysmouse
crw------- 1 root  wheel  12, 128 Feb 19 11:05 /dev/sysmouse
$
```

Here again, you can see that the mouse is considered a character device.

Disks are also accessible using UNIX character devices. The same disks can be accessed using the corresponding block device that you read about earlier. However, character raw devices (for disks) are often provided to the database engines. Database engines manage the performance of disk I/O better than the block device cache because of their intimate knowledge of the data structures being used by the database.

By convention, the character raw device name of a block device usually has the letter r in front of it. See the following FreeBSD example:

```
$ mount
/dev/wd0s2a on / (ufs, local, writes: sync 4505 async 92982)
/dev/wd0s2e on /usr (ufs, local, writes: sync 6926 async 118585)
procfs on /proc (procfs, local)
$ ls -l /dev/rwd0s2a
crw-r----- 1 root  operator   3, 0x00030000 Feb 19 11:05 /dev/rwd0s2a
$
```

The `mount(8)` command was used to discover the block device names. Note that the `ls(1)` command adds the letter r to the device name to arrive at the character raw device name of `/dev/rwd0s2a` for the root mount. The first character of the `ls(1)` output shows the letter c, confirming that this is a character device.

Named Pipes (FIFOs)

In the period between 1970 and 1972, Doug McIlroy at BTL would sketch out how he would like to connect processes by saying "who into `cat` into `grep`." In 1972, Ken Thompson finally said, "I'm going to do it!" Overnight Ken worked to implement the pipe concept. Ken also had to rework many of the tools because, at the time, the tools did not support the idea of standard input—they read from files named on the command line instead. UNIX, starting with Third

Edition, was forever changed that night. The pipe feature was so well accepted that anyone who had seen it would not give it up.

Pipes are now routinely used on the command line under UNIX for all sorts of purposes, using the | pipe (vertical bar) symbol. These are anonymous pipes, since they exist only between the processes that are communicating with each other. They disappear from the system when both ends of the pipe become closed.

It is also possible to create a *named pipe* that exists in the file system. These are also known as FIFOs, since data that is written *first in* is *first out* of the pipe. The following shows a simple example:

```
$ mkfifo myFIFO
$ ls -l
total 0
prwxr-xr-x  1 myid  mygrp  0 Apr 15 16:55 myFIFO
$ ls -l >myFIFO &
$ tr '[a-z]' '[A-Z]' <myFIFO
TOTAL 0
PRWXR-XR-X  1 MYID  MYGRP  0 APR 15 16:55 MYFIFO
[1] 77637 Exit 0              ls -l >myFIFO
$
```

The example illustrates how the ls(1) command was able to redirect its output into the FIFO myFIFO (ls was placed into the background so that another command could be started in the same session). Then the tr(1) command was started to accept input from myFIFO, translating all lowercase letters into uppercase.

Notice also that the first letter of the ls(1) output is the letter p. This is how FIFO file system objects can be identified.

Sockets

The socket was a Berkeley University concept that found its way into 4.1BSD and 4.2BSD implementations of UNIX *circa* 1982. Sockets permit processes on one UNIX host to communicate over a network with processes on a remote host. Sockets can also be used to communicate with other processes within the same host. (The BSD lpr(1) command does this to accept output for spooling to a printer.)

Local sockets can also exist within the file system. This is the type of socket that can be used only between processes within the same host. If you have the PostgreSQL database installed on your FreeBSD system, you might have a socket like this one:

```
$ ls -l /tmp/.s.PGSQL.5432
srwxrwxrwx  1 postgres  wheel  0 Mar  7 04:43 /tmp/.s.PGSQL.5432
$
```

The example shows that the ls(1) command identifies the socket with the starting letter s.

Sockets that connect to remote systems, however, do not appear anywhere in the file system.

Symbolic Links

UNIX has supported linked files for quite some time. However, the symbolic link is a relatively new concept by UNIX standards. It was added to address the limitations of the normal link, sometimes now referred to as the "hard link."

Normally, files can be linked only when both links are contained on the same file system. On some systems, the /usr file system is different from other parts of the **root** file system. An attempt to create a link on a file system that is different from the file being linked will fail:

```
$ ln /etc/hosts /usr/me/work/my_link
ln: /home/me/work/my_link: Cross-device link
$
```

The UNIX kernel tells us that these two ends of a would-be link are on different devices. The symbolic link makes it possible to overcome this limitation:

```
$ ln -s /etc/hosts /usr/me/work/my_link
$ ls -dl my_link
lrwxr-xr-x  1 me   mygrp  10 Apr 15 17:22 my_link -> /etc/hosts
$
```

Note that the ln(1) command shown here uses the -s option to request a symbolic link, as if to say, "If you list the contents of my_link you will see the contents of your /etc/hosts file." The ls(1) command output for the symbolic link shows a starting letter l.

Symbolic links work around the original problem with hard links because they are actually a special kind of file that contains a pathname. When the UNIX kernel sees that it is a symbolic link, the kernel reads this special file to find out what the real pathname is. However, it is possible that the pathname listed is yet another symbolic link. The UNIX kernel will return the error **ELOOP** if the symbolic link is a circular reference or simply has too many indirect references. Chapter 6 will examine symbolic links further.

Note

The maximum symlink recursion in FreeBSD is defined by the macro MAXSYMLINKS. The macro is defined in the include file <sys/param.h>. For FreeBSD 3.4 Release, its value is 32. Other UNIX platforms may differ.

Special Files

While you may not have realized it, you already know about special files. These are file system objects that allow access to devices. Here are some of the examples that you have seen already:

/dev/tty	Terminal device
/dev/sysmouse	Mouse
/dev/wd0s2a	Block disk device
/dev/rwd0s2a	Character disk device

These are special files because they represent only the actual device in question (FreeBSD see `intro(4)`). It is only by convention that you tend to find these devices in the /dev directory. They could be placed in other directories.

Another important quality about special files is that their existence does not imply that the device or its driver support exists. For example, on a FreeBSD 3.4 Release system you might list a device:

```
$ ls -l /dev/da0
brw-r----- 1 root  operator   4, 0x00010002 Feb 19 11:05 /dev/da0
$ ls -l /dev/rda0
crw-r----- 1 root  operator  13, 0x00010002 Feb 19 11:05 /dev/rda0
$
```

The example shows a SCSI disk block and character device. Yet, if you were to switch to **root** to access this device, you would see the following:

```
# dd if=/dev/da0 of=/dev/null
dd: /dev/da0: Device not configured
#
```

The `dd(1)` command is told that the device is not configured (on the particular system on which it was tried). The file system object /dev/da0 is just a placeholder that informs the kernel what device you want access to, if this special file is accessed.

Harking back to an earlier example

```
$ mount
/dev/wd0s2a on / (ufs, local, writes: sync 4505 async 92982)
/dev/wd0s2e on /usr (ufs, local, writes: sync 6926 async 118585)
procfs on /proc (procfs, local)
$ ls -l /dev/rwd0s2a
crw-r----- 1 root  operator   3, 0x00030000 Feb 19 11:05 /dev/rwd0s2a
$
```

The /dev/rwd0s2a device is listed as the disk device (partition) for use by the **root** file system. You can also access this same device with another special file, if you create one of your own:

```
$ mknod /usr/me/work/root c 3 0x30000
mknod: /usr/me/work/root: Operation not permitted
$ su -
Password:
# cd /usr/me/work
# mknod root c 3 0x30000
# ls -l root
crw-r--r-- 1 root  mygrp     3, 0x00030000 Apr 15 18:03 root
# rm root
# exit
$
```

The `mknod(1)` command requires **root** access (note the failed first attempt). As **root**, the `mknod(1)` command was used to create an entirely new special file /usr/me/work/root, which even used a different filename. Once that is created, you will find that you could access the same device by using either /dev/rwd0s2a or /usr/me/work/root (but I wouldn't advise that you do anything with your **root** file system!).

The special file **root** in the example was deleted also. Did that make the device disappear? No. Not only is the special file /dev/rwd0s2a still available, even if that entry was deleted, you could always re-create it with the mknod(1).

The special file entry specifies three pieces of information:

- Block or character device (**b** or **c**)

- The major number for the device

- The minor number for the device

The major number (**3** in the example above) indicates what type of device it is (based upon the kernel configuration). The minor number can be as simple as the value zero, or it can reference a particular unit within a set. For example, a minor number of **2** might choose a second partition of the disk drive, and a minor number of **0** might reference the entire disk drive.

Minor numbers can also include bit flags. Some character devices such as tape drives have a bit set to indicate that the tape drive should be rewound upon close. In all cases, special file major and minor numbers are very kernel specific. You cannot use the same special files saved on an HPUX UNIX platform and restore them to an AIX 4.3 platform. This would be a recipe for disaster!

Special files are given attention here because they are important for those system programmers who want to take up daunting challenges such as writing database engines. The writer of any new device support must also be keenly interested in the special device entry for the hardware device.

Some device entries are pseudo devices. They don't actually represent hardware, but specialized kernel services. One pair of such devices under FreeBSD is the /dev/kmem and /dev/mem devices (see mem(4)). With the correct permissions, it is possible to inspect kernel memory through these special files. For example, a writer of a ps(1) command could choose to work through kernel structures this way (there are better ways).

Permissions

It is generally assumed in this book that the reader is already familiar with the UNIX access conventions that are applied. At the risk of stating the obvious, it is often useful at this stage to restate the precise way that permissions affect certain categories of file system objects. This is important because there are some minor semantic differences that depend on the file system object type.

Access of Regular Files

This is perhaps the simplest case to consider. Files can be controlled by

- Read access

- Write access

- Execute access

These are relatively simple concepts. However, a couple of interesting combinations exist:

- A file that has read and execute access
- A file that has execute-only access

The first case is necessary for shell scripts. In order for the shell interpreter to be started by the kernel with the !/bin/ksh hack, the UNIX kernel insists that the execute permission be given on the shell script. Additionally, the shell itself must interpret the file, so it must access enough to read the script. A shell script is unsuccessful if it has only one access permission or the other.

The execute permission is necessary to load and execute a binary executable as a process. This should be nothing new. However, an executable file, for instance /usr/local/bin/gzip, cannot be copied to your home directory with only execute permission. In this case, you are able only to execute gzip, but you are unable to ftp(1) it to your friends.

On older UNIX systems, there used to be a sticky bit available, which had meaning for executable files. When set on an executable file, this would cause the kernel to attempt to keep the program text (instructions) in its memory and swap other memory out instead. This optimization was often used on frequently accessed commands.

Access of Directories

Since directories are different from files, the semantics of directory access is a bit different also:

- *Read* grants permission to list the directory's contents.
- *Write* grants permission to modify the directory's contents.
- *Execute* grants permission to search the directory's contents and open a file or change to a subdirectory within it.

The read and execute permissions are similar, but distinct. You cannot list what files or subdirectories exist in a directory without read permission on that directory. However, if you already know the name of a file under that directory and you have execute access on the directory, then you can open that file (assuming the file grants read access).

You can also change to a subdirectory of a directory with execute-only access, if you already know the subdirectory's name (if the named subdirectory itself permits it with execute permission). A subdirectory without execute permission will not permit you to change to that directory, nor will it permit you to open files within it.

Many new UNIX users have difficulty understanding write access to directories. Write access permits users to create, rename, or delete files and other file system objects in that directory. Imagine a directory that contains a read-only file granting write access. That read-only file can be deleted because of the write permission available at the directory level. To disallow deleting of files, you must withdraw write permission on the directory containing the file. This also prevents the user from creating new files or renaming the existing ones in that directory.

Many UNIX systems allow a sticky bit to be set for directories. FreeBSD 3.4 Release describes this in its man page sticky(8). This feature is necessary for dealing with shared directories such as the /tmp directory. Without the sticky bit, all users would have write access to the /tmp directory and be able to

- Rename another user's temp file

- Delete another user's temp file

- Move another user's temp file to another writable directory on the system

In short, there is room for a lot of mischief without any special treatment of the /tmp directory. Rather than customize the operating system to make special allowances for fixed directories, the sticky bit was permitted for directories. Look at your /tmp directory now. Under FreeBSD you would see:

```
$ ls -dl /tmp
drwxrwxrwt  2 root  wheel  512 Apr 15 03:33 /tmp
$
```

Notice the t where the x should go (last position in drwxrwxrwt). This indicates that both the execute bit (for others) and the sticky bit are present. The sticky bit (S_ISVTX) for directories imposes the rules that the file system object can be removed or renamed only when

- The user has write permission for the directory containing the object.

- The user is the owner of the file system object itself.

The only exception is for the root user, who is permitted to do anything. The sticky bit in this way permits only the user's own files in a given directory to be tampered with.

The sticky bit enables you to create a directory in which other users can create files of their own, but they cannot remove other users' files. Additionally, you can create read-only files for those users without worrying about those read-only files being renamed or deleted.

Working with Files Under UNIX

A file or device under UNIX is opened with the open(2) system call. Before open(2) is considered in detail, let's first examine the way UNIX references open files in general.

When you want to read from a file, such as /etc/hosts, you must indicate which file you want to read. However, if you had to name the path as a C string "/etc/hosts" each time you wanted to read part of the file, this would not only be tedious and inefficient, it would also be inflexible. How would you read from different parts of the same file? Obviously, a method by which the file can be opened more than once is much more flexible.

When you open a file under UNIX, you are given a reference to that file. You already know (since this is review) that it is a number. This is also known as a *file unit number* or a *file descriptor*. Conceptually, this number is a handle that refers back to the file that you named in the open(2) call.

File descriptors returned from an **open(2)** call allow you to name the path of the file system object once. After you have a file descriptor, you can read the /etc/hosts file one line at a time by providing the file descriptor to the **read(2)** function. The UNIX kernel then knows which file you mean, because it remembers it from the earlier **open(2)** call.

This provides flexibility also, since **open(2)** can be called a second (or *n*th) time for the same file. In this way, one part of your application can be reading one part of the file while another part is reading another. Neither read disturbs the other. The **read(2)** call can manage this because file state information is associated with each different file descriptor.

Finally, it should be apparent that an open file descriptor eventually needs to be closed. The **close(2)** function fills that need. When a process terminates because of a signal or for any other reason, including a normal exit, any file descriptors that are still open are closed by the UNIX kernel. If this were not done, the UNIX kernel would suffer from a serious memory leak, among other problems.

Less obvious is that, when an **execve(2)** is called to start a new program within a process, some file descriptors can be closed automatically, while others are left open. See **fcntl(2)** and the **F_SETFD** flag if this is of interest. The **execve(2)** call is covered in Chapter 19, "Forked Processes."

Opening and Closing Files

Files under UNIX are opened and closed with the following functions:

```
#include <sys/types.h>          /* for mode_t */
#include <sys/stat.h>           /* for mode_t */
#include <fcntl.h>              /* For open */

int open(const char *path, int flags, ... /* mode_t mode */);


#include <unistd.h>

int close(int d);
```

The **open(2)** call accepts a C string that represents the pathname of the file system object to be opened, some flags, and optionally some permission bits in the **mode** argument. The return value is either -1 (with **errno**) if the call fails or a file descriptor value that starts at the value zero.

Note

The handling of **errno** is covered in Chapter 3, "Error Handling and Reporting," if you need to know more about this variable.

The returned file descriptor is always the lowest unused file descriptor number. If you have standard input already open (file unit **0**), standard output (file unit **1**), and standard error (file unit **2**), then the next successful **open(2)** call will return file unit **3**.

When you are finished with a file descriptor (an open file system object), you must close it with a call to close(2).

Flags for open(2)

The second argument to open(2) can consist of several flag bits. These are given in Table 2.1.

TABLE 2.1   FreeBSD open(2) Flag Bits

Flag	Description
O_RDONLY	Open for read only
O_WRONLY	Open for write only
O_RDWR	Open for read and write
O_NONBLOCK	Do not block on open
O_APPEND	Append with each write
O_CREAT	Create file if necessary
O_TRUNC	Truncate file to 0 bytes
O_EXCL	Error if creating and the file already exists
O_SHLOCK	Atomically obtain a shared lock
O_EXLOCK	Atomically obtain an exclusive lock

The flag O_NONBLOCK causes the open(2) call not to block while waiting for the device to be ready. For example, opening a modem device can cause it to wait until a carrier is detected. On some UNIX platforms such as SGI's IRIX 6.5, there is also the O_NDELAY flag, which has special semantics when combined with the O_NONBLOCK flag.

The O_APPEND flag will cause each write to the file to be appended to the end of the file. This applies to all write(2) calls, not just the first one (intervening appends can be done by other processes).

The O_CREATE flag can be used to cause the file to be created, if necessary. However, when combined with the O_EXCL flag, if the file already exists, the open(2) call returns an error. A special case of this is when flags O_CREATE and O_EXCL are used and the pathname given is a symbolic link. The call will fail even if the pathname resolved by the symbolic link does not exist. Another way to state this is that if the *symbolic link* exists, the open call treats this as if the *file* already exists and returns an error.

When opening a file in order to overwrite it, you can specify the O_TRUNC flag. This causes the file to be emptied prior to open(2) returning successfully. Any prior content of the file is lost.

Flags O_SHLOCK and O_EXLOCK are permitted on FreeBSD 3.4 Release and cause certain flock(2) semantics to be applied. Chapter 5, "File Locking," will cover the topic of locking files under UNIX.

Closing Files Automatically

All files are closed when the current process terminates. However, by default they remain open across calls to the execve(2) function. If you need the open file descriptor to close prior to executing a new program (with execve(2)), then you should apply a call to fcntl(2) using the F_SETFD operation.

```
#include <fcntl.h>

int fcntl(int fd, int cmd, ...);
```

To change a file descriptor given by variable fd to close automatically before another executable is started by execve(2), perform the following:

```
int fd;                            /* Open file descriptor */
int b0;                            /* Original setting */

if ( (b0 = fcntl(fd,F_GETFD)) == -1 )  /* Get original setting */
    /* Error handling... */

if ( fcntl(fd,F_SETFD,1)) == -1 )      /* Set the flag TRUE */
    /* Error handling... */
```

Here both the fetching of the current setting and the setting of the close-on-exec flag are shown. Some platforms use a C macro to identify this bit. For example, SGI's IRIX 6.5 uses the FD_CLOEXEC macro instead of assuming it is the least significant bit.

Opening Special Files

There is actually nothing unusual about opening a special file. You open it as you would any other file. For example, if you have permission to open a disk partition, your program can use the open(2) call to open it for reading and writing. For example

```
int fd;

fd = open("/dev/wd0s2f",O_RDWR);
if ( fd == -1 )
    /* Error handling... */
```

From this point on, this sample program would have access to the entire disk or disk partition, assuming that the open call succeeded. File systems have their special files protected so that normal users cannot open them this way. If they could, they could seriously corrupt the file system.

Tip

The open(2) and close(2) functions can return the error EINTR. It is easy to overlook this fact for the close(2) function. See Chapter 15, "Signals," for a discussion of this error code.

Working with Sockets

Sockets require special treatment. They are not opened with the normal open(2) call. Instead, sockets are created with the socket(2) or socketpair(2) call. Other socket function calls are used to establish socket addresses and other operating modes. Socket programming is outside the scope of this book.

It should be noted, however, that once a socket is created and a connection is established (at least for connection-oriented protocols), reading and writing to a socket can occur like any open file, with calls to read(2) and write(2). Sockets are like bi-directional pipes, and seeking is not permitted.

Duplicating File Descriptors

UNIX provides this unique capability to have one open file descriptor available as two (or more) separate file descriptors. Additionally, it is possible to take an open file descriptor and cause it to be available on a specific file unit number, provided the number is not already in use.

The function synopses for dup(2) and dup2(2) are as follows:

```
#include <unistd.h>

int dup(int oldfd);

int dup2(int oldfd, int newfd);
```

In the case of dup(2), the returned file descriptor when successful is the lowest unused file unit number available in the current process. For dup2(2), however, the new file descriptor value is specified in the argument newfd. When dup2(2) returns successfully, the return value should match newfd.

Tip

On some UNIX platforms, the dup(2) and dup2(2) calls can return the error EINTR (known to be documented for SGI's IRIX 6.5). See Chapter 15 for a discussion of this error code.

One situation in which dup(2) is helpful is in opening FILE streams to work with an existing socket. The following example takes the socket s and creates one input stream rx and another tx stream for writing:

```
int s;                          /* Open socket */
FILE *rx;                       /* Read stream */
FILE *tx;                       /* Write stream */

...
rx = fdopen(s,"r");             /* Open stream for reading on s */
tx = fdopen(dup(s),"w");        /* Open stream for writing on s */
```

Did you spot the dup(2) call? Why is it necessary? The dup(2) call is necessary because when the fclose(3) call is later made to close the rx stream, it will also close the file descriptor (socket) s. The dup(2) call ensures that the tx stream will have its own file descriptor to use, regardless of if stream rx is still open.

If the dup(2) were omitted from the example, the final data held in the buffers for tx would fail to be written to the socket when fclose(3) was called for tx (assuming rx has been closed first). The reason is that the underlying file descriptor will already have been closed. The dup(2) call solves an otherwise thorny problem.

Changing Standard Input

If you need to change your standard input, how is this accomplished? This may be necessary for the sort(1) command for example, since it processes the data presented on its standard input.

Assume that the input file to be sorted has been opened on unit 3 and held in variable fd. You can place this open file on standard input as follows:

```
int fd;                         /* Open input file for sort(1) */

close(0);                       /* Close my standard input */
if ( dup2(fd,0) == -1 )         /* Make fd available on 0 */
    /* Error handling... */
close(fd);                      /* This fd is no longer required */
```

The basic principle here is that once you close unit 0 (standard input), you can make the file that is open on unit 3 available as unit 0 by calling dup2(2). Once you have accomplished that, you can close unit 3, since it is not needed any longer.

You can apply this principle for standard output, standard error, or any other file unit you would like to control.

Warning

Note that the example avoided testing for errors for close(2), which should be done. Test for the error EINTR, and retry the close(2) call if the EINTR error occurs.

UNIX File I/O

Many C programming texts teach the reader how to do I/O using the `stdio(3)` functions `fopen(3)`, `fgets(3)`, `fread(3)`, `fwrite(3)`, and the rest. Because UNIX supports the `stdio(3)` interface, many new UNIX programmers think of this as UNIX file I/O. However, this interface is simply the `stdio(3)` set of routines, which is layered on top of the UNIX system calls. The underlying system calls perform the real UNIX file I/O.

There will be times where you'll need to use the "bare metal calls" such as `read(2)` and `write(2)` under UNIX. These and other UNIX I/O functions will be covered in Chapter 4, "UNIX Input and Output." These ultimately give you the most control and, in some cases, relief from bugs in `stdio(3)`.

Figure 2.1 illustrates how the `stdio(3)` functions call upon the section 2 functions. The `read(2)` and `write(2)` calls are serviced by the UNIX kernel, shown at the bottom of the figure.

FIGURE 2.1

The I/O software layers.

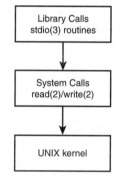

An example of a shortcoming of the `stdio(3)` routines is that they behave differently on different platforms. On some UNIX platforms, the error `EINTR` is returned when a signal handler returns, while on others this error is not returned at all. On still other UNIX platforms, the `stdio(3)` routines get confused dealing with `EINTR` and do not work correctly.

Sometimes you can live with the `stdio(3)` interface, but you'll want to perform a special control function on the open `FILE`. For example, you might need to issue an I/O control operation with `ioctl(2)` or set the close-on-exec flag using `fcntl(2)`. In these cases, you can gain access to the underlying file descriptor by using the `stdio(3)` macro `fileno(3)`. To set the close-on-exec flag on `FILE` stream `tx`, do the following:

```
FILE *tx;                                /* Opened by fopen(3) */

...
if ( fcntl(fileno(tx),F_SETFD,1)) == -1 )   /* Set the flag TRUE */
    /* Error handling... */
```

The example shows how the macro call `fileno(tx)` exposes the underlying UNIX file descriptor to the `fcntl(2)` function. This technique can sometimes be used with other functions such as `ioctl(2)`. However, be careful that what you are doing in this scenario does not upset what is being managed by the `stdio(3)` routines. For example, it might seem harmless to duplicate a file descriptor being used by `stdio(3)` and then call `lseek(2)` on the duplicated file descriptor. However, this will also change the file position for the original file descriptor. For some implementations of the `stdio(3)` library, this may cause you grief.

Summary

For many readers, this chapter has been a review. For those ramping up their knowledge to program in C under UNIX, this chapter will have exposed you to some important UNIX concepts. Perhaps you learned a few historical tidbits along the way.

Chapter 3 is another foundation-building chapter. Veterans can skip that chapter if they are in a hurry. If you are still building up your knowledge about UNIX programming, you will want to pay special attention to this chapter. It will help you master the material in the remainder of this book.

CHAPTER 3

ERROR HANDLING AND REPORTING

The UNIX operating system and its associated C libraries offer a rich set of system and function library calls, respectively. Within this set of calls there are very few functions, which cannot return an error. Reasons for errors include the incorrect use of parameters, inadequate buffer sizes, missing or misnamed file system objects, or simply a lack of access to a resource. A mechanism must exist to return an error indication to the caller of the function.

This chapter examines the error reporting mechanism used by the UNIX system and library function calls. This includes a discussion of the original error reporting mechanism that was used in the past and the implementation now in use. Additionally, it will be shown how UNIX error codes can be translated into meaningful text messages that can be reported to a user.

Determining Success or Failure

When a C function is called, the programmer is interested in two things upon its return:

- Did the function call succeed?
- If not, why did the call fail?

General Rules for Error Indication

The UNIX convention used by most system calls and library functions is that the return value indicates a general success or failure. Return values fall into two major categories:

- The return value is an integer value (int or long). Normally failure is indicated by a value of negative one (-1).
- The return value is a pointer type, such as pointers (char *), (void *) or a pointer to a structure. Failure is indicated by a null return pointer and success by a non-null pointer.

Exceptions to the General Rule

There are exceptions to the general rule just listed, but these are rare. When the functions wait(2), waitpid(2), wait3(2), and wait4(2) return an error indication, they return the integer value (pid_t)(-1). This is similar to the integer return case, except that the value -1 is returned in a process ID data type.

An exception to the pointer rule is the shmat(2) function call. When it returns an error indication, it returns the pointer value (void *)(-1).

Unusual exceptions to the general rule can be found in the functions strtol(3), strtoul(3), and strtod(3), which return special values like LONG_MIN, LONG_MAX, ULONG_MAX, +HUGE_VAL, and -HUGE_VAL. These will be covered in detail in Chapter 10, "Conversion Functions."

Classifying Successful Return Values

For integer return values, a successful return value is normally anything other than -1. Often this is a value that is greater than or equal to zero. For example, the UNIX open(2) call returns a file descriptor number that can be zero or greater.

For pointer return values, a successful return value is normally a non-null pointer. An example is the fopen(3) function, which returns a pointer to a FILE object.

As noted previously, under unusual circumstances the null pointer can indicate a successful return from certain exceptional functions (recall shmat(2)). For this reason, the best programming practice is for the programmer to test for failure indication upon return from a function. Anything that does not classify as a failure should be considered a successful indication.

Other Return Indications

Before leaving the topic of function return indications, it is worth pointing out that some functions offer a third indication, in addition to the normal success or failure. These generally fall into two categories:

- No more information exists (examples include waitpid(2), wait3(2), wait(4)).

- A timeout has occurred without returning any "interesting" event (examples include select(2), poll(2)).

In these examples, the designers of these functions have decided not to treat the "no information" or "timeout" case as an error. At the same time, these cases cannot be considered successful returns, since either no information is returned or a timeout has occurred.

This type of indication can be treated as an error by the programmer, with the exception that there will be no value provided in the global variable errno.

Determining the Reason for Failure

The foregoing discussion identifies most function calls as returning an indication of

- success

- failure

- in rare cases, no information

Once you have discovered that the function call has failed, you need to know why. For example, the UNIX `make(1)` command needs to know from `open(2)` when it fails that

- It was unable to open `makefile` because it did not exist.

- It lacked the permissions necessary to open `makefile` for reading.

The reason for the failure *might* have a bearing on the action taken by the command. For example, if it finds that file `makefile` does not exist, `make(1)` tries to open the file `Makefile` instead. However, when it discovers that it lacks permissions to open file `makefile`, some implementations of the `make(1)` command report this as an error to the user. See the following Note for variations on this theme by the different UNIX platforms tested.

Note

The `make(1)` command's behavior varies on the different UNIX platforms tested. The following platforms report an error if they lack permission to read the file `makefile`:

Linux (GNU make 3.77)

SunOS 5.6 (reports a warning and tries to open `Makefile`)

The `make(1)` command on the following platforms ignores the file access error and proceeds to open `Makefile` instead:

FreeBSD 3.4 Release

HPUX 10.2 and HPUX 11.0

AIX 4.3

The nature of a failure is clearly important to the programmer of any software or utility program. The error-reporting mechanism that early developers of UNIX chose was the special external integer variable named `errno`. Whenever a function call returned a failure indication, it would first assign a reason code for the failure to the external `errno` variable. The calling program could then examine this external variable if it cared to know the reason for the failure. When the function returned a successful indication (or "no information" indication), the value of `errno` was left unchanged.

This mechanism was suitable for early versions of UNIX. However, this older method has limitations. To remove the inherent limitations of the `errno` variable, its definition has changed somewhat in modern versions of UNIX. If it is applied correctly, this change is transparent to you as a programmer.

The Old `errno` Value

The original method that the programmer used to gain access to the error code was to declare an external reference to the `int` value `errno`:

```
extern int errno;
```

When an attempt to open a file fails, a program can simply query the external variable `errno` to determine the reason for the failure. The following example shows how the make(1) command could be written using the old `errno` method:

```
#include <errno.h>                          /* Defines ENOENT */
extern int errno;                           /* Error code */
int fd;                                     /* File descriptor */

/* Attempt to open makefile */
if ( (fd = open("makefile",O_RDONLY)) == -1 ) { /* Fail to open? */
    if ( errno == ENOENT )                  /* File does not exist? */
        fd = open("Makefile",O_RDONLY);     /* No, so try Makefile instead */
}

if ( fd == -1 ) {                           /* Did either open(2) fail? */
    /* Yes, report the open failure... */
    ...
} else {
    /* makefile or Makefile is open on file unit fd */
}
```

The example shows that if `makefile` fails to open, with the error `ENOENT`, `Makefile` is opened. The example also illustrates that the reason for the error is never returned directly by the function, nor is it returned by an argument reference. Instead, using this older external variable methodology, the programmer queries this value when a function returns a failure indication.

Note

ENOENT means No Such File or Directory. This error code indicates that the requested file system object was not found (does not exist).

Referencing Error Codes by Name

Using the `errno` external variable convention for errors required that a series of error codes be agreed on in advance. Since numeric error codes might vary on different UNIX platforms, a set of C macros is defined to refer to these error codes (for example, error code `ENOMSG` is **83** for FreeBSD 3.4, **35** for HPUX, and **42** for Linux). The symbolic macro names can be used to refer to the same error codes on different UNIX platforms. These C macros are defined in the include file `errno.h`.

```
#include <errno.h>
```

Using symbolic macro references for error codes is important, since it allows your C programs to be portable to other UNIX platforms. Only a compile is required to reference the correct numeric value for these codes on a given platform.

UNIX `errno` codes are non-zero values and usually start at 1 and work up. Zero is sometimes used to indicate "no error" (this convention is used in rare cases with the functions `strtol(3)`, `strtoul(3)`, and `strtod(3)`, for example).

Applying `errno` Correctly

There is a temptation for novice programmers to use the `errno` value to test for success. However, it is incorrect to do so because the purpose of the `errno` value is to be a central place to which to post error codes. As a general policy, never expect the `errno` value to be cleared to zero for success. *Only errors (failures) are posted to this variable.*

There are special situations that require you to clear the `errno` value to zero before making a function call (some examples are `strtol(3)`, `strtoul(3)`, `strtod(3)`, and `getpwent(3)`). This is necessary because the function will not clear the `errno` value to zero when success is returned. Under these special circumstances, if the `errno` value remains as the value `0` (presuming it was cleared prior to the call), then this indicates a successful return. This technique must only be applied to *specially indicated* functions. This technique cannot be extended for use on other functions. The special cases will be carefully indicated within this book.

Warning

The `errno` value is updated by system and library functions only after an error indication is returned. This value is never cleared to zero for a successful operation. Always test the function's return value to determine if an error has been indicated. If so, then the value of `errno` has meaning.

Testing for Failure with Integer Return Values

Earlier it was shown how functions, which return integer results, use the value of -1 to indicate that a call has failed. The following `open(2)` example indicates when the value of `errno` is valid:

```
extern int errno;          /* Old way of gaining access to errno */
int fd;                    /* File descriptor */

if ( (fd = open("makefile",O_RDONLY)) == -1 ) {
    /* Failed: errno holds a valid error code */
    ...
} else {
    /* Success: fd holds file descriptor, and errno is meaningless here */
    ...
}
```

If the `open(2)` call returns a failed indication by a return value of -1, then we know that the error code will have been posted to the integer `errno`.

Testing for Failure with Pointer Results

Other functions that report their failure by returning a null pointer can identify when to use errno as follows:

```
FILE *fp = fopen("makefile","r");           /* Attempt to open makefile */

if ( fp == NULL ) {                         /* Failed? */
    /* Open Failed: the value of errno holds an error code */
    ...
} else {
    /* Open succeeded: the value of errno has no meaningful value */
    ...
}
```

Here the fopen(3) call indicates failure by returning a null pointer (which matches the C macro value NULL). Again, only when it is determined that the function has returned a failure indication is the value errno valid and does it contain an error code.

The New errno Value

If you've been a veteran of UNIX C/C++ code for some time, then you've probably noticed some changes in the declaration of the variable errno over the years. Modern UNIX platforms have undergone some changes in order to support threads.

While threads are a welcome addition to the UNIX platform, they have required a number of internal changes to the underlying C libraries and the way in which the errno variable is defined. A thread is a separate flow of instructions within one memory environment (all threads share one memory address space). Consequently, the traditional single global integer value of errno no longer suffices, since function calls in one thread would alter the errno values being referenced in another thread.

In order to support threads without requiring all existing software to be redesigned, a new declaration has been crafted for the errno value (usually a C macro). This new definition defines a separate copy of errno for each thread. Rather than have the programmer declare this variable, it is now done by the provided include file <errno.h> instead. This change in definition should be transparent to most UNIX source code. Note that there were older releases of the GNU libraries under Linux, where the extern int errno declaration was in conflict and required removal to compile successfully. The modern GNU libraries no longer suffer from this problem.

Declaring the New errno Variable

The new errno value is now defined in a platform-dependent manner. This means that you should let the system define it for you by including the file <errno.h>. You should no longer declare it as an external integer variable.

The <errno.h> include file will define errno in a manner that is appropriate for your specific UNIX platform. This also defines the errno macro constants for the error codes.

Using the New errno Variable

Once variable errno is appropriately declared for your platform, you can still use it as you did before. For example

```
int saved_errno;
```

```
saved_errno = errno;            /* Saving errno */
printf("errno = %d\n",errno);   /* Inspecting errno */
errno = ENOENT;                 /* Changing errno */
errno = 0;                      /* Clearing errno to zero */
```

You can obtain value of errno and change its value, just as before its definition changed. The change in the way errno is defined is meant to be transparent to you.

Reporting on errno Values

When an error occurs, it is simple for the program to test for a specific case and act upon it. The problem becomes more complex when all you want to do is report the error to the user. Users do not like to memorize error codes, so a method must exist to translate an errno code into a readable message.

Meaningful error messages can be reported by a UNIX program to the user, in the following ways:

- Use the perror(3) function to generate a message from the errno value and report it to stderr.

- Use the provided sys_errlist[] array of messages (on FreeBSD this is described by the man page strerror(3)).

- Use the strerror(3) function to return a message for the error code provided in the function argument.

Using the perror(3) Function

One function provided for reporting errors is the library function perror(3). This function takes one string argument and writes that string to stderr, followed by a colon and then a message for the current errno value. The function synopsis is as follows:

```
#include <stdio.h>

void perror(const char *s);
```

This function is easily tested by simply assigning an error of our choice to errno and calling perror(3). An example is provided in Listing 3.1.

LISTING 3.1   perror.c—A Test Program for perror(3)

```
1:   #include <stdio.h>
2:   #include <errno.h>
3:
4:   int
5:   main(int argc,char **argv) {
6:
7:       errno = EIO;
8:       perror("Test EIO Message");
9:       return 0;
10:  }
```

Line 7 shows how an I/O error was assigned to the **errno** variable (the error code was arbitrarily chosen to simulate an error). Line 8 calls upon the **perror(3)** function to report the error. The test session is shown below:

```
$ make perror
cc -c -D_POSIX_C_SOURCE=199309L -Wall perror.c
cc perror.o -o perror
$ ./perror
Test EIO Message: Input/output error
$
```

The session output shows the program-supplied message, which is followed by a colon and then by an interpretation of the error code that was assigned to variable **errno**. The value, **EIO** in this example, was translated to the message Input/output error.

Evaluating the perror(3) Function

At first sight, the **perror(3)** function might appear to be a good solution. In practice, however, this function is not very useful. The first problem is that the message must go to standard error. If the message must be

- Written to a log file

- Reported to an X Window pop-up

- Reported in a different format

- Stored as a string

then the function **perror(3)** is not able to help. Another problem that often occurs is this: What if the error code is not coming from **errno** but some other variable? The **perror(3)** function seems best left to academic examples because of its simplicity.

Using the sys_errlist[] Array

If you look up the **perror(3)** function in the FreeBSD **man(1)** pages (and on most UNIX platforms), you will also see that it describes the **sys_errlist[]** array. The synopsis of this array is this:

```
#include <stdio.h>     /* Defines sys_errlist[] and sys_nerr */

extern const char *sys_errlist[];
extern const int sys_nerr;
```

Variations:

```
#include <errno.h>     /* HPUX 10.2 & 11.0 */
/* None */             /* AIX 4.3 */
/* None */             /* SunOS 5.6, Solaris 8 */
/* None */             /* UnixWare 7 */
#include <errno.h>     /* SGI IRIX 6.5 */
```

The sys_errlist[] array is an external array of pointers to string constants. Each string describes a particular error that corresponds to an errno code. The array and the error codes are structured so that the error message can be obtained by using the errno value as the subscript into the array. For example

```
errno = EIO;                    /* Simulate an error */
printf("The EIO Message is '%s'\n",sys_errlist[errno]);
```

Having access to the error message text for each error code provides much more flexibility. When the fopen(3) call fails, you can report the reason for the failure, the pathname being opened, and whether it is being opened for reading or writing:

```
FILE *fp = fopen(pathname,"r");   /* Attempt to open a file */

if ( !fp ) {                      /* Did the open fail? */
    fprintf(stderr,"%s: Unable to open %s for read.\n",
        sys_errlist[errno],       /* The error message text */
        pathname);                /* The file being opened */
    exit(13);
}
```

This example shows a typical format for error messages from UNIX programs. This typical format used can be summarized as

```
Explanation of error code: Explanation of the operation being attempted
```

Notice that this convention contradicts the format used by the perror(3) function.

Using sys_nerr to Range Check Errors

The largest error code that is provided for in the sys_errlist[] array is given by the external integer value of sys_nerr minus one. To be safe, you should technically always test the errno value before using it as a subscript:

```
int fd;                    /* File descriptor */

fd = open(pathname,O_RDONLY);   /* Attempt to open for read */
if ( fd == -1 ) {               /* Did open(2) fail? */
    /* The open(2) call failed: */
    fprintf(stderr,"%s: opening %s for read\n",
        errno < sys_nerr ? sys_errlist[errno] : "?",
        pathname);
```

In the example shown, the C operator **?** is used to test **errno** to make sure that it is less than the value of **sys_nerr**. If it is, the value of **sys_errlist[errno]** can be safely supplied to **fprintf(3)**. If the **errno** value fails to be less than the **sys_nerr** value, the C string **"?"** is supplied instead, to prevent a program abort.

Evaluating the sys_errlist[] Array Method

While range-checking **errno** with the **sys_nerr** value is the correct thing to do, it is considered tedious and pedantic by many programmers. Therefore, many programmers ignore this test completely. Because programmers fail to apply this test, the practice of using the **sys_errlist[]** array has fallen out of favor, and another way has been subsequently provided.

Note

The **man(1)** pages provided by SGI for its IRIX 6.5 operating system state "Code using **sys_errlist**, and **sys_errlist** directly, will not be able to display any **errno** greater than 152." It is unclear from this text whether it is simply stating the SGI value of **sys_nerr** or whether this is a limitation of using the array on that platform.

The tone of the message suggests that the **sys_errlist[]** array falls short of **strerror(3)** and thus should be avoided in new code. A possible reason for this is that dynamic content could be provided by the **strerror(3)** function for errors with codes greater than 152.

The strerror(3) Function

This is the last of the error code conversion methods that will be examined. The synopsis of the **strerror(3)** function is as follows:

```
#include <string.h>

char *strerror(int errnum);
```

Tip

A common mistake is to include the file **<errno.h>** instead of **<string.h>**. It is commonly assumed that the **strerror(3)** function is declared in the **<errno.h>** include file because it reports an error message. However, this function is grouped with the string functions, instead.

The **strerror(3)** function provides the flexibility afforded by the **sys_errlist[]** array, but it also performs the necessary range check on the error code being converted. If the error code is outside of the known list of error codes, an unknown error message is returned instead of a bad pointer.

Using the strerror(3) Function

Listing 3.2 shows a short program that we can use to test the **strerror(3)** function.

LISTING 3.2   strerror.c—Test Program for strerror(3)

```
 1:    #include <stdio.h>
 2:    #include <errno.h>
 3:    #include <string.h>
 4:
 5:    extern int sys_nerr;     /* Highest supported error code */
 6:
 7:    int
 8:    main(int argc,char **argv) {
 9:        int x;
10:        static int ecodes[] = { -1, EIO, 0 };
11:
12:        /* Get maximum code and add 4096 */
13:        ecodes[2] = sys_nerr + 4096;    /* A very high code */
14:
15:        for ( x=0; x<3; ++x ) {
16:            errno = ecodes[x];
17:            printf("%4d = '%s'\n",ecodes[x],strerror(errno));
18:        }
19:
20:        return 0;
21: }
```

This test program tries strerror(3) with a -1 value, EIO, and a very high error code, which should not exist.

Testing the Range Check in strerror(3)

When the program in Listing 3.2 is compiled and run, the following results are obtained under FreeBSD (3.4 Release):

```
$ make strerror
cc -c -D_POSIX_C_SOURCE=199309L -Wall strerror.c
cc strerror.o -o strerror
$ ./strerror
  -1 = 'Unknown error: -1'
   5 = 'Input/output error'
4183 = 'Unknown error: 4183'
$
```

This shows how well behaved the strerror(3) function is, despite the bad errno values that were provided to it. The error code 5 (EIO) correctly translated to the message Input/output error. The values -1 and 4183 both provided a meaningful clue to a programming problem with a message of the form Unknown error: 4183. Had this program used the sys_errlist[] array instead, a program abort may have occurred.

Applying strerror(3) Correctly

One important thing to note about using the strerror(3) function is that the pointer returned by this function is only valid until the next call to the same function is made. The following code is incorrect:

```
char *eptr1 = strerror(EIO);
char *eptr2 = strerror(ENOENT);  /*** value of eptr1 is now invalid ***/

printf("Msg1='%s', msg2='%s'\n",eptr1,eptr2);        /*** INCORRECT ***/
```

This code is not acceptable because by the time `strerror(3)` is called the second time and its return value is assigned to `eptr2`, the pointer value `eptr1` is rubbish. Even if your experimentation proves this practice to be apparently safe, code should not be written to rely on this behavior. There is a possibility that someday (if not already), `strerror(3)` may return dynamic content and cause this to fail.

Warning

The value returned by `strerror(3)` is valid only until the next call to `strerror(3)`.

Testing for Errors Using `stdio(3)`

One area that is often overlooked in various texts that describe the `stdio(3)` set of routines is the proper treatment of errors. You have already seen how to discriminate between an error return and a success return with the `fopen(3)` call. Immediately after a `fopen(3)` failure, the value of `errno` contains the reason for the open failure. However, the situation may not be so clear in other circumstances, which will be examined next.

Pitfalls of the `ferror(3)` Function

By way of review, examine the function synopsis for the `ferror(3)` function:

```
#include <stdio.h>

int ferror(FILE *stream);            /* Test stream for an error */
void clearerr(FILE *stream);         /* Clear an error indication */
```

The `ferror(3)` function returns a non-zero value (a logical `True`) when an error has occurred at some point on the `FILE` stream identified by the argument `stream`. This indicator remains `True` until the function `clearerr(3)` is called for the same stream. This in itself is not a problem.

What can be a problem is when `ferror(3)` is called to test for an error on a stream after several other `stdio(3)` calls have been made. If the value of `errno` is consulted at this later point, it may report incorrect results.

Only the indication of the occurrence of the error is saved within the stream object `FILE` by the `stdio(3)` set of routines. The `errno` value itself is valid only immediately after the `stdio(3)` call that failed (up to the point of the next `errno` modifying function call). Consequently, while `ferror(3)` can be useful in telling you that something went wrong on a `FILE` stream at some point in time, it will not provide you with the details of the error. This is because the value of `errno` may have been lost by other intervening calls.

Avoiding the `fclose(3)` Pitfall

When using `stdio(3)` function calls, you must check for errors immediately after the call that caused the error, when you want to consult `errno`. Errors can occur in surprising places when buffering is being used (see `setbuf(3)` for how to control this feature).

Data previously written by a call to `fwrite(3)` may have returned a successful indication earlier in the program. Later a failure can be reported by the `fclose(3)` function. To see why, look at the following example:

```
fwrite(buf,strlen(buf),1,fptr);    /* Write out a C string in buf[] */
if ( ferror(fptr) ) {              /* Write error occur? */
    /* Process write error */      /* Yes, process error.. */
}
if ( fclose(fptr) == EOF ) {       /* Did the close succeed? */
    /* errno = ENOSPC */           /* A failure during close occurred */
}
```

Some programmers are surprised to realize that `fclose(3)` can fail in the example provided. This can happen because the data written by `fwrite(3)` is still contained in a buffer provided by the stream `fptr`. When `fclose(3)` is finally called, it is first necessary to force the unwritten data in the buffer out to disk before closing the underlying file descriptor. If the disk is full, the `fclose(3)` call will fail and `errno` will report the error as code `ENOSPC`.

Note that in this scenario, `ferror(3)` cannot be used to test for an error because the FILE stream is destroyed by the `fclose(3)` call. Here it is essential to test the return value from `fclose(3)` and then report the reason contained within `errno` immediately upon detecting the failure.

Note

ENOSPC means No Space Left On Device. This error code is returned when there is insufficient disk space to enlarge a file. It frequently happens when `write(2)` is called and the size of the file would have increased as a result of the call, but no free space remained.

Delaying the Reporting of an Error

There are times when error reporting must wait until other steps are taken in the program to recover. Sometimes those steps can cause the value of `errno` to be lost. The following example illustrates this:

```
int z;                             /* status code */
int fd;                            /* open file descriptor */

z = write(fd,buf,n);               /* Write some data */
if ( z == -1 ) {                   /* Did this write fail? */
    unlink(pathname);              /* Yes, delete half baked file */
    fprintf(stderr,"%s: write error on %s\n",
        strerror(errno),
        pathname);
```

In this example, the program insists on calling `unlink(2)` first to remove the file that the `write` has failed to write to. It then reports the error, after the file has been deleted.

The problem is that by the time the error is reported by `fprintf(3)`, the `errno` value for the failed `write(2)` call could be lost. The `errno` value may instead contain an error from the `unlink(2)` call (if it fails) that is more recent.

At the risk of stating the obvious, the value of `errno` can be saved in another variable and then reported later. Here is the modified example:

```
int z;                         /* status code */
int fd;                        /* open file descriptor */
int e;                         /* Saved errno value */

z = write(fd,buf,n);           /* Write some data */
if ( z == -1 ) {               /* Did this write fail? */
    e = errno;                 /* Preserve the value of errno */
    unlink(pathname);          /* Delete this half baked file */
    fprintf(stderr,"%s: write error on %s\n",
        strerror(e),           /* Report e here (not errno) */
        pathname);
```

While it is true that you could simply move the `fprintf(3)` call to execute prior to the `unlink(2)` call, this is not always possible. If you must clean up something prior to opening a pop-up error message window, this might not be practical.

Summary

In this chapter, the general philosophy behind the UNIX C library method of reporting success and failure has been covered. You have studied the global variable `errno` and learned how to declare it and use it. Also very importantly, you learned when the value of `errno` is valid.

You have seen the different ways that error codes can be converted into a user-friendly message. Some of the pitfalls of error reporting were also examined, such as that of detecting an error too late with the function `ferror(3)`.

While this chapter has been a review for seasoned programmers, this material is vitally important to those that are just starting out programming for UNIX. With this foundation, you are better equipped to tackle the upcoming chapters successfully.

CHAPTER 4

UNIX INPUT AND OUTPUT

C hapter 2, "UNIX File System Objects," reviewed the open(2) and close(2) system calls. Once you have your file open on a file unit, you need some other routines that let you manipulate that file. That is largely what this chapter is all about.

However, before jumping into that topic, another topic related to open(2) should be discussed first. This is the UNIX umask(2) bits and how they affect the permissions that are established in new file system objects.

The umask(2) Function and umask Bits

When new files and directories are created, the designer of the program must decide which permissions to use. These are usually specified as quite liberal permissions. Sometimes greater security is required when you do not want to give away certain permissions to the group or to the world.

Permission Bits

Just by way of review, the permission bit scheme will be presented. Not everyone is used to working with permissions in the octal form, which is the way umask is discussed for convenience.

The data type used for permission bits in modern UNIX systems is the mode_t data type. Under older versions of UNIX, it was the int data type. The permission bits are laid out in three groups:

rwx rwx rwx

Each of the three groupings consists of bits rwx, representing

read permission	r
write permission	w
execute permission	x

respectively. From left to right, the permission groups are

owner permissions	u
group permissions	g
all others permissions	o

The letters u, g, and o are the ones used on the chmod(1) command line when octal notation is not used. Since octal notation encodes each digit with three bits, it proves to be a convenient way to specify the permissions. For example, the octal value 0740 specifies

rwx permissions for the owner	u
r permission only for the group	g
no permissions for others	o

Standards bodies are encouraging programmers not to rely on octal encoding. The C macros in Table 4.1 have been defined for use in programs:

TABLE 4.1   C Macros for Permission Bits

C Macro	Octal	Meaning
S_ISUID	04000	Set user ID on execution.
S_ISGID	020#0	Set group ID on execution if # is 7, 5, 3, or 1; enable mandatory file/record locking if # is 6, 4, 2, or 0.
S_ISVTX	01000	Save text image after execution (sticky bit).
S_IRWXU	00700	Read, write, execute by owner.
S_IRUSR	00400	Read by owner.
S_IWUSR	00200	Write by owner.
S_IXUSR	00100	Execute (search if a directory) by owner.
S_IRWXG	00070	Read, write, execute by group.
S_IRGRP	00040	Read by group.
S_IWGRP	00020	Write by group.
S_IXGRP	00010	Execute by group.
S_IRWXO	00007	Read, write, execute (search) by others.
S_IROTH	00004	Read by others.

C Macro	Octal	Meaning
S_IWOTH	00002	Write by others.
S_IXOTH	00001	Execute by others.

Based on the values in Table 4.1, the permissions **0740** would be defined in macro form as follows:

```
S_IRWXU | S_IRWXU
```

Alternatively, it can be spelled out as

```
S_IRUSR | S_IWUSR | S_IXUSR | S_IRWXU
```

The permission **S_ISVTX** (sticky bit) is not supported by FreeBSD for executables, but is supported for directories.

Understanding the Need for umask

Consider an example in which you are working in a student environment with a number of other students on the same machine. You create a program to hand in as an assignment and save it. The vi editor creates the text file with read and write permissions for the owner, the group, and the world. Another enterprising student copies your assignment to his home directory and later hands it in. He can do this because he can read your saved assignment. Because he also has write permission on your text file, he overwrites your file with something else so that you have nothing to hand in. All of this happened because vi gave the owner, the group, and the world permission to read and write the file.

The manner in which the designers of UNIX have chosen to deal with this problem is to allow program designers to specify the most liberal permissions they dare apply for the application involved. Then a mask is applied on a process-level basis to exclude permissions the user does not want to give away. In the example, the student would have been prudent to exclude group and world access to his new files.

Your UNIX process maintains a **umask** value to allow you to have control over the permissions being handed out. This is a mask value since it is used to mask out certain permission bits that you do not want to give away. To prevent the group or the world from being granted any permission on your top secret new files, you could set the **umask** value to octal **077**. This would allow the **umask** value to remove any permission at the group and world (other) levels.

Understanding the Scope of umask

The **umask** value is maintained by the UNIX kernel at the process level. The **umask** built-in command for the Korn shell sets the **umask** value for that shell process (in other words, its own process). However, whenever the shell creates a new process, that new process inherits the shell's **umask** setting. In this manner, setting the **umask** value in the shell causes it to be set for the entire user session, even in new shell processes.

The scope of the umask value is also limited to file system objects. This means that it applies to files and directories, but it does not apply to IPC objects such as semaphores, message queues, and shared memory.

Using the umask(2) Function

The umask value applies to file system objects. Therefore, whenever your current process creates a new directory or file, the umask value is applied before the final permission bits are established.

In C language terms, the umask value is computed like this:

```
actual_permissions = requested_permissions & ( ~umask );
```

The value requested_permissions represents the most liberal set of permissions that might be given in the open(2) call that was covered earlier. Note the use of the unary ~ (tilde) operator to invert the umask bits before using the binary & (and) operator. The resulting actual_permissions bits are the ones then that are actually applied when the file or directory is created.

Example Using the umask Value

If the vi editor was to create a new text file requesting permission bits 0666 (read and write for everyone), and the current umask value was 0077 (exclude group and others), the following computations would occur (successively simplifying):

1. `actual_permissions = requested_permissions & (~umask)`

2. `actual_permissions = 0666 & ( ~0077 )`

3. `actual_permissions = 0666 & 0700`

4. `actual_permissions = 0600`

The final permission bits would be computed as 0600, which represents read and write for the owner of the file but no permission for the group or for others.

The umask(2) Function

The umask setting is queried and set by the function umask(2). The function prototype is as follows:

```
#include <sys/types.h>
#include <sys/stat.h>

mode_t umask(mode_t new_umask);
```

The value provided in the argument is the new umask value that you want to apply. The value returned is the umask value that was in effect before the current call. The umask(2) function never returns an error.

In the following code, a new umask value of **077** is being established. At the same time, the original umask setting is saved in the variable **old_mask**:

```
int old_mask;

old_mask = umask(0077);
```

Setting umask **with** umask(2)

The procedure for setting the umask value is as follows:

1. Call umask(2) with the new mask value.

2. Save the old umask value if there is a possibility that you need to restore the present umask setting.

The original umask value is frequently saved because it may need to be restored later. This is often done in a library function, where the umask value may need to be temporarily changed.

Querying umask **with** umask(2)

There is no function to inquire about the umask(2) value. For this reason, you must inquire using a procedure that sets one umask value and then restores the original. This procedure is outlined as follows:

1. Call umask(2) with a new mask value. Zero will do.

2. Save the returned value as the present umask value in a variable.

3. Call umask(2) again, with the original umask value to restore it.

Listing 4.1 shows an example of a function named **query_umask()**, which performs this very process:

LISTING 4.1   umask.c—Program Example Querying the umask Value

```
 1:    /* umask.c */
 2:
 3:    #include <stdio.h>
 4:    #include <sys/types.h>
 5:    #include <sys/stat.h>
 6:
 7:    mode_t
 8:    query_umask(void) {
 9:        mode_t old_umask;
10:
11:        umask(old_umask = umask(0));
12:        return old_umask;
13:    }
14:
15:    int
16:    main(int argc,char **argv) {
17:
```

continued from previous page
```
18:       printf("umask = %04o\n",query_umask());
19:       return 0;
20:  }
```
The following session shows the compile and run of the example program:
```
$ make umask
cc -c -D_POSIX_C_SOURCE=199309L -Wall umask.c
cc umask.o -o umask
$ ./umask
umask = 0022
$ umask
0022
$
```
The program is invoked with the command ./umask, and it reports a mask value of 0022. The shell's built-in umask(1) command is then invoked, and its results agree.

The creat(2) Function

A companion function to the open(2) call is the creat(2) function. Its function synopsis is as follows:
```
#include <fcntl.h>
```
```
int creat(const char *path,mode_t mode);
```
This function is equivalent to the following open(2) function call:
```
open(path,O_CREAT|O_TRUNC|O_WRONLY,mode);
```
This means that creat(2) function will

- Create the file if necessary

- Truncate the file to zero bytes of length

- Open it for writing only

The umask(2) setting will be applied to mode to arrive at the final permissions on the regular file created.

Reading and Writing

The UNIX kernel readies a file for I/O by giving you a file descriptor, which is returned by open(2) or creat(2). The file descriptor might represent an I/O device, a socket or, most often, a regular file. The I/O semantics vary somewhat, depending on what it is that your program is interacting with. This will be noted in a few places as you are introduced to the system calls for I/O.

Introducing `read(2)` and `write(2)`

These are perhaps the most basic of all UNIX I/O system calls. Their function synopsis is as follows:

```
#include <sys/types.h>
#include <sys/uio.h>
#include <unistd.h>

ssize_t read(int fd,void *buf,size_t nbytes);

ssize_t write(int fd,const void *buf,size_t nbytes);
```

The `read(2)` and `write(2)` calls take the same arguments, with the exception that the `write(2)` function does not modify the buffer it is supplied with. Each must be supplied with an open file descriptor, which can be a socket.

The `read(2)` Function

The `read(2)` function reads into the buffer `buf[]` to a maximum of `nbytes`. The number of bytes actually read is the return value. If an error occurs, `-1` is returned (with `errno`).

A return value of zero indicates that end-of-file has been reached. There is no error code associated with end-of-file, since this is not an error.

In some read contexts, you may receive fewer bytes than requested by the `nbytes` argument. This can happen when reading from regular files, when the end-of-file is reached while trying to satisfy the count. Otherwise, when reading from a regular file, you are guaranteed that the function will not return until `nbytes` is returned.

In all other read contexts, such as when reading from a socket, the count `nbytes` serves as a maximum number. Any number of bytes from one to `nbytes` may be returned.

> **Tip**
>
> For any slow device, it is possible for `read(2)` to return the error `EINTR` if a signal handler has handled a signal. Simply retry the `read(2)` call when this error is received.
>
> A regular file is not considered a slow device.

The `write(2)` Function

The `write(2)` function writes from the supplied buffer `buf` exactly `nbytes`. It returns the number of bytes actually written. If an error occurs, the value `-1` is returned (with `errno`).

For regular files, `write(2)` should always write the requested number of bytes `nbytes`. In other write contexts, the return value indicates the actual number of bytes written.

Tip

For any slow device, it is possible for write(2) to return the error EINTR if a signal handler has handled a signal. Simply retry the write(2) call when this error is received.

A regular file is not considered a slow device.

Applying UNIX I/O

The program in Listing 4.2 shows a simple I/O example, using the basic system calls. This program opens the file /etc/motd by default and copies its contents to the standard output device (file unit 1). A different pathname can be supplied by specifying it as the first command-line argument.

LISTING 4.2   unixio.c—A Simple UNIX I/O Example Program

```
 1:    /* unixio.c */
 2:
 3:    #include <stdio.h>
 4:    #include <fcntl.h>
 5:    #include <unistd.h>
 6:    #include <errno.h>
 7:    #include <string.h>
 8:    #include <sys/types.h>
 9:    #include <sys/uio.h>
10:
11:    int
12:    main(int argc,char **argv) {
13:        int z;                          /* Return status code */
14:        int n;                          /* # of bytes written */
15:        int fd;                         /* Read file descriptor */
16:        char buf[128];                  /* I/O Buffer */
17:        char *pathname = "/etc/motd";   /* Default file to open */
18:
19:        if ( argc > 1 )
20:            pathname = argv[1];         /* Choose a different file */
21:
22:        fd = open(pathname,O_RDONLY);   /* Open /etc/motd file */
23:
24:        if ( fd == -1 ) {
25:            fprintf(stderr,"%s: opening %s for read\n",
26:                strerror(errno),pathname);
27:            return 1;                   /* Failed */
28:        }
29:
30:        for (;;) {
31:            z = read(fd,buf,sizeof buf);   /* Fill buf with read data */
32:            if ( !z )
33:                break;                  /* End of file */
34:            if ( z == -1 ) {
```

```
35:                    fprintf(stderr,"%s: reading file %s\n",
36:                        strerror(errno),pathname);
37:                    return 2;                    /* Failed */
38:                }
39:
40:            n = write(1,buf,z);                  /* Write out buffer contents */
41:            if ( n == -1 ) {
42:                fprintf(stderr,"%s: writing to stdout\n",strerror(errno));
43:                    return 3;                    /* Failed */
44:            }
45:        }
46:
47:        close(fd);                               /* Close the file */
48:
49:        return 0;
50:    }
```

The basic procedure used in Listing 4.2 is this:

1. The `pathname` variable defaults to the C string `"/etc/motd"` (line 17) or uses the command line argument (lines 19 and 20).

2. The file is opened with a call to open(2) (line 22).

3. If the open(2) call fails, the error is reported (lines 24 to 28).

4. An I/O loop is started in lines 30 to 45.

5. The read(2) call reads as many bytes as it can to fill the buffer buf[]. The maximum number of bytes read is indicated by the argument sizeof buf.

6. If there is no more data to be read, the return value will be zero, and the loop is exited (lines 32 and 33) with the break statement.

7. If a read error occurs, the error is reported (lines 34 to 38).

8. The data read into array buf[] is now written out to standard output (file unit 1 in line 40). Note that the number of bytes being written is z. This is the value returned from step 5.

9. If a write error occurs, the error is reported (lines 41 to 44).

10. When the loop is exited, the close(2) function is called (line 47).

The program in Listing 4.2 is called a simple program because it does not allow for the possibility that the write(2) call may not always write the full amount of data expected if the standard output is not a regular file. Furthermore, it does not allow for the possibility of the error EINTR, which it needs to do if there is any signal catching used in this program.

In a production quality program, the buffer size would be declared a larger size. Generally, a buffer like this should be a minimum of 1024 bytes in length to better match the I/O size that is being used by the operating system.

Seeking Within a File

The last example showed a program that sequentially read through the /etc/motd file, copying it to standard output. Sometimes it is necessary to access portions of a file randomly. Perhaps your file represents a series of a million fixed-length records that must be retrieved at random. UNIX provides this functionality in the form of the lseek(2) function.

Applying lseek(2)

The lseek(2) function is actually a dual-purpose function. It not only allows the program to seek a specified offset within the open file, but the program can also find out what the current offset is, within the specified file. The function synopsis for lseek(2) is as follows:

```
#include <sys/types.h>
#include <unistd.h>

off_t lseek(int fildes, off_t offset, int whence);
```

This function requires a file descriptor in the first argument and then a file **offset** and an integer value named **whence**. The combination of arguments **offset** and **whence** indicates how the **seek** is to be performed within the file.

Upon successful completion of the **seek** operation, the new file offset is returned. If the operation fails, an (off_t)-1 value is returned, with **errno** holding the reason for the error. Note that this function call does not return the error **EINTR**. The error code **ESPIPE** is returned if the file descriptor is for a non-seekable device.

Values for **whence** are provided in Table 4.2. These values are defined in the include file <unistd.h>.

TABLE 4.2   Values for lseek(2) Argument whence

C Macro	Meaning
SEEK_SET	The file offset is set to offset bytes.
SEEK_CUR	The file offset is set to its current location plus offset bytes.
SEEK_END	The file offset is set to the size of the file plus offset bytes.

The value **SEEK_SET** allows you to set an absolute file position, while **SEEK_CUR** lets you adjust your offset relative to your current offset. The **SEEK_END** value is usually used to position at the end of the file but, by applying a negative offset, you can establish some other position.

FIGURE 4.1

lseek(2) changes to a file offset.

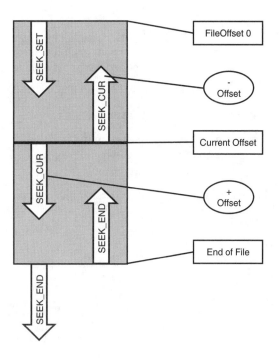

To establish a new file position at the offset of **1024**, you would code

```
off_t new_off;        /* New offset */
int fd;               /* File descriptor */

new_off = lseek(fd,1024,SEEK_SET);
if ( new_off == (off_t)(-1) )
    /* Report error */
```

To find out what your current file offset is, you could use the following form of the lseek(2) call, which does not change your current position:

```
off_t offset;         /* File offset */
int fd;               /* File descriptor */

offset = lseek(fd,0,SEEK_CUR);
```

In this form of the call, you seek **0** bytes from the current position, which changes nothing. However, the lseek(2) function tells you in the return value what the unchanged file offset is.

Truncating Files

You have already seen that the open(2) and creat(2) calls are capable of truncating an existing file. There are times when it is necessary to empty a file of its contents at some later point after the file is open. In other situations, perhaps you simply want to shorten the file because you have compacted your file. To perform these functions, you can call upon the truncate(2) and ftruncate(2) functions.

The `truncate(2)` Function

The `truncate(2)` function does not work with an open file. Instead, it allows you to truncate a file without actually opening it. The function synopsis is as follows:

```
#include <unistd.h>

int truncate(const char *path, off_t length);
```

Quite simply, you supply a pathname and the size in bytes that you want it to be (this is equivalent to specifying the `length` of the offset at which to truncate). The function returns zero if it is successful; otherwise -1 is returned (with `errno`).

To force a file to become an empty file (zero bytes), you would call

```
int z;

z = truncate(pathname,0);
if ( z == -1 )
    /* Report error */
```

Warning
On some UNIX platforms, the error `EINTR` can be returned by `truncate(2)`.

Tip
On some UNIX platforms, the function `truncate(2)` is documented under `truncate(3C)` instead.

The `ftruncate(2)` Function

The `truncate(2)` function performs the function of truncation well, but it proves to be inconvenient at times. If you have written some form of data management library, you may have the file descriptor given to your function as an argument. However, you will not have the pathname necessary for the call to `truncate(2)`. The `ftruncate(2)` function comes to the rescue, since it works with open files:

```
#include <unistd.h>

int ftruncate(int fildes, off_t length);
```

The file that is truncated is specified by the file descriptor `fildes`. Otherwise, the function is identical to the `truncate(2)` function. To force the file open on `fd` to become an empty file, you would code

```
int z;                  /* Return status */
int fd;                 /* Open file descriptor */
```

```
z = ftruncate(fd,0);
if ( z == -1 )
    /* Report Error */
```

When files are written, they are enlarged automatically by the UNIX kernel, as needed. The `truncate` system calls are the only way you can shorten the length of a file.

Sparse Files

The previous sections have focused on reading, writing, and truncating files. Now turn your attention briefly to the physical makeup of UNIX regular files. UNIX regular files have a special quality, which is supported by the kernel, that permits them to be sparsely populated.

A sparse file is a lot like the sparse matrixes that you learned about in school. The following represents a sparse matrix:

```
0 0 0 0 9
0 0 0 7 0
0 0 8 0 0
0 1 0 0 0
3 0 0 0 0
```

You can see that this matrix is made up entirely of zeros, except for the one diagonal. Storing this matrix requires 5 * 5 = 25 cells to store all the values. Yet, it would be wasteful to store this matrix with 25 cells when only 5 of them are non-zero. One form of sparse matrix might be optimized to store only the diagonal values and to supply zeros when requested for any of the non-diagonal cells.

Creating a Sparse File

Sparse files work the same way. It is possible to create a 1GB file with only a few bytes of real data in it. The program in Listing 4.3 illustrates a simple program that does this.

LISTING 4.3 `bigfile.c`—Creating a Sparse File

```
 1:    /* sparse.c */
 2:
 3:    #include <stdio.h>
 4:    #include <fcntl.h>
 5:    #include <unistd.h>
 6:    #include <errno.h>
 7:    #include <string.h>
 8:    #include <sys/types.h>
 9:    #include <sys/uio.h>
10:
11:    int
12:    main(int argc,char **argv) {
13:        int z;                              /* Return status code */
```

continued from previous page

```
14:     off_t o;                            /* Offset */
15:     int fd;                             /* Read file descriptor */
16:
17:     /*
18:      * Create/truncate sparse.dat
19:      */
20:     fd = open("sparse.dat",O_CREAT|O_WRONLY|O_TRUNC,0640);
21:     if ( fd == -1 ) {
22:         fprintf(stderr,"%s: opening sparse.dat for write\n",
23:             strerror(errno));
24:         return 1;                        /* Failed */
25:     }
26:
27:     /*
28:      * Seek to almost the 1GB mark :
29:      */
30:     o = lseek(fd,1023*1024*1024,SEEK_SET); /* Seek to ~1GB */
31:     if ( o == (off_t)(-1) ) {
32:         fprintf(stderr,"%s: lseek(2)\n",strerror(errno));
33:         return 2;
34:     }
35:
36:     /*
37:      * Write a little message :
38:      */
39:     z = write(fd,"END-OF-SPARSE-FILE",18);
40:     if ( z == -1 ) {
41:         fprintf(stderr,"%s: write(2)\n",strerror(errno));
42:         return 2;
43:     }
44:
45:     close(fd);                           /* Close the file */
46:
47:     return 0;
48: }
```

A compile-and-test session for this program is shown next:

```
$ make sparse
cc -c -D_POSIX_C_SOURCE=199309L -Wall sparse.c
cc sparse.o -o sparse
$ ./sparse
$ ls -l sparse.dat
-rw-r----- 1 me   mygrp 1072693266 Apr 17 02:36 sparse.dat
$ od -cx sparse.dat
0000000   \0  \0  \0  \0  \0  \0  \0  \0  \0  \0  \0  \0  \0  \0  \0  \0
        0000    0000    0000    0000    0000    0000    0000    0000
*
7774000000    E   N   D   -   O   F   -   S   A   R   S   E   -   F   I
        4e45    2d44    464f    532d    4150    5352    2d45    4946
7774000020    L   E
        454c
7774000022
$
```

After the program is compiled and run, the ls(1) command lists the file sparse.dat that it creates. Notice its huge size of **1072693266** bytes. You may not even have that much free space left! Yet the file exists.

Next, the od(1) command is used to dump the contents of this file in both hexadecimal and in ASCII where possible (options -cx). This command may run a very long time, since the od(1) command will read almost 1GB of zero bytes before reaching the end of the file.

Looking at the od(1) output, you can see that UNIX has provided zero bytes between the beginning of the file and the point where the seek was done, and it finally found the string "END-OF-SPARSE-FILE" that was written by the program. At the left of the output, where od(1) shows the file offset, you can see that the string was written at a very large file offset.

Now that sparse.dat exists, there is really only a small amount of disk space allocated to this file. There is no need to panic about wasted disk space, because just enough space is allocated to hold the C string that was written. Whenever any program reads other parts of this sparse file, which is largely one big hole, the UNIX kernel simply returns zero bytes.

Warning

It is probably a good idea to delete the sparse.dat file that was created by the example program. Sparse files can provide a real headache for backup programs, because many backup programs simply copy the file in question to the backup medium. If a backup is performed for your sparse.dat file, almost a gigabyte of zeros will be copied to the backup medium. For this reason, smarter backup utility programs know about sparse files and copy only the active information within them.

Sparse files can also be a problem when you copy them. If you attempt to copy your sparse.dat file to another location in your current directory, you may run out of disk space.

Forcing Data to Media

When the UNIX file system objects were reviewed in Chapter 2, it was documented that file systems use block raw devices. This is done so that disk accesses are buffered in the UNIX disk cache for performance reasons. However, a disk cache presents certain dangers for your valuable data.

When a file is opened, written to, and closed to update its contents, changes may still be sitting in disk cache in the kernel's memory for quite some time. If the system suddenly loses power or your UNIX kernel panics for some other reason, those changes may never be written to your disk media. When you examine the file after such a catastrophe, you'll discover that the file's content is not what you had thought it was. There must be a way to force critical data to be written to the intended media immediately.

The `sync(2)` Function

A popular command for those writing a lot of source code under UNIX is the `sync(8)` command (on many UNIX platforms it is `sync(1M)`). After making several changes to shell scripts or to source code, it is nice to be able to say

```
$ sync
```

and know that all your changes are being written to the disk media. After the command finishes, you can rest assured that your work will not be lost if the lights should suddenly go out.

The `sync(8)` command ends up calling the system call `sync(2)`. The function synopsis is as follows:

```
#include <unistd.h>
```

```
void sync(void);
```

As you can see, this function takes no arguments and returns no values. It couldn't be simpler to use.

If you should find that the `sync(8)` command is restricted on the system on which you have an account, you can easily write one of your own. Listing 4.4 shows how simple it is to do so.

LISTING 4.4   `sync.c`—Building Your Own `sync` Command

```
1:   /* sync.c */
2:
3:   #include <unistd.h>
4:
5:   int
6:   main(int argc,char **argv) {
7:
8:       sync();
9:       return 0;
10:  }
```

The following shows the program being compiled and run:

```
$ make sync
cc -c -D_POSIX_C_SOURCE=199309L -Wall sync.c
cc sync.o -o sync
$ ./sync
$
```

If you were running this program on your own computer, then you might have heard some disk activity when the command was invoked. Perhaps you watched the disk activity light instead. In any case, this was the result of all unwritten changes being forced out to the disk media.

The Disadvantages of `sync(2)`

The `sync(8)` command is sometimes restricted in shared UNIX environments to prevent its abuse. For example, an abusive user can issue the following command:

```
$ while true; do sync; sleep 1; done
```

This shell command would be forcing disk writes every second. Of course, this would hurt the performance of the disk cache.

Assume you have an application that updates a custom database, which is stored within a file. At certain points in the update process, you will want to make certain that these changes are forced out to disk. However, to issue a frequent call to `sync(2)` would affect other users too much. The solution is found in the `fsync(2)` function.

The `fsync(2)` Function

This function provides the power of `sync(2)` but limits the scope to one file. See the function synopsis:

```
#include <unistd.h>

int fsync(int fd);
```

This function simply accepts the file descriptor as an argument, which indicates the file for which all cached changes must be written out. Note that if several processes are modifying the same file, all changed data for that file is written out. Changes are not traced back to a particular file descriptor and kept separate.

The `fsync(2)` function returns zero if successful and `-1` if an error occurs. One of the more interesting possible errors is `EIO`, which will tell your application that an I/O error has occurred, while it was forcing the written data out to disk.

Tip

If you need to be certain that all data changes for a file have been successfully written to the disk media, call `fsync(2)` prior to calling `close(2)`. Without a call to `fsync(2)`, the `close(2)` call may succeed, since the changes remain in the disk cache. Later the UNIX kernel may discover that the cached changes cannot be written out due to a media error. By this time, your application not only is unaware of the problem, it also cannot take corrective action.

Calling `fsync(2)` prior to `close(2)` allows your application to decide what to do about media problems.

Scattered Reading and Writing

There are times when the `read(2)` and `write(2)` calls are not convenient. This happens frequently with socket programming, where data is scattered around in different buffers. To address this issue, the UNIX kernel provides scatter read and write functions.

The readv(2) and writev(2) Functions

readv(2) and writev(2) are known as the *scatter read and write* functions. This is because they can read and write a number of scattered I/O buffers. The function synopsis is as follows:

```
#include <sys/types.h>
#include <sys/uio.h>
#include <unistd.h>

ssize_t readv(int fd, const struct iovec *iov, int iovcnt);

ssize_t writev(int fd, const struct iovec *iov, int iovcnt);

struct iovec {
    char    *iov_base;  /* Base address. */
    size_t  iov_len;    /* Length. */
};
```

In addition to the file descriptor, these functions accept two other arguments:

- The I/O vector pointer iov
- The count of I/O vector items iovcnt

The argument iov is actually an array of type **struct iovec**. Each array entry points to one buffer (by iov_base) of a specific size (size iov_len). The count iovcnt indicates how many array elements the function call should use.

The return values are otherwise identical to the **read(2)** and **write(2)** calls. The number of bytes read or written is returned. If an error occurs, -1 is returned (with **errno**).

Listing 4.5 shows a simple example of using writev(2). It simply writes from three separate buffers to the standard output.

LISTING 4.5   writev.c—An Example of a writev(2) Call

```
 1:   /* writev.c */
 2:
 3:   #include <stdio.h>
 4:   #include <fcntl.h>
 5:   #include <unistd.h>
 6:   #include <errno.h>
 7:   #include <string.h>
 8:   #include <sys/types.h>
 9:   #include <sys/uio.h>
10:
11:   int
12:   main(int argc,char **argv) {
13:       int z;                                  /* Return status code */
14:       static char buf1[] = "by writev(2)";/* Middle buffer */
15:       static char buf2[] = ">>>";             /* Last buffer */
16:       static char buf3[] = "<<<";             /* First buffer */
```

```
17:     static char buf4[] = "\n";          /* Newline at end */
18:     struct iovec iov[4];                /* Handles 4 buffers */
19:
20:     iov[0].iov_base = buf3;
21:     iov[0].iov_len = strlen(buf3);
22:     iov[1].iov_base = buf1;
23:     iov[1].iov_len = strlen(buf1);
24:     iov[2].iov_base = buf2;
25:     iov[2].iov_len = strlen(buf2);
26:     iov[3].iov_base = buf4;
27:     iov[3].iov_len = strlen(buf4);
28:
29:     z = writev(1,&iov[0],4);            /* scatter write 4 buffers */
30:     if ( z == -1 )
31:         abort();                        /* Failed */
32:
33:     return 0;
34: }
```

The session for compiling and running this program is shown next:

```
$ make writev
cc -c -D_POSIX_C_SOURCE=199309L -Wall writev.c
cc writev.o -o writev
$ ./writev
<<<by writev(2)>>>
$
```

When the program ./writev is invoked, the standard output shows the result of four buffers being combined, including the trailing '\n' character that was written.

Determining Your tty Name

If your application must request input from the terminal, you can always open the special pathname "/dev/tty". This special pathname causes the UNIX kernel to open the real pathname necessary to gain access to the controlling terminal. This allows your application to request a password from the user, for example.

There are other times when you need to know if a particular file descriptor is a tty device or not. This frequently occurs when dealing with standard input, which is provided by the shell. How does the application tell when the standard input is redirected to take data from a file, or when the data is coming from a terminal? Perhaps the user prompt is to be suppressed if the input is coming from a file. The ttyname(3) and isatty(3) functions solve these thorny problems.

```
#include <unistd.h>

char * ttyname(int fd);

int isatty(int fd);
```

The `ttyname(3)` function accepts an open file descriptor as its only input argument. It returns a string pointer for the `tty` device if `isatty(3)` returns `true`. Otherwise, `ttyname(3)` will return a null pointer. The `errno` value is not affected.

Function `isatty(3)` accepts an open file descriptor as its only input argument. It returns `true` if the file descriptor represents a terminal and `false` when it is not a `tty`.

Listing 4.6 shows a simple program putting these functions to work on standard input, output, and error.

LISTING 4.6   `tty.c`—A Test Program for `ttyname(3)` and `isatty(3)`

```
 1:    /* tty.c */
 2:
 3:    #include <stdio.h>
 4:    #include <unistd.h>
 5:
 6:    void
 7:    tty_info(int fd) {
 8:        int b = isatty(fd);                    /* Test if a tty */
 9:
10:        printf("fd=%d %s a tty\n",fd,b?"is":"isn't");
11:        if ( b )
12:            printf("tty name is '%s'\n",ttyname(fd));
13:    }
14:
15:    int
16:    main(int argc,char **argv) {
17:
18:        tty_info(0);                           /* Query standard input */
19:        tty_info(1);                           /* Query standard output */
20:        tty_info(2);                           /* Query standard error */
21:        return 0;
22:    }
```

The program in Listing 4.6 tests the status of each of the shell-provided file descriptors, standard input, output, and error. The following shows a compile-and-execute session:

```
$ make tty
cc -c -D_POSIX_C_SOURCE=199309L -Wall tty.c
cc tty.o -o tty
$ ./tty
fd=0 is a tty
tty name is '/dev/ttyp2'
fd=1 is a tty
tty name is '/dev/ttyp2'
fd=2 is a tty
tty name is '/dev/ttyp2'
$ ./tty 2>/dev/null </dev/null
fd=0 isn't a tty
fd=1 is a tty
tty name is '/dev/ttyp2'
fd=2 isn't a tty
$
```

The first time `./tty` is invoked, all three file descriptors are identified as a `tty` device. The second time the program is invoked, the standard input and standard error are redirected to `/dev/null`. The program correctly identifies that file descriptors `0` (standard input) and `2` (standard error) are not terminal devices.

When running this program with standard output redirected, just keep in mind that standard output is where the program output is going.

Summary

This chapter presented an overview of the UNIX philosophy of working with file I/O. You saw how the `umask(2)` function controls how permissions are given out when new file system objects are created. The chapter also covered various aspects of performing reading, writing, seeking, truncating, and working with sparse files. UNIX truly does provide the programmer a rich environment in which to write applications.

The next chapter is going to extend this programming knowledge further. Building databases and updating files are almost trivial tasks for a system that has only one user. However, on the multiuser operating system that UNIX is, you need to be concerned about when and where certain update events occur in files being updated by more than one process. File locking is the topic of the next chapter.

CHAPTER 5

FILE LOCKING

*I*f you were in the business of selling a piano on consignment, then you would only make a profit if you could sell the piano for more than the owner required for it. However, if the owner kept raising the price of his piano every time you had a buyer for it, then you'd soon have to give up selling it or lose money on the sale.

Working with data records within a file of a multi-processing system can present the same challenge. If one process must update records while another process is doing the same, then some form of coordination is required to prevent chaos. One UNIX solution to this problem is the file locking facility.

In this chapter, you will learn about

- Lock files

- Advisory locking

- Applying region locks

- Mandatory locking

Understanding Lock Types

There are two basic forms of file locking. They are

- Lock files

- Locked regions

The first form requires that a process create and open a *lock file* before it writes to the protected data file. If a process fails to create the lock file, then it sleeps for a while and tries again.

For example, if the data file `database.dat` is the data file, then the lock file might be named `database.lck`. The contents of the lock file are not important to the procedure, and it may even be empty. When the updating process has finished with its update of `database.dat`, then the lock file `database.lck` is released. This method works only when all processes cooperate and obey this procedure.

The UNIX kernel also will permit a process to lock regions of a data file. A region consists of one or more bytes at a specified starting offset. The offset can extend beyond the end of the current file size. In this way, all processes agree to tell the kernel which regions of the file they are about to update. If a requested lock region is in conflict with presently granted locks on that file, the requesting process is put to sleep until the conflict is removed. When all processes obey this procedure, the integrity of the file is preserved. Figure 5.1 shows four processes that want to update one data file concurrently.

FIGURE 5.1

Three locked file regions and one pending request to lock a file region.

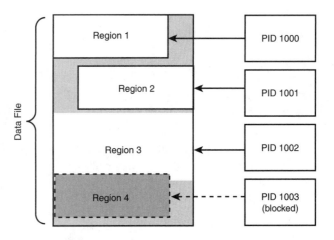

Process IDs 1000, 1001, and 1002 in Figure 5.1 have their regions locked within the data file. The UNIX kernel grants these locks because they do not overlap. This allows these three processes to update the same file concurrently. Notice that process ID 1003 has requested a lock for a region that conflicts with a presently locked Region 3, owned by process ID 1002. Consequently, process 1003 sleeps until Region 3 becomes unlocked.

File locking under UNIX occurs under one of two lock enforcement models:

Advisory locking—No enforcement
Mandatory locking—Enforced locking

The lock file and lock region methods just discussed require process cooperation to maintain the integrity of the data file. Cooperative locking methods are known as *advisory locking*. The UNIX kernel cannot enforce such cooperative methods. Consequently, when advisory locking methods are employed, processes that disobey the locking convention can corrupt the data file.

Many UNIX kernels also support *mandatory locking* of files. When a process attempts to write to a region of a file that has enforced locking enabled, all other processes are prevented from interfering. Similarly, the writing process is blocked from executing until its conflicts with other processes have vanished.

The Lock File Technique

The lock file technique is a coarse-grained locking technique, since it implies that the entire file is locked. The technique is simple, however:

1. Attempt to create and open the lock file.

2. If step 1 fails, sleep for a while and repeat step 1.

3. If step 1 succeeds, then you have successfully locked the resource.

The success of this method depends on the fact that the creation and opening of the lock file must be atomic. In other words, they must either succeed completely or fail completely.

This is easily accomplished with the UNIX open(2) call, when the options O_CREAT|O_EXCL are used together:

```
fd = open("file.lck",O_WRONLY|O_CREAT|O_EXCL,mode);
```

The O_CREAT flag tells open(2) to create the file if it does not exist. However, the flag O_EXCL tells open(2) to return an error if the file already exists when the flag O_CREAT has also been supplied. This causes the open(2) call to succeed only if the file did not already exist and it was possible to create the file.

Listing 5.1 shows how locking can be performed using a lock file.

LISTING 5.1   lockfile.c—Using a Lock File to Promote Safe Updates

```
 1:   /* lockfile.c */
 2:
 3:   #include <stdio.h>
 4:   #include <unistd.h>
 5:   #include <string.h>
 6:   #include <fcntl.h>
 7:   #include <errno.h>
 8:
 9:   /*
10:    * Lock by creating a lock file :
11:    */
12:   static void
13:   Lock(void) {
14:       int fd = -1;                 /* Lock file descriptor */
15:
16:       do {
17:           fd = open("file.lck",O_WRONLY|O_CREAT|O_EXCL,0666);
18:           if ( fd == -1 ) {
19:               if ( errno == EEXIST ) {
20:                   sleep(1);        /* Nap for a bit.. */
```

continued from previous page

```
21:                      } else {
22:                          fprintf(stderr,"%s: Creating lock file.lck\n",
23:                              strerror(errno));
24:                          abort();          /* Failed */
25:                      }
26:                  }
27:          } while ( fd == -1 );
28:
29:          close(fd);                        /* No longer need file open */
30:  }
31:
32:  /*
33:   * Unlock by releasing the lock file :
34:   */
35:  static void
36:  Unlock(void) {
37:
38:          unlink("file.lck");               /* Release the lock file */
39:  }
40:
41:  int
42:  main(int argc,char **argv) {
43:          FILE *f = NULL;
44:          int i;
45:          int ch;
46:          int lck = 1;
47:
48:          /*
49:           * If command line argument 1 is nolock or NOLOCK,
50:           * this program runs without using the Lock() and
51:           * Unlock() functions :
52:           */
53:          if ( argc >= 2 && !strcasecmp(argv[1],"NOLOCK") )
54:              lck = 0;                       /* No locking */
55:
56:          printf("Process ID %ld started with %s\n",
57:              (long)getpid(),
58:              lck ? "locking" : "no locking");
59:
60:          /*
61:           * Now create some rows of data in file.dat :
62:           */
63:          for ( i=0; i<1000; ++i ) {
64:              if ( lck )                     /* Using locks? */
65:                  Lock();                    /* Yes, get lock */
66:
67:              /*
68:               * Here we just update file.dat with new records. If
69:               * no locking is used while multiple processes do this,
70:               * some records will usually be lost. However, when
71:               * locking is used, no records are lost.
72:               *
73:               * Here we just open the file if it exists, otherwise
```

```
74:             * the file is opened for write.
75:             */
76:            f = fopen("file.dat","r+");      /* Open existing file */
77:
78:            if ( !f && errno == ENOENT )
79:                f = fopen("file.dat","w");   /* Create file */
80:
81:            if ( !f ) {
82:                fprintf(stderr,"%s: opening file.dat for r/w\n",
83:                    strerror(errno));
84:                if ( lck )
85:                    Unlock();                /* Unlock */
86:                return 1;                    /* Failed */
87:            }
88:
89:            /*
90:             * Seek to the end of the file, and add a record :
91:             */
92:            fseek(f,0,SEEK_END);             /* Seek to end of file */
93:
94:            fprintf(f,"%05ld i=%06d ",(long)getpid(),i);
95:            for ( ch=' '; ch<='z'; ++ch )
96:                fputc(ch,f);        /* A bunch of data to waste time */
97:            fputc('\n',f);
98:
99:            fclose(f);
100:
101:            if ( lck )                       /* Using locks? */
102:                Unlock();                    /* Yes, unlock */
103:        }
104:
105:        /*
106:         * Announce our completion :
107:         */
108:        printf("Process ID %ld completed.\n",(long)getpid());
109:        return 0;
110: }
```

The program in Listing 5.1 loops 1000 times to append records to the file `file.dat`. The function `Lock()` calls on `open(2)` with the `O_CREAT|O_EXCL` flags in order to exclusively open and create the file. If the create call fails, the function invokes `sleep(3)` for one second and then tries again.

Notice that `Lock()` closes the lock file after it successfully opens and creates it. The opening of the file is required only to prove that the file was created successfully by your current process and not some other. This is how the `Lock()` function determines that it has "acquired" the lock.

The procedure for unlocking the lock file is as simple as releasing the lock file (line 38 in function `Unlock()`). The `unlink(2)` function is discussed in Chapter 6, "Managing Files and Their Properties."

Compiling the program in Listing 5.1 is as follows:

```
$ make lockfile
cc -c -D_POSIX_C_SOURCE=199309L -Wall lockfile.c
cc lockfile.o -o lockfile
$
```

Next, make sure that the file `file.dat` does not exist:

```
$ rm file.dat
rm: file.dat: No such file or directory
$
```

This removal of `file.dat` is especially important if you run the test multiple times. If you prefer, you can do the following instead:

```
$ make cleanfiles
rm -f file.dat file.lck
$
```

The `make cleanfiles` command removes both the data file and the lock file if it should exist.

Next, using the compiled executable `lockfile`, run a test using three processes with no locking. This is done by providing the argument `NOLOCK` on the command line as follows:

```
$ ./lockfile NOLOCK & ./lockfile NOLOCK & ./lockfile NOLOCK &
$ Process ID 83554 started with no locking
Process ID 83556 started with no locking
Process ID 83555 started with no locking
Process ID 83556 completed.
Process ID 83555 completed.
Process ID 83554 completed.

[1] 83554 Exit 0          ./lockfile NOLOCK
[2] 83555 Exit 0          ./lockfile NOLOCK
[3] 83556 Exit 0          ./lockfile NOLOCK
$
```

It is very important that you start these processes as shown (the `&` character causes each of the commands to run in the background). If there is too much time delay between starting each of these processes, you will not see the expected problem. If this should still be a problem because of the speed of your system, change the number `1000` in line 63 of Listing 5.1 to something much larger.

In the session shown above, the three processes ran without using any locking and finished successfully. Now check the file `file.dat`, which was updated by all three:

```
$ wc -l file.dat
    2999 file.dat
$
```

The `wc(1)` command shown counted only 2999 lines, when there should have been 3000 (three times 1000 for each process). Remove `file.dat` and repeat the test. You may occasionally find that the count will change. You might get 2998, instead. This shows that you are not getting the full count.

Now repeat the test, but this time use the locking (which is the default for this program):

```
$ rm file.dat
$ ./lockfile & ./lockfile & ./lockfile &
$ Process ID 83606 started with locking
Process ID 83607 started with locking
Process ID 83608 started with locking
Process ID 83606 completed.
Process ID 83608 completed.
Process ID 83607 completed.

[1]  83606 Exit 0              ./lockfile
[2]  83607 Exit 0              ./lockfile
[3]  83608 Exit 0              ./lockfile
$ wc -l file.dat
    3000 file.dat
$
```

In this test, you can see that the final resulting line count in `file.dat` is 3000 lines, which is correct. The locking file `file.lck` prevented lost data by ensuring that only one process at a time was updating the file `file.dat`.

Limitations of the Lock File

One of the things that you probably noticed about running the program `lockfile` from Listing 5.1 was that when locks were enabled, the test took much longer to run. The reason for this has to do with the need for the `Lock()` function in line 20 to call upon `sleep(3)` when it was unsuccessful creating the lock file. While you could omit the `sleep(3)` function call, this would be unwelcome on a multiuser system.

Other functions could be used to reduce the `sleep(3)` time to less than one second, but the real problem lies in the fact that this is a polling method.

Another limitation of the lock file method is that it is reliable only on a local file system. If your lock file is created on an NFS file system, NFS cannot guarantee that your `open(2)` flags `O_CREAT|O_EXCL` will be respected (the operation may not be atomic). The operation must be atomic to be a reliable lock indicator.

Additionally, the lock file technique can only operate at a file level. Successful locking with a lock file implies that the process has access to update the entire data file. All other processes must wait, even if they want to update different parts of the same file.

Summarized, some lock file disadvantages are

- There is high latency time between failed attempts when used with `sleep(3)`.
- It is unreliable when used on NFS file systems.
- It is a coarse-grained lock (this implies that a process has locked the entire data file).

These are reasons why you should consider other file locking methods.

Using an Advisory Lock on the Entire File

An improvement over the file locking method was the creation of a UNIX kernel service that would allow a process to lock or unlock an entire file. Additionally, it was desirable to indicate when a file was being read or written. When a file is locked for reading, other processes can safely read the file concurrently. However, while the file remains read-locked, write-lock requests are blocked to ensure the safety of the data being read. Once all read locks are released, a write lock can be established on the file.

This kernel service provides the following benefits to the programmer:

- Higher performance, since `sleep(3)` is not called
- Finer lock granularity: read and write locks

The performance of the application is greatly improved because the kernel is able to resume process execution at the earliest opportunity, once the lock can be granted. This is in contrast to application calls to the `sleep(3)` function.

Granularity is finer because applications can acquire read locks or write locks. Read locks (also known as *shared locks*) allow multiple processes to read the same data regions concurrently. Write locks (also known as *exclusive locks*) are exclusive to any read locks and other write locks. This capability is in contrast to one file lock, allowing only one process to access the file at once.

Locking with `flock(2)`

The file locking service is provided by the `flock(2)` function on a BSD platform. This function provides the programmer with the following file locking capabilities:

Shared locks—for reading
Exclusive locks—for writing

Shared locks allow one or more concurrent reading processes to share access to the file. However, when an exclusive lock is obtained on the file, there can be no shared locks. Only one process is permitted to obtain an exclusive lock on the file. Consequently, exclusive locks are used when updates to the file are taking place.

The function synopsis for the `flock(2)` function is as follows:

```
#include <sys/file.h>

int flock(int fd, int operation);

#define LOCK_SH    0x01    /* shared file lock */
#define LOCK_EX    0x02    /* exclusive file lock */
#define LOCK_NB    0x04    /* don't block when locking */
#define LOCK_UN    0x08    /* unlock file */
```

The function `flock(2)` requires an open file descriptor `fd`. This open file descriptor must be open for read access to gain shared locks with `LOCK_SH`. The file descriptor must have write access in order to apply exclusive locks with `LOCK_EX`.

A shared lock is requested by using the operation `LOCK_SH` in the call. Other processes can request shared locks and succeed with existing shared locks. However, once a process establishes an exclusive lock (`LOCK_EX`), no shared lock will succeed.

When `LOCK_NB` is *not* used, a request that cannot be granted immediately causes the process to be put to sleep. When a shared lock is attempted when an exclusive lock is established, the calling process is put to sleep until the exclusive lock is released. Similarly, if a process has a shared lock and attempts to upgrade it to an exclusive lock, the calling process will sleep until the conflicting shared locks are released.

When `LOCK_NB` is used, the lock request immediately fails by returning -1, if the request cannot be granted. The value `EWOULDBLOCK` is returned in `errno`. This allows a process to attempt a lock without its execution being suspended if the request cannot be granted.

Note

Some platforms will provide a compatibility function. Sun's Solaris 8 `flock(3UCB)` documentation states that the "compatibility version of `flock()` has been implemented on top of `fcntl(2)` locking. It does not provide complete binary compatibility."

The `flock(2)` function has a few advantages over the lock file technique.

- No additional lock file is involved.
- `sleep(3)` is not called for retry attempts, providing improved performance.
- Finer-grained locking allows locks to be shared or exclusive.
- Allows locks to be held on NFS mounted file systems.

NFS can be configured to support a lock manager (`rpc.lockd(8)` under FreeBSD), to allow file locking on remote file systems. This overcomes the lock file limitation on remote file systems, where open and create are not atomic operations.

Note

According to simple tests performed under FreeBSD by the author, the `flock(2)` function does not appear to return the `EINTR` error after a signal handler return. However, the FreeBSD documentation states that "processes blocked awaiting a lock may be awakened by signals." For this reason, you might want to allow for the `EINTR` signal in your code.

Warning

Locks created by `flock(2)` are managed by file—not by file descriptors. Additional file descriptors obtained by `dup(2)` and `dup2(2)` manage the same locks.

The parent process that has `fork(2)` calls can lose locks on a file if its child process unlocks the file when it uses the open file descriptors obtained from the parent.

Record Locking

The BSD `flock(2)` approach provides improved performance over the lock file but still suffers from the fact that it locks the entire file.

Even better performance can be obtained when the regions of the file are locked instead of the entire file. System V provided the `lockf(2)` function to accomplish this. Later, POSIX defined yet another application interface using the `fcntl(2)` function.

To visualize locked regions, review Figure 5.1, in which three processes successfully obtained region locks. The execution of the fourth process was suspended because its request to lock a region overlapped with another granted lock.

Locking with `lockf(2)`

The `lockf(2)` function is not documented under FreeBSD, presumably because it was a System V development, which was superceded by the POSIX `fcntl(2)` interface. For those interested in porting existing applications that call it, the `lockf(2)` function will be presented here:

```
#include <sys/lockf.h>     /* AIX */
#include <unistd.h>

int lockf(int fd,int request,off_t size);

#define F_ULOCK   0      /* unlock a region */
#define F_LOCK    1      /* lock a region */
#define F_TLOCK   2      /* test and lock a region */
#define F_TEST    3      /* test region for lock */
```

The `lockf(2)` function uses the current offset in the file open on `fd`. The request to lock a region of the file starts at this implied offset and includes `size` bytes. If `size` is negative, the region works backward from the current offset.

Regions are locked when `request` is `F_LOCK` and unlocked when `request` is `F_ULOCK`. The operation `F_TEST` returns zero if the specified region is not locked. Otherwise, `-1` and `errno=EACCES` are returned instead.

Note

EACCES—Permission Denied. This error is returned when the permissions on an object prevent the access that is requested. In the context of calls like lockf(2), it simply means that the specified region is already locked and the request cannot be granted.

Note that the macro name EACCES is frequently misspelled: there is only one S.

The lockf(2) function requires that the file descriptor **fd** must be open for write (O_WRONLY) or for read/write (O_RDWR). A file that is open only for reading cannot obtain a locked region with lockf(2).

Note

HP-UX notes in lockf(2) that "If the calling process is a member of a group that has the PRIV_LOCKRDONLY privilege (see getprivgrp(2)), it can also use lockf(2) to lock files opened with read-only permission (O_RDONLY)."

Warning

All locks that a process owns for a given file are released when *any one* of the file descriptors associated with that file is closed with close(2). This is true even when the process may still have other dup(2) file descriptors open for the same file.

Process termination and calls to execve(2) with the close-on-exec flag set have the same effect.

When a process provides multiple lock requests for overlapping regions that are already locked, the lock regions are merged. Figure 5.2 shows two overlapping regions that merge into one larger locked region for the calling process.

FIGURE 5.2

Two overlapping lock regions merge into one.

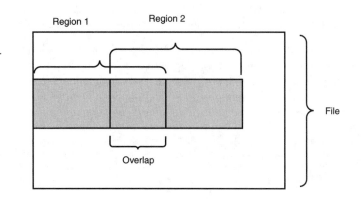

It is possible to arbitrarily unlock regions within a larger locked region. For example, the over-lapping area shown in Figure 5.2 can be subsequently unlocked if the calling application issues the request to do so.

As noted in the earlier Warning, any call to close(2) by the current process releases all of its presently held locks. There are no separately managed lock regions by file descriptor. All lock regions are managed strictly on a file basis for each process. This can sometimes present a challenge to software design.

Note

EDEADLK—Resource Deadlock Avoided. This error can be returned by lockf(2) to indicate that the operation being attempted would have been blocked indefinitely if an error had not been returned instead. This frequently occurs when two processes are locking overlapping sets of resources and each is waiting for the other to give way.

Avoiding Deadlock

Whenever the error EDEADLK is returned, your application should release all of the locks it has acquired so far and try again. Eventually your process or the other process will then acquire all of the locks needed.

The best avoidance of deadlocks is accomplished if all processes attempt to lock records in the same sequence. For example, you might have all applications lock lowest offset records first. If multiple files are involved, you might also lock the files with the lowest i-node numbers first (see Chapter 6).

Advisory Locking

Unless you take steps to enable *mandatory locking*, the lockf(2) function provides *advisory locking* only. Advisory locking works when all processes accessing the same file agree to use lockf(2) voluntarily when accessing the file. Any process that chooses to ignore this convention can still do as it pleases without regard to the locks in place.

With mandatory locking enabled, the UNIX kernel enforces locking on the file. With locking enforced, reads and writes that overlap with a locked region put the calling process to sleep until the lock is released. Enabling mandatory locking is discussed in the section "Mandatory Locking," later in this chapter.

Note

HP-UX documentation states that some system functions like execve(2) are not subject to enforcement of mandatory locks. See lockf(2).

POSIX Locking with `fcntl(2)`

The POSIX method for locking files uses the `fcntl(2)` application interface. The function synopsis for `fcntl(2)` as it applies to file locking is as follows:

```
#include <fcntl.h>

int fcntl(int fd, int cmd, struct flock *lck);
```

cmd:

F_GETLK, F_SETLK, or F_SETLKW

```
struct flock {
    off_t   l_start;   /* starting offset */
    off_t   l_len;     /* len = 0 means until end of file */
    pid_t   l_pid;     /* lock owner (F_GETLK only) */
    short   l_type;    /* F_RDLCK, F_WRLCK or F_UNLCK */
    short   l_whence;  /* SEEK_SET, SEEK_CUR or SEEK_END */
};
```

The `fcntl(2)` interface permits two different locks to be applied when the `cmd` argument is `F_SETLK` or `F_SETLKW`:

Shared locks—`F_RDLCK`

Write locks—`F_WRLCK`

The argument `lck` points to the structure `flock` where the structure member `l_type` is set to `F_RDLCK` or `F_WRLCK`. When a region of the file needs to be unlocked, the member `l_type` is set to `F_UNLCK` instead.

The `cmd` values `F_SETLK` and `F_SETLKW` differ as follows:

- When `F_SETLK` is used, the lock operation is attempted as described by the supplied structure `flock`, which is pointed to by the argument `lck`. If the operation cannot succeed because of another process's locks, an error return value of -1 is returned and `errno=EAGAIN`.

- The operation for `F_SETLKW` is the same as `F_SETLK`, except that the operation will block until the operation can succeed.

Initializing `struct flock`

The `l_start` member of the `flock` structure indicates the starting file offset of the region involved. Member `l_len` indicates in bytes how long the file region is. A value of zero for `l_len` indicates that the entire file should be locked.

The structure member `l_pid` is used only by the `fcntl(2)` command `F_GETLK`. This value is returned to the caller and will be discussed later.

The structure member `l_type` indicates what type of lock is being applied. The values possible here are `F_RDLCK` for shared locks, `F_WRLCK` to establish a write (exclusive) lock, or `F_UNLCK` to unlock the specified region.

The value of `l_whence` indicates how the offset in `l_start` should be interpreted. The values possible are `SEEK_SET`, `SEEK_CUR`, and `SEEK_END`. This follows the convention used by `lseek(2)`.

Locking a Region

The following code segment shows how a region of an open file descriptor `fd` would be locked:

```
int fd;                     /* Open file descriptor */
struct flock lck;           /* Lock structure */

lck.l_start = 0;            /* Start at beginning of file */
lck.l_len = 0;              /* Lock entire file */
lck.l_type = F_RDLCK;       /* Shared lock */
lck.l_whence = SEEK_SET;    /* Absolute offset */

if ( fcntl(fd,F_SETLKW,&lck) == -1 ) {
    /* Error handling */
```

This example locks the entire file with a shared (read) lock on the file descriptor `fd`. Since `F_SETLKW` was used, this function call will block until it is successful.

Warning

The `fcntl(2)` function will return the error `EINTR` when command `F_SETLKW` is used and the process has finished handling a signal.

When `fcntl(2)` is called with command `F_SETLK` instead of `F_SETLKW`, a return value of -1 is provided with `errno=EAGAIN` if the operation cannot immediately succeed. This prevents the process from blocking in the function call.

Note

`EAGAIN`—`Resource Temporarily Unavailable`   In the context of the `fcntl(2)` function call using `F_SETLK`, it means that some other lock currently conflicts with the request. However, retrying the operation later may yield success.

Unlocking a Region

Unlocking a region is almost identical to the lock procedure:

```
int fd;                          /* Open file descriptor */
struct flock lck;                /* Lock structure */

lck.l_start = 0;                 /* Start at beginning of file */
lck.l_len = 0;                   /* Lock entire file */
lck.l_type = F_UNLCK;            /* unlock */
lck.l_whence = SEEK_SET;         /* Absolute offset */

if ( fcntl(fd,F_SETLKW,&lck) == -1 ) {
    /* Error handling */
```

The only difference in the code shown is the line:

```
lck.l_type = F_UNLCK;            /* Shared lock */
```

The example code shown will undo the shared lock established in the previous section.

Obtaining Lock Information

The POSIX fcntl(2) lock operations permit the program to query the given file for locks using the command F_GETLK. The following shows an example:

```
int fd;                          /* Open file descriptor */
struct flock lck;                /* Lock structure */

lck.l_start = 0;                 /* Start at beginning of file */
lck.l_len = 0;                   /* Lock entire file */
lck.l_type = F_RDLCK;            /* Shared lock */
lck.l_whence = SEEK_SET;         /* Absolute offset */

if ( fcntl(fd,F_GETLK,&lck) == -1 ) {
    /* Error handling */
} else if ( lck.l_type == F_UNLCK ) {
    /* Operation F_RDLCK would have succeeded */
} else {
    printf("PID %ld is preventing F_RDLCK\n",(long)lck.l_pid);
}
```

The command F_GETLK indicates that the operation would have been successful by leaving the structure lck intact, with the exception that lck.l_type is set to F_UNLCK. However, if the request would have failed, the structure member lck.l_pid is set to the process ID of the process holding the first conflicting lock (there may be more than one conflict).

Warning

All locks that a process owns for a given file are released when *any one* of the file descriptors associated with that file is closed with close(2). This is true even when the process may still have other dup(2) file descriptors open for the same file.

Process termination and calls to execve(2) with the close-on-exec flag set have the same effect.

Note that the POSIX implementation of record locking using `fcntl(2)` suffers from the same limitations noted in the discussion of `lockf(2)`.

Mandatory Locking

The discussions so far have covered only advisory locking. As long as all processes cooperate and use the locking conventions in agreement, the integrity of the file is maintained. However, if one or more processes do not obey the locking convention established, then updates to the file can result in file corruption and data loss.

To enable mandatory locking on a file, the `setgid` bit is established for the file without the execution permission being given. More precisely, permission bit `S_ISGID` must be enabled, and `S_IXGRP` must be reset (on some systems, the macro `S_ENFMT` can be used).

Note

The functions `read(2)`, `write(2)`, `readv(2)`, `writev(2)`, `open(2)`, `creat(2)`, `mmap(2)`, `truncate(2)`, and `ftruncate(2)` are among the functions affected by mandatory locking.

Note that `truncate(2)` and `ftruncate(2)` are considered to be write actions for locking purposes.

All lock requests are still performed with the `fcntl(2)` function, as they were for advisory locks. However, with mandatory locking enabled, all read/write I/O calls will be affected as follows:

- Any write call will be blocked if another process has a conflicting region locked with a shared or exclusive lock.

- Any read attempt will be blocked if another process has a conflicting region locked with an exclusive lock.

This form of locking imposes a performance penalty, because every read and write on the file must go through lock tests within the UNIX kernel. Additionally, mandatory locking is not supported on all UNIX platforms. Mandatory locking was not part of the POSIX.1 standard, so some vendors have chosen not to support it.

Note

SGI IRIX 6.5, HPUX 10 and 11, UnixWare 7, Solaris 8, AIX 4.3, and Linux 2.1.x and later support mandatory file locking.

BSD derivatives, including FreeBSD, do not appear to support mandatory locking.

To see if your platform supports mandatory locking, look at `chmod(2)` and `stat(2)`. Most platforms that support it will define the macro `S_ENFMT`. Alternatively, look for a discussion of enforced or mandatory file locking.

Mandatory locking provides the following benefits:

- All processes are forced to synchronize their access to the file, whether they explicitly lock regions or not.

- The application does not have to issue lock and unlock requests for simple updates.

Mandatory locking suffers from the following disadvantages:

- Additional UNIX kernel overhead is required to check locks for every read and write system call on the file.

- A malicious process can hold an exclusive lock on the file indefinitely, preventing any reads or writes to the file.

- A malicious process can hold a shared lock on a mandatory lock to deny any process to write to the file.

- Mandatory locks may not be supported on NFS mounted file systems.

- Mandatory locks are not supported on all UNIX platforms.

Lower efficiency and potential lack of portability are the most serious disadvantages that you need to consider.

Note

If the file being opened with open(2) has outstanding read or write mandatory locks, and the flag O_TRUNC or O_CREAT has been supplied, the call will fail with the error EAGAIN on many UNIX platforms.

Enabling Mandatory Locking

The following example shows how you can enable mandatory locking for a file named file.dat:

```
$ ls -l file.dat
-rw-rw----  1 me    mygrp  596 Apr 24 16:55 file.dat
$ chmod g+s,g-x file.dat
$ ls -l file.dat
-rw-rwS---  1 me    mygrp  596 Apr 24 16:55 file.dat
$
```

Notice the large S in the group permissions shown for file.dat. This indicates that mandatory locking is in effect for this file.

Summary

This chapter covered the different forms of locking, from the primitive file-based locks to the more advanced region locks. The next chapter will look at the basic UNIX functions that allow your programs to manage files and to obtain property information about them.

CHAPTER 6

MANAGING FILES AND THEIR PROPERTIES

When you first started using UNIX, the first interaction you had with the system was through the shell. With the shell's help you listed, copied, linked, moved, and even removed files. All of these routine jobs were accomplished with the shell.

The purpose of this chapter is to introduce you to the C library functions that permit you to delete, link, and move files. Additionally, the very important stat(2) and fstat(2) functions that give you information about file system objects will be covered. With the exception of directories, this chapter will enable you to manage files from your C program without any help from the shell.

Removing Files

You delete files under UNIX using the unlink(2) system call. The function synopsis for it is as follows:

```
#include <unistd.h>

int unlink(const char *pathname);
```

A UNIX file can have more than one name linked to a copy of the file. When the last link is removed, the file itself is deleted and the disk space is returned to the file system for re-use.

The function returns -1 if it fails and leaves the error code in errno. Upon a successful return, the value 0 is returned.

The following example code shows how the pathname /tmp/12345.tmp is deleted from a C program:

```
if ( unlink("/tmp/12345.tmp") == -1 ) {
    fprintf(stderr,"%s: removing /tmp/12345.tmp\n",strerror(errno));
    abort();
}
```

All links to the same file must be released this way before the disk space is returned to the file system.

Warning

The unlink(2) call can take a long time to delete a large file. Time is required to update many internal file system blocks and pointers. Consequently, on some UNIX platforms the unlink(2) call can return the error EINTR (SGI IRIX 6.5 for example).

Note

Note that if any links remain for the file, the file's stat(2) value st_ctime (create time) is updated. The stat(2) values st_ctime and st_mtime (time last modified) are updated for the directory containing the link that was removed.

In addition to the unlink(2) function, the programmer has the remove(3) function, which was formalized by the ISO 9899: 1990 ("ISO C") standard. Its function synopsis is as follows:

```
#include <stdio.h>

int remove(const char *path);
```

The remove(3) function differs from unlink(2) in that it is able to remove a file or an empty directory. remove(3) calls upon unlink(2) or rmdir(2) as appropriate. When argument path is a directory, the function rmdir(2) is called. Otherwise, unlink(2) is called. rmdir(2) is described in Chapter 7, "Directory Management."

When remove(3) is successful, the value 0 is returned. Otherwise -1 is returned and the error code is left in global variable errno. For a list of error codes possible, consult the functions unlink(2) and rmdir(2).

Note

While remove(3) is able to remove a directory, it does require that it be empty. This restriction is due to limitation of rmdir(2).

Linking Files

This is accomplished by the link(2) system call:

```
#include <unistd.h>

int link(const char *oldpath, const char *newpath);
```

The function returns -1 if it fails and leaves the error code in errno. Upon a successful return, the value 0 is returned.

The following example shows how the function can be used to link the filename `a.out` to
`my_app`:

```
if ( link("a.out","my_app") == -1 ) {
    fprintf(stderr,"%s: link(2)\n",strerror(errno));
    abort();
}
```

Warning

Some UNIX platforms allow `link(2)` to return the error `EINTR` (SGI IRIX 6.5 for example).

Note

The `st_ctime` (create time) value of the file is updated upon successful completion of a `link(2)`
call. The values `st_ctime` and `st_mtime` (time of last modification) of the directory containing the
new link are updated. See the section "The `stat(2)` Function," later in this chapter.

Moving Files

The `mv(1)` command uses the `link(2)` and `unlink(2)` calls in order to move a file. However,
if the file is moved to another file system, the `mv(1)` command must copy it. Assuming that the
file is being moved within the same file system, an example command looks like this:

$ mv ./a.out ./bin/my_app

In C terms, this is accomplished as follows:

```
if ( link("./a.out","./bin/my_app") == -1 ) {
    fprintf(stderr,"%s: link(2)\n",strerror(errno));
    abort();
}
if ( unlink("./a.out") == -1 ) {
    fprintf(stderr,"%s: unlink(2)\n",strerror(errno));
    abort();
}
```

The idea behind moving a file is to create a new link and then remove the old link. This gives
the illusion of moving the file from one path to another. However, if the source and destination
pathnames are on different file systems, you will get the error `EXDEV`.

Note

EXDEV—`Cross-device link`. When `link(2)` returns this error, it indicates that the operation failed
because both pathnames were not on the same file system.

While pathnames can be moved using individual calls to link(2) and unlink(2), the operation occurs frequently enough that the rename(2) function has been provided for convenience. This simplifies your coding effort, since you have to test only one source of error instead of two. The synopsis for this function is as follows:

```
#include <stdio.h>

int rename(const char *from, const char *to);
```

The rename(2) function returns 0 if it succeeds. Otherwise the value -1 is returned and an error code is provided in errno.

It is also worth noting that if the final component of the pathname from is a symbolic link, the symbolic link is renamed—not the file or directory that the symbolic link points to.

Warning

The rename(2) function will unlink(2) the to pathname if it already exists.

Additionally, SGI IRIX 6.5 documents this function as being capable of returning EINTR if a signal is caught.

Obtaining File System Information

The UNIX kernel maintains considerable detail about every file system object. This is true whether the object is a file, a directory, a special device node, or a named pipe. Whatever the file system object is, several properties are tracked and maintained for it.

The stat(2) and fstat(2) functions return information about file system objects in a structure named stat. The synopsis for the stat structure is as follows:

```
struct stat {
    dev_t     st_dev;                      /* device */
    ino_t     st_ino;                      /* inode */
    mode_t    st_mode;                     /* protection */
    nlink_t   st_nlink;                    /* number of hard links */
    uid_t     st_uid;                      /* user ID of owner */
    gid_t     st_gid;                      /* group ID of owner */
    dev_t     st_rdev;                     /* device type (if inode dev) */
#ifndef _POSIX_SOURCE
    struct timespec st_atimespec;          /* time of last access */
    struct timespec st_mtimespec;          /* time of last data modification */
    struct timespec st_ctimespec;          /* time of last file status change */
#else
    time_t    st_atime;                    /* time of last access */
    long      st_atimensec;                /* nsec of last access */
    time_t    st_mtime;                    /* time of last data modification */
    long      st_mtimensec;                /* nsec of last data modification */
    time_t    st_ctime;                    /* time of last file status change */
    long      st_ctimensec;                /* nsec of last file status change */
```

```
#endif
    off_t      st_size;              /* file size, in bytes */
    int64_t    st_blocks;            /* blocks allocated for file */
    u_int32_t  st_blksize;           /* optimal blocksize for I/O */
    u_int32_t  st_flags;             /* user defined flags for file */
    u_int32_t  st_gen;               /* file generation number */
};

#ifndef _POSIX_SOURCE
#define st_atime st_atimespec.tv_sec
#define st_mtime st_mtimespec.tv_sec
#define st_ctime st_ctimespec.tv_sec
#endif

struct timespec {
    time_t     tv_sec;               /* seconds */
    long       tv_nsec;              /* and nanoseconds */
};
```

The definition shown is the one documented by FreeBSD Release 3.4. This definition shows the difference that exists, depending on whether or not POSIX standards are being used. When POSIX standards are *not* in use, the members **st_atimespec**, **st_mtimespec**, and **st_ctimespec** are defined in terms of the structure **timespec**. Then macros are used to equate, for example, the name **st_atime** to **st_atimespec**.

When POSIX standards are used, the **st_atime** member is defined in terms of the C type **time_t**, as has been the traditional type for this member. If finer-grained time information is required, the member **st_atimensec** can be consulted when compiling to POSIX standards.

Note

SGI's IRIX 6.5 describes the **access**, **modified**, and **create** date/time structure members in terms of the C data type **timespec_t**. Many other UNIX systems such as HPUX 10 and 11, Solaris 8, and UnixWare 7 describe the **stat** members in simple terms of the C data type **time_t**.

The stat(2) Function

The **stat(2)** function allows the programmer to supply the pathname of the file system object and retrieve file system properties. The function synopsis for **stat(2)** is as follows:

```
#include <sys/types.h>
#include <sys/stat.h>
#include <unistd.h>

int stat(const char *file_name, struct stat *buf);
```

The **stat(2)** function returns **0** when it is successful. When the call fails, -1 is returned with an error code placed in the global variable **errno**.

You can use the following code to obtain information about the executable file `bin/a.out`:

```
struct stat sbuf;

if ( stat("bin/a.out",&sbuf) == -1 ) {
    fprintf(stderr,"%s: stat(2)\n",strerror(errno));
    abort();
}
```

The code shows how the properties are returned to the structure `sbuf` for the file `a.out`. The programmer can then access the members of variable `sbuf` to work with the file properties.

Warning

`stat(2)` and `fstat(2)` under SGI IRIX 6.5 are capable of returning `EINTR` if a signal is caught.

Table 6.1 reviews the `stat` structure members in detail, complete with units.

TABLE 6.1 The stat Structure

Data Type	Member Name	Description
dev_t	st_dev	The device number for this file system.
ino_t	st_ino	The i-node number for this file system entry.
mode_t	st_mode	File system object permission bits.
nlink_t	st_nlink	The number of hard links to this file.
uid_t	st_uid	The uid number of the owning user for this file system object.
gid_t	st_gid	The gid number of the group for this file system object.
dev_t	st_rdev	The device type, if the device is an i-node device.
time_t	st_atime	The time this file system object was last accessed.
long	st_atimensec	The last access time in nanoseconds.
time_t	st_mtime	The time this file system object was last modified.
long	st_mtimensec	The time of last modification in nanoseconds.
time_t	st_ctime	The time of creation for this file system object.
long	st_ctimensec	The time of creation in nanoseconds.
off_t	st_size	The total size in bytes of this file system object.
int64_t	st_blocks	The number of blocks allocated to this file system object.
u_int32_t	st_blksize	The block size for file system I/O.

Data Type	Member Name	Description
u_int32_t	st_flags	User-defined flags for file. This appears to be a FreeBSD extension.
u_int32_t	st_gen	File generation number. This appears to be a FreeBSD extension.

The HPUX operating system also includes another useful piece of information:

```
struct stat {
    …
    uint        st_acl:1;           /* Set if the file has optional */
                                    /* access control list entries */
                                    /* HFS File Systems only */
};
```

When set, the flag bit member **st_acl** indicates that access control list (ACL) entries exist for that file. Only certain types of file systems, including HP's HFS file system, support access control list entries.

The fstat(2) Function

There are situations where it is necessary to obtain properties of the file system object that is open on a file descriptor. In this situation, you may not have the pathname for the object. The **fstat(2)** function solves this problem by allowing you to retrieve properties for the object open on the file descriptor.

```
#include <sys/types.h>
#include <sys/stat.h>
#include <unistd.h>

int fstat(int fd, struct stat *sb);
```

For a file that is open on file descriptor **fd**, the following example shows how **fstat(2)** is used:

```
int fd;                         /* Open file descriptor */
struct stat sbuf;

if ( fstat(fd,&sbuf) == -1 ) {
    fprintf(stderr,"%s: fstat(2)\n",strerror(errno));
    abort();
}
```

In this example, the structure **sbuf** receives all of the file properties for the object open on file unit **fd**.

Working with File Properties

In order to put the **stat(2)** and **fstat(2)** functions through their paces, a simple C++ object will be created to allow a few simple tests to be performed. The system call functions will be encapsulated in the object and then tested by calling upon the object methods. Listing 6.1 shows the C++ program.

LISTING 6.1 stat.cc—The Stat Class and Test Program

```
1:   // stat.cc
2:
3:   #include <iostream.h>
4:   #include <string.h>
5:   #include <errno.h>
6:   #include <sys/types.h>
7:   #include <sys/stat.h>
8:
9:
10:  //////////////////////////////////////////////////////////////
11:  // Simple Stat object :
12:  //////////////////////////////////////////////////////////////
13:
14:  class Stat : public stat {
15:
16:  private:
17:      char        *path;          // Pathname
18:      int         fd;             // File descriptor
19:
20:  public:
21:      Stat() { path = 0; fd = -1; }
22:      ~Stat();
23:
24:      Stat & examine(const char *pathname);
25:      Stat & examine(int fd);
26:      int operator==(Stat &o);
27:
28:      friend ostream & operator<<(ostream &out,Stat &o);
29:  };
30:
31:  //////////////////////////////////////////////////////////////
32:  // Destructor :
33:  //////////////////////////////////////////////////////////////
34:
35:  Stat::~Stat() {
36:      if ( path )                 // Path allocated?
37:          delete path;            // Yes, release string
38:  }
39:
40:  //////////////////////////////////////////////////////////////
41:  // stat(2) on pathname :
42:  //////////////////////////////////////////////////////////////
43:
44:  Stat &
45:  Stat::examine(const char *pathname) {
46:
47:      if ( path )                 // Is there a prior path?
48:          delete path;            // Yes, release string
49:
50:      path = strdup(pathname);    // Create a new string
51:      fd = -1;                    // Not using fd here
52:
```

```
53:        // Obtain stat info :
54:        if ( ::stat(path,this) == -1 )
55:            throw errno;              // Oops- error
56:
57:        return *this;                 // Successful
58:    }
59:
60:    /////////////////////////////////////////////////////////
61:    // Perform fstat(2) on fd :
62:    /////////////////////////////////////////////////////////
63:
64:    Stat &
65:    Stat::examine(int fd) {
66:
67:        if ( path ) {                 // Is there a path?
68:            delete path;              // Yes, release string
69:            path = 0;                 // Mark as gone
70:        }
71:
72:        this->fd = fd;                // Save fd
73:
74:        // Obtain stat info :
75:        if ( ::fstat(fd,this) == -1 )
76:            throw errno;              // Oops- error
77:
78:        return *this;                 // Successful
79:    }
80:
81:    /////////////////////////////////////////////////////////
82:    // This friend function can be called to dump the
83:    // contents of the stat structure :
84:    /////////////////////////////////////////////////////////
85:
86:    ostream &
87:    operator<<(ostream &out,Stat &o) {
88:
89:        // If there is no information, say so :
90:        if ( o.fd == -1 && !o.path ) {
91:            out << "No current information.";
92:            return out;
93:        }
94:
95:        // Otherwise, show what sort of stat() info it is:
96:        if ( o.path )
97:            cout << "stat(" << o.path << ") {\n";
98:        else
99:            cout << "fstat(" << o.fd << ") {\n";
100:
101:        // Dump all other structure members :
102:
103:        cout<< "\tst_dev =\t" << o.st_dev << ";\n"
104:            << "\tst_ino =\t" << o.st_ino << ";\n";
105:
```

continued from previous page

```
106:        cout.setf(ios::oct,ios::basefield);
107:        cout<< "\tst_mode =\t" << '0' << o.st_mode << ";\n";
108:
109:        cout.setf(ios::dec,ios::basefield);
110:        cout<< "\tst_nlink =\t" << o.st_nlink << ";\n"
111:            << "\tst_uid =\t" << o.st_uid << ";\n"
112:            << "\tst_gid =\t" << o.st_gid << ";\n"
113:            << "\tst_rdev =\t" << o.st_rdev << ";\n"
114:            << "\tst_atime =\t" << o.st_atime << ";\n"
115:            << "\tst_mtime =\t" << o.st_mtime << ";\n"
116:            << "\tst_ctime =\t" << o.st_ctime << ";\n"
117:            << "\tst_size =\t" << o.st_size << ";\n"
118:            << "\tst_blocks =\t" << o.st_blocks << ";\n"
119:            << "\tst_blksize =\t" << o.st_blksize << ";\n"
120:            << "\tst_flags =\t" << o.st_flags << ";\n"
121:            << "\tst_gen = \t" << o.st_gen << ";\n"
122:            << "\n};";
123:
124:    return out;
125: }
126:
127: ///////////////////////////////////////////////////////////////
128: // This method tests to see if two file system objects
129: // are the same one :
130: ///////////////////////////////////////////////////////////////
131:
132: int
133: Stat::operator==(Stat &o) {
134:
135:        // Does either object lack information?
136:
137:        if ( fd == -1 && !path )
138:            throw EINVAL;                   // No information here
139:        if ( o.fd == -1 && !path )
140:            throw EINVAL;                   // No information there
141:
142:        // Now test to see if these are the same objects:
143:
144:        if ( o.st_dev != st_dev          // Devices match?
145:        ||   o.st_ino != st_ino )        // Inodes match?
146:            return 0;                    // Devices or inodes don't match
147:
148:        return 1;                        // Return TRUE, they are the same
149: }
150:
151: ///////////////////////////////////////////////////////////////
152: // Test Main Program :
153: ///////////////////////////////////////////////////////////////
154:
155: int
156: main(int argc,char **argv) {
157:        int x;                           // work index
158:        Stat t;                          // stat("./stat")
```

```
159:    Stat s;                            // work stat object
160:
161:    t.examine("./stat");               // Do stat(2)
162:
163:    // Now try all command line arguments :
164:
165:    for ( x=1; x<argc; ++x ) {
166:
167:        try {
168:            s.examine(argv[x]);        // Stat this pathname
169:        } catch ( int e ) {
170:            // e is errno value :
171:            cerr << strerror(e) << ": stat(2) of "
172:                << argv[x] << '\n';
173:            continue;
174:        }
175:
176:        cout << s << '\n';             // Dump stat info
177:
178:        // Test if s is same as t :
179:
180:        cout << "'" << argv[x] << "' is "
181:            << ( s == t ? "same" : "not the same" )
182:            << " file as ./stat\n";
183:    }
184:
185:    return 0;
186: }
187:
188: // End stat.cc
```

The program in Listing 6.1 defines the class `Stat`, beginning at line 14. This class inherits from the `stat` structure and leaves the `stat` members exposed for simplicity (note the `public` keyword in line 14). Two additional `private` members, `path` and `fd`, are declared in lines 17 and 18 for tracking purposes.

Two `examine` C++ methods are declared in lines 24 and 25 to allow the object to inquire by pathname or by file descriptor. This eventually translates to a call to `stat(2)` or `fstat(2)`, respectively.

Lines 45–58 declare the implementation of the inquiry by pathname. Line 54 shows the call to `stat(2)`. Note that this method is coded to throw the `errno` value if an error is returned by `stat(2)`. Lines 64–79 likewise define the implementation of the inquiry by open file descriptor. The `fstat(2)` call appears in line 75, and again, `errno` is thrown if an error is returned.

Lines 86–125 define a `friend` function (see line 28) that allows the class `Stat` to be sent to `cout` with the `<<` operator. This provides a simple dump of the `stat` structure members.

The loop in the `main()` program in lines 165–183 performs the task of examining every pathname provided on the command line (line 168). Any error is caught in line 169 and reported in lines 171–173. If `s.examine(argv[x])` executes successfully, control passes to line 176, where the contents of the object are formatted for output.

The following session shows the program in Listing 6.1 being compiled and tested using the file `Makefile`:

```
$ make stat
cc -c -D_POSIX_C_SOURCE=199309L -Wall -fhandle-exceptions stat.cc
cc stat.o -o stat -lstdc++
$ ./stat Makefile
stat(Makefile) {
        st_dev =        196613;
        st_ino =        125953;
        st_mode =       0100644;
        st_nlink =      1;
        st_uid =        1001;
        st_gid =        1001;
        st_rdev =       525400;
        st_atime =      956797796;
        st_mtime =      956723168;
        st_ctime =      956723168;
        st_size =       378;
        st_blocks =     2;
        st_blksize =    8192;
        st_flags =      0;
        st_gen =        0;

};
'Makefile' is not the same file as ./stat
$
```

Notice that, if we verify a few attributes of the file `Makefile`, they will agree with the output shown:

```
$ ls -li Makefile
125953 -rw-r--r--  1 me    mygrp 378 Apr 26 00:26 Makefile
$
```

The file size of 378 bytes matches the value shown for `st_size`, and the permissions `-rw-r--r--` match the lower 3 octal digits of `st_mode` for permission bits. The `-i` option of the `ls(1)` command causes the i-node number to be displayed. It is shown as 125953 and agrees with the `st_ino` value shown.

Testing Links for the Same File

When the device number in `st_dev` and the i-node in `st_ino` match for two different pathnames, this indicates that these are links to the same file. The method `int operator==(Stat &o)` is defined in the class `Stat` of Listing 6.1 to allow the user of `Stat` objects to perform such a comparison test. The method is implemented in lines 132–149.

This class method is tested in the `main()` program by initially obtaining the `stat(2)` information on the executable file `./stat` in line 161. Then the command-line argument is compared against this in line 181 (note the `s == t` expression before the `?` operator).

In the earlier test run, the message

```
'Makefile' is not the same file as ./stat
```

was shown. However, if this program is tested again with `new_link` as the argument that is linked to `./stat`, then the following results are obtained:

```
$ ln ./stat new_link
$ ./stat new_link
stat(new_link) {
        st_dev =        196613;
        st_ino =        125955;
        st_mode =       0100755;
        st_nlink =      2;
        st_uid =        1001;
        st_gid =        1001;
        st_rdev =       525312;
        st_atime =      956797797;
        st_mtime =      956797797;
        st_ctime =      956798301;
        st_size =       12080;
        st_blocks =     24;
        st_blksize =    8192;
        st_flags =      0;
        st_gen =        0;
};
'new_link' is same file as ./stat
$ ls -li new_link stat
125955 -rwxr-xr-x  2 me   mygrp 12080 Apr 26 21:09 new_link
125955 -rwxr-xr-x  2 me   mygrp 12080 Apr 26 21:09 stat
$
```

After creating a link `new_link` to `./stat`, the program correctly states that the pathname `new_link` is the same file as `./stat`. This is reported from lines 180–182 of the `main()` program.

Testing for File Type

The `st_mode` member also holds information about the type of file system object. To determine the object type, use one of the following macros, where m is the `st_mode` value to be tested. The following tests and macros can be used:

symbolic link	`S_ISLNK(m)`
regular file	`S_ISREG(m)`
directory	`S_ISDIR(m)`
character special device	`S_ISCHR(m)`
block special device	`S_ISBLK(m)`
named pipe (FIFO)	`S_ISFIFO(m)`
socket	`S_ISSOCK(m)`

These macros test the high order bits in the `stat` structure member `st_mode`.

The following code shows how a function could report the type of the file system object `path` that is provided as an argument:

```
static void
report_type(const char *path) {
    struct stat sbuf;
    char *cp = "?";

    if ( stat(path,&sbuf) == -1 ) {
        /* Report stat(2) error */
        fprintf(stderr,"%s: stat(%s)\n",
            strerror(errno),path);
        return;
    }

    if ( S_ISDIR(sbuf.st_mode) )
        cp = "directory";
    else if ( S_ISREG(sbuf.st_mode) )
        cp = "regular file";
    else if ( S_ISCHR(sbuf.st_mode) )
        cp = "character raw device";
    else if ( S_ISBLK(sbuf.st_mode) )
        cp = "block raw device";
    else if ( S_ISFIFO(sbuf.st_mode) )
        cp = "named pipe (FIFO)";
    else if ( S_ISSOCK(sbuf.st_mode) )
        cp = "UNIX socket";
    else if ( S_ISLNK(sbuf.st_mode) )
        cp = "symbolic link";

    printf("Path %s is a %s\n",path,cp);
}
```

This example shows how the `stat` structure member `st_mode` is used in each of the test macro calls.

Modification, Access, and Creation Times

The time values `st_atime`, `st_mtime`, and `st_ctime` are sometimes valuable assets to the programmer. Most of the time, the value `st_mtime` is examined, which represents the last modification for the object. However, the time of last access, `st_atime`, can be extremely useful if you need to see if the object has been recently accessed. The creation time, `st_ctime`, indicates when the object was created. The data type `time_t` is discussed in Chapter 11, "UNIX Date and Time Facilities."

Note

Calling `stat(2)` or `fstat(2)` to query a file system object's properties does not alter its date and time accessed.

Testing Access to a File

Sometimes it is necessary to test the access of a file system object prior to its actual use. For example, if your application must provide the pathname of an executable to another application, you might want to make sure that you possess execute rights on that file. Testing access ahead of time may be simpler for corrective action. This is accomplished with the UNIX function access(2):

```
#include <unistd.h>

int access(const char *path, int mode);
```

mode:

F_OK, R_OK, W_OK and/or X_OK

The pathname of the object to be tested for access is provided in the first argument. The mode argument contains the bit-wise OR of the following values:

File exists	F_OK
Read access	R_OK
Write access	W_OK
Execute access	X_OK

The real user ID and group ID are used for testing the access to the file (not the *effective* user ID and group ID). If the access is not successful, -1 is returned and an appropriate error in errno is returned (EACCES if the problem is a lack of access rights). If the function succeeds, the value 0 is returned instead.

The following example shows how a program could test to see if the shell script my_script is executable:

```
if ( access("./my_script",R_OK|X_OK) == -1 )
    /* Report error */
else
    /* ./my_xeq has execute access */
```

Note

Script files must be readable and executable. Executable files require only execute access.

The value F_OK simply tests for the existence of the pathname. SGI's IRIX 6.5 and UnixWare 7 allow the additional flag bits to be supplied:

Regular executable file	EX_OK
Test using effective IDs	EFF_ONLY_OK

However, these tests are not universally available.

Warning

SGI's IRIX 6.5 and Solaris 8 document the access(2) function returning the error EINTR.

Symbolic Links

Symbolic links solve the thorny problem of providing a link to a file on another file system. They represent a file system "re-director" of sorts. In order to allow programs to work with symbolic links, the UNIX kernel provides a few system calls specific to symbolic links.

The symlink(2) Function

The symlink(2) function permits the caller to create a symbolic link, as opposed to a hard link that is created by link(2). The synopsis for symlink(2) is as follows:

```
#include <unistd.h>

int symlink(const char *path, const char *symlnk);
```

The symbolic link named by the argument symlnk is created to point to the pathname provided by the argument path. The function returns 0 if successful; otherwise -1 and a value for errno are returned. The pathname in path does not need to exist already.

The following example shows how a symbolic link named my_hosts can be created to point to the file /etc/hosts:

```
if ( symlink("/etc/hosts","./my_hosts") == -1 )
    /* Report error */
else
    /* Success */
```

FreeBSD has an extensive man(1) page describing how symbolic links work, in section seven, symlink(7).

The lstat(2) Function

There are times when your program may need status information about the symbolic link, rather than the file it points to. The lstat(2) function fills this need:

```
#include <sys/types.h>
#include <sys/stat.h>

int lstat(const char *path, struct stat *sb);
```

The structure **sb** is filled with the same type of information that is provided for **stat(2)** and **fstat(2)**. The difference, of course, is that the information is returned for the symbolic link itself. The function returns **0** when successful; otherwise **-1** and a value for **errno** are returned instead.

Warning

lstat(2) under SGI IRIX 6.5 is capable of returning **EINTR** if a signal is caught.

Reading the Contents of the Symbolic Link with readlink(2)

In order to determine what an existing symbolic link points to, you call upon the function **readlink(2)**:

```
#include <unistd.h>

int readlink(const char *path, char *buf, int bufsiz);
```

The symbolic link of interest is provided in the argument **path**. The buffer pointer **buf** indicates where the symbolic link information should be returned. The argument **bufsiz** indicates the maximum number of bytes that can be returned by **readlink(2)**.

The value returned by **readlink(2)** is the number of characters that were placed into the buffer **buf**. There is no null byte returned by **readlink(2)**. If an error occurred, **-1** is returned and **errno** holds the error code. The following example shows how to report the link information for symbolic link **my_symlink**:

```
int z;
char buf[1024];

z = readlink("my_symlink",buf,sizeof buf-1);
if ( z == -1 )
    /* Report error */
else {
    /* Success */
    buf[z] = 0;     /* Null terminate */
    printf("symlink is '%s'\n",buf);
}
```

Notice how the null byte has to be added by the caller, since **readlink(2)** does not provide one.

File Permissions and Ownership

The stat(2) family of functions allows you to inquire about a file system object's permissions and ownership. Permissions are described by the stat structure member st_mode. To alter this permission setting, you change its mode. This is covered next, using the functions chmod(2), fchmod(2), and lchmod(2).

Each user on a UNIX system *owns* files that he has created. He is the *owner* of his files and, as the owner, possesses the right to change its permissions (mode). Likewise, the user is a member of a group. Consequently, there exists group ownership on file system objects. The owner of a file (with exceptions) can give his ownership away to another user or group on the system. This is known as changing the owner or group of the file.

Changing Permissions

The chmod(2) function permits the program to alter the permission bits of a file system object. The functions chmod(2), fchmod(2), and lchmod(2) have the following synopsis:

```
#include <sys/stat.h>

int chmod(const char *path, mode_t mode);

int fchmod(int fd, mode_t mode);

int lchmod(const char *path, mode_t mode);
```

The chmod(2) function follows symbolic links to arrive at the file that will have its permissions altered. The lchmod(2) function, which is not available on all UNIX platforms, allows the caller to alter the permissions on the symbolic link itself.

Note

FreeBSD and HPUX 10 support the lchmod(2) function.

Documentation for HPUX 11 does not show support for lchmod(2). No documented support for lchmod(2) exists in IBM AIX 4.3, Solaris 8, UnixWare 7, SGI IRIX 6.5, or Linux.

The functions chmod(2) and lchmod(2) require the pathname of the file system object. Function fchmod(2) changes the permissions on the object open on the file descriptor fd.

The permission bits in argument mode replace the existing permissions on the file system object. These functions return 0 when successful or -1 with an error code in errno if they fail.

The following example shows how a C program could make the shell script my_script executable for the owner and group:

```
if ( chmod("./my_script",0550) == -1 )
    /* Report error */
else
    /* Successful */
```

Alternatively, using macro constants, this example could have been written as follows:

```
if ( chmod("./my_script",S_IRUSR|S_IXUSR|S_IRGRP|S_IXGRP) == -1 )
    /* Report error */
else
    /* Successful */
```

Calling these functions will not affect the access of objects that have already been opened.

Warning

chmod(2) and fchmod(2) under SGI IRIX 6.5, UnixWare 7, and Solaris 8 are capable of returning EINTR if a signal is caught.

Changing Ownership

In order to change the ownership of a file, the function chown(2) must be called. The synopsis for this family of functions is as follows:

```
#include <sys/types.h>
#include <unistd.h>

int chown(const char *path, uid_t owner, gid_t group);

int fchown(int fd, uid_t owner, gid_t group);

int lchown(const char *path, uid_t owner, gid_t group);
```

Function chown(2) follows the symbolic links starting with path to arrive at the file that will be changed. The function fchown(2) affects the file that is open on file descriptor fd. The lchown(2) function affects the ownership of the symbolic link itself, rather than the file it points to.

The arguments owner and group set the ownership user ID and group ID, respectively. Argument owner or group may be given the value -1 (with one exception) to leave the user ID or group ID unchanged. This is useful when changing only one of the two values of a file system object. See Chapter 12, "User ID, Password, and Group Management," for more about how to obtain user and group ID numbers.

Note

HPUX 10 and 11 documents that you should use the macro value UID_NO_CHANGE to leave the owner as is. Additionally, macro GID_NO_CHANGE is used to leave the group ownership as is.

AIX 4.3, Solaris 8, SGI IRIX 6.5, UnixWare 7, FreeBSD, and Linux document the use of -1 for leaving the owner or group as is.

Most UNIX platforms clear the set-user-ID and set-group-ID bits when these functions are called. This helps to prevent accidental or mischievous security holes in file system permissions. However, when the caller is `root`, the set-user-ID and set-group-ID bits are not reset.

The following example sets the ownership of the file `/etc/hosts` to `root` (value `0`), while leaving the group ID unchanged:

```
if ( chown("/etc/hosts",0,-1) == -1 )
    /* Report error */
else
    /* Successful */
```

Some systems may restrict these calls, since they can represent a security risk under the right conditions.

> **Tip**
>
> Whether `chown(2)` is restricted or not can be tested using `pathconf(2)` or `fpathconf(2)` and the test `_PC_CHOWN_RESTRICTED`. This is covered later in this chapter.

Named Pipes (FIFOs)

Command lines are formed regularly under UNIX to pipe information from one process to another. These pipes are anonymous. When unrelated processes want to pipe information, they usually require the help of a named pipe. Because pipes process information on a first-in, first-out basis, they are also known as FIFOs.

A FIFO can be created from a C/C++ program using the `mkfifo(2)` function. The function synopsis is as follows:

```
#include <sys/types.h>
#include <sys/stat.h>

int mkfifo(const char *path, mode_t mode);
```

The FIFO is created with the pathname `path` with permissions specified by the argument `mode`. The permission bits in `mode` are subject to the current `umask(2)` value in effect.

The function `mkfifo(2)` returns `0` when successful or `-1` with an error code in `errno` when it fails. The following shows how a named pipe, `/tmp/my_pipe`, can be created with read and write access for everyone (subject to the `umask(2)` setting):

```
if ( mkfifo("/tmp/my_pipe",0666) == -1 )
    /* Report errors */
else
    /* Successful */
```

Note

On some platforms, the `mkfifo(2)` call may be implemented in terms of another function. For example, SGI's IRIX 6.5 and Solaris 8 implement `mkfifo(2)` by calling `mknod(path,(mode|S_IFIFO),0)`.

Obtaining Size and Configuration Information

If you are writing applications for several UNIX platforms, it is wisest if your application can determine the size of certain platform-specific values. One frequently needed piece of information is the maximum length of a pathname. This is needed so that pathname buffers can be safely allocated.

The `pathconf(2)` and `fpathconf(2)` functions can answer your query about the size of a pathname buffer required. The function synopsis is as follows:

```
#include <unistd.h>

long pathconf(const char *path, int name);

long fpathconf(int fd, int name);
```

A number of configured values can be returned to the program with these functions. The tests that can be performed are summarized in Table 6.2.

Warning

When the `pathconf(2)` or `fpathconf(2)` function fails, the value `-1L` is returned, and `errno` contains reason for the error.

If the parameter queried is not supported or does not have a limit in the system, the value `-1L` is also returned, and the value of `errno` is left unchanged. To detect this, you should clear the value of `errno` before making the call.

TABLE 6.2 `pathconf(2)` and `fpathconf(2)` Tests

Test	Description
_PC_LINK_MAX	The maximum file link count.
PC_MAX_CANON	The maximum number of bytes in terminal canonical input line. Input must represent a terminal.
_PC_MAX_INPUT	The number of bytes for which space is available in a terminal input queue. Input must represent a terminal.

continued from previous page

Test	Description
_PC_NAME_MAX	The maximum number of bytes in a filename (excludes null bytes). The input must represent a directory.
_PC_PATH_MAX	The maximum number of bytes in a pathname (excludes null bytes). The input must represent a directory.
_PC_PIPE_BUF	The maximum number of bytes that will be written atomically to a pipe. Input must represent a pipe, FIFO, or directory.
_PC_CHOWN_RESTRICTED	Returns 1 if appropriate privileges are required for the chown(2) system call, 0 otherwise. Input must represent a file or directory.
_PC_NO_TRUNC	Return 1 if pathnames longer than _PC_NAME_MAX are truncated. Otherwise, long pathnames cause an error to be returned. Input must be a directory.
_PC_VDISABLE	Returns the terminal character disabling value.

Most of the time, programmers will be interested in the value **_PC_PATH_MAX**. However, a number of other useful values are provided as well, including the test **_PC_CHOWN_RESTRICTED**. A feature test program is presented in Listing 6.2.

LISTING 6.2   pathconf.c—A pathconf(2) and fpathconf(2) Test Program

```
 1:   /* pathconf.c */
 2:
 3:   #include <stdio.h>
 4:   #include <unistd.h>
 5:   #include <string.h>
 6:   #include <errno.h>
 7:
 8:   int
 9:   main(int argc,char **argv) {
10:       int x;
11:       struct  {
12:           int     test;
13:           char    *desc;
14:       } tests[] = {
15:           { _PC_LINK_MAX, "The maximum file link count." },
16:           { _PC_MAX_CANON, "The maximum number of bytes \n"
17:                   "\tin terminal canonical input line." },
18:           { _PC_MAX_INPUT, "The minimum maximum number\n"
19:                   "\tof bytes for which space is available\n"
20:                   "\tin a terminal input queue." },
21:           { _PC_NAME_MAX, "The maximum number of bytes in\n"
22:                   "\ta file name." },
23:           { _PC_PATH_MAX, "The maximum number of bytes\n"
24:                   "\tin a pathname." },
```

```
25:               { _PC_PIPE_BUF, "The maximum number of bytes\n"
26:                       "\twhich will be written atomically to a pipe." },
27:               { _PC_CHOWN_RESTRICTED, "Return 1 if appropriate\n"
28:                       "\tprivileges are required for the chown(2)\n"
29:                       "\tsystem call, otherwise 0." },
30:               { _PC_NO_TRUNC, "Return 1 if file names longer\n"
31:                       "\tthan KERN_NAME_MAX are truncated." },
32:               { _PC_VDISABLE, "Returns the terminal character\n"
33:                       "\tdisabling value." },
34:       };
35:       long lv;
36:
37:       for ( x=0; x<sizeof tests/sizeof tests[0]; ++x ) {
38:           errno = 0;                           /* Clear */
39:           lv = pathconf(".",tests[x].test);    /* Use dir . */
40:           if ( lv == -1L && errno == EINVAL )
41:               lv = fpathconf(0,tests[x].test);/* Use fd=0 */
42:
43:           if ( lv == -1L ) {                   /* Test if error */
44:               if ( errno )
45:                   printf("%s: %s\n",strerror(errno),tests[x].desc);
46:               else
47:                   printf("The value test[%d] is not supported.\n",x);
48:               continue;
49:           }
50:
51:           printf("%ld:\t%s\n",lv,tests[x].desc);
52:       }
53:
54:       return 0;
55:   }
```

The program in Listing 6.2 takes the very simple approach of calling `pathconf(2)` (line 39) using the current directory `"."` and the test macro found in array `tests[]` (lines 11–34). If the call should fail with the value `EINVAL`, then the function `fpathconf(2)` is called in line 41, using standard input instead (file unit zero). Unless the input has been redirected, this gives the program the input it needs to query certain terminal settings.

Notice that line 38 clears `errno` to zero. This allows line 44 to test if the returned value was an error or an unsupported value. Line 45 reports errors, and line 47 reports unsupported parameters.

A compile and run under FreeBSD Release 3.4 is shown:

```
$ make pathconf
cc -c -D_POSIX_C_SOURCE=199309L -D_POSIX_SOURCE -Wall pathconf.c
cc pathconf.o -o pathconf
$ ./pathconf
32767:  The maximum file link count.
255:    The maximum number of bytes
        in terminal canonical input line.
255:    The minimum maximum number
        of bytes for which space is available
        in a terminal input queue.
```

```
255:      The maximum number of bytes in
          a file name.
1024:     The maximum number of bytes
          in a pathname.
512:      The maximum number of bytes
          which will be written atomically to a pipe.
1:        Return 1 if appropriate
          privileges are required for the chown(2)
          system call, otherwise 0.
1:        Return 1 if file names longer
          than KERN_NAME_MAX are truncated.
255:      Returns the terminal character
          disabling value.
$
```

The session output shows you the various values that are obtained from `pathconf(2)` and `fpathconf(2)`. Notice in this example that the maximum filename length is 255 bytes and the maximum pathname length is 1024 bytes.

Note

Note that the maximum filename length and pathname length can vary according to the file system in question. For example, a `pathconf(2)` query on a mounted DOS floppy will return **12** for `_PC_NAME_MAX` (an 8-character filename, a dot, and a 3-character extension). Additionally, **1** is returned for `_PC_LINK_MAX`, since DOS file systems do not support links.

Summary

This chapter has covered the essential UNIX functions that manipulate and provide information about file system objects. While directories are also file system objects, they are given their own special treatment by UNIX. Consequently, the next chapter will introduce you to the essential directory-related functions.

CHAPTER 7

DIRECTORY MANAGEMENT

T he previous chapter dealt with system calls that work primarily with files. This chapter will focus on operations that are specific to directories. In this chapter you will learn how to

- Change, save, and restore a current directory
- Create and remove directories
- Open, search, and close directories
- Change the root directory

Obtaining the Working Directory

As an application writer, you will sometimes want to know what the current directory is from within your C/C++ program. The function getcwd(3) returns this information, and its synopsis is presented as follows:

```
#include <unistd.h>

char *getcwd(char *buf, size_t size);

char *getwd(char *buf);  /* FreeBSD: For compatibility only */
```

The function getwd(3) is provided by FreeBSD for compatibility and should not be used in new programs. The getwd(3) function assumes the buffer is of size MAXPATHLEN. If the supplied buffer is shorter than this, then a security breach is possible due to the buffer overrun.

A better function is the getcwd(3) function, which is supported by all modern UNIX systems. The argument buf of length size is filled with the name of the current working directory pathname. The size value must include the size of the returned pathname, *including* the null byte.

Both getcwd(3) and getwd(3) return the pointer to buf if the call is successful. A null pointer is returned when the call has failed, and the error code is left in the global variable errno.

Note

ERANGE—Result Too Large   This error is returned by getcwd(3) and getwd(3) when the pathname to be returned will not fit in the buffer provided. The buffer must allow enough space for the pathname and the terminating null byte.

Specifying a Null Buffer Argument

The buf argument can be specified as null for some UNIX platforms. FreeBSD states that the "ability to specify a NULL pointer and have getcwd() allocate memory as necessary is an extension."

When the buf argument is a null pointer, a buffer of size bytes is allocated and its pointer is returned with the pathname in it. The argument size must be specified greater than zero and one byte greater than the largest expected pathname being returned. See the following Note for the Linux extension that applies when size is negative.

Note

Under Linux, specifying argument size as -1 when the argument buf is null will cause the correct size to be allocated for the returned pathname. When size is greater than zero, size bytes are allocated for the pathname instead.

Warning

The null buf argument is an extension to the standard for getcwd(3). It should not be used for code that must be used on all UNIX platforms.

FreeBSD, Linux, SGI IRIX 6.5, UnixWare 7, HPUX-10, HPUX-11, and Solaris-8 appear to support a null buf argument when size is greater than zero. HP warns that its support of a null buf argument may be withdrawn in the future.

Linux is the only one that documents support for a null buf argument and size less than zero. With this combination, the buffer is allocated as large as required.

The pointer that is returned when buf is null must later be released with a call to free(3) when you no longer require the pathname string.

Given all the variation in the levels of support for the null buf argument, the best advice that can be given is to keep control in your own hands. Allocate your own buffer and provide its correct size in the size argument when calling getcwd(3).

Changing the Current Directory

In order to change the current directory for the program, the function chdir(2) can be used. The synopsis for this function is as follows:

```
#include <unistd.h>
```

```
int chdir(const char *path);
```

This function simply accepts the pathname of the directory that is to become the current directory. To be successful, the current process must have execute access to the directory name given. When successful, the value 0 is returned. Otherwise, -1 is returned, and errno contains the error code.

The following shows how a program can change to the games home directory:

```
if ( chdir("/home/games") == -1 ) {
    fprintf(stderr,"%s: chdir(2)\n",strerror(errno));
    exit(13);
}
```

If the chdir(2) call fails, this program reports the error and exits with status code 13. Otherwise, the program continues with the current directory set to /home/games.

Saving a Working Directory

Traditionally, programmers have written code to get the current directory in order to restore it later. This allows the program to change to some other directory for a time and return to the original later. A disadvantage of this approach is that the directory name saved may be renamed by some other process. This would make it impossible for the program to restore the original current directory.

Another approach is possible using the fchdir(2) function in combination with the open(2) function. The function synopsis for fchdir(2) is as follows:

```
#include <unistd.h>
```

```
int fchdir(int fd);
```

The input argument fd is the directory that is open on that file descriptor. In order for fchdir(2) to succeed, it must be able to search the directory. The function returns 0 when successful and -1 with an error code in errno when it fails.

The following example shows how the directory /etc can be opened and given to fchdir(2) to set it as the current directory.

```
int fd;

fd = open("/etc",O_RDONLY);    /* Open the directory */
if ( fd == -1 )
    /* Report open error */

if ( fchdir(fd) == -1 )         /* Change to directory ref'd by fd */
    /* Report error */
else
    /* Current directory is now /etc */
```

A Limitation of `fchdir(2)`

The one limitation of the approach just presented using `fchdir(2)` is that `open(2)` will not be able to open a directory that provides execute-only permission. For example

```
$ ls -dl /tmp/x_only
d--x--x--x  2 me    mygrp  512 Apr 29 14:38 /tmp/x_only
$
```

Here the directory `/tmp/x_only` can be visited with `chdir(2)` but not opened by `open(2)`. You can test `chdir(2)` using the shell

```
$ cd /tmp/x_only
$
```

You can see that the shell **cd** command, which calls `chdir(2)`, succeeds without complaint. However, `open(2)` must have read access on the directory in order to open it.

This situation does not occur often in practice, since a directory normally grants both read and execute permissions together. However, you should be aware of this limitation, since this could come back to bite you in highly secure application environments.

Making a New Directory

A C/C++ program may create a directory by calling upon the UNIX `mkdir(2)` system call. Its synopsis is as follows:

```
#include <sys/types.h>
#include <sys/stat.h>

int mkdir(const char *path, mode_t mode);
```

The argument `path` is the pathname of the new directory that is to be created. All intermediate directory names in the pathname must already exist. Only the last component of the pathname is actually created. The argument `mode` specifies the permission bits that are to be given to the new directory being created. In most cases, the `S_ISGID`, `S_ISUID`, and `S_ISVTX` bits are silently deleted from the value given in `mode`. The final permission bits assigned to the new directory are affected by applying the current `umask(2)` setting.

The function returns `0` when successful or `-1` with a code in `errno` if it fails. A number of possible errors can be returned, but `EROFS` and `EDQUOT` are introduced in the following Note.

Note

`EROFS—Read Only File System`   An attempt was made to create a directory when the file system has been mounted in read-only mode.

`EDQUOT`   The directory `create` failed because the user's quota of disk blocks on the containing file system has been exhausted. Alternatively, the user's quota of i-nodes has been exhausted on the file system.

The following example shows how a directory /tmp/my_dir could be created from a C program:

```
int z;

z = mkdir("/tmp/my_dir",S_IRWXU|S_IRWXG|S_IROTH|S_IXOTH); /* 0775 */
if ( z == -1 )
    /* report error */
```

The example gives all access to the user and the group, and all others receive only read and execute. The final permissions given to the directory will be determined by the umask(2) that is in effect at the time.

Removing a Directory

The opposite of creating a directory with mkdir(2) is the removal of a directory with rmdir(2). Its function synopsis is as follows:

```
#include <unistd.h>

int rmdir(const char *path);
```

The function returns 0 if it succeeds and -1 with the error code in errno when it fails. The directory name given by path must be empty in order to succeed. If the directory is not empty, the error ENOTEMPTY is returned.

Note

ENOTEMPTY—Directory not empty   This error indicates that the directory pathname given to rmdir(2) contains one or more files or subdirectories (or any other file system object). Files must all be released with the unlink(2) function prior to releasing the directory containing them.

Warning

HPUX documents that rmdir(2) will not remove the root directory. While it is hard to imagine a situation where this functionality would be desirable, it may be an important consideration in a specialized application.

Note

Some platforms may not permit you to remove the current working directory for the current process (for example, HPUX and SGI IRIX prevent this). See the Note about EINVAL, later in this section.

However, most UNIX platforms will permit the current directory to be deleted by a different process (HPUX, for example).

The `rmdir(2)` function is capable of returning a number of different errors. Two that will be introduced here are **EBUSY** and **EINVAL**.

> **Note**
>
> `EBUSY—Device busy` In the context of `rmdir(2)`, this error code indicates that the directory is a mount point and cannot be deleted until the file system is unmounted.
>
> `EINVAL—Invalid argument` This error return from `rmdir(2)` indicates that the directory to be removed is the current directory.

The following shows how the empty directory `/tmp/my_dir` is deleted:

```
int z;

z = rmdir("/tmp/my_dir");
if ( z == -1 )
    /* Report error */
```

Opening a Directory for Searching

It is often necessary to search a directory to determine what entries the directory contains. For example, a backup utility would need to visit all files and subdirectories as it is backing them up. A family of functions, starting with `opendir(3)`, is provided for that purpose:

```
#include <sys/types.h>
#include <dirent.h>

DIR *opendir(const char *pathname);

int dirfd(DIR *dirp);
```

In the synopsis, note the return value provided by the function `opendir(3)`. This is similar to the `fopen(3)` call in the way that it returns a pointer to a structure. Here, the `opendir(3)` function returns a pointer to the data type `DIR`. The argument `pathname` is the name of the directory to be opened for searching.

The function `opendir(3)` returns a pointer when successful and a null pointer when it fails. The error code is placed in `errno` when the function call fails.

The pointer to `DIR` cannot be used in other functions such as `fchdir(2)`, for example, so a function `dirfd(3)` is provided (this may be implemented as a macro). The following example shows how `opendir(3)` and `dirfd(3)` might be used together:

```
DIR *dirp;            /* Ptr to open directory */
int fd;               /* fd of open directory */

dirp = opendir("/etc");
if ( !dirp ) {
    /* report error */
```

```
} else {
    …    /* Do some stuff here */
    fd = dirfd(dirp);  /* Get fd of open directory */
    if ( fchdir(fd) == -1 ) {
        /* Report failed fchdir(2) */
    }
}
```

Note

The `dirfd(3)` function is not available on many UNIX platforms. FreeBSD and SGI IRIX 6.5 support this function.

IRIX 6.5 supports the `dirfd(3)` function if you include the 4.3BSD file `<sys/dir.h>` instead of the System V include file `<dirent.h>`.

The example shows how `opendir(3)` opens the directory /etc. Later, with the help of the function `dirfd(3)`, the file descriptor is fetched out of the structure pointed to by `dirp` and assigned to variable `fd`. Once `fd` is established, the function `fchdir(2)` can be called to make the open directory the current directory.

Closing a Directory

An open directory needs to be closed when the program is finished with it. The synopsis for `closedir(3)` is as follows:

```
#include <sys/types.h>
#include <dirent.h>

int closedir(DIR *dirp);
```

This function is simply called with a pointer to an open **DIR** structure. The value returned is -1 if the **close** operation fails, and the error is posted to **errno**. Otherwise, `closedir(3)` returns 0 upon success. An example is as follows:

```
DIR *dirp;                /* Ptr to open directory */

dirp = opendir("/etc");
if ( !dirp ) {
    /* report error */
} else {
    /* Close the directory now */
    if ( closedir(dirp) == -1 ) {
        /* Report closedir(3) error */
    }
}
```

The example simply opens the directory /etc and then closes it again.

Searching a Directory

Opening and closing directories might be fun, but it doesn't accomplish too much without any additional functions. The function readdir(3) allows an open directory to be searched for one directory member at a time. The function synopsis for readdir(3) is as follows:

```
#include <sys/types.h>
#include <dirent.h>

struct dirent *readdir(DIR *dirp);

struct dirent {
    /* etc. */          /* Other members are implementation specific */
    char    d_name[256]; /* Max POSIX name is 255 bytes */
};
```

The input to readdir(3) is simply a pointer to an open DIR structure provided by opendir(3). The value returned is a pointer to the structure dirent, or a null pointer if it fails or reaches the end of the directory. FreeBSD does not document any error codes being returned in errno, while Linux documents one error (EBADF). SGI's IRIX 6.5 documents several possible errors, although EINTR is not among them.

Note

The structure dirent is very implementation specific. According to the POSIX standard, you can depend upon only the member d_name[] for the directory entry name. Some implementations include a member d_ino to describe the i-node of the entry. Not all UNIX implementations provide for this, however.

In order to distinguish the difference between the end of the directory and an error, it is necessary for the caller to clear errno before calling readdir(3). The example program in Listing 7.1 demonstrates this.

LISTING 7.1   readdir.c—A Program That Lists a Directory

```
 1:    /* readdir.c */
 2:
 3:    #include <stdio.h>
 4:    #include <errno.h>
 5:    #include <sys/types.h>
 6:    #include <dirent.h>
 7:
 8:    int
 9:    main(int argc,char **argv) {
10:        DIR dirp = 0;              /* Open directory */
11:        struct dirent *dp;         /* Directory entry pointer */
12:
13:        if ( argc < 2 ) {
```

```
14:            fputs("A pathname argument is required.\n",stderr);
15:            return 1;
16:        }
17:
18:        dirp = opendir(argv[1]);     /* Open directory */
19:        if ( !dirp ) {               /* errors? */
20:            perror("opendir(3)");
21:            return 2;
22:        }
23:
24:        errno = 0;                   /* Clear errno for readdir(3) */
25:
26:        while ( (dp = readdir(dirp)) != NULL ) {
27:            printf("%s\n",dp->d_name);
28:            errno = 0;
29:        }
30:
31:        if ( errno != 0 )            /* EOF or error? */
32:            perror("readdir(3)");    /* Error occurred in readdir(3) */
33:
34:        if ( closedir(dirp) == -1 )  /* Close the directory */
35:            perror("closedir(3)");   /* Close error- report it */
36:
37:        return 0;
38:    }
```

The essential points of the program in Listing 7.1 are

- errno is cleared to zero in line 24 before the while loop in lines 26–29 begins.

- readdir(2) is called in the while clause on line 26. If a null pointer is returned, control exits the loop.

- errno is cleared to zero in line 28, to prepare for the next call to readdir(3) in the while clause on line 26.

The while loop exits when readdir(3) returns a null pointer. The errno test in line 31 tests to see if an error was encountered. If so, it is reported in line 32. If errno remained the zero value that was established in line 24 or 28, then it is known that the end of the directory was reached without encountering any errors.

Line 27 reports the directory member name using the printf(3) function. The following shows the compile and run of the program in Listing 7.1:

```
$ make readdir
cc -c -D_POSIX_C_SOURCE=199309L -D_POSIX_SOURCE -Wall readdir.c
cc readdir.o -o readdir
$ ./readdir /etc/ppp
.
..
ppp.deny
ppp.shells.sample
ppp.conf
$
```

The program requires a directory name to be provided as a command-line argument. The example shows the listing of directory /etc/ppp on a FreeBSD system.

Rewinding to the Start of a Directory

To permit a directory to be searched more than once, the open directory must be rewound. This is what the rewinddir(3) function achieves.

```
#include <sys/types.h>
#include <dirent.h>

void rewinddir(DIR *dirp);
```

When the directory is initially opened with opendir(3), it is implicitly positioned at the start of the directory. When rewinddir(3) is called, the open directory is repositioned at the start. The input argument dirp is simply the pointer to the open DIR structure that was returned by opendir(3). There is no return value for rewinddir(3), and there are no documented errors for this call.

The following shows how the function can be called:

```
DIR *dirp;              /* Open DIR pointer */

rewinddir(dirp);
```

Saving Position Within a Directory

It is possible to use the function telldir(3) to save a position within a directory. The function synopsis is as follows:

```
#include <sys/types.h>
#include <dirent.h>

long telldir(const DIR *dirp);
```

Given the input pointer dirp, which points to an open DIR structure returned by opendir(3), this function returns an offset into the directory for later use by seekdir(3). The offset returned is greater than or equal to zero if it is successful. A -1L value is returned if it fails, and the error code is found in errno.

Note

Some UNIX platforms may have a slightly different type definition for telldir(3). For example, SGI's IRIX 6.5 defines its telldir(3) as follows:

```
off_t telldir (DIR *dirp);
```

Note that the returned offset is type off_t, and that the input argument lacks the keyword const.

Restoring Position Within a Directory

In order to position the directory randomly according to information saved from a prior call to telldir(3), the function seekdir(3) must be used to restore the directory position. The function synopsis is as follows:

```
#include <sys/types.h>
#include <dirent.h>

void seekdir(DIR *dirp, long loc);
```

The seekdir(3) function simply accepts the pointer to an open DIR structure and an offset loc to restore as a directory position. No success or error indication is returned for this call.

The following example shows how telldir(3) and seekdir(3) can be used together:

```
DIR *dirp;                  /* Open DIR pointer */
long dirpos;                /* Directory offset */

dirpos = telldir(dirp);     /* Get offset in directory */
...
seekdir(dirpos);            /* Restore directory position */
```

Note

Note that some UNIX platforms such as SGI's IRIX 6.5 may use a slightly different definition of seekdir(3):

```
void seekdir(DIR *dirp, off_t loc);
```

This definition uses the data type off_t for the directory offset.

Scanning a Directory

While the family of routines (see directory(3)) starting with opendir(3) performs the functions that a programmer might need, they are somewhat tedious to code if you need them frequently enough. The scandir(3) and alphasort(3) routines assist in reducing the programmer effort required:

```
#include <sys/types.h>
#include <dirent.h>

int scandir(
    const char *dirname,
    struct dirent ***namelist,
    int (*select)(struct dirent *),
    int (*compar)(const void *, const void *));

int alphasort(const void *d1, const void *d2);
```

Function `scandir(3)` might look somewhat intimidating. However, once you spend a moment examining it, you will see that it is easy to use. The argument `dirname` is given the pathname of the directory that you want to scan. The argument `namelist` points to a (`struct dirent **`) pointer, so that a list of directory entries can be returned. The argument `select` can be left null, if you want to select all directory names. When the argument `compar` is given a null pointer, the directory entries returned are unsorted.

Upon a successful return, `scandir(3)` returns the number of entries that are returned in the `namelist` array (this may include the value `0`). The value `-1` is returned when there is an error (no `errno` values appear to be formally documented).

The function `alphasort(3)` is a function that can be supplied in the argument `compar` if you require that `namelist` be sorted alphabetically.

Note
The `namelist` array is dynamically allocated and must be freed when your program no longer requires it. You must first call `free(3)` for each entry in the array and then free the array itself by calling `free(3)`.

Declaring Your Own `select` Function for `scandir(3)`

The function pointer supplied for the `select` argument is called with one pointer to a `dirent` structure. Based on this, the function must return non-zero (true) if the entry is to be included (selected) in the final list of entries. If zero (false) is returned by this function, the entry is to be excluded. The following shows an example function that selects only the entries starting with `h`.

```
/*
 * Select only those directory entries that start with 'h'
 */
int
my_select(struct dirent *dp) {

    if ( dp->d_name[0] != 'h' )
        return 0;                       /* Don't include this */
    return 1;                           /* else include this one */
}
```

The function `my_select()` will be called for each directory entry found by `scandir(3)`. When `my_select()` returns zero, the directory entry is excluded from the final list.

Declaring Your Own `compar` Function for `scandir(3)`

The function supplied for `compar` is called with two `void` pointer arguments. The IBM AIX and FreeBSD platforms define their arguments this way. See the next section for platforms that declare these arguments differently.

The man(1) page provided by FreeBSD is not abundantly clear how you should interpret these void pointer arguments. The void pointers are actually pointers to a pointer to a dirent structure. The following example illustrates in code how they should be cast and used:

```
int
my_compar(const void *d1,const void *d2) {
    struct dirent *dir1 = *(struct dirent **)d1;
    struct dirent *dir2 = *(struct dirent **)d2;

    return strcmp(dir1->d_name,dir2->d_name);
}
```

The code shown implements what the function alphasort(3) provides. The two void pointers are cast to a (struct dirent **) and then dereferenced once to point to the struct dirent entry itself. Once this is done, then strcmp(3) can be called upon to provide a comparison result to be returned.

SysV Variations

You will find that some systems will declare the compar and alphasort(3) functions differently. These systems use the following synopsis:

```
#include <sys/types.h>
#include <dirent.h>

/* SysV Definiton : */

int scandir(const char *dirname,
    struct dirent **namelist[],
    int (*select)(struct dirent *),
    int (*compar)(struct dirent **, struct dirent **));

int alphasort(struct dirent **d1, struct dirent **d2);
```

The notable difference here is that the compar function pointer is defined in terms of a function that receives pointers to (struct dirent **) instead of (void *). In this case, you would define the function my_compar() in the following manner:

```
int
my_compar(struct dirent **d1,struct dirent **d2) {
    struct dirent *dir1 = *d1;
    struct dirent *dir2 = *d2;

    return strcmp(dir1->d_name,dir2->d_name);
}
```

Platforms that use this definition include SGI's IRIX 6.5, UnixWare-7, Sun's Solaris 8, and HPUX 11.

A scandir(3) Example

An example program making use of the scandir(3) function is provided in Listing 7.2.

LISTING 7.2   scandir.c—A Demonstration Program Using scandir(3)

```
 1:   #include <stdio.h>
 2:   #include <stdlib.h>
 3:   #include <unistd.h>
 4:   #include <errno.h>
 5:   #include <sys/types.h>
 6:   #include <dirent.h>
 7:
 8:   extern int scandir(const char *dirname, struct dirent ***namelist,
 9:       int (*select)(struct dirent *),
10:       int (*compar)(const void *, const void *));
11:
12:   extern int alphasort(const void *d1, const void *d2);
13:
14:   /*
15:    * Select only those directory entries that start with
16:    * 'h' to demonstrate the selection ability :
17:    */
18:   static int
19:   my_select(struct dirent *dp) {
20:
21:       if ( dp->d_name[0] != 'h' )
22:           return 0;                     /* Don't include this */
23:       return 1;                         /* else include this one */
24:   }
25:
26:   /*
27:    * Sort entries in reverse order for demonstration
28:    * purposes :
29:    */
30:   static int
31:   my_compar(const void *d1,const void *d2) {
32:       struct dirent *dir1 = *(struct dirent **)d1;
33:       struct dirent *dir2 = *(struct dirent **)d2;
34:
35:       /*
36:        * Reverse the comparison by reversing
37:        * dir2 with dir1 in the strcmp(3) call:
38:        */
39:       return strcmp(dir2->d_name,dir1->d_name);
40:   }
41:
42:   /*
43:    * A good test is the directory /etc :
44:    */
45:   int
46:   main(int argc,char **argv) {
47:       int x;                            /* Work index */
48:       int n;                            /* namelist[n] */
49:       struct dirent **namelist;         /* List of names */
50:
51:       if ( argc < 2 ) {
52:           fputs("A pathname argument is required.\n"
```

```
53:                      "Try /etc for the directory.\n",stderr);
54:            return 1;
55:        }
56:
57:        /*
58:         * Scan the directory given :
59:         */
60:        n = scandir(argv[1],&namelist,my_select,my_compar);
61:
62:        /*
63:         * Report the directory entries :
64:         */
65:        printf("%d entries for %s:\n",n,argv[1]);
66:        for ( x=0; x<n; ++x )
67:            printf("%3d: %s\n",x,namelist[x]->d_name);
68:
69:        if ( n > 0 ) {
70:            for ( x=0; x<n; ++x )
71:                free(namelist[x]);          /* Release entry */
72:            free(namelist);                 /* Release the array */
73:        }
74:        return 0;
75:    }
```

The main program shown in Listing 7.2 is straightforward. The scandir(3) function is called on line 60, using argv[1] as the directory that is to be scanned. The list of directory entries will be returned to the pointer namelist, which is declared in line 49. The number of entries returned by scandir(3) is stored to variable n, which is declared in line 48.

You have seen the function my_select() before, for example on page 140. The function my_compar() was altered slightly from the example shown on page 141 to sort the entries in reverse order (lines 30–40).

Finally, notice how the allocated storage is released in lines 69–73 of the main() program. First all of the array elements are released (line 71), and then the array itself (line 72).

Compiling and running the program yields the following results:

```
$ make scandir
cc -c -D_POSIX_C_SOURCE=199309L -D_POSIX_SOURCE -Wall scandir.c
cc scandir.o -o scandir
$ ./scandir /etc
5 entries for /etc:
  0: hosts.lpd
  1: hosts.equiv
  2: hosts.allow
  3: hosts
  4: host.conf
$
```

Using the directory /etc, you can see that, indeed, only the filenames starting with h were selected. Thanks to the custom sort function my_compar(), the entries were sorted in reverse alphabetical order as well.

Walking a Directory Structure

Some UNIX platforms provide the function ftw(3C) and the newer function nftw(3C) to make it simpler to perform a tree walk of a file system. These functions do not appear on the FreeBSD system, so only a cursory description of them will be provided here. The HPUX-11 ftw(3C) page provides this function synopsis:

```
#include <ftw.h>

int ftw (const char *path,
    int (*fn)(const char *obj_path,
        const struct stat *obj_stat,
        int obj_flags),
    int depth);

int nftw (const char *path,
    int (*fn)(const char *obj_path,
        const struct stat *obj_stat,
        int obj_flags,
        struct FTW obj_FTW),
    int depth,
    int flags);
```

These functions start by examining the directory provided by the argument **path**. From this point on, the directory is recursively searched for subdirectories until all file system objects under **path** have been processed.

Both of these functions also require a pointer to a function **fn** that will be called for each file system object being considered.

The **depth** argument determines how many levels deep the tree will be traversed. HP's documentation indicates that this will also be limited by "the number of file descriptors currently available for use." A negative or zero value for the **depth** argument is equivalent to specifying **depth=1**.

The nftw(3C) function accepts an additional **flags** argument. This argument accepts values like **FTW_DEPTH** to cause a depth-first tree walk to be performed. Flag **FTW_PHYS** is useful because it prevents the tree walk from following symlinks. This prevents the tree walk from visiting files more than once. See Table 7.1 for a complete list of these flags.

TABLE 7.1 Macro Names of nftw(3C) Flags

Macro Name	Description
FTW_PHYS	Causes nftw(3C) to perform a physical walk. No symbolic links are followed. Hard links are followed unless the path crosses itself. When FTW_PHYS is not given, nftw(3C) follows symbolic and hard links but does not walk a path that crosses itself.
FTW_MOUNT	The tree walk will not cross a mount point. Only files on the same mounted device as the starting path are considered.

Macro Name	Description
FTW_DEPTH	A depth-first walk is performed, causing a directory's entries to be visited before the directory itself.
FTW_CHDIR	A call to chdir(2) is performed prior to reading the directory being visited.
FTW_SERR	The tree walk normally exits with a return value of -1 if lstat(2) fails (error code in errno). When FTW_SERR is specified, a failure of lstat(2) causes the function fn to be called, and the tree walk is allowed to continue.

The ftw(3C) and nftw(3C) functions call a user-supplied function fn. The function fn that is called by ftw(3C) looks like this:

```
int fn(const char *obj_path,        /* Pathname of object */
    const struct stat *obj_stat,    /* struct stat info */
    int obj_flags);                 /* flag bits */
```

The obj_path argument contains the pathname of the object being considered, and obj_stat is a pointer to a stat structure describing the object. The additional flags in argument obj_flags are provided and contain the values shown in Table 7.2.

TABLE 7.2   Table of ftw(3C) and nftw(3C) obj_flags

Macro	Description
FTW_F	Object is a file.
FTW_D	Object is a directory.
FTW_SL	Object is a symbolic link (nftw(3C) only).
FTW_DNR	Object is a directory without read permission. Function fn will not be called for any of its descendants.
FTW_NS	lstat(2) failed to obtain information about the object, leaving the stat structure contents undefined. For ftw(3C), if the failure is because the directory containing the object could not be searched, fn is called and the walk continues. For nftw(3C), the value for errno is set, and nftw(3C) returns -1 after calling fn, instead. Other lstat(2) failures cause fn not to be called, and the value -1 is returned, with errno set. This behavior is modified by the nftw(3C) flag FTW_SERR.

The function nftw(3C) calls a slightly different user-supplied function fn. Its definition includes an additional argument named obj_FTW:

```
int fn(const char *obj_path,        /* pathname of object */
    const struct stat *obj_stat,    /* struct stat info */
    int obj_flags,                  /* flag bits */
    struct FTW *obj_FTW);           /* additional info */
```

The structure FTW contains the following members:

```
struct FTW {
    int    base;   /* Offset into pathname to the start of the basename */
    int    level;  /* Relative depth level (root is level 0) */
    /* private members.. */
};
```

The only members of **struct FTW** that should be used are the **base** and **level** members. Other members of the structure, if present, are not portable to all platforms. If function **fn** is called with the arguments **obj_path** and the argument **obj_FTW** as shown earlier, then the basename of the object can be displayed as follows:

```
printf("Basename = '%s'\n",obj_path+obj_FTW->base);
```

If your application must be portable to the widest possible range of UNIX platforms, then you would be wise to avoid the **ftw(3C)** and **nftw(3C)** functions. These will be found on most SysV-derived UNIX platforms but may not exist on a BSD-derived UNIX.

Changing Your Root Directory

The UNIX file system has one root directory, on which all other file systems are mounted. It is often desirable to limit the exposure of the entire file system to a smaller portion when dealing with potentially hostile users. This approach is commonly used by **ftp(1)** servers.

An anonymous **ftp(1)** server could be established with all of its files and subdirectories in the directory **/home/ftp**. Additionally, the directory **/home/ftp/pub** might contain public files for downloading. At startup, the **ftp(1)** server would change its root directory to the directory **/home/ftp**. From that point forward, the public directory would be known to the server as **/pub** instead of **/home/ftp/pub**. This prevents the client user from accessing anything outside of the **ftp(1)** server's root directory, which in actual fact is **/home/ftp** on the host system.

The system call **chroot(2)** allows a new root directory to be established for the current session and all subsequent child processes. The function synopsis is given as follows:

```
#include <unistd.h>

int chroot(const char *dirname);
```

The **chroot(2)** function simply accepts the pathname that will become the new effective root for the current process. The function returns **0** if it is successful and **-1** if it fails (**errno** holds the error code).

Warning

When chroot(2) returns 0 indicating success, the current directory for the current process remains unaffected. When writing programs that must be secure, make certain that you change the current directory to the new root level or to a subdirectory of the new root.

Additionally, large software projects may have other directories open on other file descriptors, which may be exploitable by fchdir(2). One way to avoid exploitable directories is to close all file descriptors prior to calling chroot(2).

The `chroot(2)` call is restricted to the `root` account for security reasons. The reason for this is simply that the ability to set a new root directory also permits a new password file to be in force, among other security problems.

Note
Once you have established a new root directory, it becomes impossible for the process to return to the original root directory.

Setting a new root directory also brings with it a number of other complications, including the need to set up hard links to support files, including shared libraries. Symbolic links cannot be used in a `chroot(2)`-ed file system to refer back to a normal non-`chroot(2)` pathname. Consequently, files in the new root file system must be copies of the original support files or hard links to them. However, hard links are not always possible when the files are on different file systems.

The program provided in Listing 7.3 shows the `chroot(2)` function in action. It calls `chroot(2)` to set directory `/tmp` as the new root file system. It then lists the current directory to demonstrate the fact that the current directory is unaffected. It follows with a listing of the new root directory (which is really the `/tmp` directory).

LISTING 7.3   `chroot.c`—A Demonstration Program for `chroot(2)`

```
1:   /* readdir.c */
2:
3:   #include <stdio.h>
4:   #include <errno.h>
5:   #include <sys/types.h>
6:   #include <dirent.h>
7:
8:   extern int chroot(const char *dirname);
9:
10:  static int
11:  ls(const char *pathname) {
12:      DIR dirp = 0;               /* Open directory */
13:      struct dirent *dp;          /* Directory entry pointer */
14:      int count = 0;              /* Count of files */
15:
16:      printf("DIRECTORY LISTING OF %s :\n",pathname);
17:
18:      dirp = opendir(pathname);   /* Open directory */
19:      if ( !dirp ) {              /* errors? */
20:          perror("opendir(3)");
21:          return -1;
22:      }
23:
24:      errno = 0;                  /* Clear errno for readdir(3) */
25:
```

continued from previous page

```
26:        while ( (dp = readdir(dirp)) != NULL ) {
27:            printf("%s\n",dp->d_name);
28:            ++count;
29:            errno = 0;
30:        }
31:
32:        if ( errno != 0 ) {          /* EOF or error? */
33:            perror("readdir(3)");    /* Error occurred in readdir(3) */
34:            return -1;
35:        }
36:
37:        if ( closedir(dirp) == -1 ) /* Close the directory */
38:            perror("closedir(3)");  /* Close error- report it */
39:
40:        printf("%6d entries\n\n",count);
41:
42:        return 0;
43:    }
44:
45:    int
46:    main(int argc,char **argv) {
47:        int z;
48:
49:        z = chroot("/tmp");
50:        if ( z == -1 ) {
51:            perror("chroot(2)");
52:            return 1;
53:        }
54:
55:        ls(".");
56:        ls("/");
57:
58:        return 0;
59:    }
```

Notice that the functions opendir(3), readdir(3), and closedir(3) were used to list the directories (function ls() in lines 10–43). This was necessary because a call to system(3) to invoke the ls(1) command will not work. The system(3) call would fail because the ls(1) command does not exist in the new root file system (/tmp), nor do any of the necessary support files such as the shared libraries.

The chroot(2) function requires root access to be successful. Consequently, the compile and run session that follows shows the user changing to the superuser account:

```
$ make chroot
cc -c -D_POSIX_C_SOURCE=199309L -D_POSIX_SOURCE -Wall chroot.c
cc chroot.o -o chroot
$ ./chroot
chroot(2): Operation not permitted
$ su root
Password:
# ./chroot
```

```
DIRECTORY LISTING OF . :
.
..
Makefile
chroot.c
chroot.o
readdir.c
chroot
scandir.c
      8 entries

DIRECTORY LISTING OF / :
.
..
.s.PGSQL.5432
psql.edit.1001.13867
t.t
      5 entries

#
```

In the session shown, the executable ./chroot was attempted without root access. This caused the error chroot(2): Operation not permitted to be reported. However, once the user switched to the **root** account, the program was able to list both the current directory and the new root directory (which was /tmp). This demonstration shows why special care needs to be exercised with the current directory. Directories currently open also present a risk, since a simple call to fchdir(2) on an open directory will allow it to become the current directory.

Summary

This chapter focused on directory functions. The next chapter will complete this coverage of files and directories by looking at functions that are specific to temporary files and their cleanup.

CHAPTER 8

TEMPORARY FILES AND PROCESS CLEANUP

A program occasionally requires temporary storage to contain unknown quantities of data. When the quantity of data is potentially large, it is stored in a temporary file. The temporary file is then released later, when the processing is complete.

In this chapter, you will learn how to

- Create temporary files
- Automatically cleanup temporary files that have been created

Creating Temporary Files

This chapter will examine a number of ways that a temporary file can be created under UNIX. Each of these has its advantages and disadvantages. The tmpnam(3) function is discouraged and is covered only because you will encounter it in existing code. The remaining functions can be used in new software.

Using the tmpnam(3) Function

The tmpnam(3) function generates a pathname for a new temporary file but does not create the temporary file itself. Its function synopsis is as follows:

```
#include <stdio.h>

char *tmpnam(char *buf);   /* Discouraged */
```

This function generates a temporary pathname in the directory given by the macro name P_tmpdir (defined in <stdio.h>). The argument buf must be null or point to a character buffer of a minimum length of L_tmpnam bytes. When the argument buf is null, the function tmpnam(3) returns a pointer to an internal static buffer containing the name of the temporary file. When buf is not null, the buffer buf is populated with the pathname of the temporary file.

When it is successful, the function returns a valid pointer to buf or to an internal buffer. A null pointer is returned when the function fails, and errno contains the reason for the error.

Note

The function `tmpnam(3)` should not be used in new code. The disadvantages of this function include the fact that the temporary directory is hard-wired to the directory `P_tmpdir` and that filename generation is subject to race conditions on some UNIX platforms.

Using `tmpnam(3)` with a Null Argument

The argument to `tmpnam(3)` is a buffer pointer, which must be a minimum of `L_tmpnam` bytes in length. However, the argument can be specified as a null pointer, as is illustrated in the example program in Listing 8.1. Note, however, that when this is done, the pointer returned is valid only until the next call to `tmpnam(3)` is performed.

LISTING 8.1   `tmpnam.c`—A Program Using `tmpnam(3)` with a Null Argument

```
 1:  /* tmpnam.c */
 2:
 3:  #include <stdio.h>
 4:  #include <stdlib.h>
 5:  #include <unistd.h>
 6:  #include <string.h>
 7:  #include <errno.h>
 8:
 9:  int
10:  main(int argc,char *argv[]) {
11:      char *tmp_pathname;      /* Temp. File Pathname */
12:      FILE *tmpf = 0;          /* Opened temp. file */
13:      char cmd[256];
14:
15:      if ( !(tmp_pathname = tmpnam(NULL)) ) {
16:          fprintf(stderr,"%s: tmpnam(3)\n",strerror(errno));
17:          abort();
18:      }
19:
20:      printf("Using temp file: %s\n",tmp_pathname);
21:
22:      if ( !(tmpf = fopen(tmp_pathname,"w")) ) {
23:          fprintf(stderr,"%s: creating temp %s\n",
24:              strerror(errno),tmp_pathname);
25:          abort();
26:      }
27:
28:      sprintf(cmd,"ls -l %s",tmp_pathname);
29:      system(cmd);
30:
31:      fclose(tmpf);              /* Close the temp file */
32:      unlink(tmp_pathname);   /* Release the temp file */
33:
34:      return 0;
35:  }
```

This program generates a temporary pathname in lines 15–18. Then the temporary file is created by calling `fopen(3)` in line 22. In lines 28–29, the temporary file is listed by a `system(3)` command, which invokes the `ls(1)` command. Finally, the temporary file is released in line 32 before the program exits.

Compiling and invoking the program yields the following results on a FreeBSD system:

```
$ make tmpnam
cc -c -D_POSIX_C_SOURCE=199309L -D_POSIX_SOURCE -Wall tmpnam.c
cc tmpnam.o -o tmpnam
$ ./tmpnam
Using temp file: /var/tmp/tmp.0.H49596
-rw-r--r--  1 me   mygrp  0 May  1 21:22 /var/tmp/tmp.0.H49596
$ ./tmpnam
Using temp file: /var/tmp/tmp.0.U49599
-rw-r--r--  1 me   mygrp  0 May  1 21:22 /var/tmp/tmp.0.U49599
$
```

The program `./tmpnam` was invoked twice to demonstrate the differences in the generated temporary filename. Note that the pathname generated for your temporary filename will differ for different UNIX platforms.

Using `tmpnam()` with a Buffer

An improved way to use the `tmpnam(3)` function is to supply a buffer to the function, so that the generated pathname can be stored there indefinitely. When the argument to `tmpnam(3)` is null, the returned pathname string is only valid until the next call to the function. Listing 8.2 shows an example program that supplies its own buffer.

LISTING 8.2   `tmpnam2.c`—A Program Using `tmpnam(3)` with a Supplied Buffer

```
 1:    /* tmpnam2.c */
 2:
 3:    #include <stdio.h>
 4:    #include <stdlib.h>
 5:    #include <unistd.h>
 6:    #include <string.h>
 7:    #include <errno.h>
 8:
 9:    int
10:    main(int argc,char *argv[]) {
11:        char tmp_pathname[L_tmpnam]; /* Temp. pathname */
12:        FILE *tmpf = 0;          /* Opened temp. file */
13:        char cmd[256];
14:
15:        if ( !tmpnam(tmp_pathname) ) {
16:            fprintf(stderr,"%s: tmpnam(3)\n",strerror(errno));
17:            abort();
18:        }
19:
20:        printf("Using temp file: %s\n",tmp_pathname);
21:
```

continued from previous page

```
22:      if ( !(tmpf = fopen(tmp_pathname,"w")) ) {
23:          fprintf(stderr,"%s: creating temp %s\n",
24:              strerror(errno),tmp_pathname);
25:          abort();
26:      }
27:
28:      sprintf(cmd,"ls -l %s",tmp_pathname);
29:      system(cmd);
30:
31:      fclose(tmpf);              /* Close the temp file */
32:      unlink(tmp_pathname);    /* Release the temp file */
33:
34:      return 0;
35: }
```

The program shown in Listing 8.2 is almost identical to the program shown in Listing 8.1. However, this time the buffer is declared in line 11 as an array with a length of L_tmpnam bytes and provided as an argument to the tmpnam(3) function in line 15.

Compiling and running the program yields the same result as before:

```
$ make tmpnam2
cc -c -D_POSIX_C_SOURCE=199309L -D_POSIX_SOURCE -Wall tmpnam2.c
cc tmpnam2.o -o tmpnam2
$ ./tmpnam2
Using temp file: /var/tmp/tmp.0.E49652
-rw-r--r--  1 wwg  wheel  0 May  1 21:37 /var/tmp/tmp.0.E49652
$
```

Using the mktemp(3) Function

Another function that is available for generating temporary filenames is the mktemp(3) function. Its synopsis is as follows:

```
#include <unistd.h>    /* <== Use for FreeBSD */
#include <stdlib.h>    /* <== Use for Solaris, AIX, Linux, HPUX, UnixWare 7 */
#include <stdio.h>     /* <== Use for SGI IRIX 6.5 */

char *mktemp(char *template);
```

The mktemp(3) function accepts as input a C string that acts as a pathname template. The last characters are specified as the character X and are replaced to generate a unique pathname. For this reason, never pass a C string constant as an argument to the function. For example, the argument **template** may contain the string "/tmp/temp.XXXX", allowing the last four X characters to be replaced to generate a unique filename.

The following example code shows how a temporary filename can be generated and displayed:

```
char template[256];             /* Holding buffer for the template */

strcpy(template,"/var/tmp/tmp.XXXX");
printf("A temp file is '%s'\n",mktemp(template));
```

The pointer value returned is the same pointer `template` that was passed as an argument if the call is successful. Otherwise, a null pointer is returned and `errno` is set.

Warning

The X characters must be at the end of the string. Placing them in other positions will not work. For example, the string `"/tmp/XXXX.tmp"` will *not* work.

Using the `mkstemp(3)` Function

The `mkstemp(3)` function goes one step further than `mktemp(3)`. It not only generates a temporary filename from the template given, but it creates and opens the temporary file. The function synopsis is as follows:

```
#include <unistd.h>    /* <== Use for FreeBSD */
#include <stdlib.h>    /* <== Use for Solaris, AIX, Linux, HPUX, UnixWare 7 */
#include <stdio.h>     /* <== Use for SGI IRIX 6.5 */

int mkstemp(char *template);
```

The rules for the template string are the same as the function `mktemp(3)`. The function returns an open file descriptor when it is successful or `-1` and an error code in `errno` if it fails.

The temporary file is created with read (`S_IRUSR`) and write (`S_IWUSR`) permissions for the owner only. The final permissions assigned are determined by the `umask(2)` value currently in effect, however. The following code shows how a temporary filename can be generated, created, and opened:

```
char template[256];        /* Holding buffer for the template */
int tmpf;                  /* Open temp. file descriptor */

strcpy(template,"/var/tmp/tmp.XXXX");
tmpf = mkstemp(template);      /* Create and open the temp. file */
```

Listing 8.3 demonstrates how the `mkstemp(3)` function can be used with the standard I/O functions.

LISTING 8.3   `mkstemp.c`—A Program Using `mkstemp(3)` to Create a Temporary File

```
 1:  /* mkstemp.c */
 2:
 3:  #include <stdio.h>
 4:  #include <stdlib.h>
 5:  #include <unistd.h>
 6:  #include <string.h>
 7:  #include <errno.h>
 8:
 9:  extern int mkstemp(char *template);
10:
```

continued from previous page

```
11:  int
12:  main(int argc,char *argv[]) {
13:      char tf_path[64];          /* Temp. File Pathname */
14:      int tfd = -1;              /* File Descriptor */
15:      FILE *tmpf = 0;            /* Opened temp FILE */
16:
17:      /*
18:       * Initialize the temp. file template :
19:       */
20:      strcpy(tf_path,"/var/tmp/tmp.XXXXXX");
21:
22:      /*
23:       * Generate temp file pathname, create and open
24:       * the temporary file on file unit tfd :
25:       */
26:      if ( (tfd = mkstemp(tf_path)) < 0 ) {
27:          fprintf(stderr,"%s: generating a temp file name.\n",
28:              strerror(errno));
29:          abort();
30:      }
31:
32:      printf("Using temp file: %s\n",tf_path);
33:
34:      /*
35:       * Use standard I/O on temp. file :
36:       */
37:      tmpf = fdopen(tfd,"w+");
38:      fprintf(tmpf,"Written by PID=%ld\n",(long)getpid());
39:      fclose(tmpf);
40:
41:      unlink(tf_path);    /* Release the temp. file */
42:
43:      return 0;
44:  }
```

The program shown in Listing 8.3 initializes the template in line 20 and then creates and opens the temporary file in line 26, where mkstemp(3) is called. To allow the standard I/O routines to be used, the function fdopen(3) is called in line 37 with the open file descriptor tfd. Then a write to the temporary file is performed in line 38 using fprintf(3).

Compiling and running the program under FreeBSD yields the following result:

```
$ make mkstemp
cc -c -D_POSIX_C_SOURCE=199309L -D_POSIX_SOURCE -Wall mkstemp.c
cc mkstemp.o -o mkstemp
$ ./mkstemp
Using temp file: /var/tmp/tmp.m49798
$
```

The temporary file generated and used for this run was the file /var/tmp/tmp.m49798, which agrees with the template used in line 20 of the program.

The program in Listing 8.3 used a temporary filename template, as shown below:

```
strcpy(tf_path,"/var/tmp/tmp.XXXXXX");
```

The characters preceding the Xs may be modified to allow more than one temporary file in your program. For example, the first and second temporary files might use the following templates instead:

```
strcpy(template01,"/var/tmp/01-XXXXXX");
strcpy(template02,"/var/tmp/02-XXXXXX");
```

This technique is not absolutely necessary for using multiple temporary files, but it can be helpful when debugging your program. When you see temporary files named in this fashion in the /var/tmp directory, you will know that the temporary file starting with 01- is the first temporary file that the application created and that 02- indicates the second.

Using the mkstemps(3) Function

FreeBSD supports the mkstemps(3) function, which permits a suffix to be appended to the temporary filename. In all other ways, it is similar to mkstemp(3). The synopsis for it is as follows:

```
#include <unistd.h>

int mkstemps(char *template, int suffixlen);
```

The template argument is the same as the template argument for mkstemp(3), except that the X characters no longer need to be at the end of the string. The argument suffixlen indicates how many characters at the end of the string represent the suffix. The following code illustrates:

```
char template[256];        /* Holding buffer for the template */
int tmpf;                  /* Open temp. file descriptor */

strcpy(template,"/var/tmp/XXXX.tmp");
tmpf = mkstemps(template,4);    /* Create and open the temp. file */
```

In this example, the last four characters form the suffix. The X characters can now be at the start or middle of the temporary file's basename.

Warning

The function mkstemps(3) is not universally available. For this reason, it is not recommended for portable code.

Using the tmpfile(3) Function

The tmpfile(3) function creates and opens a temporary file, returning a FILE stream pointer instead of a file descriptor. The following is its synopsis:

```
#include <stdio.h>

FILE *tmpfile(void);
```

Listing 8.4 shows a short program that creates a temporary file, writes one line to it, and then reads back one line from it.

LISTING 8.4   `tmpfile.c`—A Program Using the `tmpfile(3)` Function

```
 1:    /* tmpfile.c */
 2:
 3:    #include <stdio.h>
 4:    #include <unistd.h>
 5:    #include <string.h>
 6:    #include <errno.h>
 7:
 8:    int
 9:    main(int argc,char *argv[]) {
10:        FILE *tmpf = 0;      /* Opened temp. file */
11:        char buf[128];       /* Input buffer */
12:
13:        if ( !(tmpf = tmpfile()) ) {
14:            fprintf(stderr,"%s: generating a temp file name.\n",
15:                strerror(errno));
16:            abort();
17:        }
18:
19:        fprintf(tmpf,"PID %ld was here.\n",(long)getpid());
20:        fflush(tmpf);
21:
22:        rewind(tmpf);
23:        fgets(buf,sizeof buf,tmpf);
24:
25:        printf("Read back: %s\n",buf);
26:
27:        fclose(tmpf);
28:
29:        return 0;
30:    }
```

The program does not show a pathname for the temporary file, nor does it call `unlink(2)` to remove it later. This is because the file has already been deleted. Even so, it remains available to you as long as the file remains open. The disk space is automatically reclaimed by the UNIX kernel when the file is closed. This saves you from having to make sure that it is deleted later.

Compiling and running this program under FreeBSD looks like this:

```
$ make tmpfile
cc -c -D_POSIX_C_SOURCE=199309L -D_POSIX_SOURCE -Wall tmpfile.c
cc tmpfile.o -o tmpfile
$ ./tmpfile
Read back: PID 10058 was here.

$
```

Notice the extra line feed displayed following the line starting with **Read back:**. This is due to the line feed written in line 19 and then included in the buffer from the **fgets(3)** call in line 23.

Using the `tempnam(3)` Function

The last temporary file function that will be covered in this chapter is the `tempnam(3)` function. Its function synopsis is as follows:

```
#include <stdio.h>

char *tempnam(const char *dir, const char *prefix);
```

This function accepts two arguments. The second argument, `prefix`, is optional and may be supplied with a null pointer. However, when it is not null, it points to a C string that specifies up to five characters that can be used as a prefix to the temporary filename generated.

The first argument, `dir`, is more complicated. It can be specified as a null pointer, or it may point to a string specifying a directory that the programmer has chosen. Whether `dir` is null or not, the following procedure determines the final directory chosen for the temporary filename:

1. Attempt to obtain exported environment variable `TMPDIR`. If this variable is defined and it specifies a directory that is writable to the current process, then this directory will be used. In effect, the `TMPDIR` variable overrides the program's choice of directory.

2. When step 1 fails, the `dir` argument of the `tempnam(3)` call is examined. If this argument is not a null pointer, then this directory will be used if the specified directory exists.

3. When step 2 is not satisfied, the directory specified by the `stdio.h` macro `P_tmpdir` is tried.

4. As a last resort, the directory `/tmp` will be used.

Normally, step 1 or 2 specifies the directory. Steps 3 and 4 represent fallback directory names.

The returned pointer is to a dynamically allocated pathname string, or a null pointer if it fails. Be certain to free this returned pointer later, when your program is finished using this pathname. Note that no file is created; only the temporary pathname is created by `tempnam(3)`.

Listing 8.5 shows a short program that uses the `tempnam(3)` function.

LISTING 8.5 `tempnam.c`—A Program Using the `tempnam(3)` Function

```
1:   /* tempnam.c */
2:
3:   #include <stdio.h>
4:   #include <stdlib.h>
5:   #include <unistd.h>
6:   #include <string.h>
7:   #include <errno.h>
8:
9:   extern char *tempnam(const char *tmpdir, const char *prefix);
10:
11:  int
12:  main(int argc,char *argv[]) {
```

continued from previous page

```
13:        char *tf_path = NULL;        /* Temp. File Pathname */
14:        FILE *tmpf = 0;              /* Temp. File stream */
15:
16:        if ( !(tf_path = tempnam("./my_tmp","tmp-")) ) {
17:            fprintf(stderr,"%s: generating a temp file name.\n",
18:                strerror(errno));
19:            abort();
20:        }
21:
22:        printf("Temp. file name is %s\n",tf_path);
23:
24:        if ( !(tmpf = fopen(tf_path,"w+")) ) {
25:            fprintf(stderr,"%s: opening %s for I/O\n",
26:                strerror(errno),tf_path);
27:            abort();
28:        }
29:
30:        fprintf(tmpf,"PID %ld was here.\n",(long)getpid());
31:        fclose(tmpf);
32:
33:        unlink(tf_path);             /* Release the temp file */
34:        free(tf_path);               /* Free allocated string */
35:
36:        return 0;
37:    }
```

In line 16 this program uses `tempnam(3)` to generate a pathname to be used for a temporary file. The temporary file is created and opened in line 24. Notice that the pathname string must be freed, since it is dynamically allocated (see line 34).

To test the `TMPDIR` environment variable, the program can be run and tested as follows:

```
$ make tempnam
cc -c -D_POSIX_C_SOURCE=199309L -D_POSIX_SOURCE -Wall tempnam.c
cc tempnam.o -o tempnam
$ TMPDIR=/tmp ./tempnam
Temp. file name is /tmp/tmp-g50054
$
```

Note that the pathname generated uses the directory `/tmp` as was given in the `TMPDIR` environment variable. If you look at line 16, the program would normally create the temporary file in subdirectory `./my_tmp`. However, the `TMPDIR` environment variable successfully overrode that choice.

Now run the same program without `TMPDIR` defined:

```
$ unset TMPDIR
$ ./tempnam
Temp. file name is ./my_tmp/tmp-D50059
No such file or directory: opening ./my_tmp/tmp-D50059 for I/O
Abort trap - core dumped
$
```

In this case, the `fopen(3)` call failed because the subdirectory `./my_tmp` does not exist yet. If you create it now and repeat the test, you will obtain the following result:

```
$ mkdir ./my_tmp
$ ./tempnam
Temp. file name is ./my_tmp/tmp-a50061
$
```

This time, the program `./tempnam` is successful at creating a temporary file in the subdirectory `./my_tmp`. This comes from the specification in line 16 of Listing 8.5.

If you remove the permissions on your `./my_tmp` directory, you can test the fallback plans for `tempnam(3)`:

```
$ chmod 0 my_tmp
$ ./tempnam
Temp. file name is /var/tmp/tmp-w50063
$ ls -l my_tmp
ls: my_tmp: Permission denied
$
```

The `chmod(1)` command takes all permissions away from the subdirectory `my_tmp`. When the program is run, the directory `/var/tmp` is used instead for the temporary filename. This agrees with FreeBSD's `P_tmpdir` macro value.

Making Files Temporary

Once a temporary file is created, a program must release it when finished with it. Otherwise, the temporary file directory will fill with many abandoned files over time. Calling `unlink(2)` is trivial, but making sure it is done when the program prematurely exits is more of a challenge.

Using `unlink(2)` to Make Files Temporary

One way to make sure that the temporary file is released is to release it immediately after it is created and opened. This looks illogical to those who are new to UNIX, but a UNIX file can exist after it has been unlinked, as long as the file remains open. When the last open file descriptor for the file is closed, the disk space is reclaimed by the UNIX kernel.

Recall function `tmpfile(3)`, which creates temporary files with no pathname. It uses this general procedure:

1. Generate a unique temporary filename.

2. Create and open the file.

3. Call `unlink(2)` on the temporary filename. This effectively makes the file nameless, but the file itself exists as long as it remains open.

4. Call `fdopen(3)` to open a `FILE` stream, using the open file descriptor from step 2.

5. Return the `FILE` stream pointer to the caller.

This temporary but nameless file has two advantages:

- The file has already been released. No temporary file cleanup is required.

- No other process can subsequently open and tamper with the temporary file. This also provides a measure of privacy.

The second point is still subject to a window of opportunity, since the file must be created and then passed to `unlink(2)`. However, the main advantage presented here is that no matter how your program exits or aborts, the temporary file will not be left in a directory, since it has already been unlinked.

Performing Exit Cleanup

There are situations in which the `unlink(2)` approach is not convenient. If the file must be closed and then reopened, then you have no choice but to keep a name associated with the temporary file. For this reason, the C programmer must rely on other methods, such as the `atexit(3)` function.

Using the `atexit(3)` Function

The C library function `atexit(3)` allows the programmer to register a function that can be used for all types of cleanup tasks. Of primary interest here is the removal of temporary files. The function synopsis for `atexit(3)` is as follows:

```
#include <stdlib.h>

int atexit(void (*func)(void));
```

The argument provided to `atexit(3)` is simply the function pointer to a function, declared as follows:

```
void func(void) {
    /* My cleanup code… */
}
```

The function `atexit(3)` returns `0` when it registers the function successfully and returns non-zero when it fails. FreeBSD returns `-1` and an error code in `errno` when `atexit(3)` fails, but be sure to read the Warning in this section about this. For maximum portability, it is best to test for zero to see if `atexit(3)` succeeded.

The functions registered by `atexit(3)` are called in the reverse order from which they are registered.

Note

FreeBSD and UnixWare 7 document that a minimum of 32 functions may be registered. Additional entries are limited only by available memory. Linux appears to support as many registrations as remaining memory permits.

HPUX 11 and IBM's AIX 4.3 state that the `atexit(3)` function is limited to a maximum of `ATEXIT_MAX` registered functions. For HPUX, this is defined by the include file `<limits.h>`; for AIX, it is `<sys/limits.h>`.

The limit for Solaris 8 is defined by `sysconf(3C)` using the parameter `_SC_ATEXIT_MAX`.

Warning

FreeBSD documents that atexit(3) sets errno when -1 is returned (ENOMEM is one documented error returned). Linux (Red Hat 6.0) documentation states that atexit(3) returns -1 if it fails, and errno is *not* set.

SGI's IRIX 6.5, UnixWare 7, and HPUX 11 document that they return "non-zero when [they] fail." No error codes for errno are documented.

For these reasons, always test for a successful return (a 0 return) of atexit(3) for maximum portability. Additionally, the errno code should be ignored unless the specific platform is taken into account.

The program in Listing 8.6 shows an example that calls on the atexit(3) function. This causes a cleanup function to be called upon program termination.

LISTING 8.6   atexit.c—A Program Using atexit(3) to Register a Cleanup Function

```
 1:   /* atexit.c */
 2:
 3:   #include <stdio.h>
 4:   #include <stdlib.h>
 5:   #include <unistd.h>
 6:   #include <string.h>
 7:   #include <errno.h>
 8:
 9:   extern char *tempnam(const char *tmpdir,const char *prefix);
10:
11:   static char *tf_path = NULL;    /* Temp. File Pathname */
12:
13:   /*
14:    * Cleanup function :
15:    */
16:   static void
17:   mr_clean(void) {
18:
19:       puts("mr_clean() started:");
20:
21:       /*
22:        * Here we assume, that if tf_path is not NULL, that
23:        * the main program has not released the temporary
24:        * file on its own.
25:        */
26:       if ( tf_path != NULL ) {
27:           printf("unlinking temp. file %s\n",tf_path);
28:
29:           /*
30:            * Unlink the temporary file, and release the
31:            * pathname string :
32:            */
33:           if ( unlink(tf_path) == -1 )
34:               fprintf(stderr,"%s: unlink(2)\n",strerror(errno));
35:           free(tf_path);           /* Free the pathname string */
```

continued from previous page

```
36:            tf_path = NULL;           /* Indicate that this is released */
37:        }
38:
39:        puts("mr_clean() ended.");
40:  }
41:
42:  /*
43:   * Main program :
44:   */
45:  int
46:  main(int argc,char *argv[]) {
47:        FILE *tmpf = 0;               /* Temp. File stream */
48:
49:        atexit(mr_clean);             /* Register our cleanup func */
50:
51:        /*
52:         * Create a temp. file pathname :
53:         */
54:        if ( !(tf_path = tempnam("/tmp","tmp-")) ) {
55:            fprintf(stderr,"%s: creating temp file.\n",strerror(errno));
56:            abort();
57:        }
58:        printf("Temp. file is %s\n",tf_path);
59:
60:        /*
61:         * Create, open and write to the temp. file :
62:         */
63:        if ( !(tmpf = fopen(tf_path,"w+")) ) {
64:            fprintf(stderr,"%s: opening %s\n",strerror(errno),tf_path);
65:            abort();
66:        }
67:        fprintf(tmpf,"PID %ld was here.\n",(long)getpid());
68:
69:        /*
70:         * Normal program exit, without unlinking the temp file:
71:         */
72:        fclose(tmpf);                 /* Notice no unlink(2) here.. */
73:        return 0;                     /* Normal program exit */
74:  }
```

An examination of the program shows that first the `mr_clean()` function is registered with `atexit(3)`, in line 49. Lines 54–72 create a temporary file, write to it, and then close it. The program takes a normal exit in line 73.

Exiting causes the registered function `mr_clean()` to be called to release the temporary file that was created. This is demonstrated by the compile and run session shown, as follows:

```
$ make atexit
cc -c -D_POSIX_C_SOURCE=199309L -D_POSIX_SOURCE -Wall atexit.c
cc atexit.o -o atexit
$ ./atexit
Temp. file is /tmp/tmp-D52582
mr_clean() started:
```

```
unlinking temp. file /tmp/tmp-D52582
mr_clean() ended.
$
```

The program announces (line 58 of Listing 8.6) that it has created the temporary file
`/tmp/tmp-D52582` and then silently returns from the `main()` program (line 73). This causes
the registered cleanup function `mr_clean()` to be called, which then produces the last three
lines of output, indicating that it has called `unlink(2)` to remove the temporary file.

One of the major portability concerns that you should bear in mind is that some platforms will
limit the number of registered functions to a maximum of 32. This is especially critical if you
are designing a C library, where you have no direct control over how the user is using
`atexit(3)`. If the caller of your library has already used up all 32 possible registrations, then
your library will be out of luck.

One way that this problem can be circumvented is by registering one special function, which
can then invoke as many additional cleanup functions as you choose.

Using C++ Destructors

The C++ programmer has the capability to rely on destructors for cleanup operations. Listing
8.7 shows a very simple example of a class named `Temp` that makes use of a temporary file.

LISTING 8.7   `destruct.cc`—A C++ Program Using a Destructor for Temporary File Cleanup

```
 1:   // destruct.cc
 2:
 3:   #include <stdio.h>
 4:   #include <stdlib.h>
 5:   #include <unistd.h>
 6:   #include <string.h>
 7:   #include <stdarg.h>
 8:   #include <errno.h>
 9:
10:   extern "C" {
11:       extern char *tempnam(const char *tmpdir,const char *prefix);
12:   }
13:
14:   /////////////////////////////////////////////////////////////
15:   // A demonstration class, showing how a temp file can
16:   // be used within a C++ class, with automatic
17:   // destruction.
18:   /////////////////////////////////////////////////////////////
19:
20:   class Temp {
21:       char    *tf_path;           // Temp. File Pathname
22:       FILE    *tf;                // Open temp. file
23:   public:
24:       Temp();                     // Constructor
25:       ~Temp();                    // Destructor
```

continued from previous page

```
26:         Temp &printf(const char *format,...);
27:         Temp &rewind();                 // Rewind
28:         Temp &gets(char *buf,int bufsiz);
29: };
30:
31:
32: ///////////////////////////////////////////////////////////////
33: // Constructor :
34: ///////////////////////////////////////////////////////////////
35:
36: Temp::Temp() {
37:
38:     /*
39:      * Create a temp. file pathname :
40:      */
41:     if ( !(tf_path = tempnam("/tmp","tmp-")) )
42:         throw errno;                // Temp. file generation failed
43:
44:     /*
45:      * Create, open and write to the temp. file :
46:      */
47:     if ( !(tf = fopen(tf_path,"w+")) )
48:         throw errno;                // Open failed
49:
50:     printf("Created temp file: %s\n",tf_path);
51: }
52:
53: ///////////////////////////////////////////////////////////////
54: // Destructor :
55: ///////////////////////////////////////////////////////////////
56:
57: Temp::~Temp() {
58:     fclose(tf);                     // Close the open file
59:     unlink(tf_path);                // Delete the temp file
60:     delete tf_path;                 // Free pathname string
61:
62:     write(1,"Temp::~Temp() called.\n",22);
63: }
64:
65: ///////////////////////////////////////////////////////////////
66: // The printf() method :
67: //
68: // Allows the caller to write to the temp. file with the
69: // convenience of printf().
70: ///////////////////////////////////////////////////////////////
71:
72: Temp &
73: Temp::printf(const char *format,...) {
74:     va_list ap;
75:
76:     va_start(ap,format);
77:     vfprintf(tf,format,ap);
78:     va_end(ap);
79:
```

```
 80:        return *this;
 81:    }
 82:
 83:
 84:    ///////////////////////////////////////////////////////////
 85:    // Rewind the temp. file :
 86:    ///////////////////////////////////////////////////////////
 87:
 88:    Temp &
 89:    Temp::rewind() {
 90:        ::rewind(tf);                    // Rewind the temp file
 91:        return *this;
 92:    }
 93:
 94:    ///////////////////////////////////////////////////////////
 95:    // Read back one text line from the temp. file :
 96:    ///////////////////////////////////////////////////////////
 97:
 98:    Temp &
 99:    Temp::gets(char *buf,int bufsiz) {
100:        int e;
101:
102:        if ( !fgets(buf,bufsiz,tf) ) {
103:            if ( feof(tf) )          // EOF ?
104:                throw EOF;           // Indicate EOF
105:            e = errno;
106:            clearerr(tf);
107:            throw e;                 // Throw the error
108:        }
109:
110:        return *this;
111:    }
112:
113:    ///////////////////////////////////////////////////////////
114:    // Main program :
115:    ///////////////////////////////////////////////////////////
116:
117:    int
118:    main(int argc,char *argv[]) {
119:        Temp tf;                     // Create a temp file
120:        char buf[256];
121:
122:        (void) argc;
123:        (void) argv;
124:
125:        // Announce start of program :
126:        printf("PID %ld started:\n",(long)getpid());
127:
128:        // Now write one text line to the temp file :
129:        tf.printf("PID %ld was here.\n",(long)getpid());
130:
131:        tf.rewind();                 // Rewind temp file
132:
```

continued from previous page

```
133:        // Now read back the one text line from the temp file
134:
135:        try {
136:            tf.gets(buf,sizeof buf);
137:        } catch ( int e ) {
138:            fprintf(stderr,"%s: tf.gets()\n",strerror(e));
139:            exit(1);
140:        }
141:
142:        printf("Read back: %s\n",buf);
143:
144:        puts("Now exiting..");
145:        return 0;
146: }
147:
148: // End destruct.cc
```

The program shown in Listing 8.7 declares a class **Temp** in lines 20–29. The class method **Temp::printf()** allows the caller to format a text line to be written to the temporary file. Method **Temp::rewind()** rewinds the temporary file, and method **Temp::gets()** allows the caller to retrieve one text line from the temporary file.

The constructor is implemented in lines 36–51. Note the call to the C function **tempnam(3)** in line 41, and the call to **fopen(3)** in line 47 to create and open the file. The pathname is stored in private member **tf_path**, and the open **FILE** is saved in private member **tf** (declared in lines 21 and 22).

When the **Temp** object is destroyed, the destructor, which is implemented in lines 57–63, is called upon. The destructor closes the temporary file, deletes the pathname of the file, and then frees the pathname string (lines 58–60).

The **main()** program constructs one instance of the **Temp** class in line 119 (the object is named **tf**). The object is destroyed when the **main()** program exits in line 145 (the **return** statement).

Lines 129–142 simply exercise some of the methods of the object **tf**. One text line is written to the temporary file, the file is rewound, and the one text line is read back.

Compiling and running this program should yield results similar to the following:

```
$ make destruct
cc -c -D_POSIX_C_SOURCE=199309L -D_POSIX_SOURCE -Wall
➥    -fhandle-exceptions destruct.cc
cc destruct.o -o destruct -lstdc++
$ ./destruct
PID 52982 started:
Read back: Created temp file: /tmp/tmp-Q52982

Now exiting..
Temp::~Temp() called.
$
```

The line starting with **Read back:** shows how the temporary file was being exercised. The line **Temp::~Temp() called.** shows the output from the **write(2)** call in line 62 of the destructor, proving that the destructor was called. In fact, if the pathname is checked, it will be nonexistent:

```
$ ls -l /tmp/tmp-Q52982
ls: /tmp/tmp-Q52982: No such file or directory
$
```

This proves that the destructor did its job.

While this technique seems to address the cleanup issue, you should be aware that pitfalls still exist. For example, if you change the statement in line 145 that now reads **return 0;** to read **exit(0);**, you will discover that the destructor for the object **tf** is not called. If your application has calls to **exit(3)** sprinkled throughout, you may still wish to use the services of the **atexit(3)** function.

Avoiding Cleanup with _exit(2)

Sometimes it is necessary for a program to exit without invoking any cleanup at all. This is highly desirable when something has gone wrong and you want your program to leave things as they are. This allows you to keep all temporary files around so that they can be inspected for troubleshooting purposes. This can be done with the **_exit(2)** function:

```
#include <unistd.h>

void _exit(int status);
```

The function is called in the same manner as **exit(3)**, except that no **atexit(3)** processing is invoked when **_exit(2)** is called.

Summary

This completes this chapter's tour of the temporary file functions. You should now have a well-rounded knowledge of file, directory, and temporary file operations under UNIX. The **atexit(3)** and C++ techniques shown in this chapter should have provided you with some tips for managing the cleanup of temporary files. Finally, the **_exit(2)** function provides a way to skip cleanup, if required for program debugging.

The next chapter examines the very important **getopt(3)** function. This function makes it possible for you to easily parse command-line options in your applications. Furthermore, the **getopt(3)** function will make your command-line processing consistent with the many existing UNIX utilities on your system.

PART II

LIBRARY FUNCTIONS

CHAPTER 9

UNIX COMMAND-LINE PROCESSING

A nyone who has been using UNIX at the shell prompt for a time has unwittingly become acquainted with how UNIX commands work. Some of the most frequently used commands—ls(1), mv(1), cp(1), rm(1), and ln(1), for example—use the same general command-line conventions.

This level of consistency is a result of a convention being adopted by UNIX developers and a library mechanism to make it easy to adhere to. In this chapter, you will look at

- UNIX command-line conventions

- Parsing command lines with getopt(3)

- Parsing suboptions with getsubopt(3)

- Parsing command lines with the GNU's getopt_long(3)

Command-Line Conventions

The general conventions used for most UNIX commands are as follows:

```
$ command_name [-options] [arg1 [arg2 [argn]]]
```

The square brackets indicate optional item zones on the command line. Options immediately follow the command name and begin with a hyphen. Each option consists of a single character—usually a letter but possibly a number or another character. When used, arguments follow the options. The number of valid arguments is determined by the command being invoked. An example of a typical UNIX command is as follows:

```
$ rm -f core
```

The option shown is specified by the hyphen and the letter f. The option -f is then followed by one argument, the filename core in this case.

Using Multiple Options

There can be several options used on a command line. An example using multiple options is

```
$ ls -l -u b*
```

The example uses the options -l and -u. In this case, the command argument is a wildcard filename.

Combining Multiple Options

Options can be grouped together behind a hyphen. The previous command is functionally equivalent to the following:

```
$ ls -lu b*
```

This ls(1) command demonstrates that option characters can be grouped following the initial hyphen character.

Using Options with Arguments

Some options accept arguments other than the command-line arguments already shown. Examine the following tar(1) command:

```
$ tar -cvf project.tar project
```

In this FreeBSD example, the options are grouped together as -cvf. However, the tar(1) -f option must be followed by a filename, which is given as project.tar. At the end of the command line is a command-line argument project, which is the directory name to be archived. The command could also have been written this way:

```
$ tar -cv -fproject.tar project
```

In this example, the argument immediately follows the option name. Options that take an argument can have the argument value immediately follow the option letter or specified next on the command line as in a regular argument.

Identifying Options or Arguments

You might wonder how to know if what follows the option letter is an option argument or more options. This can't be determined by the appearance of the command line. This behavior is defined by the option itself, which is declared within the program.

Arguments That Look Like Options

You may have encountered a situation in which you wanted to specify an argument that started with a hyphen, and your command complained about the improper options that were being used. For example, if grep(1) were used to search a source program for the string --help, you might experience the following under FreeBSD:

```
$ grep --help tempnam.c
grep: illegal option -- -
usage: grep [-[AB] <num>] [-CEFGLVXHPRSZabchilnqsvwxy]
        [-e <expr>] [-f file] [files ...]
$
```

The problem with this grep(1) command is that the command was confused about how to treat the text --help. The following technique shows how to avoid this little problem:

```
$ grep -- --help tempnam.c
$
```

The example shows that grep(1) understood the -- (double hyphen) on the command line to indicate that there were no further options. This permitted grep(1) to understand that --help was the text being searched for in the file tempnam.c.

The getopt(3) Function

What helps to make UNIX commands consistent in their syntax is that most commands use the library function getopt(3). Its synopsis is as follows:

```
#include <unistd.h>

extern char *optarg;
extern int optind;    /* initialized to 1 */
extern int optopt;
extern int opterr;    /* initialized to 1 */
extern int optreset;  /* extension to IEEE Std1003.2 "POSIX.2" */

int getopt(int argc, char * const *argv, const char *optstring);

extern void getoptreset(void);            /* SGI IRIX 6.5 only */
```

The getopt(3) function returns the option letter that is parsed. Alternatively, -1 is returned when the end of the options has been reached. The value ? is returned when an unrecognized option character has been encountered. If the argument optstring begins with a : character, then : is returned when an option expecting an argument does not have one given.

The getopt(3) External Values

Before you can use getopt(3), you need to be aware of how the external values are used by it. The two most important of these variables are the optarg and optind variables.

The optarg External Variable

The optarg external pointer variable is set to point at the argument supplied for the option being processed. However, this is only done for those options that take arguments (this will be expanded upon later). If getopt(3) were processing the option -fproject.tar or -f project.tar, then the variable optarg would point to the C string containing project.tar when getopt(3) is returned.

The optind External Variable

The external variable optind is initially set to the value 1. It is used by getopt(3) to point to the next argv[] value to be processed. This initial value causes getopt(3) to start processing options in argv[1]. When the end of the options is reached on the command line, the value of optind indicates where on the command line the first argument is located. For example, if the following command were to be processed by getopt(3)

$ rm -f core

then the optind value after all options are processed would be 2. This indicates that argv[2] has the first command-line argument following the options that were just processed.

The opterr External Variable

The external value opterr is initialized to the value of 1 (indicating true) and is used as input to the getopt(3) function. When it is true and an unrecognized option character is encountered, getopt(3) prints an error message to stderr indicating the unrecognized option. This behavior is suppressed when opterr is set to 0 (false). This is usually necessary when your program will be doing the error reporting itself or when the error message must go somewhere other than stderr.

The optreset External Variable

The FreeBSD platform exposes the external variable optreset. This is an extension to the IEEE Std1003.2 POSIX.2 standard and is not supported by other UNIX platforms. Setting this variable to 1 allows a new scan of options to be processed. This is normally accompanied by resetting the variable optind to 1.

To cause getopt(3) to rescan the command line a second time, the following procedure is used under FreeBSD:

```
optreset = 1;          /* Restart scan in getopt(3) */
optind = 1;            /* Restart scan with argv[1] */
```

This pair of assignments readies getopt(3) to start over. SGI's IRIX 6.5, for example, provides a getoptreset(3) function instead:

```
optind = 1;            /* Restart scan with argv[1] */
getoptreset();         /* Reset getopt(3) to start over */
```

Although the IRIX 6.5 documentation states that getoptreset(3) "can be used to reset all the internal state of getopt so that it may be used again on a different set of arguments," it might be wise to set optind=1 prior to making the call.

Note

The UNIX systems UnixWare 7, HPUX-11, Solaris 8, and AIX 4.3 do not document a formal way to reset the scanning of a command line.

The getopt(3) Function Call

The getopt(3) function returns an integer value that fits into one of the following categories:

- The option character just parsed.

- The character ?, indicating that an unrecognized option character was encountered.

- The character :, indicating that an option is missing its argument (this is supported only when the argument optstring begins with a colon character).

- The value -1, indicating that no more options exist (see the Note about EOF).

Note

Prior to the IEEE Std1003.2-1992 (POSIX.2) standard, the macro EOF was documented as the return value from getopt(3) when no more options remain to be processed. Now the standard documents that the value -1 is returned, and the use of the macro EOF in this context is discouraged.

The first argument `argc` for `getopt(3)` states how many argument values we have in the second array `argv[]`. This second argument is an array of C string pointers that point to each command-line argument. The values `argc` and `argv[]` are normally taken directly from the `main()` function interface.

The last argument to `getopt(3)` is the C string that drives the processing. It tells `getopt(3)` which options are supported and which options take arguments. This single string determines the whole personality of the command line.

Defining the `optstring` Argument

To support a few options such as the `tar(1)` example earlier, the `optstring` argument would be defined as follows:

```
int main(int argc,char **argv) {
    static char optstring[] = "cvf:";
```

Note how a colon (`:`) character follows the `f` character in the string `optstring`. The colon indicates that the option `-f` requires an argument. Option order is not significant in the `optstring`. The following would be equally acceptable:

```
int main(int argc,char **argv) {
    static char optstring[] = "vf:c";
```

Whenever `getopt(3)` processes an option, it searches the `optstring` argument. If the option character is not present in `optstring`, then it is not a supported option character, and it is treated as an error (a `?` is returned). When the option character is found within `optstring`, the `getopt(3)` function checks the next immediate character in the `optstring`. If it finds a colon, then it knows that it must extract an argument to go with this option.

`optstring` can be begun with a colon character, as shown:

```
int main(int argc,char **argv) {
    static char optstring[] = ":cvf:";
```

When the `optstring` is specified with a leading colon, `getopt(3)` will return a `:` character when a valid option was parsed but no argument was found following it. This allows your program to assume some other default for the option argument.

Defining an Option-Processing Loop

Listing 9.1 shows a typical option-processing loop using `getopt(3)`. The options supported in this program are the `-c`, `-v`, and `-f` options that were demonstrated by the earlier example using `tar(1)`.

LISTING 9.1   `getopt.c`—A Typical Option-Processing Loop Using `getopt(3)`

```
1:   /* getopt.c */
2:
3:   #include <stdio.h>
4:   #include <unistd.h>
5:
6:   int
7:   main(int argc,char **argv) {
8:        int rc;
9:        int optch;
10:       static char optstring[] = "cvf:";
11:
12:       while ( (optch = getopt(argc,argv,optstring)) != -1 )
13:            switch ( optch ) {
14:            case 'c' :
15:                puts("-c processed.");
16:                break;
17:            case 'v' :
18:                puts("-v processed.");
19:                break;
20:            case 'f' :
21:                printf("-f '%s' processed.\n",optarg);
22:                break;
23:            default :   /* '?' */
24:                rc = 1; /* Usage error has occurred */
25:            }
26:
27:       for ( ; optind < argc; ++optind )
28:            printf("argv[%d] = '%s'\n",optind,argv[optind]);
29:
30:       return rc;
31:  }
```

When the program is compiled and run, the output should appear as follows:

```
$ make getopt
cc -c -D_POSIX_C_SOURCE=199309L -D_POSIX_SOURCE -Wall getopt.c
cc getopt.o -o getopt
$ ./getopt -cvf project.tar project_dir
-c processed.
-v processed.
-f 'project.tar' processed.
argv[3] = 'project_dir'
$
```

The session output shows how the various **case** statements in the program were exercised by the options -c, -v, and -f. Notice the use of the external variable `optarg` for the -f option case (lines 20–22). After all the options were processed, the `for` loop in lines 27–28 reported the remaining command-line arguments. This was shown to be the single argument `project_dir`.

The `getsubopt(3)` Function

Many UNIX platforms support suboptions. Suboptions are useful when your application has many possible parameter values and suboptions, which are best specified by name. SGI's IRIX 6.5 documents an example of suboptions using its `mount(1)` command:

```
# mount -o rw,hard,bg,wsize=1024 speed:/usr /usr
```

In this example, the `-o` represents the option, which is then followed by an argument consisting of suboptions. The argument `rw,hard,bg,wsize=1024` has several suboptions, which are separated by commas. As the example illustrates, some suboptions take arguments and others do not.

To make it easier for the application writer to parse suboptions, the function `getsubopt(3)` is provided. Its synopsis is as follows:

```
#include <stdlib.h>

extern char *suboptarg

int getsubopt(char **subopts_str, char *const *tokens, char **valuep);
```

The first argument `subopts_str` is a pointer to the string that is to be parsed. This pointer is updated with each call to the function.

The argument `tokens` is an array of token string pointers that represent valid suboption values. The last element of the array should be a null pointer, to mark the end of the array. Using the SGI `mount(1)` example shown earlier, the array could be declared and initialized as follows:

```
static char *tokens[] = {
    "rw",    /* [0] */
    "hard",  /* [1] */
    "bg",    /* [2] */
    "wsize", /* [3] */
    NULL
};
```

The last argument, `valuep`, is a pointer to a character pointer. After the `getsubopt(3)` call returns the pointer to which it points, it will be null if there was no value for the parameter, or it will point to the value string. The following shows how the third argument is used:

```
char *valuep = NULL;

x = getsubopt(&optarg,&tokens[0],&valuep);

printf("The value = '%s'\n",valuep != NULL ? valuep : "<NULL>");
```

The return value from `getsubopt(3)` is the index into the `tokens[]` array if the value is a recognized suboption. The returned pointer for the `valuep` argument will contain a pointer to the value part of the `subopt=value` in the suboption or null if no value was provided. The index value `-1` is returned when the suboption is not recognized as an option in the `tokens[]` array.

Determining the End of Suboption Processing

The suboption parsing ends when the pointer being passed into the first argument of getsubopt(3) points to a null byte. An example will illustrate this best.

Assume that you must parse the option argument string found in the getopt(3) external variable optarg. Assume further that the tokens[] array was declared as shown earlier. The general loop used for getsubopt(3) then is as follows:

```
extern char *optarg;    /* getopt(3) */

char *valuep;
int x;

while ( *optarg != 0 )
    switch ( (x = getsubopt(&optarg,tokens,&valuep)) ) {
    case 3 :  /* wsize=arg */
        printf("  %s = '%s'\n",tokens[x],valuep ? valuep : "<NULL>");
```

When the suboption wsize=1024 is parsed, the value for x that is returned by getsubopt(3) will be 3 (due to the tokens[] array). The pointer optarg is updated by getsubopt(3) to point to the next suboption. When no suboptions remain, the pointer optarg in this example will point to a null byte in the string.

Note

Platforms that support getsubopt(3) include FreeBSD, Solaris 8, AIX 4.3, HPUX-11, and SGI IRIX 6.5. Linux (Red Hat 6.0) shows no support for this option.

A Full getsubopt(3) Example

The program shown in Listing 9.2 processes command-line arguments using both getopt(3) and getsubopt(3) in order to demonstrate how they work together. It implements a few options that might be used in a hypothetical tape transport control command xmt, similar to the mt(1) that is available on most UNIX platforms. The synopsis for this hypothetical command is as follows:

```
xmt [-f /dev/tape_device] [-c suboptions]
```

where -f /dev/tape_device specifies the tape device to use and -c suboptions specifies various tape commands:

rewind Rewind the tape drive

weof=n Write file mark(s)

fsf=n   Forward space file(s)

bsf=n   Backspace file(s)

The program presented in Listing 9.2 simply parses these options and suboptions and then lists the remaining command-line arguments.

LISTING 9.2   xmt.c—An Example Using `getsubopt(3)` and `getopt(3)`

```
 1:    /* xmt.c */
 2:
 3:    #include <stdio.h>
 4:    #include <stdlib.h>
 5:    #include <unistd.h>
 6:
 7:    extern char *suboptarg;
 8:    int getsubopt(char **optionp, char * const *tokens, char **valuep);
 9:
10:    int
11:    main(int argc,char **argv) {
12:        int rc = 0;          /* Return code */
13:        int x;               /* Arg index */
14:        int n;               /* Int value */
15:        char *valuep;        /* Ptr to subopt value */
16:        int optch;           /* Option character */
17:        static char optstring[] = "f:c:";
18:
19:        /* Suboptions Table of Tokens : */
20:        static char *tokens[] = {
21: #define _SO_WEOF      0
22:            "weof",          /* Write n EOF marks */

23: #define _SO_FSF       1
24:            "fsf",           /* Forward space file */
25: #define _SO_BSF       2
26:            "bsf",           /* Back space file */
27: #define _SO_REWIND    3
28:            "rewind",        /* Rewind tape */
29:            NULL
30:        };
31:
32:        /*
33:         * Process all command line options :
34:         */
35:        while ( (optch = getopt(argc,argv,optstring)) != -1 )
36:            switch ( optch ) {
37:
38:            case 'f' :       /* -f device */
39:                printf("-f '%s' (tape device).\n",optarg);
40:                break;
41:
42:            case 'c' :       /* -c commands */
43:                /*
```

continued from previous page

```
44:                        * Process all suboptions for -c :
45:                        */
46:                  while ( *optarg != 0 )
47:                      switch ( (x = getsubopt(&optarg,tokens,&valuep)) ) {
48:
49:                      case _SO_WEOF :
50:                          n = !valuep ? 1 : atoi(valuep);
51:                          printf("Write %d EOF marks (%s=%s)\n",
52:                                  n,suboptarg,valuep);
53:                          break;
54:
55:                      case _SO_FSF :
56:                          n = !valuep ? 1 : atoi(valuep);
57:                          printf("Forward space %d file(s) (%s=%s)\n",
58:                                  n,suboptarg,valuep);
59:                          break;
60:
61:                      case _SO_BSF :
62:                          n = !valuep ? 1 : atoi(valuep);
63:                          printf("Backspace %d file(s) (%s=%s)\n",
64:                                  n,suboptarg,valuep);
65:                          break;
66:
67:                      case _SO_REWIND :
68:                          if ( valuep ) {
69:                              printf("Suboption %s does not take a arg\n",
70:                                      suboptarg);
71:                              rc = 1;      /* Flag usage error */
72:                          } else
73:                              printf("Rewind tape (%s)\n",suboptarg);
74:                          break;
75:
76:                      case -1 :
77:                          printf("Illegal suboption %s%s%s\n",
78:                                  suboptarg,
79:                                  valuep ? "=" : "",
80:                                  valuep ? valuep : "");
81:                          break;
82:
83:                      default :
84:                          abort();     /* Should never get here */
85:                      }
86:                  break;
87:
88:          default :   /* '?' */
89:              rc = 1; /* Usage error has occurred */
90:          }
91:
92:      /*
93:       * Report all arguments :
94:       */
95:      for ( ; optind < argc; ++optind )
```

```
96:            printf("argv[%d] = '%s'\n",optind,argv[optind]);
97:
98:        return rc;
99:  }
```

Compiling and running this **xmt** command produces the following session output:

```
$ make xmt
cc -c -D_POSIX_C_SOURCE=199309L -D_POSIX_SOURCE -Wall -g xmt.c
cc xmt.o -o xmt
$ ./xmt -f /dev/tape -crewind,fsf=3,weof=2
-f '/dev/tape' (tape device).
Rewind tape (rewind)
Forward space 3 file(s) (fsf=3)
Write 2 EOF marks (weof=2)
$
```

From the example, you can see that the **rewind** suboption was processed first, followed by **fsf=3** and then **weof=2** to write two end-of-file marks on the tape.

GNU Long Options Extension

A number of GNU commands like the **gcc(1)** compiler for example have a large number of options to support. Besides the fact that you can exhaust all possible characters for those options, a user just cannot remember them all. The GNU solution to this problem is the convention of *long options*.

FreeBSD 3.4 Release includes **gcc(1)**, allowing the following demonstration of a long option:

```
$ gcc --version
2.7.2.3
$
```

Long options begin with two hyphens and must be followed by one or more characters. In order to process long options, the GNU function **getopt_long(3)** must be used.

The GNU getopt_long(3) Function

The **getopt_long(3)** function will process both the traditional short options and the newer GNU long options. The synopsis for **getopt_long(3)** is as follows:

```
#include <getopt.h>

int getopt_long(int argc, char * const argv[],
    const char *optstring,
    const struct option *longopts,
    int *longindex);
```

The function prototype is almost identical to **getopt(3)**, except for the two new arguments **longopts** and **longindex**. The argument **longindex** points to an integer, where an index value is returned.

Understanding the `option` Structure

The `longopts` structure pointer points to the array of `option` structure entries. The `option` structure is composed of four members:

- `name` points to a C string containing the name of the long option, without the leading hyphens.

- `has_arg` is defined as an integer but used as a Boolean value. It must be zero (false) if there is no argument or non-zero (true) if there is an argument for this option.

- `flag` either points to an integer or is null.

- `val` is used in different ways, depending upon how `flag` is initialized.

Setting Up the `option` Structure

The last array entry in the `option` structure array must be initialized with a null pointer for its `name` member, zero for the `has_arg` member, a null pointer for the `flag` member, and zero for the `val` member. This entry indicates to `getopt_long(3)` that there are no more entries in that array. Here is an example of two long options defined in the static `option` structure `long_opts[]`.

```
static struct option long_opts[] = {
    { "help", 0, 0, 'h' },    /* name, has_arg, flag, val */
    { "version", 0, 0, 'v' }, /* name, has_arg, flag, val */
    { 0, 0, 0, 0 }
};
```

Using a Null `option.flag` Pointer

The members `flag` and `val` of the `option` structure work together as a team. The easiest way to use these is through the following procedure:

1. Set `flag` to null.

2. Set the `int` member `val` to the value that you want `getopt_long(3)` to return. Often this is the ASCII character code for the equivalent short option letter.

Making a Long Option Look Short

A common practice is to set `val` to the short option letter equivalent of the long option. For example, if a command supports both `--help` and `-h`, then `option` member `flag` would be set to a null pointer, and `val` would be set to the ASCII value `'h'`. The structure would be initialized as follows:

```
static struct option long_opts[] = {
    { "help", 0, 0, 'h' }, /* name, has_arg, flag, val */
    { 0, 0, 0, 0 }
};
```

Processing when the `option.flag` Pointer Is Null

When processing the long option --`help`, the `getopt_long(3)` function performs the following basic steps:

1. The `getopt_long(3)` scans the `long_opts[]` array, using an index that we will call `x`. It will start with `x=0`.

2. A `strcmp(3)` is done to see if our option string `"help"` matches the entry in `long_opts[x].name` (x is currently the value zero). Note that the hyphens are already stripped off the option string.

3. The `strcmp(3)` function returns zero because the strings match.

4. Now `getopt_long(3)` knows the correct index value *x*. This is returned to the caller by using the integer pointer provided in the fifth argument (`longindex`).

5. The pointer in `long_opts[x].flag` is tested for a `null` pointer. If it is `null`, then processing proceeds to the next step.

6. The value of `long_opts[x].val` is used as the return value for `getopt_long(3)`.

A C code fragment illustrates the last three steps:

```
*longindex = x;              /* 4. Return array index */
if ( !long_opts[x].flag )    /* 5. if flag is null then */
    return long_opts[x].val; /* 6. return 'h' */
```

Your options loop within your program is now tricked into thinking the -`h` option was processed instead, because the value '`h`' was returned. This is the easiest way to use long options.

Using a Non-Null `option.flag` Pointer

When the structure `option` member `flag` is a non-null pointer, something different happens. First, examine Listing 9.3.

LISTING 9.3   A Non-Null `option.flag` Member

```
1:    static int cmdopt_v = 0;      /* Initialized to false */
2:    static struct option long_opts[] = {
3:        { "help", 0, 0, 'h' },    /* name, has_arg, flag, val */
4:        { "version", 0, &cmdopt_v, 1 },
5:        { 0, 0, 0, 0 }
6:    };
```

Listing 9.3 shows how the variables and the `long_opts[]` array are declared. The following points explain the reasoning behind this code:

1. Line 1 declares our -`v` option `flag` variable `cmdopt_v`. It is initialized to false (zero).

2. Array element `long_opts[1]` is initialized to accept the long option --`version` (line 4).

3. Member `long_opts[1].flag` (line 4) is initialized with a pointer to our variable `cmdopt_v` (in line 1).

4. Member `long_opts[1].val` (line 4) is initialized with the `int` value of 1.

5. Array element `long_opts[2]` has all members initialized to null or zero. This marks the end of the long options array.

With the declarations arranged as they are in Listing 9.3, the actions of `getopt_long(3)` when it processes the `--version` option can be explained.

1. Internally to `getopt_long(3)` an array index is initialized to zero. We will call this variable `x`.

2. A `strcmp(3)` is done to see if the option string version matches the entry in `long_opts[x].name` (x is currently the value zero).

3. The `strcmp(3)` function returns non-zero, because the strings do not match (`long_opts[0].name` points to C string `"help"`).

4. The `getopt_long(3)` function increments `x` to the value 1.

5. A `strcmp(3)` is done to see if our option string version matches the entry in `long_opts[x].name` (x=1).

6. The `strcmp(3)` function returns zero, because the option string version matches `long_opts[x].name`, which also points to a string `"version"`.

7. Now `getopt_long(3)` knows the correct index value `x`. This is returned to the caller by using the integer pointer provided in argument five (`longindex`) (x=1).

8. The pointer value `long_opts[1].flag` is tested to see if it is null. It is not null, so the processing moves on to the next step.

9. The integer value from `long_opts[1].val` is fetched and then stored at the location pointed to by `long_opts[1].flag`.

10. The `getopt_long(3)` function returns the value zero to indicate that this special long option has been processed.

Steps 9 and 10 are carried out when the `flag` member is not null. Step 6 in the list from the "Processing when `option.flag` Pointer Is Null" section is used when the `flag` member is null. Note again how `getopt_long(3)` returns zero in step 10.

The following code fragment summarizes steps 7 through 10 of the procedure:

```
*longindex = x;                /* 7. Return array index */
if ( !long_opts[x].flag )      /* 8. if flag is null */
    return long_opts[x].val;   /*    return val */
/* Return val via flag ptr */
*(long_opts[x].flag) = long_opts[x].val; /* 9. Use ptr */
return 0;                       /* 10. Indicate flag use */
}
```

Note

FreeBSD does not document or include development libraries for `getopt_long(3)` when Linux extensions are not installed.

Summary

This chapter has covered the operation of the `getopt(3)` and `getsubopt(3)` functions. Additionally, the `getopt_long(3)` function was included to cover the GNU/Linux method of parsing command lines. All of these functions help keep your applications smaller, simpler, and more reliable.

The next chapter covers the very important topic of performing numeric conversions.

CHAPTER 10

CONVERSION FUNCTIONS

The need for data conversions is always present within an application program. Arithmetic is performed using int, float, and double types because it is efficient and convenient. The same data must then be converted into ASCII strings in order for it to be displayed on a terminal. Data input also must undergo conversions.

In this chapter, you will examine

- The atoi(3), atol(3), and atof(3) family
- The sscanf(3) function
- The strtol(3) and strtoul(3) functions
- The strtod(3) function

All of these functions concern themselves with conversion from ASCII to a numeric C data type.

Simple Conversion Functions

These are the simplest functions for a C programmer to use, because they require no preparation or subsequent tests for conversion errors. With the exception of atof(3) on some UNIX platforms, the entire issue of conversion errors is ignored. For this reason, they are frequently not the best choice of conversion functions available.

Before the alternatives are explored, let's examine these traditional functions more closely.

Scrutinizing the Functions atoi(3) and atol(3)

The functions atoi(3) and atol(3) have the following synopsis:

```
#include <stdlib.h>

int atoi(const char *nptr);
long atol(const char *nptr);
```

These functions simply take the starting address of a C string and return the result as an `int` or a `long` data type value. Any leading whitespace characters, as defined by the C library function `isspace(3)`, are skipped before the conversion is begun. If the conversion fails, the functions `atoi(3)` and `atol(3)` simply give up and return zero.

Using the `atoi(3)` Function

The following is a simple example of using the `atoi(3)` function:

```
char buf[32];
int i;

strcpy(buf,"23");
i = atoi(buf);
```

In this example, the string `"23"` is converted to an integer value `23` and assigned to the variable `i`. However, had the input string contained bad input, the value of `i` would not contain a meaningful result (zero).

Understanding the Conversion Error Problem

As an example, consider the problem where the function `atoi(3)` is used. Assume that there is a debug command-line option of the form `-x n`, where `n` is the debug level between 0 and 9. Within the `getopt(3)` processing loop, the `optarg` value for `-x` must be converted to an integer value.

```
switch( optch ) {
case 'x' :
    cmdopt_x = atoi(optarg); /* Get debug level */
    break;
```

Assume that the user supplied the option as `-x high` on the command line because he didn't know any better. The `atoi(3)` function will glibly return the value `0` in this case because it cannot convert `high` to an integer numeric value. The program will be unaware that there should be a debug level set because the conversion value was `0` (due to the conversion error). Consequently, the program will run without any debug level at all. This results in a program action that is not user friendly.

Converting Garbled Data

A similar problem develops when the user supplies the debug option as `-x 5oops` because he is all thumbs on the keyboard. The program will glibly accept the value `5` that `atoi(3)` was able to convert successfully. The remaining part of the string `oops` is ignored.

The functions `atoi(3)`, `atol(3)`, and `atof(3)` all lack error return information. A better indication of when the conversion succeeded or failed is required.

Knowing Where the Conversion Ended

An additional limitation of the `atoi(3)` family of functions is that the caller is not given information about where the conversion ends in the input string. If it is necessary to write a function to extract the month, day, and year from a date string, you would have a challenge using the `atoi(3)` function. Consider the following variations in date strings that might be provided as input from a terminal:

- `01/01/2000`

- `1/2/2000`

- `12/1/2000`

- `1/ 9/2000`

- `  1 / 31   /  2000`

- `6-31-2001`

The `atoi(3)` function can help only with the month extraction (assuming month/day/year format). After extracting the month, you are left with these questions: How many blanks were skipped over? How many digits were there? Were any trailing blanks present? Because no scan information is returned by `atoi(3)`, your code doesn't know where to start the extraction for the following day or year field.

The `atof(3)` Function

The `atof(3)` function is very similar to the `atoi(3)` function, except that it converts string values into floating point values. The synopsis for `atof(3)` is as follows:

```
#include <stdlib.h>

double atof(const char *nptr);
```

Its use is equally simple. The following is an example:

```
char buf[32];
double f;

strcpy(buf, "  -467.01E+02");
f = atof(buf);
```

The example shows some leading whitespace, a sign character, a decimal number, and a signed exponent. The `atof(3)` function skips over the leading whitespace and converts the remaining characters into a `double` C type value, which is assigned to variable `f`.

Again, the simplicity of this call woos many a C programmer into using this form of conversion. However, the problems that exist for `atoi(3)` and `atol(3)` also apply to the `atof(3)` function.

Most UNIX platforms implement the `atof(3)` function as a call to the function `strtod(3)`:

```
strtod(nptr, (char **)NULL);
```

The function `strtod(3)` does return the special values +HUGE_VAL, -HUGE_VAL, and 0 (zero), in conjunction with the external variable `errno` (see the section "Testing for Math Errors," later in this chapter). Since the implementation of `atof(3)` might not always be in terms of the `strtod(3)` function, you should use `strtod(3)` to test for errors.

Using sscanf(3) for Conversion and Validation

The function sscanf(3) is like a Swiss Army Knife for C input and conversion. While this mechanism is not a perfect solution for all conversions, it still enjoys simplicity of use and provides some measure of error detection.

Applying sscanf(3) to Numeric Conversion

Listing 10.1 shows a simple program that extracts the month, day, and year from a string. The input data has been deliberately made as messy as possible (lines 15–18) with lots of white-space.

LISTING 10.1   sscanf.c—Extracting Date Fields Using sscanf(3)

```
1:    /* sscanf.c */
2:
3:    #include <stdio.h>
4:    #include <stdlib.h>
5:    #include <string.h>
6:
7:    int
8:    main(int argc,char *argv[]) {
9:        int x;
10:       char *datestr;       /* Date string to parse */
11:       int nf;              /* Number of fields converted */
12:       int n;               /* # of characters scanned */
13:       int mm, dd, yyyy;    /* Month, day and year */
14:
15:       static char *sdate[] = {
16:           "  1 /  2  /  2000   ",
17:           " 03 - 9-2001,etc."
18:       };
19:
20:       for ( x=0; x<2; ++x ) {
21:           datestr = sdate[x];      /* Parse this date */
22:           printf("Extracting from '%s'\n",datestr);
23:
24:           nf = sscanf(datestr,"%d %*[/-]%d %*[/-]%d%n",&mm,&dd,&yyyy,&n);
25:
26:           printf("%02d/%02d/%04d nf=%d, n=%d\n",mm,dd,yyyy,nf,n);
27:
28:           if ( nf >= 3 )
29:               printf("Remainder = '%s'\n",&datestr[n]);
30:       }
31:
32:       return 0;
33:    }
```

The variables used in this program are as follows:

- Variable nf receives the number of the conversions that sscanf(3) successfully accomplishes (line 11).

- Variable n receives the number of characters scanned so far (line 12).

- Variables mm, dd, and yyyy are the month, day, and year extracted values, respectively (line 13).

- The character pointer array sdate[] contains the two strings that are going to be used for extraction of the date components (lines 15–18).

Testing Numeric Conversions Using sscanf(3)

Compiling and running this program yields the following results under FreeBSD:

```
$ make sscanf
cc -c -D_POSIX_C_SOURCE=199309L -D_POSIX_SOURCE -Wall sscanf.c
cc sscanf.o -o sscanf
$ ./sscanf
Extracting from '  1 / 2 /  2000  '
01/02/2000 nf=3, n=18
Remainder = '   '
Extracting from ' 03 - 9-2001,etc.'
03/09/2001 nf=3, n=12
Remainder = ',etc.'
$
```

The first example shows how the date 01/02/2000 is successfully parsed. The second result 03/09/2001 is parsed out of the date string using hyphens instead. This is possible because the sscanf(3) %[] format feature was used to accept either a slash or a hyphen (line 24). The full format specifier used was %*[/ -]. The asterisk indicates that the extracted value is not assigned to a variable (nor is it counted for the purposes of %n).

Notice that a space character precedes the %*[/ -] format specification. This causes sscanf(3) to skip over preceding spaces prior to the slash or hyphen, if spaces are present.

The extracted results are reported in line 26, along with the values nf and n. Line 28 tests the value of nf before reporting the remainder string in line 29. This is necessary because the value of n is undefined if the sscanf(3) function did not work its way to the point of the %n specification (at the end of line 24).

The remainder strings show the points where the date extractions ended in both data examples. The last example shows the parse ending at the point ,etc..

Note that there are only three conversions present in the sscanf(3) call of line 24. This is because the %n specification does not count as a conversion.

Improving the sscanf(3) Conversion

One irritation that remains in our example in Listing 10.1 is that it does not skip over the trailing whitespace. This makes it difficult to test whether the entire input string was consumed when the date was extracted. Leftover data usually indicates that not all of it was valid.

This problem is remedied by altering the sscanf(3) statement on line 24 to read

```
nf = sscanf(datestr,"%d %*[/-]%d %*[/-]%d %n",&mm,&dd,&yyyy,&n);
```

If you look carefully at the format string, you will notice that one space was inserted before the %n specifier. This coaxes sscanf(3) into skipping over more whitespace before reporting how many characters were scanned. With the whitespace skipped, the test for leftovers is simple:

```
if ( datestr[n] != 0 ) {
    printf("EEK! Leftovers = '%s'\n",&datestr[n]);
```

If the expression datestr[n] points to a null byte after the conversion, then it is known that all the input string was valid for the conversion.

The Limitations of sscanf(3)

The sscanf(3) return count indicates whether or not the conversion(s) was successful. When the %n specifier is processed, the caller can also determine where the scanning ended. However, sscanf(3) still suffers from the limitation that it does not indicate to the caller where in the string the point of failure is when the conversion fails.

The strtol(3) and strtoul(3) Functions

The function sscanf(3) calls upon the functions strtol(3) and strtoul(3) to carry out its dirty work. You can go right to the source by calling them. The synopses for strtol(3) and strtoul(3) are as follows:

```
#include <stdlib.h>
#include <limits.h>

long strtol(const char *nptr, char **endptr, int base);

unsigned long strtoul(const char *nptr, char **endptr, int base);

Macros from <limits.h> :
    LONG_MAX
    LONG_MIN
    ULONG_MAX
    LONGLONG_MAX
    LONGLONG_MIN
    ULONGLONG_MAX
```

The function strtol(3) converts a possibly signed integer within a character string to a long integer data type value. The function strtoul(3) is functionally identical, except that no sign is permitted, and the returned conversion value is an unsigned long integer.

Within this section, only the strtol(3) function will be examined in detail, with the understanding that the same principles can be applied to the strtoul(3) function.

Using the strtol(3) Function

Listing 10.2 shows a short program that attempts to convert the first signed value in a character array named snum[ ]. Not only will it extract the integer value, but it will also indicate where the conversion ended.

LISTING 10.2   strtol.c—A Conversion Program Using strtol(3)

```
 1:    /* strtol.c */
 2:
 3:    #include <stdio.h>
 4:    #include <stdlib.h>
 5:
 6:    int
 7:    main(int argc,char *argv[]) {
 8:        long lval;
 9:        char *ep;
10:        static char snum[] = " -2567,45,39";
11:
12:        lval = strtol(snum,&ep,10);
13:
14:        printf("lval = %ld, ep = '%s'\n",lval,ep?ep:"<NULL>");
15:
16:        return 0;
17:    }
```

When the program is compiled and run, the following results are observed:

```
$ make strtol
cc -c -D_POSIX_C_SOURCE=199309L -D_POSIX_SOURCE -Wall strtol.c
cc strtol.o -o strtol
$ ./strtol
lval = -2567, ep = ',45,39'
$
```

From the output, you can see that the value **lval** was assigned the converted value. The character pointer **ep** pointed to the part of the string where the conversion stopped, namely **,45,39**. Another parse could be continued after the comma is skipped, if the program were required to do this.

Testing for Errors

The **strtol(3)** and **strtoul(3)** functions return zero if the conversion fails completely. However, zero is a valid conversion value, and it should not be used as the only basis for concluding that an error took place.

If the returned pointer (variable **ep** in Listing 10.2) points to the starting point in the string, this indicates that a conversion error took place. This shows that no progress whatsoever was made in the conversion process. In Listing 10.2, you would test for the error in this manner:

```
if ( ep == snum ) {
    printf("Cannot convert value '%s'\n",snum);
```

This tests to see if the end pointer **ep** matches the starting point **snum**. If they are equal, then no progress was made in the conversion.

Testing the Conversion Pointer

It has already been demonstrated in Listing 10.2 that the return pointer **ep** shows where the conversion ended. This permits the caller to see if all of the input string was used to participate in the conversion. This can be tested as follows:

```
if ( *ep != 0 ) {
    printf("Conversion of '%s' failed near '%s'\n",snum,ep);
```

This not only tests that the conversion consumed all of the input, but it shows the point of failure if one occurs.

Performing Multiple Conversions

In Listing 10.2, three values separated by commas were used as input. A test for a successful field parse can be performed by testing for the delimiting comma:

```
if ( *ep != ',' )
    printf("Failed near '%s'\n",ep);
else {
    ++ep;      /* Skip comma */
    /* Parse next field */
```

In this example, it is known that the next character should be a comma. If it is not a comma, then an error has been encountered. Otherwise, the expected comma is skipped and the conversion proceeds with the next numeric value, using **strtol(3)**.

Using the base Argument for Radix Conversions

The **base** argument of the **strtol(3)** and **strtoul(3)** functions specifies the *radix value* of the number system. For the decimal number system, the radix value is 10.

The program shown in Listing 10.3 will allow you to run some tests with **strtol(3)** using different radix values.

LISTING 10.3   radix.c—Testing the base Argument of strtol(3)

```
1:   /* radix.c */
2:
3:   #include <stdio.h>
4:   #include <stdlib.h>
5:   #include <errno.h>
6:
7:   int
8:   main(int argc,char *argv[]) {
```

```
 9:     int i;              /* Iterator variable */
10:     char *ep;           /* End scan pointer */
11:     long base;          /* Conversion base */
12:     long lval;          /* Converted long value */
13:
14:     /*
15:      * Test for arguments :
16:      */
17:     if ( argc < 2 ) {
18:         printf("Usage: %s base 'string' [base 'string]...\n",argv[0]);
19:         return 1;
20:     }
21:
22:     /*
23:      * Process arguments :
24:      */
25:     for ( i=1; i<argc; ++i ) {
26:         /*
27:          * Get conversion base :
28:          */
29:         base = strtol(argv[i],&ep,10);
30:         if ( *ep != 0 ) {
31:             printf("Base error in '%s' near '%s'\n",argv[i],ep);
32:             return 1;
33:         } else if ( base > 36 || base < 0 ) {
34:             printf("Invalid base: %ld\n",base);
35:             return 1;
36:         }
37:         /*
38:          * Get conversion string :
39:          */
40:         if ( ++i >= argc ) {
41:             printf("Missing conversion string! Arg # %d\n",i);
42:             return 1;
43:         }
44:
45:         errno = 0;      /* Clear prior errors, if any */
46:
47:         lval = strtol(argv[i],&ep,(int)base);
48:
49:         printf("strtol('%s',&ep,%ld) => %ld; ep='%s', errno=%d\n",
50:             argv[i], base, lval, ep, errno);
51:     }
52:
53:     return 0;
54: }
```

This program is invoked with the radix (**base**) value as the first argument of a pair. The second argument of the pair is the input string that you want to convert. The following shows a compile-and-test run:

```
$ make radix
cc -c -D_POSIX_C_SOURCE=199309L -D_POSIX_SOURCE -Wall radix.c
cc radix.o -o radix
```

```
$ ./radix 10 '  +2345' 10 -456 10 '123  '
strtol('  +2345',&ep,10) => 2345; ep='', errno=0
strtol('-456',&ep,10) => -456; ep='', errno=0
strtol('123  ',&ep,10) => 123; ep='  ', errno=0
$
```

Three decimal conversions are attempted in the session shown. The first shows that the white-space was skipped successfully. The second shows that it was successful at converting a negative value. The third conversion shows how the variable **ep** points to the trailing whitespace.

Running Hexadecimal Tests

Setting the base to **16** will allow some hexadecimal conversions to be attempted:

```
$ ./radix 16 012 16 0x12 16 FFx
strtol('012',&ep,16) => 18; ep='', errno=0
strtol('0x12',&ep,16) => 18; ep='', errno=0
strtol('FFx',&ep,16) => 255; ep='x', errno=0
$
```

The first conversion converts the string **012** to **18** decimal, clearly a hexadecimal conversion. The second conversion demonstrates that the **strtol(3)** function will skip over the leading **0x** characters when the base is **16**. The third shows how **FFx** was properly converted, leaving a trailing unprocessed **x**.

Testing a Radix of Zero

When the radix is set to **0**, the function **strtol(3)** will adapt to different number bases. Numbers are considered decimal unless they are prefixed by a leading zero (such as **017**) or a leading zero and the letter **x** (such as **0xDEADBEEF** or **0XDEADBEEF**). The **0x** notation introduces a hexadecimal number, for radix **16**. If the leading zero is present without the letter **x**, then the conversion radix is set to **8**, for octal.

The following demonstrates these types of conversions:

```
$ ./radix 0 '012' 0 '0x12' 0 '12'
strtol('012',&ep,0) => 10; ep='', errno=0
strtol('0x12',&ep,0) => 18; ep='', errno=0
strtol('12',&ep,0) => 12; ep='', errno=0
$
```

The session shown tests octal, hexadecimal, and decimal conversions, in that order.

Testing Binary Conversions

Even binary conversions are possible. The following session output shows some examples in which the radix is **2**.

```
$ ./radix 2 '00001010' 2 '00010110'
strtol('00001010',&ep,2) => 10; ep='', errno=0
strtol('00010110',&ep,2) => 22; ep='', errno=0
$
```

Testing Radixes Above 16

Numbers can be represented in radixes above 16. These are not used very often, but they are available if you have the need:

```
$ ./radix 36 'BSD' 36 'FREEBSD' 36 'LINUX!' 36 'UNIX!' 36 'HPUX' 36 'SUN'
strtol('BSD',&ep,36) => 15277; ep='', errno=0
strtol('FREEBSD',&ep,36) => 2147483647; ep='', errno=34
strtol('LINUX!',&ep,36) => 36142665; ep='!', errno=0
strtol('UNIX!',&ep,36) => 1430169; ep='!', errno=0
strtol('HPUX',&ep,36) => 826665; ep='', errno=0
strtol('SUN',&ep,36) => 37391; ep='', errno=0
$
```

Above base 10, the conversion routines consider the letter A to be the digit 10, B to be the digit 11, and so on. Lowercase letters are treated the same as their uppercase counterparts. Radix 36 is the highest base supported and uses the letter Z defined as the value 35.

The radix 36 value of the string UNIX is 1430169. Others, including the value for the string FREEBSD, were reported. Could these be magic numbers in some contexts?

Testing for Overflows and Underflows

If an attempt is made to convert a very large value, the test program fails:

```
$ ./radix 10 '99999999999999999999'
strtol('99999999999999999999',&ep,10) => 2147483647; ep='', errno=34
$
```

Notice how the result 2147483647 was obtained instead of the correct decimal value of 99999999999999999999. Yet, the ep variable shows that the scan made it to the end of the string. The display of errno=34 provides a clue to the problem.

Interpreting LONG_MAX and ERANGE

Overflows are handled by a special return value LONG_MAX for strtol(3). When strtol(3) returns the value LONG_MAX, the value of errno must be tested as well. If it has the value ERANGE posted to it, then it can be concluded that an overflow has indeed occurred.

The overflow example tried in the previous section reported a return value of 2147483647. This is the value LONG_MAX (FreeBSD). Additionally, the value of errno=34 was reported. Under FreeBSD, this is the value ERANGE. Clearly, these two indications together conclude that an overflow has occurred.

The Overflow Test Procedure

Having strtol(3) return 2147483647 (LONG_MAX) whenever an overflow occurs would seem to preclude the function from ever being able to return this value normally. However, the overflow is further indicated by setting errno to ERANGE. This leads to the following procedure for testing for overflows and underflows:

1. Clear variable **errno** to zero. This is necessary because **strtol(3)** will not zero it.

2. Call **strtol(3)** to perform the conversion.

3. If the value returned is not **LONG_MAX** (and not **LONG_MIN**), then no overflow has occurred, and you are finished. Otherwise, proceed to step 4.

4. Test the value of **errno**. If it is still cleared to zero from step 1, then there was no overflow during the conversion, and the value returned truly represents the converted input value.

5. If the **errno** value is **ERANGE**, then an overflow during the conversion has occurred and the returned value **LONG_MAX** is not representative of the input value.

The same logic can be applied to testing for underflows when the value **LONG_MIN** is returned in step 3.

Proving the Overflow Test Procedure

You can prove this procedure with the test program from Listing 10.3:

```
$ ./radix 10 '99999999999999999999' 10 2147483647
strtol('99999999999999999999',&ep,10) => 2147483647; ep='', errno=34
strtol('2147483647',&ep,10) => 2147483647; ep='', errno=0
$
```

The first conversion fails and returns **LONG_MAX** (value **2147483647**) and shows an **errno** value of **34**, which is known to be the value **ERANGE** (under FreeBSD).

Notice that the second decimal conversion uses as input the maximum **long** value of **2147483647**, and it converts successfully and returns **LONG_MAX**. This time, however, **errno** is not the value of **ERANGE** but remains as zero instead. This is due to line 45 in Listing 10.3, which reads

```
errno = 0;   /* Clear prior errors, if any */
```

Recall that the **errno** value is never cleared by a successful operation. It is only used to post errors. To allow differentiation between a successful conversion and an overflow, the value **errno** must be cleared before calling **strtol(3)**. Otherwise, you will be testing a leftover error code if the conversion is successful.

Coding an Overflow/Underflow Test

If **lval** is assigned the **strtol(3)** return value, the overflow/underflow test should be written like this:

```
if ( lval == LONG_MAX || lval == LONG_MIN ) {
    /* Test for over / under flow */
    if ( errno == ERANGE ) {
        puts("Over/Under-flow occurred!");
```

This test only works if you clear **errno** to zero before calling the conversion function.

Testing for `strtoul(3)` Overflows

Function `strtoul(3)` does unsigned integer conversions. The maximum unsigned value is not the same as the maximum signed value. Consequently, the maximum value returned is `ULONG_MAX`. Otherwise, the general test procedure for overflow is quite similar to the one just covered.

1. Clear variable `errno` to zero.

2. Call `strtoul(3)` to perform the conversion.

3. If the value returned is not `ULONG_MAX`, then no overflow has occurred and you are finished. Otherwise, proceed to step 4.

4. Test the value of `errno`. If it is still cleared to zero from step 1, then there was no overflow during the conversion, and the value returned truly represents the input value.

5. If the `errno` value is `ERANGE` instead, then an overflow during conversion has occurred and the returned value `ULONG_MAX` is not truly representative of the input value.

Because `strtoul(3)` is an unsigned conversion, you have no minimum value to test like the `LONG_MIN` value for `strtol(3)`.

Large Integer Conversions

With the migration of UNIX systems to 64-bit CPUs, the C language now supports 64-bit integers. These data types are

- `long long int`

- `unsigned long long int`

or simply

- `long long`

- `unsigned long long`

With the appearance of these C data types comes the need to make conversions from strings to these 64-bit types.

Some UNIX platforms now support the `strtoll(3)` and `strtoull(3)` functions. Their synopsis is as follows:

```
#include <stdlib.h>

long long strtoll(const char *str, char **endptr, int base);

unsigned long long strtoull (const char *str, char **endptr, int base);
```

These functions work the same as their `strtol(3)` and `strtoul(3)` counterparts. The only difference is that you must use the macro `LONGLONG_MAX` or `LONGLONG_MIN` when testing for overflow/underflows for `strtoll(3)`. Use the macro `ULONGLONG_MAX` for `strtoull(3)`.

Note
Many UNIX systems of today define the C data type `long` to be the same size as the type `int`. As UNIX operating systems move to 64-bit CPU platforms, and as the application software migrates with it, the `long` data type will become 64 bits in length. When that happens, the `strtol(3)` and `strtoul(3)` functions will perform 64-bit conversions instead of the present 32-bit. Consequently, some implementations such as HPUX-11 do not provide a `strtoll(3)` function. Instead, a 32- or 64-bit data model is chosen, and the correct implementation of `strtol(3)` and `strtoul(3)` is linked in to match the data model.

BSD `strtoq(3)` and `strtouq(3)` Functions

BSD is a little different in its large integer conversions. FreeBSD supports its `strtoq(3)` and `strtouq(3)` functional equivalents of the `strtoll(3)` and `strtoull(3)` functions. The 64-bit C data types that FreeBSD uses are

Signed 64-bit	quad_t
Unsigned 64-bit	u_quad_t

The function synopsis of the conversion routines for these data types is as follows:

```
#include <sys/types.h>
#include <stdlib.h>
#include <limits.h>

quad_t strtoq(const char *nptr, char **endptr, int base);

u_quad_t strtouq(const char *nptr, char **endptr, int base);
```

The C macros that you should use with `strtoq(3)` are `QUAD_MAX` and `QUAD_MIN`, when testing for overflow and underflow, respectively. For `strtouq(3)`, you must use the C macro `UQUAD_MAX` instead. Neither of these appears in the `man(1)` pages for these routines, but they can be found in the include file `<machine/limits.h>`.

Note
It seems likely that FreeBSD will change its C data type `long` to be 64-bit in the future. This will result in the `strtol(3)` and `strtoul(3)` functions performing 64-bit conversion when that happens.

The `strtod(3)` Function

The `strtod(3)` function is used to perform string-to-floating point conversions. This function is quite similar in operation to the integer conversion functions just covered, but it has a few new wrinkles. The synopsis for `strtod(3)` is as follows:

```
#include <stdlib.h>
#include <math.h>

double strtod(const char *nptr, char **endptr);
```

Note that there is no **base** argument. No radix conversions are available for floating-point conversions other than base 10.

The input string **nptr** and the second argument **endptr** are used in precisely the same way they are used in the **strtol(3)** function.

Using the `strtod(3)` Function

The following shows how the **strtod(3)** function can be used to convert a floating-point value in a string buffer to the C **double** type:

```
static char buf[] = "-32000.009E+01";
char *ep;               /* Returned pointer */
double dval;            /* Converted value */

dval = strtod(buf,&ep); /* Convert buf to double */
```

The input string is converted and the floating-point result is returned and assigned to the variable **dval**. The point where the conversion ends is passed back to the caller by storing the pointer in pointer variable **ep**. In this example, **ep** should end up pointing to the null byte at the end of the **buf[]** array.

Testing for Math Errors

This function adds a new twist to overflow and underflow detection. In order to test for overflows and underflows, you must include the file **<math.h>**:

```
#include <math.h>
```

This include file defines the macro **HUGE_VAL**, which will be needed in the tests. Three return values from **strtod(3)** require further investigation by the program:

- +HUGE_VAL

- 0.0

- -HUGE_VAL

The test procedure will rely on the fact that the **errno** value is cleared before calling **strtod(3)**.

Testing for Overflow

When the value **+HUGE_VAL** is returned, you must check **errno** to see if the value **ERANGE** was posted there. If **errno** is set to **ERANGE**, then the conversion process had an overflow. If **errno** remains cleared to zero, then the value returned is a valid number.

Testing for Underflow

When the value -HUGE_VAL is returned, you must also check errno to see if the error ERANGE was posted there. If errno remains cleared to zero, then the returned value is a valid number.

Testing for Exponent Underflow

The function strtod(3) returns 0.0 when the converted value is extremely small in value fractionally—so small that the underlying data type cannot represent it. When zero is returned and ERANGE is posted to the errno variable, then it is known that the conversion failed because the input value was too small a fraction to represent. Another way to state this is that the exponent value underflowed.

Handling Exponent Underflow

In many cases, you might be happy just to round that small fractional value to zero and move on. However, this may not be suitable for all applications, especially scientific ones.

A scientific model may depend on the precision of that variable to represent a very small value. If precision is maintained, then that value might be later multiplied by a large value to compute a reasonable result.

However, if you simply allow the value to round to zero, then the multiplied result will be zero also—leading to an incorrect answer. Thus, it is better to abort the computation and point out that the value could not be contained with the necessary precision.

Warning

Consider any computation that leads to a small result that does not quite underflow to be unstable. A significant loss of precision is likely when operating in this extreme exponent range.

Flowchart of Math Error Tests

The entire procedure for math error testing for strtod(3) is shown in Figure 10.1 as a flowchart. This should help summarize the overflow and underflow detection logic that should be used.

FIGURE 10.1

Testing for overflow and
underflow after calling
`strtod(3)`.

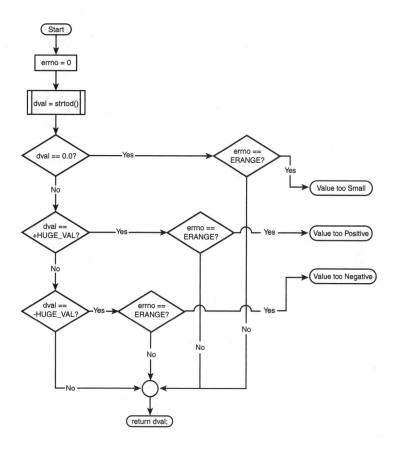

Summary

In this chapter, you learned about the limitations of the simple `atoi(3)` family of functions. The `sscanf(3)` function was discussed as a better replacement, and it was noted that some limitations remain with that approach. The remainder of the chapter covered the details of the `strtol(3)`, `strtoul(3)`, and `strtod(3)` functions.

The next chapter covers the UNIX library calls for working with dates and times. There you will learn how each user can manage his own concept of a time zone, and the system manages time for everyone. Conversions from strings to dates and dates to strings

CHAPTER 11

UNIX DATE AND TIME FACILITIES

Date and time facilities are important to nearly everything you do in UNIX. When a process starts, the time is recorded in a kernel table. When you create a new file, the creation date and time are recorded. Modification times are recorded when you edit a file. Even when you just view a file, its access time is updated.

In this chapter, you will learn about date and time management functions that are available for your use in applications. This chapter covers

- UNIX Epoch Time
- Local, GMT, and UTC time zones
- The `localtime(3)` and `gmtime(3)` functions
- The `asctime(3)` function
- The `tzset(3)` function
- The `mktime(3)` function
- the `strftime(3)` function

UNIX Epoch Time

When reading the `man(1)` pages regarding time functions for UNIX, you will frequently encounter the term *Epoch Time*. This is the beginning of time for UNIX: January 1, 1970, at 00:00:00 GMT (Greenwich Mean Time). This coincides with the value of zero for the data type `time_t`.

Time Zones

Since the UNIX kernel bases its *Epoch Time* on the Greenwich Mean Time (GMT) time standard, it is instructive to do a review of time standards in general. Then, local time zones will be covered to provide a clear understanding of how they are related to the UNIX kernel clock.

Introducing World Time Standards

Originally, the GMT time standard was the world standard. Since then, a new world standard has emerged to coordinate the precise synchronization needed for distributed computer systems.

UNIX had its beginnings when GMT was the still the world standard. Consequently, much of the UNIX literature is steeped in the references to GMT today.

The GMT Time Standard

Greenwich Mean Time is based on the prime meridian of the Earth, which in 1884 was established as passing through Great Britain's Greenwich Observatory. Since then, the observatory has moved and been renamed the Royal Greenwich Observatory. However, its original location is still used to define the prime meridian.

The precise GMT time is determined by observations of the Sun. Due to variations in the Earth's rotation and its orbit around the Sun, small corrections are computed regularly and applied to arrive at the precise time.

The UTC Time Standard

UTC is the abbreviation for the time standard named Universelle Tempes Coordinaté in French, or Coordinated Universal Time in English. This standard is based on atomic clock measurements instead of solar observations, but it still uses the prime meridian. This standard replaced the GMT in 1986.

Choosing a World Time Standard

For many people, a fraction of a second is insignificant. They can set their UNIX system clocks according to the GMT time standard or the UTC time standard. The standards are so similar that they are sometimes used interchangeably.

The correct designation to use for the world time standard today is UTC. Consequently, new software should be written to display UTC instead of GMT.

Understanding Local Time Zones

UNIX allows for those people who do not live in the UTC time zone. This is done by taking your local time zone and adding an offset to arrive at UTC. In the Eastern time zone in North America, for example, UTC time is local time plus five hours. For much of Europe, it is the local time minus one hour.

Customizing Local Time Zones

Since UNIX is a multiuser operating system, it is designed to permit a user to define his own concept of local time. The `tzset(3)` function is used internally by a number of date and time functions to determine the local time zone. This function will be examined in more detail later in this chapter. The important thing to note is that it looks for an exported environment variable `TZ` to define your preference for local time. Your `TZ` value may be different from what other users on your system are using.

Setting the TZ Variable

When the environment variable TZ is found and has a properly defined value, the tzset(3) function will configure your local time zone. This will be used by the rest of the date and time functions where necessary. If the value TZ is not defined or is incorrectly set, the tzset(3) function falls back on the following zone information file (for FreeBSD):

```
/etc/localtime
```

Failing variable TZ and the zone information file, UTC time is assumed.

To configure your session for Eastern Standard Time and no daylight saving time, you can use

```
$ TZ=EST05
$ export TZ
```

This sets the time zone name to EST. Since it is west of the prime meridian, the offset is a positive 05 hours (think of this as local time + 5 hours = UTC). Eastern Daylight Saving Time can be configured as follows:

```
$ TZ=EST05EDT
$ export TZ
```

If you need more information on time zone configuration, a good place to start is the man(1) page for tzset(3). More advanced information is found in the tzfile(5) man pages.

Defining the Date and Time Data Type

Originally, the UNIX time and date value was stored in the C data type long. As time passed, and as standardization efforts got underway, it was recognized that this was not good for long-range planning. The capacity of the long integer was going to run out someday (January 19, 2038, at 03:14:07 UTC, to be precise). The next second after that will cause the 31-bit positive number to roll over to a 32-bit value, making it a negative number.

Since the long integer data type was going to overflow in the near future, it was decided that date and time deserved its own special data type: time_t. This permits the underlying data type to be changed at a future date, requiring that applications only be recompiled.

To obtain the current system date and time from the UNIX kernel, you call upon the time(3) library function. Its synopsis is as follows:

```
#include <time.h>

time_t time(time_t *tloc);
```

The single argument provided to the time(3) function is optional (it must be null when not provided). When provided, it must point to a time_t variable that is to receive the current date and time. This will be the same value returned by the function. For example

```
time_t cur_time;

time(&cur_time);
```

If the pointer argument cur_time is invalid, the value (time_t) -1 is returned and errno is set to the value EFAULT.

While the time since Epoch Time is useful to the UNIX kernel, it must be converted into various other forms to be displayed or to work with its components. The next section examines the library functions that are available for this.

Time Conversion Functions

All date and time functions in this section require the include file <time.h>. In the remainder of this chapter, the following conversions will be examined:

- time_t values to ASCII date/time strings

- time_t values to date/time components (second, minute, hour, day, month, year, and so on)

- Date/time components to ASCII strings

- Date/time components to time_t values

In addition to looking at the various conversion functions, a simple C++ class DTime will be built and illustrated. This object has been left as simple as possible to prevent obscuring the underlying functions being discussed. For this reason, the DTime class in its present form is not entirely suitable for use in production-mode programs. The include file and the class definition for DTime are shown in Listing 11.1.

LISTING 11.1   dtime.h—The Declaration of Class DTime

```
 1:    // dtime.cc
 2:
 3:    #include <iostream.h>
 4:    #include <stdlib.h>
 5:    #include <unistd.h>
 6:    #include <string.h>
 7:    #include <errno.h>
 8:    #include <time.h>
 9:
10:    extern "C" {
11:    extern char *ctime_r(const time_t *clock, char *buf);
12:    extern struct tm *localtime_r(const time_t *clock, struct tm *result);
13:    extern struct tm *gmtime_r(const time_t *clock, struct tm *result);
14:    extern char *asctime_r(const struct tm *tm, char *buf);
15:    }
16:
17:    //////////////////////////////////////////////////////////////
18:    // Experimental DTime Class :
19:    //////////////////////////////////////////////////////////////
20:
21:    class DTime : public tm {
```

```
22:   private:
23:        time_t        dt;           // Date/time in epoch time
24:        char          buf[128];     // ctime(3)/strftime(3) buffer
25:   public:
26:        DTime();
27:        DTime &operator+=(long secs); // Add time
28:        DTime &operator-=(long secs); // Subtract time
29:        inline time_t time() { return dt; }
30:        time_t getTime();            // time(3)
31:        time_t putTime(time_t dt); // Put a time value into this->dt
32:        char *ctime();               // ctime(3)
33:        struct tm *localtime(); // localtime(3)
34:        struct tm *gmtime();     // gmtime(3)
35:        char *asctime();             // asctime(3)
36:        time_t mktime();             // mktime(3)
37:        char *strftime(const char *format); // strftime(3)
38:   };
39:
40:   extern ostream &operator<<(ostream &ostr,DTime &obj);
41:
42:   // End dtime.h
```

The class DTime inherits structure members from the public tm (line 21), which will be discussed later. Private member dt is the time_t data type that is required for several of the functions being discussed (line 23). A number of other functions require the use of a buffer. These use buf[] in line 24.

Listing 11.2 shows the constructor, the operators += and -=, and the getTime() and putTime() methods.

LISTING 11.2   gettime.cc—The Constructor and getTime() Methods of DTime

```
1:   // gettime.cc
2:
3:   #include "dtime.h"
4:
5:   ////////////////////////////////////////////////////////////
6:   // Constructor:
7:   ////////////////////////////////////////////////////////////
8:
9:   DTime::DTime() {
10:       dt = (time_t)(-1);         // No current time
11:   }
12:
13:   ////////////////////////////////////////////////////////////
14:   // Add seconds to the current time in this->dt :
15:   ////////////////////////////////////////////////////////////
16:
17:   DTime &
18:   DTime::operator+=(long secs) {
19:       dt += (time_t) secs;
20:       return *this;
```

continued from previous page

```
21:  }
22:
23:  ////////////////////////////////////////////////////////////
24:  // Subtract seconds to the current time in this->dt :
25:  ////////////////////////////////////////////////////////////
26:
27:  DTime &
28:  DTime::operator-=(long secs) {
29:      dt -= (time_t) secs;
30:      return *this;
31:  }
32:
33:  ////////////////////////////////////////////////////////////
34:  // Return current time :
35:  ////////////////////////////////////////////////////////////
36:
37:  time_t
38:  DTime::getTime() {
39:      return ::time(&dt);
40:  }
41:
42:  ////////////////////////////////////////////////////////////
43:  // Allow the caller to plug-in a time value :
44:  ////////////////////////////////////////////////////////////
45:
46:  time_t
47:  DTime::putTime(time_t dt) {
48:      return this->dt = dt;
49:  }
50:
51:  // End gettime.cc
```

The constructor initializes the member `dt` to the value `(time_t)(-1)` (lines 9–11). This is the error value that is returned by `mktime(3)`, which is used here to indicate that no time is set.

The operators `+=` and `-=` are overloaded for this class to allow the user to add or subtract time from the object (lines 17–31). This will be demonstrated later in the chapter.

The member `getTime()` retrieves the current time into member `dt` using the function `time(3)` that was discussed earlier (lines 37–40). The same value is returned.

The `putTime()` method is provided so that the user can supply a `time_t` value of his own choosing (lines 46–49).

Converting Time to String Form Using `ctime(3)`

This is perhaps the easiest of the date and time conversion functions to use. This function takes the `time_t` value as input and converts it to an ASCII string that can be displayed. The synopsis for `ctime(3)` is as follows:

```
#include <time.h>
```

```
char * ctime(const time_t *timep);
```

The `ctime(3)` function requires a pointer to the time variable that contains the time and date to be converted. The following example shows how to obtain the current system date and pass it to `ctime(3)`. The string returned is then displayed:

```
time_t td;     /* Time and Date */
```

```
time(&td);     /* Get current date */
printf("Today is %s", ctime(&td) );
```

The 26-byte string returned by `ctime(3)` is a date and time string of the form

```
Mon Jan 18 22:14:07 2038
```

The function returns a pointer to an internal static buffer, which is valid only until the next call. One annoying aspect of this returned date string is that a newline character is placed at the end.

The `ctime_r(3)` Function

The `ctime(3)` function returns a pointer to its internal static buffer. This makes it unsafe for threaded programs. A thread-safe version of this routine is available as `ctime_r(3)`:

```
#include <time.h>
```

```
char *ctime_r(const time_t *clock, char *buf);
```

The buffer supplied for argument `buf` must be at least 26 characters long. The pointer value returned is the same pointer supplied for `buf`.

The `DTime::ctime()` method is shown in Listing 11.3.

LISTING 11.3   `ctime.cc`—The Implementation of the `DTime::ctime()` Method

```
 1:   // ctime.cc
 2:
 3:   #include "dtime.h"
 4:
 5:   ///////////////////////////////////////////////////////////
 6:   // Returns the ctime(3) string for the current time_t
 7:   // value that is stored in this->dt. This routine assumes
 8:   // that this->getTime() has been previously called:
 9:   ///////////////////////////////////////////////////////////
10:
11:   char *
12:   DTime::ctime() {
13:       char *cp;
14:
15:       ::ctime_r(&dt,buf);     // Put ctime(3) string into buf[]
```

continued from previous page

```
16:        if ( (cp = strchr(buf,'\n')) != NULL )
17:            *cp = 0;              // Eliminate pesky newline character
18:        return buf;              // Return ptr to buffer
19:    }
20:
21: // End ctime.cc
```

The `DTime::ctime()` method calls on the function `ctime_r(3)`. The function `ctime_r(3)` takes the time that is in the member `dt` and converts it to ASCII form in the private buffer `buf[]` (line 15). The annoying newline character is eliminated in lines 15 and 16. Line 18 returns the pointer to the private buffer containing the string.

The `localtime(3)` and `gmtime(3)` Functions

The programmer often needs direct access to the date and time components. The `time_t` data type may be convenient for math, but it is not always convenient for all forms of date arithmetic. To extract the date components from a `time_t` value, the function `localtime(3)` or `gmtime(3)` can be used:

```
#include <time.h>

struct tm *localtime(const time_t *timep);

struct tm *gmtime(const time_t *timep);

struct tm *localtime_r(const time_t *clock, struct tm *result);

struct tm *gmtime_r(const time_t *clock, struct tm *result);
```

The `localtime(3)` function returns time and date components according to the local time. To obtain time components according to the UTC time zone, use the `gmtime(3)` function. These functions both accept a pointer to a `time_t` value that is to be converted. The result from these functions is only valid until the next call.

The functions `localtime_r(3)` and `gmtime_r(3)` are thread-safe versions of the older `localtime(3)` and `gmtime(3)` functions, respectively. They have the additional pointer argument `result`, into which the results are written. This is different from returning the results in an internal static buffer as the older `localtime(3)` and `gmtime(3)` functions do.

The returned result is a pointer to a `struct tm`, which provides access to date and time components such as the day of the month and the year. The following example obtains the current date using `time(3)` and then calls on `localtime(3)`. The returned results are copied to the structure variable `dc` in this example:

```
time_t dt;           /* Current date */
struct tm dc;        /* Date components */

time(&td);           /* Get current date */
dc = *localtime(&dt); /* convert dt -> dc */
```

A better way to place the results into the dc structure is to use the new re-entrant counterpart of localtime(3):

```
time_t dt;              /* Current date */
struct tm dc;           /* Date components */

time(&td);              /* Get current date */
localtime_r(&dt,&dc);   /* convert dt -> dc */
```

In this manner, the results are placed into dc straightaway, rather than copying the results from one structure to another.

Listing 11.4 shows the implementation of DTime::localtime() and DTime::gmtime() methods using localtime_r(3) and gmtime_r(3), respectively.

LISTING 11.4   localtime.cc—The Implementation of DTime::localtime() and DTime::gmtime()

```
 1:   // localtime.cc
 2:
 3:   #include "dtime.h"
 4:
 5:   ////////////////////////////////////////////////////////////
 6:   // Return the local time components, based upon the
 7:   // current value of this->dt; assumes that a prior
 8:   // call to getTime() has been made:
 9:   ////////////////////////////////////////////////////////////
10:
11:   struct tm *
12:   DTime::localtime() {
13:       ::localtime_r(&dt,this);
14:       return this;
15:   }
16:
17:   ////////////////////////////////////////////////////////////
18:   // Return the UTC (GMT) time components, based upon the
19:   // current value of this->dt; assumes that a prior
20:   // call to getTime() has been made:
21:   ////////////////////////////////////////////////////////////
22:
23:   struct tm *
24:   DTime::gmtime() {
25:       ::gmtime_r(&dt,this);
26:       return this;
27:   }
28:
29:   // End localtime.cc
```

In both of these methods, the DTime class itself is used in the second argument because it inherits from struct tm. The pointer to the class is returned.

The Members of the `struct tm`

This is the structure that is used by several of the date/time functions, including `localtime(3)`, `gmtime(3)`, and `mktime(3)`. The structure is defined as follows:

```
struct tm {
    int   tm_sec;     /* seconds */
    int   tm_min;     /* minutes */
    int   tm_hour;    /* hours (0-23) */
    int   tm_mday;    /* day of the month (1-31) */
    int   tm_mon;     /* month (0-11) */
    int   tm_year;    /* year 2000=100 */
    int   tm_wday;    /* day of the week (0-6) */
    int   tm_yday;    /* day in the year (0-365) */
    int   tm_isdst;   /* daylight saving time */
};
```

This C structure is defined in the file `<time.h>`. The individual members of this structure are documented in Table 11.1.

Warning

Note that member tm_mon starts at zero. To produce a month number 1–12, you must add 1 to this value.

Note also that you must add 1900 to member tm_year to arrive at the century.

Note

The member tm_isdst has three possible states:

When it is positive, daylight saving time is in effect.

When it is zero, daylight saving time is not in effect.

When it is negative, daylight saving time information is not known or is not available.

TABLE 11.1 The `struct tm` Structure Members

Member	Description
tm_sec	The number of seconds after the minute. Normally the range is 0 to 59, but this value can be as high as 61 to allow for leap seconds.
tm_min	The number of minutes after each hour; it ranges in value from 0 to 59.
tm_hour	The hour past midnight, from 0 to 23.
tm_mday	The day of the month, from 1 to 31.
tm_mon	The month of the year, from 0 to 11.

Member	Description
tm_year	The year, expressed as years since 1900. For example, the year 2010 is represented as 110.
tm_wday	The day of the week, in the range 0 to 6. Day 0 is Sunday, 1 is Monday, and so on.
tm_yday	The day of the year, in the range 0 to 365.
tm_isdst	This is a flag with three possible states. See the Note immediately prior to this table.

The class DTime that is developed in this chapter inherits from the struct tm. Consequently, the members are available to the programmer directly. (Its access is public; see line 21 of Listing 11.1.)

Conversion of Date/Time Components to Strings Using the asctime(3) Function

The asctime(3) function accepts the date and time components from the struct tm and composes an ASCII-formatted date string. Its synopsis is as follows:

```
#include <time.h>

char *asctime(const struct tm *tm_ptr);

char *asctime_r(const struct tm *tm, char *buf);
```

The single argument is a pointer to an input struct tm, which will be used to format a date string. The returned pointer from asctime(3) is to a static buffer that is valid only until the next call. Function asctime_r(3) is the re-entrant counterpart, which requires a destination buffer buf[] that is at least 26 bytes in size.

LISTING 11.5   asctime.cc—The Implementation of DTime::asctime()

```
1:  // asctime.cc
2:
3:  #include "dtime.h"
4:
5:  /////////////////////////////////////////////////////////////////
6:  // This function returns the asctime(3) string, for the
7:  // present members of this class (struct tm). This method
8:  // assumes that the present struct tm members are valid.
9:  /////////////////////////////////////////////////////////////////
10:
11: char *
12: DTime::asctime() {
13:     return ::asctime_r(this,buf);
14: }
15:
16: // End asctime.cc
```

In the implementation of this `DTime` method, the function `asctime_r(3)` is used, passing the pointer `this` as input in the first argument. This works because the class inherits from the `struct tm`. The second argument is set as `buf` in line 13 to receive the ASCII result, which is then returned.

The `tzset(3)` Function

Previously, it was indicated that the `tzset(3)` function is responsible for establishing your definition of local time. This function looks for the exported `TZ` environment variable and falls back to the system-configured zone information file if it is not defined. The synopsis for `tzset(3)` is as follows:

```
#include <time.h>

extern long int timezone;       /* Not BSD */
extern char *tzname[2];
extern int daylight;            /* Not BSD */

void tzset(void);
```

The `tzset(3)` function is called on by any of the library date functions that need to know about the configured local time for this session. For example, after the function `localtime(3)` returns, it is known that the function `tzset(3)` has been called, because it must know about local time.

Once the function `tzset(3)` has been called, it does not need to be called again. However, if you aren't certain that it has been called, there is no harm in calling it again.

The `tzset(3)` External Variables

The side effect of calling function `tzset(3)` is that certain external variables are assigned values. These indicate to the date library routines what the local time zone is. These variables are

```
extern long int timezone;       /* Not BSD */
extern char *tzname[2];
extern int daylight;            /* Not BSD */
```

Understanding the `timezone` External Variable

The value `timezone` is the number of seconds you must add to your local time to arrive at UTC time. If you are in the Eastern Standard Time zone, then you need to add five hours to the local time to arrive at UTC time. To configure the external variable `timezone`, this value should be `+18000` (seconds).

Note

FreeBSD, OpenBSD, and NetBSD do not appear to support the external variable `timezone`.

Understanding the `daylight` External Variable

The value of the `daylight` external variable indicates the following:

- When `daylight` is true (non-zero), daylight saving time is in effect.

- When `daylight` is false (zero), daylight saving time is not in effect.

Note

FreeBSD, OpenBSD, and NetBSD do not appear to support the external variable `daylight`.

Understanding the `tzname[]` External Array

The `tzname[]` array of two-character strings provides the name strings of two time zones. The normal time zone string is provided in `tzname[0]`, and the daylight saving time zone is provided in `tzname[1]`. Examples might be **EST** and **EDT** for Eastern Standard Time and Eastern Daylight Saving Time, respectively.

When daylight saving time is not in effect, array elements `tzname[0]` and `tzname[1]` will point to the same C string.

Using the `tzname[]` External Array

To display the time zone currently in effect, use the following code on a non-BSD system:

```
tzset();                /* Make sure externs are set */
printf("Zone is '%s'\n", tzname[daylight ? 1 : 0]);
```

Warning

Do not rely on the `daylight` external variable to be exactly one or zero. The documentation simply states that this value will be non-zero if daylight saving time is in effect.

Determining the Time Zone Under BSD

If you find that there is no support for the external variables `timezone` and `daylight`, the time zone can be determined by a more tedious procedure:

```
struct tm tmvals;                      /* Date/time components */
time_t td;                             /* Current time/date */
int x;                                 /* tmvals.is_dst */

time(&td);                             /* Get current time */
localtime_r(&td,&tmvals);              /* Populate tmvals */
x = tmvals.tm_isdst < 0 ? 0 : tmvals.tm_isdst;/* Assume not DST if unknown */
printf("Zone is '%s'\n",tzname[x ? 1 : 0]); /* Print time zone */
```

It must be noted that the assignment to x in the example was done because the value in `tmvals.tm_isdst` is a three-state flag. It can be negative, indicating that the time zone is not known. In the example, the code assumed that daylight saving time was not in effect, if it was not known.

Creating Epoch Time Values with the `mktime(3)` Function

If you want to construct a `time_t` value based on a specific date, you need the `mktime(3)` function. Its synopsis is as follows:

```
#include <time.h>

time_t mktime(struct tm *tm_ptr);
```

The `mktime(3)` function requires a pointer to a `struct tm`. This input/output structure contributes date and time components that are used to compute a `time_t` value, which is returned. Some values are also returned in this structure.

Testing for `mktime(3)` Errors

If the values in the `struct tm` are such that a date cannot be computed, the value `(time_t)` `(-1)` is returned. This happens when `tm_year` is set to a year before 1970 or when nonexistent dates are supplied, such as February 30 or June 35.

Setting Input Members of `struct tm` for `mktime(3)`

Not all of the `struct tm` members are used for input when passed to the `mktime(3)` function. The following members are mandatory for input and are not altered by `mktime(3)`:

- `tm_sec` (seconds: 0 to 61)
- `tm_min` (minutes: 0 to 59)
- `tm_hour` (hours: 0 to 23)
- `tm_mday` (days of month: 1 to 31)
- `tm_mon` (months: 0 to 11)
- `tm_year` (years: year 2000 is value 100)
- `tm_isdst` (positive for daylight saving time, zero if no daylight saving time in effect)

Be sure to make the `tm_mon` member a zero-based month value (`0` to `11`).

Members of `struct tm` Altered by `mktime(3)`

The following members are ignored as input but are recomputed and altered before the `mktime(3)` function returns:

- `tm_wday` is ignored as input and is recomputed for output.
- `tm_yday` is ignored as input and is recomputed for output.

The fact that these two values are recomputed allows you to plug in a date and time and call `mktime(3)`. The returned values in the structure will tell you what the weekday and day of the year are.

Tip

Do not forget to set `tm_isdst` before calling `mktime(3)`. This input value determines whether daylight saving time is in effect for the local date and time specified in the other members.

Failure to set this value correctly can allow the computed UTC `time_t` value to be incorrect by the amount of the daylight saving time difference.

Warning

Since the `tm_wday` and `tm_yday` values are replaced by recomputed values, never pass a constant or read-only structure to `mktime(3)`.

Implementing the `DTime::mktime()` Method

Listing 11.6 shows how the `DTime::mktime()` method was implemented. This method calls upon the C function `mktime(3)` to convert the current `struct tm` members that this class inherits into `time_t` values, which are returned. This method will be tested later in the chapter.

LISTING 11.6   `mktime.cc`—The Implementation of the `DTime::mktime()` Method

```
 1:   // mktime.cc
 2:
 3:   #include "dtime.h"
 4:
 5:   //////////////////////////////////////////////////////////////
 6:   // This method assumes that the struct tm members of this
 7:   // class already contain valid values (tm_wday and tm_yday
 8:   // are ignored in this case):
 9:   //////////////////////////////////////////////////////////////
10:
11:   time_t
12:   DTime::mktime() {
13:       return dt = ::mktime(this);
14:   }
15:
16:   // End mktime.cc
```

Customizing Date and Time Formats with `strftime(3)`

The string format of the date and time can vary considerably with the preference of each user. The `strftime(3)` function makes it easier for the C programmer to implement custom date and time formats. Its synopsis is as follows:

```
#include <time.h>

size_t strftime(char *buf, size_t maxsize,
    const char *format, const struct tm *timeptr);
```

The arguments `buf` and `maxsize` specify the receiving buffer and its maximum size, respectively. The argument `format` specifies a `printf(3)`-like format string. The last argument, `timeptr`, points to a `struct tm` structure that will supply all of the input date and time values. The final output string size is returned, excluding the null byte.

If the output buffer is not large enough, the value `maxsize` is returned, indicating that `maxsize` characters were placed into the buffer. However, since there is no room for the null byte when this happens, do not expect one to be there.

The `strftime(3)` Format Specifiers

The format specifiers are quite different from the `sprintf(3)` variety. Table 11.2 lists the format specifiers that are supported. Notice that each specifier starts with the percent character (`%`) and is followed by a letter. All other text in the format string is copied verbatim, in the same way that `sprintf(3)` does. To include a percent character, use two successive percent characters.

TABLE 11.2   Format Specifiers for `strftime(3)`

Specifier	Description
%a	The abbreviated weekday name is substituted according to the locale.
%A	The full weekday name is substituted according to the locale.
%b	The abbreviated month name is substituted according to the locale.
%B	The full month name is substituted according to the locale.
%c	The preferred date and time representation for the current locale.
%d	The day of the month in decimal.
%H	The hour of the day in 24-hour form (00 to 23).
%I	The hour in 12-hour form (01 to 12).
%j	The day of the year as a decimal number (001 to 365).
%m	The month as a decimal number (01 to 12).
%M	The minute as a decimal number.
%p	The string AM or PM according to the time.
%S	The second as a decimal value.

Specifier	Description
%U	The week number of the current year, expressed as a decimal number. The first Sunday is considered the first day of the first week.
%W	The week number of the current year, expressed as a decimal number. The first Monday is considered the first day of the first week.
%w	The day of the week as a decimal number (0 to 6).
%x	The preferred date representation without time, for the current locale.
%X	The preferred time representation without date, for the current locale.
%y	The year without a century (00 to 99).
%Y	The year with the century.
%Z	The time zone or zone abbreviation.
%%	A single percent character (%).

Implementing the `DTime::strftime()` Method

To enable you to try out the `strftime(3)` C function, it has been included in the class `DTime` as the method `DTime::strftime()`. This is shown in Listing 11.7.

LISTING 11.7   `strftime.cc`—The Implementation of the `DTime::strftime()` Method

```
 1:  // strftime.cc
 2:
 3:  #include "dtime.h"
 4:
 5:  /////////////////////////////////////////////////////////////
 6:  // Call strftime(3) to format a string, based upon the
 7:  // current struct tm members. This method assumes that the
 8:  // struct tm members contain valid values.
 9:  /////////////////////////////////////////////////////////////
10:
11:  char *
12:  DTime::strftime(const char *format) {
13:      size_t n = ::strftime(buf,sizeof buf-1,format,this);
14:      buf[n] = 0;               // Enforce a null byte
15:      return buf;               // Return formatted string
16:  }
17:
18:  /////////////////////////////////////////////////////////////
19:  // Output operator for the DTime object :
20:  /////////////////////////////////////////////////////////////
21:
22:  ostream &
```

continued from previous page

```
23:   operator<<(ostream &ostr,DTime &obj) {
24:
25:       if ( obj.time() == (time_t)(-1) )
26:           ostr << "[No current time]";
27:       else
28:           ostr << obj.ctime();
29:       return ostr;
30:   }
31:
32:   // End strftime.cc
```

A C++ function `operator<<()` was implemented in Listing 11.7 to make it possible to display this `DTime` class using the overloaded C++ `<<` operator. Line 25 checks to see if there is a current time for the object and, if so, the `DTime::ctime()` method is called to format a date/time string (line 28). This string is then sent to the output stream.

Testing Class `DTime`

Listing 11.8 shows a main program that will instantiate a `DTime` class and then invoke some operations on it.

LISTING 11.8   `main.cc`—The `main()` Program for Demonstrating the `DTime` Class

```
1:    // main.cc
2:
3:    #include "dtime.h"
4:
5:    int
6:    main(int argc,char **argv) {
7:        DTime obj;
8:
9:        (void) argc;
10:       (void) argv;
11:
12:       // Set and display epoch time in the local time zone :
13:       obj.putTime(0);          // Establish epoch time
14:       cout << "Local UNIX Epoch time is '" << obj << "'\n\n";
15:
16:       // Get and display the current time and date :
17:       obj.getTime();           // Get current date/time
18:       cout << "Current time is '" << obj << "'\n\n";
19:
20:       // Compute a date 30 days from today :
21:       obj += 30 * 24 * 60 * 60;
22:       cout << "30 days from now is '" << obj << "'\n";
23:
24:       // Get UTC values :
25:       obj.gmtime();            // Set struct tm values from time_t
26:       cout << "That date is " << obj.tm_mon + 1 << "/" << obj.tm_mday
27:           << "/" << obj.tm_year + 1900 << " "
```

```
28:            << obj.tm_hour << ":" << obj.tm_min << ":" << obj.tm_sec
29:            << " UTC\n\n";
30:
31:      // Reset to local time, and set to 1st of the month :
32:      obj.getTime();            // Get current time
33:      obj.localtime();          // In local time components
34:      obj.tm_mday = 1;          // Set to 1st of the month
35:      obj.tm_hour = obj.tm_min = obj.tm_sec = 0;
36:      obj.mktime();             // Now set the time_t value
37:      cout << "The 1st is '" << obj << "' in this month\n";
38:
39:      cout << "which is the same as "
40:            << obj.strftime("%A %B %d, %Y at %I:%M %p") << "\n";
41:
42:      return 0;
43:   }
```

Compiling and running this program yields output similar to the following:

```
$ make
cc -c -D_POSIX_C_SOURCE=199309L -D_POSIX_SOURCE -Wall gettime.cc
cc -c -D_POSIX_C_SOURCE=199309L -D_POSIX_SOURCE -Wall ctime.cc
cc -c -D_POSIX_C_SOURCE=199309L -D_POSIX_SOURCE -Wall asctime.cc
cc -c -D_POSIX_C_SOURCE=199309L -D_POSIX_SOURCE -Wall localtime.cc
cc -c -D_POSIX_C_SOURCE=199309L -D_POSIX_SOURCE -Wall mktime.cc
cc -c -D_POSIX_C_SOURCE=199309L -D_POSIX_SOURCE -Wall strftime.cc
cc -c -D_POSIX_C_SOURCE=199309L -D_POSIX_SOURCE -Wall main.cc
cc -o dtime gettime.o ctime.o asctime.o localtime.o mktime.o strftime.o main.o -
lstdc++
$ ./dtime
Local UNIX Epoch time is 'Wed Dec 31 19:00:00 1969'

Current time is 'Sun May  7 22:05:54 2000'

30 days from now is 'Tue Jun  6 22:05:54 2000'
That date is 6/7/2000 2:5:54 UTC

The 1st is 'Mon May  1 00:00:00 2000' in this month
which is the same as Monday May 01, 2000 at 12:00 AM
$
```

The first line of program output states your local time for UNIX Epoch Time. The example output was produced in the EST zone. Yours will differ if you are in a different time zone. This is accomplished in lines 13 and 14 of `main.cc`, shown in Listing 11.8. Line 13 sets the UNIX Epoch Time, which is the value `(time_t)(0)`.

The next line of output beginning with `Current time is` is produced by lines 17 and 18. Line 17 sets the current date and time by calling `obj.getTime()`.

Line 21 adds 30 days to the current time in `obj` using the overloaded `+=` operator. Then the object is directed to `cout` in line 22 to display the date.

Line 25 establishes UTC values in the **struct tm** members that **DTime** inherits. Lines 26–29 access the structure members to send a manually formatted UTC time to **cout**.

Line 32 obtains the current time again for object **obj**. Lines 33–35 establish the first of the current month at midnight. Method **DTime::mktime()** is invoked at line 36, and then the object is sent to **cout** in line 37, displaying what the first of the current month is.

The last test in lines 39 and 40 tests the **strftime(3)** function by calling on the method **DTime::strftime()**.

Understanding the Effects of Locale

Some of the format specifiers that **strftime(3)** supports format according to a *locale*. An example of this is the **%A** specifier (the full weekday name).

In the UNIX context, the locale represents the language and cultural rules that are used on a particular host system. It defines the language used for certain messages and the lexicographic conventions for date and time. Locale also establishes the character set that is to be used.

The locale setting will determine whether, for example, your system uses the English names for the days of the week or French names. The names of the months are also affected by locale. Lexicographical conventions such as the **%X** specifier dictate whether the time should be shown in 12- or 24-hour format, for example.

For more information about locale, view the **man(1)** page for **mklocale(1)** under FreeBSD.

Summary

This chapter covered the UNIX time management and conversion functions. The next chapter covers the subject of converting user ID and group ID names into usernames and group names, and vice versa. These are useful functions when working with **stat(2)** and **fstat(2)**, for example. In addition, the password database routines will be covered.

CHAPTER 12

USER ID, PASSWORD, AND GROUP MANAGEMENT

When you log into your UNIX system, you provide a username and a password at the login prompt. The `login(1)` program looks up that username in a database and obtains your registered password. It encrypts the password you supply at login and compares it to the one that is registered. If they are equal, the `login(1)` program lets you pass in peace.

Once you are logged in, however, you become just a number to the UNIX kernel. This user ID number simplifies user and security management for the kernel. In addition to logging in with a user ID, you log in with a group ID.

In this chapter, you will learn about the following:

- User ID functions `getuid(2)` and `geteuid(2)`
- Group ID functions `getgid(2)` and `getegid(2)`
- How to change your effective user ID and group ID
- The `/etc/password` file and its support functions
- The `/etc/group` file and its support functions
- Supplementary groups and their functions

Introduction to UNIX User Management

To find out what user ID number you are, the `id(1)` command can be used:

```
$ id
uid=1001(me) gid=2010(mygrp) groups=2010(mygrp), 2011(dev)
$
```

The `id(1)` command indicates that the user `me` is user ID number `1001` and is a member of group number `2010`. The user and group names are shown in brackets. These were obtained by looking up the user ID and group ID numbers in the password and group file databases, respectively.

Understanding Username and User ID Numbers

The id(1) command previously reported that username me was user ID 1001. Another term for the user ID number is the uid number. This is derived from the fact that UNIX systems today keep the user ID number in the C data type uid_t. The following summarizes these ideas:

Username	me
User ID (uid) number	1001

The uid number is how the UNIX kernel knows you. Files and IPC resources that you create will have the owner set to this number.

Understanding Username root

The uid number 0 is special under UNIX. It is known as the root user ID, though it need not be named root. Another term used for this user account is *super user*. The 0 (zero) uid number enjoys unrestricted access to the UNIX system as a whole. This is naturally the reason that this account is very strictly guarded.

If you administer a UNIX system (possibly your own), you can be root when you want to be. While this might be fun or convenient, you should do most of your chores in a non-root account where possible. This allows the kernel to protect itself from harm when accidents occur (and they will).

The Group Name and Group ID Numbers

In the same way that the uid number refers to a username, the group ID number is used by UNIX to refer to a group name. The C data type gid_t is used for group numbers. Consequently, the group ID number is frequently referred to as the gid number.

The group file permits one user to be a member of multiple groups. This permits more flexibility in giving out access, since users can frequently be members of several functional groups.

Understanding gid Zero

Like the uid value of zero, the gid value of zero grants unrestricted access to resources at the group level. While this is not the same as being the super user, it still grants dangerous access. Consequently, this group is usually granted only to the root account, or a special administration account.

The getuid(2) and geteuid(2) Functions

When the id(1) command runs, it needs to find out what user and group it is running under. This is accomplished by the getuid(2) and geteuid(2) functions. The function synopsis is as follows:

```
#include <unistd.h>
#include <sys/types.h>

uid_t getuid(void);

uid_t geteuid(void);
```

The `getuid(2)` function returns the real `uid` number it is operating under, while `geteuid(2)` returns the effective `uid`. There are no errors returned; these functions always succeed.

The `geteuid(2)` function returns the effective `uid` that is currently in force. UNIX processes can arrange to become other `uid` values temporarily through functions such as `setuid(2)`. For security reasons, `setuid(2)` functionality is severely restricted. The differences between a *real* user ID and an *effective* user ID will be discussed shortly.

The `getgid(2)` and `getegid(2)` Functions

The `id(1)` command must determine the `gid` it is operating under. The `getgid(2)` and `getegid(2)` functions are shown in the synopsis for this purpose:

```
#include <sys/types.h>
#include <unistd.h>

gid_t getgid(void);

gid_t getegid(void);
```

The `getgid(2)` function returns the real group ID number, and the `getegid(2)` function returns the effective group ID. There are no errors to check; these functions always succeed.

Real, Effective, and Saved User ID

The preceding functions dealt with real and effective user IDs and group IDs. There is a third level of identification known as the *saved* user ID and group ID. Three levels of user ID and group ID can be very confusing. The explanations provided for user ID in the following sections apply equally to group ID.

The Effective User ID

Although the `setuid(2)` call has not been covered yet, recall that it can change the effective user ID for a process. The effective user ID determines what level of access the current process has. When the effective user ID is zero (`root`), then the process has unrestricted access, for example.

The Real User ID

The real user ID is what it sounds like. It identifies who you really are. For example, even when you have the effective user ID of `root`, the real user ID identifies who really is performing functions under UNIX.

The real user ID is normally set only by the login(1) program and remains unchanged for the remainder of the session. The exception to this rule is that **root** can change its real user ID. This is how login(1) is able to establish your real ID.

The Saved User ID

The *saved* user ID value is established by **root** calling setuid(2) or when a new program is started by execve(2) (see Chapter 19, "Forked Processes"). When a new executable file is started, the effective user ID that is in force at the time is copied to the saved user ID.

This is helpful when the current process is running an effective user ID that is different from the real user ID. When the current process needs to call execve(2) to start a new executable, its effective user ID might be changed if the new executable has the set-user-ID bit on. By saving the effective user ID, the process is permitted to call setuid(2) to switch back to the saved user ID.

The Identification Role Summary

The following list summarizes the purpose of the various identifications that are made within the UNIX kernel and the controlling ID involved:

Real user ID	Identifies the real user
Real group ID	Identifies the real group
Effective user ID	Determines access
Effective group ID	Determines access
Supplementary groups	Determine access
Saved user ID	Saves the effective user ID
Saved group ID	Saves the effective group ID

Notice in this list that the effective user ID, effective group ID, and supplementary groups determine the access that the process has to restricted objects such as files. The discussion of supplementary groups will be deferred until the end of this chapter.

Setting User ID

The real and effective user IDs can be changed under the correct conditions. These UNIX functions are strictly controlled because they change the accountability and the access of the calling process involved.

The setuid(2) function permits the real user ID to be changed. seteuid(2) allows the effective user ID to be altered. The function synopsis for both is as follows:

```
#include <sys/types.h>
#include <unistd.h>

int setuid(uid_t uid);

int seteuid(uid_t euid);
```

These functions return **0** when successful and **-1** if they fail. The value of **errno** will be set when the call fails (errors **EPERM** or **EINVAL** can be returned).

Note

EPERM—Operation Not Permitted   This error states that the function requested an operation that is not permitted.

Table 12.1 summarizes how the **setuid(2)** function affects the various user ID values that the kernel maintains for the process. Note that a non-**root** process can change the effective user ID only for the current process.

TABLE 12.1   User ID Changes Made by **setuid(2)**

User ID	As root	As non-root
Real	Set	Unchanged
Effective	Set	Set
Saved	Set	Unchanged

Table 12.2 summarizes the ways that executing a new program affects the user ID values. Notice that the real user ID is never changed by executing a new program. The effective user ID is changed by **execve(2)** only when executables have the **set-uid** bit enabled. The saved user ID value is always the effective user ID that was in effect.

TABLE 12.2   User ID Changes Made by **execve(2)**

User ID	No set-uid Bit	With set-uid Bit
Real	Unchanged	Unchanged
Effective	Unchanged	Owner of executable file
Saved	Effective	Effective

Note

Group ID values function in the same manner as the user ID values shown in Tables 12.1 and 12.2.

The exception is that when `execve(2)` starts an executable with the `set-gid` bit on, the effective group ID comes from the group owner of the file.

Setting Group ID

Group ID values can be altered according to the same rules as user ID values. For completeness, these functions are shown in the following sections.

The functions `setgid(2)` and `setegid(2)` establish the new real and effective group ID values, respectively. The function synopsis is as follows:

```
#include <sys/types.h>
#include <unistd.h>

int setgid(gid_t gid);

int setegid(gid_t egid);
```

These functions return **0** when successful. Otherwise, **-1** is returned, and an error code is available in `errno`.

The FreeBSD Function `issetugid(2)`

Since FreeBSD release 3.0, the function `issetugid(2)` has been supported. Its synopsis is as follows:

```
#include <unistd.h>

int issetugid(void);
```

The `issetugid(2)` function returns the value **1** if the process is considered tainted and **0** otherwise. A *tainted* process is one in which the `execve(2)` call established new effective user ID and/or group ID values because of the `set-uid/gid` bits on the executable file. A process can also become tainted if any of the real, effective, or saved user ID/group ID values has changed since the executable file started its execution.

Processes inherit the tainted status when `fork(2)` is called. The tainted status can be cleared by restoring the effective user ID and group ID values to the real user ID and group ID values. Then call `execve(2)` to execute a new program that has not had the `set-uid/set-gid` bits set (or the ID values matched the real ones).

The purpose of this function is to give the library functions a reliable way to determine if the present user ID and group ID values can be trusted to identify the user.

The /etc/passwd File

The information database for the username is stored in a simple text file named /etc/passwd. This file is formatted as a number of different colon-separated fields. A small example is shown:

```
root:bbCsSRB7BZfM.:0:0:root:/root:/bin/sh
bin:*:1:1:bin:/bin:
daemon:*:2:2:daemon:/sbin:
adm:*:3:4:adm:/var/adm:
lp:*:4:7:lp:/var/spool/lpd:
mail:*:8:12:mail:/var/spool/mail:
news:*:9:13:news:/var/lib/news:
uucp:*:10:14:uucp:/var/spool/uucppublic:
man:*:13:15:man:/usr/man:
postmaster:*:14:12:postmaster:/var/spool/mail:/bin/sh
www:*:99:103:web server:/etc/httpd:/bin/sh
nobody:*:-1:100:nobody:/dev/null:
ftp:*:404:1::/home/ftp:/bin/sh
jan:/WzbqfJwMa/pA:503:100:Jan Hassebroek:/home/jhassebr:/bin/ksh
postgres:gXQrO/hNwy5IQ:506:102:Postgres SQL:/usr/local/postgres:/bin/sh
student1:6YNV6cIZxiM2E:507:104:Student 01:/home/student1:/bin/ksh
$
```

Table 12.3 describes the fields, using user jhassebr as an example.

TABLE 12.3   The /etc/passwd Fields

Field Number	Value Shown	Description
1	jan	Username
2	/WzbqfJwMa/pA	Encrypted password, if present
3	503	The user ID number for this user
4	100	The group ID number for this user
5	Jan Hassebroek	The name of the user; also known as the GECOS field
6	/home/jhassebr	The home directory
7	/bin/ksh	The shell program for this user

Notice that field 5 contains the user's full name.

Note

UNIX systems today also implement *shadow password* files. These are readable and writable only to the super user. This improves system security by keeping the encrypted passwords hidden.

If a shadow password file is being used, a single asterisk (*) or x replaces the password in the traditional /etc/passwd file.

The Comment Field

The Comment field is also known as the GECOS field, presumably due to influence from the Honeywell GECOS operating system in times past. This field can be subdivided into comma-delimited subfields, as described in Table 12.4.

TABLE 12.4   The Subfields of the Comment/GECOS Field

Field	Example	Description
1	Jan Hassebroek	User's full name
2	3rd Floor	Office location
3	x5823	Office telephone or extension number
4	905-555-1212	Home telephone number

In the /etc/passwd file, this would appear as

...:Jan Hassebroek,3rd Floor,x5823,905-555-1212:...

These extra subfields are optional. Comment subfields supply extra information to facilities like the finger(1) command does.

Using the & Feature of the Comment Field

The Comment field also supports the use of the ampersand (&) as a substitution character. When this appears, the username from field 1 is substituted and the first letter is capitalized. The Comment field could take advantage of this feature as follows:

...:& Hassebroek,3rd Floor,x5823,905-555-1212:...

Here, the username jan is substituted for the ampersand character, and the j is capitalized. After the substitution is complete, the first subfield would indicate the name is Jan Hassebroek.

The Password Database Routines

To ease the burden of searching the /etc/passwd file, the getpwent(3) function can be used:

```
#include <sys/types.h>
#include <pwd.h>

struct passwd *getpwent(void);

void setpwent(void);

void endpwent(void);
```

The getpwent(3) function will automatically open the /etc/passwd file, if it hasn't already been opened. Then a database entry with the fields already parsed and converted is returned in the structure passwd. The returned pointer is valid only until the next call to getpwent(3) is made.

If the first entry did not contain the information you wanted, you can continue to call getpwent(3) for more entries until it returns a null pointer. The null pointer indicates that it has reached the end of the file (or an error has occurred).

When you cease processing password file entries, the endpwent(3) function is called to close the implicitly opened password file. Alternatively, if you need to scan the database again, you call setpwent(3) to rewind to the start. Calling setpwent(3) is more efficient than calling endpwent(3), because endpwent(3) requires the file to be reopened the next time getpwent(3) is called.

The passwd Structure

The getpwent(3) function returns a pointer to a static structure, which looks like this:

```
struct passwd {
    char    *pw_name;      /* username */
    char    *pw_passwd;    /* user password */
    uid_t   pw_uid;        /* user id */
    gid_t   pw_gid;        /* group id */
    char    *pw_gecos;     /* comment field */
    char    *pw_dir;       /* home directory */
    char    *pw_shell;     /* shell program */
};
```

Reviewing the layout of the /etc/passwd fields, you'll see a one-to-one correspondence between them and the passwd structure. The getpwent(3) function performs all of the grunt work of converting /etc/passwd numeric fields and separating the other fields into C strings.

Error Handling for getpwent(3)

When the getpwent(3) function returns a null pointer, this can indicate that the end of the password database was reached or that an error occurred. You must check the errno value to distinguish between them. To do this, you must zero errno prior to calling getpwent(3).

```
struct passwd *pwp;

errno = 0;        /* IMPORTANT: Clear error code */
pwp = getpwent(); /* Get passwd entry */
if ( !pwp ) {
    if ( errno != 0 ) {
        perror("getpwent() failed!");
        abort();
    }
    /* Else end of password database */
}
```

It is very important to remember that you must zero the **errno** value before calling
getpwent(3).

The fgetpwent(3) Function

Sometimes it is desirable to maintain a password file separately from the system password file.
A private password file might be used to protect access to certain server resources. The
fgetpwent(3) function on some UNIX systems is available for this purpose:

```
#include <stdio.h>
#include <pwd.h>
#include <sys/types.h>

struct passwd *fgetpwent(FILE *f);
```

Notice that this function requires that you provide a **FILE** pointer. This implies that you have
opened the stream, and the pointer represents a valid open file.

The fgetpwent(3) file otherwise performs precisely the same as the getpwent(3) function.
Each successive password entry is returned by a pointer to a **passwd** structure.

Note

BSD and AIX 4.3 do not support the fgetpwent(3) function. However, SGI IRIX 6.5, UnixWare 7,
HPUX-11, and Linux do support fgetpwent(3).

The putpwent(3) Function

The naming of this function is not quite consistent with the **fgetpwent()** function, but the
putpwent(3) function is indeed its counterpart. The fgetpwent(3) function lets you scan a
password database of your choice, and the putpwent(3) function allows you to write a password database of your choice.

```
#include <stdio.h>
#include <pwd.h>
#include <sys/types.h>

int putpwent (const struct passwd *p, FILE *f);
```

The input argument **p** consists of a **passwd** structure to be written out. The second argument **f** must be an open **FILE** that is capable of writing.

The function returns the integer value **0** if the function succeeds. Otherwise, **-1** is returned and an error code can be found in **errno**.

Note

FreeBSD does not support the putpwent(3) function. SGI's IRIX 6.5, UnixWare 7, Solaris 8, AIX 4.3, HPUX-11, and Linux do support the putpwent(3) function, however.

The getpwuid(3) Function

Sequentially calling the **getpwent(3)** function to look up one user ID is not convenient to the programmer. The function **getpwuid(3)** is an improvement:

```
#include <sys/types.h>
#include <pwd.h>

struct passwd *getpwuid(uid_t uid);
```

To obtain the password entry for the current real **uid**, you could write

```
struct passwd *pwp;

if ( !(pwp = getpwuid(getgid())) )
    puts("No password entry found!");
else
    printf("real username %s\n",pwp->pw_name);
```

It can happen that there is no password entry for a user ID being looked up, so errors should be tested. Even when your current process is running under its real ID, it is possible that the database entry being sought was deleted. Always test for errors.

When you must distinguish between "not found" and an error, it is recommended that you clear **errno** prior to calling **getpwuid(3)**. Otherwise, it is impossible to make the distinction. When a null pointer is returned and **errno** remains zero, then it is likely that the entry being sought does not exist.

The **ls(1)** command is an example of a UNIX command that must map the numeric user ID from the information returned by **stat(2)** to a username that can be displayed. The **getpwuid(3)** function is used for this purpose.

The getpwnam(3) Function

Sometimes you need to look up the password entry by username, such as in the **login(1)** program, for example. The function synopsis for **getpwname(3)** is as follows:

```
#include <sys/types.h>
#include <pwd.h>

struct passwd *getpwnam(const char *name);
```

The getpwnam(3) function simply takes the C string that contains the username and performs the lookup for you. If a match in the password database is found, the pointer to the passwd structure is returned. Otherwise, a null pointer is returned (not found, or an error occurred).

To display the home directory of the mail user account, you might code

```
struct passwd *pwp;

if ( (pwp = getpwnam("mail")) != 0 )
    printf("mail HOME=%s\n",pwp->pw_dir);
```

Since a null pointer returned may indicate an error, you should clear errno before calling getpwnam(3) to make the distinction. If errno is not zero when a null pointer is returned, an error has occurred.

The Group Database

The previous section covered library functions that work with the password database. Functions that search the group database will be covered in this section.

The /etc/group File

The group database has traditionally been a simple text file /etc/group. Its format is similar to the password database, and a small example is as follows:

```
root::0:root
bin::1:root,bin,daemon
daemon::2:root,bin,daemon
sys::3:root,bin,adm
adm::4:root,adm,daemon,wwg
lp::7:lp
mem::8:
kmem::9:
mail::12:mail
news::13:news
uucp::14:uucp
man::15:man
users::100:student1,jan
postgres::102:wwg
nogroup::-1:
nobody::-1:
```

The format of the group database is illustrated in Table 12.5.

TABLE 12.5   The Group Database Fields

Field	Example	Description
1	users	Group name
2		Group password (if any—none shown here)
3	100	The group ID number
4	student1,jan	The list of usernames that belong to this group

Each text line in the /etc/group database is composed of colon-separated fields. The fourth field is a list of usernames that belong to this group, separated by commas.

Functions getgrent(3), setgrent(3), and endgrent(3)

Like the password database, the group database has its own set of functions for lookups. The function synopsis for getgrent(3), setgrent(3), and endgrent(3) is as follows:

```
#include <sys/types.h>
#include <grp.h>

struct group *getgrent(void);

int setgrent(void);

void endgrent(void);
```

The function getgrent(3) automatically opens the group database when necessary. The getgrent(3) function can be used to scan the group database by calling it until a null pointer is returned. The database is rewound by calling setgrent(3), or you can close the database by calling endgrent(3).

When getgrent(3) returns a null pointer, this can indicate that an error occurred. To distinguish between end of file and an error, you must test **errno**. This requires that **errno** be zeroed before making the call.

Understanding the group Structure

The routines just presented return the **group** structure. This structure is shown in the following synopsis:

```
struct group {
    char    *gr_name;   /* group name */
    char    *gr_passwd; /* group password */
    gid_t   gr_gid;     /* group id */
    char    **gr_mem;   /* group members */
};
```

Again, there is a correspondence between the **group** structure members and the group file fields. The **gr_name** entry points to a C string that contains the group name. The **gr_passwd** entry will point to a C string containing the group's password, if one exists. If no password is configured, this will be a pointer to an empty string (it will not be a null pointer). The **gr_gid** member holds the group ID value.

The last structure member, **gr_mem**, points to a list of C strings. The last pointer in this list is a null pointer to mark the end of the list. Each string in this list is a username that is a member of the group.

The following example shows how the entire group database can be scanned, with the group and member usernames listed as shown:

```
struct group *gp;
int x;

while ( (gp = getgrent()) != 0 ) {
    printf("gr_name='%s', gr_passwd='%s'\n",
        gp->gr_name,
        gp->gr_passwd);
    for ( x=0; gp->gr_mem[x] != 0; ++x )
        printf("  member='%s'\n",gp->gr_mem[x]);
}

endgrent(); /* Close the database */
```

Notice how the **for** loop tests for the null pointer in **gp->gr_mem[x]**.

The fgetgrent(3) Function

To allow the programmer to process private copies of a group-formatted database, the **fgetgrent(3)** function is available on some platforms. Its synopsis is as follows:

```
#include <stdio.h>
#include <grp.h>
#include <sys/types.h>

struct group *fgetgrent(FILE *stream);
```

The input argument requires an open **FILE**. The function **fgetgrent(3)** returns null if no more entries exist on the stream or an error occurs. To test for an error, clear the **errno** value prior to making the call.

Note that there is no **putgrent(3)** function or equivalent available. If you need to write group database records, you will have to write the code yourself.

Note

There is no support for fgetgrent(3) from BSD or AIX 4.3. However, IRIX 6.5, UnixWare 7, Solaris 8, HPUX-11, and Linux do support fgetgrent(3).

The `getgrgid(3)` Function

The `getgrgid(3)` function is provided for programmer convenience to allow lookup of group ID values. Its synopsis is as follows:

```
#include <sys/types.h>
#include <grp.h>

struct group *getgrgid(gid_t gid);
```

The input argument is the group ID number. The function returns a pointer to a `group` structure, or a null pointer. This pointer is valid only until the next call to `getgrgid(3)`. If the returned pointer is null, then no matching group entry was found, or an error occurred. To determine if an error occurred, the caller must clear `errno` before calling `getgrgid(3)`.

The `getgrnam(3)` Function

The `getgrnam(3)` convenience function allows the caller to look up a group database record by group name.

```
#include <grp.h>
#include <sys/types.h>

struct group *getgrnam(const char *name);
```

The input argument to `getgrnam(3)` is a C string holding the group name to look up. The returned pointer points to a structure; the pointer is valid only until the next call. If a match to the name could not be made or an error occurs, a null pointer is returned. In order to distinguish between a failed lookup and an error, you must clear the `errno` value before calling the function.

Related Re-entrant Functions

A number of functions covered in this chapter so far have re-entrant counterparts on some platforms. For example, the function synopsis for `getgrnam_r(3C)` under IRIX 6.5 is as follows:

```
#include <stdio.h>
#include <grp.h>
#include <sys/types.h>

int getgrnam_r(const char *name,   /* Group name to search */
    struct group *grent,           /* Used for storage */
    char *buffer,                  /* Used for storage */
    int bufsize,                   /* Size of buffer in bytes */
    struct group **grp);           /* Pointer to return pointer */
```

To be re-entrant, the caller must supply the function with all of its needs. In the case of `getgrnam_r(3C)` shown, argument `grent` and `buffer` are two storage areas that are provided to the function for its own internal use. The `buffer` points to an I/O buffer, and it is suggested to be BUFSIZ bytes in size. The last argument, grp, is a pointer to a pointer, which is used to return the group structure pointer of interest.

Most of the re-entrant functions work similarly to this one. These functions are preferred when they are available, because they permit multithreaded code to be used. Check the man(1) pages by appending the characters _r to the normal function name to see if you have documentation and support for them.

Note

At the time of this writing, FreeBSD and Linux do not support re-entrant functions such as getgrnam_r(3) for password and group files.

Supplementary Groups

Many people are members of several functional groups. Having access to files based on a single group designation is inconvenient. This often requires the user to switch between groups, using the newgrp(1) command, simply to gain the correct access permissions.

Supplementary groups makes it possible for a user to have access to all files at the group level, even when the groups differ. An example illustrates this problem:

- Account erin is a member of group projectx.
- Account scott is a member of group projectq.

Erin and Scott are working on similar programs within each of their own projects (projects X and Q), and they are in dispute. Laura, their supervisor, wants to compare the files to see how much they differ.

The difficulty is that Erin and Scott each own their files. However, Erin's file grants read permission to the group projectx, and Scott's file grants read permission to the group projectq. Laura cannot be in the correct group to read both of them at the same time.

Supplementary groups allow Laura to be a member of both groups at the same time. This allows her to be granted read access to both files at once, even when the groups differ. Laura is able to perform a diff(1) command without having to copy one file and then perform a newgrp(1) command.

The getgroups(2) Function

The id(1) command reports all of the supplementary groups that you are currently in. This is accomplished with a call to the getgroups(2) function. Its synopsis is as follows:

```
#include <sys/types.h>
#include <unistd.h>

int getgroups(int gidsetlen, gid_t *gidset);
```

The getgroups(2) function returns a list of group ID values in the array pointed to by gidset. The list can have no more than gidsetlen values, and the number of groups returned in the array is the return value. A return value of -1 indicates that an error has occurred (check errno). If your platform has the sysconf(2) value for _SC_NGROUPS_MAX defined as zero, then zero is returned by getgroups(2). This indicates no supplementary group support.

When the argument gidsetlen is zero, the return value indicates how many supplementary groups there are to be returned. No change is made to the set given by the gidset argument in this case. This can be used to determine how large the array should be.

Note

For many systems, the maximum possible number of supplementary groups is determined by calling sysconf(2) using _SC_NGROUPS_MAX.

An example of getgroups(2) is found in Listing 12.1.

LISTING 12.1   getgroups.c—An Example Using getgroups(2)

```
1:    /* getgroups.c */
2:
3:    #include <stdio.h>
4:    #include <stdlib.h>
5:    #include <unistd.h>
6:    #include <sys/types.h>
7:    #include <grp.h>
8:    #include <errno.h>
9:
10:   int
11:   main(int argc,char **argv,char **envp) {
12:       int x;                                  /* Index */
13:       int n;                                  /* groups returned */
14:       struct group *grp;                      /* /etc/group entry */
15:       int setlen = sysconf(_SC_NGROUPS_MAX);  /* Max # groups */
16:       gid_t *gidset = 0;                      /* sup. grp array */
17:
18:       printf("setlen = %d\n",setlen);         /* Print max # groups */
19:       if ( setlen < 1 )
20:           exit(1);                            /* Quit if we have none */
21:
22:       /*
23:        * Allocate the set to maximum size :
24:        */
25:       gidset = (gid_t *) malloc(setlen * sizeof *gidset);
26:
27:       /*
28:        * Obtain the list of supplementary groups :
29:        */
```

continued from previous page

```
30:        n = getgroups(setlen,gidset);
31:
32:        /*
33:         * Display the supplementary groups found :
34:         */
35:        for ( x=0; x<n; ++x ) {
36:            grp = getgrgid(gidset[x]);
37:            printf("Supplemental group: %5d  %s\n",
38:                gidset[x],
39:                grp ? grp->gr_name : "?");
40:        }
41:
42:        return 0;
43:    }
```

The program in Listing 12.1 first calls on `sysconf(2)` to determine what the maximum number of supplementary groups is for this system (line 15). Once that value is known (variable `setlen`), then the array `gidset` is allocated, in line 25, by calling `malloc(3)`. An alternative would have been to call `getgroups(2)` with a zero value for the array length. This would have indicated how many group ID values to expect.

After the `getgroups(2)` function is called in line 30, the entries are displayed in the `for` loop in lines 35–40. Notice the use of `getgrgid(3)` in line 36 to convert the group ID number into a name (displayed in line 39).

Compiling and running the program on your system should return results similar to this:

```
$ make
cc -c -D_POSIX_C_SOURCE=199309L -D_POSIX_SOURCE -Wall getgroups.c
cc -o getgroups getgroups.o
$ ./getgroups
setlen = 16
Supplemental group:  1001   me
Supplemental group:  2010   mygrp
$
```

On this FreeBSD system, you can see that a maximum of 16 supplementary groups is supported. Two supplementary groups are returned and reported here.

Setting Groups with `setgroups(2)`

The `login(1)` program, which determines the groups to which your account belongs, must call on a function to establish your list of supplementary groups. This is accomplished with the `setgroups(2)` function:

```
#include <sys/param.h>
#include <unistd.h>

int setgroups(int ngroups, const gid_t *gidset);
```

The number of groups being established is given in ngroups, and the array of values is given by the pointer gidset. This function returns 0 upon success or -1 if an error occurs. Expect to get the error EPERM if you call this function without being the super user, because only the super user is permitted to set supplementary groups.

Setting Groups for a Specific Username

The function initgroups(3) is a convenience function that might be used by login(1) instead of building its own array of groups. The FreeBSD and AIX synopsis for initgroups(3) is as follows:

```
/* FreeBSD and IBM AIX 4.3 */

#include <unistd.h>

int initgroups(const char *name, int basegid);
```

There is considerable variation of this on other UNIX platforms. Variation occurs with the include files used and the type of the second argument. The synopsis for HPUX-11 is as follows:

```
/* HPUX-11 */

#include <unistd.h>

int initgroups(char *name, gid_t basegid);
```

The next synopsis is valid for UnixWare 7, Solaris 8, and Linux:

```
/* UnixWare 7, Solaris 8, and Linux */

#include <grp.h>
#include <sys/types.h>

int initgroups(char *name, gid_t basegid);
```

The last synopsis is for SGI IRIX 6.5. There is no <grp.h> file included.

```
/* SGI IRIX 6.5 */

#include <sys/types.h>

int initgroups(char *name, gid_t basegid);
```

With this function, a program such as login(1) needs only to supply the user's name in argument name and a current group ID basegid. The function initgroups(3) builds an array of all groups to which the named user belongs and calls on setgroups(2) to make it so.

The function returns 0 when successful or -1 when it fails (check errno). Since initgroups(3) calls on setgroups(2), only a super user will be successful in making this call.

Summary

In this chapter, you learned about usernames, user ID numbers, group names, and group ID numbers. The password and group database access routines were covered in detail. You now should have a clear understanding of the role of real, effective, and saved user ID and group ID identifiers. The chapter concluded with supplementary groups and how to control them.

The next chapter digs into the topic of library functions. You'll start with static libraries and then leap into the exciting functionality of shared and dynamically loaded libraries.

CHAPTER 13

STATIC AND SHARED LIBRARIES

*I*n the early days of computer programming, a program was written completely from scratch, because there was no code to reuse. Each program was new and unique. Since then, programmers have recognized the value of subroutines and collected them into libraries of one form or another.

UNIX C libraries come in two basic forms: static and shared. Each of these formats has its own advantages. In this chapter you will learn how to

- Create and maintain static libraries

- Create and maintain shared libraries

- Define shared library search paths

- Load and execute shared libraries on demand

The Static Library

A static library is a collection of object modules that are placed together in an archive file. Think of it as a repository of code, which is linked with your object code at link time, rather than at runtime. In this section, you will examine how to create, use, and maintain a static library.

Examining the Process Memory Image

Figure 13.1 shows how a small program memory image is allocated in FreeBSD and Linux. Other UNIX platforms will use similar arrangements, but their addresses will be different.

The addresses indicated in Figure 13.1 are only approximate. In the uppermost region of memory are the environment variables. Below them is the top of the stack, which grows downward for most UNIX platforms. At the bottom of the stack is a slack area of unallocated memory.

At the left side of the figure is a series of boxes that represent static library modules and program object modules that are used as input to the linking process. The arrows show how the linker brings them together to form a memory image, which begins at `0x80000000` and works its way up to `0x80049F18`. This collection of regions forms what is stored in the executable file.

FIGURE 13.1

The composition of a process memory image.

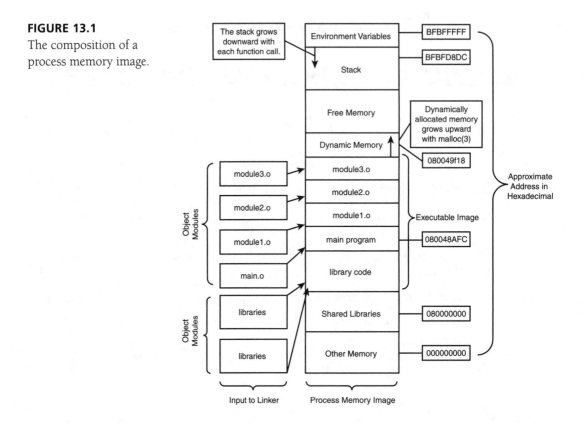

The region below `0x80000000` is reserved for any dynamic (shared) libraries that may need to be brought into memory when the program begins its execution. This area is also used for attaching to shared data regions of memory.

The library code, which is linked to the executable image and resides beneath the main program in Figure 13.1, is called *static library code*. It is static because once it is linked to the program, it never changes. This is in contrast to shared library modules, which are loaded at execution time beneath the address `0x80000000`. If you change the shared libraries, it is the changed libraries that are loaded and executed with your program. The participating static library code never changes once the executable file has been written.

Implementing a Static Library

To demonstrate the use of a static library, a small project that implements a `Passwd` class is used. This project reinforces the concepts that were covered in Chapter 12, "User ID, Password, and Group Management." Listing 13.1 shows the class definition.

LISTING 13.1   passwd.h—The Include File for the `Passwd` Class Example

```
 1:   // passwd.h
 2:
 3:   #include <sys/types.h>
 4:   #include <pwd.h>
 5:
 6:   class Passwd : public passwd {
 7:       enum {
 8:           undefined,                  // object has no content
 9:           defined                     // object has content
10:       }       state;                  // This object's state
11:       int     e;                      // Last errno
12:   protected:
13:       void _dispose();                // Dispose of current content
14:       void _import(struct passwd *p); // Import new contents
15:   public:
16:       Passwd()                        // Constructor
17:           { state = undefined; e = 0; }
18:       ~Passwd()                       // Destructor
19:           { _dispose(); }
20:       inline int isValid()
21:           { return state == defined ? 1 : 0; }
22:       inline int getError()           // Get errno value
23:           { return e; }
24:       char *getuid(uid_t uid);        // Lookup uid, return name
25:       int getnam(const char *name);   // Lookup name, return Boolean
26:   };
27:
28:   // End passwd.h
```

The code in Listing 13.2 implements the methods for `Passwd_getuid()` and `Passwd::getnam()`.

LISTING 13.2   getuid.cc—The Implementation of `Passwd:getuid()` and `Passwd::getnam()` Methods

```
 1:   // getuid.cc
 2:
 3:   #include <errno.h>
 4:   #include "passwd.h"
 5:
 6:   ///////////////////////////////////////////////////////////
 7:   // LOOKUP UID VALUE:
 8:   //      Returns ptr to this->pw_name
 9:   //      Throws errno if call fails
10:   ///////////////////////////////////////////////////////////
11:
12:   char *
13:   Passwd::getuid(uid_t uid) {
14:       passwd *p = 0;
15:
```

continued from previous page

```
16:         if ( state == defined )
17:             _dispose();                 // Dispose of content
18:
19:         e = errno = 0;                  // Clear errno
20:         p = ::getpwuid(uid);            // Look up uid
21:
22:         if ( !p ) {
23:             if ( !errno )
24:                 e = ENOENT;             // Use ENOENT for "not found"
25:             else
26:                 e = errno;              // Capture errno
27:             throw e;                    // throw the error
28:         }
29:
30:         _import(p);                     // Copy to this object
31:         return this->pw_name;           // Return login name
32:     }
33:
34:     //////////////////////////////////////////////////////////
35:     // LOOKUP LOGIN NAME :
36:     //      Returns uid_t value
37:     //      Throws errno if call fails
38:     //////////////////////////////////////////////////////////
39:
40:     int
41:     Passwd::getnam(const char *name) {
42:         passwd *p = 0;
43:
44:         if ( state == defined )
45:             _dispose();                 // Dispose of content
46:
47:         e = errno = 0;                  // Clear errno
48:         p = ::getpwnam(name);           // Look up uid
49:
50:         if ( !p ) {
51:             if ( !errno )
52:                 e = ENOENT;             // Use ENOENT for "not found"
53:             else
54:                 e = errno;              // Else capture errno
55:             throw e;                    // Throw the error
56:         }
57:
58:         _import(p);                     // Copy to this object
59:         return p->pw_uid;               // Return uid #
60:     }
61:
62:     // End getuid.cc
```

Listing 13.3 shows code that implements the protected methods `Passwd::_import()` and `Passwd::_dispose()`. These methods manage dynamic string memory allocation and destruction.

LISTING 13.3   `import.cc`—The Implementation of the Protected `Passwd::_import()` and `Passwd::_dispose()` Methods

```
1:   // import.cc
2:
3:   #include "passwd.h"
4:   #include <string.h>
5:
6:   extern "C" char *strdup(const char *str);
7:
8:   /////////////////////////////////////////////////////////////
9:   // DISPOSE OF OBJECT'S CONTENTS (IF ANY):
10:  //      1. Check state (if defined)
11:  //      2. Delete all allocated strings
12:  //      3. Set state to "undefined"
13:  /////////////////////////////////////////////////////////////
14:
15:  void
16:  Passwd::_dispose() {
17:      if ( state == defined ) {
18:          delete pw_name;     pw_name = 0;
19:          delete pw_passwd;   pw_passwd = 0;
20:          delete pw_gecos;    pw_gecos = 0;
21:          delete pw_dir;      pw_dir = 0;
22:          delete pw_shell;    pw_shell = 0;
23:      }
24:      state = undefined;
25:  }
26:
27:  /////////////////////////////////////////////////////////////
28:  // IMPORT A STRUCT PW INTO THIS OBJECT :
29:  //      1. Dispose of current contents
30:  //      2. Copy and strdup(3) member components
31:  //      3. Set state to "defined"
32:  /////////////////////////////////////////////////////////////
33:
34:  void
35:  Passwd::_import(passwd *pw) {
36:
37:      if ( state == defined )
38:          _dispose();                    // Dispose of present content
39:
40:      pw_name = strdup(pw->pw_name);
41:      pw_passwd = strdup(pw->pw_passwd);
42:      pw_uid = pw->pw_uid;
43:      pw_gid = pw->pw_gid;
44:      pw_gecos = strdup(pw->pw_gecos);
45:      pw_dir = strdup(pw->pw_dir);
46:      pw_shell = strdup(pw->pw_shell);
47:
48:      state = defined;                   // Set into defined state
49:  }
50:
51:  // End import.cc
```

In order to test the `Passwd` class that is implemented in Listings 13.1 to 13.3, a `main()` program is provided in Listing 13.4.

LISTING 13.4   `main.cc`—The `main()` Test Program for the `Passwd` Class

```
 1:    // main.cc
 2:
 3:    #include <iostream.h>
 4:    #include <string.h>
 5:    #include "passwd.h"
 6:
 7:    int
 8:    main(int argc,char **argv) {
 9:        unsigned ux;
10:        Passwd pw;
11:        const char *accts[] = { "uucp", "xyzzy", "games" };
12:
13:        (void) argc;
14:        (void) argv;
15:
16:        // Report root's home directory :
17:
18:        try {
19:            pw.getuid(0);            // Lookup root
20:            cout << "Root's home dir is " << pw.pw_dir << ".\n";
21:        } catch ( int e ) {
22:            cerr << strerror(e) << ": looking up uid(0)\n";
23:        }
24:
25:        // Try a few accounts :
26:
27:        for ( ux=0; ux<sizeof accts/sizeof accts[0]; ++ux )
28:            try {
29:                pw.getnam(accts[ux]);    // Lookup account
30:                cout << "Account " << accts[ux]
31:                    << " uses the shell " << pw.pw_shell << ".\n";
32:            } catch ( int e ) {
33:                cerr << strerror(e) << ": looking up account "
34:                    << accts[ux] << ".\n";
35:            }
36:
37:        return 0;
38:    }
```

The `main()` program instantiates the `Passwd` class in line 10 of Listing 13.4. The first test (lines 18–23) simply looks up `root`'s home directory and reports it (line 20).

The second group of tests are performed in the **for** loop of lines 27–35. This loop looks up the account names **uucp**, **xyxxy**, and **games**. The shell program for each is listed if the account exists. Account **xyzzy** is not expected to exist on most systems and is provided as a test of the error exception raised by the object **pw**.

The result of compiling and running this test should be something like this:

```
$ make getuid
cc -c -D_POSIX_C_SOURCE=199309L -D_POSIX_SOURCE -Wall -fPIC
➥-fhandle-exceptions -g import.cc
cc -c -D_POSIX_C_SOURCE=199309L -D_POSIX_SOURCE -Wall -fPIC
➥-fhandle-exceptions -g getuid.cc
ar -r libpasswd.a import.o getuid.o
cc -c -D_POSIX_C_SOURCE=199309L -D_POSIX_SOURCE -Wall -fPIC
➥-fhandle-exceptions -g main.cc
cc -o getuid main.o -L/home/wwg/book3-code/13 -lpasswd -lstdc++
$ ./getuid
Root's home dir is /root.
Account uucp uses the shell /usr/libexec/uucp/uucico.
No such file or directory: looking up account xyzzy.
Account games uses the shell /sbin/nologin.
$
```

To aid you with following the upcoming text, please remove the archive file, which the make file above has produced:

```
$ rm libpasswd.a
```

The project, when compiled, consists of the following object files, which form input to the linker:

The main program	main.o
Some protected methods	import.o
Methods getuid and getnam	getuid.o

The object module main.o is not a reusable piece of code, but the import.o and getuid.o modules implement a class that can be used by other projects. These two object modules will be placed into a static library for general use.

Using the ar(1) Command to Create an Archive

The ar(1) command is used to create and maintain archive files. Since a static library is a special form of an archive, then the ar(1) command can be used to create a static library.

If you have the object modules import.o and getuid.o, the static library libpasswd.a can be created as follows:

```
$ ar r libpasswd.a import.o getuid.o
```

The ar(1) command is one of those UNIX commands that break from the traditional getopt(3) processing standard. However, most UNIX platforms today now support a leading hyphen character for this command, allowing it to be given as follows:

```
$ ar -r libpasswd.a import.o getuid.o
```

The -r (or simply r) that follows the command name is an option letter that causes the archive libpasswd.a to be created if necessary and replaces the listed object modules if they already exist. If they do not exist in the archive, the listed object modules are added to it.

The normal convention for a library is that it begins with the three letters lib. Archives use the suffix .a. Following these conventions, you end up with a static library named libpasswd.a.

Archives can be updated after their initial creation. If you discover that the getuid.o module has bugs in it, you can replace it with the fixed and recompiled version of the object module, as follows:

```
$ ar -r libpasswd.a getuid.o
```

This type of update is generally performed only for large libraries. Smaller archives are usually re-created from scratch by the make file. The following example shows how a make file creates the static library libpasswd.a:

```
$ make libpasswd.a
cc -c -D_POSIX_C_SOURCE=199309L -D_POSIX_SOURCE -Wall -fhandle-exceptions
➥import.cc
cc -c -D_POSIX_C_SOURCE=199309L -D_POSIX_SOURCE -Wall -fhandle-exceptions
➥getuid.cc
ar -r libpasswd.a import.o getuid.o
$
```

At the completion of this session, the static library libpasswd.a is ready to be used by other projects.

Listing the Contents of an Archive

You can list the contents of an existing archive by performing the following:

```
$ ar -t libpasswd.a
import.o
getuid.o
$
```

The option -t (or simply t) causes ar(1) to list the table of contents for the archive named.

Obtaining a Verbose Listing of an Archive

More information can be displayed by adding the option letter v for a verbose table of contents:

```
$ ar -tv libpasswd.a
rw-r----- 1001/2010    2536 May 11 12:18 2000 import.o
rw-r----- 1001/2010    2948 May 11 12:18 2000 getuid.o
$
```

The leftmost column shows the permission bits that were present when the module was added to the archive. These are displayed in the same form as the ls(1) command. The numbers 1001 and 2010 in the example represent the user ID and group ID numbers, respectively. The date and time are also shown, just left of the module filenames.

Linking with Static Libraries

The link step for shared libraries is easy to accomplish. The filename of the static library can be placed on the link command line like any object module. Alternatively, you can place the library in a certain directory and link with it using the -l option. The following example shows the former method of specifying the filename:

```
$ cc -o getuid main.o libpasswd.a -lstdc++
```

In the command shown, the file libpasswd.a is simply specified on the command line, where any *.o object file could have been given. In larger projects, it's often desirable to place the shared library in a central directory, /usr/local/lib, for example. When this is done, you need to tell the linker where this special directory is, using the -L option. One or more library can then be specified using the -l option. The following is a simple example:

```
$ make getuid
cc -c -D_POSIX_C_SOURCE=199309L -D_POSIX_SOURCE -Wall -fhandle-exceptions
→main.cc
cc -o getuid main.o -L/home/me/myproject -lpasswd -lstdc++
$
```

In this example, the link step specified -L/home/me/myproject to indicate that libraries will be found there. The option -lpasswd caused the linker to look for the library libpasswd.a, in the indicated directory (in addition to system standard directories).

The highlights of the linking process are shown in Figure 13.2.

FIGURE 13.2
The static library linking process.

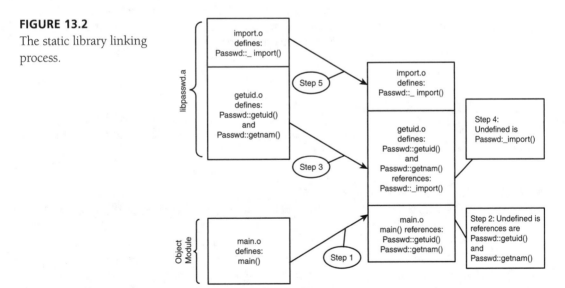

The steps used in the linking process can be summarized as follows:

1. The linking process begins with the loading of the `main.o` module (in this example).

2. Then, the linker notes that there are undefined references to symbols `Passwd:getuid()` and `Passwd::getnam()` referenced by the `main()` function.

3. Since a library has been provided (`libpasswd.a`), this archive file is searched for an object module that defines the symbol `Passwd::getuid`. The linker locates a function named `Passwd:getnam()` in the object module `getuid.o`, which is contained within the archive file. The linker then extracts module `getuid.o` from the archive file and loads it. In the process of doing this, the symbol `Passwd::getnam()` is resolved as well, since it is also contained in the same object module.

4. The linker reviews its list of unresolved symbols. The symbol `Passwd::_import()` is now unresolved. This new reference is from the object module `getuid.o` that the linker just loaded.

5. Working from the top of the list, the linker searches the archive `libpasswd.a` again and determines that it must extract and load module `import.o`. This satisfies the symbol `Passwd::_import()`.

This is an oversimplification of the linking process, since references to the C library functions such as `free(3)` were ignored (for the `delete` C++ keyword). However, this illustrates what happens when a static library is involved in the linking process.

From this process, it has been demonstrated that object modules are brought in by the linker only as required. This bodes well for those who wish to use only a few functions in a large collection of functions. After all, you do not want to link with every object module if you need only a small part of the library.

The Shared Library

In this section, you'll learn how to create and use shared libraries. You've already seen hints about the shared library, in Figure 13.1.

Limitations of Static Libraries

Figure 13.2 shows how the linker automatically extracts object modules from an archive and loads them as required. Although linking only what you need with your program provides a certain amount of economy, there is still duplication when looking at the system-wide picture. Imagine a huge hypothetical static library that contains 90% of the functions used by the Netscape Web browser. Netscape is then linked with this library, producing perhaps a 5MB executable file. Approximately 90% of this executable file will be a copy of what was contained in the static library.

Assume that you want to build a Web-enabled program that creates a Netscape X Window from within your application. Your 200KB object module links with this Netscape static library, and the resulting executable program is written out with a size of 4.5MB. Now you have a 5MB Netscape executable and a 4.5MB program, but 90% of both programs is the same code.

Consider further that five users running Netscape and three users running your custom application consume a large amount of memory within the system. Add more users, and the UNIX kernel will start doing some serious swapping.

Shared libraries provide a mechanism that allows a single copy of code to be shared by several instances of programs in the system.

Creating a Shared Library

In times past, shared library creation and maintenance required some real hand waving by UNIX system administration wizards. To create a shared library for your own use under FreeBSD or Linux, you can simply use the -shared option of the gcc(1) command. Using the earlier example, the shared library for the class Passwd is created as follows:

```
$ cc -o libshared.so import.o getuid.o -shared
```

The gcc(1) command is executed with the -shared option, causing the output file to be written as a shared library rather than an executable file. In this case, file libshared.so is the library created. The suffix .so is used to indicate shared library files under FreeBSD and Linux.

Linking with a Shared Library

Using the shared library is straightforward, but there can be some complications. First, examine how the link step is performed:

```
$ gcc main.o -o getuid -L. -lshared -lstdc++
```

Note the use of the -L and -l options. The -L option specifies an additional directory to search for a shared library. The -lshared option tells it the name of the library to search (the prefix lib and the suffix .so are added for shared libraries, resulting in libshared.so being searched). Because the linker knows that methods Passwd:getuid() and Passwd::getnam() are in the shared library, the linker simply "makes a note" about this in the final executable file that is written. These notes allow the shared library to be loaded when the program is executed.

Choosing Static or Dynamic Libraries

When both shared and static libraries are available, gcc(1) normally will choose the shared library. However, if you specify the option -static on the gcc(1) command line, the link phase will use static libraries instead where possible.

Listing Shared Library References

Under FreeBSD and Linux, you can check the new executable file `getuid`, to see if it is referencing the new shared library that was created earlier:

```
$ ldd ./getuid
./getuid:
        libshared.so => not found (0x0)
        libstdc++.so.2 => /usr/lib/libstdc++.so.2 (0x28063000)
        libc.so.3 => /usr/lib/libc.so.3 (0x2809a000)
        libm.so.2 => /usr/lib/libm.so.2 (0x2811b000)
$
```

From the output shown, it can be seen that `./getuid` is indeed referencing a shared library named `libshared.so`. The `not found` message indicates that `ldd(1)` cannot locate the library. Running the program under these conditions would confirm this:

```
$ ./getuid
/usr/libexec/ld-elf.so.1: Shared object "libshared.so" not found
$
```

Why didn't the dynamic loader find the shared library? To find out why, you need to understand more about the dynamic loader.

The Dynamic Loader

Shared libraries require more attention than do static libraries. This is because shared libraries must be found and loaded on demand.

When `ldd(1)` was used earlier, the dynamic loader was used to test each referenced library found in the executable. This dynamic loader is used to perform the loading and dynamic linking of other shared libraries.

Searching for Shared Libraries

In order for the shared library to be loaded at runtime, the dynamic loader must know where to locate it at runtime. Just as the shell must have a search path for commands, the dynamic loader needs a search mechanism for its libraries.

FreeBSD and Linux both share a *cache file* that indicates where libraries can be found. The following lists where the cache files are located:

FreeBSD `a.out` cache	`/var/run/ld.so.hints`
FreeBSD ELF cache	`/var/run/ld-elf.so.hints`
Linux cache	`/etc/ld.so.cache`

These cache files are updated by the `ldconfig(8)` command under FreeBSD and Linux.

Other UNIX platforms use environment variables to select custom library directories. FreeBSD and Linux also support these environment variables. Among the different UNIX platforms, there are three search path variables in use. Table 13.1 lists these variables and the platforms that use them.

TABLE 13.1   Shared Library Search Path Variables

Environment Variable	UNIX Platforms
LD_LIBRARY_PATH	Solaris, UnixWare, IRIX, Alpha OSF, FreeBSD, and Linux
LIBPATH	AIX
SHLIB_PATH	HPUX

All of these environment variables work in the same fashion as the **PATH** variable. A colon-separated list of directories to be searched is provided.

Using the LD_LIBRARY_PATH **Variable**

Since FreeBSD inspects the **LD_LIBRARY_PATH** variable, the examples given will use it. Recall the example that was shown earlier:

```
$ ldd ./getuid
./getuid:
        libshared.so => not found (0x0)
        libstdc++.so.2 => /usr/lib/libstdc++.so.2 (0x28063000)
        libc.so.3 => /usr/lib/libc.so.3 (0x2809a000)
        libm.so.2 => /usr/lib/libm.so.2 (0x2811b000)
$
```

To fix the search difficulty with your newly created shared library, the **LD_LIBRARY_PATH** variable can be modified to include your current directory (using the shell variable $PWD):

```
$ LD_LIBRARY_PATH=$PWD
$ export LD_LIBRARY_PATH
$ ldd ./getuid
./getuid:
        libshared.so => /home/me/myproject/libshared.so (0x28063000)
        libstdc++.so.2 => /usr/lib/libstdc++.so.2 (0x28065000)
        libc.so.3 => /usr/lib/libc.so.3 (0x2809c000)
        libm.so.2 => /usr/lib/libm.so.2 (0x2811d000)
$
```

Notice that, with the **LD_LIBRARY_PATH** modified to include your current directory, the dynamic loader is able to locate your shared library file `libshared.so`. If you have other directories already included in the present **LD_LIBRARY_PATH** variable, this is a better approach:

```
$ LD_LIBRARY_PATH=$LD_LIBRARY_PATH:$PWD
```

This simply appends your current directory to the values you already have in effect.

Testing the `LD_LIBRARY_PATH` Variable

With the `LD_LIBRARY_PATH` variable properly set, you can now run the test program, as follows:

```
$ ./getuid
Root's home dir is /root.
Account uucp uses the shell /usr/libexec/uucp/uucico.
No such file or directory: looking up account xyzzy.
Account games uses the shell /sbin/nologin.
$
```

If you download the source code for this project, you will see that the output reflects a successful run for this test program. The `No such file or directory:` error message was supposed to occur as part of this test.

Position-Independent Code

There is one small matter that has been overlooked, which is important to shared libraries. For a shared library to be effective at sharing its code with several programs, it should be compiled in *position-independent code* form.

When a program is compiled in position-independent code form, it can be executed from any memory location without regard to its starting address. This makes it possible for the same physical memory segments to be shared virtually at different relative positions in each process that references it.

Figure 13.3 shows Program_A and Program_B, two programs that call upon the same shared library. The shaded areas in the memory images show where in the address space the shared code appears. Notice that the shared library code in Program_A is lower than it is in Program_B. Only one physical copy of this code exists in the system's physical memory, which is managed by the UNIX kernel. The shaded areas represent virtual memory mappings of the same shared code in both processes.

For shared library code to execute in the way Figure 13.3 shows, the code must be compiled as position-independent code. If this is not done, the dynamic loader must create multiple copies of the same library in memory, with different starting addresses.

To compile a module as position-independent code, the `gcc(1)` compile option `-fPIC` can be used under FreeBSD and Linux:

```
$ cc -c -D_POSIX_C_SOURCE=199309L -D_POSIX_SOURCE -Wall -fPIC
➥-fhandle-exceptions import.cc
$ cc -c -D_POSIX_C_SOURCE=199309L -D_POSIX_SOURCE -Wall -fPIC
➥-fhandle-exceptions getuid.cc
```

These commands compile the given modules into position-independent code that can be made into a shared library.

FIGURE 13.3
A shared library compiled
as position-independent
code.

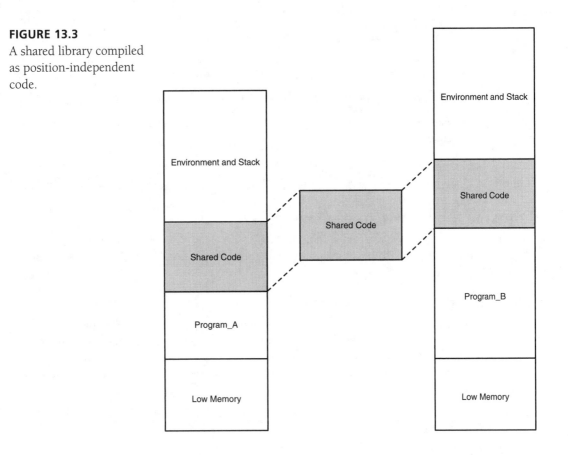

Controlling What Is Shared

When you make a UNIX shared library, you must control what is externally visible to the user of your library. By default, whatever remains external in the normal sense of executables will also be visible externally to the user of your shared library. If you have functions internal to your library, it is a good idea to define them as static functions wherever possible. This keeps them private.

Likewise, it is a good practice to have no unnecessary global variables or common storage. They will be visible from your shared library, also. Sloppiness in this area can cause programs to invoke functions or global variables in your shared library that you did not intend to release to the general public.

Comparing Static and Shared Libraries

Now is a good time to review what you have learned, and compare the pros and cons of each type of library.

The Benefits of Static Libraries

Static libraries cannot eliminate duplicated code in the system. However, there are other benefits to using static libraries. Some of these benefits are as follows:

- Static libraries are simple to use.

- The executable does not depend on related external components (shared libraries). The executable contains everything it needs.

- There are no environmental or administrative issues for static libraries.

- The static library code does not need to be position-independent code.

Enjoying the Ease of Static Linking

Ease of use is often the reason for choices in the early stages of project development. Later, when the project is reviewed, the developer might make the switch to shared libraries if this approach makes sense.

The Independence of Static Linking

This is probably the strongest point in favor of static libraries. Once an executable is linked statically, the program has everything it needs in its own executable file. This is important when you want to install a program on another system, where the versions of shared libraries that you need may or may not be present. This is also desirable if the shared libraries are always being updated.

Examples of this principle at work can be found in your FreeBSD /sbin directory. The following illustrates:

```
$ ldd /sbin/mount
ldd: /sbin/mount: not a dynamic executable
$
```

If the mount(1) command requires a shared library in /usr/lib, but /usr has not been mounted yet, then the mount(1) command would fail.

Installing Made Simpler

Statically linked programs do not require any environment variables like LD_LIBRARY_PATH to be set up (nor would you have to choose LIBPATH or SHLIB_PATH when the code was ported to any UNIX platform). This makes things easier for unsophisticated administrators and users to install.

Linking when Shared Libraries Are Not Supported

Statically linking a program is important if you are running UNIX on a platform that does not support shared libraries. This may happen on platforms in which Linux or FreeBSD is ported to a new platform. You will also want to revert to static linking, in which the code is not compiled as position-independent code.

Avoiding Licensing Restrictions

Sometimes static libraries are used only to avoid licensing issues. For example, a suite of programs that is statically linked to a MOTIF library can be legally released. However, it cannot be released using the shared library mechanism, because each site installing this software would have to buy a MOTIF library license. The original developer licensed and paid for the use of the library product, but he is not permitted to redistribute it.

The Benefits of Shared Libraries

Shared libraries have their own advantages:

- Code sharing saves system resources.

- Several programs that depend on a common shared library can be fixed all at once by replacing the common shared library.

- The environment can be modified to use a substitute shared library.

- Programs can be written to load dynamic libraries without any prior arrangement at link time. For example, Netscape can be told about a plug-in, which it is immediately able to load and execute without any recompiling or linking.

Enjoying the Savings with Shared Memory

Code sharing is the shared library's main claim to fame. A properly implemented shared library means that you'll have only a small amount of real memory assigned in the system to the library code being used. The programs using the shared library require little or no additional memory from the system. The benefit is greatest for large libraries, such as those dealing with the X Window system.

Centralizing Code in a Shared Library

Centralizing code in a shared library is both an advantage and a disadvantage. Only you can decide which it is for your application.

Favoring Centralized Code

If you are running production-level code in several executables, and you discover a bug in the common shared library that they use, fixing that library will instantly fix all programs that use it. None of the executables that use that common shared library require recompiling or re-linking.

Discouraging Centralized Code

At the same time, a working set of production-level executable programs can be busted by a single change in the common shared library. Be especially critical of changes to include files that change the structure and class definitions and macros. Existing programs calling on shared libraries may need to be recompiled to reference the correct member offsets within structures and classes.

Redirecting Shared Libraries

The use of shared libraries allows you to control which library is used by a program by changing the LD_LIBRARY_PATH variable. This allows you to substitute libraries without recompiling and linking the executable. For example, you might try different versions of a shared library for quality assurance testing. This type of substitution would require relinking the executables if you were using static libraries.

Linking Dynamically at Runtime

This is something you simply cannot do with a static library. Your program can indicate a shared library filename and function entry-point name, and the dynamic loader will take care of loading the shared library module and pass control to it. This allows your program to call on library modules without any prior arrangement.

Dynamic Library Loading

Most shared libraries are loaded dynamically when the program is started (on some platforms this behavior can be customized). However, when Netscape starts up, it does not know, for example, that it is going to need the Adobe Acrobat plug-in. The user does not want to wait while Netscape loads every possible plug-in at program startup. Consequently, only when Netscape has determined that it needs Adobe Acrobat support does it call on the dynamic library loader.

Opening the Shared Library

Opening a shared library causes a search for the library file to be performed. Then it is loaded into shared memory and made available for use. The function that accomplishes all of this is the dlopen(3) function:

```
#include <dlfcn.h>

void *dlopen(const char *path, int mode);
```

When calling dlopen(3), argument *mode* must be specified as RTLD_LAZY or RTLD_NOW. This determines how references are resolved within the shared library itself.

The pointer returned by dlopen(3) is a handle to the open shared library. The path argument specifies the name of the shared library.

Mode RTLD_LAZY

When a shared library is loaded into memory, it may have shared library dependencies of its own. For example, a shared library may need to call on printf(3), which is in another shared library.

When the mode argument is given as RTLD_LAZY, these references are resolved as the execution encounters them. For example, when printf(3) is called from within the shared library, the call will automatically reference the shared library that contains that code (it may or may not already be loaded).

Mode `RTLD_NOW`

This mode causes all outstanding references to the shared library to be resolved immediately upon being loaded. For example, if the shared library calls `printf(3)`, this reference will be resolved before the execution of the shared library begins.

This is useful when you don't want the execution to proceed if any of the other shared libraries cannot be found and loaded. This method can lead to faster execution, because the dynamic symbols are resolved all at once. Otherwise, `RTLD_LAZY` is preferred for its efficiency.

Reporting Errors

The `dlopen(3)` call returns a null pointer when it fails. To provide a meaningful error message to the user, you call on the `dlerror(3)` function:

```
#include <dlfcn.h>

const char *dlerror(void);
```

The `dlerror(3)` function returns a string pointer describing the last error that occurred. It is only valid until the next call to any of the dynamic library functions is made.

Obtaining a Shared Reference Pointer

Once the shared library is open, you can obtain a pointer to a function or a data structure by calling on `dlsym(3)`:

```
#include <dlfcn.h>

void *dlsym(void *handle, const char *symbol);
```

The first argument `handle` is the `(void *)` pointer returned from the function `dlopen(3)`. The argument `symbol` is the C string containing the name of the function or external data structure that you are interested in. If `dlh` contains a valid handle, you can call `printf(3)` dynamically as follows:

```
void *dlh;                          /* handle from dlopen(3) */
int (*f)(const char *format, ...);     /* Function pointer */

f = (int(*)(const char *,…))dlsym(dlh,"printf"); /* Get reference */

f("The dlsym(3) call worked!\n");      /* Call printf(3) now */
```

Since the function `dlsym(3)` returns a `(void *)` pointer, be very careful to code the correct cast operator when assigning the returned pointer (`f` in the example). If the symbol could not be located in the shared library, a null pointer is returned.

Closing a Shared Library

When your application knows that it no longer requires the services of the shared library, it may call upon dlclose(3):

```
#include <dlfcn.h>

int dlclose(void *handle);
```

The dlclose(3) function simply accepts a handle that was returned by dlopen(3) in a previous call. Reference counts are maintained by dlopen(3) and dlclose(3). When the reference count drops to zero, the shared library is unloaded and the resources are freed.

Initialization and Destruction

When a shared library is loaded for the first time by dlopen(3), the symbol _init() is called, if it exists. When the shared library is being unloaded, the symbol _fini() is called, if it exists. The function prototypes for these functions are as follows:

```
void _init(void);      /* Called by dlopen(3) */
void _fini(void);      /* Called by dlclose(3) */
```

This mechanism allows a shared library to initialize itself and clean up.

Applying Dynamic Loading

To apply your knowledge of dynamically loaded libraries, a dynamic library and a main program will be used. The program presented in Listing 13.5 is a simple subroutine that will be dynamically loaded and exercised.

LISTING 13.5   dyn001.c—A Dynamically Loaded Shared Library

```
 1:    /* dyn001.c */
 2:
 3:    #include <stdio.h>
 4:    #include <stdlib.h>
 5:    #include <stdarg.h>
 6:
 7:    int
 8:    sum_ints(int n,...) {
 9:        va_list ap;
10:        int x;
11:        int sum = 0;
12:
13:        va_start(ap,n);
14:
15:        for ( ; n>0; --n ) {
16:            x = va_arg(ap,int);
17:            sum += x;
18:        }
19:
```

```
20:        va_end(ap);
21:
22:        return sum;
23:   }
24:
25:   /* End dyn001.c */
```

The program in Listing 13.5 is a simple test function that sums a variable number of arguments. The program in Listing 13.6 is the `main()` program, which will invoke it.

LISTING 13.6   `dlmain.c`—An Example Program That Dynamically Loads and Calls a Function

```
1:    /* dlmain.c */
2:
3:    #include <stdio.h>
4:    #include <stdlib.h>
5:    #include <string.h>
6:    #include <dlfcn.h>
7:
8:    extern int strcasecmp(const char *s1, const char *s2);
9:
10:   int
11:   main(int argc,char **argv) {
12:       int isum = 0;                 // Sum variable
13:       void *dlh = 0;                // Dynamic library handle
14:       int (*sum_ints)(int n,...);  // Dynamic function pointer
15:
16:       if ( argc <= 1 || strcasecmp(argv[1],"DONT_LOAD") != 0 ) {
17:           dlh = dlopen("libdyn001.so",RTLD_LAZY);
18:           if ( !dlh ) {
19:               fprintf(stderr,"%s: loading ./libdyn001.so\n",dlerror());
20:               return 1;
21:           }
22:       }
23:
24:       sum_ints = (int (*)(int,...)) dlsym(dlh,"sum_ints");
25:       if ( !sum_ints ) {
26:           fprintf(stderr,"%s: finding symbol sum_ints()\n",dlerror());
27:           return 1;
28:       }
29:
30:       /*
31:        * Call the dynamically loaded function :
32:        */
33:       isum = sum_ints(5,1,2,3,4,5);
34:       printf("isum = %d\n",isum);
35:
36:       if ( dlh )
37:           dlclose(dlh);
38:
39:       return 0;
40:   }
41:
42:   /* End dlmain.c */
```

An examination of Listing 13.6 reveals that the main() program uses the following basic steps:

1. A test is made in line 16 to see if any arguments were supplied on the command line. If not, or if the argument was not DON'T_LOAD, then the function dlopen(3) is called to open the shared library libdyn001.so, using RTLD_LAZY.

2. The symbol sum_ints is looked up in line 24. It is expected to be a pointer to a function int (*)(int,...).

3. The pointer from step 2 is tested. If null, it means that the function was not known to the shared library, and an error message is reported (line 26).

4. The dynamically loaded function sum_ints() is called in line 33.

5. The shared library is closed and unloaded in lines 36 and 37.

Compiling the program is accomplished as follows:

```
$ make dlmain
cc -c -D_POSIX_C_SOURCE=199309L -D_POSIX_SOURCE -Wall dlmain.c
cc -c -D_POSIX_C_SOURCE=199309L -D_POSIX_SOURCE -Wall dyn001.c
cc -o libdyn001.so -shared dyn001.o
cc -o dlmain dlmain.o
$
```

Create a new login session, or log out and log in again. This will bring LD_LIBRARY_PATH to your system default value again. Now invoke ./dlmain:

```
$ ./dlmain
Shared object "libdyn001.so" not found: loading ./libdyn001.so
$
```

Note that the error message is the one produced by the code in line 19 of Listing 13.6. This tells you that library libdyn001.so does not exist in the system standard library directories or in any directories listed in the current LD_LIBRARY_PATH variable. Now add one entry to your variable as follows:

```
$ LD_LIBRARY_PATH=$LD_LIBRARY_PATH:$PWD
$ export LD_LIBRARY_PATH
$
```

Now run the program again with the LD_LIBRARY_PATH modified:

```
$ ./dlmain
isum = 15
$
```

This session demonstrates that the library was loaded, and the function executed successfully. To prove that your dlopen(3) call is doing the work, run the program one more time as follows:

```
$ ./dlmain dont_load
Undefined symbol "sum_ints": finding symbol sum_ints()
$
```

If you look at line 16 of Listing 13.6, you'll see that the argument dont_load causes the program to skip the dlopen(3) call. This is the reason the error message is reported instead.

HPUX 10.2 Dynamic Library Loading

Some UNIX platforms provide similar dynamic library functionality in a different API. As an example, the HPUX 10.2 API will be briefly presented. Only the important functions will be discussed from the function synopsis:

```
#include <dl.h>

shl_t shl_load(const char *path, int flags, long address);

int shl_findsym(
    shl_t *handle,
    const char *sym,
    short type,
    void *value
);

int shl_definesym(
    const char *sym,
    short type,
    long value,
    int flags
);

int shl_getsymbols(
    shl_t handle,
    short type,
    int flags,
    void *(*memory) (),
    struct shl_symbol **symbols,
);

int shl_unload(shl_t handle);

int shl_get(int index, struct shl_descriptor **desc);

int shl_gethandle(shl_t handle, struct shl_descriptor **desc);

int shl_get_r(int index, struct shl_descriptor *desc);

int shl_gethandle_r(shl_t handle, struct shl_descriptor *desc);
```

A functional equivalence table showing the HPUX 10.2 functions with the **dlopen(3)** follows:

shl_load(3X)	dlopen(3)
shl_findsym(3X)	dlsym(3)
shl_unload(3X)	dlclose(3)

The HP `shl_load(3X)` function requires the `path` of the shared library. The `flags` argument accepts one of these values:

`BIND_IMMEDIATE`	Resolve the symbol references when the library is loaded. This is equivalent to `RTLD_NOW`.
`BIND_DEFERRED`	Resolve when the symbol is referenced. This is similar to `RTLD_LAZY`.

In addition to the above flags, a number of additional flags can be ORed with the above. These include

- `BIND_FIRST`
- `BIND_NONFATAL`
- `BIND_NOSTART`
- `BIND_VERBOSE`
- `BIND_RESTRICTED`
- `DYNAMIC_PATH`
- `BIND_TOGETHER`

The `address` argument of `shl_load(3X)` allows the value `0L` to be used. This recommended practice directs the function to choose an appropriate address at which to load the library. Otherwise, the caller must have an intimate knowledge of the memory address space and supply a suitable address.

The function `shl_load(3X)` returns a handle to the library loaded, or `NULL` is returned when it fails. The `shl_load(3X)` function sets the value of `errno` when it fails. Errors can be reported with `strerror(3)`, as usual. This is in contrast to the `dlerror(3)` routine discussed earlier.

The `shl_findsym(3X)` function is similar to the `dlsym(3)` function call. The `handle` and `sym` arguments specify the shared library handle and the symbol to look up, respectively. The `handle` argument can be null, which causes all currently loaded libraries to be searched for the symbol. The return pointer value is passed via argument pointer `value`, and `NULL` is returned if the symbol search is unsuccessful.

Argument `type` in the `shl_findsym(3X)` call must be one of these:

- `TYPE_PROCEDURE`
- `TYPE_DATA`
- `TYPE_STORAGE`
- `TYPE_TSTORAGE`
- `TYPE_UNDEFINED`

The value TYPE_UNDEFINED is useful when you don't want type-checking rules to be applied. In fact, HP's own documentation further states that the "first four constants may not be supported in future 64-bit HP-UX releases."

The function shl_findsym(3X) returns an integer result of 0 if it is successful. Otherwise -1 is returned, and errno is set. However, note that errno is set to 0 if the symbol could not be found. If the symbol was found but other symbol references on which it depends could not be satisfied, the errno value will be ENOSYM.

Finally, shl_unload(3X) performs a function equivalent to dlclose(3). The handle provided by shl_load(3X) is used in the call to shl_unload(3X) to close and unload the shared library.

The following is a simple example that uses the HPUX 10.2 shared library functions:

```
shl_t h;                     /* HP handle to shared library */
int (*f)(int arg1,...);      /* Function pointer for sum_int() */
int sum ;                    /* Sum variable */

if ( (h = shl_load("libdyn001.sl",BIND_DEFERRED,0L)) == NULL )
    { perror("shl_load()"); abort(); }

if ( shl_findsym(h,"sum_ints",TYPE_UNDEFINED,&f) == -1 )
    { perror("shl_findsym()"); abort(); }

sum = f(5,1,2,3,4,5);        /* Sum 5 arguments */

shl_close(h);                /* Close shared library */
```

This was a brief look at the HPUX 10.2 shared library functions. You are encouraged to view the shl_load(3X) manual pages on the HP system to learn more about them. This brief coverage allows you to plan your porting to HPUX 10.2, if you need to support it. HPUX 11 supports the dlopen(3) functions, which you'll find on most other UNIX platforms today.

Summary

In this chapter, you learned about the differences between static and shared libraries, how to create and maintain them, and how shared libraries can be loaded and called dynamically. The dynamic library support for HPUX 10.2 was also discussed to expand your knowledge for porting purposes.

The next chapter will discuss the NDBM database routines, which are available on most UNIX systems today. These routines allow you to manage large collections of application data within a compact and efficient database.

CHAPTER 14

DATABASE LIBRARY ROUTINES

Applications often manage large collections of data. The larger the data set, the more difficult it is to retrieve information quickly. Applications today can use relational database management systems (RDBMS), but for small applications, this may not be the most practical choice. For this reason, this chapter will explore a set of functions designed to provide lightweight database services.

Ken Thompson produced the original Data Base Management (DBM) library at Bell Labs. A description of the original DBM routines is found in the UNIX Seventh Edition documentation at `http://plan9.bell-labs.com/7thEdMan/index.html`.

Visit the link `vol1/man3.bun - libraries` and search for "DBM". The original implementation consisted of the following API set:

`int dbminit(char *file)`
`int dbmclose(void)`
`datum fetch(datum key)`
`int store(datum key,datum content)`
`int delete(datum key)`
`datum firstkey(void)`
`datum nextkey(datum key)`

The severest limitation of this API set was that there could be only one database open at one time. To overcome this and other limitations, a newer implementation, known as *NDBM* (New DBM), was developed by the University of California, Berkeley. This API is available on most UNIX platforms.

The Free Software Foundation (FSF) has since improved upon the NDBM routines with the GDBM (GNU DBM) set of routines. Software for GDBM can be downloaded and compiled on most UNIX platforms without a hitch.

In this chapter, you will focus on the NDBM routine that is most common. This will help you understand how existing code uses it and will allow you to use the software you have. Only a small effort is required to graduate to GDBM, once the NDBM routines have been mastered.

In this chapter, you will learn about

- Concurrency limitations of the NDBM database.
- How to create, open, and close an NDBM database.
- How to insert, replace, and delete records.
- How to retrieve records.
- How to process all record keys.

The NDBM Database

Before you design your application program around a NDBM database, you need to answer the following questions:

- Will readers and writer(s) need access at the same time?
- How many writers will there be at one time?

Having multiple readers is not a problem when there is no write activity occurring. However, the NDBM routines do not provide any protection against readers and writers in conflict. For example, one process might delete a key that conflicts with another process that is visiting all the keys in the database. Additionally, these routines do not permit multiple writers to the database at one time. Despite these limitations, the NDBM routines still find many uses in standalone and single-user solutions.

Error Handling

With the exception of `dbm_close(3)`, all NDBM functions return an indication of success or failure. Some functions return zero for success. A negative value is returned for failure. Other cases are unique. These will be detailed as you review them in the upcoming sections.

You can test for errors using the call to `dbm_error(3)`. This function returns a non-zero value when an error has occurred. However, this function continues to return an error indication until `dbm_clearerr(3)` is called. A function synopsis is provided as follows:

```
#include <ndbm.h>

int dbm_error(DBM *db);

int dbm_clearerr(DBM *db);
```

The NDBM routines will influence the `errno` value, but there are no standardized errors documented for them. For portability reasons, you should rely on only the `dbm_error(3)` and `dbm_clearerr(3)` routines and avoid interpreting `errno`.

Note

Most UNIX systems will provide man(1) pages for NDBM routines under ndbm(3) or ndbm(3X). FreeBSD does not provide any documentation for these routines. This is perhaps because dbopen(3) is being promoted as its replacement.

Documentation for ndbm(3) can be found on the Internet, however, at the URL

http://www.opengroup.org/public/pubs/online/7908799/xsh/dbm_open.html

While FreeBSD lacks documentation on routines such as dbm_open(), this book will use section three, as in dbm_open(3). Sun Solaris places its documentation for these routines in section 3, while others place it in section 3X or 3C.

Opening an NDBM Database

The dbm_open(3) function is used to create or open a database for use. Its synopsis is as follows:

```
#include <ndbm.h>

DBM *dbm_open(const char *file, int open_flags, int file_mode);
```

The first argument, file, specifies the pathname of the database. Note that some implementations append a suffix to this name (FreeBSD adds .db). Other implementations may create two files with different suffixes appended. The string supplied in the argument file remains unchanged.

The argument open_flags specifies flag bits that would be supplied to the open(2) call. These include

- O_RDONLY
- O_RDWR
- O_CREAT
- O_EXCL

The behavior for some flags, such as the O_APPEND flag, will not be defined for this function call.

The third argument, mode, forms the permission bits to apply to the creation of the new file(s). These are passed onto the open(2) call and are subject to the current umask(2) setting.

The return value is a pointer to a DBM object if the call is successful or the value (DBM *)0 if it fails. The following example shows how a database might be created:

```
DBM *db;

db = dbm_open("mydatabase",O_RDWR|O_CREAT,0666);
```

Under FreeBSD, this creates a database file named mydatabase.db and opens it for reading and writing.

Closing an NDBM Database

An open database should always be closed before the program exits. This is accomplished with the **dbm_close(3)** function:

```
#include <ndbm.h>

void dbm_close(DBM *db);
```

There is no error return from this function. The input argument **db** must point to an open database or a fault may occur.

Storing Information

To insert a new record or to update an existing record, the **dbm_store(3)** function is used. Its function synopsis is as follows:

```
#include <ndbm.h>

typedef struct {
    char    *dptr;        /* Pointer to data */
    int     dsize;        /* Byte length of data */
} datum;

int dbm_store(DBM *db, datum key, datum content, int store_mode);
```

The first argument, **db**, specifies the open database into which to store the record. The arguments **key** and **content** are described by the C data type **datum**. The **key** argument defines the start of the key and its length. The **content** argument defines the record content and its length.

The final argument **store_mode** must contain one of the following values:

- DBM_INSERT
- DBM_REPLACE

When **store_mode** is equal to **DBM_INSERT**, the new record is inserted into the database, even if a record already exists with a matching **key** value. When **store_mode** is equal to **DBM_REPLACE**, an existing record with a matching **key** is replaced with the content being supplied. Otherwise, a new record is simply inserted.

The return value from the **dbm_store(3)** call is **0** or **1** when successful. A negative value represents a failure. The **dbm_store(3)** function returns a **1** when **store_mode** equals **DBM_INSERT** and the function finds an existing record with a matching **key** value.

The following example shows how a phone number acting as a key and an address acting as the data record are supplied to the **dbm_store(3)** function:

```
DBM *db;                    // Open database
int z;                      // Status return code
```

```
char phone_no[20];             // Phone #
datum key;                     // Key datum
char address[64];              // Record data (address information)
datum content;                 // Content datum

key.dptr = phone_no;           // Point to key value
key.dsize = strlen(phone_no);  // Set key length
content.dptr = address;        // Point to record content
content.dsize = strlen(address); // Set record length

z = dbm_store(db,key,content,DBM_REPLACE); // Replace if exists
if ( z < 0 ) {
    // Handle error
    dbm_clearerr(db);
```

The example shown will replace the record if a match is made on the telephone number in the database. Duplicate keys can be inserted by changing the DBM_REPLACE macro to DBM_INSERT.

Fetching Information

Once information is stored, it is necessary to retrieve it quickly. The function dbm_fetch(3) performs this function:

```
#include <ndbm.h>

datum dbm_fetch(DBM *db, datum key);
```

The dbm_fetch(3) function accepts a db argument, which specifies the database to search. The key argument specifies the key value to look up.

The return value from dbm_fetch(3) is a datum type. A successful search is indicated by returning a datum, which contains a non-null member, dptr. The following example illustrates:

```
DBM *db;                       // Open database
char phone_no[20];             // Phone #
datum key;                     // Key datum
char address[64];              // Record data (address information)
datum content;                 // Content datum

key.dptr = phone_no;           // Point to key value
key.dsize = strlen(phone_no);  // Set key length

content = dbm_fetch(db,key);   // Lookup phone #
if ( !content.dptr ) {
    // Key was not found in database
} else {
    // Content was returned:
    strncpy(address,content.dptr,
        min(sizeof address-1,content.dsize));
    address[sizeof address-1] = 0; // Null terminate
}
```

The example shows how the telephone address is extracted from the returned datum content.

Deleting Information

Data that has been created must sometimes be destroyed later. This includes when the key changes: The record must be deleted and inserted again with the new key. The synopsis of the `dbm_delete(3)` function is as follows:

```
#include <ndbm.h>

int dbm_delete(DBM *db, datum key);
```

The function call setup is identical to the `dbm_fetch(3)` function. The database is chosen by argument `db`, and the key value is given by the **key** argument. The return value is zero if the call is successful and is negative if the call fails.

The following example deletes a telephone entry from a telephone database of addresses:

```
DBM *db;                            // Open database
char phone_no[20];                  // Phone #
datum key;                          // Key datum

key.dptr = phone_no;                // Point to key value
key.dsize = strlen(phone_no);       // Set key length

if ( dbm_delete(db,key) < 0 )   // Delete phone #
    // Key was not found in database
} else {
    // Record was deleted
}
```

Visiting All Keys

All records managed by a NDBM database are stored and managed by key values. Effective hashing algorithms are applied to keys to make accessing specific records very efficient. However, it often happens that you need to examine all or most records in the database. In these situations, you may not know all the key values in advance.

The functions `dbm_firstkey(3)` and `dbm_nextkey(3)` allow you to iterate through the keys stored within your database. The key values will be presented in an unsorted sequence, however. This is because hashing algorithms are used for the index. Hashed indexes cannot offer sorted keys like the B-tree indexing algorithm, for example. If you need a sorted list, you must first visit all the keys and then sort them in a temporary file.

The `dbm_firstkey(3)` and `dbm_nextkey(3)` synopsis is as follows:

```
#include <ndbm.h>

datum dbm_firstkey(DBM *db);
datum dbm_nextkey(DBM *db);
```

The functions both require one argument db as input. The function dbm_firstkey(3), as its name implies, returns the first database key. Once that function has been invoked successfully, successive calls should be made to dbm_nextkey(3) to retrieve the remaining keys.

To visit all keys within a database, the general loop construct is as follows:

```
DBM *db;                    // Open database
datum key;                  // Key datum

for ( key=dbm_firstkey(db); key.dptr != NULL; key=dbm_nextkey(db) ) {
    // Process key
}
```

The functions dbm_firstkey(3) and dbm_nextkey(3) can both indicate the end of the keys, by returning a datum, which has a null dptr pointer. When dbm_firstkey(3) returns null in the datum member dptr, this indicates that there are no keys in the database.

Deleting Keys with dbm_nextkey(3)

Special attention should be paid to modifications to the database during key visits. If you have a loop constructed as in the previous example and you use the key value to delete entries in the database, you will encounter trouble. The following shows what not to do:

```
DBM *db;                    // Open database
datum key;                  // Key datum

// DO NOT DO THIS:
for ( key=dbm_firstkey(db); key.dptr != NULL; key=dbm_nextkey(db) ) {
    dbm_delete(db,key);        // Delete this key
    if ( dbm_error(db) )
        abort();               // Something failed
}
```

The example runs into trouble because the routines dbm_firstkey(3) and dbm_nextkey(3) assume that no changes to keys will occur while the loop runs. When keys are deleted, the hash index blocks are modified, which may affect the way the next key is retrieved (these are implementation-specific problems.)

If you need to perform the function just shown, another approach works:

```
DBM *db;                    // Open database
datum key;                  // Key datum

for ( key=dbm_firstkey(db); key.dptr != NULL; key=dbm_firstkey(db) ) {
    dbm_delete(db,key);        // Delete this key
    if ( dbm_error(db) )
        abort();               // Something failed
}
```

The change is subtle, but important. The next key is fetched by calling upon dbm_firstkey(3) instead. This works because the loop always deletes the first key. By calling dbm_firstkey(3) again, you get the next "first" key.

An NDBM Database Example

An example of a small application employing a NDBM database is presented in the upcoming listings. The purpose of the application is to tree walk one or more directory names, calling lstat(2) on each file system object. Then the lstat(2) information is stored in the snapshot database and indexed by the device number and i-node number. The application has been named SnapShot.

Once a snapshot has been taken, it is possible to invoke the application again with different command-line options. With the -c option provided, the SnapShot program will then walk the named directories, comparing each file system's lstat(2) information to what is stored in the database. Any differences are then reported. This provides similar functionality to the Tripwire[r] file integrity software.

Directory Software

In order to perform the directory tree walk, a C++ class named Dir was created. Listing 14.1 shows the Dir.h include file, which declares the class.

LISTING 14.1   Dir.h—The Dir Class Definition Source File

```
 1:    // dir.h
 2:
 3:    #ifndef _dir_h_
 4:    #define _dir_h_
 5:
 6:    #include <sys/types.h>
 7:    #include <dirent.h>
 8:
 9:    ////////////////////////////////////////////////////////////
10:    // A Directory class object :
11:    ////////////////////////////////////////////////////////////
12:
13:    class Dir {
14:        DIR     *dir;
15:        char    *name;
16:        int     error;
17:    public:
18:        Dir();
19:        ~Dir();
20:        Dir &open(const char *path);
21:        Dir &rewind();
22:        Dir &close();
23:        char *read();
24:        inline int getError() { return error; }
25:        inline char *getEntry() { return name; }
26:    };
27:
28:    #endif // _dir_h_
29:
30:    // End dir.h
```

The class shown in Listing 14.1 implements methods to open a directory (`Dir::open()`),rewind it (`Dir::rewind()`), read entries (`Dir::read()`), and close it (`Dir::close()`). Additional inline methods `Dir::getError()` and `Dir::getEntry()` are provided. The destructor takes care of automatically closing the directory if necessary.

Listing 14.2 shows how the class is implemented.

LISTING 14.2   `Dir.cc`—The Implementation of the `Dir` Class

```
 1:   // dir.cc
 2:
 3:   #include "Dir.h"
 4:   #include <errno.h>
 5:   #include <string.h>
 6:
 7:   extern "C" char *strdup(const char *str);
 8:
 9:   //////////////////////////////////////////////////////////////
10:   // Dir Constructor :
11:   //////////////////////////////////////////////////////////////
12:
13:   Dir::Dir() {
14:       dir = 0;
15:       name = 0;
16:   }
17:
18:   //////////////////////////////////////////////////////////////
19:   // Dir Destructor :
20:   //////////////////////////////////////////////////////////////
21:
22:   Dir::~Dir() {
23:       if ( dir )
24:           close();
25:   }
26:
27:   //////////////////////////////////////////////////////////////
28:   // Open a directory :
29:   //////////////////////////////////////////////////////////////
30:
31:   Dir &
32:   Dir::open(const char *path) {
33:
34:       if ( dir )
35:           throw error = EINVAL;   // Object is already open
36:
37:       dir = ::opendir(path);      // Attempt to open directory
38:       if ( !dir )
39:           throw error = errno;    // Open failed
40:
41:       return *this;
42:   }
```

continued from previous page

```
43:
44:    //////////////////////////////////////////////////////////
45:    // Close a directory :
46:    //////////////////////////////////////////////////////////
47:
48:    Dir &
49:    Dir::close() {
50:        int z;
51:
52:        if ( !dir )
53:            throw error = EINVAL;    // Nothing to close
54:        if ( name ) {
55:            delete name;
56:            name = 0;               // No name now
57:        }
58:        z = ::closedir(dir);
59:        dir = 0;                    // No dir now
60:        if ( z == -1 )
61:            throw error = errno;
62:        return *this;
63:    }
64:
65:    //////////////////////////////////////////////////////////
66:    // Read a directory :
67:    //////////////////////////////////////////////////////////
68:
69:    char *
70:    Dir::read() {
71:        dirent *p;
72:
73:        if ( !dir )
74:            throw error = EINVAL;    // Nothing to read
75:        if ( name ) {
76:            delete name;
77:            name = 0;
78:        }
79:
80:        p = readdir(dir);            // Read the next entry
81:        if ( !p )
82:            return name;             // End of directory
83:
84:        return name = strdup(p->d_name);
85:    }
86:
87:    //////////////////////////////////////////////////////////
88:    // Rewind a directory :
89:    //////////////////////////////////////////////////////////
90:
91:    Dir &
92:    Dir::rewind() {
93:
```

```
94:     if ( !dir )
95:         throw error = EINVAL;    // Nothing to rewind
96:     ::rewinddir(dir);           // Rewind directory
97:     return *this;
98: }
99:
100: // End dir.cc
```

The methods in the Dir class throw errno values if errors are detected. An example of this is in lines 38 and 39 of Listing 14.2. If the opendir(3) call fails, the value in errno is thrown in line 39. The error EINVAL is thrown if the directory is not open, and an operation such as Dir::read() is attempted (lines 73 and 74, for example).

The implementation of this class should be review, since Chapter 7, "Directory Management," covered the directory functions in detail. Only the file system object name is returned by the Dir::read() method (see line 84).

The Dbm Class

The Dbm class is declared in the include file Dbm.h, which is shown in Listing 14.3. This class wraps the NDBM functions in a C++ object for convenience and simplicity. Additionally, this approach allows exceptions and destructors to be used. The object destructor ensures that the database is properly closed.

LISTING 14.3   Dbm.h—The Dbm Class Definition

```
1:  // Dbm.h
2:
3:  #ifndef _Dbm_h_
4:  #define _Dbm_h_
5:
6:  #include <sys/types.h>
7:  #include <unistd.h>
8:  #include <ndbm.h>
9:  #include <fcntl.h>
10:
11: ////////////////////////////////////////////////////////////
12: // A Class for the DBM Routines :
13: ////////////////////////////////////////////////////////////
14:
15: class Dbm {
16:     int     flags;          // Open flags
17:     char    *path;          // Pathname of database
18:     DBM     *db;            // Open database
19: protected:
20:     int     error;          // Last error
21: public:
22:     Dbm();
23:     ~Dbm();
24:     Dbm &open(const char *path,int flags=O_RDWR,int mode=0666);
```

continued from previous page

```
25:        Dbm &close();
26:        datum fetch(datum key);
27:        Dbm &store(datum key,datum content,int flags);
28:        Dbm &deleteKey(datum key);
29:        datum firstKey();
30:        datum nextKey();
31:        inline int getError() { return error; }
32:        inline int getFlags() { return flags; }
33:        inline char *getPath() { return path; }
34:    };
35:
36:    #endif // _Dbm_h_
37:
38:    // End Dbm.h
```

The **Dbm** object manages private members **flags**, **path**, and **db**. The **flags** and **path** members can be examined with the inline member functions **getFlags()** and **getPath()**. The protected member **error** holds the last **errno** value thrown and can be examined with the inline function **getError()**.

The member functions **open()**, **close()**, **fetch()**, **store()**, **deleteKey()**, **firstKey()**, and **nextKey()** are simply wrapper methods for the various **NDBM** routines you have learned about in this chapter. The method **deleteKey()** could not be named **delete()**, since this conflicts with the reserved C++ keyword **delete**.

Listing 14.4 shows the implementation of the **Dbm** class.

LISTING 14.4   Dbm.cc—The Implementation of the **Dbm** Class

```
1:     // Dbm.cc
2:
3:     #include <string.h>
4:     #include <errno.h>
5:     #include "Dbm.h"
6:
7:     /////////////////////////////////////////////////////////////////
8:     // Constructor :
9:     /////////////////////////////////////////////////////////////////
10:
11:    Dbm::Dbm() {
12:        flags = 0;           // No flags
13:        path = 0;            // No path
14:        db = 0;              // No database
15:        error = 0;           // No logged errors
16:    }
17:
18:    /////////////////////////////////////////////////////////////////
19:    // Destructor :
20:    /////////////////////////////////////////////////////////////////
21:
22:    Dbm::~Dbm() {
```

```
23:        if ( db )
24:            close();              // Close database
25:    }
26:
27:    ////////////////////////////////////////////////////////////
28:    // Open/Create a Database :
29:    // NOTES:
30:    //   flags        O_RDWR, O_RDONLY, O_CREAT etc. (see open(2))
31:    //   mode         Permission bits
32:    ////////////////////////////////////////////////////////////
33:
34:    Dbm &
35:    Dbm::open(const char *path,int flags,int mode) {
36:
37:        if ( db )
38:            throw error = EPERM;      // Database already open
39:
40:        db = ::dbm_open(path,this->flags = flags,mode);
41:        if ( !db )
42:            throw error = EIO;        // Open failed
43:
44:        path = strdup(path);          // Save pathname
45:
46:        return *this;
47:    }
48:
49:    ////////////////////////////////////////////////////////////
50:    // Close the open database :
51:    ////////////////////////////////////////////////////////////
52:
53:    Dbm &
54:    Dbm::close() {
55:
56:        if ( !db )
57:            throw error = EPERM;      // Database is not open
58:
59:        dbm_close(db);                // Close Database
60:        db = 0;
61:        delete path;                  // Free pathname
62:        path = 0;
63:
64:        return *this;
65:    }
66:
67:    ////////////////////////////////////////////////////////////
68:    // Fetch data by key :
69:    ////////////////////////////////////////////////////////////
70:
71:    datum
72:    Dbm::fetch(datum key) {
73:        datum content;
74:
75:        if ( !db )
```

continued from previous page

```
 76:            throw error = EPERM;     // No database
 77:
 78:         content = ::dbm_fetch(db,key);
 79:         if ( dbm_error(db) ) {
 80:             dbm_clearerr(db);
 81:             throw error = EIO;
 82:         }
 83:         if ( !content.dptr )
 84:             throw error = ENOENT;    // Not found
 85:
 86:         return content;              // Found content
 87:    }
 88:
 89:    /////////////////////////////////////////////////////////
 90:    // Replace or Insert new data by key :
 91:    /////////////////////////////////////////////////////////
 92:
 93:    Dbm &
 94:    Dbm::store(datum key,datum content,int flags) {
 95:
 96:         if ( !db )
 97:             throw error = EPERM;     // No database
 98:
 99:         if ( ::dbm_store(db,key,content,flags) < 0 ) {
100:             dbm_clearerr(db);
101:             throw error = EIO;       // Failed
102:         }
103:         return *this;
104:    }
105:
106:    /////////////////////////////////////////////////////////
107:    // Delete data by key :
108:    /////////////////////////////////////////////////////////
109:
110:    Dbm &
111:    Dbm::deleteKey(datum key) {
112:
113:         if ( !db )
114:             throw error = EPERM;     // No database
115:         if ( ::dbm_delete(db,key) < 0 ) {
116:             dbm_clearerr(db);
117:             throw error = EIO;       // Failed
118:         }
119:         return *this;
120:    }
121:
122:    /////////////////////////////////////////////////////////
123:    // Retrieve the first data key :
124:    /////////////////////////////////////////////////////////
125:
126:    datum
127:    Dbm::firstKey() {
```

```
128:        datum d;
129:
130:        if ( !db )
131:            throw error = EPERM;      // No database
132:
133:        d = ::dbm_firstkey(db);
134:
135:        if ( dbm_error(db) ) {
136:            dbm_clearerr(db);
137:            throw error = EIO;        // Database error
138:        }
139:
140:        return d;
141: }
142:
143: ///////////////////////////////////////////////////////////
144: // Retrieve the next data key :
145: ///////////////////////////////////////////////////////////
146:
147: datum
148: Dbm::nextKey() {
149:        datum d;
150:
151:        if ( !db )
152:            throw error = EPERM;      // No database
153:
154:        d = ::dbm_nextkey(db);
155:
156:        if ( dbm_error(db) ) {
157:            dbm_clearerr(db);
158:            throw error = EIO;        // Database error
159:        }
160:
161:        return d;
162: }
163:
164: // End Dbm.cc
```

The destructor `Dbm::~Dbm()` in Listing 14.4 calls upon `Dbm::close()` if it finds that private member `db` is not null. This allows the database to be closed automatically, when the `Dbm` object is destroyed. However, the user may call upon `Dbm::close()` himself. This allows him to re-use the object by calling the `Dbm::open()` method to open a different database.

The methods `Dbm::fetch()`, `Dbm::store()`, `Dbm::deleteKey()`, `Dbm::firstKey()`, and `Dbm::nextKey()` all use the `datum` data type in the same manner as the `ndbm(3)` routines. The `InoDb` class that inherits from `Dbm` will tailor the interfaces to the application, as you will see in listings later in this chapter.

Similar to the implementation of the `Dir` class, the `Dbm` class throws an error (`EPERM`) when the database is not open and an operation is attempted on it. Unlike the `Dir` class, the error thrown after a failed `ndbm(3)` call is always `EIO`. This was done because there are no documented errors given for `ndbm(3)` routines. Literature indicates that only `dbm_error(3)` can be trusted, and it is only an indication of error. The values of `errno` are not consistently returned for different UNIX platforms. The method `Dbm::fetch()` shows an example of this in lines 79–82.

The remainder of the implementation provides a wrapper around the `ndbm(3)` routines.

The `InoDb` Class

The `Dbm` class is a foundation class. The `SnapShot` database uses a device number and an i-node number as a key for each record. Furthermore, each record is simply the `struct stat` data type. A new class, inheriting from the `Dbm` class, could then provide convenient interfaces for the application involved. That is what was done with the `InoDb` class, which is presented in Listing 14.5.

LISTING 14.5   `InoDb.h`—The `InoDb` Class Declaration

```
 1:  // InoDb.h
 2:
 3:  #ifndef _InoDb_h_
 4:  #define _InoDb_h_
 5:
 6:  #include <sys/types.h>
 7:  #include <sys/stat.h>
 8:  #include "Dbm.h"
 9:
10:  /////////////////////////////////////////////////////////////
11:  // Specialized Database Class for an Inode Database :
12:  /////////////////////////////////////////////////////////////
13:
14:  class InoDb : public Dbm {
15:  public:
16:      struct Key {
17:          dev_t   st_dev;      // Device number
18:          ino_t   st_ino;      // Inode number
19:      };
20:  protected:
21:      Key         ikey;        // Internal key
22:  public:
23:      InoDb &fetchKey(Key &key,struct stat &sbuf);
24:      InoDb &insertKey(Key &key,struct stat &sbuf);
25:      InoDb &replaceKey(Key &key,struct stat &sbuf);
26:      InoDb &deleteKey(Key &key);
27:      Key *firstKey();
28:      Key *nextKey();
29:  };
30:
31:  #endif _InoDb_h_
32:
33:  // End InoDb.h
```

Line 14 of Listing 14.5 shows how the class `InoDb` inherits from the class `Dbm`. The type definition `InoDb::Key` is made publicly available in lines 15–19. A protected internal key member `ikey` is declared in line 21.

Lines 23–28 implement new methods that feature an API that is convenient for the application. In each case, the key is using the `InoDb::Key` type. Where data content is involved, a `struct stat` is referred to.

The implementation of the `InoDb` class is shown in Listing 14.6.

LISTING 14.6   `InoDb.cc`—The Implementation of the `InoDb` Class

```
 1:   // InoDb.cc
 2:
 3:   #include <errno.h>
 4:   #include "InoDb.h"
 5:
 6:   //////////////////////////////////////////////////////////////
 7:   // Fetch stat info by inode number :
 8:   //////////////////////////////////////////////////////////////
 9:
10:   InoDb &
11:   InoDb::fetchKey(Key &key,struct stat &sbuf) {
12:       datum d, f;
13:
14:       d.dptr = (char *)&key;
15:       d.dsize = sizeof key;
16:       f = fetch;
17:
18:       if ( f.dsize != sizeof (struct stat) )
19:           throw error = EINVAL;    // Corrupt database
20:       memcpy(&sbuf,f.dptr,sizeof sbuf);
21:
22:       return *this;
23:   }
24:
25:   //////////////////////////////////////////////////////////////
26:   // Add new stat info by inode number :
27:   //////////////////////////////////////////////////////////////
28:
29:   InoDb &
30:   InoDb::insertKey(Key &key,struct stat &sbuf) {
31:       datum k, c;
32:
33:       k.dptr = (char *)&key;
34:       k.dsize = sizeof key;
35:       c.dptr = (char *)&sbuf;
36:       c.dsize = sizeof sbuf;
37:       store(k,c,DBM_INSERT);
38:       return *this;
39:   }
```

continued from previous page

```
40:
41:    //////////////////////////////////////////////////////////
42:    // Replace stat info by inode number :
43:    //////////////////////////////////////////////////////////
44:
45:    InoDb &
46:    InoDb::replaceKey(Key &key,struct stat &sbuf) {
47:        datum k, c;
48:
49:        k.dptr = (char *)&key;
50:        k.dsize = sizeof key;
51:        c.dptr = (char *)&sbuf;
52:        c.dsize = sizeof sbuf;
53:        store(k,c,DBM_REPLACE);
54:        return *this;
55:    }
56:
57:    //////////////////////////////////////////////////////////
58:    // Delete stat info by inode number :
59:    //////////////////////////////////////////////////////////
60:
61:    InoDb &
62:    InoDb::deleteKey(Key &key) {
63:        datum k;
64:
65:        k.dptr = (char *)&key;
66:        k.dsize = sizeof key;
67:        Dbm::deleteKey(k);
68:        return *this;
69:    }
70:
71:    //////////////////////////////////////////////////////////
72:    // Retrieve the first key entry :
73:    //////////////////////////////////////////////////////////
74:
75:    InoDb::Key *
76:    InoDb::firstKey() {
77:        datum k;
78:
79:        k = Dbm::firstKey();
80:        if ( !k.dptr )
81:            return 0;                      // Return NULL for EOF
82:
83:        if ( k.dsize != sizeof ikey )
84:            throw error = EINVAL;          // Corrupt?
85:        memcpy(&ikey,k.dptr,sizeof ikey);
86:        return &ikey;                      // Return pointer to key
87:    }
```

```
88:
89:  ////////////////////////////////////////////////////////////
90:  // Retrieve the last key entry :
91:  ////////////////////////////////////////////////////////////
92:
93:  InoDb::Key *
94:  InoDb::nextKey() {
95:      datum k;
96:
97:      k = Dbm::nextKey();
98:      if ( !k.dptr )
99:          return 0;                      // Return NULL for EOF
100:
101:      if ( k.dsize != sizeof ikey )
102:          throw error = EINVAL;       // Corrupt?
103:      memcpy(&ikey,k.dptr,sizeof ikey);
104:      return &ikey;                    // Return pointer to key
105: }
106:
107: // End InoDb.cc
```

Much of the code presented in Listing 14.6 simply makes the application interface conform to the Dbm class interface. For example, examine the code for InoDb::fetchKey() (lines 10–23). The datum value d is prepared to point to the key (line 14) and establish the key size (line 15). Then the datum value f is set by the call to fetch() (which is actually a call to Dbm::fetch()).

Upon return from Dbm::fetch(), the size of the returned data is checked (line 18), and EIN-VAL is thrown if is not correct (line 19). Otherwise, the data pointed to by f.dptr is copied to the receiving struct stat buffer (line 20) that the application has provided as argument sbuf. The argument sbuf is provided by reference, so the value is passed back to the caller in this way.

The method InoDb::insertKey() is similar (lines 29–39), with the exception that the datum c is setup to provide the calling argument sbuf as input to the Dbm::store() call (line 37). Notice that the value DBM_INSERT is used in line 37, causing duplicate keys to be ignored.

The method InoDb::replaceKey() is identical to InoDb::insertKey(), with the exception that Dbm::store() is called using the value DBM_REPLACE in line 53.

The methods InoDb::firstKey() and InoDb::nextKey() return a null (Key *) value if they reach the end of the keys (lines 98 and 99). The returned key is copied to the protected internal key ikey in line 103. The address of ikey is returned in line 104.

The SnapShot Application

Listing 14.7 shows the SnapShot.cc application source listing. This listing shows how the Dir and InoDb objects are put to use.

LISTING 14.7   SnapShot.cc—The SnapShot Application Program

```
 1:    // SnapShot.cc
 2:
 3:    #include <stdio.h>
 4:    #include <stdlib.h>
 5:    #include <unistd.h>
 6:    #include <errno.h>
 7:    #include <string.h>
 8:    #include <sys/types.h>
 9:    #include <sys/stat.h>
10:    #include <pwd.h>
11:    #include <grp.h>
12:
13:    #include "Dir.h"
14:    #include "InoDb.h"
15:
16:    static int rc = 0;              // return code
17:    static int cmdopt_i = 0;        // -i
18:    static int cmdopt_c = 0;        // -c
19:    static int cmdopt_v = 0;        // -v
20:    static int cmdopt_h = 0;        // -h
21:
22:    ////////////////////////////////////////////////////////
23:    // RETURN BASENAME OF A PATHNAME :
24:    ////////////////////////////////////////////////////////
25:
26:    char *
27:    Basename(char *path) {
28:        char *bname = strrchr(path,'/');
29:
30:        return !bname ? path : bname + 1;
31:    }
32:
33:    ////////////////////////////////////////////////////////
34:    // COMPARE CURRENT VS PRIOR STAT(2) INFO :
35:    ////////////////////////////////////////////////////////
36:
37:    char *
38:    Compare(struct stat is,struct stat was) {
39:        static char cmpmsg[512];    // Compare() message buffer
40:        static char dtbuf[64];      // Date time format buffer
41:        struct passwd *pw;          // /etc/password lookup
42:        struct group *gr;           // /etc/group lookup
43:
44:        // DID THE FILE SIZE CHANGE?
45:        if ( is.st_size != was.st_size ) {
46:            sprintf(cmpmsg,"Size has changed (was %ld bytes)",
47:                (long)was.st_size);
48:            return cmpmsg;
49:        }
50:
51:        // DID THE FILE MODIFICATION TIME CHANGE?
52:        if ( is.st_mtime != was.st_mtime ) {
```

```
53:            strftime(dtbuf,sizeof dtbuf,"%x %X",localtime(&was.st_mtime));
54:            dtbuf[sizeof dtbuf-1] = 0;
55:            sprintf(cmpmsg,"Modification time has changed (was %s)",dtbuf);
56:            return cmpmsg;
57:        }
58:
59:        // DID THE FILE MODE CHANGE?
60:        if ( is.st_mode != was.st_mode ) {
61:            sprintf(cmpmsg,"File mode changed (was 0%03o)",was.st_mode);
62:            return cmpmsg;
63:        }
64:
65:        // DID THE OWNERSHIP OF THE FILE CHANGE?
66:        if ( is.st_uid != was.st_uid ) {
67:            if ( !(pw = getpwuid(was.st_uid)) )
68:                sprintf(cmpmsg,"File ownership has changed (was uid %d)",
69:                    was.st_uid);
70:            else
71:                sprintf(cmpmsg,"File ownership has changed (was %s)",
72:                    pw->pw_name);
73:            return cmpmsg;
74:        }
75:
76:        // DID THE GROUP CHANGE?
77:        if ( is.st_gid != was.st_gid ) {
78:            if ( !(gr = getgrgid(was.st_gid)) )
79:                sprintf(cmpmsg,"Group ownership changed (was gid %d)",
80:                    was.st_gid);
81:            else
82:                sprintf(cmpmsg,"Group ownership changed (was %s)",
83:                    gr->gr_name);
84:            return cmpmsg;
85:        }
86:
87:        // DID THE NUMBER OF LINKS TO THIS FILE CHANGE?
88:        if ( is.st_nlink != was.st_nlink ) {
89:            sprintf(cmpmsg,"Number of links changed (was %ld)",
90:                (long)was.st_nlink);
91:            return cmpmsg;
92:        }
93:
94:        return NULL;
95:    }
96:
97:    //////////////////////////////////////////////////////////////
98:    // UPDATE DATABASE OR CHECK AGAINST DATABASE :
99:    //////////////////////////////////////////////////////////////
100:
101: void
102: Process(InoDb &inodb,const char *fullpath,struct stat &sbuf) {
103:     struct stat pbuf;
104:     InoDb::Key key;
105:     char *msg;
```

continued from previous page

```
106:
107:     if ( !strcmp(fullpath,"/proc") )
108:         return;                 // Ignore pseudo directories
109:
110:     if ( lstat(fullpath,&sbuf) == -1 ) {
111:         fprintf(stderr,"%s: stat(%s)\n",
112:             strerror(errno),fullpath);
113:         rc |= 4;                // Error, but non-fatal
114:         return;
115:     }
116:
117:     // READY THE DATABASE KEY:
118:     key.st_dev = sbuf.st_dev;
119:     key.st_ino = sbuf.st_ino;
120:
121:     if ( !cmdopt_c ) {
122:         // CREATE or UPDATE DB RECORD:
123:         inodb.replaceKey(key,sbuf);
124:     } else {
125:         // LOOKUP LAST SNAPSHOT :
126:         try {
127:             inodb.fetchKey(key,pbuf);
128:         } catch ( int e ) {
129:             if ( e == ENOENT ) {
130:                 fprintf(stderr,"New %s: %s\n",
131:                     S_ISDIR(sbuf.st_mode)
132:                         ? "directory"
133:                         : "object",
134:                     fullpath);
135:                 return;
136:             } else {
137:                 fprintf(stderr,"%s: fetchKey(%s)\n",
138:                     strerror(e),fullpath);
139:                 abort();         // Fatal DB error
140:             }
141:         }
142:
143:         // COMPARE CURRENT STAT VS STORED STAT INFO :
144:         msg = Compare(sbuf,pbuf);
145:         if ( msg ) {
146:             printf("%s: %s\n",msg,fullpath);
147:             rc |= 8;
148:         }
149:     }
150: }
151:
152: /////////////////////////////////////////////////////////////////
153: // WALK A DIRECTORY :
154: /////////////////////////////////////////////////////////////////
155:
156: void
157: walk(InoDb &inodb,const char *dirname,int inclDir=0) {
```

```
158:        Dir dir;
159:        char *ent;
160:        long pathmax;
161:        struct stat sbuf;
162:
163:        // AVOID CERTAIN PSEUDO FILE SYSTEMS :
164:        if ( !strcmp(dirname,"/proc") )
165:            return;
166:
167:        if ( cmdopt_v )
168:            fprintf(stderr,"Examining: %s\n",dirname);
169:
170:        // OPEN DIRECTORY :
171:        try {
172:            dir.open(dirname);
173:        } catch ( int e ) {
174:            fprintf(stderr,"%s: opening directory %s\n",
175:                strerror(e),dirname);
176:            rc |= 2;
177:            return;                      // Non-fatal
178:        }
179:
180:        // INCLUDE TOP LEVEL DIRECTORIES :
181:        if ( inclDir )
182:            Process(inodb,dirname,sbuf);
183:
184:        // DETERMINE MAXIMUM PATHNAME LENGTH :
185:        if ( (pathmax = pathconf(dirname,_PC_PATH_MAX)) == -1L ) {
186:            fprintf(stderr,"%s: pathconf('%s',_PC_PATH_MAX)\n",
187:                strerror(errno),dirname);
188:            abort();
189:        }
190:
191:        char fullpath[pathmax+1];   // Full pathname
192:        int bx;                     // Index to basename
193:
194:        strcpy(fullpath,dirname);
195:        bx = strlen(fullpath);
196:        if ( bx > 0 && fullpath[bx-1] != '/' ) {
197:            strcat(fullpath,"/");   // Append slash
198:            ++bx;                   // Adjust basename index
199:        }
200:
201:        // PROCESS ALL DIRECTORY ENTRIES:
202:        while ( (ent = dir.read()) ) {
203:            if ( !strcmp(ent,".") || !strcmp(ent,"..") )
204:                continue;            // Ignore these
205:            strcpy(fullpath+bx,ent);
206:
207:            Process(inodb,fullpath,sbuf);
208:
209:            // IF OBJECT IS A DIRECTORY, DESCEND INTO IT:
210:            if ( S_ISDIR(sbuf.st_mode) )
```

continued from previous page

```
211:                walk(inodb,fullpath);
212:        }
213:
214:        // CLOSE DIRECTORY:
215:        dir.close();
216: }
217:
218: ////////////////////////////////////////////////////////////
219: // PROVIDE USAGE INSTRUCTIONS :
220: ////////////////////////////////////////////////////////////
221:
222: static void
223: usage(char *cmd) {
224:        char *bname = Basename(cmd);
225:
226:        printf("Usage:  %s [-c] [-i] [-v] [-h] [dir...]\n",bname);
227:        puts("where:");
228:        puts("    -c      Check snapshot against file system");
229:        puts("    -i      (Re)Initialize the database");
230:        puts("    -v      Verbose");
231:        puts("    -h      Help (this info)");
232: }
233:
234: ////////////////////////////////////////////////////////////
235: // MAIN PROGRAM :
236: ////////////////////////////////////////////////////////////
237:
238: int
239: main(int argc,char **argv) {
240:        InoDb inodb;
241:        int optch;
242:        const char cmdopts[] = "hicv";
243:
244:        // PROCESS COMMAND LINE OPTIONS:
245:        while ( (optch = getopt(argc,argv,cmdopts)) != -1 )
246:            switch ( optch ) {
247:            case 'i' :
248:                cmdopt_i = 1;   // -i (initialize database)
249:                break;
250:            case 'c' :          // -c (check snapshot)
251:                cmdopt_c = 1;
252:                break;
253:            case 'v' :
254:                cmdopt_v = 1;   // -v (verbose)
255:                break;
256:            case 'h' :          // -h (give help)
257:                cmdopt_h = 1;
258:                break;
259:            default :
260:                rc = 1;
261:            }
262:
```

```
263:        if ( cmdopt_i && cmdopt_c ) {
264:            fputs("You cannot use -i and -c together\n",stderr);
265:            exit(1);
266:        }
267:
268:        if ( cmdopt_h || rc ) {
269:            usage(argv[0]);
270:            exit(rc);
271:        }
272:
273:        // IF -i THEN DELETE DATABASE, TO RECREATE
274:        if ( cmdopt_i && unlink("snapshot.db") == -1 )
275:            if ( errno != ENOENT ) {
276:                fprintf(stderr,"%s: unlink(snapshot.db)\n",
277:                    strerror(errno));
278:                exit(13);
279:            }
280:
281:        // OPEN EXISTING DATABASE (snapshot.db) :
282:        try {
283:            inodb.open("snapshot");
284:        } catch ( int e ) {
285:            // IF -c OPTION, DO NOT CREATE DB :
286:            if ( !cmdopt_c && e == EIO ) {
287:                // FILE NOT FOUND: CREATE DATABASE
288:                try {
289:                    inodb.open("snapshot",O_RDWR|O_CREAT);
290:                } catch ( int e ) {
291:                    fprintf(stderr,"%s: creating snapshot db\n",
292:                        strerror(e));
293:                    exit(1);
294:                }
295:            } else {
296:                // REPORT DB OPEN ERROR :
297:                fprintf(stderr,"%s: creating snapshot db\n",strerror(e));
298:                exit(1);
299:            }
300:        }
301:
302:        // WALK ALL DIRECTORIES GIVEN ON COMMAND LINE :
303:        for ( int x=optind; x<argc; ++x )
304:            walk(inodb,argv[x],1);
305:
306:        inodb.close();
307:
308:        return rc;
309: }
310:
311: // End SnapShot.cc
```

The `main()` program begins in line 239 of Listing 14.7. Command-line options are processed in lines 245–271. Line 274 checks to see if the option -i was present on the command line. If so, it deletes the database snapshot.db by calling unlink(2).

The database is opened in line 283. However, if the database does not exist, the error EIO will be thrown, and execution continues at line 286. If the -c option is not present on the command line, the database is created in line 289.

Once the database is open, the remaining command-line arguments are processed in lines 303 and 304. After the for loop exits, the database is closed in line 306.

The Tree Walk

The function walk() is implemented in lines 156–216. The argument inclDir in line 157 defaults to zero (false). However, when called from the main() program, the inclDir argument is true. This causes the directory dirname to be processed in addition to the directory members that it contains (lines 181 and 182).

Certain directories should not be included, and /proc is one of them. Consequently, a test is included in lines 164 and 165 to bypass /proc if it should be encountered.

The -v command-line option causes the directory being processed to be displayed on stderr (lines 167 and 168). This is useful when you want to see the progress of a lengthy operation.

The directory dirname is opened in line 172. Lines 185–191 determine the maximum pathname length and allocate a buffer named fullpath[]. Variable bx (lines 192 and 195) indicates where the basename of the pathname is in the buffer fullpath[].

Lines 202–212 form the directory-processing loop. For each entry encountered, the function Process() is invoked. Furthermore, if the object is a directory, walk() is called recursively on this new directory (lines 210 and 211).

Processing for walk() ends in line 215, where the directory is closed.

The Process() Function

The interesting database functionality exists in lines 101–150. Line 107 tests to see if the pathname in argument fullpath matches the directory /proc. If it matches, the return statement (line 108) is executed, which causes the /proc directory to be ignored.

Line 110 performs a lstat(2) call on the object fullpath. The function lstat(2) is used because you want to know if symbolic links have changed, not just the files to which they point.

The key is prepared in lines 118 and 119 to indicate the device and i-node entry. If option -c is not supplied, then the application is taking a snapshot of the file system, and the lstat(2) information is saved (line 123). The method used is InoDb::replaceKey(), since if this is run on an existing database, the record should be updated.

If the option -c is provided, then a lookup is attempted by device and i-node number in line 127 instead. If the exception is ENOENT, then the entry does not exist, and the object is reported as being a new object (lines 130–135). If the entry is found, then the present lstat(2) information in sbuf is compared to the prior lstat(2) information in pbuf. This is accomplished by calling upon the function `Compare()` in line 144. If `Compare()` returns a message pointer, then the difference is reported in lines 146 and 147. Otherwise, the function `Process()` exits quietly.

The Application Function `Compare()`

The function `Compare()` is implemented in lines 37–95. The `lstat(2)` information in variables `is` and `was` is compared in lines 45–92. The following comparison tests are made:

- The sizes of the object (line 45)

- The modification times (line 52)

- The permissions of the object (line 60)

- The ownership of the object (line 66)

- The group ownership of the object (line 77)

- The number of links to the object (line 88)

If no differences are found in these tests, a null pointer is returned in line 94.

Running the SnapShot Application

To compile the program, SnapShot and its companion executable `EmptyDb` perform the following:

```
$ make
cc -c  -Wall -fhandle-exceptions Dir.cc
cc -c  -Wall -fhandle-exceptions Dbm.cc
cc -c  -Wall -fhandle-exceptions InoDb.cc
cc -c  -Wall -fhandle-exceptions SnapShot.cc
cc -o SnapShot SnapShot.o Dir.o Dbm.o InoDb.o -lstdc++
cc -c  -Wall -fhandle-exceptions EmptyDb.cc
cc -o EmptyDb EmptyDb.o Dir.o Dbm.o InoDb.o -lstdc++
$
```

This should create the executables `SnapShot` and `EmptyDb`.

Note

On many UNIX systems, the NDBM routines are included in a separate library. For this reason, you may need to add the linking option `-lndbm` to link with the NDBM library.

Under FreeBSD, the NDBM functions are included in the standard C library `/usr/lib/libc.so`. Consequently, under FreeBSD you have no special linking requirements, since `libc.so` is searched by default.

You should now be able to provoke usage information from the executable `SnapShot`:

```
$ ./SnapShot -h
Usage:  SnapShot [-c] [-i] [-v] [-h] [dir...]
```

```
where:
     -c        Check snapshot against file system
     -i        (Re)Initialize the database
     -v        Verbose
     -h        Help (this info)
$
```

To create a SnapShot database (`snapshot.db` in the current directory), do not include the `-c` option. The `-i` option is used when you want to re-initialize an existing database. Perform this simple experiment:

```
$ ./SnapShot /tmp
$
```

If all went well, the program should quickly run through your `/tmp` directory, making notes in the database. To compare the `/tmp` directory against your database, enter the command

```
$ ./SnapShot -c /tmp
$
```

If you have a relatively quiet system, you'll not likely see any changes. Now make a change or two—perhaps this:

```
$ ls -ltr >/tmp/dummy.file
$ ./SnapShot -c /tmp
Modification time has changed (was 05/14/00 20:37:35): /tmp
New object: /tmp/dummy.file
$
```

Because you created a new file `/tmp/dummy.file`, it was not in the database. Hence, it is reported as a new file. However, note that the `/tmp` directory's modification time changed, and so it was reported. This tells you that a file was added, renamed, or deleted in that directory.

Now try something more adventuresome:

```
$ ./SnapShot -i /etc /var /tmp
Permission denied: opening directory /etc/isdn
Permission denied: opening directory /etc/uucp
Permission denied: opening directory /var/cron/tabs
Permission denied: opening directory /var/spool/opielocks
Permission denied: opening directory /var/games/hackdir
$
```

Since this was not run from a **root** account, there were some permission problems. These can be ignored for our purposes, as follows:

```
$ ./SnapShot -i /etc /var /tmp 2>/dev/null
$
```

Now keep that database for a while and test it later. After an hour of using a FreeBSD system with one user on it, the following changes were observed:

```
$ ./SnapShot -c /etc /var /tmp 2>/dev/null
Modification time has changed (was 05/14/00 16:15:38): /etc/ntp
Modification time has changed (was 05/14/00 16:15:38): /etc/ntp/drift
Size has changed (was 94415 bytes): /var/cron/log
```

```
Modification time has changed (was 05/14/00 02:02:03): /var/log
Modification time has changed (was 05/14/00 15:28:26): /var/log/lastlog
Size has changed (was 3784 bytes): /var/log/wtmp
Size has changed (was 359 bytes): /var/log/maillog.0.gz
Modification time has changed (was 05/14/00 15:28:35): /var/run/utmp
Modification time has changed (was 05/14/00 16:32:48): /var/tmp
$
```

This output shows what files had changed on the system (for the directories tested). The system that this ran on had the daemon xntpd(8) running to keep the clock synchronized. Consequently, directory /etc/ntp and file /etc/ntp/drift were updated.

Visiting All Keys and Deletion

To test the key visitation feature and the delete capability, the program EmptyDb.cc is provided in Listing 14.8.

LISTING 14.8   EmptyDb.cc—Emptying the Database with InoDb::deleteKey()

```
 1:   // EmptyDb.cc
 2:
 3:   #include <stdio.h>
 4:   #include <stdlib.h>
 5:   #include <unistd.h>
 6:   #include <errno.h>
 7:   #include <string.h>
 8:   #include <sys/types.h>
 9:   #include <sys/stat.h>
10:
11:   #include "InoDb.h"
12:
13:   /////////////////////////////////////////////////////////////
14:   // MAIN PROGRAM :
15:   //
16:   // If the first command line argument is the word "LIST"
17:   // the keys will be listed only. Otherwise the records
18:   // are deleted.
19:   //
20:   // This test program deletes all entries from the database
21:   // to demonstrate key traversal and delete operations.
22:   /////////////////////////////////////////////////////////////
23:
24:   int
25:   main(int argc,char **argv) {
26:       InoDb inodb;
27:       InoDb::Key *key;
28:
29:       (void)argc;
30:       (void)argv;
31:
32:       // OPEN EXISTING DATABASE (snapshot.db) :
```

continued from previous page

```
33:        try {
34:            inodb.open("snapshot");
35:        } catch ( int e ) {
36:            fprintf(stderr,"%s: creating snapshot db",strerror(e));
37:            exit(1);
38:        }
39:
40:        // LIST THE KEYS ONLY :
41:        if ( argc == 2 && !strcasecmp(argv[1],"LIST") ) {
42:            for (key=inodb.firstKey(); key != NULL;
43:                key=inodb.nextKey() ) {
44:                printf("Key %d:%d from db.\n",
45:                    key->st_dev,key->st_ino);
46:            }
47:            return 0;
48:        }
49:
50:        // DELETE ALL ENTRIES IN DB :
51:        while ( (key = inodb.firstKey()) != NULL ) {
52:            printf("Delete: Inode %d:%d from db.\n",
53:                key->st_dev,key->st_ino);
54:            inodb.deleteKey(*key);   // DELETE ENTRY
55:        }
56:
57:        // CLOSE DB :
58:        inodb.close();
59:
60:        return 0;
61:    }
62:
63:    // End SnapShot.cc
```

Listing 14.8 simply opens the database in line 34 of the `main()` program (it must already exist). If the first argument on the command line is `LIST`, then the `for` loop in lines 42–46 exercise the database using `InoDb::firstKey()` and `InoDb::nextKey()`. The key values are reported in lines 44 and 45.

If no argument `LIST` is given, the delete loop in lines 51–55 is exercised instead. The `InoDb::deleteKey()` method is invoked in line 54.

Running the `EmptyDb` command in list mode is done as follows (with some output omitted):

```
$ ./EmptyDb LIST
Key 196608:142861 from db.
Key 196608:166656 from db.
Key 196608:198403 from db.
Key 196608:206340 from db.
Key 196608:63493 from db.
Key 196608:63509 from db.
Key 196608:63525 from db.
...
$
```

Running `EmptyDb` again to delete records is done as follows (with some output omitted):

```
$ ./EmptyDb
Delete: Inode 196608:142861 from db.
Delete: Inode 196608:166656 from db.
Delete: Inode 196608:198403 from db.
Delete: Inode 196608:206340 from db.
Delete: Inode 196608:63493 from db.
Delete: Inode 196608:63509 from db.
Delete: Inode 196608:63525 from db.
...
$
```

Using `LIST` on it now should yield no results:

```
$ ./EmptyDb LIST
$
```

Summary

In this chapter, you learned about the `ndbm(3)` set of routines. With the working SnapShot program and the `Dbm` and `InoDb` classes, you saw how the NDBM database routines were applied to a real-world application. The NDBM routines are ideal for small applications where multiuser contention is not an issue.

The next chapter covers the topic of UNIX signals. Signals permit you to process asynchronous events in your program.

PART III

ADVANCED CONCEPTS

CHAPTER 15

SIGNALS

The execution of a program normally proceeds synchronously, with each step following the previous one. Sometimes actions must be executed immediately by interrupting this flow of execution. This may be a request to terminate the program or to process some new action. UNIX provides for this capability with *signals*.

In this chapter you will learn how to

- Create and manage signal sets
- Catch signals
- Suspend signals
- Raise signals

Understanding UNIX Signals

A signal is an asynchronous software interrupt. The asynchronous nature of the signal prevents your program from anticipating when it will arrive. Consequently, a signal action must be registered before the signal's arrival.

A signal will suspend the execution of the program. The signal handling procedure then invokes the registered function or action. The function that is called to handle a signal is known as a *signal handler*.

When you want to interrupt a program that is executing, you interrupt it with the signal **SIGINT**. Another way of expressing this is to say that the signal **SIGINT** is *raised*. For many people, this is accomplished by entering Ctrl+C, but the character you use may be configured differently. To determine what your interrupt character is, the following command gets the result shown:

```
$ stty -a
speed 9600 baud; 0 rows; 0 columns;
lflags: icanon isig iexten echo echoe -echok echoke -echonl echoctl
        -echoprt -altwerase -noflsh -tostop -flusho pendin -nokerninfo
        -extproc
iflags: -istrip icrnl -inlcr -igncr ixon -ixoff ixany imaxbel -ignbrk
        brkint -inpck -ignpar -parmrk
oflags: opost onlcr -oxtabs
```

```
cflags: cread cs8 -parenb -parodd hupcl -clocal -cstopb -crtscts -dsrflow
        -dtrflow -mdmbuf
cchars: discard = ^O; dsusp = ^Y; eof = ^D; eol = <undef>;
        eol2 = <undef>; erase = ^H; intr = ^C; kill = ^U; lnext = ^V;
        min = 1; quit = ^\; reprint = ^R; start = ^Q; status = ^T;
        stop = ^S; susp = ^Z; time = 0; werase = ^W;
$
```

The example shown is the output from the FreeBSD stty(1) command. The output of the stty(1) command may vary on your UNIX platform. Look for the clause intr = ^C in the output. The example shows that the Ctrl+C (^C) character sends the signal SIGINT (intr).

The interrupt character raises the signal SIGINT in the executing program. Every defined UNIX signal has a default action associated with it. By default, the SIGINT signal causes the executing process to terminate. This signal is used for demonstration purposes in this chapter.

Reliable and Unreliable Signals

The original UNIX signal handling design using signal(3) contained a race condition. When a signal was caught by a program, the signal's registered action reverted to its default. To maintain the same registered action, the signal handler was forced to immediately re-register its required action. This left a small window of opportunity for the default action to be exercised by bad timing. This is why the signal(3) API is considered unreliable.

A new set of functions, including the function sigaction(2), has been added to the list of system calls. These form the reliable signals API. All new program development should use this API set. However, when the signal(3) API is discussed next, you will see that there are still a few cases where the older API can be used for its simplicity.

Note

BSD release 4.3 and later do not implement the System V behavior of changing the registered action to SIG_DFL. Consequently, the FreeBSD 3.4 release does not exhibit a race condition.

Registering the actions SIG_DFL and SIG_IGN can be done safely with the function signal(3). However, you should avoid the signal(3) function otherwise.

The Unreliable signal(3) API

The signal(3) function forms the basis for the unreliable signals interface. Its function synopsis is as follows:

```
#include <signal.h>

void (*signal(int sig, void (*func)(int)))(int)
```

```
/* Alternatively */

typedef void (*sig_t)(int);

sig_t signal(int sig, sig_t func);
```

The first synopsis is rather difficult to decipher. The FreeBSD man(1) page offers a second interpretation of the first. The signal(3) function's first argument sig identifies the signal for which the caller wants to register an action. The second argument func identifies the action or the function pointer.

The return value from signal(3) is the previous action that was established at the time of the call. Alternatively, the value SIG_ERR indicates that an error has occurred and the variable errno should be examined for the cause.

The argument sig identifies the signal to be prepared. Table 15.1 shows some of the more commonly used signals available under UNIX.

TABLE 15.1 Commonly Used Signals

Signal	Description
SIGHUP	The terminal line has hung up. This refers to when a modem line experiences a hangup due to a loss of carrier. However, it also applies to any terminal device when it is closed for logout(1).
SIGINT	The terminal line has received the interrupt character.
SIGQUIT	The terminal line has received the quit character. The default action produces a core file.
SIGUSR1	User-defined signal 1.
SIGUSR2	User-defined signal 2.
SIGTERM	The process is being terminated (often the result of the kill(1) command).
SIGCHLD	A child process has terminated.
SIGPIPE	A write to a half-closed pipe has occurred.
SIGALRM	The timer for function alarm(3) has expired.

The argument func allows the caller to register the action that is required for the given signal. There are three possible values for the argument func. They are

SIG_DFL	Default signal action
SIG_IGN	Ignore the signal
function pointer	The signal handler

The SIG_DFL macro causes the system default action for the named signal to be registered. The default action is not the same for all signals. For SIGINT, the default action causes the program to terminate. Alternatively, the default action for SIGCHLD is to ignore the signal.

The SIG_IGN macro allows the programmer to indicate that the signal is to be ignored. Once this action is registered, it remains in effect for the indicated signal sig until it is changed.

Note

Calling signal(3) with SIG_DFL or SIG_IGN is considered reliable. These actions can be registered reliably by signal(3) because they do not change after a signal is raised.

The programmer may also choose to register a signal handler to be called when a signal is received. This is accomplished by providing the function's pointer in the func argument. This practice is now discouraged, because this part of the signal(3) API is unreliable on non-BSD platforms.

The program shown in Listing 15.1 shows a simple demonstration program using the unreliable signal API.

LISTING 15.1 ursig1.c—A Simple signal(3) Example Program

```
 1:    /* ursig1.c */
 2:
 3:    #include <stdio.h>
 4:    #include <signal.h>
 5:    #include <unistd.h>
 6:
 7:    static int count = 0;
 8:
 9:    void
10:    handler(int signo) {
11:
12:        signal(SIGINT,handler);     /* Re-instate handler */
13:        ++count;                    /* Increment count */
14:        write(1,"Got SIGINT\n",11); /* Write message */
15:    }
16:
17:    int
18:    main(int argc,char **argv) {
19:
20:        signal(SIGINT,handler);     /* Register function */
21:
22:        while ( count < 2 ) {
23:            puts("Waiting for SIGINT..");
24:            sleep(4);               /* Snooze */
25:        }
26:        puts("End.");
27:        return 0;
28:    }
```

Line 12 of Listing 15.1 is necessary for non-BSD systems. Otherwise, only the first SIGINT signal will be caught by the function handler(), because the signal reverts to its default action.

Compiling and running this program under FreeBSD yields the following result:

```
$ make ursig1
cc -c -D_POSIX_C_SOURCE=199309L -D_POSIX_SOURCE -Wall ursig1.c
cc -o ursig1 ursig1.o
$ ./ursig1
Waiting for SIGINT..
^CGot SIGINT
Waiting for SIGINT..
^CGot SIGINT
End.
$
```

In the example session shown, the loop in lines 22–24 causes the message Waiting for SIGINT.. to appear. Then the user presses Ctrl+C, which is shown as ^C in the session output. Immediately after Ctrl+C is pressed, the message Got SIGINT is displayed. Later, another Ctrl+C is pressed to demonstrate that the signal can be caught more than once. The program terminates normally after it notices that SIGINT has been received twice (see line 22). The message Got SIGINT comes from line 14 of Listing 15.1, demonstrating that the signal handler was executed.

The Reliable Signal API

To use the reliable signal API, you must work with *signal sets*. These allow you to work with signal collections. Alternatively, signal sets can be used as masks that enable or disable collections of signals.

The data type that is used for constructing signal sets is sigset_t. This type is manipulated by the following functions:

```
#include <signal.h>

int sigemptyset(sigset_t *set);
int sigfillset(sigset_t *set);
int sigaddset(sigset_t *set,int signum);
int sigdelset(sigset_t *set,int signum);

int sigismember(const sigset_t *set,int signum);
```

The functions sigemptyset(3), sigfillset(3), sigaddset(3), and sigdelset(3) all manipulate the sigset_t data type. The last function, sigismember(3), allows you to test the sigset_t data type.

The first four functions return a value of 0 if the operation was successful. If the call failed, -1 is returned, and errno will contain the error code. The function sigismember(3) will be examined later in this chapter.

> **Warning**
>
> No signal set should be used unless `sigemptyset(3)` or `sigfillset(3)` has been called to initialize the set. Any signal set function can be applied after initialization has been performed.

Emptying a Signal Set

The function `sigemptyset(3)` is used to initialize a signal set to the state of "no signal members." Initialization is necessary because a declared variable of type `sigset_t` has undefined content. Consequently, `sigemptyset(3)` is often called before the programmer adds one or more signals to the set with `sigaddset(3)`.

The function `sigemptyset(3)` accepts a pointer to the set to initialize. The following shows how it is used to initialize a new set:

```
sigset_t my_sigs;          /* Signal set declaration */

sigemptyset(&my_signals); /* Clear set */
```

This example initializes the signal set `my_sigs` to contain no signals.

Filling a Signal Set

The function `sigfillset(3)` is similar to `sigemptyset(3)`, except that it fills a signal set with all possible signals. This is often required when a signal mask is being created. After filling the set with all possible signals, the programmer will delete one or more signals to be excluded from the mask.

This function is used in the same manner as the `sigemptyset(3)` function. The following example shows how to create a set with all possible signals in it:

```
sigset_t all_sigs;

sigfillset(&all_sigs);
```

The signal set `all_sigs` is initialized to contain every possible signal.

Adding Signals to a Signal Set

The function `sigaddset(3)` is used to add a new signal to a signal set. This function is often used to add a new signal after the set has been emptied. The function prototype is as follows:

```
#include <signal.h>

int sigaddset(sigset_t *set,int signum);
```

The following example shows how to declare and initialize a signal set to contain two signals:

```
sigset_t two_sigs;

sigemptyset(&two_sigs);         /* Initialize as empty */
```

```
sigaddset(&two_sigs,SIGINT);   /* Add SIGINT to set */
sigaddset(&two_sigs,SIGPIPE); /* Add SIGPIPE to set */
```

The function `sigemptyset(3)` initializes the set `two_sigs`. The signals `SIGINT` and `SIGPIPE` are then added by calling the function `sigaddset(3)`.

Removing Signals from a Signal Set

Signals are removed from a signal set with the function `sigdelset(3)`. This function is often used after using `sigfillset(3)` to remove one or more signals from the set. Its function prototype is as follows:

```
#include <signal.h>

int sigdelset(sigset_t *set,int signum);
```

In the example that follows, the `sig_msk` set is filled with all possible signals by calling `sigfillset(3)`. Function `sigdelset(3)` is then used to remove `SIGINT` from this set:

```
sigset_t sig_msk;

sigfillset(&sig_msk);        /* Initialize with all sigs */
sigdelset(&sig_msk,SIGINT);    /* Del SIGINT from set */
```

The resulting signal set `sig_msk` includes all signals except `SIGINT`.

Testing for Signals in a Set

The function `sigismember(3)` is used to test if the signal is a member of the given signal set. The function prototype is as follows:

```
#include <signal.h>

int sigismember(const sigset_t *set,int signum);
```

The function `sigismember(3)` returns the value 1 if the signal given in argument `signum` is a member of the given signal set in argument `set`. Otherwise, 0 is returned to indicate that the signal is not a member of the set. The following code illustrates its use:

```
sigset_t myset;

sigemptyset(&myset);                /* Clear the set */
sigaddset(&myset,SIGINT);           /* Add SIGINT to set */

if ( sigismember(&myset,SIGINT) )  /* Test for SIGINT */
    puts("HAS SIGINT");
if ( sigismember(&myset,SIGPIPE) ) /* Test for SIGPIPE */
    puts("HAS SIGPIPE");
```

In the code shown, the message HAS SIGINT will be displayed, but since the SIGPIPE signal is not a member of the set, the message HAS SIGPIPE will not be shown.

Setting Signal Actions

Function `sigaction(2)` is used to query and set signal actions when using reliable signals. This function replaces the older `signal(3)` function that you have seen before. The function synopsis for `sigaction(2)` is as follows:

```
#include <signal.h>

struct sigaction {
    void     (*sa_handler)();    /* signal handler */
    sigset_t sa_mask;            /* signal mask to apply */
    int      sa_flags;           /* see signal options below */
};

int sigaction(int signum,         /* Signal number */
    const struct sigaction *act,  /* New actions */
    struct sigaction *oldact);    /* Old actions */
```

The function `sigaction(2)` returns `0` when successful and `-1` if an error occurs (check `errno`). Function argument `signum` is the signal number that is to be queried or modified.

The argument `oldact` allows the programmer to obtain the original handler state. This is ideal for when the new handler is temporary, such as within a library function. Before the library function returns, the original signal action can be restored precisely as it was.

The argument `act` establishes the action that is to be taken by the UNIX kernel when the specified signal `signum` is received by the current process. A detailed description of each member of the `sigaction` structure is given in Table 15.2.

TABLE 15.2   The Members of the `sigaction` Structure

Structure Member	Data Type	Description
sa_handler	void (*)(int)	The address of the signal handler. This may also be the value SIG_DFL to indicate the default action or SIG_IGN to indicate that the signal should be ignored.
sa_mask	sigset_t	This represents the set of other signals that should be blocked while the current signal is being processed. In addition, the signal being processed will be blocked unless the SA_NODEFER or SA_NOMASK flag is used.
sa_flags	int	This integer value specifies a set of flags that modify the signal handling process.

The value of `sa_handler` can also be specified as the value `SIG_DFL` to specify the system default signal handling instead of a user-supplied function address. Another value that can be used is `SIG_IGN`, which indicates that the signal is to be ignored.

The `sigaction(2)` function allows you to query the current signal action without modifying the current action for the indicated signal. Simply specify the second argument **act** as a null pointer, as shown:

```
struct sigaction sa_old;

sigaction(SIGINT,0,&sa_old);
```

The following code segment shows how you could report what the current setting for SIGINT is:

```
struct sigaction sa_old;                  /* Queried signal set */

sigaction(SIGINT,0,&sa_old);              /* Query SIGINT */

if ( sa_old.sa_handler == SIG_DFL )
    puts("SIG_DFL");                      /* System Default */
else if ( sa_old.sa_handler == SIG_IGN )
    puts("SIG_IGN");                      /* Ignore signal */
else                                      /* Function Pointer */
    printf("sa_handler = 0x%08lX;\n",(long)sa_old.sa_handler);
```

The code presented will print the message SIG_DFL, indicating the current state of the signal SIGINT.

Signal Action Flags

Within the structure **sigaction**, the **sa_flags** member allows a number of options to be specified. Table 15.3 outlines the signal-processing flags that UNIX supports.

TABLE 15.3 sigaction sa_flags

Flag	Description
SA_ONESHOT or SA_RESETHAND	These flags cause the signal action to revert to the default (SIG_DFL) when a signal is caught. Note that this is equivalent to using unreliable signals. The AT&T SVID document uses the macro SA_RESETHAND for this flag.
SA_NOMASK or SA_NODEFER	These flags prevent the signal being processed from being blocked automatically when it is processed. This allows recursive signals of the same type to occur.
SA_RESTART	This flag permits the automatic retry BSD semantic for interrupted system calls. The error EINTR is suppressed when this flag is in effect.
SA_NOCLDSTOP	This flag is applicable only for the signal SIGCHLD. When used with SIGCHLD, no notification occurs when the child process is stopped.

continued from previous page

Flag	Description
SA_NOCLDWAIT	This flag is applicable only for the signal SIGCHLD. The UNIX kernel will not leave zombie processes when child processes of the calling process terminate. If the calling process issues a wait(2) or equivalent call, it sleeps until all child processes have terminated (wait(2) will return -1 with an errno value of ECHILD).
SA_ONSTACK	With this flag set, the signal will be delivered to the process using an alternate signal stack (see sigaltstack(2)).

Flags SA_NOMASK or SA_NODEFER are noteworthy because they allow a signal handler to be called recursively. When a signal is caught, further signals of the same signal number normally are blocked until the present signal finishes processing.

Flag SA_NOCLDSTOP prevents the parent process from being notified every time a child process is stopped. SA_NOCLDWAIT prevents zombie processes, if the parent process does not call wait(2) or its equivalent (see Chapter 19, "Forked Processes," for more information about zombie processes).

The flag SA_RESTART permits system calls to not return the error code EINTR when the specified signal is received. Those system calls are automatically retried, instead. This flag may be useful for signal handlers that never post results for the application to test.

Applying Reliable Signals

The program shown in Listing 15.2 is a modified version of Listing 15.1, using the sigaction(2) function.

LISTING 15.2 rsig1.c—An Example Using sigaction(2)

```
 1:  /* rsig1.c */
 2:
 3:  #include <stdio.h>
 4:  #include <signal.h>
 5:  #include <unistd.h>
 6:
 7:  static int count = 0;
 8:
 9:  void
10:  handler(int signo) {
11:
12:      signal(SIGINT,handler);     /* Re-instate handler */
13:      ++count;                    /* Increment count */
14:      write(1,"Got SIGINT\n",11); /* Write message */
15:  }
16:
17:  int
```

continued from previous page

```
18:  main(int argc,char **argv) {
19:      struct sigaction sa_old;    /* Old signal actions */
20:      struct sigaction sa_new;    /* New signal actions */
21:
22:      sa_new.sa_handler = handler;    /* Point to our function */
23:      sigemptyset(&sa_new.sa_mask);   /* Clear mask */
24:      sa_new.sa_flags = 0;            /* No special flags */
25:      sigaction(SIGINT,&sa_new,&sa_old);
26:
27:      while ( count < 2 ) {
28:          puts("Waiting for SIGINT..");
29:          sleep(4);                   /* Snooze */
30:      }
31:
32:      sigaction(SIGINT,&sa_old,0);    /* Restore signal actions */
33:
34:      puts("End.");
35:      return 0;
36:  }
```

The `signal(3)` call is replaced by lines 19–25 of Listing 15.2. Line 22 defines the address of the function to be invoked when **SIGINT** is raised. Line 23 clears the signal mask, and line 24 indicates no special flag bits will be used.

Compiling and running the program gives the following result:

```
$ make rsig1
cc -c -D_POSIX_C_SOURCE=199309L -D_POSIX_SOURCE -Wall rsig1.c
cc -o rsig1 rsig1.o
$ ./rsig1
Waiting for SIGINT..
^CGot SIGINT
Waiting for SIGINT..
^CGot SIGINT
End.
$
```

The program works just as the program in Listing 15.1 did.

Notice that a call to `sigaction(2)` was added in line 32. This was not necessary for this program, but it demonstrates how a program can restore signal-handling actions. The actions for **SIGINT** were saved when line 25 was executed, by saving the settings in variable `sa_old`. Line 32 restores the actions for **SIGINT** by using variable `sa_old`.

Controlling Signals

The previous sections demonstrate how you can define actions for signals and process them within your programs. Sometimes it is necessary to control more closely when a signal is allowed to be raised. The following sections will show you how this is accomplished under UNIX.

Blocking Signals

When the sigaction(2) function was discussed, it was noted that certain signals could be blocked during the call to the signal handler. For example, when SIGINT is handled by the signal handler, further SIGINT signals are prevented from taking place until the present handler returns (unless flag SA_NOMASK or SA_NODEFER is used).

In a similar fashion, your application can enter a critical piece of code where signals could cause it problems. An example of this might be keeping track of child process termination status information in a linked list. However, if the program is updating the linked list, you do not want the signal handler to be called until the linked list has been completely updated. Otherwise, corruption of the list would result.

Critical sections of code can block certain signals from taking place. Once the critical section is completed, then the selected signals can be enabled. This functionality is supported by the function sigprocmask(2), which manipulates the current signal mask. Its function synopsis is as follows:

```
#include <signal.h>

int sigprocmask(int how, const sigset_t *set, sigset_t *oldset);
```

The function sigprocmask(2) returns 0 when called successfully. Otherwise, -1 is returned, and the error code is left in external variable errno.

The sigprocmask(2) argument how determines how the signal action is to be modified. It can be one of the following values:

SIG_BLOCK	The specified set indicates additional signals to be blocked (disabled).
SIG_UNBLOCK	The specified set indicates signals that are to become unblocked (enabled).
SIG_SETMASK	The specified set replaces the current mask representing blocked signals.

The macros SIG_BLOCK and SIG_UNBLOCK modify the current signal mask. Macro SIG_SETMASK allows the caller to completely replace the current signal mask.

The argument set is the new set that is to be used in modifying the current process signal mask. Argument oldset can be provided so that the caller can receive a copy of the current process mask settings.

The following example shows how to block signals SIGINT and SIGPIPE from being received:

```
sigset_t blk;                   /* Signals to block */
sigset_t sigsv;                 /* Saved signal mask */

sigemptyset(&blk);              /* clear set */
sigaddset(&blk,SIGINT);         /* add SIGINT */
sigaddset(&blk,SIGPIPE);        /* add SIGPIPE */
```

```
sigprocmask(SIG_BLOCK,&blk,&sigsv);  /* Block sigs */

    /* CRITICAL CODE HERE */

sigprocmask(SIG_SETMASK,&sigsv,0);  /* Restore mask */
```

The first call to sigprocmask(2) adds signals SIGINT and SIGPIPE to the list of signals to be blocked (note how the how argument is given as SIG_BLOCK). Once the critical code has finished, the next call to sigprocmask(2) restores the mask value that was saved in the variable sigsv.

Obtaining Pending Signals

When signals are blocked by sigprocmask(2), they become pending signals, rather than being lost. A program can inquire if a signal is pending by using the function sigpending(2). Its function synopsis is as follows:

```
#include <signal.h>

int sigpending(sigset_t *set);
```

The function sigpending(2) returns 0 if the call is successful. Otherwise, the value -1 is returned, and the error code is found in the variable errno.

The set of pending signals is copied to the set provided in argument set. The following example assumes that signal SIGPIPE is blocked and illustrates how to test if the same signal is pending:

```
sigset_t pendg;                    /* Pending signal set */

sigpending(&pendg);                /* Inquire of pending signals */

if ( sigismember(&pendg,SIGPIPE) ) {
    puts("SIGPIPE is pending.");
```

The sigpending(2) function is useful when a program is in a critical code loop and needs to test for a pending signal.

The sigsuspend(2) Function

After noting that a signal is pending with a call to sigpending(2), you need a reliable way to unblock that signal and allow the signal to be raised. The function for this job is sigsuspend(2):

```
#include <signal.h>

int sigsuspend(const sigset_t *mask);
```

The sigsuspend(2) function temporarily applies the signal mask supplied in argument mask and then waits for the signal to be raised. If the mask permits the signal you know to be pending, the signal action will take place immediately. Otherwise, the program will pause indefinitely until an unblocked signal is received.

Once the signal action is carried out, the original signal mask is re-established. This provides a safe and reliable method to control when a signal is raised.

Using the example presented with `sigpending(2)`, you can extend that to raise and handle the signal when you know it is pending. This example assumes that `SIGPIPE` is currently blocked:

```
sigset_t pendg;              /* Pending signal set */
sigset_t notpipe;            /* All but SIGPIPE */

sigfillset(&notpipe);        /* Set to all signals */
sigdelset(&notpipe,SIGPIPE); /* Remove SIGPIPE */

sigpending(&pendg);          /* Query which signals are pending */

if ( sigismember(&pendg,SIGPIPE) ) { /* Is SIGPIPE pending? */
    sigsuspend(&notpipe);    /* Yes, allow SIGPIPE to be raised */
```

In the example shown, signal set `notpipe` is initialized so that all signals are set except for `SIGPIPE`. This is done so that the mask presented to `sigsuspend(2)` is the set of signals to block. In this manner, when the function `sigsuspend(&notpipe)` is called, the signal `SIGPIPE` is temporarily unblocked and allows the signal to be processed. However, when the signal handler returns, the original signal mask is restored.

The returned value from `sigsuspend(2)` is always `-1`, and the `errno` value is set to the value `EINTR`. This reflects the fact that a signal was handled.

When `sigsuspend(2)` is called, your program is suspended indefinitely until a signal is raised. Sometimes this is the desired behavior, when the program has no work to perform, and it is waiting for a signal to arrive.

Applying the `alarm(3)` Function

The `alarm(3)` function is related to signals. It is useful as a simple timer and is used for signal demonstrations in this chapter. The function synopsis is as follows:

```
#include <unistd.h>

unsigned int alarm(unsigned int seconds);
```

The `alarm(3)` function returns the previous alarm setting in seconds and establishes a new timer if the argument `seconds` is greater than zero. After the call is made and the specified time elapses, the signal `SIGALRM` is raised. This signal indicates the expiration of the timer. If `alarm(3)` is called before `SIGALRM` is raised, the current timer is canceled and a new timer is started. Specifying a value of zero to `alarm(3)` cancels the timer in progress without starting a new one.

Note

There is only one `alarm(3)` timer per process.

The program in Listing 15.3 shows how a signal handler processes signals SIGINT and SIGALRM.

LISTING 15.3   intalrm.c—An Example Using alarm(3) and sigsuspend(2)

```
 1:   #include <stdio.h>
 2:   #include <stdlib.h>
 3:   #include <unistd.h>
 4:   #include <signal.h>
 5:
 6:   /*
 7:    * Signal Catcher :
 8:    */
 9:   static void
10:   catch_sig(int signo) {
11:
12:       if ( signo == SIGINT ) {
13:           alarm(0);                           /* Cancel the timer */
14:           write(1,"CAUGHT SIGINT.\n",15);
15:       } else if ( signo == SIGALRM )
16:           write(1,"CAUGHT SIGALRM.\n",16);
17:   }
18:
19:   int
20:   main(int argc,char *argv[]) {
21:       sigset_t sigs;                          /* SIGINT + SIGALRM */
22:       struct sigaction sa_old;                /* Saved signals */
23:       struct sigaction sa_new;                /* New signals */
24:
25:       sa_new.sa_handler = catch_sig;          /* Signal handler */
26:       sigemptyset(&sa_new.sa_mask);           /* Empty mask */
27:       sigaddset(&sa_new.sa_mask,SIGALRM);     /* Add SIGALRM */
28:       sigaddset(&sa_new.sa_mask,SIGINT);      /* Add SIGINT */
29:       sa_new.sa_flags = 0;                    /* No flags */
30:
31:       sigaction(SIGINT,&sa_new,&sa_old);      /* Catch SIGINT */
32:       sigaction(SIGALRM,&sa_new,0);           /* Catch SIGALRM */
33:
34:       sigfillset(&sigs);                      /* All signals */
35:       sigdelset(&sigs,SIGINT);                /* Exclude SIGINT */
36:       sigdelset(&sigs,SIGALRM);               /* Exclude SIGALRM */
37:
38:       puts("You have 3 seconds to SIGINT:");
39:
40:       alarm(3);                        /* Timeout in 3 seconds */
41:       sigsuspend(&sigs);               /* Wait for SIGINT or SIGALRM */
42:
43:       puts("Done.");
44:       return 0;
45:   }
```

The main() program is shown in lines 19–45 of Listing 15.3. The signal handler is established as catch_sig() (line 25), the signal mask (lines 26–28) and the signal action flags (line 29).

The actions for **SIGINT** and **SIGALRM** are registered in lines 31–32. At this point, the signal handler is ready.

Lines 34–36 establish a signal mask consisting of the signals **SIGINT** and **SIGALRM**. This is used in line 41 in the call to **sigsuspend(2)**. Line 40 starts a three-second timer, which will cause **SIGALRM** to be raised if the timer is allowed to expire. The call to **sigsuspend(2)** puts the process to sleep until one of the signals **SIGINT** or **SIGALRM** arrives.

The signal mask sa_new is carefully established in lines 26–28 to block **SIGINT** and **SIGALRM** when a signal is being handled. Consequently, if **SIGINT** is being handled by the function **catch_sig()**, **SIGALRM** is blocked until the signal handler returns. Alternatively, when **SIGALRM** is being processed by **catch_sig()**, the signal **SIGINT** cannot be raised. Furthermore, neither signal can interrupt itself.

Note how, when **SIGINT** is processed by **catch_sig()**, it cancels the timer by calling on **alarm(3)** in line 13. However, there is a small possibility of the **SIGALRM** being raised once the signal handler returns. This is because the timer may expire before it is canceled in line 13.

Compile and run the example program as follows, allowing the timer to expire:

```
$ make intalrm
cc -c -D_POSIX_C_SOURCE=199309L -D_POSIX_SOURCE -Wall intalrm.c
cc -o intalrm intalrm.o
$ ./intalrm
You have 3 seconds to SIGINT:
CAUGHT SIGALRM.
Done.
$
```

The program successfully catches the **SIGALRM** signal when the timer expires. Now run the program and interrupt it (Ctrl+C) before three seconds is up:

```
$ ./intalrm
You have 3 seconds to SIGINT:
^CCAUGHT SIGINT.
Done.
$
```

In this example, when Ctrl+C is pressed, the signal is caught and the **alarm(3)** timer is canceled.

Warning

Note that the function **sleep(3)** calls on the function **alarm(3)** internally. Do not mix calls to **alarm(3)** and **sleep(3)**, since there is only one **SIGALRM** timer.

Calling Functions from a Signal Handler

The signal is an asynchronous event. Consequently, a signal such as **SIGINT** can arrive while your program is in the middle of executing a call to **malloc(3)**, **sprintf(3)**, or your own code. This creates some program integrity issues that you will need to plan for.

If malloc(3) is being executed, linked lists of free memory areas may be only partially updated when the signal arrives. Thus, when the signal handler is executing, the memory heap is in an unstable state. If the signal handler were itself to call upon malloc(3), it is likely that data corruption or a program fault would follow. The function malloc(3) cannot tolerate this sequence of events, because it is not designed to be re-entrant code.

One characteristic of re-entrant code is that it does not save any state information within itself in static or global areas. Instead, the caller in an argument list provides all data items. Contrast this to the function malloc(3), which relies on a global heap, with global state data.

The asynchronous nature of signals is such that you must call only re-entrant functions from within your signal handler. Otherwise, you may end up spending many hours removing the occasional bug that shows up.

The following are the POSIX.1 standard re-entrant functions. The entries marked with an asterisk are not listed in the POSIX.1 standard, but were listed as re-entrant by the AT&T SVID standard. Check these with your local documentation before they are used in a signal handler.

_exit	fork	read	tcdrain
abort*	fstat	rename	tcflow
access	getegid	rmdir	tcflush
alarm	geteuid	setgid	tcgetattr
cfgetispeed	getgid	setpgid	tcgetpgrp
cfgetospeed	getgroups	setsid	tcsendbreak
cfsetispeed	getpgrp	setuid	tcsetattr
cfsetospeed	getpid	sigaction	tcsetpgrp
chdir	getppid	segaddset	time
chmod	getuid	segdelset	times
chown	kill	sigemptyset	umask
chroot*	link	sigfillset	uname
close	longjmp	sigismember	unlink
creat	lseek	signal*	ustat*
dup	mkdir	sigpending	utime
dup2	mkfifo	sigprocmask	wait
execle	open	sigsuspend	waitpid
execve	pathconf	sleep	write
exit*	pause	stat	
fcntl	pipe	sysconf	

Avoiding Re-entrant Code Issues

The reliable signal interface permits you to control when certain signals are raised. This can be used to your advantage when a signal handler must call functions that are not re-entrant. This method is applied in the following steps:

1. Block the signal of interest using `sigprocmask(2)`.

2. At certain points within your application, test if the signal is pending using `sigpending(2)`.

3. Call `sigsuspend(2)` at a safe point to allow the signal to be raised.

By calling `sigsuspend(2)` at a controlled point in your application, you eliminate the fact that functions such as `malloc(3)` were executing at the time of the signal. This procedure ensures that it is safe to call upon functions that are not re-entrant.

Re-entrancy Issues with `errno` in a Signal Handler

Technically, many of the functions listed previously are not purely re-entrant. Many have the capability to modify the value of the global external variable `errno`. Consequently, you must be careful to preserve `errno` within a signal handler.

Warning

Many re-entrant functions are capable of modifying the external variable `errno`. To maintain pure re-entrancy, be sure to save and restore `errno` in the signal handler.

A failure to observe this rule can lead to some obscure and difficult-to-diagnose bugs.

The signal-catching function code found in Listing 15.2 is repeated here, as follows:

```
void
handler(int signo) {

    ++count;                  /* Increment count */
    write(1,"Got SIGINT\n",11); /* Write message */
}
```

This function is not purely re-entrant, because the `errno` value could be disturbed by the call to `write(2)`. This is easily corrected by inserting a save and restore statement:

```
void
handler(int signo) {
    int e = errno;            /* Save errno */

    ++count;                  /* Increment count */
    write(1,"Got SIGINT\n",11); /* Write message */
    errno = e;                /* Restore errno */
}
```

Saving and restoring `errno` prevents the application from seeing a changed `errno` value when the signal handler returns. This type of problem can be extremely difficult to debug, because it will often depend upon timing.

Applying the `EINTR` Error Code

Except when the `sigsuspend(2)` technique is used, a signal can be caught by a signal handler at any time. This restricts the choice of available functions to those that are re-entrant. Consequently, when non–re-entrant functions must be called, a different technique must be used.

A signal handler can post a result to a global flag variable, which is later polled by the application. Using this technique, no re-entrancy issues arise because the event is synchronous (polled) instead of being asynchronous. The following example shows a signal handler that posts a true result to the flag variable `gotSIGINT`:

```
static int gotSIGINT = 0;    /* True when SIGINT arrives */

static void
catch_SIGINT(int signo) {
    gotSIGINT = 1;           /* Post the flag */
}
```

This part of the application is simple, and no re-entrancy issues arise. The difficulty is that, when the program is blocked waiting for a system call to complete, it never gets a chance to poll for the posted `SIGINT` event. The following statement illustrates another part of the program that will wait indefinitely until data arrives on standard input:

```
int z;
char buf[256];

z = read(0,buf,sizeof buf);   /* Obtain terminal input */
```

When the program is waiting for input, the signal handler can still post its event by assigning 1 to variable `gotSIGINT`. However, the application cannot break out of the `read(2)` function to test if the event occurred. Instead, the application will wait indefinitely until all of the data arrives or an end-of-file is received.

To avoid this difficulty, the designers of UNIX offered the following solution: When a signal handler returns, certain system calls immediately return the error code `EINTR`. This allows the calling application to regain control from its blocked state and have a chance to poll for any events that may have been posted by a signal handler.

The value of the variable `gotSIGINT` can be tested in the example given earlier. If no event was detected by the calling application, it can simply ignore the error and retry the system call. The following illustrates this procedure in code:

```
int z;
char buf[256];
```

```
do {
    z = read(0,buf,sizeof buf);       /* Obtain terminal input */
    if ( gotSIGINT )                  /* Was SIGINT posted? */
        process_SIGINT();             /* Yes, Process the SIGINT event */
} while ( z == -1 && errno == EINTR );  /* Repeat while EINTR */
```

This loop is typical of many that process the `EINTR` error code. The system call `read(2)` is attempted, which may block indefinitely (for terminal input). If an error occurs, the code tests to see if `SIGINT` was posted by looking at global variable `gotSIGINT`. If `gotSIGINT` is true, then function `process_SIGINT()` will perform the actions that the signal handler was unable to perform. The loop repeats at the `while` clause as long as an error is reported by `z` and the error code in `errno` is equal to `EINTR`.

Note

`EINTR—Interrupted system call`   This error is returned by a number of system calls to indicate that a signal handler was executed as a result of receiving a signal. This is done to permit the calling application to become unblocked by a blocking system call, so that action may be executed for a received signal.

Many people in various UNIX Usenet newsgroups have complained about this behavior over the years. However, this behavior is a feature of the operating system and is not a defect. You should get into the habit of thinking about blocking system calls when you write applications.

If a function might block the execution of your program for a long time, then you may have to be concerned with `EINTR` processing loops. The general rule is if the system call may block for long or indefinite periods, then `EINTR` is possible. Note for example that `read(2)` will not return `EINTR` for file reads, since this type of call is not considered long. However, when `read(2)` is used to read terminal input or a socket, the error `EINTR` can be returned.

Always check the `man(1)` pages of system calls to see if `EINTR` is possible. If your code must be portable, be sure to check the `man(1)` pages of the other platforms as well. Some platforms, particularly SGI's IRIX 6.5, will return `EINTR` when the others do not.

Raising Signals

A UNIX signal can be raised from your application by the use of the `kill(2)` system call. Its synopsis is as follows:

```
#include <sys/types.h>
#include <signal.h>

int kill(pid_t pid, int sig);
```

This function raises the signal `sig` in the process `pid` (by process ID). You must have permission to raise the signal in the indicated process to succeed. To raise the signal `SIGUSR1` in your own application, you can code:

```
kill(getpid(),SIGUSR1); /* Raise SIGUSR1 in current process */
```

The value **0** is returned for success and **-1** if it fails (check **errno**).

The value of **sig** is permitted to be **0**. When it is, **kill(2)** allows your process to detect if the process **pid** exists. For example

```
pid_t PID = 1234;     /* Process ID 1234 */

if ( kill(PID,0) == -1 ) {
    if ( errno == ESRCH )
        puts("Process 1234 is not executing.");
    else
        perror("kill(2)");
} else
    puts("Process 1234 is executing.");
```

When **kill(2)** returns success in the example, then the program has determined that process ID **1234** existed at the time of the test. The **errno** code **ESRCH** indicates that no process matching argument **pid** exists.

Note

ESRCH—No such process   This error is returned by kill(2) when the process indicated does not exist.

The argument **pid** can be given as 0. When it is, all processes within your process group are signaled with the signal **sig**.

When **kill(2)** argument **pid** is **-1**, the signal is sent to all but system processes if the caller has super user privileges. When the caller does not have super user privileges, the signal is delivered to all processes with a real user ID that matches the caller's effective user ID. The calling process is not signaled, however.

Note

There is also a raise(3) function, which can be used to send a signal to the current process.

```
#include <signal.h>
```

```
int raise(int sig);
```

This function is implemented in terms of calls to getpid(2) and kill(2):

```
kill(getpid(),sig);
```

Since this is easily written, raise(3) is perhaps unnecessary.

Summary

This chapter has shown the signal handling functions and some of their pitfalls. The next chapter will show you how to write code that can efficiently handle input and output for many open file descriptors. This is an essential skill for writing server programs.

CHAPTER 16

EFFICIENT I/O SCHEDULING

M any applications are written to be interactive with one user. For these, it is a simple matter to be responsive to the whims of that one user. However, when you design server programs, each user of that server must receive immediate responses, as if there were only one user. This becomes impossible if your server is waiting for input from another user, within a system call. Consequently, a different design strategy is required when performing I/O with multiple clients.

In this chapter, you will examine how to perform

- Non-blocking I/O
- I/O using `select(2)`
- I/O using `poll(2)`

Non-Blocking I/O

A process is put to sleep when performing I/O for one or more of the following reasons:

- A read request must wait for input data to arrive.
- A write request must wait until previously written data has been written to the media.
- A device must be opened, such as a modem terminal line waiting for a carrier or a FIFO waiting for a reader.
- Mandatory locking is enabled on files, causing a wait for locking on a read or a write system call.

Conceptually, the simplest solution to this problem is to not put the process to sleep. When the I/O cannot be completed, the system call returns an error indicating that it cannot succeed at this time. This is non-blocking I/O.

Opening Files in Non-Blocking Mode

One method of specifying to the UNIX kernel that you want to use non-blocking I/O is to open with the O_NONBLOCK flag:

```
#include <fcntl.h>
int open(const char *path, int flags, ...);
```

where the **flags** argument is set to include O_NONBLOCK, to open in non-blocking mode.

The O_NONBLOCK flag prevents the open(2) call from suspending the execution of the calling process if it must wait for some reason. This can happen, for example, when opening a terminal line that must have a modem carrier. With the O_NONBLOCK flag provided, the open call returns success immediately.

Subsequently, after an open(2) has been accomplished with the O_NONBLOCK flag, other I/O operations are also subject to the non-blocking rule. This is explained further in upcoming sections.

The following shows how a process can open its terminal line in non-blocking I/O mode:

```
int fd;                    // Terminal file descriptor

fd = open("/dev/tty",O_RDWR|O_NONBLOCK);
if ( fd == -1 ) {
    perror("open(2)");    // Report error
    abort();              // Abort run.
}
// fd is open in non-blocking I/O mode
```

Once the file descriptor is open in this manner, a call to read(2) will no longer suspend the program's execution while waiting for input.

Setting Non-Blocking Mode

Another method of choosing non-blocking I/O mode is to call upon the services of fcntl(2) after the file or device is already open:

```
#include <fcntl.h>
int fcntl(int fd, int cmd, ...);
```

where **cmd** is one of the following:

F_GETFL	Get flags
F_SETFL	Set flags

The command F_SETFL allows you to enable the flag O_NONBLOCK after the file has been opened. However, to do this, you will usually want to use the command F_GETFL to obtain the current flags in effect.

The following example shows how to enable O_NONBLOCK on an open file descriptor fd:

```
int fd;      /* Open file descriptor */
int fl;      /* Flags for fd */

fl = fcntl(fd,F_GETFL,0);
if ( fl == -1 ) {
    perror("fcntl(F_GETFL)");     /* Report failure */
    exit(13);
}

if ( fcntl(fd,F_SETFL,fl|O_NONBLOCK) == -1 ) {
    perror("fcntl(F_SETFL)");     /* Report failure */
    exit(13);
}
```

Notice how the flag O_NONBLOCK was ORed with the flags received in variable fl in the call to fcntl(2) using the F_SETFL command.

Performing Non-Blocking I/O

Once the file descriptor is in non-blocking I/O mode, you can use it with regular calls to read(2) and write(2). When no input is ready to be returned by read(2) or no output can be written by write(2), the returned error code in errno will be EAGAIN.

Note

EAGAIN—Resource temporarily unavailable   This error is returned when using non-blocking I/O to indicate that no input was available for reading or that the output could not be written at this time.

Listing 16.1 presents a program that uses non-blocking I/O on a FIFO.

LISTING 16.1   nblockio.c—A Program That Reads a FIFO in Non-Blocking I/O Mode

```
1:    /* nblockio.c */
2:
3:    #include <stdio.h>
4:    #include <unistd.h>
5:    #include <fcntl.h>
6:    #include <errno.h>
7:
8:    int
9:    main(int argc,char **argv) {
10:       int z;          /* # of bytes returned */
11:       int fd;         /* File descriptor */
12:       char buf[256];  /* I/O buffer */
13:
14:       fd = open("./fifo",O_RDWR|O_NONBLOCK);
15:       if ( fd == -1 ) {
```

continued from previous page

```
16:            perror("open(2)");
17:            exit(13);
18:        }
19:
20:        while ( (z = read(fd,buf,sizeof buf)) == -1 && errno == EAGAIN )
21:            ;
22:
23:        if ( z >= 0 ) {
24:            buf[z] = 0;
25:
26:            printf("GOT INPUT! '%s'\n",buf);
27:        } else
28:            perror("read(2)");
29:
30:        return 0;
31:    }
```

Compiling the program with the make(1) file provided also creates this FIFO:

```
$ make nblockio
mkfifo ./fifo
cc -c  -Wall nblockio.c
cc -o nblockio nblockio.o
$
```

The program in Listing 16.1 opens the FIFO in line 14 in non-blocking mode (note the flag O_NONBLOCK). Once the FIFO is open, the program loops in line 20 as long as the error EAGAIN is returned from the read(2) call. The error EAGAIN tells the caller that no input is available for reading.

Once input is returned, the loop is exited, and the error or the data is reported in lines 23–28. The loop in lines 20–21 is very unfriendly to the system, and it will consume all available CPU trying to obtain input. However, in a real product, there would be other program events being performed in this loop instead.

Warning

The loop in lines 20–21 of Listing 16.1 consumes all available CPU. Do not run this demonstration program for long if you are sharing a host with other users!

Additionally, make certain that you do not accidentally leave it running.

Run the program in the background, so that you can use another command to put input into the FIFO. The following shows a sample session:

```
$ ./nblockio &
$ echo BOO >./fifo
$ GOT INPUT! 'BOO
'

[1] 19449 Exit 0              ./nblockio
$
```

The first command starts the program nblockio and places it in the background. At this point, it is chewing up CPU because of its non-blocking I/O loop.

The `echo` command is entered to feed the letters **BOO** and a linefeed character into the FIFO `./fifo`, which the program is trying to read. Once that is done, the nblockio program reports that it got input, and it exits. You will need to press Return again to cause the job termination status to appear. The session output demonstrates that the nblockio program did read the input that was written to the FIFO.

The Problem with Non-Blocking I/O

The preceding demonstration shows how non-blocking I/O could be applied. However, if you were to run the program again and watch the system CPU usage with a resource-monitoring tool such as `top(1)`, you would immediately recognize that the nblockio program was not a good UNIX citizen. It was using as much CPU as it could obtain from the kernel (this may not be as extreme, if you have other program functions to perform within the loop).

You would be forced to avoid using CPU time by calling a function such as `sleep(3)`. Even if you use a more fine-grained timer such as `nanosleep(2)`, you as the server designer will always be forced to compromise between latency and CPU overhead. As the sleep time is increased, the latency increases. As the sleep time is reduced, the CPU overhead increases.

An ideal solution for both your server and the rest of the host is to have your process awakened at the right time by the UNIX kernel. The kernel knows when it has data for your process to read on one of its open file descriptors. The kernel also knows when it can accommodate a write to one of the file descriptors belonging to your process.

In this fashion, the kernel suspends your server process from executing until there is something for it to perform. This allows precious CPU time to be used by other processes while your server process waits for something to happen. The kernel will awaken your process the moment it has pending I/O to perform. This is how efficiency is maintained within the host system while keeping server latency to a minimum.

I/O Scheduling Functions

In order for the UNIX kernel to know when your process should be awakened for I/O, your process must first register the I/O events that it is interested in. This is accomplished with the system call `select(2)` or `poll(2)`. Because these calls are so similar, some UNIX systems implement one of the calls in terms of the other.

The `select(2)` system call will be presented first in this chapter. However, before you can use the `select(2)` function, you must first get to know file descriptor sets and the `timeval` structure that it uses.

File Descriptor Sets and Their Macros

In order to work with the `select(2)` system call, you must work with file descriptor sets. These are collections of file descriptors that make it easier to specify a number of file descriptors at once. The following synopsis shows the macros that are available for working with file descriptor sets:

```
#include <sys/types.h>

FD_ZERO(fd_set *set)            /* Macro */
FD_SET(int fd, fd_set *set)     /* Macro */
FD_CLR(int fd, fd_set *set)     /* Macro */
int FD_ISSET(int fd, fd_set *set) /* Macro returning int */
FD_SETSIZE /* Defines the maximum value for argument fd */
```

You must initialize a file descriptor set before using it. This is accomplished with the `FD_ZERO()` macro:

```
fd_set fdset1;      /* File descriptor set 1 */

FD_ZERO(&fdset1);   /* Initialize fdset1 */
```

Initialization of a file descriptor set by `FD_ZERO()` causes it to contain the "empty set." That is, no file descriptors are contained in the set.

The highest number file descriptor in the set is the value `FD_SETSIZE`. The behavior of the `FD_SET()`, `FD_CLR()`, and `FD_ISSET()` macros is undefined if the file descriptor number exceeds this value or is negative.

To add a file descriptor to the set, you use the `FD_SET()` macro. To add file descriptor `fd` to set `fdset1`, you would write

```
int fd = 1;         /* File descriptor: Standard output */

FD_ZERO(&fdset1);   /* Initialize fdset1 */
FD_SET(fd,&fdset1); /* Add file descriptor to fdset1 */
```

A file descriptor can be removed from the set using the `FD_CLR()` macro. To remove `fd` from the set, you would write

```
FD_CLR(fd,&fdset);  /* Remove fd from fdset1 */
```

Sometimes it is necessary to test if a particular file descriptor is a member of the set. This is performed using the `FD_ISSET()` macro. The following tests to see if file unit `2` (standard error) is a member of `fdset1`:

```
if ( FD_ISSET(2,&fdset1) ) {
    puts("Standard error (unit 2) is part of fdset1");
} else {
    puts("Standard error (unit 2) is not in fdset1");
}
```

The macro call `FD_ISSET(2,&fdset1)` will return a non-zero value if the file unit `2` is a member of the set `fdset1`.

The `timeval` Structure

Another important element of using the `select(2)` function is the capability to specify a `timeout` parameter. This is specified with the use of the structure `timeval`:

```
#include <sys/time.h>

struct timeval {
    long    tv_sec;     /* seconds */
    long    tv_usec;    /* microseconds */
};
```

The following example shows how you would define a `timeout` value of 1.25 seconds:

```
struct timeval timeout;     /* 1.25 second timeout */

timeout.tv_sec = 1;         /* 1 second */
timeout.tv_usec = 250000;   /* 250000 microseconds = 0.25 seconds */
```

While the timer values suggest a very precise value for a timeout, the UNIX system that you are using might not be quite so accurate. The actual precision used may be as low as .01 second. However, as CPU technology gets faster, precision often improves with it.

The `select(2)` Function

The `select(2)` function is what you have been working up to. Here is its function synopsis:

```
#include <sys/types.h>
#include <sys/time.h>
#include <unistd.h>

int select(int nfds,            /* # of file descriptors */
    fd_set *readfds,            /* Read descriptor set */
    fd_set *writefds,           /* Write descriptor set */
    fd_set *exceptfds,          /* Exception descriptor set */
    struct timeval *timeout);   /* Timeout value */
```

The argument `timeout` indicates when the `select(2)` call should give up and return **0**. Zero indicates that no interesting events have occurred. If you do not require a timeout, the argument `timeout` should be a null pointer. This will cause `select(2)` to wait forever unless a signal is caught, in which case the error `EINTR` is returned.

If a `timeout` argument is supplied but the members indicate a total time of zero seconds, then `select(2)` will return immediately without suspending the execution of the program. This allows the caller to poll several file descriptors for interesting events without actually suspending the program.

The file descriptor set `readfds` specifies all the file descriptors that the calling process wants to read data from. For example, if your program were expecting input on standard input (file descriptor **0**) and a FIFO to be open on file unit **3**, then `readfds` would include the descriptors **0** and **3** in the set. This orders the `select(2)` function to block the execution of your calling process until input arrives on one or both of these file descriptors.

When control returns to your process, you then test the set `readfds` to see which file descriptors have input available. For example, the following code tests for file units **0** or **3** for input pending:

```
if ( FD_ISSET(0,&readfds) ) {
    // Read input data from unit 0
}
if ( FD_ISSET(3,&readfds) ) {
    // Read input data from unit 3
}
```

The value returned by `select(2)` is one of the following:

- **-1** if the call failed (check `errno`)

- **0** if a timeout occurred

- Less than zero, indicating the number of file descriptors that have events registered

When an error is returned, including the error `EINTR`, the file descriptor sets will be left unmodified. Documentation does not spell out clearly what happens for the `timeout` argument when this happens. Consequently, you should assume that it has been modified and that it requires re-initialization.

Note

The file descriptor sets `readfds`, `writefds`, and `exceptfds` are modified by the function `select(2)`. Be certain to re-establish the file descriptor sets prior to the next call to `select(2)`.

Note also that the time values in the `timeout` argument are updated *on some UNIX platforms* to reflect the time remaining. Be sure to reset the time values in this argument prior to the next call to `select(2)`.

When zero is returned, no events are registered in the file descriptor sets. The file descriptor sets will be empty. Consequently, you will need to re-establish the file descriptor sets and the `timeout` argument prior to calling `select(2)` again.

When a value greater than zero is returned, this indicates the total number of events that have been returned in the file descriptor sets. For example, the return value **6** may indicate that you have three read events, two write events, and one exception event, registered in the sets `readfds`, `writefds`, and `exceptfds`, respectively. To find the specific file unit numbers, you will need to iterate through each of the sets using the `FD_ISSET()` macro.

The only input argument to `select(2)`, which is not modified, is the value `nfds`. This argument is copied by value. It specifies the highest number of file descriptors to process in the specified sets. For example, if file descriptor **3** is the highest file descriptor present in any of the given sets, then `nfds` must be specified as **4**. The value **1** must be added because file descriptors start at zero. The descriptor range of **0** to **3** represents a total of four file descriptors.

Note

Keep the value of `nfds` as small as possible in a call to `select(2)`. This helps the UNIX kernel process your request more efficiently.

The arguments `readfds`, `writefds`, and `exceptfds` represent sets of file descriptors to process for read events, write events, and exception events, respectively. If you have no interest in a particular set of events, you can supply a null pointer in that argument position. For example, if you do not care about write or exception events, the `writefds` and `exceptfds` arguments can be supplied by a null pointer.

Read Events

A read event is when a file descriptor in the set `readfds` has input data available for reading. This may include only one byte of data, or it may include a block of bytes. Timing plays a big role in arrival of input data.

A read event can also include a client program connecting to your server on a socket. For example, if you have a socket open on file unit **4** and `listen(2)` has been called on it, then a read event will occur when a connection has been established by the client program using `connect(2)`. Upon receiving such an event, your server program then should call `accept(2)` if the client connection is to be accepted.

Finally, a read event can also occur when end-of-file is reached. For example, this occurs when connected sockets have been closed at the remote end.

Warning

Not all devices are "pollable." Some devices may immediately return a ready status. A subsequent `read(2)` call may return **0** bytes or block the execution of the program. This often happens due to a third-party driver for a particular device.

Write Events

The execution of a process can be suspended if a `write(2)` call is made when the data being supplied cannot be accepted at the current time. For example, a process writing to a pipe will block on many UNIX hosts if more than 5120 (5K) bytes is written before the reading process has read the data from the pipe. A write event is an indication that it is safe to write some data to the file descriptor without blocking.

Note

When `select(2)` indicates that writing may begin to a file descriptor, there is no implied size guarantee. The execution of the process will be suspended if it writes an excessively large block.

To avoid blocked execution, use non-blocking I/O for writing. The return value from `write(2)` will indicate the number of bytes that were successfully accepted by the UNIX kernel.

Exception Events

Exception events are chosen by a separate file descriptor set. Exception events include

- Reception of out-of-band data on a socket
- Certain conditions occurring on a pseudo-terminal
- Reception of auxiliary error data on a socket

All of these conditions are outside the scope of this chapter. These special events are not classified as read or write data events.

Using the `select(2)` Function

The program in Listing 16.2 creates a pipe to two shell processes that will list a directory. The output of one process is converted to uppercase and the other is converted to lowercase to make them easier to distinguish. Since one or both processes may have output ready for the current process, the `select(2)` function can help.

LISTING 16.2   select.c—A Program Using `select(2)`

```
1:   /* select.c */
2:
3:   #include <stdio.h>
4:   #include <stdlib.h>
5:   #include <stdarg.h>
6:   #include <unistd.h>
7:   #include <fcntl.h>
8:   #include <errno.h>
9:   #include <string.h>
10:  #include <sys/types.h>
11:  #include <sys/time.h>
12:  #include <sys/stat.h>
13:
14:  static void
15:  quit(int rc,const char *fmt,...) {
16:      va_list ap;
17:
18:      if ( errno != 0 )   /* Report errno */
19:          fprintf(stderr,"%s: ",strerror(errno));
20:
21:      va_start(ap,fmt);   /* Format error message */
22:      vfprintf(stderr,fmt,ap);
23:      va_end(ap);
24:      fputc('\n',stderr);
25:
26:      exit(rc);                /* Exit with return code */
27:  }
28:
29:  int
30:  main(int argc,char **argv) {
31:      int z;               /* General status code */
```

```
32:     int f1;              /* Open fifo 1 */
33:     int f2;              /* Open fifo 2 */
34:     fd_set rxset;        /* Read fd set */
35:     int nfds;            /* Number of file descriptors */
36:     struct timeval tv;   /* Timeout */
37:     char buf[200+1];     /* I/O Buffer */
38:     FILE *p1, *p2;       /* Pipes from popen(3) */
39:
40:     /*
41:      * Pipes :
42:      */
43:     if ( !(p1 = popen("ls -l|tr '[a-z]' '[A-Z]'","r")) )
44:         quit(1,"popen(3) failed for p1");
45:
46:     if ( !(p2 = popen("ls -l|tr '[A-Z]' '[a-z]' && sleep 8","r")) )
47:         quit(1,"popen(3) failed for p2");
48:
49:     /*
50:      * Obtain the underlying file descriptors :
51:      */
52:     f1 = fileno(p1);
53:     f2 = fileno(p2);
54:     printf("BEGUN: f1=%d, f2=%d\n",f1,f2);
55:
56:     /*
57:      * Enter a select loop :
58:      */
59:     do  {
60:         FD_ZERO(&rxset);         /* Clear set */
61:         if ( f1 >= 0 )
62:             FD_SET(f1,&rxset);   /* Check f1 */
63:         if ( f2 >= 0 )
64:             FD_SET(f2,&rxset);   /* Check f2 */
65:
66:         nfds = (f1 > f2 ? f1 : f2) + 1;
67:         tv.tv_sec = 3;           /* 3 seconds */
68:         tv.tv_usec = 500000;     /* + 0.5 seconds */
69:
70:         do  {
71:             z = select(nfds,&rxset,0,0,&tv);
72:         } while ( z == -1 && errno == EINTR );
73:
74:         if ( z == -1 )           /* Error? */
75:             quit(13,"select(2)");
76:
77:         if ( z == 0 ) {
78:             printf("TIMEOUT: f1=%d, f2=%d\n",f1,f2);
79:             continue;
80:         }
81:
82:         /*
83:          * Control is here if f1 or f2 has data
84:          * available to be read.
85:          */
```

continued from previous page

```
86:                 if ( f1 >= 0 && FD_ISSET(f1,&rxset) ) {
87:                     z = read(f1,buf,sizeof buf-1);
88:                     if ( z == -1 )
89:                         quit(6,"read(2) of f1.");
90:                     if ( z > 0 ) {
91:                         buf[z] = 0;
92:                         printf("*** read %d bytes <<<%s>>> from f1;\n",z,buf);
93:                     } else {
94:                         puts("read EOF from f1;");
95:                         pclose(p1);
96:                         f1 = -1;
97:                     }
98:                 }
99:
100:                 if ( f2 >= 0 && FD_ISSET(f2,&rxset) ) {
101:                     z = read(f2,buf,sizeof buf-1);
102:                     if ( z == -1 )
103:                         quit(6,"read(2) of f2.");
104:                     if ( z > 0 ) {
105:                         buf[z] = 0;
106:                         printf("*** read %d bytes <<<%s>>> from f2;\n",z,buf);
107:                     } else {
108:                         puts("read EOF from f2;");
109:                         pclose(p2);
110:                         f2 = -1;
111:                     }
112:                 }
113:
114:         } while ( f1 >= 0 || f2 >= 0 );
115:
116:         puts("End select.");
117:
118:         return 0;
119: }
```

Lines 43–47 open pipes to processes that will list the current directory. Note how the tr(1) command is used to translate the output into uppercase or lowercase for each process. This will make separating the process output in the example easier.

The select(2) function requires the use of file descriptors, and these are extracted from the FILE pointers p1 and p2 using the fileno(3) macro in lines 52 and 53.

Lines 59–114 form the select(2) loop. Lines 60–64 initialize the read file descriptor set rxset. The if statements in lines 61 and 63 are necessary because f1 and f2 are closed once the end-of-file is detected (see lines 95, 96, 109, and 110). Once the file descriptor is closed, it is not included in the read file descriptor set.

The value of nfds is computed at line 66. It must be 1 higher than the highest file descriptor considered in the file descriptor sets. Lines 67 and 68 set the timeout to 3.5 seconds.

The loop in lines 70–72 demonstrates how to code the select(2) call while considering the error EINTR. In this program there is no special processing required when EINTR is detected, so the select(2) system call is simply retried.

Line 74 tests for an error return from `select(2)`. The error is reported by the static function `quit()`, which appears earlier in the listing.

A timeout is tested for in line 77. When `z` equals `0`, this indicates that the `select(2)` call timed out without anything interesting happening. Notice that in line 46 the `sleep(1)` command has been invoked in the piped command to demonstrate the timeout capability of `select(2)`.

Lines 86–98 performs a test for file descriptor `f1` (on behalf of pipe `p1`). If the file descriptor has not been closed (it is not `-1`) and it appears in the file descriptor set `rxset`, then a `read(2)` call is performed in line 87. This will not block because the `select(2)` function promises that there will be some data waiting to be read. The returned value `z` will indicate the number of bytes read, or it will be `0`, indicating that the end of the file has been reached. If `z` is greater than zero, the buffer `buf` is dumped to standard output in line 92.

When end-of-file is reported in line 94, the pipe `p1` is closed in line 95 (you must close a `popen(3)` pipe with `pclose(3)`). This closes the underlying file descriptor `f1`. Variable `f1` is then set to `-1` in line 96 to mark it as closed, so that it will not be included in the next call to `select(2)`.

Lines 100–112 repeat the same operations for file descriptor `f2`. The `do { } while` loop is continued until both `f1` and `f2` are marked as closed (line 114).

Now compile the program:

```
$ make select
cc -c  -Wall -g select.c
cc -o select select.o
$
```

Your results will vary, depending on the contents of your current directory. To run the example program, simply invoke it:

```
$ ./select
```

An example session output is as follows (line numbers were added at left for ease of reference):

```
 1:    BEGUN: f1=3, f2=4
 2:    *** read 200 bytes <<<TOTAL 28
 3:    -RW-R----- 1 EAG  GRP    481 JUN  6 21:52 MAKEFILE
 4:    -RW-R----- 1 EAG  GRP    589 JUN  4 22:09 NBLOCKIO.C
 5:    -RWXR-X--- 1 EAG  GRP  12756 JUN  6 22:03 SELECT
 6:    -RW-R----- 1 EAG  GRP   3063 JUN  >>> from f1;
 7:    *** read 116 bytes <<<6 22:01 SELECT.C
 8:    -RW-R----- 1 EAG  GRP  10172 JUN  6 22:03 SELECT.O
 9:    -RW-R----- 1 EAG  GRP      0 JUN  6 22:03 T.T
10:    >>> from f1;
11:    read EOF from f1;
12:    *** read 200 bytes <<<total 28
13:    -rw-r----- 1 eag  grp    481 jun  6 21:52 makefile
14:    -rw-r----- 1 eag  grp    589 jun  4 22:09 nblockio.c
15:    -rwxr-x--- 1 eag  grp  12756 jun  6 22:03 select
16:    -rw-r----- 1 eag  grp   3063 jun  >>> from f2;
```

continued from previous page

```
17:  *** read 116 bytes <<<6 22:01 select.c
18:  -rw-r-----  1 eag  grp  10172 jun  6 22:03 select.o
19:  -rw-r-----  1 eag  grp      0 jun  6 22:03 t.t
20:  >>> from f2;
21:  TIMEOUT: f1=-1, f2=4
22:  TIMEOUT: f1=-1, f2=4
23:  read EOF from f2;
24:  End select.
```

Line 1 of the session output shows that the file descriptors that are open to the piped commands are units **3** and **4**. Figure 16.1 shows the values present in **fd_set rxset** for the first call to **select(2)**. It also illustrates why **nfds** is the value **5**.

FIGURE 16.1

The **fd_set rxset** for Listing 16.2.

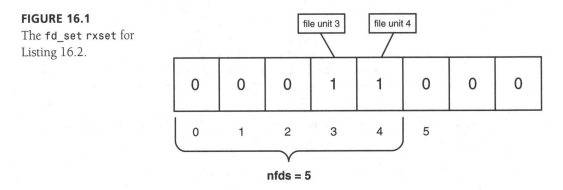

Lines 2–6 of Listing 16.2 show that 200 bytes was read from the first pipe (note the uppercase output). Lines 7–10 show that another 116 bytes was read from the first pipe. This shows that the output from the second pipe was not ready at the time that the **do {} while** loop started. Line 11 shows that the end of the file was detected in pipe **p1**.

Lines 12–16 show that 200 bytes was read from pipe **p2** (note the lowercase). Lines 17–20 show another 116 bytes that was read from pipe **p2**.

Lines 21 and 22 show that two timeouts occurred. The values show that pipe **p1** is closed, because file descriptor **f1** is marked as closed by its value of -**1**. Pipe **p2** is still open on unit **4** when the timeouts occur.

The timeouts occur because of the **sleep(1)** command in line 46. The **sleep(1)** command stalls from closing the pipe. The timeout value used in lines 67 and 68 is 3.5 seconds, and this permits two timeouts to occur before the pipe **p2** is finally closed. Once both pipes are closed, as reflected in **f1** and **f2**, the **while** clause ends the loop in line 114.

I/O Polling

The function **poll(2)** represents another way to perform efficient I/O scheduling. It was originally developed by AT&T to be used for STREAMS file descriptors. However, **poll(2)** now accepts all file descriptors. The function synopsis for **poll(2)** is as follows:

```
/*
 * UnixWare 7, SGI IRIX 6.5 :
 */
#include <stropts.h>
#include <poll.h>

/*
 * HP-UX 11.x, Solaris 8 :
 */
#include <poll.h>

/*
 * IBM AIX 4.3 :
 */
#include <sys/poll.h>
#include <sys/select.h>
#include <sys/types.h>

/*
 * FreeBSD :
 */
#include <sys/types.h>
#include <poll.h>

int poll(struct pollfd *fds, unsigned int nfds, int timeout);
struct pollfd {
    int    fd;         /* file descriptor */
    short  events;     /* events to look for */
    short  revents;    /* returned events */
};
```

As you can see, the necessary include files vary considerably, depending on the platform on which you are compiling. The poll(2) function uses an array of structure pollfd to drive the I/O polling operation (argument fds). Each element of this array specifies a file descriptor (fd) and the events (events) that are to be reported. When poll(2) returns with a value greater than zero, the member revents will contain bits that represent events that have occurred for the file descriptor. The argument nfds indicates how many array elements are participating in the call.

Note

When the fd member of the structure pollfd is negative, the member events is ignored and the revents member is set to zero.

Setting fd to -1 is an effective way to indicate to poll(2) to ignore that entry.

The value returned by poll(2) is in one of three value categories:

- Negative (-1), to indicate an error has occurred (check errno).

- Zero, to indicate that a timeout has occurred with no events being reported.

- Greater than zero, to indicate how many file descriptors have reported events.

The `timeout` argument specifies in milliseconds the minimum period to wait for an event to occur. If the `timeout` value is specified as the macro `INFTIM` (or `-1`), then an infinite timeout is assumed. If the `timeout` argument is `0`, then `poll(2)` will return immediately, even if there are no events to report.

Note
The function `poll(2)` can return the error `EINTR` after a signal has been processed.

Poll Events

The `events` member of the `pollfd` array must be initialized to describe the events that are to be reported. There are three categories of these event bit macros:

- Macros that describe `event` and `revent` flags concerning input (see Table 16.1)
- Macros that describe `event` and `revent` flags concerning output (see Table 16.2)
- Macros that describe only `revent` flags for information that is returned (see Table 16.3)

Table 16.1 describes the input bit masks that can be ORed together to indicate read events to be polled.

TABLE 16.1 Read Event Bit Masks for `poll(2)`

Macro	Event
POLLIN	Data other than high priority data may be read without blocking.
POLLRDNORM	Normal data may be read without blocking.
POLLRDBAND	Data with a non-zero priority may be read without blocking.
POLLPRI	High priority data may be read without blocking.

Table 16.2 is additional bit masks that describe write events.

TABLE 16.2 Write Event Bit Masks for `poll(2)`

Macro	Event
POLLOUT	Normal data can be written without blocking.
POLLWRNORM	Same as `POLLOUT`.
POLLWRBAND	Data with a non-zero priority may be written without blocking.

Table 16.3 lists macros, which represents bits that are only returned in the `revents` member of the `pollfd` array member.

TABLE 16.3   Returned `revent` Bit Masks for `poll(2)`

Macro	Event
POLLERR	An exceptional condition has occurred on the device or socket.
POLLHUP	The device or socket has been disconnected. Note that the POLLHUP and POLLOUT flags are mutually exclusive (they will not appear at the same time in `revent`).
POLLNVAL	The file descriptor is not open. Note that when the file descriptor is negative, this bit is not returned.

Poll Priorities

The poll(2) documentation presented so far mentions priorities and priority bands. The manual page for `poll(2)` will also make mention of this. Priority bands are part of the System V implementation of STREAMS, which was a generalization for communicating with device drivers.

Unless you are performing STREAMS programming, you can simply ignore the priority bands and use the normal macros for input and output. This means that you can use `POLLIN` or `POLLRDNORM` for input and `POLLOUT` or `POLLWRNORM` for output.

A `poll(2)` Example

Listing 16.3 shows the source listing for `poll.c`, which is a `poll(2)` adaptation of the `select.c` program in Listing 16.2.

LISTING 16.3   `poll.c`—An Example Program Using `poll(2)`

```
 1:    /* poll.c */
 2:
 3:    #include <stdio.h>
 4:    #include <stdlib.h>
 5:    #include <stdarg.h>
 6:    #include <unistd.h>
 7:    #include <fcntl.h>
 8:    #include <errno.h>
 9:    #include <string.h>
10:    #include <sys/types.h>
11:    #include <sys/time.h>
12:    #include <sys/stat.h>
13:    #include <poll.h>
14:
```

continued from previous page

```
15:  static void
16:  quit(int rc,const char *fmt,...) {
17:      va_list ap;
18:
19:      if ( errno != 0 )    /* Report errno */
20:          fprintf(stderr,"%s: ",strerror(errno));
21:
22:      va_start(ap,fmt);   /* Format error message */
23:      vfprintf(stderr,fmt,ap);
24:      va_end(ap);
25:      fputc('\n',stderr);
26:
27:      exit(rc);            /* Exit with return code */
28:  }
29:
30:  int
31:  main(int argc,char **argv) {
32:      int z;                /* General status code */
33:      int f1;               /* Open fifo 1 */
34:      int f2;               /* Open fifo 2 */
35:      struct pollfd fds[2]; /* Poll events */
36:      int nfds;             /* Number of file descriptors */
37:      char buf[200+1];      /* I/O Buffer */
38:      FILE *p1, *p2;        /* Pipes from popen(3) */
39:
40:      /*
41:       * Pipes :
42:       */
43:      if ( !(p1 = popen("ls -l|tr '[a-z]' '[A-Z]'","r")) )
44:          quit(1,"popen(3) failed for p1");
45:
46:      if ( !(p2 = popen("ls -l|tr '[A-Z]' '[a-z]' && sleep 8","r")) )
47:          quit(1,"popen(3) failed for p2");
48:
49:      /*
50:       * Obtain the underlying file descriptors :
51:       */
52:      f1 = fileno(p1);
53:      fds[0].fd = f1;              /* File descriptor to poll.. */
54:      fds[0].events = POLLIN;      /* for input events */
55:
56:      f2 = fileno(p2);
57:      fds[1].fd = f2;              /* File descriptor to poll.. */
58:      fds[1].events = POLLIN;      /* for input events */
59:
60:      nfds = 2;                    /* nfds is fds[2] array size */
61:
62:      printf("BEGUN: f1=%d, f2=%d\n",f1,f2);
63:
64:      /*
65:       * Enter a poll loop :
66:       */
```

```
67:     do  {
68:         do  {
69:             z = poll(fds,nfds,3500); /* Timeout is 3.5 seconds */
70:         } while ( z == -1 && errno == EINTR );
71:
72:         if ( z == -1 )              /* Error? */
73:             quit(13,"poll(2)");
74:
75:         if ( z == 0 ) {
76:             printf("TIMEOUT: f1=%d, f2=%d\n",f1,f2);
77:             continue;
78:         }
79:
80:         /*
81:          * Control is here if f1 or f2 has data
82:          * available to be read.
83:          */
84:         if ( fds[0].revents & POLLIN ) {
85:             z = read(f1,buf,sizeof buf-1);
86:             if ( z == -1 )
87:                 quit(6,"read(2) of f1.");
88:             if ( z > 0 ) {
89:                 buf[z] = 0;
90:                 printf("*** read %d bytes <<<%s>>> from f1;\n",z,buf);
91:             } else {
92:                 puts("read EOF from f1;");
93:                 pclose(p1);
94:                 fds[0].fd = f1 = -1;
95:             }
96:         }
97:
98:         if ( fds[1].revents & POLLIN ) {
99:             z = read(f2,buf,sizeof buf-1);
100:            if ( z == -1 )
101:                quit(6,"read(2) of f2.");
102:            if ( z > 0 ) {
103:                buf[z] = 0;
104:                printf("*** read %d bytes <<<%s>>> from f2;\n",z,buf);
105:            } else {
106:                puts("read EOF from f2;");
107:                pclose(p2);
108:                fds[1].fd = f2 = -1;
109:            }
110:        }
111:
112:    } while ( f1 >= 0 || f2 >= 0 );
113:
114:    puts("End poll.");
115:
116:    return 0;
117: }
```

Examination of Listing 16.3 reveals that the code is almost the same as Listing 16.2. However, the following differences are worth noting:

- For FreeBSD, the include file <poll.h> was added in line 13.

- An array of structure pollfd replaced the fd_set definitions in line 35.

- The array elements of fds[0] and fds[1] were initialized once in lines 53–54 and again in 57–58.

- The variable nfds is set to the size of the array pollfd[] in line 60.

- The function poll(2) is called in place of select(2) in line 69.

- The events are tested differently in lines 84 and 98. In this program, the flag bit POLLIN is tested in array member revents.

- The pollfd member fd is set to -1 to cause that array member to be ignored when the file descriptor is closed (lines 94 and 108).

One additional difference between Listing 16.3 and 16.2 is that you establish the events that you are interested in only once (see lines 52–58). In Listing 16.2 it was necessary to re-establish the file descriptors in variable rxset prior to each call to select(2). Only the revents member of the pollfd structure is updated by the function poll(2).

Compiling the program gives the following session results:

```
$ make poll
cc -c  -Wall -g poll.c
cc -o poll poll.o
$
```

Running the program provides these results:

```
$ ./poll
BEGUN: f1=3, f2=4
*** read 200 bytes <<<TOTAL 32
-RW-R-----  1 EAG  GRP    524 JUN  7 21:47 MAKEFILE
-R--------  1 EAG  GRP    589 JUN  4 22:09 NBLOCKIO.C
-RWXR-X---  1 EAG  GRP  12570 JUN  7 21:51 POLL
-RW-R-----  1 EAG  GRP   3117 JUN  7 >>> from f1;
*** read 115 bytes <<<21:50 POLL.C
-RW-R-----  1 EAG  GRP  10028 JUN  7 21:51 POLL.O
-R--------  1 EAG  GRP   3063 JUN  6 22:01 SELECT.C
>>> from f1;
read EOF from f1;
*** read 200 bytes <<<total 32
-rw-r-----  1 eag  grp    524 jun  7 21:47 makefile
-r--------  1 eag  grp    589 jun  4 22:09 nblockio.c
-rwxr-x---  1 eag  grp  12570 jun  7 21:51 poll
-rw-r-----  1 eag  grp   3117 jun  7 >>> from f2;
*** read 115 bytes <<<21:50 poll.c
-rw-r-----  1 eag  grp  10028 jun  7 21:51 poll.o
-r--------  1 eag  grp   3063 jun  6 22:01 select.c
>>> from f2;
```

```
TIMEOUT: f1=-1, f2=4
TIMEOUT: f1=-1, f2=4
read EOF from f2;
End poll.
```

The session output is almost identical to the previous example. The differences are due to the presence of different filenames. Notice that the `poll(2)` function also demonstrated its timeout capability near the end.

Summary

This chapter has provided you with the background necessary to use the UNIX system calls `select(2)` and `poll(2)`. Additionally, you will now be able to use non-blocking I/O, particularly for writing to a file descriptor in concert with `select(2)` or `poll(2)`.

The next chapter will explore the wonderful world of UNIX timers.

## CHAPTER 17

TIMERS

*I*n Chapter 15, "Signals," you were introduced to the alarm(3) function, which enables you to create and cancel a timer. This function provides a timer service that has its time resolution measured in seconds.

This chapter will begin with a hypothetical implementation of the sleep(2) function call. This will provide additional insight into why there is a conflict between the use of alarm(3) and sleep(2). Later you'll learn that the conflict may extend to other UNIX functions.

This chapter also will introduce you to

- Fine-grained timers such as usleep(3) and nanosleep(2)
- The interval timer functions

The Sleep Functions

Chapter 15 stated that the sleep(3) function is often implemented in terms of the alarm(3) function. You will look at one such hypothetical implementation of sleep(3) in this section. The function synopsis for sleep(3) is as follows:

```
#include <unistd.h>

unsigned int sleep(unsigned int seconds);
```

The function accepts a time value in seconds to pause the execution of the calling process. If the sleep(3) call is interrupted because a signal was received, the remaining time in seconds is returned to the caller. The return value 0 indicates that the full sleep time has elapsed.

Listing 17.1 shows a simple program that calls on sleep(3). The program simply reports the starting time, sleeps for five seconds, and then reports the ending time of the program run.

LISTING 17.1   sleep.c—A Simple Demonstration of sleep(3)

```
1:   /* sleep.c */
2:
3:   #include <stdio.h>
4:   #include <stdlib.h>
5:   #include <unistd.h>
6:   #include <signal.h>
7:   #include <time.h>
8:
```

continued from previous page

```
 9:   int
10:   main(int argc,char **argv) {
11:       time_t dt;
12:
13:       time(&dt);
14:       printf("%s begun at:\t%s",__FILE__,ctime(&dt));
15:
16:       puts("Zzz...(5 seconds)...");
17:       sleep(5);
18:
19:       time(&dt);
20:       printf("%s completed at:\t%s",__FILE__,ctime(&dt));
21:       return 0;
22:   }
```

A compile and run session is as follows:

```
$ make sleep
cc -c  -Wall sleep.c
cc -o sleep sleep.o
$ ./sleep
sleep.c begun at:      Sat Jun 10 11:22:23 2000
Zzz...(5 seconds)...
sleep.c completed at:  Sat Jun 10 11:22:28 2000
$
```

This is very simple indeed. However, the implementation of sleep(3) is a little more involved. The design of the sleep(3) function requires the following basic steps:

1. Arrange to catch the signal SIGALRM.

2. Start a timer using alarm(3).

3. Wait for any signal to occur.

4. Restore signal handling for SIGALRM.

5. Return the time remaining, if any.

The UNIX Implementation of sleep(3)

Using the basic steps listed previously, you can write your own version of the library sleep(3) function. Listing 17.2 shows one possible implementation.

LISTING 17.2 impsleep.c—An Example of an Implementation of sleep(3)

```
 1:   /* impsleep.c */
 2:
 3:   #include <stdio.h>
 4:   #include <stdlib.h>
 5:   #include <unistd.h>
 6:   #include <signal.h>
 7:   #include <time.h>
 8:
 9:   /*
10:    * Signal handler for SIGALRM :
```

```
11:    */
12:   static void
13:   h_sigalrm(int signo) {
14:
15:       return;                              /* Just return */
16:   }
17:
18:   /*
19:    * An emulated sleep(2) function :
20:    */
21:   static unsigned
22:   Sleep(unsigned seconds) {
23:       time_t dt0, dt1;                     /* Start and end times */
24:       unsigned e;                          /* Elapsed seconds */
25:       struct sigaction old_sigalrm;        /* Old signal action */
26:       struct sigaction new_sigalrm;        /* New signal action */
27:       sigset_t nosigs;                     /* The empty set */
28:
29:       sigemptyset(&nosigs);                /* The empty set */
30:
31:       /*
32:        * Establish the signal action required for SIGALRM :
33:        */
34:       new_sigalrm.sa_handler = h_sigalrm;
35:       sigemptyset(&new_sigalrm.sa_mask);
36:       new_sigalrm.sa_flags = 0;
37:
38:       sigaction(SIGALRM,&new_sigalrm,&old_sigalrm);
39:
40:       /*
41:        * Get start time, start timer, pause, and get end time :
42:        */
43:       time(&dt0);                          /* Get start time in seconds */
44:       alarm(seconds);                      /* (re)start timer */
45:       sigsuspend(&nosigs);                 /* Wait for any signal */
46:       alarm(0);                            /* Cancel timer */
47:       time(&dt1);                          /* Get end time in seconds */
48:       e = (unsigned)(dt1 - dt1);   /* Elapsed time in seconds */
49:
50:       /*
51:        * Restore SIGALRM action, and return time remaining :
52:        */
53:       sigaction(SIGALRM,&old_sigalrm,NULL);
54:       if ( e >= seconds )          /* Did we use up the time? */
55:           return 0;                /* No time remaining.. */
56:       return seconds - e;          /* Return time remaining */
57:   }
58:
59:   int
60:   main(int argc,char **argv) {
61:       time_t dt;
62:
63:       time(&dt);
64:       printf("%s begun at:\t%s",__FILE__,ctime(&dt));
65:
66:       puts("Zzz...(5 seconds)...");
```

continued from previous page

```
67:        Sleep(5);
68:
69:        time(&dt);
70:        printf("%s completed at\t%s",__FILE__,ctime(&dt));
71:        return 0;
72: }
```

In Listing 17.2, the `sleep(3)` function is given the name `Sleep()`. The following basic steps are traced back to the code:

1. Arrange to catch the signal **SIGALRM** (lines 31–38).

2. Start a timer using `alarm(3)` (line 44).

3. Wait for any signal to occur (lines 29 and 45).

4. Restore the signal handling for **SIGALRM** (line 53).

5. Return the time remaining, if any (lines 43, 47, 48, and 54–56).

Compiling and running the program is as follows:

```
$ make impsleep
cc -c  -Wall impsleep.c
cc -o impsleep impsleep.o
$ ./impsleep
impsleep.c begun at:    Sat Jun 10 11:34:09 2000
Zzz...(5 seconds)...
impsleep.c completed at Sat Jun 10 11:34:14 2000
$
```

The session output confirms that your `Sleep()` function substituted well for the `sleep(3)` function. Knowing the nature of the implementation for `sleep(3)` makes it easy to appreciate why `alarm(3)` should not be used in concert with `sleep(3)`. If a program had called on `alarm(3)` prior to calling on `sleep(3)`, it is obvious that the `alarm(3)` call within `sleep(3)` would cancel the application's timer.

However, it must be stressed that this is only one possible implementation for `sleep(3)`. As newer releases of UNIX become available, the implementation may vary. Later in this chapter, you will read about interval timers. Solaris 8 and UnixWare 7, for example, state that you should not mix calls to `setitimer(2)` (an interval timer) with calls to `sleep(3)`. This suggests that the implementation of `sleep(3)` may use an interval timer instead (especially since they also state that `setitimer(2)` is independent of the `alarm(3)` system call).

Note

When you design a UNIX application, it is wise to choose in advance one of the following groups of functions:

- `sleep(3)`, `usleep(3)`, or `nanosleep(2)`
- `alarm(3)`, `getitimer(2)`, or `setitimer(2)`

If you must use conflicting groups of timing routines, you must take care to invoke them at times when they will not conflict with each other.

Sleeping in Microsecond Units

The sleep(3) call permits the process to sleep in terms of seconds. However, as hardware speed increases and processes become more sophisticated, this is often inadequate. The usleep(3) function helps to overcome the low resolution problem:

```
#include <unistd.h>

int usleep(unsigned int microseconds);
```

The input argument to usleep(3) is in microseconds. The return value of usleep(3) differs from sleep(3) in that 0 is returned if the call is successful. Otherwise, -1 is returned and an error code is found in errno. The errno value of EINTR indicates that a signal was raised. There is no indication of whether the entire sleep time elapsed.

Listing 17.3 shows a program that calls on the usleep(3) function.

LISTING 17.3   usleep.c—A Demonstration of the usleep(3) Function

```
 1:    /* usleep.c */
 2:
 3:    #include <stdio.h>
 4:    #include <stdlib.h>
 5:    #include <unistd.h>
 6:    #include <time.h>
 7:
 8:    extern int usleep(unsigned int microseconds);
 9:
10:    static unsigned
11:    test(unsigned usec) {                       /* Microseconds to sleep */
12:        unsigned Zzz = 5;                       /* Sleep time in seconds */
13:        long count = 0L;                        /* Interation Counter */
14:        unsigned avg;                           /* Average time interval */
15:        long sb_count = (Zzz * 1000000) / usec;
16:        time_t t0, t1;
17:
18:        time(&t0);
19:        printf("%s started at:\t%s",__FILE__,ctime(&t0));
20:
21:        for ( ; time(&t1) - t0 < Zzz; ++count ) {
22:            usleep(usec);
23:        }
24:
25:        printf("%s ended at:\t%s",__FILE__,ctime(&t1));
26:
27:        printf("Elapsed time is %u seconds\n",(unsigned)(t1-t0));
28:        printf("Counter reached %ld, should be %ld\n",count,sb_count);
29:        avg = (unsigned) (((long)(t1-t0))*1000000 / (long)count);
30:        printf("The average time was %u usec.\n",avg);
31:
32:        return avg;
33:    }
34:
35:    int
```

continued from previous page

```
36:  main(int argc,char **argv) {
37:      short x;
38:      unsigned a;
39:      unsigned usec = ~0U;
40:      unsigned usleep_times[] = {
41:          1000000, 100000, 10000, 1000, 100
42:      };
43:
44:      for ( x=0; x<5; ++x ) {
45:          printf("TESTING USLEEP(%u) :\n",usleep_times[x]);
46:          a = test(usleep_times[x]);
47:          putchar('\n');
48:
49:          if ( a < usec )
50:              usec = a;          /* Save shortest avg time */
51:      }
52:
53:      printf("Shortest usleep(3) time is %u usec.\n",usec);
54:
55:      return 0;
56:  }
```

Some explanation is required for this program: Five sleep times are tried, and then the usleep(3) call is performed as many times as possible within the allotted time (5 seconds). Then an average sleep time is computed to see how well the function delivered.

The test function is composed of lines 10–33. The start time and end time are recorded in lines 18 and 25, respectively. The counter count is initially 0 in line 13. The loop in lines 21–23 continues until Zzz seconds have elapsed (Zzz is initialized to 5 seconds in line 12). The results are then computed and returned in lines 25–32.

Compiling and running the program provides the following session output on a FreeBSD machine, using an AMD-K6 CPU (450MHz):

```
$ make usleep
cc -c  -Wall usleep.c
cc -o usleep usleep.o
$ ./usleep
TESTING USLEEP(1000000) :
usleep.c started at:    Sat Jun 10 12:13:47 2000
usleep.c ended at:      Sat Jun 10 12:13:52 2000
Elapsed time is 5 seconds
Counter reached 5, should be 5
The average time was 1000000 usec.

TESTING USLEEP(100000) :
usleep.c started at:    Sat Jun 10 12:13:52 2000
usleep.c ended at:      Sat Jun 10 12:13:57 2000
Elapsed time is 5 seconds
Counter reached 43, should be 50
The average time was 116279 usec.

TESTING USLEEP(10000) :
usleep.c started at:    Sat Jun 10 12:13:57 2000
```

```
usleep.c ended at:    Sat Jun 10 12:14:02 2000
Elapsed time is 5 seconds
Counter reached 250, should be 500
The average time was 20000 usec.

TESTING USLEEP(1000) :
usleep.c started at:    Sat Jun 10 12:14:02 2000
usleep.c ended at:    Sat Jun 10 12:14:07 2000
Elapsed time is 5 seconds
Counter reached 250, should be 5000
The average time was 20000 usec.

TESTING USLEEP(100) :
usleep.c started at:    Sat Jun 10 12:14:07 2000
usleep.c ended at:    Sat Jun 10 12:14:12 2000
Elapsed time is 5 seconds
Counter reached 250, should be 50000
The average time was 20000 usec.

Shortest usleep(3) time is 20000 usec.
```

The first results for 1,000,000 microseconds (1 second) show that the usleep(3) call returned five times during the 5-second period. This is as expected.

The next section shows the results for a test that was performed using the value of 100,000 microseconds in calls to usleep(3). While the elapsed time was still 5 seconds, note that the counter reported that only 43 iterations of the loop in lines 21–23 were executed. Ideally, there should have been 50 iterations.

The third test shows the results for 10,000 microsecond sleeps. The counter reached only 250 instead of the theoretical 500. The average time was computed as being 20,000 microseconds.

The increasingly shorter usleep(3) times do not yield corresponding higher loop counts. This suggests that the combination of timer resolution and CPU overhead prevents the application from getting resolution any finer than 20,000 microseconds (20 milliseconds).

Note

Although the function usleep(3) accepts sleep time in units of microseconds, the resolution provided may be much coarser and is specific to the implementation.

Sleeping in Nanosecond Units

It was demonstrated in the preceding section that the usleep(3) function delivered a resolution of approximately 20 milliseconds on the system used. The UNIX operating system can exist on nimble hardware. Consequently, resolution greater than one microsecond is often required on faster hardware. The nanosleep(2) function, which is currently defined by the IEEE POSIX P1003.4 standard, draft 14, makes this possible:

```
#include <time.h>

int nanosleep(const struct timespec *rqtp, struct timespec *rmtp);

struct timespec {
    time_t   tv_sec;    /* seconds */
    long     tv_nsec;   /* and nanoseconds */
};
```

The function accepts two arguments, both of which point to the structure type `timespec`:

- `rqtp` is a pointer to a `timespec` structure that defines how long the calling process is to sleep. The content of this structure must be defined and is used for input to `nanosleep(2)`.

- `rmtp` is an optional pointer to a `timespec` structure. When this pointer argument is not null, the structure will receive results from the call to `nanosleep(2)`.

The result returned via the `rmtp` argument is the amount of time remaining, if any.

The `nanosleep(2)` call returns the value `0` if the time requested has elapsed. The actual time elapsed may be longer than requested, but it is never shorter. This is due to the implementation's resolution of the timer used.

The `nanosleep(2)` function will return `-1` when an error occurs or the call is interrupted by a signal. The value of `errno` is `EINTR` when a signal has been received with the time via the `rmtp` argument, reflecting the amount of time that was remaining. The error code `ENOSYS` is returned when the system does not support the `nanosleep(2)` call. Note that the error code `EINVAL` is returned when the `rqtp` member `tv_nsec` exceeds 1 billion nanoseconds.

Note

ENOSYS—Function Not Implemented   For the `nanosleep(2)` call, this indicates that this system call is not implemented. The calling program should resort to `usleep(3)` instead.

`nanosleep(2)` is not supported by UnixWare 7 or Linux, but it is supported by SGI IRIX 6.5, HPUX 11, and Solaris 8. Documentation for IBM's AIX 4.3 mentions `nanosleep(2)` but does not provide a manual page for it.

Warning

Processing `EINTR` for `nanosleep(2)` requires careful consideration. If it is important to maintain the same total elapsed time for the original call with or without interruptions, you must copy the remaining time values to the input of the retried system call. If the total elapsed time is unimportant, you may want simply to retry the system call with the original sleep time instead.

Listing 17.4 shows a demonstration program using `nanosleep(2)` instead of `usleep(3)`. Note the similarity between this program and Listing 17.3.

LISTING 17.4   `nanosleep.c`—A Demonstration of the `nanosleep(2)` Function

```
 1:    /* nanosleep.c */
 2:
 3:    #include <stdio.h>
 4:    #include <stdlib.h>
 5:    #include <unistd.h>
 6:    #include <time.h>
 7:
 8:    int nanosleep(const struct timespec *rqtp,struct timespec *rmtp);
 9:
10:    static unsigned
11:    test(unsigned usec) {                       /* Microseconds to sleep */
12:        unsigned Zzz = 5;                       /* Sleep time in seconds */
13:        long count = 0L;                        /* Interation Counter */
14:        unsigned avg;                           /* Average time interval */
15:        long sb_count = (Zzz * 1000000) / usec;
16:        time_t t0, t1;
17:        struct timespec rqt;                    /* Requested time */
18:
19:        rqt.tv_sec = usec / 1000000;            /* Seconds */
20:        rqt.tv_nsec = ( usec % 1000000 ) * 1000;/* Nanoseconds */
21:
22:        time(&t0);
23:        printf("%s started at:\t%s",__FILE__,ctime(&t0));
24:
25:        for ( ; time(&t1) - t0 < Zzz; ++count ) {
26:            nanosleep(&rqt,NULL);
27:        }
28:
29:        printf("%s ended at:\t%s",__FILE__,ctime(&t1));
30:
31:        printf("Elapsed time is %u seconds\n",(unsigned)(t1-t0));
32:        printf("Counter reached %ld, should be %ld\n",count,sb_count);
33:        avg = (unsigned) (((long)(t1-t0))*1000000 / (long)count);
34:        printf("The average time was %u usec.\n",avg);
35:
36:        return avg;
37:    }
38:
39:    int
40:    main(int argc,char **argv) {
41:        short x;
42:        unsigned a;
43:        unsigned usec = ~0U;
44:        unsigned nanosleep_times[] = {
45:            1000000, 100000, 10000, 1000, 100
46:        };
47:
48:        for ( x=0; x<5; ++x ) {
49:            printf("TESTING NANOSLEEP(%u) :\n",nanosleep_times[x]);
50:            a = test(nanosleep_times[x]);
51:            putchar('\n');
52:
```

continued from previous page

```
53:            if ( a < usec )
54:                usec = a;        /* Save shortest avg time */
55:        }
56:
57:        printf("Shortest nanosleep(3) time is %u usec.\n",usec);
58:
59:        return 0;
60:  }
```

The program is essentially the same as the preceding one, except that the requested time is set up on a structure in lines 19 and 20. Then nanosleep(2) is substituted for usleep(3) in line 26. Notice how this program uses a null pointer in argument two of the nanosleep(2) call.

Compiling and running this program under FreeBSD using an AMD-K6 CPU (450MHz) yielded the following:

```
$ make nanosleep
cc -c  -Wall nanosleep.c
cc -o nanosleep nanosleep.o
$ ./nanosleep
TESTING NANOSLEEP(1000000) :
nanosleep.c started at:  Sat Jun 10 13:14:33 2000
nanosleep.c ended at:    Sat Jun 10 13:14:38 2000
Elapsed time is 5 seconds
Counter reached 5, should be 5
The average time was 1000000 usec.

TESTING NANOSLEEP(100000) :
nanosleep.c started at:  Sat Jun 10 13:14:38 2000
nanosleep.c ended at:    Sat Jun 10 13:14:43 2000
Elapsed time is 5 seconds
Counter reached 39, should be 50
The average time was 128205 usec.

TESTING NANOSLEEP(10000) :
nanosleep.c started at:  Sat Jun 10 13:14:43 2000
nanosleep.c ended at:    Sat Jun 10 13:14:48 2000
Elapsed time is 5 seconds
Counter reached 248, should be 500
The average time was 20161 usec.

TESTING NANOSLEEP(1000) :
nanosleep.c started at:  Sat Jun 10 13:14:48 2000
nanosleep.c ended at:    Sat Jun 10 13:14:53 2000
Elapsed time is 5 seconds
Counter reached 250, should be 5000
The average time was 20000 usec.

TESTING NANOSLEEP(100) :
nanosleep.c started at:  Sat Jun 10 13:14:53 2000
nanosleep.c ended at:    Sat Jun 10 13:14:58 2000
Elapsed time is 5 seconds
```

```
Counter reached 250, should be 50000
The average time was 20000 usec.

Shortest nanosleep(3) time is 20000 usec.
```

Notice how the results agreed with the `usleep(3)` results for this platform, with a resolution of approximately 20 milliseconds.

Interval Timer Functions

The release of BSD4.2 UNIX introduced interval timers. This new facility provided the programmer the capability to create

- A realtime timer
- A virtual timer
- A system virtual (profile) timer

These timers provided three different ways to measure time. The realtime timer measures elapsed time in the same way as the `alarm(3)` function. The virtual timer measures CPU time used while the process executes in user mode.

The system virtual timer, however, measures the time of execution for the current process in system and user modes. The system mode time measured is the execution time spent within the kernel on behalf of the current process. This timer is intended to assist interpreters in measuring the CPU profile of an interpreted program.

The new realtime timer provides additional advantages over the older `alarm(3)` function:

- It allows microsecond resolution if the platform supports it.
- It is capable of repeating.

The Interval Timer API

The new timer functionality came in the form of two functions: `getitimer(2)` and `setitimer(2)`. These allow the caller to query and configure the timers, respectively.

```
#include <sys/time.h>
#define ITIMER_REAL        0          /* Realtime timer (SIGALRM) */
#define ITIMER_VIRTUAL     1          /* User time timer (SIGVTALRM) */
#define ITIMER_PROF        2          /* System + user time (SIGPROF) */

int getitimer(int which, struct itimerval *ovalue);

int setitimer(int which,              /* timer selection */
    const struct itimerval *value,    /* new timer settings */
    struct itimerval *ovalue);        /* old timer settings */

struct timeval {
        long    tv_sec;               /* seconds */
```

```
        long    tv_usec;                /* and microseconds */
};

struct itimerval {
        struct  timeval it_interval; /* timer interval */
        struct  timeval it_value;    /* current value */
};
```

The getitimer(2) and setitimer(2) functions require the programmer to choose one of the values ITIMER_REAL, ITIMER_VIRTUAL, or ITIMER_PROF for the argument which. The ovalue argument receives a copy of the settings in the selected timer. In setitimer(2), where the timer settings are changed, the ovalue argument receives the former timer values. The new timer values are supplied by the value argument. Both functions return 0 when they succeed and -1 with an errno code if they fail.

Each timer generates a signal, as follows:

ITIMER_REAL	SIGALRM
ITIMER_VIRTUAL	SIGVTALRM
ITIMER_PROF	SIGPROF

Note

Interval timers are not inherited by the child process after a fork(2) call. Interval timers do continue after an exec(2) call is made, however.

The itimerval structure has two members. The member it_value represents the time remaining until the next timer expiry. If this value is specified as 0, the timer is canceled. The member it_interval specifies the value to be loaded into the timer with the next timer expiry. If this value specifies zero time, then the timer is not reactivated.

The following specifies a timer that will expire once, 5.25 seconds after activation:

```
struct itimerval tmr;

tmr.it_value.tv_sec = 5;
tmr.it_value.tv_usec = 250000;
tmr.it_interval.tv_sec = 0;
tmr.it_interval.tv_usec = 0;
```

The next example shows how to define a timer that will expire after 3.75 seconds and repeat every 4.25 seconds thereafter:

```
struct itimerval tmr;

tmr.it_value.tv_sec = 3;
tmr.it_value.tv_usec = 750000;
tmr.it_interval.tv_sec = 4;
tmr.it_interval.tv_usec = 250000;
```

Interval Timer Macros

The manual page for `setitimer(2)` usually mentions three helpful macros.

- `timerclear(tvp)` clears the timer value.
- `timerisset(tvp)` indicates if the timer value is non-zero.
- `timercmp(tvp,uvp,cmp)` comparestwo timer values.

The following example shows how `timerclear()` can be used to clear a time value:

```
struct itimerval tmr;

timerclear(&tmr);                 /* Clear time value tmr */
```

The following tests to see if timer value `tmr` is zero:

```
if ( timerisset(&tmr) )
    /* tmr is non-zero */
```

The last example tests to see if variables `tm1` and `tm2` represent the same timer values:

```
struct itimerval tm1;
struct itimerval tm2;

if ( timercmp(&tm1,&tm2,=) )
    /* Values are equal */
```

The following tests to see if the variable `tm1` represents less time than `tm2`:

```
struct itimerval tm1;
struct itimerval tm2;

if ( timercmp(&tm1,&tm2,<) )
    /* tm1 < tm2 */
```

Interval Timer Restrictions

Most UNIX platforms insist that the microsecond component of the interval time specification (`tv_usec`) not exceed one second (1,000,000 microseconds). Otherwise, an error will be reported.

A programmer that is striving for maximum UNIX platform portability should keep a few other things in mind when designing programs around interval timers. While `setitimer(2)` may be independent of the `alarm(3)` function call (UnixWare 7), you may not always be able to depend on this. Additionally, the `sleep(3)` function may be implemented in terms of `alarm(3)`, or it may be implemented in terms of the `ITIMER_REAL` interval timer. HPUX 11 documents that "interaction between `setitimer()` and any of `alarm()`, `sleep()` or `usleep()` [functions] is unspecified."

The granularity of the timer will be very platform specific. While the specification permits the programmer to specify units of microseconds, your platform may round the time specifications to a less precise value. If your application is time critical, you may need to test your interval timer before relying on a particular level of precision.

Linux documents that generation and delivery of the timer signal are separate. This means that under severe conditions it is possible for realtime timer signals to be lost if they occur too soon to be handled. They are not stacked or counted.

Note

Some UNIX platforms document additional interval timers. For example, Solaris 8 documents the timer ITIMER_REALPROF, which delivers the same signal SIGPROF but has different semantics.

Note also that the ITIMER_PROF is capable of causing interrupted system calls, because the signal can be raised while executing in system mode. This means that your application must properly plan for the EINTR error code from system calls.

Creating One-Shot Timers

Listing 17.5 illustrates the use of the interval timer. This program establishes a simple one-shot realtime timer that raises the signal SIGALRM and then exits.

LISTING 17.5   r1shot.c—A Simple One-Shot Realtime Timer Demonstration

```
 1:  /* r1shot.c */
 2:
 3:  #include <stdio.h>
 4:  #include <stdlib.h>
 5:  #include <unistd.h>
 6:  #include <signal.h>
 7:  #include <errno.h>
 8:  #include <sys/time.h>
 9:
10:  static int count = 0;               /* Counter */
11:
12:  /*
13:   * Signal handler :
14:   */
15:  static void
16:  handler(int signo) {
17:      int e = errno;                  /* Save errno */
18:
19:      ++count;                        /* Increment count */
20:      write(1,"<<<SIGALRM>>>\n",14);
21:      errno = e;                      /* Restore errno */
22:  }
23:
24:  /*
25:   * Main program :
26:   */
27:  int
28:  main(int argc,char **argv) {
29:      int z;                          /* Status return code */
```

```
30:        struct sigaction new_sigalrm;    /* New signal action */
31:        struct itimerval old_timer;      /* Old timer values */
32:        struct itimerval new_timer;      /* New timer values */
33:
34:        /*
35:         * Establish the signal action required for SIGALRM :
36:         */
37:        new_sigalrm.sa_handler = handler;
38:        sigemptyset(&new_sigalrm.sa_mask);
39:        new_sigalrm.sa_flags = 0;
40:        sigaction(SIGALRM,&new_sigalrm,NULL);
41:
42:        /*
43:         * Establish a one-shot realtime timer :
44:         */
45:        new_timer.it_interval.tv_sec = 0;
46:        new_timer.it_interval.tv_usec = 0;
47:        new_timer.it_value.tv_sec = 5;
48:        new_timer.it_value.tv_usec = 250000;    /* 5.25 seconds */
49:
50:        puts("Starting ITIMER_REAL...");
51:
52:        z = setitimer(ITIMER_REAL,&new_timer,&old_timer);
53:        if ( z ) {
54:            perror("setitimer(ITIMER_REAL)");
55:            return 1;
56:        }
57:
58:        /*
59:         * A loop :
60:         */
61:        do  {
62:            /* Do Work...*/ ;
63:        } while ( count < 1 );
64:
65:        printf("ITIMER_REAL count is %d.\n",count);
66:        return 0;
67:    }
```

The program in Listing 17.5 establishes a signal handler for the signal **SIGALRM** in lines 34–40. The function **handler()** is called when the signal is raised, and it simply increments variable **count** in line 19 and reports a message in line 20.

The one-shot timer is configured in lines 45–52. Notice that the **it_interval** member values are **0**, causing the timer to not restart when the initial value expires.

Warning

The program in Listing 17.5 uses a CPU-intensive loop in lines 61–63. Out of courtesy to others, do not invoke this program often in a multiuser environment.

Compiling and running the program should yield the following:

```
$ make r1shot
cc -c  -Wall r1shot.c
cc -o r1shot r1shot.o
$ ./r1shot
Starting ITIMER_REAL...
<<<SIGALRM>>>
ITIMER_REAL count is 1.
$
```

You will see the message <<<SIGALRM>>> raised 5.25 seconds after the program starts. Then the program reports the final value of **count** and exits normally.

Establishing Repeating Timers

The program shown in Listing 17.6 is more interesting. It starts realtime, virtual, and profile timers all at once.

LISTING 17.6   `timers.c`—A Program That Uses Realtime, Virtual, and Profile Timers

```
 1:  /* timers.c */
 2:
 3:  #include <stdio.h>
 4:  #include <stdlib.h>
 5:  #include <unistd.h>
 6:  #include <signal.h>
 7:  #include <errno.h>
 8:  #include <sys/time.h>
 9:
10:  static int count = 0;                /* Counter */
11:
12:  /*
13:   * Signal handler :
14:   */
15:  static void
16:  handler(int signo) {
17:      int e = errno;                   /* Save errno */
18:      char *signame = "?";             /* Signal name */
19:
20:      switch( signo ) {
21:      case SIGALRM :                   /* Realtime timer expired */
22:          ++count;                     /* Increment counter */
23:          signame = "<<<SIGALRM>>>\n";
24:          break;
25:      case SIGVTALRM :                 /* Virtual timer expired */
26:          signame = "<<<SIGVTALRM>>>\n";
27:          break;
28:      case SIGPROF :                   /* System virtual timer expired */
29:          signame = "<<<SIGPROF>>>\n";
30:          break;
31:      }
32:
```

```
33:         write(1,signame,strlen(signame));
34:         errno = e;                       /* Restore errno */
35:     }
36:
37:     /*
38:      * Main program :
39:      */
40:     int
41:     main(int argc,char **argv) {
42:         int z;                          /* Status return code */
43:         struct sigaction new_sigalrm;   /* New signal action */
44:         struct itimerval real_timer;    /* Real timer values */
45:         struct itimerval virt_timer;    /* User mode timer */
46:         struct itimerval prof_timer;    /* System+User mode timer */
47:         struct itimerval timer_values;  /* Timer values */
48:
49:         /*
50:          * Establish the signal action required for SIGALRM :
51:          */
52:         new_sigalrm.sa_handler = handler;
53:         sigemptyset(&new_sigalrm.sa_mask);
54:         new_sigalrm.sa_flags = 0;
55:
56:         sigaction(SIGALRM,&new_sigalrm,NULL);
57:         sigaction(SIGVTALRM,&new_sigalrm,NULL);
58:         sigaction(SIGPROF,&new_sigalrm,NULL);
59:
60:         /*
61:          * Establish a realtime timer :
62:          */
63:         real_timer.it_interval.tv_sec = 3;
64:         real_timer.it_interval.tv_usec = 500000; /* 3.5 seconds */
65:         real_timer.it_value.tv_sec = 3;
66:         real_timer.it_value.tv_usec = 500000;
67:
68:         virt_timer.it_interval.tv_sec = 0;
69:         virt_timer.it_interval.tv_usec = 500000; /* 0.5 seconds */
70:         virt_timer.it_value.tv_sec = 0;
71:         virt_timer.it_value.tv_usec = 500000;
72:
73:         prof_timer.it_interval.tv_sec = 0;
74:         prof_timer.it_interval.tv_usec = 500000; /* 0.5 seconds */
75:         prof_timer.it_value.tv_sec = 0;
76:         prof_timer.it_value.tv_usec = 500000;
77:
78:         puts("Starting ITIMER_REAL...");
79:         z = setitimer(ITIMER_REAL,&real_timer,NULL);
80:         if ( z ) {
81:             perror("setitimer(ITIMER_REAL)");
82:             return 1;
83:         }
84:
85:         puts("Starting ITIMER_VIRTUAL...");
86:         z = setitimer(ITIMER_VIRTUAL,&virt_timer,NULL);
```

continued from previous page

```
87:      if ( z ) {
88:          perror("setitimer(ITIMER_VIRTUAL)");
89:          return 1;
90:      }
91:
92:      puts("Starting ITIMER_PROF...");
93:      z = setitimer(ITIMER_PROF,&prof_timer,NULL);
94:      if ( z ) {
95:          perror("setitimer(ITIMER_PROF)");
96:          return 1;
97:      }
98:
99:      /*
100:      * A loop :
101:      */
102:      do  {
103:          /* Perform work which involves system time */
104:          getitimer(ITIMER_PROF,&timer_values);
105:          (void) timer_values;
106:      } while ( count < 2 );
107:
108:      printf("ITIMER_REAL count is %d.\n",count);
109:      return 0;
110: }
```

Lines 52–58 establish a single handler function `handler()` to process signals `SIGALRM`, `SIGVTALRM`, and `SIGPROF`. The counter variable `count` is incremented only when `handler()` receives the signal `SIGALRM` (see line 22).

The three timers are configured in lines 63–76. The timers themselves are started in lines 78–97.

After the program begins executing, the `do { } while` loop in lines 102–106 repeatedly calls on `getitimer(2)` to read the current timer values for `ITIMER_PROF`. This is performed so that much of the CPU time expended in this demonstration will be in system mode.

Note

The program in Listing 17.6 is very CPU intensive. To be courteous to other users of the same system, do not run this program frequently.

Compiling and running this program on a FreeBSD system yielded the following:

```
$ make timers
cc -c  -Wall timers.c
cc -o timers timers.o
$ ./timers
Starting ITIMER_REAL...
Starting ITIMER_VIRTUAL...
Starting ITIMER_PROF...
<<<SIGPROF>>>
<<<SIGPROF>>>
```

```
<<<SIGPROF>>>
<<<SIGVTALRM>>>
<<<SIGPROF>>>
<<<SIGPROF>>>
<<<SIGPROF>>>
<<<SIGPROF>>>
<<<SIGALRM>>>
<<<SIGVTALRM>>>
<<<SIGPROF>>>
<<<SIGPROF>>>
<<<SIGPROF>>>
<<<SIGVTALRM>>>
<<<SIGPROF>>>
<<<SIGPROF>>>
<<<SIGPROF>>>
<<<SIGALRM>>>
ITIMER_REAL count is 2.
$
```

You can see the names of the different signals that were raised when the timers expired. Note how the timers kept working in this example.

Note also that the signal `SIGPROF` occurs more frequently than the signal `SIGVTALRM`. This should tell you that more CPU time was being spent in system mode in the `do { } while` loop than in user mode.

The `SIGALRM` signal occurred twice because the `while` clause exits after the counter `count` reaches `2`. Since the realtime timer was configured to expire at 3.5 seconds, the entire output represents approximately 7 seconds of time.

Summary

This chapter has explored the use of using sleep functions and interval timers. The realtime timer provides your application with the capability to act with elapsed time. The virtual and profile interval timers allow your application to act when a certain amount of CPU time has been consumed by the current process. Frequently these are useful for interpreted languages.

The next chapter will look at how you can create new processes using pipes and the `system(3)` call.

## CHAPTER 18

PIPES AND PROCESSES

One of the strengths of UNIX is its ability to reuse different process components. The shell demonstrates this by connecting the output of one process to the input of another, using pipes in an almost effortless manner. This chapter will focus on how programs create pipes to other processes using **popen(3)** and how to use the **system(3)** function to invoke external processes.

UNIX Pipes

A pipe between two processes is similar to a tubular piece of plumbing. When a UNIX pipe is created, a data pipeline is formed between a writing process and a reading process. The UNIX pipe can become plugged if the reading process does not continue to receive the piped data. Unlike a physical pipe, however, some versions of UNIX insist that the data must flow in one direction: from its source to its destination.

In Chapter 2, "UNIX File System Objects," you read about FIFOs, which are also known as named pipes. This chapter, however, will be concerned with *nameless* pipes. Unlike FIFOs, nameless pipes are created in the open state and only exist between processes.

Creating UNIX Pipes

The system call that is responsible for creating nameless pipes is the function **pipe(2)**. Its function synopsis is as follows:

```
#include <unistd.h>
```

```
int pipe(int fildes[2]);
```

The **pipe(2)** call returns one pair of file descriptors that represent both ends of the pipe. When the function is successful, the array **fildes[]** is populated with two open file descriptors, and the value **0** is returned. Otherwise **-1** is returned, and an error code is left in the external variable **errno**.

Note

The close-on-exec flag is not set on the two file descriptors that are returned by **pipe(2)**.

Systems that only support unidirectional pipes will provide `fildes[0]` as a file descriptor capable of reading only. The descriptor `fildes[1]` will be capable of writing only. Data written to `fildes[1]` can be read at the opposite end of the pipe with file descriptor `fildes[0]`.

Systems that support STREAMS-based pipes allow reading and writing to both ends. Data written to `fildes[0]` is read via descriptor `fildes[1]`. Data written to `fildes[1]` is read via descriptor `fildes[0]`. In this respect, the STREAMS-based pipe is similar to a connected socket (the curious may read about `socketpair(2)`).

The following example shows how a pipe is created:

```
int z;                          /* General status code */
int fildes[2];                  /* Pair of file descriptors */

if ( (z = pipe(&fildes[0])) == -1 ) {
    perror("pipe(2)");          /* Report the error */
    exit(13);
)
printf("fildes[0] = %d, for reading\n",fildes[0]);
printf("fildes[1] = %d, for writing\n",fildes[1]);
```

This example shows how a pipe is created and how its file descriptors are reported (a unidirectional pipe is assumed in this example).

Note

The value `st_size` returned by `fstat(2)` is the number of bytes available for reading. For systems that support only unidirectional pipes, the same value `st_size` is returned for either file descriptor `fildes[0]` or `fildes[1]`.

For STREAMS-based pipes, the `st_size` value returned by `fstat(2)` is the number of bytes available for reading at the specified end of the pipe. Descriptor `fildes[0]` or `fildes[1]` specifies which end of the pipe to query.

The creation of a pipe within one process may not appear to be useful. However, when you couple this functionality with the `fork(2)` system call, which is covered in Chapter 19, "Forked Processes," this becomes a powerful tool.

Because `fork(2)` is covered in the next chapter, this discussion will now turn to the `popen(3)` call. The `pipe(2)` function was introduced here because the `popen(3)` function calls upon it internally.

Note

FreeBSD release 3.4, UnixWare 7, and Solaris 8 support STREAMS-based pipes (bi-directional).

SGI IRIX 6.5 and HPUX 10.0 and later can be configured to use STREAMS-based (bi-directional) or unidirectional pipes. SGI also permits STREAMS-based pipe support to be chosen at program link time.

Only the unidirectional pipe is supported by Linux and IBM's AIX 4.3.

Opening Pipes to Other Processes

The C standard I/O library `popen(3)` makes it easy for the application programmer to open a pipe to an external process. It makes the necessary call to `pipe(2)` and then calls upon `fork(2)` to start a new process, which is attached to a pipe. The function synopsis for `popen(3)` is as follows:

```
#include <stdio.h>

FILE *popen(const char *command, const char *mode);

int pclose(FILE *stream);
```

The `popen(3)` function arguments are similar to the `fopen(3)` function except that the first argument is a command rather than a pathname. The argument `command` must be a command that is acceptable to the UNIX shell.

The second argument `mode` must be the C string `"r"` for reading or `"w"` for writing. No other combination, such as `"w+"`, is acceptable. A `popen(3)` pipe must be opened for reading from a process or writing to a process, but never for both. When `popen(3)` is successful, a valid `FILE` pointer is returned. Otherwise, a null pointer is returned and the error is posted to `errno`.

Successfully opened pipes must be later closed by a call to `pclose(3)`. The return value for `pclose(3)` is the termination status of the shell process.

Warning

Calling `popen(3)` from a set-user-ID program is dangerous. The `popen(3)` function uses `fork(2)` and `exec(2)` to invoke the new shell, and consequently it is possible for a security leak to occur (the current effective user and group ID values are saved by `exec(2)`). The shell and the commands invoked are subject to environment variable settings such as PATH and SHELL.

The C string given as argument `command` to `popen(3)` must be acceptable to the shell. This is because the `popen(3)` function invokes a shell process first. The entire pipe creation process can be described as follows:

1. The `popen(3)` function creates a nameless pipe with a call to `pipe(2)`.

2. The `popen(3)` function calls functions `fork(2)` and `execve(2)` to start the shell.

3. The shell interprets your `command` string that was provided in the call to `popen(3)`.

4. The shell starts your `command` if it is able to. If not, the shell returns an error to the `popen(3)` call.

The command process started by `popen(3)` is referred to as the *child* process of your current process. The current process that has called `popen(3)` is known as the *parent* process. This terminology helps to identify the process relationships involved.

Because the `command` string is passed to the shell, you have considerable flexibility in the features at your disposal. This includes the ability to use command lines that use wildcard filenames and shell input and output redirection operators. Additionally, you may use the pipe symbol to create additional pipes to other processes.

Warning

If you write programs that use the popen(3) function and that must be portable to other UNIX operating systems, keep in mind the limitations of the shell. Different shell programs are used on some UNIX platforms, with varying capabilities.

The current process environment is important to the shell that is invoked by the popen(3) call to start your command. This means that any commands that you expect it to invoke are subject to the usual PATH directory searches.

Reading from Pipes

The short program in Listing 18.1 shows a simple program that opens a pipe to the ps(1) command. After the pipe is opened, the program reads from the pipe until end-of-file is reached. All read data is displayed on standard output.

LISTING 18.1   popen.c—Demonstration of popen(3) and Reading ps(1) Output

```
 1:   /* popen.c */
 2:
 3:   #include <stdio.h>
 4:   #include <stdlib.h>
 5:
 6:   int
 7:   main(int argc,char **argv) {
 8:       char buf[256];                      /* Input buffer */
 9:       FILE *p;                            /* Input pipe */
10:
11:       /*
12:        * Open pipe to ps(1) command for reading :
13:        */
14:       p = popen("ps -l","r");
15:
16:       if ( !p ) {
17:           perror("popen(3)");
18:           return 13;
19:       }
20:
21:       /*
22:        * Read the output of the pipe:
23:        */
24:       while ( fgets(buf,sizeof buf,p) != 0 )
25:           fputs(buf,stdout);
26:
27:       if ( pclose(p) ) {
28:           perror("pclose(3)");
29:           return 13;
30:       }
31:
32:       return 0;
33:   }
```

The program begins by opening a read pipe to the command `ps -l` in line 14. Once the pipe has been opened successfully, the program reads each text line in the loop in lines 24 and 25, until end-of-file is reached. Then the `pclose(3)` function is called to properly close the pipe `p` (line 27).

The following FreeBSD compile and run session is provided as follows:

```
$ make popen
cc -c  -Wall popen.c
cc -o popen popen.o
$ ./popen
  UID   PID  PPID CPU PRI NI  VSZ  RSS WCHAN  STAT  TT       TIME COMMAND
 1001  7590     1   0  10  0  596  344 wait   Is    p0    0:00.05 -sh (sh)
 1001  7593  7592   1  10  0  596  344 wait   Ss    p1    0:00.22 -sh (sh)
 1001  7813  7593   1  -6  0  780  408 piperd S+    p1    0:00.01 ./popen
 1001  7814  7813   1  10  0  496  332 wait   S+    p1    0:00.00 sh -c ps -l
 1001  7815  7814   1  28  0  376  244 -      R+    p1    0:00.00 ps -l
$
```

The last three lines of output show the processes involved (the preceding ones are for the `xterm(1)` session that was being used). Process **7813** is the process used to execute the program `./popen`. However, note how the `popen(3)` call has created two new processes:

- Process **7814** is the shell that has been started to execute the command.
- Process **7815** is the command process itself (the `ps(1)` command).

Although you cannot see the single quotes that were used, you can see how the `popen(3)` process created the command process using the shell process **7814**. If you could see the single quotes, you would see:

```
sh -c 'ps -l'
```

This demonstrates the work that the `popen(3)` function has performed for you by calling upon `pipe(2)`, `fork(2)`, and `execve(2)`. The functions `fork(2)` and `execve(2)` are discussed in Chapter 19.

Note

The command-line options for the `ps(1)` command differ for different UNIX platforms. The examples presented in this chapter assume FreeBSD release 3.4.

Writing to Pipes

When a pipe is being written to by the current process, another process at the other end of the pipe is reading that data from its standard input. To illustrate that procedure, look at the example program provided in Listing 18.2.

LISTING 18.2   `pmail.c`—A Program That Writes to a `popen(3)` Pipe

```
 1:    /* pmail.c */
 2:
 3:    #include <stdio.h>
 4:    #include <stdlib.h>
 5:    #include <unistd.h>
 6:    #include <pwd.h>
 7:    #include <sys/types.h>
 8:
 9:    int
10:    main(int argc,char **argv) {
11:        struct passwd *pw = 0;        /* Password info */
12:        char cmd[256];                /* Command buffer */
13:        FILE *p = 0;                  /* mailx pipe */
14:
15:        /*
16:         * Lookup our userid:
17:         */
18:        if ( !(pw = getpwuid(geteuid())) ) {
19:            perror("getpwuid()");
20:            return 13;
21:        }
22:
23:        /*
24:         * Format command :
25:         */
26:        sprintf(cmd,"mail -s 'A message from process ID %ld' %s",
27:            (long)getpid(),          /* Process ID */
28:            pw->pw_name);            /* User name */
29:
30:        /*
31:         * Open a pipe to mailx:
32:         */
33:        if ( !(p = popen(cmd,"w")) ) {
34:            perror("popen(3)");
35:            return 13;
36:        }
37:
38:        /*
39:         * Now write our message:
40:         */
41:        fprintf(p,"This is command %s speaking.\n",argv[0]);
42:        fprintf(p,"I am operating in the account for %s\n",pw->pw_gecos);
43:
44:        if ( getuid() != 0 ) {
45:            fprintf(p,"I'd like to operate in root instead.\n");
46:            fprintf(p,"I could do more damage there. :)\n\n");
47:        } else {
48:            fprintf(p,"I'd like to operate in a non-root ID instead.\n");
49:            fprintf(p,"I would be safer there.\n");
50:        }
51:
```

```
52:        fprintf(p,"Sincerely,\n  Process ID %ld\n",(long)getpid());
53:
54:        if ( pclose(p) == -1 ) {
55:            perror("pclose(3)");
56:            return 13;
57:        }
58:
59:        printf("Message sent to %s\n",pw->pw_name);
60:        return 0;
61:    }
```

This program looks up your user ID in lines 18–21. Then it forms a command to start an email to your current account in lines 26–28. A write pipe is created by calling **popen(3)** in line 33. The message text lines are written to lines 41–52. The message text is completed by sending end-of-file to the **mail(1)** command by calling **pclose(3)** in line 54.

Compiling and running this command under FreeBSD yields the following result:

```
$ make pmail
cc -c  -Wall pmail.c
cc -o pmail pmail.o
$ ./pmail
Message sent to ehg
$
```

Checking the mailbox yields results similar to this:

```
$ mail
Mail version 8.1 6/6/93.  Type ? for help.
"/var/mail/ehg": 1 message 1 new
>N  1 ehg       Mon Jun 19 23:20  20/588  "A message from process ID 7943"
& 1
Message 1:
From ehg Mon Jun 19 23:20:24 2000
Date: Mon, 19 Jun 2000 23:20:24 -0400 (EDT)
From: "Earl Grey" <ehg>
To: ehg
Subject: A message from process ID 7943

This is command ./pmail speaking.
I am operating in the account for Earl Grey
I'd like to operate in root instead.
I could do more damage there. :)

Sincerely,
  Process ID 7943

& d 1
& q
$
```

This demonstrated how your C program could write data to another external process through a pipe.

Closing a Pipe

After a pipe is opened for reading or writing, the pipe must be closed by a call to `pclose(3)`. This allows a number of important concluding operations to take place:

- The `wait(2)` function (or equivalent) must be called to pause the execution of the current process until the child process terminates.

- Obtain success or failure information from `wait(2)` about the child process that has terminated.

- Destroy the `FILE` control block.

The `wait(2)` call is necessary to obtain termination status about the child process. This is fully discussed in the next chapter.

Because `popen(3)` returns a pointer to `FILE`, there is a strong urge by programmers to close the open pipe with a call to `fclose(3)`. However, close `popen(3)` pipes with `pclose(3)` only. On some platforms, using `fclose(3)` on a `popen(3)` `FILE` stream will cause the program to abort.

Warning

Always use function `pclose(3)` to close a pipe opened with `popen(3)`. Failure to obey this rule will result in undetected process errors, possible memory leaks and, on some UNIX platforms, aborts.

Furthermore, this practice can result in zombie processes while your program continues to run. For more about zombie processes, see Chapter 19.

Handling a Broken Pipe

When a program has opened a pipe to another process for writing, and that other process has aborted, the read end of the pipe becomes closed. At that point, the pipe is half closed and there is no hope for it to be emptied of data—there is no process reading from it. This causes the UNIX kernel to raise the signal `SIGPIPE` in the process that is attempting to write to the pipe. This indicates to the writer that the pipe is *broken*.

The signal `SIGPIPE` is not always desirable for this purpose. You can elect to ignore the signal `SIGPIPE` and simply allow the `write(2)` function to return an error when this condition arises (error code `EPIPE`).

For example, you could alter Listing 18.2 as follows:

```
1:    /* pmail.c */
2:
3:    #include <stdio.h>
4:    #include <stdlib.h>
5:    #include <unistd.h>
6:    #include <pwd.h>
```

```
 7:    #include <sys/types.h>
 8:
 9:    int
10:    main(int argc,char **argv) {
11:        struct passwd *pw = 0;      /* Password info */
12:        char cmd[256];              /* Command buffer */
13:        FILE *p = 0;                /* mailx pipe */
14:
15:        signal(SIGPIPE,SIG_IGN);    /* Ignore SIGPIPE */
```

Line 15 adds a call to `signal(3)` that requests the action `SIG_IGN` for signal `SIGPIPE`. The
default action for signal `SIGPIPE` is to terminate the process. Consequently, you must be prepared for this signal in programs that work with pipes.

Note

EPIPE—Broken pipe   This error indicates that the calling process is not able to perform a
`write(2)` (or equivalent) operation on a file descriptor because it is writing to a pipe with no reading
processes.

External Processes Without Pipes

The previous section demonstrated an easy method to create a pipe to an external process and
either read its output or feed it input. It often happens, however, that C programs need only to
invoke another process, without using a pipe. The standard C library provides the `system(3)`
function for this purpose.

```
#include <stdlib.h>

int system(const char *command);
```

In general, there are two ways to use the `system(3)` function: with a null argument or with a
non-null `command` string argument.

Almost all systems document the fact that when `system(3)` is called with a null `command`
pointer, the function call checks on the availability of the shell that would normally be used to
carry out the command (`system(3)` for HPUX-11 does not mention this feature). The shell is
considered available if it exists and is executable. If the shell is available, `system(3)` returns
non-zero to indicate true. Otherwise, `0` indicates that no shell is available.

When the argument `command` is not a null pointer, it is expected to point to a null terminated
C string containing a shell command to be executed as a child process. The function
`system(3)` does not return until the indicated command has completed. The return status for
this type of `system(3)` call is somewhat complicated, and is explained in full in Table 18.1
later in the chapter.

The shell program that is checked or invoked by the system(3) call varies somewhat with the UNIX platform. The following gives a partial list:

FreeBSD release 3.4	/bin/sh
SGI IRIX 6.5	/sbin/sh
HPUX-11	/usr/bin/sh
UnixWare 7	$SHELL or /bin/sh
Solaris 8 (native)	/usr/bin/sh
Solaris 8 (standard)	/usr/bin/ksh
IBM AIX 4.3	/usr/bin/sh
IBM AIX 4.3 (trusted)	/usr/bin/tsh
Linux	/bin/sh

The actual shell used on some platforms depends upon certain conditions. UnixWare 7 looks for the existence of the environment variable SHELL and uses that pathname for the shell. Otherwise it falls back to the default of /bin/sh. The choice for Solaris 8 depends upon whether it was compiled and linked to a particular standard. IBM's AIX 4.3 has a Trusted Computing Base for certain file system objects. If this feature is installed and enabled, the trusted shell /usr/bin/tsh can be invoked under some circumstances. Linux normally has /bin/sh linked to the GNU bash(1) shell.

Note

On some platforms, the signals SIGINT and SIGQUIT are ignored for the duration of the system(3) call. Furthermore, the signal SIGCHLD may be blocked until system(3) returns. IBM AIX 4.3 and HPUX-11 document this behavior.

Warning

Calling system(3) from a set-user-ID program is dangerous. The system(3) function uses fork(2) and exec(2) to invoke the new shell, and consequently it is possible for a security leak to occur (the current effective user and group ID values are saved by exec(2)). The shell and the commands invoked are subject to environment variable settings such as PATH and SHELL.

Review Table 12.2 in Chapter 12, "User ID, Password, and Group Management," if you are unclear how the current effective user and group ID values are affected by the exec(2) family of functions.

Interpreting `system(3)` Return Values

The return value for `system(3)` is complex when the `command` string is not null. It requires care to arrive at the correct conclusion. Table 18.1 contains a summary of the return values from `system(3)` when the `command` argument is not null. The `errno` value must be cleared to zero before calling `system(3)` to use this table. This permits the distinction between a failure to start the command and a command returning an exit code of 127.

TABLE 18.1   The `system(3)` Function Return Values

Return Value	Check `errno`	Description
0	No	The function call was successful launching the command and `command` exited with a 0 exit status.
-1	Yes	An error has occurred. Check the value of `errno` to determine the reason for failure.
127	Maybe	If `errno` was cleared to 0 prior to calling `system(3)` and it is not 0 after the call, then an error has occurred while starting the new process. Check `errno` for the reason that the process could not be started. Otherwise, if `errno` has remained 0, then `command` executed and has returned exit code 127.
1-126	No	These are return codes from `command` that has executed.
128-255	No	These are return codes from `command` that has executed.

Invoking Commands

To illustrate the `system(3)` function and its complex return values, a program has been provided in Listing 18.3.

LISTING 18.3   `smail.c`—Example Program Using the `system(3)` Function

```
1:   /* smail.c */
2:
3:   #include <stdio.h>
4:   #include <stdlib.h>
5:   #include <unistd.h>
6:   #include <errno.h>
7:   #include <string.h>
8:   #include <pwd.h>
9:   #include <sys/types.h>
10:
11:  int
```

continued from previous page

```
12:   main(int argc,char **argv) {
13:       struct passwd *pw = 0;        /* Password info */
14:       char cmd[256];                /* Command buffer */
15:       int rc;                       /* Command return code */
16:
17:       /*
18:        * Lookup our userid:
19:        */
20:       if ( !(pw = getpwuid(geteuid())) ) {
21:           fprintf(stderr,"%s: unknown userid\n",strerror(errno));
22:           return 13;
23:       }
24:
25:       /*
26:        * Format command :
27:        */
28:       sprintf(cmd,"ps -l|mail -s 'PID %ld' %s",
29:           (long) getpid(),     /* Process ID */
30:           pw->pw_name);        /* User name */
31:
32:       /*
33:        * Run the command :
34:        */
35:       errno = 0;               /* Clear errno */
36:       rc = system(cmd);        /* Execute the command */
37:
38:       if ( rc == 127 && errno != 0 ) {
39:           /* Command failed to start */
40:           fprintf(stderr,"%s: starting system(%s)\n",
41:               strerror(errno),cmd);
42:       } else if ( rc == -1 ) {
43:           /* Other errors occurred */
44:           fprintf(stderr,"%s: system(%s)\n",
45:               strerror(errno),cmd);
46:       } else {
47:           printf("Command '%s'\n  returned code %d\n",cmd,rc);
48:           puts("Check your mail.");
49:       }
50:
51:       return 0;
52:   }
```

The `smail.c` program looks up your effective user ID in lines 20–23. Then a command is formatted into character array `cmd[]` to list your current processes and email it to you (lines 28–30). The actual process list and mailing occurs in lines 35 and 36, where `cmd` is carried out. Lines 38–49 show how to make sense of the return code from `system(3)`.

When the program in Listing 18.3 is compiled and executed under FreeBSD, the following results are obtained:

```
$ make smail
cc -c  -Wall smail.c
cc -o smail smail.o
$ ./smail
```

```
Command 'ps -l|mail -s 'PID 10424' ehg'
  returned code 0
Check your mail.
$
```

At this point, the program is telling you that mail has been sent. Now check your mail with the mail(1) command (the output lines from ps(1) have been shortened for readability):

```
$ mail
Mail version 8.1 6/6/93.  Type ? for help.
"/var/mail/ehg": 1 message 1 new
>N  1 ehg    Wed Jun 21 21:56  20/931    "PID 10424"
& 1
Message 1:
From ehg Wed Jun 21 21:56:26 2000
Date: Wed, 21 Jun 2000 21:56:26 -0400 (EDT)
From: "Earl H. Grey" <ehg>
To: ehg
Subject: PID 10424

  UID   PID  PPID CPU PRI NI  TIME     COMMAND
 1001 10200     1   0  10  0  0:00.05 -sh (sh)
 1001 10203 10202   0  10  0  0:00.20 -sh (sh)
 1001 10424 10203   1  10  0  0:00.01 ./smail
 1001 10425 10424   2  10  0  0:00.01 sh -c ps -l|mail -s 'PID 10424'
 1001 10426 10425   1  28  0  0:00.00 ps -l
 1001 10427 10425   2  28  0  0:00.00 sh -c ps -l|mail -s 'PID 10424'

& d 1
& q
$
```

Your message content may vary somewhat from the message shown here. The timing is always such that it appears that two processes are executing the command sh -c ps -l|mail -s 'PID 10424'. In fact, what you see here is a snapshot of how things appear after fork(2) has created a new process, but before it has been able to perform an exec(2) call. The following explains what you see in the message:

- Process 10424 is the initial ./smail program that was started.

- Process 10425 is the shell process that has been started because of the system(3) call. This shell process must execute the command ps -l|mail -s ehg.

- Process 10426 is the ps(1) command that has been started by the shell (note its parent process ID is 10425).

- Process 10427 was to be the mail(1) command. However, it shows the command line of the shell because the shell had not yet carried out the call to exec(2) before the ps(1) command took a snapshot. Had the exec(2) call taken place, you would have seen the command mail -s 'PID 10424' ehg instead.

If you are unfamiliar with fork(2) and exec(2) this may be difficult to understand. Chapter 19 will cover fork(2) and exec(2) in detail.

Scrutinizing the `system(3)` Function

Although the `system(3)` function is quite easy to use, it has drawbacks. One of them is the complex set of return values when the `command` string is not a null pointer (review Table 18.1).

The `system(3)` call is also considered a security risk, especially for programs that are `setuid(2)` or `setgid(2)`. If this applies to your application, you would be wise to shun the `system(3)` call, and carefully craft `fork(2)` and `exec(2)` calls directly.

Summary

This chapter focused on the creation of other processes with and without pipes. Pipes allow your current process to read or write data to another process. The `system(3)` function also permits your process to start other processes without using a pipe.

The next chapter discusses the system calls that make other processes available. There you will learn what you need to master the use of the `fork(2)` and `exec(2)` family of functions.

CHAPTER 19

FORKED PROCESSES

*I*n the previous chapter, you learned how to create new processes with the help of the popen(3) and system(3) function calls. These functions end up calling upon the system calls fork(2) and exec(2), however. This chapter will enable you to call fork(2) and exec(2) directly from your programs, giving you complete and total control over process creation.

Overview of the UNIX Fork Process

Every process under UNIX is created using the fork(2) system call. UNIX pioneered this concept of creating two nearly identical processes from one original process. The original process is known as the parent process and the new process is the child process. Figure 19.1 shows how three processes are related in this manner.

FIGURE 19.1
The parent-child relationship between processes.

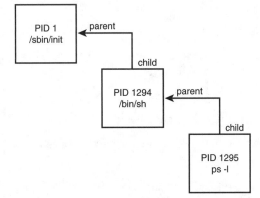

In Figure 19.1, the shell process ID **1294** lost its parent process, because it terminated. All orphaned processes are inherited by the init(8) process, and its process ID is always **1**. Consequently, the shell's parent becomes process ID **1**. When the ps(1) command is typed in at the shell prompt, a fork(2) and a execve(2) are performed, resulting in the process ID **1295** being created as a child process of the shell.

Conceptually, the fork(2) call is like meeting a fork in the road. Initially there is one process executing. Upon successful return from the fork(2) function are two nearly identical processes. The difference is that one has the child process ID returned from `fork(2)`, whereas the child process has the value **0** returned instead.

The two processes share the following characteristics:

- Process group ID
- Current working directory
- Root directory
- `umask(2)` bits
- Real and effective user ID values
- Real and effective group ID values
- Set-user-ID flag and set-group-ID flag
- Session ID
- Controlling terminal, if any
- Signal mask and registered actions
- Close-on-exec flag for open file descriptors
- Environment variables
- Attached shared memory
- Resource limits

The parent and child processes have the following differences, however:

- The return value from `fork(2)` is different. The parent has the child process ID returned. The child process has zero returned.
- The process ID values are different.
- The parent process ID values are different.
- The execution time charged for system and user CPU time starts at zero for the child process (see `getrusage(2)`).
- File locks held by the parent are not inherited by the child process.
- Child processes do not inherit alarms and timers from the parent process (`alarm(2)` and `setitimer(2)`). Pending alarms are cleared.
- Pending signals for the child process are set to the empty set.

The open file descriptors for the child process are duplicated. This is similar to calling `dup(2)` for each open file descriptor and giving the duplicated units to the child process. If the child process performs an `lseek(2)` on an open file unit, it changes the file offset for both the parent and child processes for the same file unit. The same interaction occurs from the parent process on the child's file units.

The operation of the `fork(2)` system call can be summarized as follows:

1. The kernel makes the current process memory space available virtually in the new process. Memory pages that are not read-only are marked for "copy-on-write." Both processes initially share the same physical memory, marked as read-only by the kernel. When one or the other process attempts to alter that page of memory, the kernel copies the page and gives each process its own writable page.

2. Open file descriptors are duplicated and made available as the same file units in the child process.

3. Other shareable resources such as attached shared memory segments are made available to the child process.

4. Other values for the child process are reset (execution time, pending signal set is cleared, and so on).

5. The `fork(2)` function establishes the value it is going to return to each process. The parent process will have the child process ID returned. The child process will have zero returned.

At this point, before `fork(2)` returns, the process that will execute first is not defined. This may be determined by the design of the UNIX scheduler or may be influenced by the number of processors and load on the system.

The `fork(2)` Function

The synopsis for the `fork(2)` system call is as follows:

```
#include <sys/types.h>
#include <unistd.h>

pid_t fork(void);
```

There are no arguments to the `fork(2)` system call. When the call is successful, the parent process receives the process ID of the child process that was created. The child process, however, receives the return value **0** instead. The child process is always able to obtain the parent process ID by calling upon `getppid(2)`.

The caller should always anticipate errors, however. The `fork(2)` call returns the value `(pid_t)(-1)` if the function fails. The value of `errno` will hold the reason for the error. Possible reasons for failure include `EAGAIN` when the system-imposed limit for the number of processes has been exceeded. `ENOMEM` is returned if the system cannot supply its memory needs.

Note

ENOMEM—Insufficient memory   When this error is returned by `fork(2)`, it means that the system is lacking the virtual memory resources (or swap space) required for starting a new process.

Applying fork(2)

The program in Listing 19.1 illustrates a simple example program that creates one child process using the fork(2) system call.

LISTING 19.1   fork.c—An Example Using fork(2) to Create a New Process

```
 1:   /* fork.c */
 2:
 3:   #include <stdio.h>
 4:   #include <unistd.h>
 5:   #include <string.h>
 6:   #include <errno.h>
 7:   #include <sys/types.h>
 8:
 9:   int
10:   main(int argc,char **argv) {
11:       pid_t pid;               /* Process ID of the child process */
12:
13:       pid = fork();            /* Create a new child process */
14:
15:       if ( pid == (pid_t)(-1) ) {
16:           fprintf(stderr,"%s: Failed to fork()\n",strerror(errno));
17:           exit(13);
18:
19:       } else if ( pid == 0 ) {
20:           printf("PID %ld: Child started, parent is %ld.\n",
21:               (long)getpid(),     /* Current child PID */
22:               (long)getppid());   /* Parent PID */
23:
24:       } else {
25:           printf("PID %ld: Started child PID %ld.\n",
26:               (long)getpid(),     /* Current parent PID */
27:               (long)pid);         /* Child's PID */
28:       }
29:
30:       sleep(1);                /* Wait one second */
31:       return 0;
32:   }
```

The program in Listing 19.1 shows fork(2) being invoked at line 13. Upon return from this function, if successful, two processes are executing. The if statement in line 15 tests to see if the function call failed.

Line 19 tests to see if the return value from fork(2) was zero. If so, then lines 20–22 are executed by the child process. The else statement in line 24 indicates that the returned process ID value pid is non-zero, and not -1 (because of line 15). Lines 25–28 are executed by the parent process only.

The remaining lines of code (lines 30 and 31) are executed by both the parent and child processes. The sleep(3) call is included here to allow both the parent and child processes to exist long enough that the other can see them. Otherwise, it is possible for the parent or the child process to execute and terminate before the other process gets to execute, following the fork(2) call.

Compiling and running the example program under FreeBSD looks like this:

```
$ make fork
cc -c -Wall fork.c
cc -o fork fork.o
$ ./fork
PID 1294: Started child PID 1295.
PID 1295: Child started, parent is 1294.
$
```

Based upon the output shown, it would seem that the parent process returned from fork(2) first. While the parent process was in the sleep(3) call, the child process executed and then reported the message PID 1295: Child started, parent is 1294.

Waiting for Process Completion

The example program of Listing 19.1 simply called upon sleep(3) to pause its execution until the other process had time to execute. A better method would be to have the parent process wait until the child process completes.

Other parent programs may continue to execute after starting several different child processes over time. Consequently, these processes need to be able to inquire about the child process's termination at some point.

The UNIX kernel provides the wait(2) family of system calls to allow a process to wait for the completion of a child process. Furthermore, these wait(2) system calls permit the parent process to answer the following questions:

- What was the process exit code?

- Did the process exit normally?

- Was the process killed (signaled)?

- Did the process abort?

- Was a core file written?

The UNIX kernel also needs the parent process to inquire about its child processes. Until the parent process inquires about its child process's termination status, it must keep the status in the process table. Once the parent process obtains this information, the kernel can free the process table entry.

Zombie Processes

Parent processes are responsible for their children. When a child process terminates for any reason, the parent process is expected to inquire about its termination status using one of the wait(2) system calls. If this fails to happen, the child process continues to show in the process table as a *zombie* process.

The UNIX kernel releases memory and closes all files of a terminated process. The one resource that remains is the process table entry for the terminated child process. This table entry is identified by process ID and keeps the termination status until the parent process fetches it. Once the parent process has obtained this status, the UNIX kernel can make both the process ID and the process table entry available for a new process.

The program in Listing 19.2 shows a parent process that creates a zombie process and reports it to standard output with the help of the ps(1) command and the function system(3).

LISTING 19.2   zombie.c—A Program That Creates a Zombie

```
 1:    /* zombie.c */
 2:
 3:    #include <stdio.h>
 4:    #include <unistd.h>
 5:    #include <stdlib.h>
 6:    #include <string.h>
 7:    #include <errno.h>
 8:    #include <sys/types.h>
 9:
10:    int
11:    main(int argc,char **argv) {
12:        pid_t pid;                  /* Process ID of the child process */
13:
14:        pid = fork();               /* Create a new child process */
15:
16:        if ( pid == (pid_t)(-1) ) {
17:            fprintf(stderr,"%s: Failed to fork()\n",strerror(errno));
18:            exit(13);
19:
20:        } else if ( pid == 0 ) {
21:            printf("PID %ld: Child started, parent is %ld.\n",
22:                (long)getpid(),     /* Current child PID */
23:                (long)getppid());   /* Parent PID */
24:            return 0;               /* Child process just exits */
25:
26:        }
27:
28:        /*
29:         * Parent process :
30:         */
31:        printf("PID %ld: Started child PID %ld.\n",
32:            (long)getpid(),         /* Current parent PID */
33:            (long)pid);             /* Child's PID */
34:        sleep(1);                   /* Wait one second */
35:
36:        /*
```

```
37:        * By this time, our child process should have terminated:
38:        */
39:       system("ps -l");        /* List the zombie */
40:
41:       return 0;
42:  }
```

The program in Listing 19.2 differs slightly from the former listing in that the child process exits immediately with the **return** statement in line 24. Only the parent process executes lines 28–42.

The parent process waits for one second in line 34 by calling **sleep(3)**. This gives ample time for the child process to start and terminate. Because the parent process never calls on **wait(2)**, the call to **system(3)** in line 39 causes the **ps(1)** command to list the zombie process.

The following shows a compile and run session under FreeBSD:

```
$ make zombie
cc -c -D_ -Wall zombie.c
cc -o zombie zombie.o
$ ./zombie
PID 1367: Started child PID 1368.
PID 1368: Child started, parent is 1367.
  UID   PID PPID CPU PRI NI   VSZ  RSS WCHAN STAT TT TIME    COMMAND
 1001  1231    1   0  10  0   596  344 wait  Is   p0 0:00.07 -sh (sh)
 1001  1234 1233   0  10  0   596  344 wait  Ss   p1 0:00.17 -sh (sh)
 1001  1367 1234   0  10  0   824  404 wait  S+   p1 0:00.01 ./zombie
 1001  1368 1367   1  28  0     0    0 -     Z+   p1 0:00.00 (zombie)
 1001  1369 1367   1  10  0   496  332 wait  S+   p1 0:00.00 sh -c ps -l
 1001  1370 1369   1  28  0   380  244 -     R+   p1 0:00.00 ps -l
$
```

The output shows the program **./zombie** as process ID **1367**. The process **1368** is the child process that was created from the call to **fork(2)** in line 14. The output provided by the **ps(1)** command (processes **1369** and **1370**) shows that the child process **1368** is a zombie (note the "**(zombie)**" shown at the right).

The **wait(2)** Function

The **wait(2)** function suspends the calling process until a child process has terminated or a signal has been received. The function synopsis is as follows:

```
#include <sys/types.h>
#include <sys/wait.h>

pid_t wait(int *status);
```

The argument **status** must be a pointer to an **int** status variable, which will receive the child termination status. The return value from **wait(2)** is the process ID that matches the returned termination status. Otherwise, the value **(pid_t)(-1)** is returned and the error is posted to the variable **errno**. Errors include the error code **EINTR** when a signal has been received.

The program in Listing 19.3 shows a modified version of the previous example. In this example, the sleep(3) call is replaced by the wait(2) system call.

LISTING 19.3   wait.c—Example Program Calling wait(2) Without Zombie Processes

```
 1:  /* wait.c */
 2:
 3:  #include <stdio.h>
 4:  #include <unistd.h>
 5:  #include <stdlib.h>
 6:  #include <string.h>
 7:  #include <errno.h>
 8:  #include <sys/types.h>
 9:  #include <sys/wait.h>
10:
11:  int
12:  main(int argc,char **argv) {
13:      pid_t pid;              /* Process ID of the child process */
14:      pid_t wpid;             /* Process ID from wait(2) */
15:      int status;            /* Status code from wait(2) */
16:
17:      pid = fork();          /* Create a new child process */
18:
19:      if ( pid == (pid_t)(-1) ) {
20:          fprintf(stderr,"%s: Failed to fork()\n",strerror(errno));
21:          exit(13);
22:
23:      } else if ( pid == 0 ) {
24:          printf("PID %ld: Child started, parent is %ld.\n",
25:              (long)getpid(),      /* Current child PID */
26:              (long)getppid());    /* Parent PID */
27:          return 0;              /* Child process just exits */
28:
29:      }
30:
31:      /*
32:       * Parent process :
33:       */
34:      printf("PID %ld: Started child PID %ld.\n",
35:          (long)getpid(),      /* Current parent PID */
36:          (long)pid);          /* Child's PID */
37:
38:      /*
39:       * Wait for the child process to exit, and obtain
40:       * its termination status :
41:       */
42:      wpid = wait(&status);    /* Wait for child process to exit */
43:      if ( wpid == (pid_t)(-1) )
```

```
44:            perror("wait(2)");   /* Report wait(2) error */
45:
46:      /*
47:       * There should be no trace of the child process in
48:       * this particular display :
49:       */
50:      system("ps -l");           /* List the processes */
51:
52:      return 0;
53:  }
```

The variables **wpid** and **status** are declared in lines 14 and 15. These are used in the call to wait(2) in lines 42–44. The wait(2) call causes the parent process to suspend its execution until the child process terminates. By the time that the **ps(1)** command is executed in line 50, there should be no trace of the terminated child process.

The compile and run session under FreeBSD provides the following results:

```
$ make wait
cc -c -Wall wait.c
cc -o wait wait.o
$ ./wait
PID 1463: Started child PID 1464.
PID 1464: Child started, parent is 1463.
  UID   PID  PPID CPU PRI NI   VSZ  RSS WCHAN  STAT  TT  TIME      COMMAND
 1001  1231     1   0  10  0   596  344 wait   Is    p0  0:00.07 -sh (sh)
 1001  1234  1233   3  10  0   600  348 wait   Ss    p1  0:00.24 -sh (sh)
 1001  1463  1234   8  10  0   824  404 wait   S+    p1  0:00.01 ./wait
 1001  1465  1463   8  10  0   496  332 wait   S+    p1  0:00.00 sh -c ps -l
 1001  1466  1465   9  29  0   376  244 -      R+    p1  0:00.00 ps -l
$
```

In this session, notice that the child process is reported to be **1464** by the parent process (**1463**). However, looking at the **ps(1)** output, you will not see any child process **1464** listed. This happens because the parent process has received the termination status of its child process by calling wait(2). The system call wait(2) causes the process table entry to be freed by the UNIX kernel, and so no zombie process remains.

Interpreting the Exit Status

The status returned by wait(2) has more in it than a program exit code. It records whether the program exited normally, was aborted, was killed (signaled), or stopped. The programmer is expected to use macros to test for these differences in status, since this is the only portable way to write code using this status information. Table 19.1 identifies macros that can be used by the programmer.

TABLE 19.1   Table of Status Test Macros

Macro	Description
WIFEXITED(status)	This macro returns true if the status indicates that the process exited normally. An exit code for this process is available using macro WEXITSTATUS(status), which returns an 8-bit exit code.
WIFSIGNALED(status)	This macro returns true if the status indicates that the process received a signal that it did not catch, and caused its termination. The macro WTERMSIG(status) is available to extract the signal number from status that caused the termination. The macro WCOREDUMP(status) is available, which indicates true if a core file was created.
WIFSTOPPED(status)	This macro returns true if the status indicates that the process is currently stopped. The macro WSTOPSIG(status) is available to extract the signal number of the signal that caused the child process to stop.

The following example shows how to test for a normal program exit and display its exit code:

```
int status;                    /* Status from wait(2) */

if ( WIFEXITED(status) ) {
    printf("Exited with return code %d;\n",
        (int)WEXITSTATUS(status));
}
```

The example tests for a normal exit with the WIFEXITED() macro. When this returns true, the value returned by WEXITSTATUS() provides the exit code from that process. This is the exit code that the shell reports with its built-in variable $?.

To test if the process aborted, or was signaled, you could use the following tests:

```
int status;                    /* Status from wait(2) */

if ( WIFSIGNALED(status) ) {
    printf("Terminated with signal %d;\n",
        (int)WTERMSIG(status));
    if ( WCOREDUMP(status) )
        printf("A core file was written.\n");
}
```

This example tests if the process was signaled with the macro WIFSIGNALED(). If this tests true, then the macros WTERMSIG() and WCOREDUMP() have meaning, and WTERMSIG() is used to extract the signal number. The WCOREDUMP() indicates that a core file was written when it tests true.

Other Wait System Calls

Other members of the wait(2) family provide additional features. These additional members are shown in the following synopsis:

```
#include <sys/types.h>
#include <sys/wait.h>

pid_t waitpid(pid_t wpid, int *status, int options);

#include <sys/time.h>
#include <sys/resource.h>

pid_t wait3(int *status, int options, struct rusage *rusage);

pid_t wait4(pid_t wpid, int *status, int options, struct rusage *rusage);
```

The function waitpid(2) is the POSIX extension of wait(2) that has the capability to return with no data, if there is no data to report. Contrast this to the wait(2) system call that always blocks execution of the calling process until there is information to report. The waitpid(2) system call can also wait on a specific child process ID. This is sometimes useful when the parent process has more than one child process outstanding.

Note

The functions wait(2) and waitpid(2) are supported by all modern UNIX platforms. However, Solaris 8 does not support the BSD functions wait3(2) and wait4(2).

The wait3(2) system call is supported by IBM AIX 4.3, SGI IRIX 6.5, HPUX 11, and UnixWare 7.

Linux and BSD support the functions wait(2), waitpid(2), wait3(2), and wait4(2).

The wait3(2) and wait4(2) system calls permit the resource utilization of the child process to be returned in addition to the status. The wait3(2) call permits options to be specified like the waitpid(2) call. The wait4(2) system call is the most flexible within the family, because it includes the ability to wait for a specific child process in addition to the features supported by the other calls.

The options argument supports the following bitwise macros:

WNOHANG	Return immediately if nothing to report
WUNTRACED	Report child processes signaled with SIGTTIN, SIGTTOU, SIGTSTP, or SIGSTOP

The WNOHANG option is used with waitpid(2), wait3(2), or wait4(2) when execution must not be suspended. This permits the parent process to query the status of a child process without giving up control. The option WUNTRACED is used for shell job control, and is beyond the scope of this text.

The calls waitpid(2) and wait4(2) allow the caller to indicate a specific child process ID in the argument wpid. Specifying a value of -1 for wpid causes these system calls to wait for any child process, as the wait(2) and wait3(2) calls would have done.

All system calls in the wait(2) family return the process ID of the return information when the call is successful. The value (pid_t)(-1) is returned when an error is reported, with the error code posted to errno. When the option argument includes the WNOHANG bit, a return value of (pid_t)(0) indicates that no information is available.

An error return is possible with the error code ECHILD if a wait(2) family system call is made and there are no outstanding child processes to be reported upon. This happens, for example, if the current process has not started any child processes. This differs from the (pid_t)(0) return value (used with the WNOHANG option), which indicates at least one child process is executing.

Note

ECHILD—No child processes   This value is returned from wait(2), waitpid(2), wait3(2), or wait4(2) when there are no child processes running for the calling parent process.

ECHILD is also reported when the argument wpid does not represent a child process of the calling process.

The resource utilization structure varies according to UNIX platform. FreeBSD defines it as illustrated in the following synopsis:

```
struct  rusage {                        /* FreeBSD 3.4 release */
    struct timeval ru_utime;     /* user time used */
    struct timeval ru_stime;     /* system time used */
    long           ru_maxrss;    /* max resident set size */
    long           ru_ixrss;     /* integral shared memory size */
    long           ru_idrss;     /* integral unshared data " */
    long           ru_isrss;     /* integral unshared stack " */
    long           ru_minflt;    /* page reclaims */
    long           ru_majflt;    /* page faults */
    long           ru_nswap;     /* swaps */
    long           ru_inblock;   /* block input operations */
    long           ru_oublock;   /* block output operations */
    long           ru_msgsnd;    /* messages sent */
    long           ru_msgrcv;    /* messages received */
    long           ru_nsignals;  /* signals received */
    long           ru_nvcsw;     /* voluntary context switches */
    long           ru_nivcsw;    /* involuntary " */
};
```

The common resource values supported on UNIX platforms that support wait3(2) or wait4(2) are members ru_utime and ru_stime. These represent the user and system CPU time, respectively. Other members of this structure are likely to be platform specific.

Executing New Programs

While the fork(2) system call starts a clone of the current process, the programmer is still left needing a way to start a new executable program. The exec(2) family of functions fills this need.

When a new program is executed, the following general steps are performed:

1. The kernel opens the new executable file for reading (and checks that the executable bit is set). An error is immediately returned to the caller if this fails.

2. The same process ID and addressable memory is retained, while the current execution becomes suspended.

3. The new program instructions are loaded from the executable file that has been opened by the kernel.

4. Certain process flags and registers are reset (for example the stack pointer is reset).

5. The execution of the new process begins.

The overall effect of an exec(2) call is to replace the currently executing process with a new program, within the same process memory. When the exec(2) system call is successful, it never returns control to the calling process.

There are a number of functions that provide the ability to start a new program within the exec(2) family, but the execve(2) function will be described first:

```
#include <unistd.h>

int execve(const char *pathname, char *const argv[], char *const envp[]);
```

This function takes three arguments:

- The pathname of the executable program or interpreter script.

- The argv[] array to be passed to the main() program.

- The envp[] array of environment variables to export.

When the function execve(2) is successful, it does not return (your current program is replaced). If the call fails, the returned value is -1 and the value of errno will contain the error code.

The pathname argument must represent an ordinary file that has execute permission bits for the current effective user or group. The pathname argument may be an executable file image or it may be a file that is read by an interpreter (that is, a script file). Interpreted files may start with the following initial content:

```
#! interpreter [arg]
```

The space between the ! character and the interpreter pathname is optional. The pathname interpreter, however, must be the pathname of an existing regular file that can be loaded as the interpreter for the script file. The script file must have read permissions for the current effective user or group ID.

The [arg] represents an optional argument. This argument becomes the command name (argv[0] value) of the interpreter when it runs. When this argument is absent, the argv[0] value is derived from the interpreter pathname instead.

On some UNIX systems, this initial script line is limited in length. Under Linux, for example, the initial line is only inspected for a maximum of 32 characters. Anything beyond this limit is ignored.

The arguments argv[] and envp[] are arrays containing character string pointers. The end of each array is marked by an array element containing a null pointer. The argv[] array specifies the command name in argv[0] and any command-line arguments starting with argv[1]. Note that for scripts (for interpreted files), argv[0] will be ignored since this information comes from the initial text line of the executable file.

The array envp[] lists all of the environment variables that you want to export to the new program. The strings must all be in the form

```
VARIABLE=VALUE
```

For example, you might use the following:

```
PATH=/bin:/usr/bin
```

Programmers often simply pass the current environment to the new process. This can easily be done by using the pointer environ:

```
extern char **environ;
```

When the external variable environ is declared as shown, you can simply pass environ in place of the envp[] array.

To illustrate the use of the execve(2) call, Listing 19.4 shows a program that starts the ps(1) command without any assistance from the shell. In a limited sense, this program performs the same steps that a shell would use.

LISTING 19.4   exec.c—Example Using exec(2) to Start the ps(1) Command

```
 1:   /* exec.c */
 2:
 3:   #include <stdio.h>
 4:   #include <unistd.h>
 5:   #include <string.h>
 6:   #include <errno.h>
 7:   #include <sys/types.h>
 8:   #include <sys/wait.h>
 9:
10:   /*
11:    * If the ps(1) command is not located at /bin/ps on your system,
12:    * then change the pathname defined for PS_PATH below.
13:    */
14:   #define PS_PATH "/bin/ps"        /* PS(1) */
15:
```

```
16:    extern char **environ;          /* Our environment */
17:
18:    /*
19:     * EXEC(2) the PS(1) Command :
20:     */
21:    static void
22:    exec_ps_cmd(void) {
23:        static char *argv[] = { "ps", "-l", NULL };
24:
25:        /*
26:         * Exec the ps command: ps f
27:         */
28:        execve(PS_PATH,argv,environ);
29:
30:        /*
31:         * If control reaches here, then the execve(2)
32:         * call has failed!
33:         */
34:        fprintf(stderr,"%s: execve(2)\n",strerror(errno));
35:    }
36:
37:    /*
38:     * Main program :
39:     */
40:    int
41:    main(int argc,char **argv) {
42:        pid_t pid;              /* Process ID of the child process */
43:        pid_t wpid;             /* Process ID from wait() */
44:        int status;            /* Exit status from wait() */
45:
46:        /*
47:         * First create a new child process :
48:         */
49:        pid = fork();
50:
51:        if ( pid == -1 ) {
52:            /*
53:             * Fork failed to create a process :
54:             */
55:            fprintf(stderr,"%s: Failed to fork()\n",strerror(errno));
56:            exit(13);
57:
58:        } else if ( pid == 0 ) {
59:            /*
60:             * This is the child process running :
61:             */
62:            exec_ps_cmd();              /* Start the ps command */
63:
64:        }
65:
66:        /*
67:         * This is the parent process running :
68:         */
```

continued from previous page

```
69:          printf("PID %ld: Started child PID %ld.\n",
70:              (long)getpid(),     /* Our PID */
71:              (long)pid);         /* Child's PID */
72:
73:      /*
74:       * Wait for the child process to terminate :
75:       */
76:      wpid = wait(&status);    /* Child's exit status */
77:      if ( wpid == -1 ) {
78:          /*
79:           * The wait() call failed :
80:           */
81:          fprintf(stderr,"%s: wait(2)\n",strerror(errno));
82:          return 1;
83:
84:      } else if ( wpid != pid ) {
85:          /* Should never happen in this program: */
86:          abort();
87:      }
88:
89:      /*
90:       * The child process has terminated:
91:       */
92:      if ( WIFEXITED(status) ) {
93:          /*
94:           * Normal exit -- print status
95:           */
96:          printf("Exited: $? = %d\n",WEXITSTATUS(status));
97:
98:      } else if ( WIFSIGNALED(status) ) {
99:          /*
100:          * Process abort, kill or signal:
101:          */
102:          printf("Signal: %d%s\n",
103:              WTERMSIG(status),
104:              WCOREDUMP(status) ? " with core file." : "");
105:
106:      } else {
107:          /*
108:           * Stopped child process :
109:           */
110:          puts("Stopped child process.");
111:      }
112:
113:      return 0;
114: }
```

Listing 19.4 starts by calling upon fork(2) to create a child process. The parent process reports the process ID values in lines 69–71 and then calls wait(2) to suspend its execution until the child process terminates in line 76.

While the parent process is waiting for the child process to terminate, the child process executes line 62, which causes the function exec_ps_cmd() to be called. This is declared in lines 21–35. The argv[] array is declared in line 23, where it supplies one command-line argument, -1. This will cause the command ps -1 to be executed. The function execve(2) is called in line 28. If the function call is successful, line 34 is never executed.

The following shows a compile and run session under FreeBSD for this program:

```
$ make exec
cc -c   -Wall exec.c
cc -o exec exec.o
$ ./exec
PID 1744: Started child PID 1745.
  UID   PID  PPID CPU PRI NI  VSZ  RSS WCHAN  STAT  TT  TIME     COMMAND
 1001  1231     1   0  10  0  596  344 wait   Is    p0  0:00.07 -sh (sh)
 1001  1234  1233   0  10  0  600  348 wait   Ss    p1  0:00.43 -sh (sh)
 1001  1744  1234   1  10  0  824  396 wait   S+    p1  0:00.01 ./exec
 1001  1745  1744   2  28  0  376  244 -      R+    p1  0:00.00 ps -1
Exited: $? = 0
$
```

The parent process starts by reporting its process ID as **1744** and its child process as **1745**. Then the remaining lines displayed are the result of the ps(1) command being executed successfully. This display shows the parent process as ./exec and the ps(1) command as ps -1. The last line reported shows that the ps(1) command exited normally with a return code of 0.

Other exec(2) Family Members

There are a number of other exec(2) family member functions that act as front-end functions to the execve(2) function. Their synopsis follows:

```
#include <unistd.h>

int execl(const char *path, const char *arg, ...);

int execlp(const char *file, const char *arg, ...);

int execle(const char *path, const char *arg, ...);

int exect(const char *path, char *const argv[], char *const envp[]);

int execv(const char *path, char *const argv[]);

int execvp(const char *file, char *const argv[]);
```

The functions that accept an argument named path indicate the specific regular file to be executed by this argument as a pathname. The functions that define an argument named file (execlp(3) and execvp(3)) will search the PATH variable for the file in the same way that the shell searches for a command. If there is no environment variable PATH defined, the value /bin:/usr/bin is used by default.

The functions `execl(2)`, `execlp(2)`, and `execle(2)` allow the programmer to specify `argv[]` values as individual arguments instead of using an array. The last argument in the argument list must be a null pointer, however. For example, Listing 19.4 could have used

```
execlp("ps","ps","-l",NULL);
```

in place of calling `execve(2)`. Note, however, the `argv[0]` is specified first, and in this example repeats the filename `"ps"`.

The `execle(3)` function needs special attention because it requires an array of environment variables as the last argument. The following is an example `execle(3)` function call:

```
extern char **environ;

execle("/bin/ps","ps","-l",NULL,environ);
```

Notice that the array of environment variables follows the `NULL` argument, which marks the end of the command line.

Warning

Forgetting to specify the null pointer after the last command argument to `execl(3)`, `execlp(3)`, or `execle(3)` is a common cause of program aborts during program development.

Note also that `execle(3)` requires an array of environment variables as the very last argument.

The `exect(2)` system call executes a program with program tracing facilities enabled. See `ptrace(2)` for more information about this facility. The functions `execv(2)` and `execvp(2)` use the current environment settings when starting the new program.

Figure 19.2 provides a feature grid of the various function calls.

FIGURE 19.2
A feature grid for the various `exec()` function calls.

	Pathname	Search file in $PATH	Arguments...	Argument array	Environment array	Environment from extern char **environ	Trace Facilities
execve(2)	X			X	X		
execl(3)	X		X			X	
execlp(3)		X	X			X	
execle(3)	X		X		X		
exect(3)	X			X	X		X
execv(3)	X			X		X	
execvp(3)		X	X			X	

Summary

This chapter discussed how the `fork(2)` function is able to create new UNIX processes. The `wait(2)` family of functions permits you to find out how your child processes terminate. Finally, the `exec(2)` family of functions provides you with the ability to start a new executable program or interpreted script.

In addition to starting new commands, a shell process must usually perform wildcard expansion for filenames on the command line. The next chapter will look at the pattern matching facilities that are used by the shell for this purpose.

CHAPTER 20

PATTERN MATCHING

T he UNIX shell must usually expand wildcard filenames for user or shell script commands. Under UNIX, this wildcard expansion is always performed before the command is executed. This simplifies the command, because it sees only the finalized arguments. It also helps to make all commands work consistently, because wildcard expansion is performed in one place only—the shell process.

However, the UNIX environment is a rich environment. If you don't like one shell, you usually can choose from other shell programs. Going a step further, you might choose to write your own. To assist in making these different shell programs behave in the same way for wildcard filenames, two groups of function calls are provided:

- Functions that match string patterns
- Functions that search directories with pattern matching applied

The function `fnmatch(3)` is provided under UNIX for matching strings in a shell-like manner.

Shell Patterns

While most users learn shell pattern matching behavior early in their exposure to UNIX, it is useful to review it here before introducing the functions that implement it.

A shell pattern can consist of normal characters and meta-characters. Normal characters represent themselves, and meta-characters have a special meaning for pattern matching. The set of meta-characters for shell patterns is relatively small. They are

*	Star (asterisk)
?	Question mark
[and]	Square brackets
!	Bang (in [])
-	Hypen (in [])
\	Backslash

Each meta-character is described in the subsections that follow.

The * Meta-Character

The * character can match zero or more characters. The following shell experiment on a FreeBSD system illustrates this meta-character at work:

```
$ cd /etc
$ ls -l hosts.*
-rw-r--r--  1 root  wheel  2278 Dec 20  1999 hosts.allow
-rw-r--r--  1 root  wheel   115 Dec 20  1999 hosts.equiv
-rw-r--r--  1 root  wheel   103 Dec 20  1999 hosts.lpd
$
```

The shell matches all files that begin with `hosts.` and are followed by zero or more characters. Consequently, the filenames `hosts.allow`, `hosts.equiv`, and `hosts.lpd` match on this particular system. The meta-character may be used in any position of the pattern, as the following example illustrates:

```
$ cd /etc
$ ls -l *lpd
-rw-r--r--  1 root  wheel  103 Dec 20  1999 hosts.lpd
$
```

This example matches any filename that is prefixed by zero or more characters and ends in the string `lpd`.

The ? Meta-Character

Unlike the `*`, the `?` meta-character matches only one character. If there is no character in that position, there is no match. The following example shows how the `?` meta-character can be used multiple times to effect a particular pattern match:

```
$ ls -l /etc/hosts.?????
-rw-r--r--  1 root  wheel  2278 Dec 20  1999 /etc/hosts.allow
-rw-r--r--  1 root  wheel   115 Dec 20  1999 /etc/hosts.equiv
$
```

In this example, only the filenames `host.allow` and `hosts.equiv` match. The filename `hosts.lpd` does not match because the last two `??` in the pattern did not have characters to match with.

The [and] Meta-Characters

The `[` and `]` meta-characters work together to specify a class of characters. The following example lists any file that has the letter `x`, `y`, or `z` within it:

```
$ ls -d *[xyz]*
exports          newsyslog.conf  skeykeys          ttys
gettytab         security        syslog.conf
$
```

The `*` meta-characters to the left and right of `[xyz]` permit zero or more characters to exist to the left and right of the middle pattern. However, the middle pattern `[xyz]` insists that a letter `x`, `y`, or `z` exist. In this case, there weren't any filenames with the letter `z` in them.

You can specify ranges of characters, as is shown in the following example:

```
$ ls -d *[x-z]*
exports         newsyslog.conf  skeykeys        ttys
gettytab        security        syslog.conf
$
```

The pattern `[x-z]` is equivalent to specifying the letters individually as `[xyz]`. Multiple ranges can also be specified: `[x-za-c]` allows any of the characters a, b, c, x, y, and z.

If you specify an unmatched pair of `[` and `]` characters, the character is taken literally, as the following example demonstrates:

```
$ >']'
$ ls -l ]
-rw-r-----  1 ehg  wheel  0 Jun 26 14:59 ]
$
```

The first command creates a file named `]` by using quotes. Then the file is listed using `ls(1)`. This same behavior also exists for the closing square bracket:

```
$ >'['
$ ls -l [
-rw-r-----  1 ehg  wheel  0 Jun 26 14:59 [
$
```

The next example shows how `[` and `]` can be used in reverse order to cause them to be interpreted as they appear.

```
$ ls -l ] [
-rw-r-----  1 ehg  wheel  0 Jun 26 14:59 [
-rw-r-----  1 ehg  wheel  0 Jun 26 14:59 ]
$
```

The ! Meta-Character

The `!` meta-character has special meaning only within the `[` and `]` meta-character pair, and only if it occurs as the first character within a range. It is known as the "not" character in this context. For example, compare the difference between the first `ls(1)` command and the second:

```
$ cd /tmp
$ ls *[0-9]
psql.edit.1001.13867    tmp-I53052      tmp-d53036      tmp-s52935
tmp-D52798              tmp-M53211      tmp-f53114      win98
tmp-G52945              tmp-d52925      tmp-o53048
$ ls *[!0-9]
c.t             dummy.file
$
```

The first `ls(1)` command lists only files and directories that end in a numeric digit (range `[0-9]`). The second `ls(1)` command, however, lists only those that do *not* end in a numeric digit (range `[!0-9]`).

In any other position within the range or outside of it, the ! character represents itself and is not special. The following example confirms this:

```
$ >'!'
$ ls -l !
-rw-r-----  1 ehg  wheel  0 Jun 26 15:10 !
$
```

Escaping Characters with \

There are times where meta-characters get in the way. To disable special treatment of meta-characters, you can escape them with the backslash character:

```
$ >'***FILE***'
$ ls
***FILE***              tmp-D52798      tmp-d52925      tmp-s52935
c.t                     tmp-G52945      tmp-d53036      win98
dummy.file              tmp-I53052      tmp-f53114
psql.edit.1001.13867    tmp-M53211      tmp-o53048
$ ls -l \*\*\*FILE\*\*\*
-rw-r-----  1 ehg  wheel  0 Jun 26 15:14 ***FILE***
$
```

The above example shows how a file with the unusual name of ***FILE*** was created. Then the ls(1) command is invoked to confirm its existence. Then another ls(1) command shows how the backslashes can be used to remove the special meaning from the * meta-character.

String Pattern Functions

To simplify program development of shells and other related functions that require this pattern matching capability, the function fnmatch(3) was developed. The function synopsis for it is as follows:

```
#include <fnmatch.h>

int fnmatch(const char *pattern, const char *string, int flags);
```

The argument **pattern** is the input pattern string, which is compared with the input argument **string**. The argument **pattern** contains the meta-characters, if any. The argument **string** is the string that you want to test for a match. The argument **flags** enables and disables certain features of the fnmatch(3) function.

The return value from fnmatch(3) is zero if a match is made. Otherwise, the value FNM_NOMATCH is returned instead.

Note

When the argument **pattern** is the C string "*" and the argument **string** is the null string "", function fnmatch(3) considers this to be a match.

The `flags` argument of the `fnmatch(3)` function accepts the following macros for various bit definitions, which may be ORed together:

FNM_NOESCAPE	Treat \ as a normal character (no quoting is performed).
FNM_PATHNAME	Slashes (/) in string must match slashes in pattern.
FNM_PERIOD	Leading periods (.) in string must only be matched by leading periods in pattern. This is affected by FNM_PATHNAME.
FNM_LEADING_DIR	Match the leading directory pattern, but ignore all text that follows the trailing slash (/) in pattern.
FNM_CASEFOLD	Ignore case distinctions in the pattern and string arguments.

Each of these option flags will be discussed in detail in the sections that follow. To aid in discussing and experimenting with these flags, the program in Listing 20.1 will be used.

LISTING 20.1   `fnmatch.c`—A Program to Exercise the `fnmatch(3)` Function

```
1:   /* fnmatch.c */
2:
3:   #include <stdio.h>
4:   #include <unistd.h>
5:   #include <fnmatch.h>
6:
7:   /*
8:    * Provide command usage instructions :
9:    */
10:  static void
11:  usage(void) {
12:
13:      puts("Usage: fnmatch [options] <pattern> <strings>...");
14:      puts("\nOptions:");
15:      puts("\t-n\tShow non-matches");
16:      puts("\t-e\tFNM_NOESCAPE");
17:      puts("\t-p\tFNM_PATHNAME");
18:      puts("\t-P\tFNM_PERIOD");
19:      puts("\t-d\tFNM_LEADING_DIR");
20:      puts("\t-c\tFNM_CASEFOLD");
21:  }
22:
23:  /*
24:   * Report the flag bits in use as confirmation :
25:   */
26:  static void
27:  report_flags(int flags) {
28:
29:      fputs("Flags:",stdout);
30:      if ( flags & FNM_NOESCAPE )
31:          fputs(" FNM_NOESCAPE",stdout);
```

continued from previous page

```
32:        if ( flags & FNM_PATHNAME )
33:            fputs(" FNM_PATHNAME",stdout);
34:        if ( flags & FNM_PERIOD )
35:            fputs(" FNM_PERIOD",stdout);
36:        if ( flags & FNM_LEADING_DIR )
37:            fputs(" FNM_LEADING_DIR",stdout);
38:        if ( flags & FNM_CASEFOLD )
39:            fputs(" FNM_CASEFOLD",stdout);
40:        if ( !flags )
41:            puts(" NONE");
42:        else
43:            putchar('\n');
44: }
45:
46: /*
47:  * Main program :
48:  */
49: int
50: main(int argc,char **argv) {
51:        int x;                      /* Interator variable */
52:        int z;                      /* General status variable */
53:        int flags = 0;              /* fnmatch(3) flags argument */
54:        int cmdopt_n = 0;           /* When true, report non-matches */
55:        char *pattern;              /* Pattern string for fnmatch(3) */
56:        const char cmdopts[] = "epPdchn"; /* Supported command options */
57:
58:        /*
59:         * Process any command options :
60:         */
61:        while ( (z = getopt(argc,argv,cmdopts)) != -1 )
62:            switch ( z ) {
63:            case 'e' :
64:                flags |= FNM_NOESCAPE;        /* -e */
65:                break;
66:            case 'p' :
67:                flags |= FNM_PATHNAME;        /* -p */
68:                break;
69:            case 'P' :
70:                flags |= FNM_PERIOD;          /* -P */
71:                break;
72:            case 'd' :
73:                flags |= FNM_LEADING_DIR;     /* -d */
74:                break;
75:            case 'c' :
76:                flags |= FNM_CASEFOLD;        /* -c */
77:                break;
78:            case 'n' :
79:                cmdopt_n = 1;                 /* -n ; Show non-matches */
80:                break;
81:            case 'h' :
82:            default :
83:                usage();
84:                return 1;
```

```
 85:          }
 86:
 87:      /*
 88:       * We must have a pattern and at least one trial string :
 89:       */
 90:      if ( optind + 1 >= argc ) {
 91:          usage();
 92:          return 1;
 93:      }
 94:
 95:      /*
 96:       * Pick the pattern string and report the flags that
 97:       * are in effect for this run :
 98:       */
 99:      pattern = argv[optind++];
100:      report_flags(flags);
101:
102:      /*
103:       * Now try pattern against all remaining command
104:       * line arguments :
105:       */
106:      for ( x=optind; x<argc; ++x ) {
107:          z = fnmatch(pattern,argv[x],flags);
108:          /*
109:           * Report matches, or report all, if -n
110:           * option was used :
111:           */
112:          if ( !z || cmdopt_n )
113:              printf("%s: fnmatch('%s','%s',flags)\n",
114:                  !z ? "Matched" : "No match",
115:                  pattern,
116:                  argv[x]);
117:      }
118:
119:      return 0;
120: }
```

The first portion of the main program parses the command line for options (lines 58–93) and prepares for the test run (lines 99 and 100). The `report_flags()` function simply reports the flag option bits in effect as a confirmation.

The interesting code is in lines 106–117 where the function `fnmatch(3)` is called to test each command-line argument. By default, only the matches are reported unless the -n option has been supplied.

The following shows how to compile the program and provoke a usage display with the -h option:

```
$ make fnmatch
cc -c  -Wall fnmatch.c
cc -o fnmatch fnmatch.o
```

```
$ ./fnmatch -h
Usage: fnmatch [options] <pattern> <strings>...

Options:
          -n       Show non-matches
          -e       FNM_NOESCAPE
          -p       FNM_PATHNAME
          -P       FNM_PERIOD
          -d       FNM_LEADING_DIR
          -c       FNM_CASEFOLD
$
```

From the output you can see that all options except -n apply additional fnmatch(3) flag bits. Initially no flags are in effect.

To make it simpler to perform some of the tests in this chapter, alter your PATH variable as follows:

```
$ PATH=$PWD:$PATH
```

Repeating one of the earlier tests, we can use our fnmatch command in place of ls(1):

```
$ cd /etc
$ fnmatch '*[xyz]*' *
Flags: NONE
Matched: fnmatch('*[xyz]*','exports',flags)
Matched: fnmatch('*[xyz]*','gettytab',flags)
Matched: fnmatch('*[xyz]*','newsyslog.conf',flags)
Matched: fnmatch('*[xyz]*','security',flags)
Matched: fnmatch('*[xyz]*','skeykeys',flags)
Matched: fnmatch('*[xyz]*','syslog.conf',flags)
Matched: fnmatch('*[xyz]*','ttys',flags)
$
```

Please notice two important things here:

- The pattern is in single quotes.

- The remaining arguments are expanded by the shell before our fnmatch command is executed.

If you add the option -n to the command line, you will list all of the entries that did not match the output. Only the command is shown here:

```
$ fnmatch -n '*[xyz]*' *
```

Any command-line options must appear before the pattern. After the options, the pattern must be the first command-line argument. All remaining arguments are tested against the pattern.

The FNM_NOESCAPE Flag

The FNM_NOESCAPE flag bit disables the fnmatch(3) capability to escape meta-characters. To test this, first change to the /tmp directory and create an empty test file named [file]:

```
$ cd /tmp
$ >'[file]'
```

Now test the `fnmatch` command using the escape characters:

```
$ fnmatch '\[file\]' *
Flags: NONE
Matched: fnmatch('\[file\]','[file]',flags)
$
```

From all of the files in the `/tmp` directory, it matched the pattern literally with filename `[file]`. The pattern `\[file\]` matches because the escape characters indicate that the following meta-characters should be treated as normal characters. Adding the flag `FNM_NOESCAPE` (option `-e`) changes things:

```
$ fnmatch -e '\[file\]' *
Flags: FNM_NOESCAPE
$
```

In this case, no match is attained. This happens because the leading backslash must now match part of the string. The remainder of the pattern is now a range, since the backslashes are not acting as escape characters when `FNM_NOESCAPE` is used.

The `FNM_CASEFOLD` Flag

The `FNM_CASEFOLD` allows the programmer to specify that `fnmatch(3)` ignore the case of the letters when performing the pattern match. This is confirmed with the help of the test program (option `-c` used):

```
$ cd /etc
$ fnmatch -c 'HOSTS*' *
Flags: FNM_CASEFOLD
Matched: fnmatch('HOSTS*','hosts',flags)
Matched: fnmatch('HOSTS*','hosts.allow',flags)
Matched: fnmatch('HOSTS*','hosts.equiv',flags)
Matched: fnmatch('HOSTS*','hosts.lpd',flags)
$
```

In this example, the pattern `HOSTS*` matches the file `hosts`, although the case differs.

Warning

The `FNM_CASEFOLD` flag appears to be a GNU C library feature and is not available on other UNIX platforms. This feature is supported by FreeBSD and Linux, however.

The `FNM_PATHNAME` Flag

The `FNM_PATHNAME` flag adds some pathname semantics to the `fnmatch(3)` function. This option requires that slashes (/) occurring in patterns must match slashes in the supplied input string. This makes it possible to perform directory and file pattern matches more intelligently. To perform this test, first create a temporary directory in `/tmp` as follows:

```
$ make one
mkdir /tmp/one
mkdir /tmp/one/log
```

```
mkdir /tmp/one/two
mkdir /tmp/one/two/log
date >/tmp/one/log/date1.log
date >/tmp/one/log/.date3
date >/tmp/one/two/log/date2.log
$
```

From this, you can see that a number of subdirectories are created, and two log files were created with the date(1) command. Now perform the following:

```
$ fnmatch '/tmp/*/log/*.log' `find /tmp/one`
Flags: NONE
Matched: fnmatch('/tmp/*/log/*.log','/tmp/one/log/date1.log',flags)
Matched: fnmatch('/tmp/*/log/*.log','/tmp/one/two/log/date2.log',flags)
$
```

If you look at this output carefully, you will see that one match is not intended. The first match makes sense because the subdirectory **one** matches the first *, and the filename **date1** matches the second *.

In the second case, however, the first * actually matches the string **one/two**, and the second * matches the **date2** in **date2.log**. The spirit of this match suggests that there should have only been one directory level between /tmp/ and /log/*.log.

To accomplish this, the FNM_PATHNAME flag (option -p) must be enabled:

```
$ fnmatch -p '/tmp/*/log/*.log' `find /tmp/one`
Flags: FNM_PATHNAME
Matched: fnmatch('/tmp/*/log/*.log','/tmp/one/log/date1.log',flags)
$
```

The results now agree with what was expected.

> **Note**
>
> FNM_FILE_NAME is provided on some UNIX platforms as a synonym for FNM_PATHNAME.

The FNM_PERIOD Flag

This flag causes strings that have leading periods to match only when the pattern has leading periods. Another way to say this is that * and ?, for example, will not match a leading period in the string with the flag FNM_PERIOD enabled. This also applies to ranges.

Usually the FNM_PERIOD flag is used in combination with the FNM_PATHNAME flag. The FNM_PATHNAME flag causes a period to be considered a leading period, if it follows a slash (/) character. Assuming that you still have the directory /tmp/one from the last experiment, perform the following pattern test using only the FNM_PATHNAME (-p) option:

```
$ fnmatch -p '/tmp/*/log/*' `find /tmp/one`
Flags: FNM_PATHNAME
Matched: fnmatch('/tmp/*/log/*','/tmp/one/log/date1.log',flags)
```

```
Matched: fnmatch('/tmp/*/log/*','/tmp/one/log/.date3',flags)
$
```

Notice that in this experiment the pattern specifies * for the last filename component. Using this pattern, two files matched: `date1.log` and `.date3`. Adding the `FNM_PERIOD` flag (option `-P`), causes the following results to be displayed instead:

```
$ fnmatch -pP '/tmp/*/log/*' `find /tmp/one`
Flags: FNM_PATHNAME FNM_PERIOD
Matched: fnmatch('/tmp/*/log/*','/tmp/one/log/date1.log',flags)
$
```

In this output, `fnmatch(3)` does not permit the leading period in `.date3` to match with the * pattern character. If your object was the files prefixed with periods, then you would alter the match string:

```
$ fnmatch -pP '/tmp/*/log/.*' `find /tmp/one`
Flags: FNM_PATHNAME FNM_PERIOD
Matched: fnmatch('/tmp/*/log/.*','/tmp/one/log/.date3',flags)
$
```

In this example, the period (`.`) was added to the pattern string in order to effect a match to `.date3`.

The FNM_LEADING_DIR Flag

This option causes the pattern match to occur on a directory component level. After the pattern match, anything that follows starting with a slash (`/`) is ignored for pattern matching purposes.

```
$ cd /tmp
$ fnmatch -d 'on*' `find one`
Flags: FNM_LEADING_DIR
Matched: fnmatch('on*','one',flags)
Matched: fnmatch('on*','one/log',flags)
Matched: fnmatch('on*','one/log/date1.log',flags)
Matched: fnmatch('on*','one/log/.date3',flags)
Matched: fnmatch('on*','one/two',flags)
Matched: fnmatch('on*','one/two/log',flags)
Matched: fnmatch('on*','one/two/log/date2.log',flags)
$
```

The documentation does not suggest that `FNM_PATHNAME` is required. Experiments suggest that `FNM_LEADING_DIR` works with or without the `FNM_PATHNAME` flag.

Warning

The `FNM_LEADING_DIR` flag appears to be a GNU C library feature and is not available on other UNIX platforms. This feature is supported by FreeBSD and Linux, however.

The `glob(3)` Function

The `glob(3)` function represents another way that a process can gather a list of file and directory name objects. Unlike the `fnmatch(3)` function, the `glob(3)` function actually performs directory searches. The function synopsis for `glob(3)` and `globfree(3)` is as follows:

```
#include <glob.h>

int glob(
    const char *pattern,
    int flags,
    int (*errfunc)(const char *, int),
    glob_t *pglob);

void globfree(glob_t *pglob);

typedef struct {
    int     gl_pathc;       /* count of total paths so far */
    int     gl_matchc;      /* count of paths matching pattern */
    int     gl_offs;        /* reserved at beginning of gl_pathv */
    int     gl_flags;       /* returned flags */
    char    **gl_pathv;     /* list of paths matching pattern */
} glob_t;
```

The first argument `pattern` for `glob(3)` is a shell pattern, like the patterns used by `fnmatch(3)`. However, the argument `flags` uses a different set of flags that will be described shortly. Argument `errfunc` is an optional function pointer and must be a null pointer when it is not used. The final argument `pglob` is a pointer to a `glob_t` structure.

The function `globfree(3)` should be called after a successful call to `glob(3)` has been made, and the information contained in the structure `glob_t` is no longer required. This function releases memory occupied by the array member `gl_pathv` and perhaps other implementation-defined storage.

The `glob_t` structure member `gl_pathv` is a returned array of matching filenames. The member `gl_pathc` is a count of how many string pointers are contained in `gl_pathv`. When `gl_pathc` is zero, there is no `gl_pathv` array allocated, and it should not be referenced. When the `gl_pathv` array is allocated, the last member of the array is followed by a null pointer.

The member `gl_flags` is used by `glob(3)` to return flag bits. Flag bit **GLOB_MAGCHAR** is one flag that may be returned in this member to indicate that the `pattern` argument contained at least one meta-character.

The member `gl_matchc` contains the current number of matched pathnames for the current `glob(3)` call. Since `glob(3)` can be called to append to the `gl_pathv` array, `gl_matchc` is useful for determining how many paths were appending with the current function call.

The member `gl_offs` must be initialized prior to the first call to `glob(3)` for the given `glob_t` structure used, when the flag **GLOB_DOOFFS** is set. This member indicates how many initial `gl_pathv` array entries to reserve as null pointers. If you do not need to reserve any array entries, then initialize this value to zero (not using flag **GLOB_DOOFFS** also will work).

The flag `GLOB_ERR` causes `glob(3)` to stop the directory scan at the first sign of trouble. By default, `glob(3)` ignores directory scan errors and attempts to match as much as possible. Using flag `GLOB_ERR` changes this behavior so that `glob(3)` will exit with the first error encountered.

Multiple calls to `glob(3)` are permitted, to gather additional member entries. The `GLOB_ERR` flag applied in an earlier call will influence later calls when the same `pglob` argument is used. This is the result of the `GLOB_ERR` flag being saved in the `gl_flags` member of the `glob_t` structure.

Return Values for `glob(3)`

When `glob(3)` returns normally, the value zero is returned. However, when an error occurs, the value `GLOB_NOSPACE` or `GLOB_ABEND` is returned instead.

When `GLOB_NOSPACE` is returned, this indicates that `glob(3)` was unable to allocate or reallocate memory. This might be a sign that you are failing to call `globfree(3)`.

The return value `GLOB_ABEND` indicates that the directory scan was stopped. An error may have occurred while scanning the directory and flag bit `GLOB_ERR` was set. Alternatively, the `errfunc` function may have returned non-zero to cause the scan to be stopped.

Before the individual `glob(3)` flags are discussed, an example program is presented in Listing 20.2. This program will permit you to experiment with the various `glob(3)` flags and patterns.

LISTING 20.2   `glob.c`—Exerciser for the `glob(3)` and `globfree(3)` Functions

```
 1:    /* glob.c */
 2:
 3:    #include <stdio.h>
 4:    #include <stdlib.h>
 5:    #include <unistd.h>
 6:    #include <errno.h>
 7:    #include <string.h>
 8:    #include <glob.h>
 9:
10:    /*
11:     * Provide command usage instructions :
12:     */
13:    static void
14:    usage(void) {
15:
16:        puts("Usage: glob [options] pattern...");
17:        puts("Options:");
18:        puts("\t-a\tGLOB_APPEND");
19:        puts("\t-c\tGLOB_NOCHECK");
20:        puts("\t-o n\tGLOB_DOOFFS");
21:        puts("\t-e\tGLOB_ERR");
22:        puts("\t-m\tGLOB_MARK");
23:        puts("\t-n\tGLOB_NOSORT");
```

continued from previous page

```
24:            puts("\t-B\tGLOB_BRACE");
25:            puts("\t-N\tGLOB_NOMAGIC");
26:            puts("\t-Q\tGLOB_QUOTE");
27:            puts("\t-T\tGLOB_TILDE");
28:    }
29:
30:    /*
31:     * Report the flag bits in use as confirmation :
32:     */
33:    static void
34:    report_flags(int flags) {
35:
36:            fputs("Flags:",stdout);
37:            if ( flags & GLOB_APPEND )
38:                fputs(" GLOB_APPEND",stdout);
39:            if ( flags & GLOB_DOOFFS )
40:                fputs(" GLOB_DOOFFS",stdout);
41:            if ( flags & GLOB_ERR )
42:                fputs(" GLOB_ERR",stdout);
43:            if ( flags & GLOB_MARK )
44:                fputs(" GLOB_MARK",stdout);
45:            if ( flags & GLOB_NOSORT )
46:                fputs(" GLOB_NOSORT",stdout);
47:            if ( flags & GLOB_NOCHECK )
48:                fputs(" GLOB_NOCHECK",stdout);
49:            if ( flags & GLOB_BRACE )
50:                fputs(" GLOB_BRACE",stdout);
51:            if ( flags & GLOB_MAGCHAR )
52:                fputs(" GLOB_MAGCHAR",stdout);
53:            if ( flags & GLOB_NOMAGIC )
54:                fputs(" GLOB_NOMAGIC",stdout);
55:            if ( flags & GLOB_QUOTE )
56:                fputs(" GLOB_QUOTE",stdout);
57:            if ( flags & GLOB_TILDE )
58:                fputs(" GLOB_TILDE",stdout);
59:            if ( !flags )
60:                puts(" NONE");
61:            else
62:                putchar('\n');
63:    }
64:
65:    /*
66:     * Error callback function :
67:     */
68:    static int
69:    errfunc(const char *path,int e) {
70:        printf("%s: %s\n",strerror(e),path);
71:        return 0;
72:    }
73:
74:    /*
75:     * Report the glob_t results :
76:     */
```

```
77:  static void
78:  report_glob(glob_t *gp) {
79:      int x;
80:      int g_offs = 0;                  /* glob offset */
81:
82:      if ( gp->gl_pathc < 1 ) {
83:          puts("There are no glob results.");
84:          return;
85:      }
86:      printf("There were %d matches returned:\n",gp->gl_pathc);
87:
88:      if ( gp->gl_flags & GLOB_DOOFFS )
89:          g_offs = gp->gl_offs;    /* Allow for offset */
90:
91:      for ( x=0; x < gp->gl_pathc + g_offs; ++x )
92:          printf("%3d: %s\n",
93:              x,
94:              gp->gl_pathv[x] ? gp->gl_pathv[x] : "<NULL>");
95:
96:      report_flags(gp->gl_flags);
97:      putchar('\n');
98:  }
99:
100: /*
101:  * Main program :
102:  */
103: int
104: main(int argc,char **argv) {
105:     int z;                          /* General status */
106:     glob_t g;                       /* The glob area */
107:     int flags = 0;                  /* All other flags */
108:     int a = 0;                      /* GLOB_APPEND flag */
109:     int offs = 0;                   /* Offset */
110:     const char cmdopts[] = "aco:emnBNQTh";
111:
112:     /*
113:      * Process any command options :
114:      */
115:     while ( (z = getopt(argc,argv,cmdopts)) != -1 )
116:         switch ( z ) {
117:         case 'a' :
118:             a = GLOB_APPEND;
119:             break;
120:         case 'o' :
121:             flags |= GLOB_DOOFFS;
122:             offs = atoi(optarg);
123:             break;
124:         case 'e' :
125:             flags |= GLOB_ERR;
126:             break;
127:         case 'm' :
128:             flags |= GLOB_MARK;
129:             break;
```

continued from previous page

```
130:            case 'n' :
131:                flags |= GLOB_NOSORT;
132:                break;
133:            case 'c' :
134:                flags |= GLOB_NOCHECK;
135:                break;
136:            case 'B' :
137:                flags |= GLOB_BRACE;
138:                break;
139:            case 'N' :
140:                flags |= GLOB_NOMAGIC;
141:                break;
142:            case 'Q' :
143:                flags |= GLOB_QUOTE;
144:                break;
145:            case 'T' :
146:                flags |= GLOB_TILDE;
147:                break;
148:            case 'h' :
149:            default :
150:                usage();
151:                return 1;
152:            }
153:
154:        /*
155:         * We must have at least one pattern :
156:         */
157:        if ( optind >= argc ) {
158:            usage();
159:            return 1;
160:        }
161:
162:        /*
163:         * Pick the pattern string and report the flags that
164:         * are in effect for this run :
165:         */
166:        report_flags(flags|a);
167:
168:        /*
169:         * Now try pattern against all remaining command
170:         * line arguments :
171:         */
172:        for ( ; optind < argc; ++optind, flags |= a ) {
173:            /*
174:             * Invoke glob(3) to scan directories :
175:             */
176:            g.gl_offs = offs;        /* Offset, if any */
177:            z = glob(argv[optind],flags,errfunc,&g);
178:            if ( z ) {
179:                if ( z == GLOB_NOSPACE )
180:                    fputs("glob(3) ran out of memory\n",stderr);
181:                else if ( z == GLOB_ABEND )
182:                    fputs("glob(3): GLOB_ERR/errfunc\n",stderr);
```

```
183:              return 1;
184:          }
185:
186:          /*
187:           * Report glob(3) findings, unless GLOB_APPEND :
188:           */
189:          if ( !a ) {              /* If not GLOB_APPEND */
190:              report_glob(&g);     /* Report matches */
191:              globfree(&g);        /* Free gl_pathv[] etc. */
192:          } else {
193:              /*
194:               * GLOB_APPEND requested. Just accumulate
195:               * glob(3) results, but here we report the
196:               * number of matches made with each pattern:
197:               */
198:              printf("Pattern '%s' got %d matches\n",
199:                  argv[optind],
200:                  g.gl_matchc);
201:          }
202:      }
203:
204:      /*
205:       * If GLOB_APPEND used, then report everything at
206:       * the end :
207:       */
208:      if ( a ) {                  /* If GLOB_APPEND */
209:          report_glob(&g);        /* Report appended matches */
210:          globfree(&g);           /* Free gl_pathv[] etc. */
211:      }
212:
213:      return 0;
214: }
```

The program in Listing 20.2 is similar in many respects to Listing 20.1. Lines 115–160 have to do with parsing the command-line options, which enable various glob(3) flags. Note that option -a causes flag bit GLOB_APPEND to be stored into variable a, which is initialized as zero in line 108. This flag is kept separate from the other flags, which are stored as variable **flags** because GLOB_APPEND cannot be used the first time that glob(3) is called (line 177). However, the for loop causes a to be ORed to **flags** at the end of each loop, ensuring that GLOB_APPEND is used in successive iterations.

After all options are parsed from the command line, the flags in effect are reported in line 166 (note the input argument is **flags|a** so that GLOB_APPEND is included.

The int variable optind will point to the first non-option command-line argument after the getopt(3) loop has completed. These remaining command-line arguments are used as input patterns to glob(3) in the for loop of lines 172–202.

If the offset option -o is used, the variable offs contains this offset. Line 176 assigns this offset value to g.gl_offs. This assignment is significant only if the GLOB_DOOFFS flag is set in variable flags, when the -o option is processed from the command line.

The function glob(3) is called in line 177. The return value z is tested and reported in lines 178–184. Line 189 tests to see if variable a is zero. When a is zero, this indicates that no GLOB_APPEND is being used, and the report of each glob(3) pattern is reported immediately after each call (lines 190 and 191). Otherwise, when GLOB_APPEND has been requested, only the number of matches made for the current glob(3) call are reported in lines 198–200. The GLOB_APPEND results are reported at the end of the for loop in lines 209 and 210 instead.

Now examine the report_glob() function in lines 77–98. The if statement in line 82 is important, because if the glob_t member gl_pathc is zero, then gl_pathv is not allocated and should not be referenced. The program executes the return statement in line 84, when there are no results to report.

Note also in line 88 that the if statement tests for flag GLOB_DOOFFS. If it is present, you must allow for the offset when iterating through the gl_pathv array of pointers. Notice how the for loop allows for the offset g_offs in its test. This allowance is necessary because the loop starts at x=0.

To compile and provoke usage information from the program in Listing 20.2, perform the following:

```
$ make glob
cc -c  -Wall glob.c
cc -o glob glob.o
$ ./glob -h
Usage: glob [options] pattern...
Options:
            -a       GLOB_APPEND
            -o n     GLOB_DOOFFS
            -e       GLOB_ERR
            -m       GLOB_MARK
            -n       GLOB_NOSORT
            -B       GLOB_BRACE
            -N       GLOB_NOMAGIC
            -Q       GLOB_QUOTE
            -T       GLOB_TILDE
$
```

Lowercase option letters represent standard flags that are available for glob(3). Uppercase options represent extension flags or non-universal ones. Option -o is the only option that takes an argument. It represents a numeric offset to be used with GLOB_DOOFFS. The -e option adds the GLOB_ERR flag, but this is not explored in the examples that follow. It is there for your own experimentation.

Flag GLOB_DOOFFS

This flag indicates that glob_t member gl_offs is being used to reserve a number of null pointers at the start of the gl_pathv array (allocated by glob(3)). When flag GLOB_DOOFFS is used, you must initialize gl_offs prior to calling glob(3).

This sounds like a strange thing to do, but it makes a lot of sense when you are about to invoke execvp(2) to start a new command. The following prepares to execute the command cc -c -g *.c:

```
glob_t g;

g.gl_offs = 3;
glob("*.c",GLOB_DOOFFS,NULL,&g);

g.gl_pathv[0] = "cc";
g.gl_pathv[1] = "-c";
g.gl_pathv[2] = "-g";

execvp("cc",g.gl_pathv);
```

The variable g is the glob_t structure being used. Three entries are reserved in the g.gl_pathv array by assigning the value 3 to g.gl_offs (flag GLOB_DOOFFS is present in the flags argument). The call to glob(3) searches the directory for the pattern *.c.

The focus here is that g.gl_pathv[0] to g.gl_pathv[2] has been reserved for your own use. In this example, these reserved elements are used for the C compiler's first three arguments. This makes the result convenient to use with the system call execvp(2).

Try one experiment without using GLOB_DOOFFS so that you can then compare results with the next experiment. Make sure to enclose your patterns in single quotes to keep the shell from expanding them:

```
$ ./glob '*.c'
Flags: NONE
There were 2 matches returned:
  0: fnmatch.c
  1: glob.c
Flags: GLOB_MAGCHAR

$
```

This example uses no command-line options and provides one pattern '*.c'. In this result, you see two filenames were returned with the glob_t member gl_flags containing the flag GLOB_MAGCHAR. The GLOB_MAGCHAR flag, when returned, indicates that at least one meta-character was found in the pattern.

Now try the same experiment, but add an offset using the -o option. This experiment uses an offset of 3:

```
$ ./glob -o3 '*.c'
Flags: GLOB_DOOFFS
There were 2 matches returned:
  0: <NULL>
  1: <NULL>
  2: <NULL>
```

```
   3: fnmatch.c
   4: glob.c
Flags: GLOB_DOOFFS GLOB_MAGCHAR

$
```

Notice how three null pointers were reserved at the start of the `gl_pathv` array for your own use. The `gl_flags` member also reports the additional flag `GLOB_DOOFFS` that was supplied as input to `glob(3)`.

The GLOB_APPEND Flag

The flag `GLOB_APPEND` indicates that the `glob_t` structure is to have new matched pathnames appended to it instead of initializing it. The following example shows how this is done:

```
glob_t g;

g.gl_offs = 3;
glob("*.c",GLOB_DOOFFS,NULL,&g);
glob("*.C",GLOB_DOOFFS|GLOB_APPEND,NULL,&g);
```

The first call to `glob(3)` initializes the `glob_t` variable `g` and adds pathnames that match the pattern `*.c`. The second call with the flag `GLOB_APPEND` causes `glob(3)` to assume that `g` has already been initialized. Matches to `*.C` are then appended to the existing collection in `g.gl_pathv`.

Now test this feature as follows:

```
$ ./glob -a '*.c' '*.o'
Flags: GLOB_APPEND
Pattern '*.c' got 2 matches
Pattern '*.o' got 1 matches
There were 3 matches returned:
  0: fnmatch.c
  1: glob.c
  2: glob.o
Flags: GLOB_APPEND GLOB_MAGCHAR

$
```

The output shows how the first pattern `'*.c'` collected two matches, and the pattern `'*.o'` appended one more match. The result of all matches is reported at the end, and you can see that three final pathnames are reported.

The GlOB_MARK Flag

The `GLOB_MARK` flag marks directory entries by appending a slash (/) to them. Files are left as they are. The following example illustrates (note the -m option):

```
$ ./glob -am '/b*' '/etc/hosts'
Flags: GLOB_APPEND GLOB_MARK
Pattern '/b*' got 2 matches
Pattern '/etc/hosts' got 1 matches
There were 3 matches returned:
```

```
 0: /bin/
 1: /boot/
 2: /etc/hosts
Flags: GLOB_APPEND GLOB_MARK
```

```
$
```

Directories /bin and /boot were marked with a trailing slash. The filename /etc/hosts was
not.

The GLOB_NOSORT Flag

The GLOB_NOSORT flag disables the sort feature of glob(3). The following example shows the
default sorted result:

```
$ ./glob '/etc/h*'
Flags: NONE
There were 5 matches returned:
  0: /etc/host.conf
  1: /etc/hosts
  2: /etc/hosts.allow
  3: /etc/hosts.equiv
  4: /etc/hosts.lpd
Flags: GLOB_MAGCHAR
```

```
$
```

Adding the GLOB_NOSORT flag by using the -n option yields unsorted results:

```
$ ./glob -n '/etc/h*'
Flags: GLOB_NOSORT
There were 5 matches returned:
  0: /etc/hosts
  1: /etc/hosts.allow
  2: /etc/host.conf
  3: /etc/hosts.equiv
  4: /etc/hosts.lpd
Flags: GLOB_NOSORT GLOB_MAGCHAR
```

```
$
```

However, note that sorting and not sorting affect only the current glob(3) call when
GLOB_APPEND is used. Consequently, while the default is to sort, appended results are not
sorted ahead of earlier results. You can test this for yourself:

```
$ ./glob -a '/etc/h*' '/b*'
Flags: GLOB_APPEND
Pattern '/etc/h*' got 5 matches
Pattern '/b*' got 2 matches
There were 7 matches returned:
  0: /etc/host.conf
  1: /etc/hosts
  2: /etc/hosts.allow
  3: /etc/hosts.equiv
```

```
    4: /etc/hosts.lpd
    5: /bin
    6: /boot
Flags: GLOB_APPEND GLOB_MAGCHAR

$
```

Although the default suggests that the gl_pathv array should be sorted, it is sorted only within pattern groups. The first pattern matches for '/etc/h*' are sorted, but the later matches for pattern '/b*' are not sorted ahead of the earlier match set.

The GLOB_QUOTE Flag

By default, there is no quoting capability in glob(3). Applying the flag GLOB_QUOTE allows glob to interpret a backslash (\) as a quote meta-character. The quote character causes the character following to be treated literally, even if it is a meta-character. The example illustrates this:

```
$ date >'*.c'
$ ./glob '*.c'
Flags: NONE
There were 3 matches returned:
  0: *.c
  1: fnmatch.c
  2: glob.c
Flags: GLOB_MAGCHAR

$
```

The example has carefully created a file named *.c that contains the current date and time. Without any special options, the ./glob program picks up all files ending in the suffix .c. If you need quoting capability, to select only the file *.c you need GLOB_QUOTE (option -Q):

```
$ ./glob -Q '\*.c'
Flags: GLOB_QUOTE
There were 1 matches returned:
  0: *.c
Flags: GLOB_QUOTE

$
```

Here, glob(3) interprets the asterisk (*) literally, because it is preceded by the quote character backslash (\) while the option GLOB_QUOTE is active.

The GLOB_NOCHECK Flag

Normally, when a pattern does not match, no results are returned. If you want to have the pattern returned as a result when no matches are found, add the GLOB_NOCHECK flag (option -c below):

```
$ ./glob '*.xyz'
Flags: NONE
There are no glob results.
```

```
$ ./glob -c '*.xyz'
Flags: GLOB_NOCHECK
There were 1 matches returned:
  0: *.xyz
Flags: GLOB_NOCHECK GLOB_MAGCHAR

$
```

In the first example, notice how no matches were found. Adding option -c causes the pattern itself (*.xyz) to be returned instead of no results.

The GLOB_ALTDIRFUNC Flag

This flag is documented by FreeBSD as an extension to glob(3) to enable programs such as restore(8) to provide globbing from directories stored on other media. The following additional glob_t members can be initialized with function pointers. When the flag GLOB_ALTDIRFUNC is used, these function pointers will be used in place of the glob(3) default functions for searching directories:

```
void *(*gl_opendir)(const char * name);
struct dirent *(*gl_readdir)(void *);
void (*gl_closedir)(void *);
int (*gl_lstat)(const char *name, struct stat *st);
int (*gl_stat)(const char *name, struct stat *st);
```

The program in Listing 20.2 does not support the GLOB_ALTDIRFUNC flag.

The GLOB_BRACE Flag

The GLOB_BRACE flag enables glob(3) to support csh(1) pattern groups that are specified between braces. The following example illustrates GLOB_BRACE (option -B):

```
$ ./glob -B '{*.c,*.o}'
Flags: GLOB_BRACE
There were 4 matches returned:
  0: fnmatch.c
  1: glob.c
  2: fnmatch.o
  3: glob.o
Flags: GLOB_BRACE GLOB_MAGCHAR

$
```

By using the GLOB_BRACE flag and the pattern '{*.c,*.o}', the glob(3) function was able to combine two patterns into one result. Notice that only the individual pattern results are sorted.

The GLOB_MAGCHAR Flag

The GLOB_MAGCHAR flag is never used as input to glob(3). However, it is returned in the glob_t member gl_flags when at least one meta-character exists in the pattern.

The GLOB_NOMAGIC Flag

The **GLOB_NOMAGIC** flag causes no results to be returned if the pattern did not make any matches and the pattern had meta-characters present. However, if no meta-characters exist in the pattern, then the pattern is returned in the same manner as **GLOB_NOCHECK** when no results are found. The following session shows the difference between **GLOB_NOMAGIC** (option -N) and **GLOB_NOCHECK** (option -c):

```
$ ./glob -N '*.z'
Flags: GLOB_NOMAGIC
There are no glob results.
$ ./glob -c '*.z'
Flags: GLOB_NOCHECK
There were 1 matches returned:
  0: *.z
Flags: GLOB_NOCHECK GLOB_MAGCHAR

$
```

The first command shows **GLOB_NOMAGIC** and a pattern with meta-characters present. The run with **GLOB_NOMAGIC** did not return any results, while the run with **GLOB_NOCHECK** returned the pattern *.z as a result. Now examine another experiment:

```
$ ./glob -N 'z.z'
Flags: GLOB_NOMAGIC
There were 1 matches returned:
  0: z.z
Flags: GLOB_NOMAGIC

$
```

In this experiment, flag **GLOB_NOMAGIC** causes pattern z.z to be returned, although this was not a match. The flag **GLOB_NOCHECK** would return the same result in this case.

The GLOB_TILDE Flag

This flag is used to enable glob(3) to interpret the Korn shell tilde (~) feature. The following illustrates (using option -T):

```
$ ./glob -T '~postgres/*'
Flags: GLOB_TILDE
There were 9 matches returned:
  0: /home/postgres/bin
  1: /home/postgres/data
  2: /home/postgres/errlog
  3: /home/postgres/include
  4: /home/postgres/lib
  5: /home/postgres/odbcinst.ini
  6: /home/postgres/pgsql-support.tar.gz
  7: /home/postgres/postgresql-7.0beta1.tar.gz
  8: /home/postgres/psqlodbc-025.tar.gz
Flags: GLOB_MAGCHAR GLOB_TILDE

$
```

In this example, the `glob(3)` function looked up the home directory for the `postgres` account and searched that home directory `/home/postgres`.

Summary

The pattern matching functions that were covered in this chapter are shell pattern matching functions. They provide the capability to expand wildcard filenames and perform `case` statement selection. When these are combined with the `fork(2)` and `exec(2)` functions of the last chapter, you have a good foundation for building a new shell.

The next chapter will delve into regular expressions. This is a more powerful pattern-matching tool that is well equipped to search for text within a file or a text editor's buffer.

CHAPTER 21

REGULAR EXPRESSIONS

T he patterns supported by the fnmatch(3) and glob(3) functions are useful for filename matches because they are simple and easily understood. Text searches, however, often require something more powerful. This chapter examines regular
expressions and the support that exists for them.

Understanding Regular Expressions

While it is assumed that the reader is familiar with regular expressions, it is useful to review.
This will ensure that the terminology is understood, and it may encourage you to use features
that you've not been using.

Like shell patterns, regular expressions match on a character-by-character basis unless a meta-
character is encountered in the pattern. Regular expressions have more meta-characters than
shell patterns, which makes them more powerful. It also makes them more difficult to master.

Anchors

When searching for text within a file, it is often necessary to use anchors. An *anchor* is a meta-
character that can cause a pattern to be attached to another entity. Regular expressions define
two anchors:

The beginning	^
The end	$

The anchors may be attached to the beginning and end of a line or to the beginning and end
of a string. The context of the anchor depends on the application.

The egrep(1) command uses regular expressions and can be used to illustrate. In the following example, only those lines that start with the letters ftp are displayed from the file
/etc/services:

```
$ egrep '^ftp' /etc/services
ftp-data        20/tcp     #File Transfer [Default Data]
ftp-data        20/udp     #File Transfer [Default Data]
ftp             21/tcp     #File Transfer [Control]
ftp             21/udp     #File Transfer [Control]
```

```
ftp-agent        574/tcp     #FTP Software Agent System
ftp-agent        574/udp     #FTP Software Agent System
$
```

The egrep(1) pattern '^ftp' causes lines starting with ftp to be selected. The regular expression used here is ^ftp. The ^ anchor indicates that the pattern match can only succeed if ftp starts the text line. Without the anchor, other lines would have matched, including, for example, lines starting with tftp.

The next example matches lines ending with the text system:

```
$ egrep 'system$' /etc/services
#                24/tcp     any private mail system
#                24/udp     any private mail system
remotefs         556/tcp    rfs rfs_server      # Brunhoff remote filesystem
remotefs         556/udp    rfs rfs_server      # Brunhoff remote filesystem
mshnet           1989/tcp   #MHSnet system
mshnet           1989/udp   #MHSnet system
$
```

The $ anchor causes the pattern system$ to succeed only when the pattern ends at the end of the line. The anchors can also be used together:

```
$ egrep '^#$' /etc/services
#
#
#
#
$
```

In this example, the anchors in the pattern ^#$ were used to select only those lines in which # is the only character on the line. The ^ and $ anchors lose their special meaning when used in places other than the beginning and end of a pattern. For example, the pattern $#^ has no meta-characters in it.

Sets

A set is a collection of characters between the meta-characters [and]. Sets work the same as they do in shell patterns. The following egrep(1) command shows a set of two characters:

```
$ egrep '^[tm]ftp' /etc/services
tftp             69/tcp     #Trivial File Transfer
tftp             69/udp     #Trivial File Transfer
mftp             349/tcp
mftp             349/udp
$
```

The first character on the line matches a t or m from the specified set [tm] in the regular expression.

When the character ^ occurs as the first character of the set, it becomes a meta-character. It reverses the sense of the set. For example the pattern [^tm] matches any character except t or m. If the ^ character occurs in any other place within the set, it is not special. For example, the pattern [tm^] matches the characters t, m, or ^.

To include the] character within the set, make it the first character of the set (or immediately following the ^ character). The following example searches for a line that starts with <abc> or [abc].

```
$ egrep '^[[<]abc[]>]' file
```

Range

A *range* is an extension of the set idea. A range is specified within the meta-characters [and] and has the hyphen character used between the extremes. For example, the range pattern [A-Z] specifies the set of all uppercase letters.

Ranges can be grouped together. For example, the range [A-Za-z] allows you to select any letter, without regard to case. They may also be combined with sets. The range pattern [A-Z01] will match any uppercase character or the digits 0 or 1.

Like sets, the ^ character reverses the sense of the set if it occurs as the first character. For example, the pattern [^A-Z] matches any character except uppercase alphabetic characters.

Character Classes

Regular expressions also include character classes. These use the meta-character pair [: and :]. An example of a character class is [:digit:], which represents any numeric digit. Valid class names are as follows and are listed in ctype(3):

alnum	digit	punct
alpha	graph	space
blank	lower	upper
cntrl	print	xdigit

These class names correspond to the ctype(3) macros isalnum(3), isdigit(3), ispunct(3), and so on.

The . Meta-Character

The . meta-character matches any single character. The following example shows a pattern in which any first character is accepted as a match:

```
$ egrep '^.ftp' /etc/services
tftp            69/tcp      #Trivial File Transfer
tftp            69/udp      #Trivial File Transfer
sftp            115/tcp     #Simple File Transfer Protocol
sftp            115/udp     #Simple File Transfer Protocol
bftp            152/tcp     #Background File Transfer Program
bftp            152/udp     #Background File Transfer Program
mftp            349/tcp
mftp            349/udp
$
```

Parenthesized Match Subexpression

A regular expression can be included within the parenthesis characters (and), which perform a grouping function. The following egrep(1) command illustrates a simple example:

```
$ egrep '^™(ftp)' /etc/services
tftp            69/tcp     #Trivial File Transfer
tftp            69/udp     #Trivial File Transfer
mftp           349/tcp
mftp           349/udp
$
```

Parenthesized matches cause substrings to be extracted from a matching operation. This and other uses of the parenthesis will become clearer as the chapter progresses.

Atoms

An *atom* is a unit that participates in pattern matching. The following are atoms within regular expressions:

- Any single non–meta-character

- A single anchor (^ or $)

- A set (such as [abc])

- A range (such as [A-Z])

- A character class (such as [:digit:])

- A parenthesized match (such as (abc[de]))

Atoms are important to understanding how a piece works in regular expressions.

Piece

A *piece* is an atom followed by the meta-character *, +, or ?. These meta-characters influence the matching process in the following ways:

*	Matches zero or more atoms
+	Matches one or more atoms
?	Matches zero or one atom

The pattern A* will match any of the following:

" "	Null string
A	One A
AA	Two As
AAA	Three As

The pattern A+ insists that at least one A be matched. Alternatively, the pattern A? matches the null string or a single A character.

The pattern (abc)+ shows a parenthesized expression. This pattern matches any of the following:

abc	The + matches one () expression.
abcabc	The + matches two () expressions.
abcabcabc	The + matches any number of () expressions.

The possibilities are nearly endless when you include sets and ranges within the parentheses.

Branch

A *branch* of a regular expression is a pattern component that is separated by the pipe symbol |. It is used to specify alternative patterns to be matched. The following example shows two branches in the pattern:

```
$ egrep '^ftp|^telnet' /etc/services
ftp-data        20/tcp      #File Transfer [Default Data]
ftp-data        20/udp      #File Transfer [Default Data]
ftp             21/tcp      #File Transfer [Control]
ftp             21/udp      #File Transfer [Control]
telnet          23/tcp
telnet          23/udp
ftp-agent       574/tcp     #FTP Software Agent System
ftp-agent       574/udp     #FTP Software Agent System
telnets         992/tcp
$
```

The example selects those lines that begin with the text ftp or telnet. Branches can be used within parenthesized subexpressions:

```
$ egrep '^ftp(-agent)?' /etc/services
ftp-data        20/tcp      #File Transfer [Default Data]
ftp-data        20/udp      #File Transfer [Default Data]
ftp             21/tcp      #File Transfer [Control]
ftp             21/udp      #File Transfer [Control]
ftp-agent       574/tcp     #FTP Software Agent System
ftp-agent       574/udp     #FTP Software Agent System
$
```

In this example, the line must start with the letters ftp. The subexpression (-agent) indicates what the subexpression should match. This is modified, however, by the following ? operator, which says that zero or one of these subexpressions must match. Consequently, lines are selected that start with ftp, ftp-data, or ftp-agent.

Expression Bounds

You have already seen how the *, +, and the ? meta-characters affect the preceding atom. It is also possible to specify a bound instead. A *bound* consists of an opening brace character ({), an unsigned integer, a comma (,), another unsigned integer, and a closing brace (}). The fully specified bound {2,5} indicates that at least 2 atoms must match but no more than 5.

The second component of the bound is optional. For example, a bound of the form {3} indicates that exactly 3 matches must be made.

A bound may also be specified with a missing second count. For example, the bound {2,} specifies that 2 or more matches can be made.

The valid range for unsigned integers is between 0 and the value RE_DUP_MAX (which is 255 on most platforms). The following example demonstrates how to select those lines with a 6 followed by at least three zeros (the egrep(1) option -E is required to enable the bounds feature):

```
$ egrep -E '60{3,}' /etc/services
netviewdm1      729/tcp     #IBM NetView DM/6000 Server/Client
netviewdm1      729/udp     #IBM NetView DM/6000 Server/Client
netviewdm2      730/tcp     #IBM NetView DM/6000 send/tcp
netviewdm2      730/udp     #IBM NetView DM/6000 send/tcp
netviewdm3      731/tcp     #IBM NetView DM/6000 receive/tcp
netviewdm3      731/udp     #IBM NetView DM/6000 receive/tcp
#x11            6000-6063/tcp    X Window System
#x11            6000-6063/udp    X Window System
$
```

Quoted Characters

Given the number of meta-characters used in regular expressions, it is often necessary to quote meta-characters to remove their special meaning. The quote character used in regular expressions is the backslash (\) character. Any character that follows this backslash is interpreted literally; it is not treated as a meta character.

For example, if you want to match a pattern that includes parentheses, you need to quote the parenthesis characters. The expression \(abc\) matches the string (abc).

The Regular Expression Library

From the preceding discussion, you can appreciate that implementing regular expression searches on your own is less than trivial. However, regular expressions can be part of your programs with the help of the C library.

Compiling Regular Expressions

For efficiency, a regular expression is first compiled into an opaque data type `regex_t`. The function synopsis for compiling a regular expression is as follows:

```
#include <sys/types.h>
#include <regex.h>

int regcomp(regex_t *preg, const char *pattern, int cflags);

typedef struct {
    int         re_magic;
    size_t      re_nsub;    /* number of parenthesized subexpressions */
    const char  *re_endp;   /* end pointer for REG_PEND */
    struct re_guts *re_g;   /* opaque */
} regex_t;
```

`pattern` is the string representing the regular expression that is to be compiled. The argument `preg` points to a data type declared as `regex_t`. This is where the compiled result is placed by the call. The argument `cflags` may have one or more of the following bitmasks ORed together:

REG_EXTENDED	Compile an extended regular expression, rather than the obsolete reg-ular expression that is the default.
REG_NOSPEC	Disable all meta-characters. None of the pattern characters will be considered special when performing a match.
REG_ICASE	Ignore case when performing matching operations.
REG_NOSUB	Compile the pattern such that the matched expressions are not tracked. When matching is performed, only a success or failure will be reported.
REG_NEWLINE	Compile the pattern for newline sensitivity. Normally, when a newline appears in the string to be matched, it is not given special treatment.
REG_PEND	Compile the pattern such that the regular expression does not end with the first null byte encountered. The regular expression ends before the byte pointed to by `preg->re_endp`. This allows null bytes to be included in the regular expression.

An additional macro is defined as `REG_BASIC` (FreeBSD), which is declared as the value zero. You can use this macro when you have no other flags to specify.

Note

FreeBSD 3.4 release and Linux support all of the flag options `REG_EXTENDED`, `REG_NOSPEC`, `REG_ICASE`, `REG_NOSUB`, `REG_NEWLINE`, and `REG_PEND`.

SGI IRIX 6.5, IBM AIX 4.3, UnixWare 7, and Solaris 8 do not support `REG_NOSPEC` and `REG_PEND`.

HPUX-11 does not support `REG_NOSPEC`, `REG_NOSUB`, and `REG_PEND`.

When successful, the regcomp(3) function returns zero, after filling the preg argument with the compiled result. Other return values represent error codes. These can be passed to the function regerror(3) to produce an error message.

Note
When the flag bit REG_NOSUB is not used, you can query the re_nsub member of the regex_t argument preg to find out how many subexpressions were present in the pattern argument.

The following demonstrates how to compile a regular expression:

```
int z;
regex_t reg;

z = regcomp(&reg,pattern,REG_EXTENDED);
if ( z != 0 )
    /* Report regcomp(3) error */
```

Once the regcomp(3) routine has returned successfully, the compiled expression in reg is ready for regexec(3) to use.

Reporting Errors

The function regcomp(3) and regexec(3) return different error codes from the rest of the UNIX library and system calls. FreeBSD documents these error codes, but you may find others on other UNIX platforms:

REG_NOMATCH	regexec(3) failed to match
REG_BADPAT	invalid regular expression
REG_ECOLLATE	invalid collating element
REG_ECTYPE	invalid character class
REG_EESCAPE	\ applied to unescapable character
REG_ESUBREG	invalid back-reference number
REG_EBRACK	brackets [ ] not balanced
REG_EPAREN	parentheses ( ) not balanced
REG_EBRACE	braces { } not balanced
REG_BADBR	invalid repetition count(s) in { }
REG_ERANGE	invalid character range in [ ]
REG_ESPACE	ran out of memory
REG_BADRPT	?, *, or + operand invalid

REG_EMPTY	empty (sub)expression
REG_ASSERT	you found a bug
REG_INVARG	invalid argument

To turn these error codes into a meaningful error message, call on the regerror(3) function:

```
#include <sys/types.h>
#include <regex.h>

size_t regerror(
    int errcode,
    const regex_t *preg,
    char *errbuf,
    size_t errbuf_size);
```

The regerror(3) function accepts the error code from regcomp(3) or regexec(3) in the argument errcode. The message is created in buffer errbuf for a maximum length of errbuf_size bytes. The length of the formatted message in bytes is returned. The function regerror(3) will return zero if the function is not implemented on some platforms.

The argument preg of type pointer to regex_t must be supplied. This will be the compiled result from a prior regcomp(3) call to provide the regerror(3) function with the necessary context it needs to format the message.

The following example shows how a regcomp(3) error can be reported using regerror(3):

```
int z;                          /* Error code */
regex_t reg;                    /* Compiled regexpr */
char ebuf[128];                 /* Error message buffer */

z = regcomp(&reg,pattern,REG_NOSUB|REG_EXTENDED);
if ( z != 0 ) {
    /* Report regcomp(3) error */
    regerror(z,&reg,ebuf,sizeof ebuf);
    printf("%s: regcomp(3)\n",ebuf);
    exit(1);
}
```

Freeing Regular Expressions

When you no longer require your compiled regular expression, you should use regfree(3) to free the storage it uses. The following shows the synopsis for regfree(3):

```
#include <sys/types.h>
#include <regex.h>

void regfree(regex_t *preg);
```

regfree(3) does not return a result. It accepts the argument preg, which must point to a compiled result in a data type regex_t. This will be a result previously established by regcomp(3). The last statement in the following example shows how regfree(3) is invoked:

```
int z;
regex_t reg;

z = regcomp(&reg,pattern,REG_EXTENDED);
if ( z != 0 )
    /* Report regcomp(3) error */

/* do stuff with regexec(3) here... */
regfree(&reg);                   /* Free compiled regexpr */
```

Matching Regular Expressions

Once you have successfully compiled your regular expression with the function regcomp(3), you are ready to perform some pattern matching with regexec(3):

```
#include <sys/types.h>
#include <regex.h>

int regexec(
    const regex_t *preg,
    const char *string,
    size_t nmatch,
    regmatch_t pmatch[],
    int eflags);

typedef struct {
    regoff_t  rm_so;      /* start of match offset */
    regoff_t  rm_eo;      /* end of match offset */
} regmatch_t;
```

The first argument preg is a pointer to the previously compiled regular expression, initialized by regcomp(3). The function returns 0 when successful, but it may return error codes such as REG_NOMATCH when unsuccessful. On platforms where regexec(3) is not implemented, the value REG_ENOSYS is returned (this macro is not always defined, however, for those systems that do support regexec(3)).

The argument string is the string that you want to match. The arguments nmatch and pmatch are used to return matched patterns to your calling program. This will be expanded upon later. Finally, the eflags argument may contain zero or an ORed combination of the following option flags:

REG_NOTBOL	The first character in string is not to be considered the start of the line. This prevents the anchor ^ from matching before the first string character. (This does not affect flag REG_NEWLINE; see regcomp(3).)
REG_NOTEOL	The null character that terminates the argument string is not to be considered the end of the line. This prevents anchor $ from matching at the end of string. (This does not affect flag REG_NEWLINE; see regcomp(3).)

REG_STARTEND	Process the argument string starting at byte offset pmatch[0].rm_so and consider the string ended before offset pmatch[0].rm_eo. The value of argument nmatch is ignored. FreeBSD documents that "this is an extension, compatible with but not specified POSIX 1003.2, and should be used with caution in software intended to be portable to other systems."

When the flag REG_NOSUB is not used in the call to regcomp(3), the arguments nmatch and pmatch allow the caller to receive information about where the pattern matches occurred. There is a performance penalty associated with this, however and, if the pattern strings are not required, the REG_NOSUB flag is recommended for efficiency.

The pmatch argument points to an array of type regmatch_t. This defines an array of starting and ending offsets into the original string argument for each matched pattern. The argument nmatch specifies to regexec(2) how many array elements to fill in array pmatch.

Array element pmatch[0] identifies the starting and ending offsets of the pattern that was found in string. Offsets in pmatch[1] identify the starting and ending offsets for the first parenthesized subexpression found in the argument string. Element pmatch[2] contains the offsets for the second subexpression, and so on.

The following example shows how to define nmatch and a pmatch array to hold a maximum of 10 match strings.

```
const size_t nmatch = 10;    /* The size of array pm[] */
regmatch_t pm[10];           /* Pattern matches 0-9 */
```

Upon successful return from the regexec(3) function, the first character of the match is found at byte string+pmatch[0].rm_so. The last character of the match is found before the byte string+pmatch[0].rm_eo. The first byte of the first subexpression is found at string+pmatch[1].rm_so and ends before the byte string+pmatch[1].rm_eo.

Applying Regular Expressions

To give you some experience with the regular expression routines, the program in Listing 21.1 is provided:

LISTING 21.1   regexpr.c—A Program Using the regexpr(3) Routines

```
1:  /* regexpr.c */
2:
3:  #include <stdio.h>
4:  #include <stdlib.h>
5:  #include <unistd.h>
6:  #include <string.h>
7:  #include <sys/types.h>
8:  #include <regex.h>
9:
```

continued from previous page

```
10:  /*
11:   * Provide usage instructions :
12:   */
13:  static void
14:  usage(void) {
15:
16:      puts("Usage:\tregexpr [options] pattern <file");
17:      puts("Options:");
18:      puts("\t-e\tREG_EXTENDED");
19:      puts("\t-b\tREG_BASIC");
20:      puts("\t-n\tREG_NOSPEC");
21:      puts("\t-i\tREG_ICASE");
22:      puts("\t-s\tREG_NOSUB");
23:  }
24:
25:  /*
26:   * Perform a substring operation :
27:   */
28:  static char *
29:  substr(const char *str,unsigned start,unsigned end) {
30:      unsigned n = end - start;
31:      static char stbuf[256];      /* Local static buffer */
32:
33:      strncpy(stbuf,str+start,n); /* Copy substring */
34:      stbuf[n] = 0;                /* Null terminate */
35:      return stbuf;                /* Return static buffer */
36:  }
37:
38:  /*
39:   * Main program :
40:   */
41:  int
42:  main(int argc,char **argv) {
43:      int z;                       /* General status code */
44:      int x;                       /* Loop iterator */
45:      int lno = 0;                 /* Line number */
46:      int cmdopt_h = 0;            /* -h ; usage option */
47:      int cflags = 0;              /* Compile flags */
48:      regex_t reg;                 /* Compiled regular expression */
49:      char *pattern;               /* Regular expression */
50:      const size_t nmatch = 10;    /* The size of array pm[] */
51:      regmatch_t pm[10];           /* Pattern matches 0-9 */
52:      char ebuf[128];              /* Error message buffer */
53:      char lbuf[256];              /* Line buffer */
54:      const char cmdopts[] = "hebnis";
55:
56:      while ( (z = getopt(argc,argv,cmdopts)) != -1 )
57:          switch ( z ) {
58:          case 'b' :
59:              cflags |= REG_BASIC;
60:              break;
61:          case 'e' :
62:              cflags |= REG_EXTENDED;
```

```
63:               break;
64:          case 'n' :
65:               cflags |= REG_NOSPEC;
66:               break;
67:          case 'i' :
68:               cflags |= REG_ICASE;
69:               break;
70:          case 's' :
71:               cflags |= REG_NOSUB;
72:               break;
73:          case 'h' :
74:          default  :
75:               cmdopt_h = 1;
76:          }
77:
78:     if ( optind + 1 != argc || cmdopt_h ) {
79:          usage();
80:          return 1;
81:     }
82:
83:     /*
84:      * Compile the regular expression :
85:      */
86:     pattern = argv[optind];
87:
88:     z = regcomp(&reg,pattern,cflags);
89:
90:     if ( z != 0 ) {
91:          regerror(z,&reg,ebuf,sizeof ebuf);
92:          fprintf(stderr,"%s: pattern '%s'\n",ebuf,pattern);
93:          return 1;
94:     }
95:
96:     /*
97:      * Report the number of subexpressions :
98:      */
99:     if ( !(cflags & REG_NOSUB) )
100:         printf("There were %d subexpressions.\n",reg.re_nsub);
101:
102:     /*
103:      * Now process each line for matches :
104:      */
105:     while ( fgets(lbuf,sizeof lbuf,stdin) ) {
106:          ++lno;                        /* Increment the line number */
107:          if ( (z = strlen(lbuf)) > 0 && lbuf[z-1] == '\n' )
108:              lbuf[z-1] = 0;            /* Eliminate newline character */
109:
110:          /*
111:           * Now apply regular expression matching to this line :
112:           */
113:          z = regexec(&reg,lbuf,nmatch,pm,0);
114:
115:          if ( z == REG_NOMATCH )
```

continued from previous page

```
116:                continue;
117:            else if ( z != 0 ) {
118:                regerror(z,&reg,ebuf,sizeof ebuf);
119:                fprintf(stderr,"%s: regcomp('%s')\n",ebuf,lbuf);
120:                return 2;
121:            }
122:
123:            for ( x=0; x<nmatch && pm[x].rm_so != -1; ++x ) {
124:                if ( !x )   /* Print the matching line number */
125:                    printf("%04d: %s\n",lno,lbuf);
126:                printf("  $%d='%s'\n",
127:                    x,                       /* Report substring $x */
128:                    substr(lbuf,pm[x].rm_so,pm[x].rm_eo));
129:            }
130:        }
131:
132:        regfree(&reg);                       /* Free compiled regexpr */
133:        return 0;
134: }
```

This program is designed to accept command-line arguments to establish certain regcomp(3) option flags. After options, if any, the regular expression pattern string is taken from the command line. The pattern is then applied to data that is supplied to the program on standard input.

Compiling and invoking the usage information from the program are performed as follows:

```
$ make
cc -c  -Wall regexpr.c
cc -o regexpr regexpr.o
$ ./regexpr -h
Usage:  regexpr [options] pattern <file
Options:
           -e       REG_EXTENDED
           -b       REG_BASIC
           -n       REG_NOSPEC
           -i       REG_ICASE
           -s       REG_NOSUB
$
```

In lines 56–76 the program applies the various flags as the command-line options are parsed. The pattern string is established in line 86.

The pattern is compiled in line 88. If an error occurs, it is reported in lines 90–94. If the flag REG_NOSUB was not used, the value of reg.re_nsub is reported in line 100.

Standard input is read in the while loop at line 105. The newline character is removed in line 108 for convenience. The recexec(3) function is called in line 113. If no match is reported, the continue statement skips the remaining processing of the loop (line 116). Errors are reported in lines 117–121.

The `for` loop in lines 123–129 reports the matches returned from `regexec(3)`. Line 125 reports the text line that brought about the match (when `x=0` only). The match results are displayed as values `$0` through `$9` in lines 126–128. The `$0` value is the match string, and `$1` to `$9` represent matched subexpressions, if any. However, if the starting offset is the value `-1`, the `for` loop exits (see line 123).

The following example uses the `-e` option for `REG_EXTENDED` and the `-i` option for `REG_ICASE` flags. Applying this to the source file `regexpr.c`, the following result was obtained:

```
$ ./regexpr -ei '([a-z]+)( *)\|= *REG_([a-z]+);' <regexpr.c
There were 3 subexpressions.
0059:               cflags |= REG_BASIC;
  $0='cflags |= REG_BASIC;'
  $1='cflags'
  $2=' '
  $3='BASIC'
0062:               cflags |= REG_EXTENDED;
  $0='cflags |= REG_EXTENDED;'
  $1='cflags'
  $2=' '
  $3='EXTENDED'
0065:               cflags |= REG_NOSPEC;
  $0='cflags |= REG_NOSPEC;'
  $1='cflags'
  $2=' '
  $3='NOSPEC'
0068:               cflags |= REG_ICASE;
  $0='cflags |= REG_ICASE;'
  $1='cflags'
  $2=' '
  $3='ICASE'
0071:               cflags |= REG_NOSUB;
  $0='cflags |= REG_NOSUB;'
  $1='cflags'
  $2=' '
  $3='NOSUB'
$
```

The subexpression was designed to capture the C variable and the flag name without the `REG_` prefix, for the `|=` assignments. The `$0` display for each line shows the extent of the entire match. The `$1` match string shows the extracted C variable name `cflags`. The `$2` subexpression was thrown in for good measure, to demonstrate the space characters that were matched by the subexpression (`*`). The `$3` match string shows the extractions without the `REG_` prefix.

The next example shows how a bound expression extracted a string constant with two or more leading spaces in it:

```
$ ./regexpr -e '" {2,}' <regexpr.c
There were 0 subexpressions.
0126:               printf("  $%d='%s'\n",
  $0='"   '
$
```

You are encouraged to apply other options and regular expressions to the `./regexpr` test program. Using this program as a testing tool, you can use regular expression routines in your application confidently.

Summary

This chapter has looked at regular expressions in depth. The `regexp(3)` set of routines truly enhances programs that need the flexible pattern matching that regular expressions provide.

The next chapter introduces interprocess communications. This will lead you into the topics of message queues, semaphores, and shared memory.

CHAPTER 22

INTERPROCESS COMMUNICATIONS

*L*arge programming efforts often use separate processes to manage complexity and risks. Sometimes, separate processes provide enhanced performance on multiprocessor systems. Client/server processes are separate by their very nature. However, once applications become separate processes, there exists a gulf between them when they need to share data. This chapter discusses interprocess communications (IPC) concepts as they exist on UNIX platforms.

Types of IPC

You have already seen some forms of interprocess communication used in this book, including

- Regular files with locking
- FIFOs (named pipes)
- Anonymous pipes
- Sockets
- Signals

Regular files, when used with the appropriate lock techniques, can be used to communicate between processes. FIFOs and anonymous pipes can also be used to form pipelines between separate processes. Sockets allow communication with local or remote processes. Finally, processes can notify each other by using signals.

This chapter discusses three other forms of IPC, which is expanded upon in the following three chapters. These additional forms are the following:

- Message queues
- Shared memory
- Semaphores

These forms of IPC establish a new group of facilities because you create and control them in a different manner than the preceding forms. Except for signals, all preceding forms used file descriptors to access and to control them. Message queues, shared memory, and semaphores use different handles.

The Message Queue

The UNIX message queue implements a priority-based queue of messages. The message is simply a short block of memory holding an application-defined message. When a message is queued, it is stored within kernel memory so that it can be later retrieved by another process. Figure 22.1 illustrates how messages are queued, stored, and retrieved.

FIGURE 22.1

The Message Queue Store within the kernel.

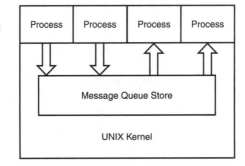

The figure shows three processes queuing messages and one process receiving messages. Message queues in general, however, can by queued by many processes and received by many processes.

Every queued message has a message priority. UNIX documentation calls this a message type (see `msgsnd(3)`). This message type, however, determines the priority of the message when it is queued. Figure 22.2 shows a series of messages from **A** to **J** being queued. The number preceding each message letter indicates the priority of the message. For example, **3C** indicates message **C** was queued at priority **3**.

FIGURE 22.2

Priority messages placed in a message queue.

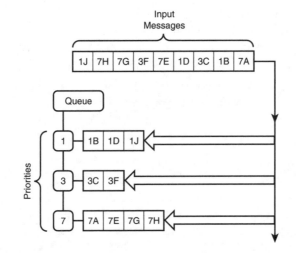

The UNIX kernel queues each message into a sub-queue that corresponds to the message priority. If no process is removing messages from the queue, Figure 22.2 shows how the nine messages would be sorted according to their message priority. The lowest numbers indicate the highest priority in message queues.

When the receiving process retrieves a message, it has several choices. These are

- Receive a message of priority x, or receive no messages if no messages exist with priority x.

- Receive the lowest numbered (highest priority) message that is less than or equal to priority x.

- Receive the first message on the queue in a first-in, first-out manner, without regard to priority.

While Figure 22.2 shows that all messages are queued by priority, the UNIX kernel also maintains another linked list that allows it to fetch messages on a FIFO basis. In this manner, a process may choose to ignore the priority of messages and simply fetch the earliest message that was queued.

Since messages can be retrieved for a specific message priority, it is possible to use the message priority (message type) to address a message to one of several receiving processes. The message priority is a 31-bit value (the sign-bit cannot be used). Consequently, some applications have used the message type for the process ID. Each receiving process simply fetches messages that correspond to its process ID. Figure 22.3 shows an illustration of this.

FIGURE 22.3

Processes reading messages by process ID.

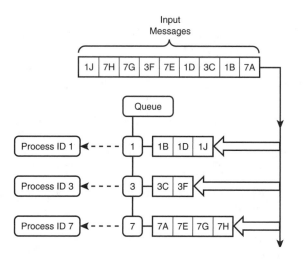

Each process selects its own messages in Figure 22.3 by using its process ID as the message priority. Readers should be cautioned, however, that as UNIX moves toward 64-bit platforms, process ID values might expand in size. This will allow the kernel to accommodate higher numbers of processes.

Shared Memory

When multiple processes cooperate, they often need to share tables of data. UNIX provides for this in the form of the shared memory facility. Figure 22.4 shows how one shared memory region can be shared by three processes.

FIGURE 22.4

A memory region shared
with three processes.

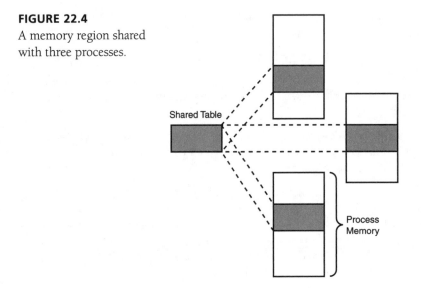

Although the concept of sharing memory is a simple one, a number of complications can occur. For example, in Figure 22.4, the shared region may be attached to each process' memory space at a different memory address. This means that if memory addresses are used within the shared table, they will not be usable in all processes. Memory offsets must be used instead. This is the reason that shared libraries must be compiled to use position-independent code.

Another complication is the problem of synchronization between the three processes. If multiple processes are changing areas of the shared memory region, how can a given process know that a particular component of data is complete? Even the process of replacing an integer value is not atomic on many CPU platforms.

Although message queues could be used for synchronization, most application designers turn to the semaphore for this purpose.

Semaphores

A UNIX semaphore keeps track of a count and notifies the interested processes when the count changes. The simplest semaphore is the binary semaphore, which can only hold the count of 0 or 1. A mutex is a simple form of a binary semaphore, which is used when programming with threads.

Other semaphores allow you to track *n* instances of a particular resource. For example, if you have three transaction servers available to serve client processes, you would initialize the semaphore to the count of **3**. As clients attach to and reserve a transaction server, you would decrement this count. When the count reaches zero, the semaphore indicates that no remaining resources exist at this time. Later, when a client finishes with a transaction server, it increments the semaphore count. When all clients complete, the count increments to the initial count of **3**. In this manner, the semaphore tracks the number of available resources.

The act of decrementing a semaphore count is known as *waiting on the semaphore*. This makes sense when you consider that when the count reaches zero, the requestor must wait for the resource to become available.

The act of incrementing a semaphore count is known as *notifying the semaphore*. The increment of the count causes processes that are waiting for a free resource to be notified that it is now available.

Individual semaphores work well for controlling individual resources. However, obtaining several resources at once is often required. Imagine a small bowling alley that has 50 pairs of bowling shoes, 30 bowling balls, and 6 bowling alleys available. To bowl, a patron needs one pair of shoes, a bowling ball, and an alley. However, a patron cannot bowl if any of the resources—shoes, balls, or alley—are unavailable. A semaphore set permits the caller to request all of the resources at once. In this way, there is no potential for deadlocks, since the request either completely succeeds or it fails (waits).

Figure 22.5 illustrates a semaphore set, which tracks 30 bowling balls, 50 pairs of bowling shoes, and 12 bowling alleys.

FIGURE 22.5

A semaphore set.

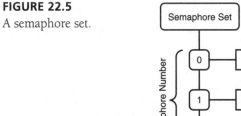

The figure illustrates one semaphore set. Within the set, semaphore **0** controls the resource "bowling balls," semaphore **1** controls the resource "bowling shoes," and semaphore **2** controls "bowling alleys." It is not necessary to request all of the resources in a semaphore set. A patron may choose to bring his own shoes or bowling ball. A group of patrons usually shares a bowling alley, and so the total number shoes, bowling balls, and one bowling alley would be requested.

The benefit of grouping these resources into one set is that the caller can obtain all resources needed in one system call, without worrying about deadlock situations. If any of the requested resources are not available, the caller simply waits until all resources become available.

Referencing IPC Resources

The UNIX kernel provides IPC ID values for processes to refer to specific instances of message queues, shared memory, and semaphore sets. The IPC ID is an integer value that is determined by the kernel, and is not known by the calling process until it has been returned in a create call. The IPC ID can be zero or positive, but it is never negative. The IPC ID is similar to a file descriptor for a specific IPC resource.

Although the IPC ID value is a convenient handle for resources once they are created, they are not well suited for a prearranged rendezvous. If three different processes must attach to a shared memory region, how do the two processes that did not create the shared region find out what the IPC ID of that resource is? To solve this difficulty, the UNIX kernel also provides facilities for working with IPC key values.

The IPC Key Value

The IPC key value is defined by the C data type `key_t`. This permits a system-wide 32-bit key value to be specified. Although files use a hierarchical file system, IPC key values are not hierarchical. The 32-bit key applies to the host system on a system-wide basis. The IPC key is like a filename, whereas the IPC ID is like an open file descriptor.

If your software and another software package choose the same IPC key value, they will be in conflict. To choose a key that is not in use, you can use the `ipcs(1)` command to list the keys that are in use (older versions of Linux do not show the key values).

Once you have chosen an IPC key value, it is possible for a process to gain access to a message queue, shared memory region, or semaphore set by specifying it. As long as all of your processes agree on this key in advance, they will locate the common IPC resource. Once the access is granted, the kernel returns the IPC ID value that is used for that resource. The IPC key is only required for the initial rendezvous.

Creating an IPC Resource

You create IPC resources with system calls named after the type of the resource. The function `msgget(3)` creates a message queue, while `shmget(2)` and `semget(2)` create shared memory regions and semaphores, respectively. The `msgget(3)` function is the simplest of these, and so its synopsis is shown as follows:

```
#include <sys/types.h>
#include <sys/ipc.h>
#include <sys/msg.h>

int msgget(key_t key, int flags);
```

The `msgget(3)` function accepts an IPC key value `key` and some flags in `flags`. All IPC create functions have a `key` argument and a `flags` argument.

To create an IPC resource, the flags argument must have the bit `IPC_CREAT` provided, in addition to the permission bits required. Otherwise, the function will attempt to gain access to the existing resource, if any. The `key` argument can have one of two possible values:

- `IPC_PRIVATE`

- A non-zero IPC key value

The IPC key must be non-zero because most UNIX systems implement `IPC_PRIVATE` as the value `(key_t)(0)`. Often, the IPC key value is specified in hexadecimal. The following example shows how a message queue with IPC key `0xFEEDBEEF` is created:

```
int mqid;                        /* Message Queue IPC ID */
```

```
mqid = msgget(0xFEEDBEEF,IPC_CREAT|0600);
```

From this point forward, the IPC ID `mqid` is used to reference the created message queue.

Private message IPC resources can also be created by using the IPC key `IPC_PRIVATE`. The following shows how a private message queue is created:

```
int mqid;                        /* Message Queue IPC ID */
```

```
mqid = msgget(IPC_PRIVATE,IPC_CREAT|0600);
```

The `IPC_PRIVATE` key does not imply privacy, however. What it does imply is that there is no IPC key associated with this created resource. This is similar to a file that is open on a file unit, but has no name because `unlink(2)` has been called on it. As long as the process knows the IPC ID (`mqid` in the example) of the resource, there is no need for an IPC key.

`IPC_PRIVATE` is useful when you want to avoid key clashes with other software on your system. A large software package, such as a relational database, could arrange to use one IPC key to allow access to a shared memory table. Within that table, the IPC ID values for all other IPC resources created using key `IPC_PRIVATE` could be stored there. Using this method, all external processes need only to gain access to the initial shared memory table with the one IPC key. All other resources can be referenced directly by the IPC ID values found within the table.

Accessing by IPC Key

Processes that do not create the shared resource must look it up to discover the IPC ID. This can be performed using the same system call that is used for creation. The following looks up the message queue that was created earlier:

```
int mqid;                        /* Message Queue IPC ID */
```

```
mqid = msgget(0xFEEDBEEF,0);
```

Observe that the `IPC_CREAT` flag bit is absent from the `flags` argument. The permission bits are also absent, since they are not required when the resource has already been created.

Once the IPC ID value in `mqid` is known, the IPC key is no longer required for access to the resource.

Accessing by IPC ID

When the IPC ID for a resource is known, the resource can be accessed directly. Unlike files, which must be opened, IPC resources can be accessed immediately when the IPC ID is known. The one exception to this rule is that shared memory must be attached to your process memory space before it can be referenced (see `shmat(2)`).

Destroying IPC Resources

IPC resources can outlive your process. When a process terminates for any reason, all files are closed and its shared memory is detached, but its IPC resources will continue to exist. If IPC resources are no longer required, they must be explicitly destroyed.

There are system calls to perform this function:

- `msgctl(3)` for message queues
- `semctl(2)` for semaphores
- `shmctl(2)` for shared memory

The following chapters cover the specifics of these operations. There are, however, some system-wide implications of destroying IPC resources that should be noted here.

When a message queue or a semaphore set is destroyed, they are destroyed immediately. Since IPC resources are not opened like files, they do not stay open until closed. When a message queue or semaphore set is destroyed, the UNIX kernel immediately discards them. If a message queue or semaphore operation is subsequently attempted on the destroyed IPC ID, the error `EIDRM` is returned.

Note

`EIDRM—Identifier removed`   This error is returned when an IPC ID is used in an IPC operation after the resource has been destroyed.

Shared memory is handled differently. When shared memory is used, it must be attached to the current process at a specific address. When the shared region is no longer required, or when the process terminates, the shared region is detached from the current process. Due to this behavior, when a process destroys shared memory, the shared memory region exists until the last process detaches it.

The following general points can now be summarized:

- IPC resources exist until destroyed.

- Message queues and semaphores are immediately destroyed.

- When shared memory is destroyed, its destruction occurs when the last process detaches from it.

Note

Under many operating systems, the IPC resources discussed in this chapter are optional. They are available only if they are configured or compiled into the kernel.

Additionally, note that IPC resources normally have system-configured limits for the number of messages queued, the maximum size of a message, the maximum number of semaphores in a set, the maximum amount of shared memory available, and so on.

Check your system documentation to find out how to configure these values to suit your application needs.

Tip

When you are debugging programs that fail to destroy IPC resources when they should, use the `ipcs(1)` command to display the resources and the `ipcrm(1)` command to remove them.

Summary

This chapter has been an overview of the IPC facilities as they exist under UNIX. The next three chapters will explore these IPC resources in detail.

## CHAPTER 23

MESSAGE QUEUES

M essage queues provide the IPC facility that permits unrelated processes to pass messages between them. This chapter will look at the message facility in detail. A C++ object is developed around the message queue facility and used in a demonstration.

Controlling a Message Queue

The initial examination of the message queue will concern control functions such as message queue creation, modification, and destruction. Message sending and receiving is covered later.

Creating Message Queues

The last chapter provided a sneak peek at the message queue creation process. The function synopsis is repeated here for your convenience:

```
#include <sys/types.h>
#include <sys/ipc.h>
#include <sys/msg.h>

int msgget(key_t key, int flags);
```

The argument `key` must have the value `IPC_PRIVATE` or a valid IPC key value.

The `flags` argument must contain the permission bits for the new queue and `IPC_CREAT` if the queue is being created. The flag `IPC_EXCL` can be added to cause `msgget(3)` to return an error if the message queue already exists. Otherwise, `IPC_CREAT` attempts to create the queue but will use the existing one that matches `key`, if it already exists.

The function returns the IPC ID of the message queue when it is successful, which is a zero or positive value. The value `-1` is returned when an error occurs, and the variable `errno` contains the error code.

Accessing a Message Queue

To locate an existing message queue, do not specify the `IPC_CREAT` flag. An error is returned in this case if the queue does not already exist. You may specify zero for the `flags` argument when a queue is not being created, since the permission bits are ignored.

Destroying a Message Queue

To perform control operations on a message queue, including its destruction, you must invoke the msgctl(3) function:

```
#include <sys/types.h>
#include <sys/ipc.h>
#include <sys/msg.h>

int msgctl(int msqid, int cmd, struct msqid_ds *buf);
```

The first argument, msqid, is the message queue IPC ID. The argument cmd is a command constant, and the last argument, buf, is a pointer to a structure.

The function msgctl(3) returns 0 when it is successful. When -1 is returned, errno holds the error code.

The operation commands accepted by this function include

IPC_RMID	Destroy the message queue.
IPC_STAT	Query the message queue for information.
IPC_SET	Change certain message queue attributes.

The command IPC_RMID is the one that you are interested in for queue destruction. The argument buf is not used for this command, and is permitted to be a null pointer. The following example shows how a queue can be destroyed:

```
int z;

z = msgctl(msqid,IPC_RMID,0);
if ( z == -1 )
    perror("msgctl(3)")
```

Obtaining Message Queue Information

The stat(2) call is available to obtain information about files. The msgctl(3) command IPC_STAT performs a similar function for message queues. In this case, the third argument must point to a struct msqid_ds to receive the results. The structure definition is shown in the synopsis:

```
struct msqid_ds {
    struct ipc_perm msg_perm;   /* msg queue permission bits */
    struct msg *msg_first;      /* first message in the queue */
    struct msg *msg_last;       /* last message in the queue */
    u_long  msg_cbytes;         /* number of bytes in use on the queue */
    u_long  msg_qnum;           /* number of msgs in the queue */
    u_long  msg_qbytes;         /* max # of bytes on the queue */
    pid_t   msg_lspid;          /* pid of last msgsnd() */
    pid_t   msg_lrpid;          /* pid of last msgrcv() */
    time_t  msg_stime;          /* time of last msgsnd() */
```

```
    time_t  msg_rtime;        /* time of last msgrcv() */
    time_t  msg_ctime;        /* time of last msgctl() */
};
```

There are a number of informational members in this structure, including the number of messages in the queue (`msg_qnum`) and time stamps.

Structure member `msg_perm` is important for controlling access to your message queue. Its structure is described in the following synopsis:

```
struct ipc_perm {
    ushort  cuid;             /* creator user id */
    ushort  cgid;             /* creator group id */
    ushort  uid;              /* user id */
    ushort  gid;              /* group id */
    ushort  mode;             /* r/w permission */
    ushort  seq;              /* sequence # (to generate unique msg/sem/shm id) */
    key_t   key;              /* user specified msg/sem/shm key */
};
```

The members `cuid` and `cgid` are the user and group IDs of the creator of the queue. The members `uid` and `gid` are the current owner user and group ID values for the message queue. The member `mode` specifies the permission bits for this queue.

The only members that can be altered after a queue has been created are the members `uid`, `gid`, `mode`, and the `msqid_ds` member `msg_qbytes`. You must be the creator of the message queue, have an effective user ID that matches the current `uid` value, or be superuser to be permitted to make changes.

The following example shows how the `IPC_STAT` command is used:

```
int z;
struct msqid_ds stbuf;

z = msgctl(msqid,IPC_STAT,&stbuf);
if ( z == -1 )
    perror("msgctl(3)");
```

Altering a Message Queue

You may occasionally need to change the ownership of your message queue, or otherwise modify the permission on it. The `msgctl(3)` command `IPC_SET` enables you to do this.

The following example queries the current message queue to fill in the structure `stbuf`. Then it looks up the `uid_t` value for the login `postgres`. Finally, the owner user ID is changed in `stbuf`, and `msgctl(3)` is called with `IPC_SET` to establish the new owner of this message queue:

```
int z;
struct msqid_ds stbuf;
struct passwd *pw;
```

```
// Obtain status info :
z = msgctl(msqid,IPC_STAT,&stbuf);
if ( z == -1 )
    abort();

// lookup postgres uid_t value :
pw = getpwnam("postgres");
if ( !pw )
    abort();

// Change owner to postgres
stbuf.msg_perm.uid = (ushort)pw->pw_uid;

z = msgctl(msqid,IPC_SET,&stbuf);
if ( z == -1 )
    perror("msgctl(IPC_SET)");
```

Note that although the owner of the message queue is changed here, the creator user and group ID values do not change.

Sending and Receiving Messages

Once you have a message queue to operate with, and the permissions are properly established, you can read and write messages to them. This section describes the msgsnd(3) and msgrcv(3) functions.

Sending Messages

Messages are sent using the msgsnd(3) function. Its function synopsis is given as follows:

```
#include <sys/types.h>
#include <sys/ipc.h>
#include <sys/msg.h>

int msgsnd(int msqid, void *msgp, size_t msgsz, int msgflg);
```

The first argument msqid is the IPC ID of the message queue to send the message on. The argument msgp points to a message structure to be sent. The size of the message msgsz is the message size, not including the message type value. The msgflg argument is specified as 0 unless the flag IPC_NOWAIT is used.

The IPC_NOWAIT allows the msgsnd(3) function to return immediately with the error EAGAIN if the operation would block. Sending a message can block if the message queue has reached its maximum limit for messages or memory use. Sending can also block when the kernel's message resources are limited.

The msgsnd(3) function returns 0 when successful. When -1 is returned, the error is found in the variable errno.

The format of the message structure is shown in the next synopsis:

```
struct msgbuf {          /* Message Structure */
    long  mtype;         /* message type */
    char  mtext[1];      /* body of message */
};
```

The first member of the message structure must be a `long` member to hold the message type (message priority). The actual message itself is shown starting with member `mtext[0]`.

Computing the `msgsz` argument requires some care. This size argument does not include the `mtype` member of the structure passed in argument `msgp`.

The following example shows a message being sent, which contains a simple pathname member `path[256]`:

```
int z;
struct {
    long     mtype;
    char     path[256];
} msg;
int msz;

msz = sizeof msg - sizeof msg.mtype;
z = msgsnd(msqid,&msg,msz,0);
if ( z == -1 )
    perror("msgsnd(3)");
```

Notice that the variable `msz` receives the size of the message without counting the size of the message type `mtype`.

Warning

The function `msgsnd(3)` returns the error `EINTR` when signals are received.

Receiving Messages

Messages are received with the function `msgrcv(3)`. The synopsis for it is as follows:

```
#include <sys/types.h>
#include <sys/ipc.h>
#include <sys/msg.h>

int msgrcv(int msqid, void *msgp, size_t msgsz, long msgtyp, int msgflg);
```

The argument `msqid` is the IPC ID of the message queue to receive the message from. The pointer argument `msgp` must point to a receiving buffer large enough to hold the received message. The argument `msgsz` indicates the maximum size of the received message, not including the size of the `mtype` member. The `msgtyp` and `msgflg` members hold the message type (priority) and option flags for this call, respectively.

The `msgflg` argument can be composed of the following flags:

- The flag `IPC_NOWAIT` indicates that the function `msgrcv(3)` will return the error code `ENOMSG` if there are no messages to receive. Normally, the program is suspended until a message arrives.

- The flag `MSG_EXCEPT`, when used with the `msgtyp` argument greater than zero, causes the first message that differs from `msgtyp` to be received.

- The flag `MSG_NOERROR` indicates that the message should be truncated if necessary to fit the receiving buffer. The error `E2BIG` is returned when this option is used and the message cannot fit into the buffer.

Warning

The function `msgrcv(3)` returns the error `EINTR` when signals are received.

Table 23.1 lists the variations that are possible for the `msgtyp` argument.

TABLE 23.1   The `msgrcv(3)` Message Type Variations

msgtyp	msgflg	Explanation
> 0	0	The `msgrcv(3)` function will return a message only where the `msgtyp` argument matches the message type value of the message.
> 0	MSG_EXCEPT	The `msgrcv(3)` function will return a message only where the `msgtyp` argument does not match the message type of the message.
0	ignored	The `msgrcv(3)` function will return the first message that has been queued.
< 0	ignored	The `msgrcv(3)` function will return the message with the lowest message type that is <= `abs(msgtyp)`.

When `msgrcv(3)` is successful, it returns the number of bytes received (excluding the size of the message type member). Otherwise, `-1` is returned and the error code is found in variable `errno`.

The following example shows how to receive a message.

```
int z;
struct {
    long    mtype;
    char    path[256];
} msg;
int msz;
```

```
msz = sizeof msg - sizeof msg.mtype;

z = msgrcv(msqid,&msg,msz,0,0);
if ( z == -1 )
    perror("msgrcv(3)");
```

This example chooses to receive the first available message without regard to priority (argument `msgtyp` is equal to `0`). The value of `msz` is computed to include the maximum size of the receiving structure, but not to include the size for `msg.mtype`.

Applying Message Queues

A client and server program that uses message queues is presented here. The client issues the request, and the server receives the message and responds. The server simply performs a `stat(2)` or `lstat(2)` call, and returns the results to the client by a message.

The client and server programs both use a C++ object that has been created to make using message queues a little friendlier. The C++ object and its implementation will be presented first.

Listing 23.1 shows the file `msq.h`, which defines the C++ class `Msq`.

LISTING 23.1   `msq.h`—The `Msq` Class Definition File

```
 1:    // msq.h :
 2:    //
 3:    // Message Queue Class :
 4:
 5:    #include <sys/types.h>
 6:    #include <sys/ipc.h>
 7:    #include <sys/msg.h>
 8:
 9:    struct Msg {
10:        long    msgtyp;      // Message type/priority
11:    };
12:
13:    class Msq {
14:        enum state { ready, notReady };
15:        key_t   key;         // IPC Key
16:        int     msqid;       // IPC ID
17:        int     error;       // Last errno
18:
19:    protected:
20:        void _verify(state s);
21:
22:    public:
23:        Msq();
24:        Msq &create(key_t key,int flags);
25:        Msq &access(key_t key);
26:        Msq &dispose();
```

continued from previous page

```
27:        Msq &destroy();
28:        msqid_ds &stat(msqid_ds &stbuf);
29:        Msq &change(msqid_ds &stbuf);
30:        int send(Msg &msg,size_t size,int flags=0);
31:        int recv(Msg &msg,size_t &size,size_t maxsz,long msgtyp,int flags=0);
32:        inline int getError() { return error; }
33:        inline key_t getKey() { return key; }
34:    };
35:
36:    // End msq.h
```

Lines 9–11 define the basic message structure that can be used with C++ inheritance for building application messages from. The `Msq` class is declared starting in line 13. The `Msq` object maintains copies of the IPC key, the IPC ID, and the last error code encountered. The IPC key and the last error are accessed through the inline methods `Msq::getError()` and `Msq::getKey()` if required.

The private `Msq::_verify()` member checks the state of the `Msq` object. It raises the error `EINVAL` if the object is in the wrong state for the operation being attempted. The methods `Msq::create()` and `Msq::access()` require the object to be in a "not ready" state. Other methods such as `Msq::send()` and `Msq::recv()` expect the object to be in the "ready" state.

With the exception of the `Msq::send()` and `Msq::recv()` methods when the flag `IPC_NOWAIT` is used, all methods throw `errno` values when an error condition is encountered. As noted earlier, if the object is in the wrong state for a method call, the error `EINVAL` is raised.

The default constructor creates the `Msq` object in the "not ready" state. The `Msq` object is designed so that it can be re-used for a different message queue by calling its `Msq::dispose()` or `Msq::destroy()` methods, and then calling `Msq::create()` or `Msq::access()`.

Object method `Msq::create()` creates a new message queue. Method `Msq::access()`, on the other hand, tries to access an existing message queue.

The method `Msq::dispose()` reinitializes the object to its initial "not ready" state. In other words, it disposes of its current context. The `Msq::destroy()` method destroys the underlying message queue and then calls `Msq::dispose()` to initialize the object to its initial "not ready" state.

The method `Msq::stat()` allows the caller to receive information about the message queue. The `Msq::change()` method allows message queue parameters to be changed using the `IPC_SET` command.

The methods `Msq::send()` and `Msq::recv()` are wrapper functions around the `msgsnd(3)` and `msgrcv(3)` functions. They provide the extra functionality of handling the `EINTR` error when signals are received.

Now look at Listing 23.2.

LISTING 23.2   msqveri.cc—The Implementation of `Msq::_verify()`, `Msq::dispose()`, and the Constructor `Msq::Msq()`

```
 1:    // msqveri.cc :
 2:
 3:    #include <stdlib.h>
 4:    #include <errno.h>
 5:    #include "msq.h"
 6:
 7:    /////////////////////////////////////////////////////////////
 8:    // (private) Msq::_verify :
 9:    //
10:    //   Checks to see that the object is in a ready or
11:    //   not ready state. If the state is not correct
12:    //   the error EINVAL is thrown.
13:    /////////////////////////////////////////////////////////////
14:
15:    void
16:    Msq::_verify(state s) {
17:        if ( s == ready && msqid < 0 )
18:            throw error = EINVAL;   // Object is not open
19:        if ( s != ready && msqid >= 0 )
20:            throw error = EINVAL;   // Object is open!
21:    }
22:
23:    /////////////////////////////////////////////////////////////
24:    // Msq::dispose :
25:    //
26:    //   Disposes of the current message queue reference, if
27:    //   any. The object is re-initialized to the not-ready
28:    //   state.
29:    /////////////////////////////////////////////////////////////
30:
31:    Msq &
32:    Msq::dispose() {
33:
34:        key = IPC_PRIVATE;
35:        msqid = -1;
36:        return *this;
37:    }
38:
39:    /////////////////////////////////////////////////////////////
40:    // Msq::Msq :
41:    //
42:    //   Constructor. This constructor calls upon the
43:    //   method Msq::dispose() to initialize the object.
44:    /////////////////////////////////////////////////////////////
45:
46:    Msq::Msq() {
47:        Msq::dispose();    // Initialize this object
48:    }
49:
50:    // End msqveri.cc
```

The method `Msq::_verify()` uses the enumerated data type **state** for its argument **s**. When **s** is equal to **ready**, the private member **msqid** must be less than zero to indicate that the object is in a not ready state. If this test fails, the error **EINVAL** is thrown in line 18. All thrown errors are preserved in the private member **error** for later retrieval.

When **s** is not equal to **ready**, then **EINVAL** is thrown if the test shows that the object currently holds a valid IPC ID in the member **msqid** (lines 19 and 20).

The `Msq::dispose()` function simply initializes the object into a not ready state (lines 34 and 35). The default constructor `Msq::Msq()` simply calls upon `Msq::dispose()` to initialize the object.

Listing 23.3 shows the implementation of the `Msq::create()` method.

LISTING 23.3   msqcr.cc—The Implementation of the `Msq::create()` Method

```
1:   // msqcr.cc :
2:
3:   #include <stdlib.h>
4:   #include <errno.h>
5:   #include "msq.h"
6:
7:   /////////////////////////////////////////////////////////////
8:   // Msq::create :
9:   //
10:  // ARGUMENTS:
11:  //   key          IPC Key of the message queue or IPC_PRIVATE
12:  //   flags        The permission bits, and possibly IPC_EXCL
13:  //
14:  //   This method creates a message queue. Object must be
15:  //   in a not-ready state.
16:  /////////////////////////////////////////////////////////////
17:
18:  Msq &
19:  Msq::create(key_t key,int flags) {
20:
21:      _verify(notReady);  // Object must not be open
22:
23:      flags |= IPC_CREAT; // Force a create symantic
24:
25:      /*
26:       * Attempt to create the message queue :
27:       */
28:      msqid = msgget(this->key = key,flags);
29:      if ( msqid == -1 )
30:          throw error = errno;
31:
32:      return *this;
33:  }
34:
35:  // End msqcr.cc
```

Like many methods within the `Msq` class, the state of the object is tested first (line 21). Since this method call implies creation of the message queue, the flag `IPC_CREAT` is or-ed in with the `flags` argument in line 23. Line 28 invokes the `msgget(3)` call to create the queue. Unless the `flags` argument included `IPC_EXCL`, the `Msq::create()` method will return an existing message queue if it already exists. If an error is encountered, it is thrown in line 30.

Listing 23.4 shows the implementation of the `Msq::access()` method.

LISTING 23.4   `msqac.cc`—The Implementation of the `Msq::access()` Method

```
 1:    // msqac.cc :
 2:
 3:    #include <stdlib.h>
 4:    #include <errno.h>
 5:    #include "msq.h"
 6:
 7:    /////////////////////////////////////////////////////////////
 8:    // Msq::access :
 9:    //
10:    // ARGUMENTS:
11:    //   key           IPC Key of the message queue or IPC_PRIVATE
12:    //
13:    //   This method accesses a message queue. Object must be
14:    //   in a not-ready state.
15:    /////////////////////////////////////////////////////////////
16:
17:    Msq &
18:    Msq::access(key_t key) {
19:
20:        _verify(notReady);  // Object must not be open
21:
22:        /*
23:         * Attempt to create the message queue :
24:         */
25:        msqid = msgget(this->key = key,0);
26:        if ( msqid == -1 )
27:            throw error = errno;
28:
29:        return *this;
30:    }
31:
32:    // End msqac.cc
```

The `Msq::access()` is very similar to the `Msq::create()` method. Note, however, that the `flags` argument in the `msgget(3)` function call (line 25) is the value zero, indicating that the message queue must already exist.

Listing 23.5 shows the implementation of the `Msq::destroy()` method.

LISTING 23.5 msqdest.cc—The Implementation of the Msq::destroy() Method

```
1:   // msqdest.cc
2:
3:   #include <stdlib.h>
4:   #include <errno.h>
5:   #include "msq.h"
6:
7:   ////////////////////////////////////////////////////////////
8:   // Msq::destroy :
9:   //
10:  //   Destroys the message queue. The object must be in a
11:  //   ready state. The object is placed into a not-ready
12:  //   state upon successful completion.
13:  ////////////////////////////////////////////////////////////
14:
15:  Msq &
16:  Msq::destroy() {
17:
18:      _verify(ready);       // Object must be open
19:
20:      if ( msgctl(msqid,IPC_RMID,0) == -1 )
21:          throw error = errno;
22:
23:      Msq::dispose();       // Re-initialize this object
24:      return *this;         // Return in not-ready state
25:  }
26:
27:  // End msqdest.cc
```

The Msq::destroy() method calls upon msgctl(3) with the command IPC_RMID in line 20. If this call succeeds, the Msq::dispose() method is called to initialize the object back to its not ready state in line 23.

Listing 23.6 illustrates the Msq::stat() method, which obtains the message queue status information from the kernel.

LISTING 23.6 msqstat.cc—The Implementation of the Msq::stat() Method

```
1:   // msqstat.cc
2:
3:   #include <stdlib.h>
4:   #include <errno.h>
5:   #include "msq.h"
6:
7:   ////////////////////////////////////////////////////////////
8:   // Msq::stat :
9:   //
10:  // ARGUMENTS :
11:  //   stbuff      The struct msqid_ds structure to populate
12:  //               with message queue information.
13:  //
14:  //   This method fills the supplied buffer with status
```

```
15:    //   information about the current queue. The object must
16:    //   be in the ready state.
17:    //////////////////////////////////////////////////////////////
18:
19:    msqid_ds &
20:    Msq::stat(msqid_ds &stbuf) {
21:
22:        _verify(ready);        // Object must be open
23:
24:        if ( msgctl(msqid,IPC_STAT,&stbuf) == -1 )
25:            throw error = errno;
26:
27:        return stbuf;
28:    }
29:
30:    // End msqstat.cc
```

In the `Msq::stat()` method, the function `msgctl(3)` is called with the command `IPC_STAT` in line 24. The argument `stbuf` is passed by reference in this method, so the results are passed back by this argument as well. If no error is encountered, the reference to the argument `stbuf` is the returned result.

Listing 23.7 shows the implementation of the `Msq::change()` method. Using this method, it is possible to change the owner, group, and permission bits.

LISTING 23.7   `msqchg.c`—The Implementation of the `Msq::change()` Method

```
1:    // msqchg.cc
2:
3:    #include <stdlib.h>
4:    #include <errno.h>
5:    #include "msq.h"
6:
7:    //////////////////////////////////////////////////////////////
8:    // Msq::change :
9:    //
10:   // ARGUMENTS :
11:   //   stbuff      The struct msqid_ds structure containing
12:   //               the changes to be made.
13:   //
14:   //   Only the values msg_perm.uid, msg_perm.gid, msg_perm.mode
15:   //   and msg_qbytes values can be changed. The value
16:   //   msg_qybytes can only be increased by the superuser.
17:   //   Object must be in the ready state.
18:   //////////////////////////////////////////////////////////////
19:
20:   Msq &
21:   Msq::change(msqid_ds &stbuf) {
22:
23:       _verify(ready);        // Object must be open
24:
25:       if ( msgctl(msqid,IPC_SET,&stbuf) == -1 )
```

continued from previous page

```
26:           throw error = errno;
27:
28:       return *this;
29:   }
30:
31:   // End msqchg.cc
```

The function msgctl(3) is called from line 25 with the command IPC_SET. Again, the argument stbuf is passed by reference in Msq::change().

The Msq::send() implementation is shown in Listing 23.8.

LISTING 23.8   msgsend.cc—The Implementation of the Msq::send() Method

```
1:    // msqsend.cc :
2:
3:    #include <stdlib.h>
4:    #include <errno.h>
5:    #include "msq.h"
6:
7:    /////////////////////////////////////////////////////////////
8:    // Msq::send :
9:    //
10:   // ARGUMENTS :
11:   //   msg          The message to be sent
12:   //   size         The total size of the message
13:   //   flags        zero or IPC_NOWAIT (optional)
14:   //
15:   // RETURNS:
16:   //   0            No message sent (with IPC_NOWAIT)
17:   //   1            Message was sent
18:   //
19:   //   Sends a message of size bytes to the message queue.
20:   //   The size must include the total size of the message,
21:   //   including the message type. The object must be in a
22:   //   ready state.
23:   /////////////////////////////////////////////////////////////
24:
25:   int
26:   Msq::send(Msg &msg,size_t size,int flags) {
27:       int z;
28:       size_t msgsz = size - sizeof msg.msgtyp;
29:
30:       _verify(ready);
31:
32:       do {
33:           z = msgsnd(msqid,&msg,msgsz,flags);
34:       } while ( z == -1 && errno == EINTR );
35:
36:       if ( z ) {
37:           if ( flags & IPC_NOWAIT && errno == EAGAIN )
38:               return 0;    // Not sent
39:
40:           // Other fatal error:
```

```
41:          throw error = errno;
42:      }
43:
44:      return 1;              // Succeeded
45:  }
46:
47:  // End msqsend.cc
```

The `Msq::send()` method has the message `msg` passed by reference (line 26). The size of the entire message is passed into argument `size`. The real size is computed internally on line 28 and placed in the variable `msgsz`.

The loop in lines 32–34 takes care of handling the error `EINTR`. This would be unsatisfactory, however, if you needed to do something after a signal within this loop (some code modification would be required).

If `flags` include `IPC_NOWAIT` and the error `EAGAIN` is returned, then the value `0` is returned instead of raising an exception (lines 37 and 38). When `IPC_NOWAIT` is used, this exit condition is likely to occur frequently and so the costly exception mechanism is avoided. The value `1` is returned when the send operation is successful (line 44).

`Msq::recv()` is illustrated in Listing 23.9.

LISTING 23.9   `msqrecv.cc`—The Implementation of the `Msq::recv()` Method

```
1:   // msqrecv.c :
2:
3:   #include <stdlib.h>
4:   #include <errno.h>
5:   #include "msq.h"
6:
7:   //////////////////////////////////////////////////////////
8:   // Msq::recv :
9:   //
10:  // ARGUMENTS :
11:  // msg          The receiving buffer for the message
12:  // size         The returned size of the message
13:  // maxsz        The maximum size of the returned message
14:  // msgtyp       The message type to use (priority)
15:  // flags        Flags IPC_NOWAIT, IPC_EXCEPT and
16:  //              IPC_NOERROR (optional)
17:  //
18:  // RETURNS :
19:  // 0            No message returned (with IPC_NOWAIT)
20:  // 1            Message was returned
21:  //
22:  // This method receives a message from the message queue.
23:  // Object must be in a ready state.
24:  //////////////////////////////////////////////////////////
25:
26:  int
27:  Msq::recv(Msg &msg,size_t &size,size_t maxsz,long msgtyp,int flags) {
28:      int z;
```

continued from previous page

```
29:        size_t msgsz = maxsz - sizeof msg.msgtyp;
30:
31:        _verify(ready);
32:
33:        do {
34:            z = msgrcv(msqid,&msg,msgsz,msgtyp,flags);
35:        } while ( z == -1 && errno == EINTR );
36:
37:        if ( z == -1 ) {
38:            if ( flags & IPC_NOWAIT && errno == EAGAIN )
39:                return 0;                // No message read
40:            throw error = errno;         // Error occurred
41:        }
42:
43:        size = z + sizeof msg.msgtyp;    // Return size
44:        return 1;                        // Successful
45: }
46:
47: // End msqrecv.cc
```

Like `Msq::send()`, the `Msq::recv()` method computes the correct message size internally, at line 29. The `msgrcv(3)` function is called in the loop to handle **EINTR** (lines 33–35). The message is returned via the argument `msg`, which is passed by reference. The `size` argument, which is also passed by reference, is updated in line 43 and adjusted to include the size of the message type. The argument `msgtyp` is used in the call to `msgrcv(3)` to select the type of message to be received.

Again, when `flag` bit `IPC_NOWAIT` is used, the value `0` is returned when there is no message instead of throwing an exception. Any unusual error is thrown, however. The value `1` is returned if a message was received.

Now you can turn your attention to the client and server programs. First, examine Listing 23.10, which shows the declaration of the message structure `StatMsg`.

LISTING 23.10   `statmsg.h`—The Declaration of the `StatMsg` Message Structure

```
1:  // statmsg.h
2:
3:  struct StatMsg : Msg {
4:      enum {
5:          stat,                   // stat a pathname
6:          lstat,                  // lstat a pathname
7:          stop                    // stop the server
8:      }           request;        // Request type
9:      int         error;          // zero if successful
10:     pid_t       PID;            // Requesting Process ID
11:     union {
12:         char    path[256];      // Pathname to stat
13:         struct stat stbuf;      // stat(2) or lstat(2) info
14:     }           u;              // union
15: };
16:
17: // End statmsg.h
```

The structure `StatMsg` uses C++ inheritance to inherit from the structure `Msg` that was shown in Listing 23.1. The `Msg` structure adds the message type member `msgtyp`.

The enumerated member `request` allows the client to request a `stat(2)`, `lstat(2)`, or server stop operation. The `error` member is used by the server to return an error code, or zero if the request succeeded.

Member `PID` is filled with the client's process ID. This allows the server to direct the reply back to the client process. All server requests go to message type `1`. The replies go back to the client's by using the process ID as the message type. This allows many clients to use the server concurrently.

The remainder of the message is declared by a `union` in lines 11–14. The request passes a pathname in member `u.path[]`, while responses return information in `u.stbuf`.

Listing 23.11 shows the source listing for the `statsrv` server.

LISTING 23.11   statsrv.cc—The `statsrv` Server Listing

```
 1:   // statsrv.cc :
 2:
 3:   #include <stdio.h>
 4:   #include <unistd.h>
 5:   #include <stdlib.h>
 6:   #include <errno.h>
 7:   #include <string.h>
 8:   #include <sys/types.h>
 9:   #include <sys/stat.h>
10:
11:   #include "msq.h"
12:   #include "statmsg.h"
13:
14:   int
15:   main(int argc,char **argv) {
16:       int quit = 0;              // True when stop received
17:       Msq q;                     // Message queue object
18:       StatMsg m;                 // Message buffer
19:       size_t msz;                // Message size
20:       char pathname[256+1];      // Local copy of pathname
21:       msqid_ds mstat;            // Message queue info
22:
23:       (void) argc;
24:       (void) argv;
25:
26:       /*
27:        * Create the server message queue :
28:        */
29:       try {
30:           q.create(0xFEEDF00D,0600);
31:       } catch ( int e ) {
32:           errno = e;
```

continued from previous page

```
33:            perror("Creating a queue");
34:        }
35:
36:        /*
37:         * Obtain queue information :
38:         */
39:        try {
40:            q.stat(mstat);
41:        } catch ( int e ) {
42:            errno = e;
43:            perror("q.stat()");
44:        }
45:
46:        printf("Queue permissions were: %04o\n",mstat.msg_perm.mode);
47:
48:        /*
49:         * For demonstration purposes,
50:         * make the queue read & writable to all :
51:         */
52:        mstat.msg_perm.mode = 0666;
53:
54:        try {
55:            q.change(mstat);
56:        } catch ( int e ) {
57:            errno = e;
58:            perror("q.change()");
59:        }
60:
61:        printf("Queue permissions now : %04o\n",mstat.msg_perm.mode);
62:
63:        /*
64:         * Server message loop :
65:         */
66:        do  {
67:            /*
68:             * Receive a message of type 1 :
69:             */
70:            try {
71:                q.recv(m,msz,sizeof m,1,0);
72:            } catch ( int e ) {
73:                errno = e;
74:                perror("Receiving from queue");
75:                return 1;
76:            }
77:
78:            /*
79:             * Process message :
80:             */
81:            switch ( (int) m.request ) {
82:            case StatMsg::stat :    // stat(2) request :
83:                strncpy(pathname,m.u.path,sizeof pathname);
84:                pathname[sizeof pathname-1] = 0;
```

```
 85:               m.error = stat(pathname,&m.u.stbuf) ? errno : 0;
 86:               break;
 87:
 88:           case StatMsg::lstat :    // lstat(2) request :
 89:               strncpy(pathname,m.u.path,sizeof pathname);
 90:               pathname[sizeof pathname-1] = 0;
 91:               m.error = lstat(pathname,&m.u.stbuf) ? errno : 0;
 92:               break;
 93:
 94:           case StatMsg::stop :    // stop server :
 95:               quit = 1;           // Stop the server
 96:               m.error = 0;        // Ack request
 97:               break;
 98:
 99:           default :               // Unknown request :
100:               m.error = EINVAL;
101:           }
102:
103:           /*
104:            * Reply to client :
105:            */
106:           m.msgtyp = m.PID;        // Reply to this process
107:
108:           try {
109:               q.send(m,sizeof m);
110:           } catch ( int e ) {
111:               errno = e;
112:               perror("q.send()");
113:               return 1;
114:           }
115:       } while ( !quit );
116:
117:       /*
118:        * Destroy the message queue :
119:        */
120:       q.destroy();
121:       return 0;
122: }
123:
124: // End statsrv.cc
```

The message queue object **q** is declared in line 17. The message queue is created in lines 29–34. To demonstrate the `Msq::stat()` and `Msq::change()` methods, the code in lines 36–59 changes the message queue to allow every user to read or write from this queue (permission **0666** in line 52).

The server loop itself occurs in lines 66–115, until the integer variable **quit** is set true. Messages are received in lines 70–76. The message is interpreted and processed in lines 81–101. Line 85 calls `stat(2)`, while line 91 calls `lstat(2)` instead. If a stop request is received, the **quit** variable is made true in line 95. Bogus messages simply get the **m.error** value returned as **EINVAL** in line 100.

The message is returned to the client by setting the message type to the client's process ID in line 106. The message is sent to the message queue in lines 108–114.

When the server is told to stop by a client, the execution falls out of the do { } while loop and q.destroy() before the server program exits. This destroys the message queue.

Listing 23.12 lists the source code for the client program statcln.

LISTING 23.12 statcln.cc—The Source Listing for the statcln Client Program

```
 1:  // statcln.cc :
 2:
 3:  #include <stdio.h>
 4:  #include <unistd.h>
 5:  #include <stdlib.h>
 6:  #include <errno.h>
 7:  #include <string.h>
 8:  #include <sys/types.h>
 9:  #include <sys/stat.h>
10:
11:  #include "msq.h"
12:  #include "statmsg.h"
13:
14:  int
15:  main(int argc,char **argv) {
16:      int x;
17:      Msq q;                      // Message queue object
18:      StatMsg m;                  // Message buffer
19:      size_t msz;                 // Message size
20:      char *pathname;             // Pathname to query
21:
22:      (void) argc;
23:      (void) argv;
24:
25:      /*
26:       * Access the queue :
27:       */
28:      try {
29:          q.access(0xFEEDF00D);
30:      } catch ( int e ) {
31:          errno = e;
32:          perror("Accessing statsrv queue");
33:      }
34:
35:      /*
36:       * Issue server requests for each command line
37:       * argument. If the argument starts with '$', then
38:       * request a lstat(2) instead of stat(2) :
39:       */
40:      for ( x=1; x<argc; ++x ) {
41:          /*
42:           * Form the server request :
43:           */
```

```
44:            if ( !strcasecmp(argv[x],"STOP") )
45:                // STOP SERVER REQUEST :
46:                m.request = StatMsg::stop;
47:            else {
48:                // STAT(2) or LSTAT(2) REQUEST :
49:                if ( argv[x][0] == '$' ) {
50:                    m.request = StatMsg::lstat;
51:                    pathname = argv[x] + 1;   // Skip '$'
52:                } else {
53:                    m.request = StatMsg::stat;
54:                    pathname = argv[x];       // Pathname
55:                }
56:                strncpy(m.u.path,pathname,sizeof m.u.path);
57:            }
58:
59:            /*
60:             * Initialize other message components :
61:             */
62:            m.error = 0;                    // Clear
63:            m.PID = getpid();              // Our process ID
64:            m.msgtyp = 1;                  // Send to the server
65:
66:            /*
67:             * Send the request to the server :
68:             */
69:            try {
70:                q.send(m,sizeof m);        // Send the message
71:            } catch ( int e ) {
72:                errno = e;
73:                perror("s.send()");
74:                return 1;                  // Bail out
75:            }
76:
77:            /*
78:             * If the request is to stop, then exit loop :
79:             */
80:            if ( m.request == StatMsg::stop )
81:                break;                     // There will be no reply
82:
83:            /*
84:             * Wait for the response :
85:             */
86:            try {
87:                q.recv(m,msz,sizeof m,getpid(),0);
88:            } catch ( int e ) {
89:                errno = e;
90:                perror("Receiving from queue");
91:                return 1;
92:            }
93:
94:            /*
95:             * Report response :
96:             */
```

continued from previous page

```
 97:            printf("RESPONSE %14s :   ",pathname);
 98:
 99:        if ( m.error != 0 )
100:            printf(" ERROR: %s\n",strerror(m.error));
101:        else
102:            printf(" SIZE:  %ld bytes\n",(long)m.u.stbuf.st_size);
103:    }
104:
105:    /*
106:     * Exit client program :
107:     */
108:    q.dispose();                        // Reset object
109:    return 0;
110: }
111:
112: // End statcln.cc
```

The **statcln** program accesses the existing message queue that the server created in the **Msq::access()** call in lines 28–33. Then the client program iterates through all of its command-line arguments in lines 40–103.

The command-line argument is tested for the caseless string **STOP** in line 44. If the string matches **STOP**, then a simple request to stop the server is created in line 46. Otherwise, the first character of the command-line argument is tested for a **$** character. If the argument starts with **$**, a **lstat(2)** server request is made (lines 50 and 51) instead of the usual **stat(2)** request (lines 53 and 54). The pathname of the request is copied in line 56.

The process ID of the client must be passed to the server so that it can reply. This is done in line 63. The message type is set to **1** to send this message to the server. Lines 69–75 send the message.

If the request is to stop the server, the loop is exited in line 81 at the **break** statement. This is done because the server will not reply.

Lines 86–92 wait for a server reply on the message queue. The response is reported in lines 97–102. If the request succeeded, the **stat(2)** or **lstat(2)** information reported is the member **st_size**. This displays the file size and confirms that the operation succeeded.

Prior to the client program's exit, it calls **q.dispose()** to forget its knowledge of the message queue it used. However, this does not remove the queue—that is left for the server to do when it shuts down.

The following shows how to make the server and client programs:

```
$ make
cc -c  -Wall -fhandle-exceptions msqveri.cc
cc -c  -Wall -fhandle-exceptions msqcr.cc
cc -c  -Wall -fhandle-exceptions msqac.cc
cc -c  -Wall -fhandle-exceptions msqdest.cc
cc -c  -Wall -fhandle-exceptions msqstat.cc
cc -c  -Wall -fhandle-exceptions msqchg.cc
cc -c  -Wall -fhandle-exceptions msqsend.cc
cc -c  -Wall -fhandle-exceptions msqrecv.cc
```

```
ar r libmsq.a msqveri.o msqcr.o msqac.o msqdest.o msqstat.o msqchg.o
➥ msqsend.o msqrecv.o
cc -c  -Wall -fhandle-exceptions statsrv.cc
cc -o statsrv statsrv.o -L. -lmsq -lstdc++
cc -c  -Wall -fhandle-exceptions statcln.cc
cc -o statcln statcln.o -L. -lmsq -lstdc++
$
```

Once the executables are prepared, you can start up the server program as follows:

```
$ ./statsrv &
$ Queue permissions were: 0600
Queue permissions now : 0666
```

The misplaced **$** character is due to the shell issuing a prompt to the user before the server program wrote its output to the terminal. The server displays before (**0600**) and after (**0666**) sets of permission bits.

With the server ready for requests, you can now issue requests on the **./statcln** command line:

```
$ ./statcln /etc/hosts STOP
RESPONSE    /etc/hosts :   SIZE:  118 bytes
[1] 12935 Exit 0              ./statsrv
$ ls -l /etc/hosts
-rw-r--r--  1 root  wheel  118 May 23 21:10 /etc/hosts
$
```

In this example, the first argument **/etc/hosts** requested a **stat(2)** of the **hosts** file from the server. The response from the server shows that the file's size was 118 bytes. This was verified by the **ls(1)** command. The **STOP** argument caused the program **./statcln** to request the server to shut down, which it did.

Summary

You have examined the message queue operations in this chapter. Message queue creation, destruction, modification, queries, and sending and receiving of messages was tested. The next chapter explores the semaphore IPC resource.

## CHAPTER 24

SEMAPHORES

W hen you have multiple processes running concurrently, there is a frequent need for synchronization. This is particularly true for using shared memory when it is being updated. Whereas Chapter 22, "Interprocess Communication," covered the concepts behind semaphores, this chapter will focus on the system calls available under UNIX for using semaphores.

Semaphore Utility Program

A semaphore utility program is presented in this chapter to facilitate the discussion of semaphore operations. The source code will be presented in modules as each subject area is introduced. This utility will allow you to manipulate all aspects of a semaphore set, including its creation and destruction.

The program will be compiled and tested before the source modules are introduced to allow you to experiment with the topics as the chapter progresses. The remaining additional source for the program will be illustrated at the end of the chapter.

The program is compiled as follows:

```
$ make
cc -c  -Wall -DHAVE_SEMUN ctlget.c
cc -c  -Wall -DHAVE_SEMUN semop.c
cc -c  -Wall -DHAVE_SEMUN semchmod.c
cc -c  -Wall -DHAVE_SEMUN semget.c
cc -c  -Wall -DHAVE_SEMUN semgetall.c
cc -c  -Wall -DHAVE_SEMUN semgetval.c
cc -c  -Wall -DHAVE_SEMUN semrmid.c
cc -c  -Wall -DHAVE_SEMUN semsetall.c
cc -c  -Wall -DHAVE_SEMUN semsetval.c
cc -c  -Wall -DHAVE_SEMUN semstat.c
cc -c  -Wall -DHAVE_SEMUN usage.c
cc -c  -Wall -DHAVE_SEMUN convrt.c
cc -c  -Wall -DHAVE_SEMUN report.c
cc -c  -Wall -DHAVE_SEMUN semchown.c
cc -c  -Wall -DHAVE_SEMUN main.c
cc -o semop ctlget.o semop.o semchmod.o semget.o  semgetall.o semgetval.o
➡ semrmid.o  semsetall.o semsetval.o semstat.o usage.o  convrt.o
➡ report.o semchown.o main.o
$
```

If you have trouble compiling this utility on your platform because the union semun is not defined, then modify the Makefile to remove the option -DHAVE_SEMUN from the compile command line. This will be explained when the include file semop.h is presented.

Now invoke the usage display of the program for help:

```
$ ./semop -h
Usage:  semop [options]
Options:
        -k key  IPC Key for -a or -c option.
        -a              Access existing set based on -k key
        -c n            Create set of n semaphores using -k key
        -i ID           Access existing set by IPC ID
        -o <sops>       semop(n) for wait/zero/notify
        -s              semctl(IPC_STAT)
        -m mode         semctl(IPC_SET) with new permissions
        -x userid       semctl(IPC_SET) with new userid
        -y group        semctl(IPC_SET) with new group
        -d              semctl(IPC_RMID)
        -g n            semctl(GETVAL) for semaphore n
        -G              semctl(GETALL)
        -v n=x          semctl(SETVAL) set semaphore n to x
        -V m,n,o        semctl(SETALL)
        -p n            semctl(GETPID) for semaphore n
        -P              Report semctl(GETPID) for all semaphores
        -n x            semctl(GETNCNT) for semaphore x
        -z x            semctl(GETZCNT) for semaphore x
        -u              No SEM_UNDO (default)
        -U              Use SEM_UNDO
        -R              Report SEM_UNDO flags

<sops> :
        <semaphore#>=<semop>[{u|U}],...
where:
        <semaphore#>    Is the semaphore # (starting from zero)
        <semop>         Semaphore operation: -n, 0 or +n
                        Negative waits, Postive notifies
                        while zero waits for zero.
        u               Do not use SEM_UNDO
        U               Apply SEM_UNDO
        Example: -o 0=-4U,2=+1u,1=2
$
```

This utility program has several command-line options. Each option will be explained as you progress through the chapter.

Note

All semop utility numeric values provided on the command line can be specified in any radix. Octal values are preceded by zero, hexadecimal by 0x, and all other values are interpreted as decimal.

Creating and Accessing Semaphore Sets

A semaphore set is created or accessed by using the semget(2) system call. Its function synopsis is as follows:

```
#include <sys/types.h>
#include <sys/ipc.h>
#include <sys/sem.h>

int semget(key_t key, int nsems, int flags);
```

The semget(2) function requires an IPC key value in the argument key, and permissions and flags in the argument flag. The argument nsems indicates how many semaphores you want to create in this set.

Like msgget(3), the key argument may be an IPC key or the value IPC_PRIVATE for a set of semaphores without a key value.

The flags argument should contain the permission bits to assign to the created set and the flag bit IPC_CREAT. The flag IPC_EXCL will force an error to be returned if the set already exists.

When accessing an existing set, you can specify zero for the flag argument. The permission bits are ignored when you are not creating semaphore sets.

The function semget(2) returns an IPC ID if the call is successful. Otherwise, -1 is returned with an error code left in errno.

Note

Note that semget(2) does not apply the process umask(2) value when creating a new set. The permission value specified in the flag argument is the final mode for the set.

Warning

Applications should always initialize the semaphore values immediately after creating the semaphore sets for maximum portability. The default values for semaphores vary according to UNIX platform.

Listing 24.1 shows the source code used by the utility program to create or access a semaphore set.

LISTING 24.1   semget.c—Source Module That Creates and Accesses a Semaphore Set

```
1:    /* semget.c */
2:
3:    #include "semop.h"
4:
```

continued from previous page

```
5:   void
6:   get_set(int optch,key_t key,int createflg) {
7:       int z;
8:       mode_t um;
9:       mode_t mode;                /* Create permissions */
10:      int flags;                  /* semget(2) flags */
11:
12:      if ( createflg )
13:          flags = IPC_CREAT|IPC_EXCL; /* Create set */
14:      else
15:          flags = 0;              /* Access existing set */
16:
17:      um = umask(077);            /* Query umask */
18:      umask(um);                  /* Restore umask */
19:      mode = 0666 & ~um;          /* Create permissions */
20:
21:      /*
22:       * Create a set of n_sem semaphores :
23:       */
24:      z = semget(key,n_sem,flags|mode);
25:      if ( z == -1 ) {
26:          fprintf(stderr,"%s: -%c\n",strerror(errno),optch);
27:          exit(1);
28:      }
29:
30:      semid = z;                  /* Semaphore IPC ID */
31:
32:      printf("  -%c 0x%X => IPC ID %d\n",optch,(int)key,semid);
33:      if ( key == IPC_PRIVATE )
34:          printf("  WARNING: IPC_PRIVATE used.\n");
35:      fflush(stdout);
36:  }
```

The function get_set() sets the variable **flags** to **IPC_CREAT|IPC_EXCL** when the set is to be created (line 13). Otherwise, **flags** is set to zero (line 15).

Since the function semget(2) does not use the umask(2) value, the current mask is looked up and applied to the default permissions **0666** line in lines 17–19.

Line 24 calls semget(2) to access or create the set, depending upon the value of its **flags** variable. The number of semaphores to create (when **flags** contains **IPC_CREAT**) is determined by a global variable n_sem. If the function call succeeds, the global variable **semid** is assigned the IPC ID in line 30.

Warning

Note that the key value used for some of the examples in this chapter uses hexadecimal values. The key value FEEDF00D uses zeros. Do not type the letter O when typing this key value.

The following example shows how to create a simple semaphore set of three, using the utility program ./semop:

```
$ ./semop -k0xFEEDF00D -c3
  -c 0xFEEDF00D => IPC ID 131072
  -c 3 : Created semaphore set -k 0xFEEDF00D
$
```

The -k0xFEEDF00D option specifies the key, which is followed by the create option -c3. The value 3 indicates that three semaphores are to be created in the set. To confirm that the set was created, invoke the ipcs(1) command. Under FreeBSD, the display appears as follows:

```
$ ipcs
Message Queues:
T    ID    KEY           MODE        OWNER     GROUP


Shared Memory:
T    ID    KEY           MODE        OWNER     GROUP


Semaphores:
T    ID     KEY          MODE        OWNER     GROUP
s 131072   -17960947   --rw-r-----    ehg       ehg

$
```

The FreeBSD ipcs(1) command displays the key value as a signed decimal value. Hence, 0xFEEDF00D becomes the decimal value -17960947 in the display. Notice that the IPC ID value is shown as 131072 in this display (your IPC ID may differ).

The created set can be accessed by the utility by IPC key or IPC ID. The following shows how the set is accessed by the key value:

```
$ ./semop -k0xFEEDF00D -a
  -a 0xFEEDF00D => IPC ID 131072
  There are 3 semaphores in this set.
$
```

The -a option directs the utility program to access the semaphore set by the last -k key value provided. The same set can also be accessed more directly by use of the IPC ID:

```
$ ./semop -i131072 -R
  -i 131072 : There are 3 semaphores in this set.
  -R : key     0xFEEDF00D
  -R : IPC ID 131072
  -R : 0 has no SEM_UNDO
  -R : 1 has no SEM_UNDO
  -R : 2 has no SEM_UNDO
$
```

The option -i131072 identifies the IPC ID of the set, and is enough on its own. The -R option was added so that the IPC key value would be reported along with some other information.

Destroying Semaphore Sets

When a semaphore set is no longer required, it must be explicitly destroyed. This is necessary because semaphores are not destroyed when a process exits. This is accomplished with the semctl(2) function:

```
#include <sys/types.h>
#include <sys/ipc.h>
#include <sys/sem.h>

int semctl(int semid, int semnum, int cmd, ...);
```

The argument semid contains the IPC ID of the semaphore set that was created or accessed by semget(2). The argument semnum identifies which semaphore in the set to operate upon when only one semaphore is being accessed. The argument cmd must contain a valid command macro constant that specifies the operation to be performed on the semaphore or semaphore set. The fourth argument is required for some semctl(2) command operations. In the man(1) pages, it is often referred to as the argument arg.

For commands that operate upon the entire set of semaphores, the argument semnum is ignored. For these occasions, semnum can be specified as 0.

The following is a list of valid semctl(2) commands:

IPC_STAT	Obtains status information about the semaphore set.
IPC_SET	Changes certain attributes of the semaphore set. The sem_perm.uid, sem_perm.gid, and sem_perm.mode values are the only values that may be altered.
IPC_RMID	Removes the semaphore set.
GETVAL	Returns the value of one semaphore in the set.
SETVAL	Changes one semaphore's value in the set. The value is supplied by the semun member val.
GETPID	Returns the process ID of the last process to perform an operation on a specific semaphore within the set. If no operations have been performed, zero is returned.
GETNCNT	Returns the number of processes waiting for a notify on a specific semaphore within the set.
GETZCNT	Returns the number of processes waiting for a zero condition on a specific semaphore within the set.

GETALL	Fetches all semaphore values from the set. The values are returned to an array pointed to by the semun member array. The receiving array must be greater than or equal to the number of semaphores in the set.
SETALL	Sets all semaphore values in the set to new values given by the semun member array. The array is expected to contain enough values to initialize all semaphores contained within the set.

When the command is GETVAL, GETNCNT, or GETZCNT, the function semctl(2) returns the corresponding value when it is successful. Otherwise, -1 is returned with errno holding the error code.

For all other command values, semctl(2) returns 0 for success. Otherwise, -1 is returned with errno holding the error code.

Listing 24.2 shows a source module that uses the semctl(2) system call to destroy a semaphore set.

LISTING 24.2   semrmid.c—Source Module That Removes a Semaphore Set

```
 1:   /* semrmid.c */
 2:
 3:   #include "semop.h"
 4:
 5:   void
 6:   ctl_rmid(int optch) {
 7:       int z;
 8:
 9:       z = semctl(semid,0,IPC_RMID);
10:       if ( z == -1 ) {
11:           fprintf(stderr,"%s: semctl(semid=%d,IPC_RMID)\n",
12:               strerror(errno),semid);
13:           exit(1);
14:       }
15:
16:       semid = -1;                      /* This resource is gone now */
17:
18:       printf("  -%c\n",optch);
19:       fflush(stdout);
20:   }
```

In Listing 24.2 the IPC_RMID command is executed in line 9. Notice no fourth argument is required, and the semnum argument is specified as zero since it is ignored.

The semaphore set from the preceding section can be removed by IPC key or by IPC ID. The following shows how it can be done for IPC ID:

```
$ ./semop -i131072 -d
  -i 131072 : There are 3 semaphores in this set.
  -d
$
```

The -d option causes the code in Listing 24.2 to be invoked to remove the previously identified set. Use the ipcs(1) command to verify that the set is gone:

```
$ ipcs
Message Queues:
T    ID    KEY        MODE        OWNER      GROUP

Shared Memory:
T    ID    KEY        MODE        OWNER      GROUP

Semaphores:
T    ID    KEY        MODE        OWNER      GROUP

$
```

Controlling Semaphores

The previous sections showed how semaphore sets could be created and accessed. This section will show you how you can query the set that you have and make changes to it.

Querying Semaphore Sets

The semctl(2) function provides the IPC_STAT command to allow you to retrieve information about the semaphore set. Of particular interest is the value that indicates how many semaphores are in the set and the permission information. Information for IPC_STAT is returned in the structure semid_ds, which is shown in the following synopsis:

```
struct semid_ds {
    struct ipc_perm sem_perm;   /* operation permission struct */
    struct sem *sem_base;       /* pointer to first semaphore in set */
    u_short sem_nsems;          /* number of sems in set */
    time_t  sem_otime;          /* last operation time */
    time_t  sem_ctime;          /* last change time */
};
```

The structure definition for ipc_perm is repeated for your convenience, as follows:

```
struct ipc_perm {
    ushort   cuid;        /* creator user id */
    ushort   cgid;        /* creator group id */
    ushort   uid;         /* user id */
    ushort   gid;         /* group id */
    ushort   mode;        /* r/w permission */
    ushort   seq;         /* sequence # (to generate unique msg/sem/shm id) */
    key_t    key;         /* user specified msg/sem/shm key */
};
```

In order to receive this information, you must make use of the fourth argument, of type semun. The POSIX standard states that you must define the union semun in your own code. Many releases of UNIX define it for you in the include files. The union is defined in the include file semop.h for the utility, which is shown in Listing 24.3.

LISTING 24.3   semop.h—The Include File That Is Used by the semop Utility Program

```
 1:  /* semop.h */
 2:
 3:  #include <stdio.h>
 4:  #include <stdlib.h>
 5:  #include <unistd.h>
 6:  #include <string.h>
 7:  #include <errno.h>
 8:  #include <sys/types.h>
 9:  #include <pwd.h>
10:  #include <grp.h>
11:  #include <sys/stat.h>
12:  #include <sys/ipc.h>
13:  #include <sys/sem.h>
14:
15:  #ifndef HAVE_SEMUN            /* Does sys/sem.h define this? */
16:
17:  union semun {
18:      int    val;              /* Value */
19:      struct semid_ds *buf;    /* IPC_STAT info */
20:      u_short *array;          /* Array of values */
21:  };
22:
23:  #endif
24:
25:  #define MAX_NSET   16         /* Max value for n_sem */
26:
27:  extern int semid;            /* Semaphore IPC ID */
28:  extern int n_sem;            /* # of semaphores to a set */
29:  extern struct semid_ds sembuf;  /* The last IPC_STAT info */
30:
31:  extern void get_set(int optch,key_t key,int createflg);
32:  extern void ctl_semop(int optch,const char *optarg,
33:      int sems[],int array[],int flags[],int n);
34:  extern void ctl_stat(int optch,int rptflag);
35:  extern void ctl_chmod(int optch,mode_t mode);
36:  extern void ctl_chown(int optch,const char *user_id);
37:  extern void ctl_chgrp(int optch,const char *group);
38:  extern void ctl_rmid(int optch);
39:  extern void ctl_getval(int optch,int semx);
40:  extern void ctl_getall(int optch);
41:  extern void ctl_setval(int optch,int semx,int value);
42:  extern void ctl_setall(int optch,int array[]);
43:  extern void ctl_get(int optch,int cmd,int semx);
44:
45:  extern void usage(void);
46:  extern int cvt2ulong(const char *str,unsigned long *ulp);
47:  extern int cvt2array(const char *str,int array[],const char *delim);
48:  extern int cvt2semops(const char *str,int sems[],int array[],int flags[]);
49:  extern void report(int optch,key_t key,int flags[]);
50:
51:  /* End semop.h */
```

The union is only compiled if the C macro HAVE_SEMUN is not defined. This is defined in the Makefile as the compiler command-line argument -DHAVE_SEMUN. Remove this option if you need the union defined.

Listing 24.4 shows the how the semctl(2) function is called for the IPC_STAT command.

LISTING 24.4 semstat.c—Source Module That Uses the IPC_STAT Command of semctl(2)

```
 1:  /* semstat.c */
 2:
 3:  #include "semop.h"
 4:
 5:  struct semid_ds sembuf;     /* Used for IPC_STAT/IPC_SET */
 6:
 7:  /*
 8:   * Return user ID string :
 9:   */
10:  static char *
11:  user_id(uid_t uid) {
12:      struct passwd *pw = getpwuid(uid);
13:
14:      return !pw ? "?" : pw->pw_name;
15:  }
16:
17:  /*
18:   * Return group ID string :
19:   */
20:  static char *
21:  group_id(gid_t gid) {
22:      struct group *gr = getgrgid(gid);
23:
24:      return !gr ? "?" : gr->gr_name;
25:  }
26:
27:  /*
28:   * Get status on semaphore set :
29:   */
30:  void
31:  ctl_stat(int optch,int reportflg) {
32:      int z;
33:      union semun un;
34:
35:      un.buf = &sembuf;
36:
37:      z = semctl(semid,0,IPC_STAT,un);
38:      if ( z == -1 ) {
39:          fprintf(stderr,"%s: semctl(semid=%d,IPC_STAT)\n",
40:              strerror(errno),semid);
41:          exit(1);
42:      }
43:
44:      if ( reportflg == 1 ) {
```

```
45:            printf("  -%c {\n"
46:                "        sem_nsems = %d\n"
47:                "        sem_perm {\n"
48:                "            cuid = %d (%s)\n"
49:                "            cgid = %d (%s)\n",
50:                optch,
51:                (int)sembuf.sem_nsems,
52:                (int)sembuf.sem_perm.cuid,
53:                user_id(sembuf.sem_perm.cuid),
54:                (int)sembuf.sem_perm.cgid,
55:                group_id(sembuf.sem_perm.cgid));
56:            printf(
57:                "            uid  = %d (%s)\n"
58:                "            gid  = %d (%s)\n"
59:                "            mode = 0%03o\n"
60:                "            key  = 0x%08lX\n"
61:                "        };\n"
62:                "   };\n",
63:                (int)sembuf.sem_perm.uid,
64:                user_id(sembuf.sem_perm.uid),
65:                (int)sembuf.sem_perm.gid,
66:                group_id(sembuf.sem_perm.gid),
67:                (int)sembuf.sem_perm.mode & 0777,
68:                (long)sembuf.sem_perm.key);
69:            fflush(stdout);
70:        }
71:
72:        /*
73:         * Check that our idea of set size agrees with actual :
74:         */
75:        if ( reportflg == -1 )          /* -a option call? */
76:            n_sem = sembuf.sem_nsems;   /* Yes, adjust for actual count */
77:
78:        else if ( n_sem != sembuf.sem_nsems ) {
79:            fflush(stdout);
80:            fprintf(stderr," WARNING: # semaphores in set is %d\n",
81:                sembuf.sem_nsems);
82:            fflush(stderr);
83:            n_sem = sembuf.sem_nsems;   /* Adjust for actual count */
84:        }
85:    }
```

The section of code that is important to the discussion is found in lines 31–42. The union named un is declared in line 33. The address of the external buffer of type struct semid_ds is pointed to in the union in line 35. The union un is passed as the fourth argument to the semctl(2) function in line 37.

The struct semid_ds sembuf is declared externally in this module in line 5. The values placed here are also used by other modules that perform the IPC_SET operation.

The following example uses the utility program ./semop to create a new semaphore set, and invokes IPC_STAT on it.

```
$ ./semop -k0xFEEDF00D -c3 -s
  -c 0xFEEDF00D => IPC ID 196608
  -c 3 : Created semaphore set -k 0xFEEDF00D
  -s {
    sem_nsems = 3
    sem_perm {
      cuid = 1001 (ehg)
      cgid = 1001 (ehg)
      uid  = 1001 (ehg)
      gid  = 1001 (ehg)
      mode = 0640
      key  = 0xFEEDF00D
    };
  };
$
```

The options -k and -c create the set. Option -s requests the IPC_STAT command, and the most important values are reported to standard output. The mode value was affected by the current umask(2) in effect, due to the umask(2) calls that were made in lines 17–19 of Listing 24.1. The mask that was in effect was

```
$ umask
0027
$
```

Keep this semaphore set around for the subsequent sections.

Changing Semaphore Access

After the semaphore set is created, it may be necessary to modify the ownership of the semaphore or change its permission bits. The IPC_SET command of the semctl(2) function allows you to make these changes. Listing 24.5 shows how IPC_SET is used.

LISTING 24.5 semchmod.c—Source Module That Uses the IPC_SET Command of semctl(2)

```
1:  /* semchmod.c */
2:
3:  #include "semop.h"
4:
5:  void
6:  ctl_chmod(int optch,mode_t mode) {
7:      int z;
8:      union semun un;
9:
10:     un.buf = &sembuf;                    /* Pointer to buffer */
11:     sembuf.sem_perm.mode = mode;         /* Change the mode */
12:
13:     z = semctl(semid,0,IPC_SET,un);      /* Change mode value */
14:     if ( z == -1 ) {
15:         fprintf(stderr,"%s: semctl(semid=%d,IPC_SET)\n",
16:             strerror(errno),semid);
17:         exit(1);
```

```
18:        }
19:
20:        printf("  -%c 0%03o\n",optch,mode);
21:        fflush(stdout);
22:  }
```

The function `ctl_chmod()` is called upon to change the permission bits (`mode`) of the semaphore set within the utility. Again, the `union` is declared in line 8, and the buffer pointer is established in line 10. The permission bits in the external variable `sembuf` are altered in line 11. Line 13 invokes the `semctl(2)` function to cause the permission bit changes to occur.

The following example accesses the previous semaphore set and changes the permissions using the -m option. Note the careful use of the leading zero in `0600` to specify the value in octal notation. The -s option follows to display the new values for this set:

```
$ ./semop -k0xFEEDF00D -a -m 0600 -s
  -a 0xFEEDF00D => IPC ID 196608
  There are 3 semaphores in this set.
  -m 0600
  -s {
    sem_nsems = 3
    sem_perm {
      cuid = 1001 (ehg)
      cgid = 1001 (ehg)
      uid  = 1001 (ehg)
      gid  = 1001 (ehg)
      mode = 0600
      key  = 0xFEEDF00D
    };
  };
$
```

Indeed the output shows that the new `mode` value is `0600`. Additional source code for the utility that allows the owner and group to be altered is shown in Listing 24.6.

LISTING 24.6   semchown.c—Source Code That Changes Owner and Group of a Semaphore Set

```
1:   /* semchown.c */
2:
3:   #include "semop.h"
4:
5:   static uid_t
6:   srch_uid(const char *user_id) {
7:       struct passwd *pw = getpwnam(user_id);
8:
9:       if ( !pw )
10:          return (uid_t)(-1);
11:      return pw->pw_uid;
12:  }
13:
14:  void
15:  ctl_chown(int optch,const char *user_id) {
```

continued from previous page

```
16:        uid_t uid = srch_uid(user_id);
17:
18:        if ( uid == (uid_t)(-1) ) {
19:            fprintf(stderr,"Unknown userid: -%c %s\n",optch,user_id);
20:            exit(1);
21:        }
22:
23:        sembuf.sem_perm.uid = uid;   /* Change userid */
24:
25:        /* Cheat: change uid by using ctl_chmod() */
26:        ctl_chmod(optch,sembuf.sem_perm.mode);
27:    }
28:
29:    static gid_t
30:    srch_gid(const char *group_id) {
31:        struct group *gr = getgrnam(group_id);
32:
33:        if ( !gr )
34:            return (gid_t)(-1);
35:        return gr->gr_gid;
36:    }
37:
38:    void
39:    ctl_chgrp(int optch,const char *group) {
40:        gid_t gid = srch_gid(group);
41:
42:        if ( gid == (gid_t)(-1) ) {
43:            fprintf(stderr,"Unknown group: -%c %s\n",optch,group);
44:            exit(1);
45:        }
46:
47:        sembuf.sem_perm.gid = gid;   /* Change group */
48:
49:        /* Cheat: change gid by using ctl_chmod() */
50:        ctl_chmod(optch,sembuf.sem_perm.mode);
51:    }
```

The functions ctl_chown() and ctl_chgrp() are called for the utility options -x and -y, respectively. The actual changes are made in lines 23 and 47. The function calls in lines 26 and 50 cheat by pretending to change the mode value, but pass the existing mode value instead. This causes the changes in variable sembuf to be written to the semaphore set using IPC_SET.

Querying the Value of a Semaphore

The semctl(2) command GETVAL allows a program to query the current value of a specific semaphore within a set. Listing 24.7 shows a source module that performs this function for the semop utility program.

LISTING 24.7   semgetval.c—Source Module That Uses GETVAL with semctl(2)

```
 1:   /* semgetval.c */
 2:
 3:   #include "semop.h"
 4:
 5:   void
 6:   ctl_getval(int optch,int semx) {
 7:       int z;
 8:       union semun un;
 9:
10:       z = semctl(semid,semx,GETVAL,un);
11:       if ( z == -1 ) {
12:           fprintf(stderr,"%s: -%c %d\n",strerror(errno),optch,semx);
13:           exit(1);
14:       }
15:
16:       printf("  -%c %d => %d\n",optch,semx,z);
17:       fflush(stdout);
18:  }
```

The ctl_getval() function is called by the -g n option of the utility. The value n represents the zero-based semaphore number within the set, which is passed to ctl_getval() in the argument semx in Listing 24.7. The semctl(2) call is made in line 10. Since the semaphore value cannot be negative, the value -1 represents an error return value, which is tested for in line 11. Otherwise, the semaphore number and its value are reported in line 16.

The following example reports the values of semaphore 0 and semaphore 2:

```
$ ./semop -k0xFEEDF00D -a -g0 -g2
  -a 0xFEEDF00D => IPC ID 196608
  There are 3 semaphores in this set.
  -g 0 => 0
  -g 2 => 0
$
```

Query the Entire Semaphore Set of Values

Querying any semaphore is a snapshot view of the values, since these values could be changing. If you need a snapshot of all of the semaphores, the GETALL control function provides a consistent result. Listing 24.8 shows how the GETALL command is used.

LISTING 24.8   semgetall.c—Source Module That Uses the GETALL Command with semctl(2)

```
 1:   /* semgetall.c */
 2:
 3:   #include "semop.h"
 4:
 5:   void
 6:   ctl_getall(int optch) {
 7:       int z;
 8:       int x;
```

continued from previous page

```
 9:        u_short array[MAX_NSET];
10:        union semun un;
11:
12:        un.array = &array[0];
13:        z = semctl(semid,0,GETALL,un);
14:        if ( z == -1 ) {
15:            fprintf(stderr,"%s: -%c\n",strerror(errno),optch);
16:            exit(1);
17:        }
18:
19:        for ( x=0; x<n_sem; ++x )
20:            printf("  -%c : semaphore # %d = %u\n",optch,x,array[x]);
21:
22:        fflush(stdout);
23: }
```

The function `ctl_getall()` is called when the `./semop` option `-G` is encountered. An array is declared in line 9 to receive all of the semaphore values. The `semun union` is pointed to this array in line 12. The `GETALL` command is invoked in line 13. If the call succeeds, the results are reported in lines 19 and 20.

The following shows `GETALL` in action:

```
$ ./semop -k0xFEEDF00D -a -G
 -a 0xFEEDF00D => IPC ID 196608
 There are 3 semaphores in this set.
 -G : semaphore # 0 = 0
 -G : semaphore # 1 = 0
 -G : semaphore # 2 = 0
$
```

Since you have not yet initialized this set of semaphores with values, you know that these are the default values for new semaphores under FreeBSD. Some UNIX platforms use different defaults, however.

Change the Value of a Semaphore

Sometimes it is necessary to adjust a specific semaphore to a specific value. This can be accomplished with the `semctl(2)` `SETVAL` command, as you can see in Listing 24.9.

LISTING 24.9   semsetval.c—Source Module That Invokes the `semctl(2)` `SETVAL` Command

```
1:    /* semsetval.c */
2:
3:    #include "semop.h"
4:
5:    void
6:    ctl_setval(int optch,int semx,int value) {
7:        int z;
8:        union semun un;
9:
```

```
10:        un.val = value;
11:        z = semctl(semid,semx,SETVAL,un);
12:        if ( z == -1 ) {
13:            fprintf(stderr,"%s: -%c %d=%d\n",
14:                strerror(errno),optch,semx,value);
15:            exit(1);
16:        }
17:
18:        printf("  -%c %d=%d\n",optch,semx,value);
19:        fflush(stdout);
20:  }
```

The ctl_setval() function is invoked when the -v n=x option is encountered. The semaphore number n is passed as the argument semx, while the value x is passed as the argument value. The union has the value assigned to its val member, which is then passed in the call in line 11. An example of the SETVAL being used is shown as follows:

```
$ ./semop -k0xFEEDF00D -a -v2=13 -G
 -a 0xFEEDF00D => IPC ID 196608
 There are 3 semaphores in this set.
 -v 2=13
 -G : semaphore # 0 = 0
 -G : semaphore # 1 = 0
 -G : semaphore # 2 = 13
$
```

Using the -v option, semaphore 2 in the set was assigned the new value of 13. This was reported by the -G option, which followed on the command line.

Change the Entire Semaphore Set of Values

The semctl(2) function allows the application writer to establish the values of all semaphores in one atomic operation, using the SETALL command. This command is used in Listing 24.10.

LISTING 24.10   semsetall.c—Source Module That Uses the semctl(2) SETALL Command

```
1:   /* semsetall.c */
2:
3:   #include "semop.h"
4:
5:   void
6:   ctl_setall(int optch,int array[]) {
7:       int z;
8:       int x;
9:       u_short ua[MAX_NSET];
10:      union semun un;
11:
12:      for ( x=0; x<n_sem; ++x )
13:          ua[x] = (u_short)array[x];
14:
15:      un.array = &ua[0];
16:      z = semctl(semid,0,SETALL,un);
```

continued from previous page

```
17:        if ( z == -1 ) {
18:            fprintf(stderr,"%s: -%c %d,%d,%d\n",
19:                strerror(errno),optch,array[0],array[1],array[2]);
20:            exit(1);
21:        }
22:
23:        printf("   -%c %d,%d,%d\n",optch,array[0],array[1],array[2]);
24:        fflush(stdout);
25:    }
```

The ./semop utility calls ctl_setall() when the option -V is encountered. This option is fol-lowed by a comma-separated list of initial values for the entire semaphore set. The number of values must exactly match the set. The array of values is passed in the argument **array** in line 6. A conversion from **int** type to **u_short** type is made in lines 12 and 13 for the purpose of the semctl(2) call in line 16. The address of the array is established in the **union** member **array** (line 15).

The following example changes all three semaphores in the existing set that you have been using:

```
$ ./semop -k0xFEEDF00D -a -V9,8,7 -G
  -a 0xFEEDF00D => IPC ID 196608
  There are 3 semaphores in this set.
  -V 9,8,7
  -G : semaphore # 0 = 9
  -G : semaphore # 1 = 8
  -G : semaphore # 2 = 7
$
```

The option -V9,8,7 sets the values for semaphores 0, 1, and 2 in the set of three.

Querying the Process ID for a Semaphore

When you are debugging a complex set of applications that modify a set of semaphores, it is sometimes useful to be able to determine which process was the last one to modify a sema-phore. The GETPID command of the semctl(2) system call performs this function. The source code in Listing 24.11 combines code that uses GETPID and some other information return commands.

LISTING 24.11   ctlget.c—Source That Uses the GETPID Command of semctl(2)

```
1:    /* ctlget.c */
2:
3:    #include "semop.h"
4:
5:    void
6:    ctl_get(int optch,int cmd,int semx) {
7:        int z;
8:        union semun un;
9:
10:       z = semctl(semid,semx,cmd,un);
```

```
11:        if ( z == -1 ) {
12:            fprintf(stderr,"%s: -%c %d\n",
13:                strerror(errno),
14:                optch,
15:                semx);
16:            exit(1);
17:        }
18:
19:        printf("  -%c %d => %d\n",optch,semx,z);
20:        fflush(stdout);
21:   }
```

The command GETPID is passed in the argument cmd of function ctl_get() in line 6 when the
-p or -P options are used on the command line. The specific semaphore number is specified in
the argument semx, which is later used in the call to semctl(2) in line 10. Since the value
being returned for all acceptable commands cannot be negative, the value -1 still identifies an
error return in line 11. The returned value is reported in line 19, when the semctl(2) call is
successful.

The following example shows how to report the process ID for semaphore number 2 and 0
using the -p option:

```
$ ./semop -k0xFEEDF00D -a -p2 -p0
  -a 0xFEEDF00D => IPC ID 196608
  There are 3 semaphores in this set.
  -p 2 => 2347
  -p 0 => 2346
$
```

If you are following along and doing these commands on your system, you may see zeros
reported instead. Zero values indicate that no process has done a wait, zero, or notify operation on your semaphore (you will do this later in the chapter). This example was preceded by
a few semaphore operations to provide non-zero process ID results.

The following example uses the -P convenience option to invoke GETPID on each semaphore
in the set:

```
$ ./semop -k0xFEEDF00D -a -P
  -a 0xFEEDF00D => IPC ID 196608
  There are 3 semaphores in this set.
  -p 0 => 2346
  -p 1 => 2348
  -p 2 => 2347
$
```

Query the Number of Processes Waiting for Notifies

The GETNCNT command allows your process to query how many processes are waiting on a
particular semaphore. Some applications may be able to make use of this information in order
to gauge the workload being processed.

The GETNCNT requests are invoked with the -n option. The module shown in Listing 24.11 handles this information request. The following command lists how many processes are waiting on the third semaphore (semaphore number 2):

```
$ ./semop -k0xFEEDF00D -a -n2
  -a 0xFEEDF00D => IPC ID 196608
  There are 3 semaphores in this set.
  -n    => 0
$
```

The returned value of zero indicates that no processes are currently waiting on this semaphore.

Query the Number of Processes Waiting for Zero

In addition to waiting and notifying semaphores, a process can also perform a wait for zero operation. This might be used to report that a particular resource is exhausted, for example. The GETZCNT command allows the caller to determine how many processes are waiting for zero on a particular semaphore. The GETZCNT operation is also handled by the code shown in Listing 24.11. The following example shows how the -z option is used to report the number of processes waiting for zero on semaphore 0:

```
$ ./semop -k0xFEEDF00D -a -z0
  -a 0xFEEDF00D => IPC ID 196608
  There are 3 semaphores in this set.
  -z    => 0
$
```

In this example, there are no processes waiting for a zero on semaphore 0 of this set.

Using Semaphores

The previous section focused on affecting changes in the semaphore and set attributes, and on obtaining information. This section will cover the aspects of using semaphores to perform the following:

- Wait operations
- Notify operations
- Wait for zero operations

These operations work on the entire set of semaphores or on a subset. You can also operate on individual semaphores in the set according to your application needs.

Semaphore operations are performed by the semop(2) system call. Its function synopsis is as follows:

```
#include <sys/types.h>
#include <sys/ipc.h>
#include <sys/sem.h>

int semop(int semid, struct sembuf array[], unsigned nops);
```

The argument `semid` contains the IPC ID of the semaphore set, which is returned by the `semget(2)` function. The `array[]` argument contains the set of semaphore operations that are to be performed, while `nops` indicates how many elements exist in the `array[]`.

The `semop(2)` function returns `0` when successful. The value `-1` is returned when an error code is returned in `errno`.

Semaphore operations are described in the structure `sembuf`, which is shown in the following synopsis:

```
struct sembuf {
    u_short   sem_num;        /* semaphore number */
    short     sem_op;         /* semaphore operation */
    short     sem_flg;        /* operation flags */
};
```

The member `sem_num` selects the semaphore number within the set. There is no requirement that semaphores be accessed in any particular order. The member `sem_op` determines the semaphore operation to be performed. This signed number affects the semaphore as follows:

`sem_op < 0`	Wait on the semaphore
`sem_op = 0`	Wait for zero to occur
`sem_op > 0`	Notify the semaphore

For example, if one semaphore represents bowling balls, you would use the value `-1` to obtain one. If you want to obtain four at one time, then you would use `-4` as the sem_op value. In this manner, if there were only three available, you would wait until at least four bowling balls became available.

Conversely, to return four bowling balls, your `sem_op` value would be the value `+4`. If you were returning only one ball, then `+1` would be the `sem_op` value. This operation may notify other processes that their wait request has now been satisfied.

A process may choose to wait for the zero count to be reached. If you have written an application that monitors the number of free bowling balls available, then a `sem_op` value of zero would cause the `semop(2)` call to return only when the count has reached zero. This would then allow your application to warn you that there are now no free bowling balls available.

The `sem_flg` member allows you to specify additional option flags for each semaphore operation. These include

`0`	No flags.
`IPC_NOWAIT`	Does not suspend execution of the calling program if this semaphore operation cannot be satisfied. Error `EAGAIN` is returned if the operation was unsuccessful.
`SEM_UNDO`	Adjusts the undo structure for this semaphore when the operation succeeds.

The `IPC_NOWAIT` flag allows your application to attempt the operation, but not have its execution suspended if it must wait. While the flag applies to individual semaphores, the returned error `EAGAIN` indicates that no semaphore operations succeeded, although only one semaphore may have used the `IPC_NOWAIT` flag.

The `SEM_UNDO` flag allows you to plan for semaphore recovery, and will be discussed later in the chapter.

Waiting on Semaphores

A wait operation decrements the count of the semaphore counter. If the count reaches zero, then the request suspends the execution of the process (unless the flag `SEM_NOWAIT` is used for the semaphore(s) in question).

The source module in Listing 24.12 performs all semaphore operations for the `./semop` utility program for the `-o` option.

LISTING 24.12   `semop.c`—Source Module That Performs `semop(2)` Operations

```
 1:    /* ctlsem.c */
 2:
 3:    #include "semop.h"
 4:
 5:    void
 6:    ctl_semop(
 7:      int optch,
 8:      const char *optarg,
 9:      int sems[],
10:      int array[],
11:      int flags[],
12:      int n) {
13:        int z;
14:        int x;                                  /* Iterator */
15:        int semx;                               /* Semaphore number */
16:        struct sembuf ops[MAX_NSET];
17:
18:        for ( x=0; x<n; ++x ) {
19:            ops[x].sem_num = semx = sems[x];    /* Semaphore # */
20:            ops[x].sem_op = array[x];           /* Semaphore operation */
21:            if ( semx >= 0 && semx < n_sem )
22:                ops[x].sem_flg = semx < n_sem   /* In range ? */
23:                    ? flags[semx]               /* Semaphore flags */
24:                    : 0;                        /* else use zero */
25:        }
26:
27:        z = semop(semid,ops,n);
28:        if ( z == -1 ) {
29:            fprintf(stderr,"%s: -%c %s\n",strerror(errno),optch,optarg);
30:            exit(1);
31:        }
32:
```

```
33:        printf(" -%c %s =>",optch,optarg);
34:
35:        for ( x=0; x<n; ++x )
36:            printf(" {%d,%+d,%s}",
37:                ops[x].sem_num,
38:                ops[x].sem_op,
39:                ops[x].sem_flg ? "SEM_UNDO" : "0");
40:        putchar('\n');
41:
42:        fflush(stdout);
43:    }
```

The `ctl_semop()` function receives the list of semaphores to act upon in the argument `sems[]` (line 9). The `array[]` argument contains the list of semaphore operations to perform. The argument `flags[]` (line 11) contains a list of flags in semaphore set order, while the last argument `n` indicates how many operations there are to perform.

The semaphore operations array is declared in line 16, named `ops[]`. The loop in lines 18–25 populates this structured array. Line 19 assigns the semaphore number within the set. Line 20 assigns the semaphore operation. Line 21 makes certain that the semaphore number is in range, and then retrieves the flags value and assigns it to the `sem_flg` member.

Once the `ops[]` array is ready, it is passed to the `semop(2)` function in line 27, along with the count value `n`. Lines 33–42 display the operation performed for the benefit of the utility program.

The `./semop` utility program uses the following format for specifying semaphore operations, after the initial `-o` option:

`<semaphore_number>=<semaphore_op>[{u|U}]`

To wait for 4 bowling balls, using semaphore 0, with no SEM_UNDO, the following option would be given:

`-o 0=-4u`

Or you can rely on the current "flags" value, and specify

`-o 0=-4`

To combine operations, separate them by commas:

`-o 0=-4,2=-1U,1=-1`

This option specifies to wait with count 4 on semaphore 0 using its current flags value, wait with count 1 on semaphore 2 using SEM_UNDO and wait with count 1 on semaphore 1 with its current flags value.

Flags for each semaphore are maintained by the utility and default to 0 (no SEM_UNDO). This can be checked using the `-R` option:

```
$ ./semop -k0xFEEDF00D -a -R
 -a 0xFEEDF00D => IPC ID 196608
 There are 3 semaphores in this set.
 -R : key    0xFEEDF00D
```

```
-R : IPC ID 196608
-R : 0 has no SEM_UNDO
-R : 1 has no SEM_UNDO
-R : 2 has no SEM_UNDO
$
```

Once **SEM_UNDO** has been applied to a semaphore, the utility program remembers this until you disable it again by a following -u option or semaphore -o operation using the trailing u.

For the following examples, initialize your semaphores as shown here:

```
$ ./semop -k0xFEEDF00D -a -V10,5,11 -G
 -a 0xFEEDF00D => IPC ID 196608
 There are 3 semaphores in this set.
 -V 10,5,11
 -G : semaphore # 0 = 10
 -G : semaphore # 1 = 5
 -G : semaphore # 2 = 11
$
```

The semaphore values should be **10**, **5**, and **11** for semaphores **0**, **1**, and **2**, respectively. The -G option permits you to check the current value of the semaphores.

The following wait operations will request **3** from semaphore **0**, and **2** from semaphore **1**, and leave semaphore **2** as it is (do not use **SEM_UNDO** here):

```
$ ./semop -k0xFEEDF00D -a -o 0=-3,1=-2 -G
 -a 0xFEEDF00D => IPC ID 196608
 There are 3 semaphores in this set.
 -o 0=-3,1=-2 => {0,-3,0} {1,-2,0}
 -G : semaphore # 0 = 7
 -G : semaphore # 1 = 3
 -G : semaphore # 2 = 11
$
```

The -o option requests a **semop(2)** call, while the final -G option shows us the final results. Notice how semaphore **0** was decremented by **3**, and semaphore **1** was decremented by **2** as requested. The display shows in { } the semaphore operations that were submitted to **semop(2)**.

Open a second terminal session, and try the following semaphore wait:

```
$ x/semop -k0xFEEDF00D -a -o 0=-6,1=-4 -G
 -a 0xFEEDF00D => IPC ID 196608
 There are 3 semaphores in this set.
```

If your semaphore values match what was shown in the previous example, your utility program should appear to hang here. This happens because you have requested **4** from semaphore **1**, but its current count is **3**. While that application waits, in another terminal session, execute the following:

```
$ ./semop -k0xFEEDF00D -a -o 1=+2
 -a 0xFEEDF00D => IPC ID 196608
 There are 3 semaphores in this set.
 -o 1=+2 => {1,+2,0}
$
```

When this command executes, semaphore 1 is notified with a count of +2 putting the semaphore count up to 5 from the current value of 3. The value 5 will satisfy the other request, so your waiting process is able to return from semop(2) successfully, as shown below:

```
$ ./semop -k0xFEEDF00D -a -o 0=-6,1=-4 -G
  -a 0xFEEDF00D => IPC ID 196608
  There are 3 semaphores in this set.
  -o 0=-6,1=-4 => {0,-6,0} {1,-4,0}
  -G : semaphore # 0 = 1
  -G : semaphore # 1 = 1
  -G : semaphore # 2 = 11
$
```

Notifying Semaphores

Adding a count to the semaphore notifies the semaphore list. The UNIX kernel maintains a list of all processes that are waiting for notification. Recall that the semctl(2) operation GETNCNT returns the number of processes on this list. When a notify occurs, the entire list of processes is re-tested to see if the semaphore operation for that process can succeed.

Warning

Applications that have a large number of processes waiting on a given semaphore may suffer system performance problems. Each notify operation on a semaphore awakens each process to re-test the semaphore. With a high number of processes and swapping, this can create poor system performance.

When possible, design your application so that only a few processes will wait on a given semaphore.

The preceding section showed a simple notify. You can also notify multiple semaphores at once, as shown here:

```
$ ./semop -k0xFEEDF00D -a -o 2=1,0=3 -G
  -a 0xFEEDF00D => IPC ID 196608
  There are 3 semaphores in this set.
  -o 2=1,0=3 => {2,+1,0} {0,+3,0}
  -G : semaphore # 0 = 4
  -G : semaphore # 1 = 1
  -G : semaphore # 2 = 12
$
```

This example adds +1 to semaphore 2 (the + sign does not have to be entered), and +3 to semaphore 0. The -G option reports the final results.

Waiting for Zero

Processes that want to be notified when the semaphore count reaches zero can specify 0 for the semaphore operation. Note, however, that this operation is different from other operations because it is just a snapshot notification. By the time the execution returns from a zero notification, another process may have notified the semaphore again.

The `./semop` command can wait for a zero count by specifying the `0` for the semaphore operation:

```
$ ./semop -k0xFEEDF00D -a -o 1=0
 -a 0xFEEDF00D => IPC ID 196608
 There are 3 semaphores in this set.
```

This process will appear to hang until you perform enough waits to bring the semaphore count to `0` for semaphore `1` of this set.

Semaphore Undo Processing

Semaphore counts manage a count of a particular resource. To keep this count accurate, each wait on a semaphore must eventually be matched by a corresponding notify. For example, if you have 30 bowling balls managed by one semaphore, eventually when no bowling balls are in use, the count must increase back to 30. Otherwise, your application will lose track of its resources.

When a process runs, however, an unexpected abort or exit can occur. If your bowling ball reservation program performed a semaphore wait for **4** balls and then aborted, your semaphore count will be left short by **4** balls. You would need to manually tweak the semaphore using the `./semop` utility to recover from this problem.

The UNIX kernel maintains `SEM_UNDO` structures for each process. This permits a process to clean up its semaphore faux pas. The use of `SEM_UNDO` must, however, be explicitly requested as a flag in `sem_flg` of the semaphore operation. When `SEM_UNDO` is enabled, each semaphore wait causes a corresponding `SEM_UNDO` count to be incremented. Each notify is tracked by a negative `SEM_UNDO` count. If the program should exit before restoring the semaphores used with `SEM_UNDO`, these recovery values are applied to the semaphores upon process termination.

For example, assume the following initial semaphore states

```
$ ./semop -k0xFEEDF00D -a -V30,20,6 -G
 -a 0xFEEDF00D => IPC ID 196608
 There are 3 semaphores in this set.
 -V 30,20,6
 -G : semaphore # 0 = 30
 -G : semaphore # 1 = 20
 -G : semaphore # 2 = 6
$
```

There are **30** bowling balls, **20** pairs of bowling shoes, and **6** bowling alleys. Now run a semaphore wait operation, requesting **4** bowling balls, **4** pairs of shoes, and **1** bowling alley, with the `SEM_UNDO` flag enabled (using -U):

```
$ ./semop -k0xFEEDF00D -a -U -o 0=-4,1=-4,2=-1 -G
 -a 0xFEEDF00D => IPC ID 196608
 There are 3 semaphores in this set.
 -U : 0 uses SEM_UNDO
 -U : 1 uses SEM_UNDO
 -U : 2 uses SEM_UNDO
 -o 0=-4,1=-4,2=-1 => {0,-4,SEM_UNDO} {1,-4,SEM_UNDO} {2,-1,SEM_UNDO}
```

```
-G : semaphore # 0 = 26
-G : semaphore # 1 = 16
-G : semaphore # 2 = 5
$
```

The -U option sets SEM_UNDO as the default for all semaphore operations. Notice how the wait operation successfully returned, and the -G option reported the final counts of 26, 16, and 5 for the semaphores. However, now check the semaphores again with the -G option:

```
$ ./semop -k0xFEEDF00D -a -G
-a 0xFEEDF00D => IPC ID 196608
There are 3 semaphores in this set.
-G : semaphore # 0 = 30
-G : semaphore # 1 = 20
-G : semaphore # 2 = 6
$
```

The counts have been restored after the prior ./semop process terminated. This was done by the UNIX kernel because the SEM_UNDO counts were being maintained. Think of SEM_UNDO keeping opposite counts for each semaphore operation.

If a wait operation of -4 is performed, +4 is added to the SEM_UNDO value. If a notify of +3 is performed, the value -3 is added to the SEM_UNDO value (subtracting 3). If these were the last operations performed, the final SEM_UNDO value at process termination would be +1, requiring the kernel to perform a notify of +1 to restore the semaphore.

As convenient as the SEM_UNDO feature may be, it is not always wise to use it. When a binary semaphore is being used to lock a shared memory table, for example, is it wise to have the table unlocked when the lock holding process aborts? The aborting process may have left the shared memory table in an unusable state. It may be preferable to have other processes hang rather than proceed. In this manner, the administrator can take corrective action and restart the application from a known and trusted state.

The semop Utility Program

The next few listings complete the source listings for the utility program semop. Listing 24.13 lists the main program.

LISTING 24.13   main.c—The Main Program Source Listing for the semop Utility

```
 1:   /* main.c */
 2:
 3:   #include "semop.h"
 4:
 5:   int semid = -1;              /* No default IPC ID */
 6:   int n_sem = 3;              /* Default # semaphores in a set */
 7:
 8:   /*
 9:    * semop utility main program :
10:    *
11:    * Use './semop -h' for help.
12:    */
```

continued from previous page

```
13:   int
14:   main(int argc,char **argv) {
15:       int z;                          /* Option character/status */
16:       int x;                          /* Iterator */
17:       int rc = 0;                     /* Return code */
18:       int n;                          /* # of values in array */
19:       key_t key = 0xFEEDF00D;         /* Default IPC key */
20:       int sems[MAX_NSET];             /* Array of semaphore numbers */
21:       int array[MAX_NSET];            /* Array of integer values */
22:       int flags[MAX_NSET];            /* Flags for each semaphore */
23:       unsigned long ul;               /* unsigned value */
24:       const char cmdopts[] = "hk:ac:i:o:sm:dg:Gv:V:p:Pn:z:uURx:y:";
25:
26:       for ( x=0; x<MAX_NSET; ++x )
27:           flags[x] = 0;               /* Initialize with no SEM_UNDO */
28:
29:       while ( !rc && (z = getopt(argc,argv,cmdopts)) != -1 )
30:           switch ( z ) {
31:           case 'h' :                  /* -h              ; usage info */
32:               usage();
33:               return 0;
34:
35:           case 'k' :                  /* -k IPCkey[,n] ; IPC Key, n_sem */
36:               if ( cvt2ulong(optarg,&ul) )
37:                   goto badcvt;
38:               key = (key_t) ul;
39:               break;
40:
41:           case 'a' :                  /* -a              ; access set */
42:               get_set(z,key,0);   /* Locate IPC ID */
43:               ctl_stat(z,-1);     /* Just fill sembuf & fix n_sem */
44:               printf("  There are %d semaphores in this set.\n",
45:                   n_sem);
46:               break;
47:
48:           case 'c' :                  /* -c n            ; create set */
49:               if ( cvt2ulong(optarg,&ul) )
50:                   goto badcvt;
51:               n_sem = (int)ul;
52:               get_set(z,key,1);   /* Create set */
53:               ctl_stat(z,0);      /* Just fill sembuf */
54:               printf("  -c %d : Created semaphore set -k 0x%08lX\n",
55:                   n_sem,(long)key);
56:               break;
57:
58:           case 'i' :                  /* -i IPCID      ; IPC ID      */
59:               if ( cvt2ulong(optarg,&ul) )
60:                   goto badcvt;
61:               semid = (int) ul;
62:               ctl_stat(z,-1);     /* Just report failure */
63:               printf("  -i %d : There are %d semaphores in this set.\n",
64:                   semid,n_sem);
65:               break;
```

```
66:
67:            case 'o' :                  /* -o m[,n[,o]] ; semop(2)    */
68:                if ( (n = cvt2semops(optarg,sems,array,flags)) < 1 )
69:                    goto badcvt;
70:                ctl_semop(z,optarg,sems,array,flags,n);
71:                break;
72:
73:            case 's' :                  /* -s           ; IPC_STAT    */
74:                ctl_stat(z,1);
75:                break;
76:
77:            case 'm' :                  /* -m mode      ; IPC_SET     */
78:                if ( cvt2ulong(optarg,&ul) )
79:                    goto badcvt;
80:                ctl_chmod(z,(mode_t)ul);
81:                break;
82:
83:            case 'x' :                  /* -x userid    ; IPC_SET     */
84:                ctl_chown(z,optarg);
85:                break;
86:
87:            case 'y' :                  /* -g group     ; IPC_SET     */
88:                ctl_chgrp(z,optarg);
89:                break;
90:
91:            case 'd' :                  /* -d           ; IPC_RMID    */
92:                ctl_rmid(z);
93:                break;
94:
95:            case 'g' :                  /* -g n         ; IPC_GETVAL  */
96:                if ( cvt2ulong(optarg,&ul) )
97:                    goto badcvt;
98:                ctl_getval(z,(int)ul);
99:                break;
100:
101:            case 'G' :                  /* -G           ; IPC_GETALL */
102:                ctl_getall(z);
103:                break;
104:
105:            case 'v' :                  /* -v n=x       ; IPC_SETVAL */
106:                if ( (n = cvt2array(optarg,array,"=")) != 2 )
107:                    goto badcvt;
108:                ctl_setval(z,array[0],array[1]);
109:                break;
110:
111:            case 'V' :                  /* -V m,n,o     ; IPC_SETALL */
112:                if ( (n = cvt2array(optarg,&array[0],",")) != n_sem )
113:                    goto badcvt;
114:                ctl_setall(z,array);
115:                break;
116:
117:            case 'p' :                  /* -p n         ; GETPID */
118:                if ( cvt2ulong(optarg,&ul) )
```

continued from previous page

```
119:                    goto badcvt;
120:                    ctl_get(z,GETPID,(int)ul);
121:                    break;
122:
123:            case 'P' :
124:                    for ( x=0; x<n_sem; ++x )
125:                        ctl_get('p',GETPID,x);
126:                    break;
127:
128:            case 'n' :                  /* -n            ; GETNCNT */
129:                    if ( cvt2ulong(optarg,&ul) )
130:                        goto badcvt;
131:                    ctl_get(z,GETNCNT,(int)ul);
132:                    break;
133:
134:            case 'z' :                  /* -z            ; GETZCNT */
135:                    if ( cvt2ulong(optarg,&ul) )
136:                        goto badcvt;
137:                    ctl_get(z,GETZCNT,(int)ul);
138:                    break;
139:
140:            case 'u' :                  /* -u            ; No SEM_UNDO */
141:                    for ( x=0; x<n_sem; ++x )
142:                        flags[x] &= ~SEM_UNDO;
143:                    report(z,key,flags);
144:                    break;
145:
146:            case 'U' :                  /* -U            ; SEM_UNDO    */
147:                    for ( x=0; x<n_sem; ++x )
148:                        flags[x] |= SEM_UNDO;
149:                    report(z,key,flags);
150:                    break;
151:
152:            case 'R' :
153:                    report(z,key,flags);
154:                    break;
155:
156:            default  :                  /* Unknown option */
157:                rc = 1;
158:            }
159:
160:        /*
161:         * Command line arguments are ignored :
162:         */
163:        for ( ; optind < argc; ++optind, rc=2 )
164:            printf("Ignored argument '%s'\n",argv[optind]);
165:
166:        return rc;
167:
168:        /*
169:         * Bad numeric conversion :
170:         */
171: badcvt:
```

```
172:          fprintf(stderr,"Bad numeric: -%c %s\n",z,optarg);
173:          return 1;
174: }
```

The loop in lines 26 and 27 initializes the flags for the semaphore set to 0. The -U option ORs in the flag SEM_UNDO to all members of the flags[] array, whereas the -u option removes this flag. The -o option individually enables and disables the SEM_UNDO flag, as you find convenient to do. With no trailing u or U specified in a semaphore operation, the default is taken from the current value in the flags[] array.

The remainder of the main program is the getopt(3) loop starting in line 29. Each option invokes the semaphore operation as it is encountered. Command-line arguments are ignored, and warnings of this are issued in lines 163 and 164. It is easy to forget a hyphen.

Listing 24.14 shows the programming used to perform the various string-to-numeric conversions. These functions support the semaphore option argument parsing operations.

LISTING 24.14   convrt.c—The Source Listing for Conversions for the semop Utility

```
1:    /* convrt.c */
2:
3:    #include "semop.h"
4:
5:    /*
6:     * Convert string to unsigned long (any radix) :
7:     */
8:    int
9:    cvt2ulong(const char *str,unsigned long *ulp) {
10:        char *ep;
11:        unsigned long ul;
12:
13:        ul = strtoul(str,&ep,0);
14:        if ( *ep != 0 )
15:            return -1;          /* Failed */
16:
17:        if ( ulp )
18:            *ulp = ul;
19:        return 0;               /* Success */
20:    }
21:
22:    /*
23:     * Parse and convert up to n_sem values to array :
24:     */
25:    int
26:    cvt2array(const char *str,int array[],const char *delim) {
27:        char *cp;                       /* Token pointer */
28:        int n = 0;                      /* # of values extracted */
29:        int m = *delim == '=' ? 2 : n_sem; /* only 2 if using '=' */
30:        unsigned long ul;               /* converted ulong value */
31:
32:        for ( cp=(char *)str; n<m && *cp; ++n ) {
33:            ul = strtoul(cp,&cp,0);     /* Convert to ulong */
```

continued from previous page

```
34:               if ( *cp && !strchr(delim,*cp) )
35:                   return -1;               /* Failed conversion */
36:               array[n] = (int)ul;         /* Save ulong value in array */
37:               if ( *cp )
38:                   ++cp;                    /* Skip delimiter */
39:           }
40:
41:       return n;                            /* Return # of values */
42:   }
43:
44:   /*
45:    * -o 0=-1u,2=-3U,1=1
46:    *
47:    * Translates to:
48:    *
49:    * Semaphore 0 does a wait of 1, with no SEM_UNDO
50:    * Semaphore 2 does a wait of 3, with SEM_UNDO
51:    * Semaphore 1 does a notify of 1, with current SEM_UNDO flag
52:    */
53:   int
54:   cvt2semops(const char *str,int sems[],int array[],int flags[]) {
55:       int x = 0;
56:       int semx;                            /* Semaphore index */
57:       char *ep = (char *)str;
58:       unsigned long ul;
59:       long lg;
60:
61:       for ( x=0; *ep && x<n_sem; ++x ) {
62:           /*
63:            * Extract the semaphore # :
64:            */
65:           ul = strtoul(ep,&ep,0);
66:           if ( *ep != '=' )
67:               return -1;                   /* Bad format */
68:           semx = sems[x] = (int) ul;       /* Semaphore # */
69:           ++ep;                            /* Skip '=' */
70:
71:           /*
72:            * Extract the Semaphore operation :
73:            */
74:           lg = strtol(ep,&ep,0);
75:           if ( *ep != 0 && *ep != ',' && *ep != 'u' && *ep != 'U' )
76:               return -1;                   /* Bad format */
77:           array[x] = (int) lg;             /* Semaphore operation */
78:
79:           /*
80:            * Process optional trailing 'u'|'U' for flags[] :
81:            */
82:           if ( *ep == 'u' ) {
83:               flags[semx] &= ~SEM_UNDO;/* Remove SEM_UNDO */
84:               ++ep;                        /* Skip 'u' */
85:           } else if ( *ep == 'U' ) {
```

```
86:                    flags[semx] |= SEM_UNDO;/* Add SEM_UNDO */
87:                    ++ep;                   /* Skip 'U' */
88:                 }
89:
90:                 /*
91:                  * Check current delimiter :
92:                  */
93:                 if ( *ep != 0 ) {
94:                     if ( *ep != ',' )
95:                         return -1;          /* Bad format */
96:                     ++ep;                   /* Skip delimiter */
97:                 }
98:             }
99:
100:        return x;
101: }
```

Listing 24.15 shows the module that performs the reporting when the -R option is used.

LISTING 24.15   report.c—The -R Reporting Function of the semop Utility

```
1:    /* report.c */
2:
3:    #include "semop.h"
4:
5:    /*
6:     * Report SEM_UNDO status :
7:     */
8:    void
9:    report(int optch,key_t key,int flags[]) {
10:       int x;
11:
12:       if ( optch == 'R' ) {
13:           /*
14:            * This report only performed for -R option :
15:            */
16:           printf("  -%c : key    0x%08lX\n",optch,(long)key);
17:           printf("  -%c : IPC ID %d\n",optch,semid);
18:       }
19:
20:       for ( x=0; x<n_sem; ++x )
21:           printf("  -%c : %d %s SEM_UNDO\n",
22:               optch,
23:               x,
24:               flags[x] & SEM_UNDO ? "uses" : "has no");
25:           fflush(stdout);
26:       fflush(stdout);
27:    }
```

Finally, Listing 24.16 shows the usage() function for completeness.

LISTING 24.16   usage.c—The usage() Function for the semop Utility Program

```
 1:    /* usage.c */
 2:
 3:    #include "semop.h"
 4:
 5:    /*
 6:     * Display usage instructions :
 7:     */
 8:    void
 9:    usage(void) {
10:
11:        puts("Usage:  semop [options]");
12:        puts("Options:");
13:        puts("\t-k key\tIPC Key for -a or -c option.");
14:        puts("\t-a\t\tAccess existing set based on -k key");
15:        puts("\t-c n\t\tCreate set of n semaphores using -k key");
16:        puts("\t-i ID\t\tAccess existing set by IPC ID");
17:        puts("\t-o <sops>\tsemop(n) for wait/zero/notify");
18:        puts("\t-s\t\tsemctl(IPC_STAT)");
19:        puts("\t-m mode\t\tsemctl(IPC_SET) with new permissions");
20:        puts("\t-x userid\tsemctl(IPC_SET) with new userid");
21:        puts("\t-y group\tsemctl(IPC_SET) with new group");
22:        puts("\t-d\t\tsemctl(IPC_RMID)");
23:        puts("\t-g n\t\tsemctl(GETVAL) for semaphore n");
24:        puts("\t-G\t\tsemctl(GETALL)");
25:        puts("\t-v n=x\t\tsemctl(SETVAL) set semaphore n to x");
26:        puts("\t-V m,n,o\tsemctl(SETALL)");
27:        puts("\t-p n\t\tsemctl(GETPID) for semaphore n");
28:        puts("\t-P\t\tReport semctl(GETPID) for all semaphores");
29:        puts("\t-n x\t\tsemctl(GETNCNT) for semaphore x");
30:        puts("\t-z x\t\tsemctl(GETZCNT) for semaphore x");
31:        puts("\t-u\t\tNo SEM_UNDO (default)");
32:        puts("\t-U\t\tUse SEM_UNDO");
33:        puts("\t-R\t\tReport SEM_UNDO flags");
34:        puts("\n<sops> :");
35:        puts("\t<semaphore#>=<semop>[{u|U}],...");
36:        puts("where:");
37:        puts("\t<semaphore#>\tIs the semaphore # (starting from zero)");
38:        puts("\t<semop>\t\tSemaphore operation: -n, 0 or +n");
39:        puts("\t\t\tNegative waits, Postive notifies");
40:        puts("\t\t\twhile zero waits for zero.");
41:        puts("\tu\t\tDo not use SEM_UNDO");
42:        puts("\tU\t\tApply SEM_UNDO");
43:        puts("\tExample: -o 0=-4U,2=+1u,1=2");
44:    }
```

That completes the source code listings for the **semop** utility program.

Summary

This chapter examined every aspect of semaphore operation under UNIX. You will be able to apply this knowledge to the next chapter, which explores shared memory.

CHAPTER 25

SHARED MEMORY

Whether the data exists in the form of a table or some other format, separate processes can share data using the shared memory resource. This chapter will look at the mechanics of how processes share memory—how it is created, established, and destroyed.

A utility program dubbed globvar is presented in module form to illustrate the use of shared memory in an actual application. This utility is designed to permit shell programs to share global variables using shared memory. This differs from the exported shell environment variables, which cannot be altered by child processes of the shell. Any process using globvar may inquire or alter the value of a global variable.

The globvar Utility Program

To permit the use of the utility while you progress through this chapter, compile the globvar utility now. The following shows a FreeBSD make(1) session:

```
$ make
cc -c  -Wall -DHAVE_SEMUN -g globat.c
cc -c  -Wall -DHAVE_SEMUN -g globcr.c
cc -c  -Wall -DHAVE_SEMUN -g globget.c
cc -c  -Wall -DHAVE_SEMUN -g globlk.c
cc -c  -Wall -DHAVE_SEMUN -g globset.c
cc -c  -Wall -DHAVE_SEMUN -g globvar.c
cc -c  -Wall -DHAVE_SEMUN -g globdest.c
cc -c  -Wall -DHAVE_SEMUN -g globun.c
cc -o globvar globat.o globcr.o globget.o globlk.o globset.o  globvar.o
➥ globdest.o globun.o
$
```

The usage information display is available with the -h option:

```
$ ./globvar -h
globvar [-i] [-s size] [-e] [-u] [-r] [-c] var... var=value...
Options:
    -i           Initialize new globvar pool
    -s size      Size of this pool, in bytes
    -e           Dump all values (after changes)
    -u           Unset all named variables
    -r           Remove this pool of values
```

```
   -c          Clear all variables
   -h          This info.
You must use -i or define environment variable GLOBVAR.
$
```

The remaining subsections will briefly explain how to use the utility and its options.

Creating Global Variable Pools

To use the `globvar` utility program, you must initially create a global memory pool. This is done using the -i option (the option -s can be added to change the default memory segment size of 4KB):

```
$ ./globvar -i
393216
$ ipcs
Message Queues:
T    ID    KEY          MODE          OWNER      GROUP

Shared Memory:
T    ID    KEY          MODE          OWNER      GROUP
m 393216          0 --rw-------       wwg        wwg

Semaphores:
T    ID    KEY          MODE          OWNER      GROUP
s 393216          0 --rw-------       wwg        wwg

$
```

The use of the -i option causes a private shared memory region to be created and displays the IPC ID on standard output. The `ipcs(1)` command confirms that a shared memory region and a semaphore set were created (they both have the same IPC ID by coincidence).

Private shared memory regions eliminate any possibility of IPC key clashes. It will require, however, that you pass the IPC ID of your global variable pool to those other shell programs that need access to it. Notice also in the `ipcs(1)` output that the permission is established so that only the owner of the shared memory has access to it. This keeps the values of your global pool safe from other users.

Destroying Global Variable Pools

A global variable pool can be destroyed using the -r option. The GLOBVAR environment variable names the IPC ID of the global memory pool that you are working with:

```
$ GLOBVAR=393216 ./globvar -r
```

This session destroys the global memory pool for IPC ID 393216. You can check this for yourself using the `ipcs(1)` command.

The GLOBVAR Environment Variable

Normally, the initialization of a global memory pool is performed so that the IPC ID is recorded in the exported shell environment variable GLOBVAR as follows:

```
$ GLOBVAR=`./globvar -i`
$ export GLOBVAR
$
```

Establishing the IPC ID in the exported shell variable GLOBVAR allows all future globvar command accesses to contact the correct instance of the global memory pool, which was just created. Changes to the GLOBVAR environment variable will permit you to work with different collections of global variables if you need to.

Creating Global Variables

Once the shell variable GLOBVAR is initialized, global variables can be added to the global memory pool as follows:

```
$ ./globvar VARIABLE=XYZ VAR2=ABC
$
```

This shows the variables VARIABLE and VAR2 being created.

Accessing Global Variables

The values contained in the global memory pool can be individually fetched or dumped in bulk with the -e option:

```
$ ./globvar VARIABLE
XYZ
$ ./globvar VAR2
ABC
$ ./globvar -e
VARIABLE=XYZ
VAR2=ABC
$
```

To copy a global variable to a shell variable, you can use the usual shell syntax for this (two methods are shown):

```
$ COPY_VARIABLE=`./globvar VARIABLE`
$ COPY_VAR2=$(./globvar VAR2)
$ echo $COPY_VARIABLE
XYZ
$ echo $COPY_VAR2
ABC
$
```

Global variables can naturally be altered by the utility:

```
$ ./globvar VAR2="A different value."
$ ./globvar -e
```

```
VARIABLE=XYZ
VAR2=A different value.
$
```

The new value of VAR2 is displayed by the -e option here.

Removing Global Variables

The -u option "unsets" each global variable named, similar to the shell built-in command unset. The following command removes the variable named VARIABLE:

```
$ ./globvar -u VARIABLE
$ ./globvar -e
VAR2=A different value.
$
```

Notice that global variable VARIABLE is absent from the -e display.

Clearing Global Variable Pools

The -c option clears the global memory pool, so that no variables remain (the -e option always displays the contents of the global pool after all changes are made):

```
$ ./globvar -c -e
$
```

Shared Memory System Calls

The sections that follow will explore the shared memory system calls and discuss how they were applied to this utility program. The discussion covers the following areas:

- Creating and Accessing Shared Memory
- Obtaining Information about Shared Memory
- Changing Shared Memory Attributes
- Attaching Shared Memory
- Detaching Shared Memory
- Destroying Shared Memory

Shared memory must be created, or it must be located if another process has already created it. The program is given an IPC ID to refer to when it has been created or located. Once you have this IPC ID, it is possible to inquire about the shared memory region attributes and change some of them, such as the ownership and permissions.

Before shared memory can be read from or written to, it must be attached to the memory space of your current process. This involves the selection of a starting address for your shared memory region.

When a process is finished with a shared memory region, it is able to detach it from its memory space. Once all processes have finished with the shared memory region and detached it, the region can be destroyed to give the memory back to the kernel.

Creating and Accessing Shared Memory

Shared memory is created and accessed if it already exists using the `shmget(2)` function. Its function synopsis is as follows:

```
#include <sys/types.h>
#include <sys/ipc.h>
#include <sys/shm.h>

int shmget(key_t key, int size, int flag);
```

The argument `key` is the value of the IPC key to use, or the value `IPC_PRIVATE`. The `size` argument specifies the minimum size of the shared memory region required. The actual size created will be rounded up to a platform-specific multiple of a virtual memory page size. The `flag` option must contain the permission bits if shared memory is being created. Additional flags that may be used include `IPC_CREAT` and `IPC_EXCL`, when shared memory is being created.

The return value is the IPC ID of the shared memory region when the call is successful (this includes the value zero). The value -1 is returned if the call fails, with `errno` set.

Listing 25.1 shows the source module that calls upon `shmget(2)` to create or access shared memory. This code is executed when the `-i` option is used to create shared memory.

LISTING 25.1   `globcr.c`—The `globvar` Source Module That Calls `shmget(2)` to Create Shared Memory

```
 1:    /* globcr.c */
 2:
 3:    #include "globvar.h"
 4:
 5:    /*
 6:     * Create a new shared memory variable pool :
 7:     */
 8:    void
 9:    create_vars(int shm_size) {
10:        int z;                      /* Status code */
11:        int semid;                  /* Semaphore IPC ID */
12:        int offset;                 /* Byte offset */
13:        union semun un;             /* Union of semctl() args */
14:        struct shmid_ds shminfo;    /* Shared memory info */
15:
16:        /*
17:         * Create shared memory region :
18:         */
19:        z = shmget(IPC_PRIVATE,shm_size,IPC_CREAT|0600);
20:
21:        if ( z == -1 ) {
```

continued from previous page

```
22:                   fprintf(stderr,"%s: shmmget(,%d,IPC_CREAT)\n",
23:                       strerror(errno),shm_size);
24:                   exit(1);
25:           }
26:
27:           shmid = z;                      /* IPC ID */
28:
29:           /*
30:            * Create semaphore for this region :
31:            */
32:           z = semget(IPC_PRIVATE,1,IPC_CREAT|0600);
33:
34:           if ( z == -1 ) {
35:               fprintf(stderr,"%s: semget(,IPC_CREAT)\n",strerror(errno));
36:               exit(1);
37:           }
38:
39:           semid = z;                      /* IPC ID */
40:
41:           /*
42:            * Discover the actual size of the region :
43:            */
44:           z = shmctl(shmid,IPC_STAT,&shminfo);
45:
46:           if ( z == -1 ) {
47:               fprintf(stderr,"%s: shmctl(%d,IPC_STAT)\n",
48:                   strerror(errno),shmid);
49:               exit(1);
50:           }
51:
52:           shm_size = shminfo.shm_segsz;   /* Actual size of the memory region */
53:
54:           /*
55:            * Initialize binary semaphore to value of 1 :
56:            */
57:           un.val = 1;
58:
59:           z = semctl(semid,0,SETVAL,un.val);
60:
61:           if ( z == -1 ) {
62:               fprintf(stderr,"%s: semctl(%d,0,SETVAL)\n",
63:                   strerror(errno),semid);
64:               exit(1);
65:           }
66:
67:           /*
68:            * Attach shared memory, and initialize it :
69:            */
70:           attach_vars();                  /* Attach shared memory */
71:           globvars->semid = semid;        /* Place semaphore ID into shared memory */
72:
73:           offset = (int) ( &globvars->vars[0] - (char *)globvars );
74:           globvars->size = shm_size - offset;
75:           globvars->vars[0] = globvars->vars[1] = 0;
76:   }
```

The `shmget(2)` call in line 19 creates a private shared memory region by using the `IPC_PRIVATE`. The flag `IPC_CREAT` causes the shared memory region to be created, while the bits `0600` causes the region to be created so that the owner alone can read and write to it.

Lines 32–39 create a semaphore set (of one), which will be used to lock the shared memory region for safe concurrent access to it. Lines 59–65 initialize the semaphore to the value of 1 (unlocked).

After the shared memory is attached by the function `attach_vars()` (to be shown later), the semaphore's IPC ID and the actual size of the shared memory region is stored in it, using the shared memory pointer `globvars` (lines 73 and 74). The variable pool is initialized as empty in line 75.

Obtaining Information About Shared Memory

Attributes of the shared memory, including its permissions and actual size, are obtained using the `shmctl(2)` system call. Its function synopsis is as follows:

```
#include <sys/types.h>
#include <sys/ipc.h>
#include <sys/shm.h>

int shmctl(int shmid, int cmd, struct shmid_ds *buf);
```

The argument `shmid` specifies the shared memory IPC ID, which is obtained from `shmget(2)`. The `cmd` is a `shmctl(2)` command value, while `buf` is an argument used with certain commands. The valid commands for `shmctl(2)` are

IPC_STAT	Obtains information about the shared memory region. The information is copied to the structure pointed by argument `buf`.
IPC_SET	Changes the values of members `shm_perm.uid`, `shm_perm.gid`, and `shm_perm.mode`. The calling process must have an effective user ID that matches the `shm_perm.cuid` (creator) or the current `shm_perm.uid` value. The values are supplied by pointer argument `buf`.
IPC_RMID	Destroys the shared memory referenced by `shmid`. The memory will undergo destruction when the last process using it detaches it with `shmdt(2)`. Argument `buf` is ignored.

Note

Some platforms also support the `SHM_LOCK` and `SHM_UNLOCK` commands, which lock and unlock shared memory, respectively. This operation can only be performed by the superuser and prevents the shared memory from swapping.

SGI IRIX 6.5, HPUX-11, UnixWare 7, Solaris 8, and Linux support this feature. FreeBSD 3.4 release and IBM AIX 4.3 do not support this feature.

The function shmctl(2) returns 0 when successful. The value -1 is returned with errno set when the call fails.

The following shows a segment from Listing 25.1, which illustrates how shmctl(2) was used:

```
14:       struct shmid_ds shminfo;      /* Shared memory info */

41:       /*
42:        * Discover the actual size of the region :
43:        */
44:       z = shmctl(shmid,IPC_STAT,&shminfo);
45:
46:       if ( z == -1 ) {
47:           fprintf(stderr,"%s: shmctl(%d,IPC_STAT)\n",
48:               strerror(errno),shmid);
49:           exit(1);
50:       }
```

This call to shmctl(2) was made in Listing 25.1 to determine the actual amount of memory allocated since the requested size is rounded up to a multiple of the memory page size when the region is created.

The structure declaration for shmid_ds is shown in the following synopsis:

```
struct shmid_ds {
    struct ipc_perm shm_perm;    /* operation permission structure */
    int             shm_segsz;   /* size of segment in bytes */
    pid_t           shm_lpid;    /* process ID of last shared memory op */
    pid_t           shm_cpid;    /* process ID of creator */
    short           shm_nattch;  /* number of current attaches */
    time_t          shm_atime;   /* time of last shmat() */
    time_t          shm_dtime;   /* time of last shmdt() */
    time_t          shm_ctime;   /* time of last change by shmctl() */
};
```

The structure definition for ipc_perm is repeated for your convenience, as follows:

```
struct ipc_perm {
    ushort  cuid;          /* creator user id */
    ushort  cgid;          /* creator group id */
    ushort  uid;           /* user id */
    ushort  gid;           /* group id */
    ushort  mode;          /* r/w permission */
    ushort  seq;           /* sequence # (to generate unique msg/sem/shm id) */
    key_t   key;           /* user specified msg/sem/shm key */
};
```

Changing Shared Memory Attributes

Permission aspects of the shared memory region can be changed after it is created. This is accomplished using the IPC_SET command in the shmctl(2) call. The following example shows how to modify access to allow everyone to read and write your shared memory region:

```
int z'
struct shmid_ds shminfo;     /* Shared memory info */

shminfo.shm_perm.mode = 0666; /* Make Read/Writable by all */

z = shmctl(shmid,IPC_STAT,&shminfo);

if ( z == -1 ) {
    fprintf(stderr,"%s: shmctl(%d,IPC_SET)\n",strerror(errno),shmid);
    exit(1);
}
```

To make this change, however, your effective user ID must match the user that created the memory region, or match the current user ID value in shm_perm.uid.

Attaching Shared Memory

Shared memory must be attached to your process memory space before you can use it as memory. This is performed by calling upon shmat(2):

```
#include <sys/types.h>
#include <sys/ipc.h>
#include <sys/shm.h>

void * shmat(int shmid, void *addr, int flag);
```

The argument shmid specifies the IPC ID of the shared memory that you want to attach to your process. The argument addr indicates the address that you want to use for this. A null pointer for addr specifies that the UNIX kernel should pick the address instead. The flag argument permits the option flag SHM_RND to be specified. Specify 0 for flag if no options apply.

When shmat(2) succeeds, a (void *) address is returned that represents the starting address of the shared memory region. If the function fails, the value (void *)(-1) is returned instead.

The combination of the addr and the flag option SHM_RND allow three possible ways for the memory region to be attached:

addr=0		The kernel decides upon an unused area of memory at which to attach the segment.
addr != 0	flag=0	The shared memory is attached at the specified addr value, if it is suitable.
addr != 0	flag=SHM_RND	The final addr used is rounded down by the nearest multiple of SHMLBA.

The first choice is the most portable way to attach shared memory. However, if you use pointers within your shared memory region, then you will likely need to specify a memory address using one of the last two methods shown.

Tip

Specifying a null **addr** value is a good way for your program to arrive at a trial value for attaching shared memory at a fixed location for a given platform.

Listing 25.2 shows the source module used by `globvar` that attaches shared memory to its process memory.

LISTING 25.2   `globat.c`—The Source Module That Calls `shmat(2)` to Attach Shared Memory

```
 1:   /* globat.c */
 2:
 3:   #include "globvar.h"
 4:
 5:   /*
 6:    * Attach the shared variable pool :
 7:    */
 8:   void
 9:   attach_vars(void) {
10:
11:       /*
12:        * Attach shared memory region :
13:        */
14:       globvars = (GlobVars *)shmat(shmid,0,0);
15:
16:       if ( (void *)(globvars) == (void *)(-1) ) {
17:           fprintf(stderr,"%s: shmat(%d,0,0)\n",strerror(errno),shmid);
18:           exit(1);
19:       }
20:   }
```

No option flags or attach address is specified in line 14. By specifying a null address, the kernel is permitted to choose a suitable place to attach it for you. Notice how the error is tested for in line 16. The returned pointer must be compared with **(void *)(-1)** and not the null pointer.

Warning

Test for failure from `shmat(2)` by comparing the returned pointer to **(void *)(-1)**. A common blunder is to assume that the null pointer is returned for this purpose.

Detaching Shared Memory

Detaching shared memory is automatically performed when your process terminates. However, if you need to detach it before it terminates, you accomplish that with the `shmdt(2)` function:

```
#include <sys/types.h>
#include <sys/ipc.h>
#include <sys/shm.h>

int shmdt(void *addr);
```

The shmdt(2) function simply accepts the address of the shared memory, as it was attached by shmat(2), in argument addr. The return value is 0 when successful. Otherwise, -1 is returned and errno holds the error code. The code in Listing 25.3 demonstrates this function call.

LISTING 25.3   globdest.c—The Source Module That Calls shmdt(2) and Destroys the Shared Memory

```
 1:    /* globdest.c */
 2:
 3:    #include "globvar.h"
 4:
 5:    /*
 6:     * Destroy the shared memory variable pool :
 7:     */
 8:    void
 9:    destroy_vars(void) {
10:        int z;                          /* Status code */
11:        int semid;                      /* Semaphore IPC ID */
12:        union semun un;                 /* Union of semctl() args */
13:
14:        /*
15:         * Lock the shared memory region :
16:         */
17:        glob_lock();
18:        semid = globvars->semid;        /* Semaphore IPC ID */
19:
20:        /*
21:         * Destroy locking semaphore :
22:         */
23:        z = semctl(semid,0,IPC_RMID,un);
24:
25:        if ( z == -1 ) {
26:            fprintf(stderr,"%s: semctl(%d,0,IPC_RMID)\n",
27:                strerror(errno),semid);
28:            exit(1);
29:        }
30:
31:        /*
32:         * Detach shared memory :
33:         */
34:        z = shmdt(globvars);
35:
36:        if ( z == -1 ) {
37:            fprintf(stderr,"%s: shmdt(2)\n",strerror(errno));
38:            exit(1);
39:        }
40:
```

continued from previous page

```
41:        /*
42:         * Destroy shared memory :
43:         */
44:        z = shmctl(shmid,IPC_RMID,NULL);
45:
46:        if ( z == -1 ) {
47:            fprintf(stderr,"%s: shmctl(%d,IPC_RMID)\n",
48:                strerror(errno),shmid);
49:            exit(1);
50:        }
51:    }
```

The shmdt(2) call is shown in line 34.

This module is called when the globvar option -r is used. The semaphore is locked by calling glob_lock() in line 17. The semaphore set is then destroyed by lines 20–29. The shared memory is detached in line 34, although it was not mandatory to do so. The IPC_RMID command in lines 44–50 would still succeed, and the actual destruction would occur when the process terminated (when the last process detached it).

Destroying Shared Memory

Listing 25.3 shows the IPC_RMID command of shmctl(2) being used. The critical lines of code are repeated here for your convenience:

```
41:        /*
42:         * Destroy shared memory :
43:         */
44:        z = shmctl(shmid,IPC_RMID,NULL);
45:
46:        if ( z == -1 ) {
47:            fprintf(stderr,"%s: shmctl(%d,IPC_RMID)\n",
48:                strerror(errno),shmid);
49:            exit(1);
50:        }
```

Notice that argument three (buf) is not required by the IPC_RMID command for shmctl(2). This code is exercised by the -r option of the globvar utility.

Using Shared Memory

Once the shared memory is attached, your process can use it like any other region of memory. However, since multiple processes can see this same region of memory, care must be exercised when changing its content.

In the globvar utility, one semaphore is used as the locking semaphore. Whenever the shared memory is searched or modified, the globvar utility waits on the semaphore first (recall that it was initialized to the value of 1). This ensures that no more than one process at a time will be working with the shared memory. When the task has been completed, the semaphore is notified to release the lock.

It should be noted that some values were accessed in the shared memory without the locking semaphore. Examine lines 15–19 in Listing 25.4. These lines declare the structure used for the global memory.

LISTING 25.4   `globvar.h`—The Global `globvar` Utility Definitions

```
 1:  /* globvar.h */
 2:
 3:  #include <stdio.h>
 4:  #include <stdlib.h>
 5:  #include <unistd.h>
 6:  #include <string.h>
 7:  #include <errno.h>
 8:  #include <sys/types.h>
 9:  #include <sys/ipc.h>
10:  #include <sys/shm.h>
11:  #include <sys/sem.h>
12:
13:  #define GLOBVARENV  "GLOBVAR"    /* Environment variable */
14:
15:  typedef struct {
16:      int    semid;              /* Semaphore's IPC ID */
17:      int    size;               /* Size of the vars[] array */
18:      char   vars[1];            /* Start of variable storage */
19:  } GlobVars;
20:
21:  extern int shmid;              /* IPC ID of shared memory region */
22:  extern int shm_size;           /* Size of shared memory region */
23:  extern GlobVars *globvars;     /* Shared memory region */
24:  extern int semid;              /* IPC ID of the locking semaphore set */
25:
26:  extern void create_vars(int shm_size);
27:  extern void attach_vars(void);
28:  extern char *get_var(const char *varname);
29:  extern void set_var(const char *varname,const char *value);
30:  extern void destroy_vars(void);
31:  extern void glob_lock(void);
32:  extern void glob_unlock(void);
33:  extern void unset_var(const char *varname);
34:
35:  #ifndef HAVE_SEMUN            /* Does sys/sem.h define this? */
36:
37:  union semun {
38:      int    val;              /* Value */
39:      struct semid_ds *buf;    /* IPC_STAT info */
40:      u_short *array;          /* Array of values */
41:  };
42:
43:  #endif
44:
45:  /* End globvar.h */
```

The members `semid` and `size` are established when the global pool is initially created. After this, these values never change. Because these values never change, they are safe to reference without a locking semaphore. Dynamic content begins at the member `vars[]` within the `GlobVars` structure. To access its content safely, you must use the locking semaphore in the utility program.

The source module `globlk.c` is shown in Listing 25.5, which implements the shared memory locking routines.

LISTING 25.5 `globlk.c`—The Semaphore Locking Routines

```
 1:  /* globlk.c */
 2:
 3:  #include "globvar.h"
 4:
 5:  static struct sembuf wait = { 0, -1, SEM_UNDO };
 6:  static struct sembuf notify = { 0, +1, SEM_UNDO };
 7:
 8:  /*
 9:   * Perform a semaphore operation :
10:   */
11:  static void
12:  do_semop(struct sembuf *op) {
13:      int z;                       /* status code */
14:
15:      do  {
16:          z = semop(globvars->semid,op,1);
17:      } while ( z == -1 && errno == EINTR );
18:
19:      if ( z ) {
20:          fprintf(stderr,"%s: semop(2)\n",strerror(errno));
21:          exit(1);
22:      }
23:  }
24:
25:  /*
26:   * Wait on semaphore to lock shared memory :
27:   */
28:  void
29:  glob_lock(void) {
30:
31:      do_semop(&wait);
32:  }
33:
34:  /*
35:   * Notify semaphore to unlock shared memory :
36:   */
37:  void
38:  glob_unlock(void) {
39:
40:      do_semop(&notify);
41:  }
```

Lines 5 and 6 define the semaphore lock (`wait`) and unlock (`notify`) operations. The function `do_semop()` performs the actual semaphore operation by calling upon `semop(2)` in line 16. The functions `glob_lock()` and `glob_unlock()` are simply wrapper routines for the `do_semop()` function.

Listing 25.6 shows the module `globget.c` that fetches the value of a global variable.

LISTING 25.6   `globget.c`—The Source Module That Looks Up a Global Variable in Shared Memory

```
 1:   /* globget.c */
 2:
 3:   #include "globvar.h"
 4:
 5:   /*
 6:    * Return the string pointer for a variable's value :
 7:    */
 8:   char *
 9:   get_var(const char *varname) {
10:       char *cp;                      /* Scanning pointer */
11:       int nlen = strlen(varname); /* Length of variable name */
12:
13:       for ( cp = &globvars->vars[0]; *cp; cp += strlen(cp) + 1 )
14:           if ( !strncmp(varname,cp,nlen) && cp[nlen] == '=' )
15:               return cp + nlen + 1; /* Pointer to it's value */
16:
17:       return NULL;                   /* Variable not found */
18:   }
```

The `main()` program calls the `glob_lock()` routine before calling `get_var()` shown in Listing 25.6. The function `get_var()` then searches the shared memory for the variable requested in `varname`. The global variables are stored in shared memory as a list of null terminated strings, in the form `VARIABLE=VALUE`. The end of the variable list is marked by an additional null byte.

Listing 25.7 shows the `main()` program that calls `get_var()`.

LISTING 25.7   `globvar.c`—The Main Program for the `globvar` Utility

```
 1:   /* globvar.c */
 2:
 3:   #include "globvar.h"
 4:
 5:   int shmid = -1;                 /* IPC ID of shared memory */
 6:   GlobVars *globvars = NULL;      /* Shared memory region */
 7:
 8:   /*
 9:    * Usage instructions :
10:    */
11:   static void
12:   usage(void) {
13:
```

continued from previous page

```
14:        puts("globvar [-i] [-s size] [-e] [-u] [-r] [-c]"
15:             " var... var=value...");
16:        puts("Options:");
17:        puts("    -i         Initialize new globvar pool");
18:        puts("    -s size    Size of this pool, in bytes");
19:        puts("    -e         Dump all values (after changes)");
20:        puts("    -u         Unset all named variables");
21:        puts("    -r         Remove this pool of values");
22:        puts("    -c         Clear all variables");
23:        puts("    -h         This info.");
24: }
25:
26: /*
27:  * Main program :
28:  */
29: int
30: main(int argc,char **argv) {
31:        int rc = 0;                  /* Return code */
32:        int optch;                   /* Option character */
33:        int cmdopt_i = 0;            /* -i to create var pool */
34:        int cmdopt_c = 0;            /* -c to clear variables */
35:        int cmdopt_r = 0;            /* -r to remove pool */
36:        int cmdopt_e = 0;            /* -D to dump the variables */
37:        int cmdopt_u = 0;            /* -u to unset named variables */
38:        int cmdopt_h = 0;            /* -h usage option */
39:        int cmdopt_s = 4096;         /* Default for -s */
40:        char *cp, *ep;               /* Character pointers */
41:        unsigned long ul;            /* Converted ulong */
42:        const char cmdopts[] = "hirs:ecu";
43:
44:        /*
45:         * Parse command line options :
46:         */
47:        while ( (optch = getopt(argc,argv,cmdopts)) != -1 )
48:            switch ( optch ) {
49:            case 'c' :               /* -c to clear variables */
50:                cmdopt_c = 1;
51:                break;
52:
53:            case 'i' :               /* -i initialize a new pool */
54:                cmdopt_i = 1;
55:                break;
56:
57:            case 'e' :               /* -e to dump all variables like env */
58:                cmdopt_e = 1;
59:                break;
60:
61:            case 'r' :               /* -r to remove the pool */
62:                cmdopt_r = 1;
63:                break;
64:
65:            case 's' :               /* -s size; affects -i */
66:                ul = strtoul(optarg,&ep,0);
```

```
67:               if ( *ep ) {
68:                   fprintf(stderr,"Bad size: -s %s\n",optarg);
69:                   rc = 1;
70:               } else
71:                   cmdopt_s = (int) ul;
72:               break;
73:
74:           case 'u' :                /* -u to unset all listed variables */
75:               cmdopt_u = 1;
76:               break;
77:
78:           case 'h' :                /* -h to request help */
79:               cmdopt_h = 1;
80:               break;
81:
82:           default  :
83:               rc = 1;
84:           }
85:
86:       /*
87:        * Give usage display if errors or -h :
88:        */
89:       if ( cmdopt_h || rc ) {
90:           usage();
91:           if ( rc )
92:               return rc;
93:       }
94:
95:       /*
96:        * Create/Access global variable pool :
97:        */
98:       if ( cmdopt_i ) {
99:           /*
100:           * Create a new shared memory variable pool :
101:           */
102:          create_vars(cmdopt_s);
103:          printf("%d\n",shmid);
104:
105:      } else if ( (cp = getenv(GLOBVARENV)) != NULL ) {
106:          /*
107:           * Extract IPC key from GLOBVAR environment variable :
108:           */
109:          ul = strtoul(cp,&ep,0);
110:          if ( *ep ) {
111:              fprintf(stderr,"%s has bad IPC key\n",cp);
112:              return 1;
113:          }
114:
115:          shmid = (int)ul;
116:          attach_vars();
117:      }
118:
119:      /*
```

continued from previous page

```
120:         * Do we have enough information to find the pool?
121:         */
122:        if ( !globvars ) {
123:            fprintf(stderr,"You must use -i or define"
124:                " environment variable %s.\n",GLOBVARENV);
125:            return 1;
126:        }
127:
128:        /*
129:         * -c clears all variables :
130:         */
131:        if ( cmdopt_c ) {
132:            glob_lock();
133:            globvars->vars[0] = globvars->vars[1] = 0;
134:            glob_unlock();
135:        }
136:
137:        /*
138:         * Now process variable requests :
139:         */
140:        for ( ; optind < argc; ++optind ) {
141:            cp = strchr(argv[optind],'=');
142:
143:            glob_lock();
144:
145:            if ( !cp ) {
146:                /*
147:                 * Just have a variable name, so return value or unset :
148:                 */
149:                if ( !cmdopt_u ) {
150:                    if ( (cp = get_var(argv[optind])) != NULL ) {
151:                        puts(cp);    /* Just emit value of variable */
152:                    } else {
153:                        fprintf(stderr,"Variable %s not found\n",argv[optind]);
154:                        rc = 1;
155:                    }
156:                } else
157:                    unset_var(argv[optind]);
158:
159:            } else {
160:                /*
161:                 * Change the variable's value :
162:                 */
163:                *cp = 0;
164:                set_var(argv[optind],++cp);
165:            }
166:
167:            glob_unlock();
168:        }
169:
170:        /*
171:         * Dump all variables (for debugging) :
172:         */
```

```
173:        if ( cmdopt_e ) {
174:            glob_lock();
175:            for ( cp=&globvars->vars[0]; *cp; cp+=strlen(cp)+1 )
176:                puts(cp);
177:            glob_unlock();
178:        }
179:
180:        /*
181:         * If -r option, destroy the global variable pool :
182:         */
183:        if ( cmdopt_r )
184:            destroy_vars();
185:
186:        return rc;
187: }
```

The get_var() function is called when a variable name is listed on the command line by itself (lines 150 and 151). Note that the shared memory is locked in line 143 and unlocked in line 167. Using the locking semaphore permits several processes to update the same global variable pool without corruption.

Listing 25.8 shows the module globset.c that implements the variable assignment functions.

LISTING 25.8   globset.c—The Implementation of the globvar Variable Assignment Functions

```
 1:    /* globset.c */
 2:
 3:    #include "globvar.h"
 4:
 5:    /*
 6:     * Change the value of a global variable :
 7:     */
 8:    void
 9:    set_var(const char *varname,const char *value) {
10:        int z;                              /* status code */
11:        char *var = get_var(varname);       /* Locate variable if it exists */
12:        char *cp;                           /* utility char pointer */
13:        int nlen = strlen(varname);         /* Length of variable name */
14:        int vlen = strlen(value);           /* Length of variable's value */
15:        int in_use = 0;                     /* Bytes in use */
16:        int avail = globvars->size;         /* Bytes available */
17:
18:        if ( var ) {                        /* Does variable exist? */
19:
20:            in_use = (int)( var - &globvars->vars[0] ) + 1;
21:            avail -= in_use;                /* Bytes available for new value */
22:
23:            z = strlen(var + nlen + 1); /* Length of current string */
24:            if ( vlen > avail + z )
25:                goto nospc;                 /* Insufficient space */
26:
27:            /*
```

continued from previous page

```
28:                     * Now delete the variable :
29:                     */
30:                    var = var - nlen - 1;        /* Point to start of entry */
31:
32:                    for ( cp=var+strlen(var)+1; *cp; var += z, cp += z ) {
33:                        z = strlen(cp) + 1;       /* Length of next value */
34:                        memmove(var,cp,z);        /* Move it up */
35:                    }
36:
37:          } else {
38:              /*
39:               * Find end of global storage :
40:               */
41:              for ( var = &globvars->vars[0]; *var; var += strlen(var) + 1 )
42:                  ;
43:
44:              in_use = (int)( var - &globvars->vars[0] ) + 1;
45:              avail -= in_use;                /* Bytes available for new value */
46:
47:              if ( nlen + 1 + vlen > avail )
48:                  goto nospc;
49:          }
50:
51:          /*
52:           * Append VARIABLE=VALUE\0 to end of shared region :
53:           */
54:          strcpy(var,varname);       /* Variable name */
55:          var += nlen;               /* Point past variable name */
56:          *var++ = '=';              /* The equal sign */
57:          strcpy(var,value);         /* The variable's value */
58:          var[vlen+1] = 0;           /* 2 null bytes mark the end */
59:
60:          return;                    /* Successful */
61:
62:          /*
63:           * Insufficient space to store this variable :
64:           */
65: nospc:
66:          fprintf(stderr,"%s: %s='%s'\n",strerror(ENOSPC),varname,value);
67:          exit(1);
68: }
```

The set_var() routine first looks up the variable in line 11. If the variable exists in the pool, the space for the new value is computed in lines 20 and 21. If the new value fits into the space remaining, the current variable is deleted by a memory move loop in lines 32–35. After this point, the remaining code treats the variable as if it were a new value.

If the variable does not exist yet, the space calculations are performed in lines 44–48. The new variable and value is appended to the shared memory region in lines 54–57. Line 58 puts a second null byte at the end to mark the end of the variables list.

Listing 25.9 shows the module that is responsible for removing a variable by name, invoked by the globvar -u option.

LISTING 25.9   `globun.c`—The Unset Feature of `globvar` Is Implemented by `globun.c`

```
 1:   /* globun.c */
 2:
 3:   #include "globvar.h"
 4:
 5:   /*
 6:    * Unset a variable :
 7:    */
 8:   void
 9:   unset_var(const char *varname) {
10:       int z;                              /* status code */
11:       char *var = get_var(varname);       /* Locate variable if it exists */
12:       char *cp;                           /* utility char pointer */
13:       int nlen = strlen(varname);         /* Length of variable name */
14:
15:       if ( !var )
16:           return;                         /* Variable is already unset */
17:
18:       /*
19:        * Now delete the variable :
20:        */
21:       var = var - nlen - 1;        /* Point to start of entry */
22:
23:       for ( cp=var+strlen(var)+1; *cp; var += z, cp += z ) {
24:           z = strlen(cp) + 1;      /* Length of next value */
25:           memmove(var,cp,z);       /* Move it up */
26:       }
27:
28:       *var = 0;                    /* two nulls mark the end of vars */
29:
30:       return;                      /* Successful */
31:   }
```

The variable name is searched in line 11. If it is not found, the function returns in line 16. Otherwise, the `for` loop of lines 23–26 moves the strings to replace the area formerly occupied by the deleted variable. Line 28 adds the second null byte to mark the new end of the variable list.

Summary

The `globvar` utility provides a simple means for shell programs running under your account to share dynamic information with each other, using shared memory. You saw how a semaphore was used to provide concurrency protection. Yet you also observed that certain static items like the semaphore IPC ID in the shared memory could be safely accessed without locks. As an exercise, you may want to enhance the utility further by adding a `-k` IPC key option. This would eliminate the need to communicate the IPC ID values between unrelated processes.

You have completed the tour of the IPC communication set, which included message queues, semaphores, and shared memory. The next chapter examines the ability of the UNIX kernel to map memory to files.

CHAPTER 26

MEMORY-MAPPED FILES

C hapter 25, "Shared Memory," showed how shared memory could be used to share information between processes. A more modern feature of the UNIX kernel permits memory to be mapped to a regular file or a character device. This technique allows unrelated processes to share information as well, but adds a number of new features to the programmer's repertoire.

All executable files under modern UNIX kernels are mapped to virtual memory pages. These pages of memory are marked as being executable only within the process memory (on many platforms, this often implies that they are readable as well). In this manner, only those memory pages needed are actually paged into memory upon demand. For large programs, this is more efficient than loading the entire program into memory at startup.

Memory mapping simply extends this idea to application data files. Figure 26.1 shows how a memory-mapped file might be accessed from within a process's memory space.

The figure shows that the mapping may be larger than the actual file itself. This is often true because the virtual memory management performed by the UNIX kernel must use a fixed page size. Thus, Figure 26.1 shows that there is an extra region above the file's mapping. These extra bytes will be zeroed when the mapping is established.

When your application examines memory within the mapped region, pages of data are retrieved from the file as necessary to make the memory cells available. Likewise, if memory cells are modified, the changes are written back out to the file (depending upon options selected) at a time determined by the kernel. There are methods to control this behavior and its timing.

FIGURE 26.1
A file is mapped to
process memory.

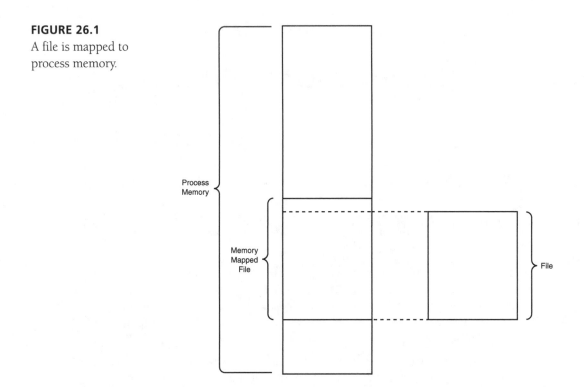

Determining the Page Size

Memory functions performed by the UNIX kernel are restricted to operating in multiples of the virtual memory (VM) page size. You have already seen this behavior when attaching shared memory. A portable program needs a way to determine what the system's VM page size is, because it varies on different UNIX platforms. The `getpagesize(3)` function returns this information. The function synopsis for it is as follows:

```
#include <unistd.h>

int getpagesize(void);
```

The function `getpagesize(3)` returns the size in bytes of the system page size used.

> **Note**
>
> The page size returned by `getpagesize(3)` is the size of the system's page size. The page size used by the hardware for virtual memory paging may be different in size.

Listing 26.1 shows a simple program that calls upon `getpagesize(3)` and reports the value returned.

LISTING 26.1   `pagesize.c`—A Program That Determines the System Page Size by Calling `getpagesize(3)`

```
 1:    /* pagesize.c */
 2:
 3:    #include <stdio.h>
 4:    #include <unistd.h>
 5:
 6:    int
 7:    main(int argc,char **argv) {
 8:
 9:        printf("Page size is %d bytes\n",getpagesize());
10:        return 0;
11:    }
```

The following shows the program being compiled and run:

```
$ make pagesize
cc -c  -Wall -DHAVE_SEMUN pagesize.c
cc -o pagesize pagesize.o
$ ./pagesize
Page size is 4096 bytes
$
```

From this FreeBSD example, you can see that the kernel is using a page size of 4096 bytes.

Creating Memory Mappings

A memory mapping is established with the help of the `mmap(2)` function call. The function synopsis for it is as follows:

```
#include <sys/types.h>
#include <sys/mman.h>

void *mmap(void *addr,size_t len,int prot,int flags,int fd,off_t offset);
```

The argument `addr` is normally specified as a null pointer unless a specific mapping address must be used. When `addr` is null, the `mmap(2)` call returns the system-selected memory address.

When `addr` is not null, the argument `flags` influences the final result: The `MAP_FIXED` flag indicates that the specified address must be used, or an error indication is to be returned instead. When the flag `MAP_FIXED` is not present and `addr` is not null, the `mmap(2)` function will attempt to accommodate the requested address. Otherwise, it will substitute another address if the requested address cannot be successful.

Argument `len` is the size of the mapping in bytes. This usually corresponds to the length of the mapped file when files are involved. This length may be larger than the mapped file, but accesses beyond the last allocated page will cause a `SIGBUS` (bus error) signal to occur.

The prot argument indicates the type of memory protection required for this memory region. With the exception of PROT_NONE, which must be specified alone, the prot argument is specified with the following macros ORed together:

PROT_NONE	Region grants no access (this flag is used exclusively of the other flags.)
PROT_READ	Region grants read access.
PROT_WRITE	Region grants write access.
PROT_EXEC	Program instructions may be executed in the memory-mapped region.

Argument flags specifies a number of optional features for the mmap(2) function call. The portable flag bits are

MAP_FIXED	Map to the address specified in argument addr or return an error if this cannot be satisfied. Normally when addr is not null, a different mapping address is substituted if the requested one is not acceptable.
MAP_PRIVATE	Modifications to the mapped file are kept private. Unmodified pages are shared by all processes mapping the same file. When one of these memory pages is modified, a private page is created as a copy of the original, which is referenced only by the current process.
MAP_SHARED	Modifications to the mapped file are eventually written back to the file. All processes share the changes.

Normally, the fd argument must be an open file descriptor (except with flag MAP_ANON). This represents the regular file or character special file to be mapped to memory. Once the mmap(2) call has returned, however, you may close the file descriptor, since the kernel maintains its own reference to that open file.

The argument offset is normally specified as 0. When other offsets are used, it must be a multiple of the page size returned by the function getpagesize(3). Otherwise, the error EINVAL is returned.

When mmap(2) is successful, the starting address for the mapping of at least len bytes is returned. Otherwise, the value MAP_FAILED is returned instead, with the error code deposited into errno.

FreeBSD mmap(2) supports additional features, which are selected by the following flag bits:

MAP_ANON	Creates mapped memory that is not associated with any file. The file descriptor parameter must contain the value -1, and the offset argument is ignored.
MAP_INHERIT	Allows a process to retain the memory mapping after an execve(2) system call.

MAP_HASSEMAPHORE	Notifies the UNIX kernel that the memory-mapped region may have semaphores present. This allows the kernel to take special precaution for mutexes.
MAP_STACK	Requests a stack region that grows downward to be created that is at most len bytes in size. The top of the stack is the returned pointer plus len bytes. This flag implies MAP_ANON and insists that the fd argument is -1, and offset must be 0. The prot argument must include at least PROT_READ and PROT_WRITE.

The flag value MAP_ANON is not supported directly by all UNIX platforms. Linux and IBM AIX 4.3 use the macro name MAP_ANONYMOUS instead.

Tip

To perform the equivalent of MAP_ANON for platforms without this mmap(2) feature, memory-map device /dev/zero using the MAP_PRIVATE flag.

The MAP_INHERIT flag allows you to retain a memory mapping after the execve(2) system call has successfully completed. This is a slick way to pass data from one executable program to another within the same process but suffers from the fact that other UNIX platforms do not support this feature.

The MAP_HASSEMAPHORE flag allows the programmer to hint to the kernel that mutex flags are present in the memory mapping. This allows the kernel to change its handling of the mapping, affecting the way changes are synchronized and perhaps the swapping status of the pages. This is a BSD UNIX feature.

The MAP_STACK flag bit allows you to create stack regions that have memory pages allocated as the stack grows downward. Many platforms, including HPUX 11 and UnixWare 7 do not support this option.

Note

On some hardware platforms, specifying a protection of PROT_EXEC also grants PROT_READ. This is due to platform hardware restrictions.

Table 26.1 shows a cross-referenced list of flag values that are supported by the various UNIX platforms.

TABLE 26.1   A Cross-Referenced Table of Supported `mmap(2)` Features

nmap(2) Flag	Platform						
	FreeBSD	*SGI IRIX 6.5*	*HPUX 11*	*UnixWare 7*	*Solaris 8*	*IBM AIX 4.3*	*Linux*
MAP_SHARED	X	X	X	X	X	X	X
MAP_PRIVATE	X	X	X	X	X	X	X
MAP_FIXED	X	X	X	X	X	X	X
MAP_ANON	X				X		
MAP_ANONYMOUS						X	X
MAP_HASSEMAPHORE	X						
MAP_INHERIT	X						
MAP_STACK	X						
MAP_GROWSDOWN							X
MAP_AUTOGROW		X					
MAP_NORESERVE					X		
MAP_AUTORESRV		X					
MAP_LOCKED							X
MAP_ADDR32			X				
MAP_LOCAL		X					
MAP_FILE						X	
MAP_VARIABLE						X	

Listing 26.2 shows a program that uses memory-mapped files to select the language of system error messages.

LISTING 26.2   `messages.c`—A Program That Uses `mmap(2)` to Select Messages by Language

```
 1:  /* messages.c */
 2:
 3:  #include <stdio.h>
 4:  #include <unistd.h>
 5:  #include <stdlib.h>
 6:  #include <fcntl.h>
 7:  #include <errno.h>
 8:  #include <string.h>
 9:  #include <sys/types.h>
10:  #include <sys/stat.h>
```

```
11:    #include <sys/mman.h>
12:
13:    #define MAX_MSGS    12              /* Limit of univ_errlist[] */
14:
15:    const char *univ_errlist[MAX_MSGS]; /* Universal sys_errlist[] */
16:    const char *univ_maclist[MAX_MSGS]; /* A list of errno macro names */
17:
18:    static void *msgs = 0;              /* Pointer to the mapping */
19:    static size_t msgs_len = 0;         /* Size of the mapping */
20:
21:    /*
22:     * Parse error messages from the memory mapped file, that
23:     * begins at address msgs for msgs_len bytes :
24:     */
25:    static void
26:    parse_messages() {
27:        char *mp = (char *)msgs;        /* Mapped messages address */
28:        char *macro, *error, *msg;
29:        int e;
30:
31:        mp[msgs_len] = 0;               /* Store a null byte at the end */
32:
33:        for ( ;; mp = NULL ) {
34:
35:            macro = strtok(mp," ");     /* Extract macro name */
36:            if ( !macro )
37:                break;
38:
39:            error = strtok(NULL," ");   /* Extract error # */
40:            if ( !error )
41:                break;
42:            if ( (e = atoi(error)) < 0 || e >= MAX_MSGS )
43:                break;                  /* Bad errno value */
44:
45:            msg = strtok(NULL,"\n");    /* Extract message */
46:            if ( !msg )
47:                break;
48:
49:            univ_errlist[e] = msg;      /* Store message */
50:            univ_maclist[e] = macro;    /* Macro name */
51:        }
52:    }
53:
54:    /*
55:     * Map the messages file to memory, and establish
56:     * pointers to them by calling parse_messages() :
57:     */
58:    static void
59:    load_messages() {
60:        int x;                              /* Iterator */
61:        char *lang = getenv("MSG_LANG");    /* Get language */
62:        char path[256];                     /* File name */
63:        struct stat sbuf;                   /* stat(2) info */
```

continued from previous page

```
64:      int fd = -1;                        /* Open file descriptor */
65:
66:      /*
67:       * Load default messages :
68:       */
69:      for ( x=0; x<MAX_MSGS; ++x ) {
70:          univ_errlist[x] = sys_errlist[x];
71:          univ_maclist[x] = "?";
72:      }
73:
74:      /*
75:       * Get message file's size :
76:       */
77:      sprintf(path,"./errors.%s",lang ? lang : "english");
78:
79:      if ( stat(path,&sbuf) != 0 )
80:          return;      /* Cannot stat(2) file, so use default msgs */
81:      msgs_len = sbuf.st_size;
82:
83:      /*
84:       * Open the message file for reading :
85:       */
86:      if ( (fd = open(path,O_RDONLY)) == -1 )
87:          return;      /* Cannot open(2) file, so use default msgs */
88:
89:      /*
90:       * Map the language file to memory :
91:       */
92:      msgs = mmap(NULL,msgs_len+1,PROT_READ|PROT_WRITE,MAP_PRIVATE,fd,0);
93:
94:      if ( msgs == (void *) MAP_FAILED ) {
95:          fprintf(stderr,"%s: mmap('%s')\n",strerror(errno),path);
96:          close(fd);
97:          return;      /* Failed, use default */
98:      }
99:
100:     close(fd);       /* no longer require file to be open */
101:
102:     /*
103:      * Now parse the messages :
104:      */
105:     parse_messages();
106: }
107:
108: /*
109:  * Main program :
110:  */
111: int
112: main(int argc,char **argv) {
113:     int x;
114:
115:     /*
```

```
116:        * Memory map the language file :
117:        */
118:       load_messages();
119:
120:       /*
121:        * Report messages :
122:        */
123:       for ( x=1; x<MAX_MSGS; ++x )
124:           printf("errno=%d (%s) : %s\n",
125:               x,univ_maclist[x],univ_errlist[x]);
126:
127:       return 0;
128: }
```

The `main()` program starts by calling upon `load_messages()` to select and load the error messages file in line 118. The `load_messages()` function initially attempts to find environment variable `MSG_LANG` by calling `getenv(3)` in line 61. This variable influences the language being used by the error messages and defaults to English (see line 77).

Only the first 12 system error messages are used in this demonstration program, and the limit is established by the macro value `MAX_MSGS` in line 13. This macro also defines the pointer array length of `univ_errlist[]` and macro name array `univ_maclist[]`. Lines 69–72 initialize defaults for the arrays `univ_errlist[]` and `univ_maclist[]`. These defaults are used if no memory mapping succeeds.

The pathname of the message file to be mapped is formed in line 77. The size of the file is determined by a call to `stat(2)` in lines 79–81. If the file cannot be `stat(2)`, then the function simply returns, causing the defaults for the error messages to be used (line 80).

The message file is opened for reading in line 86. The file is mapped by calling `mmap(2)` in line 92. Since no address was given, the kernel will select a suitable address, which will be assigned to variable `msgs`. The mapped region was specified to be at least `msgs_len+1` bytes in length. The extra byte was requested so that the program can plug in a terminating null byte to simplify the code.

The access to the region will allow both reading and writing. The flag `MAP_PRIVATE` was used so that any changes made by the program would be kept separate from both the file and other processes mapping this file. The reason for allowing write access will be clear when the function `parse_messages()` is explained.

Line 100 closes the message file, since it no longer needs to be open. The UNIX kernel maintains its own reference to the file after a successful `mmap(2)` call, so your application is free to close the file.

Now examine the function `parse_messages()` in lines 25–52. Line 27 casts the `(void *)` pointer `msgs` into the character pointer `mp` in line 27. This points to the beginning of our mapped file. Line 31 places a null byte at the end of the file to simplify the work in this routine. Note that this extra byte was allowed for in the original `mmap(2)` call.

Before looking at how the code is parsed, look at a sample message file in English first:

```
$ cat errors.english
EPERM 1 Operation not permitted
ENOENT 2 No such file or directory
ESRCH 3 No such process
EINTR 4 Interrupted system call
EIO 5 Input/output error
ENXIO 6 Device not configured
E2BIG 7 Argument list too long
ENOEXEC 8 Exec format error
EBADF 9 Bad file descriptor
ECHILD 10 No child processes
EDEADLK 11 Resource deadlock avoided
$
```

Each line of the message file is divided into a macro name field, an `errno` value, and the text of the message itself. Only the first 12 codes are covered in this demonstration.

The first time `strtok(3)` is called, in line 35, the argument `mp` is not null. This starts the entire parsing process, but note that successive iterations provide a null pointer here (see the `for` loop in line 33). Lines 35–47 parse the three fields of the input line. Lines 49–50 store pointer references to these messages.

The protection `PROT_WRITE` was necessary for this application because `strtok(3)` modifies the memory it is parsing. Recall that it places a null byte at the end of the token found. However, to prevent these changes from being written back to the messages file, the flag `MAP_PRIVATE` keeps the changes local to the process memory.

An improvement would be to use one application to create a message image file that does not require parsing. Then the second application could simply map the resulting generated memory image into its memory with read-only access. This will be left for you as an exercise.

Compiling the program in Listing 26.2 and invoking it without any language setting causes it to display its defaults:

```
$ make messages
cc -c  -Wall messages.c
cc -o messages messages.o
$ ./messages
errno=1 (EPERM) : Operation not permitted
errno=2 (ENOENT) : No such file or directory
errno=3 (ESRCH) : No such process
errno=4 (EINTR) : Interrupted system call
errno=5 (EIO) : Input/output error
errno=6 (ENXIO) : Device not configured
errno=7 (E2BIG) : Argument list too long
errno=8 (ENOEXEC) : Exec format error
errno=9 (EBADF) : Bad file descriptor
errno=10 (ECHILD) : No child processes
errno=11 (EDEADLK) : Resource deadlock avoided
$
```

The default is to assume the English language, so the message file `errors.english` is used in this example run. If you change the environment variable `MSG_LANG` to the German language, you get different results:

```
$ MSG_LANG=german ./messages
errno=1 (EPERM) : Operation nicht die Erlaubnis gehabt
errno=2 (ENOENT) : Keine solche Datei oder Verzeichnis
errno=3 (ESRCH) : Kein solches Prozeß
errno=4 (EINTR) : Unterbrochener Systemaufruf
errno=5 (EIO) : Input/Output Fehler
errno=6 (ENXIO) : Einheit nicht konfiguriert
errno=7 (E2BIG) : Argumentliste zu lang
errno=8 (ENOEXEC) : Formatfehler Exec
errno=9 (EBADF) : Falscher Dateibeschreiber
errno=10 (ECHILD) : Keine Kindprozesse
errno=11 (EDEADLK) : Hilfsmittelsystemblockade vermieden
$
```

In this example, the input file `errors.german` was mapped to memory instead. This file has the following content:

```
$ cat errors.german
EPERM 1 Operation nicht die Erlaubnis gehabt
ENOENT 2 Keine solche Datei oder Verzeichnis
ESRCH 3 Kein solches Prozeß
EINTR 4 Unterbrochener Systemaufruf
EIO 5 Input/Output Fehler
ENXIO 6 Einheit nicht konfiguriert
E2BIG 7 Argumentliste zu lang
ENOEXEC 8 Formatfehler Exec
EBADF 9 Falscher Dateibeschreiber
ECHILD 10 Keine Kindprozesse
EDEADLK 11 Hilfsmittelsystemblockade vermieden
$
```

With the help of the following, you could create yet another message file, such as for French:

```
http://babelfish.altavista.com/raging/translate.dyn
```

Another use for memory-mapped files might be to save your application's workspace. For example, with memory-mapped files, the shared global variables in the `globvar` utility discussed in Chapter 25 could be saved to a file for future use after a system reboot. Regions for just-in-time executable code can be placed into executable memory regions. This would be performed without actually using a file (recall that the flag `MAP_ANON` or the mapping of `/dev/zero` effectively provides this capability).

If memory-mapped regions are used for interprocess communication, keep in mind that synchronization is still required. You may need the assistance of a semaphore set, for example.

Controlling Memory-Mapped Regions

A memory-mapped region often requires its attributes to be queried or changed in some fashion. This section looks at four system calls designed for this purpose:

mprotect(2)	Change the access of the indicated memory pages.
madvise(2)	Advise the UNIX kernel how you intend to use your memory region.
mincore(2)	Determine if pages of mapped memory are currently in memory.
msync(2)	Where modifications exist, indicate what regions of memory should be updated to the mapped files.

Changing the Access Protection

A memory-mapped region, entirely or in part, may have its access protections changed by the mprotect(2) system call. Its function synopsis is as follows:

```
#include <sys/types.h>
#include <sys/mman.h>

int mprotect(const void *addr, size_t len, int prot);
```

The function mprotect(2) allows the application to change the region starting at address addr for a length of len bytes, so as to use the protection specified by the argument prot. The prot flags permitted are

PROT_NONE	Region grants no access (this flag excludes use of the other flags).
PROT_READ	Region grants read access.
PROT_WRITE	Region grants write access.
PROT_EXEC	Program instructions may be executed in the memory-mapped region.

The function mprotect(2) returns the value 0 when successful. Otherwise, -1 is returned, and the error code is found in errno.

Warning

Not all UNIX implementations permit the caller to change memory region protection on a page-by-page basis. For maximum portability, the entire memory region should be specified.

The messages.c program was modified to call mprotect(2) in the file mprotect.c. The changes made to the program are shown in the context diff(1) form in Listing 26.3.

LISTING 26.3 `mprotect.c`—Changes to `messages.c` to Make Message Text Read-Only

```
$ diff -c messages.c mprotect.c
*** messages.c  Sun Jul  9 18:11:00 2000
--- mprotect.c  Sun Jul  9 18:59:19 2000
***************
*** 1,4 ****
! /* messages.c */

  #include <stdio.h>
  #include <unistd.h>
--- 1,4 ----
! /* mprotect.c */

  #include <stdio.h>
  #include <unistd.h>
***************
*** 103,108 ****
--- 103,114 ----
        * Now parse the messages :
        */
       parse_messages();
+
+      /*
+       * Make the message text read only now :
+       */
+      if ( mprotect(msgs,msgs_len+1,PROT_READ) )
+          fprintf(stderr,"%s: mprotect(PROT_READ)\n",strerror(errno));
  }

  /*
$
```

The `mprotect(2)` call follows the `parse_messages()` function call in Listing 26.3. At this point, it is desirable to use a read-only status, since this will prevent buggy code from altering the message text. If an attempt is made to change the error message text, a **SIGBUS** signal will be raised instead.

Advising the Kernel About Memory Use

To achieve maximum performance, you may find it desirable for your application to inform the UNIX kernel about the status of a memory region or about its usage patterns. The system call `madvise(2)` permits this to be accomplished:

```
#include <sys/types.h>
#include <sys/mman.h>

int madvise(void *addr, size_t len, int behavior);
```

The `madvise(2)` function returns **0** when successful. The value **-1** is returned when the call fails, leaving the error code in the variable `errno`.

The `madvise(2)` system call allows you to hint to the kernel about the memory region starting at `addr` for a length of `len` bytes. The behavior is specified by one of the following values:

MADV_NORMAL	Normal behavior; no special treatment is required.
MADV_RANDOM	Expect memory pages to be referenced at random. Sequential prefetching is to be discouraged.
MADV_SEQUENTIAL	Expect memory pages to be referenced sequentially. This encourages prefetching and decreases the priority of previously fetched pages.
MADV_WILLNEED	Indicates a range of memory pages that should temporarily have a higher priority, since they will be needed.
MADV_DONTNEED	Indicates a range of memory pages that are no longer required (their priority is reduced). It is likely that future references to these pages will incur a page fault.
MADV_FREE	Indicates that the modifications in the memory pages indicated do not need to be saved. Furthermore, this permits the kernel to release the physical memory pages used. The next time the page is referenced, it may be zeroed, or it may still contain the original data.

In addition to these, some platforms support the following behavior:

MADV_SPACEAVAIL	Ensures that the necessary resources are reserved.

Linux and UnixWare 7 do not support the `madvise(2)` function at all. Table 26.2 provides a cross-reference grid of supported behaviors.

TABLE 26.2 A Cross-Reference Guide to `madvise(2)` Behavior Support on Different Platforms

madvise(2) Behavior	Platform						
	FreeBSD	*SGI IRIX 6.5*	*HPUX 11*	*UnixWare 7*	*Solaris 8*	*IBM AIX 4.3*	*Linux*
MADV_NORMAL	X		X		X	X	
MADV_RANDOM	X		X		X	X	
MADV_SEQUENTIAL	X		X		X	X	
MADV_WILLNEED	X		X		X	X	
MADV_DONTNEED	X	X			X	X	
MADV_FREE	X				X		
MADV_SPACEAVAIL			X			X	

Listing 26.4 shows a context `diff(1)` listing, illustrating the changes between `mprotect.c` and `madvise.c`. In `madvise.c`, calls to `madvise(2)` have been added.

LISTING 26.4   `madvise.c`—Changes Made to `mprotect.c` to Indicate Access Behavior Patterns to the Kernel

```
*** mprotect.c     Sun Jul  9 18:59:19 2000
--- madvise.c      Sun Jul  9 19:40:33 2000
***************
*** 1,4 ****
! /* mprotect.c */

  #include <stdio.h>
  #include <unistd.h>
--- 1,4 ----
! /* madvise.c */

  #include <stdio.h>
  #include <unistd.h>
***************
*** 100,105 ****
--- 100,111 ----
      close(fd);        /* no longer require file to be open */

      /*
+      * Advise kernel of sequential behavior :
+      */
+     if ( madvise(msgs,msgs_len+1,MADV_SEQUENTIAL) )
+         fprintf(stderr,"%s: madvise(MADV_SEQUENTIAL)\n",strerror(errno));
+
+     /*
       * Now parse the messages :
       */
      parse_messages();
***************
*** 109,114 ****
--- 115,126 ----
      */
      if ( mprotect(msgs,msgs_len+1,PROT_READ) )
          fprintf(stderr,"%s: mprotect(PROT_READ)\n",strerror(errno));
+
+     /*
+      * Advise kernel of random behavior :
+      */
+     if ( madvise(msgs,msgs_len+1,MADV_RANDOM) )
+         fprintf(stderr,"%s: madvise(MADV_SEQUENTIAL)\n",strerror(errno));
  }

  /*
```

The first madvise(2) call occurs before the error message file is parsed, to indicate sequential access with MADV_SEQUENTIAL. Recall that the parsing of the messages is sequential from the start to the end of the mapped message file.

Once the messages have been parsed, however, the access pattern changes to that of a random nature, since any error message may be called upon demand. Hence, the second call to madvise(2) selects behavior MADV_RANDOM.

Querying Pages in Memory

It is possible to query the kernel to determine which memory pages are currently in memory. This is accomplished by the mincore(2) system call, and its synopsis is as follows:

```
#include <sys/types.h>
#include <sys/mman.h>

int mincore(const void *addr, size_t len, char *vec);
```

The mincore(2) function accepts a starting address **addr** and a length of **len** bytes. All pages within this range are then reported by setting values in the **vec** character array. The array **vec** is expected to be large enough to contain all the values that must be reported. Each byte receives 1 if the page is in memory or 0 if the page is not in memory. The number of bytes required depends on the length of the region and the page size returned by the function getpagesize(3).

When successful, the value 0 is returned by mincore(2). Otherwise, -1 is returned, and the error is found in the variable errno.

The following shows a call to mincore(2):

```
char vec[32];                   /* Reports for up to 32 pages */

if ( mincore(addr,len,&vec[0]) == -1 )
    perror("mincore(2)");       /* Report error */
```

Table 26.3 shows that support for mincore(2) is not available on many platforms. Also, note that the argument **addr** is type caddr_t on non-BSD platforms.

TABLE 26.3   A Cross-Reference Chart for mincore(2) Support on Different Platforms

mincore(2) Support	Platform						
	FreeBSD	SGI IRIX 6.5	HPUX 11	UnixWare 7	Solaris 8	IBM AIX 4.3	Linux
mincore(2)	X			X	X	X	
const void *addr	X						
caddr_t addr				X	X	X	

Synchronizing Changes

When changes are made to writable mapped regions of memory, there are various timing choices for recording changes into the file. The msync(2) system call provides a degree of control over this choice. Its function synopsis is as follows:

```
#include <sys/types.h>
#include <sys/mman.h>

int msync(void *addr, size_t len, int flags);
```

The msync(2) call affects the region starting at addr for a length of len bytes. When len is 0, all of the pages of the region are affected. Argument flags determines what synchronization choice is to take effect:

MS_ASYNC	Request all changes to be written out, but return immediately. (Not implemented for FreeBSD release 3.4.)
MS_SYNC	Perform synchronous writes of all outstanding changes.
MS_INVALIDATE	Immediately invalidate all cached modifications to pages. Future references to these pages require the pages to be fetched from the file.

The MS_SYNC flag is similar to calling fsync(2) on an open file descriptor. It forces all changes out to the disk media and returns once this has been accomplished. The MS_INVALIDATE flag allows the application to discard all changes that have been made. This saves the kernel from synchronizing the memory region with the file.

The function msync(2) returns 0 when successful. Otherwise, -1 is returned with the error code deposited in errno. The following shows an example of a msync(2) call to cause all changes to be immediately written to the file:

```
if ( msync(addr,0,MS_SYNC) == -1 )
    perror("msync(2)");
```

Table 26.4 shows the support available for msync(2) on the different platforms.

TABLE 26.4   A Cross-Reference Chart of msync(2) Support on Different Platforms

msync(2) Support	Platform						
	FreeBSD	SGI IRIX 6.5	HPUX 11	UnixWare 7	Solaris 8	IBM AIX 4.3	Linux
MS_ASYNC		X	X	X	X	X	X
MS_SYNC	X	X	X	X	X	X	X
MS_INVALIDATE	X	X	X	X	X	X	X
void *addr	X	X	X		X	X	

continued from previous page

msync(2) Support	Platform						
	FreeBSD	*SGI IRIX 6.5*	*HPUX 11*	*UnixWare 7*	*Solaris 8*	*IBM AIX 4.3*	*Linux*
const void *addr							X
caddr_t addr				X			

Destroying Memory Mappings

With the exception of the MAP_INHERIT flag for FreeBSD, the memory-mapped regions are unmapped automatically by the kernel when execve(2) is called or when the process terminates. It may occur in an application, however, that the memory-mapped file is needed only temporarily. The munmap(2) system call is used to unmap it:

```
#include <sys/types.h>
#include <sys/mman.h>

int munmap(void *addr, size_t len);
```

The memory region to be unmapped is specified as the region starting at **addr** for a length of **len** bytes. The function munmap(2) returns **0** when successful. Otherwise, **-1** is returned, with an error code left in **errno**. It should be noted that this system call does not cause pending changes to be written out to the file. If this is important, you must make appropriate use of the msync(2) system call prior to calling on munmap(2).

Referencing memory after it has been unmapped will cause the signal **SIGSEGV** or **SIGBUS** to occur. Some UNIX platforms can return either, depending on the nature of the memory access.

Note

Unfortunately, no platform documents that len can be specified as zero. This forces the application programmer to keep track of the memory region size, so that it can be unmapped successfully at a later time.

This restriction is especially painful when MAP_INHERIT is used with execve(2) to execute a new program. Unless the size of the region has been stored in the memory region itself (or communicated some other way), the new program will not know the correct length to use in a munmap(2) call.

To unmap a region of memory in the Listing 26.2 program (**messages.c**), the following function call could be added prior to the **return** statement on line 127:

```
if ( munmap(msgs,msgs_len+1) == -1 )
    perror("munmap(2)");
```

In this example, recall that one byte was added to the file's size when it was mapped. Consequently, **msgs_len+1** is necessary in the munmap(2) call.

Warning

The munmap(2) system call does not cause pending changes to be written out to the file. If this is important, you must make appropriate use of the msync(2) system call prior to calling munmap(2).

Summary

This chapter looked at the UNIX facility that is available for memory-mapped files. This facility provides some interesting new choices to the application programmer.

However, be aware that memory mapping is often restricted to files and memory regions of less than 2GB (FreeBSD release 3.4 restriction). On any given platform, you are restricted to the process memory image size.

If you use memory-mapped files to share information between separate processes, remember that semaphores and calls to msync(2) may be required for synchronization. If you use some of the more exotic mmap(2) features, your application may not be portable to other UNIX platforms.

Despite these challenges, memory-mapped files can be an extremely efficient way to work with data in memory and keep copies of it in a disk file.

The next chapter takes a departure into the world of X Window programming. This will provide an introduction to graphical programming under UNIX and an example of event-driven processing.

CHAPTER 27

X WINDOW PROGRAMMING

Non-graphical programs tend to follow the programmer's choice of events, accepting user input only when it is convenient for the program. An update process will chug through a database and wait for the user's input only when it has called fgets(3), for example. Once control has returned from fgets(3) with the input, however, any additional user input is ignored as the update proceeds.

Another program that puts up a text-based screen is also program directed. The user must provide input that is suitable for the field where the cursor is. As the cursor moves to other input fields, the input data provided must obey content rules for those fields. These are examples of a program telling the user what input to provide and when it must be provided.

Graphical user interfaces use a different processing paradigm. Event-driven programming has a program constantly waiting for user input events. Processing occurs briefly only after these user-input events have been received by the program. The user is able to choose where to input text with a mouse click or a tab key. Alternatively, the user may use the mouse to draw, causing numerous input events to occur.

This chapter will examine event-driven programming as it applies to X Window graphics. The intention of this chapter is to

- Illustrate event-driven programming
- Introduce X Window graphics programming

Event-Driven Programming

Figure 27.1 shows a program that progresses from time T0 to T6 in two states: a processing state in which program instructions are executed and an input state in which program execution is suspended until user input arrives.

After some program initialization starting at time T0, the program ignores user input until it reaches time T1. At T1, the execution of the program is suspended until fgets(3) receives input (using an underlying read(2) system call). At time T1 the program is attentive to the user.

At time T2, however, the program is busy executing instructions that pertain to database queries and other non-input activities. The user cannot direct the flow of the program at this point.

FIGURE 27.1

Non–event-driven states from time T0 to T6.

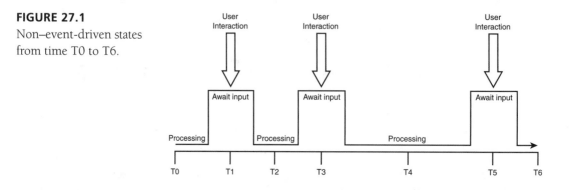

At time T3, the program is willing to listen to the user again, providing the user some measure of control. However, after this input is received, at time T4 the program completely ignores the user as it chugs away.

Time T5 allows the user one more opportunity for input before ignoring the user again at time T6. Throughout the entire execution of the program, it has only allowed user control over it at a few defined points.

An Event-Driven Model

Figure 27.2 shows how an event-driven model behaves.

FIGURE 27.2

Event-driven states from time T0 to T6.

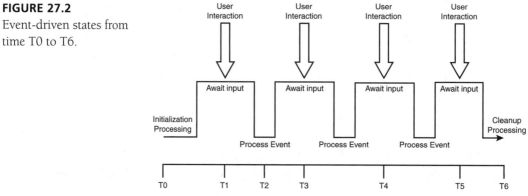

In this program, there is some initialization starting at time T0. However, from time T1 to T5 the program is preoccupied with obtaining input events from the user. Only after an input event occurs does the program ignore input briefly to process the action required by the event.

The fact that event-driven models also ignore input briefly highlights one important aspect of graphical programming: Event processing must be brief. Otherwise, the user will cease to have control. Note that, like character mode programs, graphical events are queued for the event-driven program. This allows event programs to process events without losing them as it performs processing for the preceding events.

Client/Server Processing

The X Window graphic software is flexible enough to allow programs to draw graphics on the local screen or to a remote computer's screen instead. The X Window server is the process that manages the input devices and the one or more display screens. The client is the program that wants to draw on the screen and receive input from the input devices, such as the mouse and keyboard. Figure 27.3 shows an X Window server running on host `alpha` and clients running on all three hosts.

FIGURE 27.3

Four X Window client programs using one X Window server.

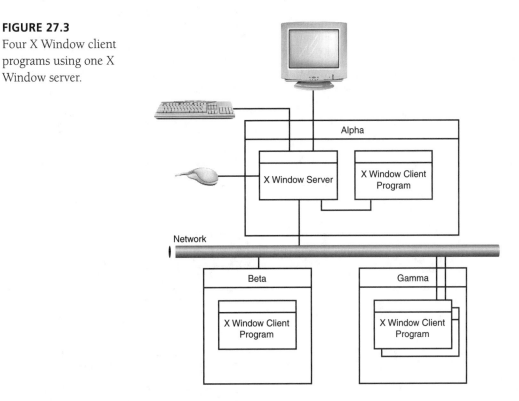

The X Window server running on host `alpha` controls the graphics display screen, the keyboard, and the mouse. On the same host, a client program is making use of these facilities through a local socket connection to the server.

On host `beta`, one client is accessing the `alpha` X Window server through the network. Host `gamma` has two client programs accessing the `alpha` X Window server through the network.

The user sitting at the display has four different windows open. Each window sends input events to the specific client program that created the window.

Software Layers

Graphical programming tends to be complex. To make the software easier to design and manage, the X Window software has been designed in layers. Figure 27.4 shows a conceptual view of this.

FIGURE 27.4
X Window software layers.

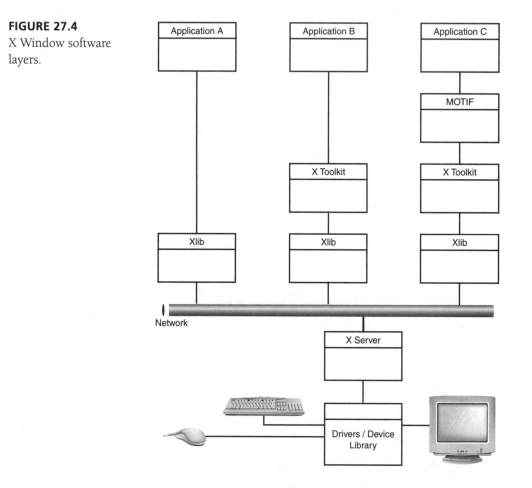

Figure 27.4 shows three client program perspectives. These are common configurations for X Window clients but not the only ones available. Application program A uses the basic X Window library Xlib. This library eliminates the need for the client program to know the X Window protocol. The Xlib library allows the programmer to concentrate on the input and the drawing events instead.

Application program B uses an X Toolkit library, which then calls upon the Xlib library. The Toolkit library provides a basic framework for X Window widget support and uses Xlib to provide lower-level support. This simplifies the application's handling of menus, buttons, and other widgets.

Application program C uses the MOTIF library, which calls upon the X Toolkit and the Xlib libraries. The MOTIF library provides a fully functional set of widgets with a 3D look and includes support for other languages.

Application program C is the simplest program to write if the application involves pushbuttons, list boxes, text entry fields, and so on. However, if your application requires only drawing facilities, the Xlib support may be all you need.

The example program presented in this chapter will be of the application A variety. Using the Xlib library is sufficient for demonstrating event-driven programming and requires the least amount of explanation. The serious X Window programmer is encouraged to read more about the X Toolkit and MOTIF libraries, however.

An Xlib Client Program

Listing 27.1 shows the listing of the include file that is used by the source modules xeg.c and events.c.

LISTING 27.1 xeg.h—Common Include File for xeg.c and events.c

```
 1:    /* xeg.h */
 2:
 3:    #include <stdio.h>
 4:    #include <strings.h>
 5:    #include <X11/Xlib.h>
 6:    #include <X11/Xutil.h>
 7:
 8:    typedef unsigned long Ulong;
 9:
10:    #define B1        1           /* Left button */
11:    #define B2        2           /* Middle button */
12:    #define B3        4           /* Right button */
13:
14:    extern Display *disp;         /* Display */
15:    extern int scr;              /* Screen */
16:
17:    extern Ulong bg;             /* Background color */
18:    extern Ulong fg;             /* Foreground color */
19:
20:    extern Ulong wht;            /* White */
21:    extern Ulong blk;            /* Black */
22:
23:    extern Ulong red;            /* red */
24:    extern Ulong green;          /* green */
25:    extern Ulong blue;           /* blue */
26:
27:    extern Window xwin;          /* Drawing window */
28:
29:    extern void event_loop(void);
30:
31:    /* End xeg.h */
```

The file includes the usual `<stdio.h>` and `<strings.h>` definitions to define the macro NULL and `strerror(3)`, respectively. It should be noted that one of the great features of UNIX graphics programming is that you can send output to standard output, in addition to graphics on the X Window server. This often assists greatly in debugging efforts.

The include file `<X11/Xlib.h>` (line 5) is required to define a number of Xlib functions and macros. Include file `<X11/Xutil.h>` (line 6) is needed to define the type XSizeHints, which is used in this example program.

The `typedef` Ulong is declared in line 8 for programming convenience, since the type `unsigned long` is used frequently. Macros B1, B2, and B3 are mouse button bits that define bits 0, 1, and 2, respectively, where 0 is the least significant bit. These macros are used in the event processing loop.

The remainder of the include file (lines 14–27) defines global values that are initialized by the `main()` program.

Listing 27.2 shows the source listing for the `main()` program.

LISTING 27.2   `xeg.c`—The `main()` Function of the Xlib Client Program

```
 1:    /* xeg.c */
 2:
 3:    #include "xeg.h"
 4:
 5:    Display *disp;              /* Display */
 6:    int scr;                    /* Screen */
 7:
 8:    Ulong bg;                   /* Background color */
 9:    Ulong fg;                   /* Foreground color */
10:
11:    Ulong wht;                  /* White */
12:    Ulong blk;                  /* Black */
13:
14:    Ulong red;                  /* red */
15:    Ulong green;                /* green */
16:    Ulong blue;                 /* blue */
17:
18:    Window xwin;                /* Drawing window */
19:
20:    int
21:    main(int argc,char **argv) {
22:        Colormap cmap;          /* Color map */
23:        XColor approx;          /* Approximate color */
24:        XColor exact;           /* Precise color */
25:        XSizeHints hint;        /* Initial size hints */
26:
27:        /*
28:         * Open display (connection to X Server) :
29:         */
30:        if ( !(disp = XOpenDisplay(NULL)) ) {
31:            fprintf(stderr,"Cannot open display: check DISPLAY variable\n");
```

```
32:            exit(1);
33:        }
34:
35:        scr = DefaultScreen(disp);  /* Obtain default screen */
36:        cmap = DefaultColormap(disp,scr);
37:
38:        /*
39:         * Obtain color information :
40:         */
41:        XAllocNamedColor(disp,cmap,"red",&exact,&approx);
42:        red = approx.pixel;
43:
44:        XAllocNamedColor(disp,cmap,"green",&exact,&approx);
45:        green = approx.pixel;
46:
47:        XAllocNamedColor(disp,cmap,"blue",&exact,&approx);
48:        blue = approx.pixel;
49:
50:        /*
51:         * Get black and white pixel values :
52:         */
53:        wht = WhitePixel(disp,scr); /* White pixel */
54:        blk = BlackPixel(disp,scr); /* Black pixel */
55:
56:        /*
57:         * Choose colors for foreground and background :
58:         */
59:        fg = wht;                       /* use white foreground */
60:        bg = blk;                       /* use black background */
61:
62:        /*
63:         * Set Hint Information for Window placement :
64:         */
65:        hint.x = 100;                 /* Start x position */
66:        hint.y = 150;                 /* Start y position */
67:        hint.width = 550;             /* Suggested width */
68:        hint.height = 400;            /* Suggested height */
69:        hint.flags = PPosition | PSize; /* pgm specified position, size */
70:
71:        /*
72:         * Create a window to draw in :
73:         */
74:        xwin = XCreateSimpleWindow(
75:            disp,                     /* Display to use */
76:            DefaultRootWindow(disp),/* Parent window */
77:            hint.x, hint.y,           /* Start position */
78:            hint.width, hint.height,/* Window Size */
79:            7,                        /* Border width */
80:            fg,                       /* Foreground color */
81:            bg);                      /* Background color */
82:
83:        /*
84:         * Specify the window and icon names :
85:         */
```

continued from previous page

```
86:        XSetStandardProperties(
87:            disp,                    /* X Server connection */
88:            xwin,                    /* Window */
89:            "xegwin",                /* Window name */
90:            "xeg.c",                 /* icon name */
91:            None,                    /* pixmap for icon */
92:            argv,argc,               /* argument values */
93:            &hint);                  /* sizing hints */
94:
95:        /*
96:         * Map the window, and ensure it is the topmost
97:         * window :
98:         */
99:        XMapRaised(disp,xwin);
100:
101:       /*
102:        * Process the event loop :
103:        */
104:       event_loop();
105:
106:       /*
107:        * Cleanup :
108:        */
109:       XDestroyWindow(disp,xwin);        /* Release and destroy window */
110:       XCloseDisplay(disp);              /* Close connection to X Server */
111:
112:       return 0;
113: }
```

The `main()` program takes care of the initialization and cleanup for the X Window demonstration. Much of this initialization is common to most X Window programs. The overall steps used by the main program are as follows:

1. Open the display on the X Window server (lines 30–33). This call creates a socket and connects to the X Window server, which may be a local or remote hosted server.

2. Select the default screen (line 35). X Window servers are capable of supporting more than one display screen. Here the application simply chooses the default screen.

3. A color map is obtained (line 36). X Window graphics operations used in this program require the use of a color map. A color map is associated with a specific screen and server connection (`scr` and `disp`, respectively).

4. The color red is allocated in the color map `cmap` (line 41). The approximate value for red is used in line 42, since the actual color is not critical for this application.

5. The colors green and blue are allocated in lines 44–48. Again, approximate colors are acceptable to this application.

6. Pixel values for white and black are determined and assigned to the variables `wht` and `blk`, respectively (lines 53 and 54). These colors will be used to establish default foreground and background colors.

7. Pixel values for foreground and background are established in variables `fg` and `bg` (lines 59 and 60).

8. This program establishes "hint" information about where the window should be created (lines 65–69). Line 69 indicates that the program wants to select the position and size of the window.

9. A simple drawing window is created in lines 74–81. Argument `disp` specifies the connection to the server. Note that it is possible for a program to establish connections to multiple X Window servers.

10. A call to `XSetStandardProperties(3X11)` (lines 86–93) is made to specify the window's name, its icon name, a pixmap for the icon if any, resource setting arguments (from the command line), and sizing hints.

11. Function `XMapRaised(3X11)` is called in line 99 to cause the created window to be mapped (displayed). Until this point, the X Window server has just kept notes about the window specified by `xwin`.

Once those steps have been accomplished, it is possible to invoke the function `event_loop()` that is in source module `events.c`. When the function `event_loop()` returns, however, this indicates that it is time for this client program to terminate. Termination consists of destroying the window that was created (`xwin`) and closing the connection to the X Window server (`disp`). The `main()` program then terminates at the `return` statement in line 112.

A number of important X Window concepts have been glossed over here to get you to the most important aspect of this chapter, which is the event-processing loop. However, even with a rudimentary understanding, you could clone other X Window graphics program clients from this main program. As your understanding grows, you can expand upon the code presented here.

The feature piece of this chapter is the event-processing loop contained within the source module `events.c`. Before examining the code for it, compile and try the program to see what it is supposed to do. The following shows a compile session under FreeBSD:

```
$ make
cc -c  -Wall -I/usr/X11R6/include xeg.c
cc -c  -Wall -I/usr/X11R6/include events.c
cc -o xeg xeg.o events.o -L/usr/X11R6/lib -lX11
$
```

It is often necessary to indicate where the include files and the X Window libraries are. If you compile this program on a different UNIX platform, you may need to adjust the options `-I/usr/X11R6/include` and `-L/usr/X11R6/lib` to point to where your include and library files are.

Normally, you start the program and place it into the background when you are using an `xterm(1)` session. This allows you to continue using the `xterm(1)` window for other things while your client program runs:

```
$ ./xeg &
$
```

Soon after the program starts, you should see a window like that shown in Figure 27.5.

FIGURE 27.5

The startup X Window
created by client program
`./xeg`.

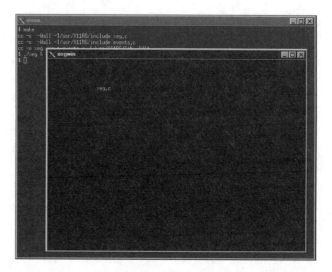

A black background window should be created with the white-lettered message `xeg.c`. Using the mouse now, it is possible to draw in different colors. To exit the window, press the lower-case *q* key to quit (the window must have the focus for the *q* key to work).

Using the left, middle, or right mouse button, you can draw in the window with the colors red, green, and blue, respectively. If you have a two-button mouse and middle button emulation enabled, press the right and left buttons simultaneously to get the color green. Figure 27.6 shows the author's attempt to write `xeg.c` on the window using the mouse.

FIGURE 27.6

The X Window with
`xeg.c` hand drawn with
the mouse.

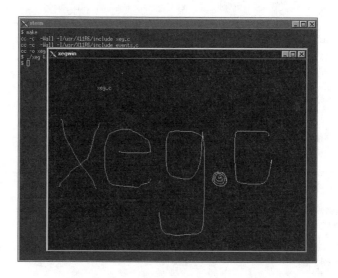

One other feature of this program is activated with the Shift+click of the mouse. When the Shift key is held down, a different drawing technique causes a starburst effect, as shown in Figure 27.7.

FIGURE 27.7

A starburst drawn in the X Window with Shift+click.

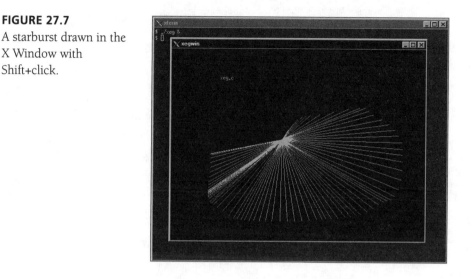

Figure 27.7 shows the mouse starting at the 2 o'clock position and circling around to 8 o'clock, while holding down the Shift key and mouse button at the same time. The way this is accomplished is explained when the code in Listing 27.3 is discussed.

LISTING 27.3   `events.c`—The Event-Processing Loop

```
 1:    /* events.c */
 2:
 3:    #include "xeg.h"
 4:
 5:    /*
 6:     * The X Window Event Loop :
 7:     */
 8:    void
 9:    event_loop(void) {
10:        int x0, y0;                 /* Prior position */
11:        GC gc;                      /* Graphics context */
12:        XEvent evt;                 /* X Event */
13:        char kbuf[8];               /* Key conv buffer */
14:        KeySym key;                 /* Key symbol */
15:        int kcount;                 /* Key count */
16:        int b = 0;                  /* Buttons Pressed */
17:        int star = False;           /* Draw stars when True */
18:        Bool quit = False;          /* Quit event loop when True */
19:
20:        /*
```

continued from previous page

```
21:        * Choose the XEvents that we want to process :
22:        */
23:       XSelectInput(disp,xwin,
24:           KeyPressMask | ExposureMask |
25:           ButtonPressMask | ButtonReleaseMask |
26:           Button1MotionMask | Button2MotionMask | Button3MotionMask);
27:
28:       /*
29:        * Create a Graphics Context :
30:        */
31:       gc = XCreateGC(disp,xwin,0,0);
32:       XSetBackground(disp,gc,bg); /* Set background color of gc */
33:       XSetForeground(disp,gc,fg); /* Set foreground color of gc */
34:
35:       /*
36:        * Process X Events :
37:        */
38:       while ( quit != True ) {
39:           /*
40:            * Fetch an X Event :
41:            */
42:           XNextEvent(disp,&evt);
43:
44:           /*
45:            * Process the X Event :
46:            */
47:           switch ( evt.type ) {
48:
49:           case Expose :
50:               /*
51:                * Window has been exposed :
52:                */
53:               if ( evt.xexpose.count == 0 )
54:                   XDrawImageString(evt.xexpose.display,
55:                       evt.xexpose.window,
56:                       gc,
57:                       105, 65,
58:                       "xeg.c", 5);
59:               break;
60:
61:           case ButtonPress :
62:               /*
63:                * A button has been pressed:
64:                *
65:                * Set the bit corresponding to the mouse button that
66:                * is pressed :
67:                */
68:               switch ( evt.xbutton.button ) {
69:               case Button1 :
70:                   b |= B1;
71:                   break;
72:               case Button2 :
73:                   b |= B2;
74:                   break;
```

```
75:                default :
76:                    b |= B3;
77:                }
78:
79:                if ( evt.xbutton.state & ShiftMask )
80:                    star = True;
81:                else
82:                    star = False;
83:
84:                /*
85:                 * Save the current position :
86:                 */
87:                x0 = evt.xbutton.x;
88:                y0 = evt.xbutton.y;
89:
90:                /*
91:                 * Establish the drawing color based upon the leftmost
92:                 * mouse button that is pressed :
93:                 */
94:                if ( b & B1 )
95:                    fg = red;
96:                else if ( b & B2 )
97:                    fg = green;
98:                else
99:                    fg = blue;
100:
101:                XSetForeground(disp,gc,fg); /* Set foreground color of gc */
102:                break;
103:
104:            case ButtonRelease :
105:                /*
106:                 * A button has been released :
107:                 *
108:                 * Unset the bit corresponding to the released color :
109:                 */
110:                switch ( evt.xbutton.button ) {
111:                case Button1 :
112:                    b &= ~B1;
113:                    break;
114:                case Button2 :
115:                    b &= ~B2;
116:                    break;
117:                default :
118:                    b &= ~B3;
119:                }
120:
121:                /*
122:                 * Set the color based upon the leftmost mouse button :
123:                 */
124:                if ( b & B1 )
125:                    fg = red;
126:                else if ( b & B2 )
127:                    fg = green;
128:                else
129:                    fg = blue;
```

continued from previous page

```
130:                    XSetForeground(disp,gc,fg); /* Set foreground color of gc */
131:                    break;
132:
133:                case MotionNotify :
134:                    /*
135:                     * Motion with a button down :
136:                     *
137:                     * Draw a line from the last know position, to the current :
138:                     */
139:                    XDrawLine(disp,xwin,gc,x0,y0,evt.xmotion.x,evt.xmotion.y);
140:
141:                    /*
142:                     * When drawing lines, we must save the last position that
143:                     * we have drawn a line segment to :
144:                     */
145:                    if ( star == False ) {
146:                        x0 = evt.xmotion.x;     /* Save x for next line segment */
147:                        y0 = evt.xmotion.y;     /* Save y for next line segment */
148:                    }
149:                    break;
150:
151:                case MappingNotify :
152:                    XRefreshKeyboardMapping(&evt.xmapping);
153:                    break;
154:
155:                case KeyPress :
156:                    /*
157:                     * A key was pressed; check for 'q' to quit :
158:                     */
159:                    kcount = XLookupString(&evt.xkey,kbuf,sizeof kbuf,&key,0);
160:                    if ( kcount == 1 && kbuf[0] == 'q' )
161:                        quit = True;
162:                }
163:        }
164:
165:    XFreeGC(disp,gc);                           /* Release graphics context */
166: }
```

Before X Window events are processed in the event loop, a call to **XSelectInput(3X11)** is performed to select the events that are of interest (lines 23–26). **disp** and **xwin** specify the connection and the window to modify. The events selected are the following:

KeyPressMask	Key press events
ExposureMask	Window expose events
ButtonPressMask	Mouse button press events
ButtonReleaseMask	Mouse button release events
Button1MotionMask	Pointer motion events when button 1 is down
Button2MotionMask	Pointer motion events when button 2 is down
Button3MotionMask	Pointer motion events when button 3 is down

Since drawing is required, a graphics context is needed to draw with. This specifies the attributes of the drawing pen, such as the foreground and background colors. Line 31 creates a graphics context with a call to XCreateGC(3X11). Line 32 selects the background color of the context by calling XSetBackground(3X11). A similar call to XSetForeground(3X11) is made in line 33 to set the foreground color of the graphics context. You will recall that the main() program established pixel values of white in variable fg and black in bg.

The event loop itself begins with the while statement in line 38 and ends at line 163. Bool variable quit is initialized as False in line 18. Consequently, the while loop continues until quit changes to True.

The function call that drives this event loop is the function XNextEvent(3X11) in line 42. The function synopsis for the function is as follows:

```
#include <X11/Xlib.h>

XNextEvent(display, event_return)
Display *display;
XEvent *event_return;
```

Notice that the X Window function is defined in the older C function syntax. This is due to the early start that X Window development had. For compatibility with older software, it has not made the change to the ANSI C function prototypes.

The argument display provides the information about the connection to the X Window server (specifically the socket). Argument event_return is used to return the event information that has been received.

If there are no events to process, XNextEvent(3X11) forces any buffered server requests to be written to the server. Execution is suspended within the function until an interesting event arrives (those events that are not masked out). Once an interesting event is received, the event information is copied to the area pointed to by the event_return argument, and the function returns to the caller.

The definition of the XEvent data type is a large union of event structures. The following synopsis is a subset of the full XEvent definition:

```
typedef union _XEvent {
    int             type;      /* Event type */
    XAnyEvent       xany;      /* Common event members */
    XKeyEvent       xkey;      /* Key events */
    XButtonEvent    xbutton;   /* Mouse button events */
    XMotionEvent    xmotion;   /* Mouse motion events */
    XExposeEvent    xexpose;   /* Window expose events */
    XMappingEvent   xmapping;  /* Key/Button mapping change events */
    /* etc. */
} XEvent;
```

The XEvent type definition is a union of the many member types within it. The most basic member of all is the member type, which identifies the type of the event that is being described.

The member `xany` defines a number of additional members that are common to almost any event:

```
typedef struct {
    int             type;       /* Event type */
    unsigned long   serial;     /* # of last request processed by server */
    Bool            send_event; /* true if from a SendEvent request */
    Display         *display;   /* Display the event was read from */
    Window          window;     /* window event was requested in event mask */
} XAnyEvent;
```

In the `XAnyEvent` structure definition, you see that the `type` of the event is included first in the structure. Each X Window request has a serial number assigned to it, and the event indicates the event number in the `serial` member. The member `send_event` is `True` when an event is artificially sent to a window with a function such as `XSendEvent(3X11)`. When this value is `False`, the event came from the X Window server. The `display` and `window` members identify the X Window server connection and the participating window.

The other `XEvent` union members will be discussed as the code is examined. When an event is received, the `switch` statement on line 47 dispatches the execution of the program to the correct `case` statement to process it.

The X Window server makes no guarantee that it will preserve a window when it is obscured. Consequently, when a window is uncovered or made viewable for the first time, one or more `Expose` event is generated. This permits the client program to restore the image in the newly exposed areas of the window.

`Expose` events often occur as regions of the full window. Clients that can take advantage of the efficiency achieved by restoring only small portions of an exposed window can do so with these events. For simpler client programs, the entire window must be refreshed instead.

The illustrated demo program simply draws a string of text `xeg.c` on the new window (lines 54–58). This is done in response to the `Expose` event, starting with the `case` statement on line 49. No attempt to restore the current drawing is performed. Consequently, you will find that when you obscure the `xeg` window and re-expose it, you will only find the text `xeg.c` redrawn. All other drawn information will be lost.

The synopsis of the `XExposeEvent` structure is as follows:

```
typedef struct {
    int             type;
    unsigned long   serial;
    Bool            send_event;
    Display         *display;
    Window          window;
    int             x;          /* Upper left x of region */
    int             y;          /* Upper left y of region */
    int             width       /* Width of region */
    int             height;     /* Height of region */
    int             count;      /* # of subsequent Expose events */
} XExposeEvent;
```

In addition to the members described by the union member XAnyEvent, the XExposeEvent type defines members x, y, width, and height. The x and y members describe the upper-left corner of the region of the window. The width and height members describe the width and height of the region that has been exposed and needs redrawing. The last member count describes how many subsequent Expose events follow.

If your client program is unable to redraw the exposed areas of the window region by region, then all Expose events where count is greater than zero should be ignored. Eventually, the count value will be decremented to zero in a subsequent event, indicating that no more Expose events remain for this window. Simple programs should therefore redraw the entire window only when this count reaches zero. Otherwise, needless repetition of the redraw operations will be performed. Since the demonstration program has been kept simple, it draws xeg.c only when this count reaches zero (line 53).

The case statement on line 61 handles the ButtonPress events. The type definition for XButtonEvent is as follows:

```
typedef struct {
    int             type;
    unsigned long   serial;
    Bool            send_event;
    Display         *display;
    Window          window;
    Window          root;       /* root window that the event occurred on */
    Window          subwindow;  /* child window */
    Time            time;       /* milliseconds */
    int             x, y;       /* pointer x, y coordinates in event window */
    int             x_root, y_root; /* coordinates relative to root */
    unsigned        int state;  /* key or button mask */
    unsigned        int button; /* detail */
    Bool            same_screen;/* same screen flag */
} XButtonEvent;
```

Member button is consulted in the switch statement on line 68. Depending upon whether Button1, Button2, or any other button has been pressed, bits are set in variable b (lines 70, 73, or 76). Depending on the bits set in b, a color is chosen in lines 94–99 for the foreground. The graphics context is modified to use this color in line 101 with XSetForeground(3X11).

However, member state of this event indicates other important things such as whether the Shift key was pressed at the time of the mouse button press. If the Shift key is pressed at the time of the button down event (line 79), the variable star is set to True. Otherwise, normal drawing is performed when star is set to False in line 82 (more about this later).

Lines 87 and 88 save the coordinates of the mouse when the button was pressed. These coordinates will be required later to draw a line when the mouse moves with the button held down.

When the mouse button is released, event ButtonRelease is processed by the case statement in line 104. The switch statement in lines 110–119 removes the bit that corresponds to the mouse button in variable b. Again, the color is modified by changing the fg variable in lines 124–129. The graphics context gc is then modified in line 130 to reflect this new choice in foreground color.

As the mouse moves with a button held down, `MotionNotify` events are delivered (line 133). The `XMotionEvent` type definition is given in the following synopsis:

```
typedef struct {
    int            type;
    unsigned long  serial;
    Bool           send_event;
    Display        *display;
    Window         window;
    Window         root;       /* root window that the event occurred on */
    Window         subwindow;  /* child window */
    Time           time;       /* milliseconds */
    int            x, y;       /* pointer x, y coordinates in event window */
    int            x_root, y_root; /* coordinates relative to root */
    unsigned       int state;  /* key or button mask */
    char           is_hint;    /* detail */
    Bool           same_screen;/* same screen flag */
} XMotionEvent;
```

The `xeg` program simply draws a line from the last saved `x0` and `y0` positions to the new location specified in the `XMotionEvent` structure members `x` and `y` (line 139). This is performed using the `XDrawLine(3X11)` function, using the color attributes assigned to the graphics context `gc`.

For normal drawing (no Shift key), the current mouse coordinates are then saved at lines 146 and 147. The next `MotionNotify` then causes the next line to be drawn from the previous mouse position to the current, effectively drawing a line as a pen would.

When the Shift key is pressed, the coordinates in lines 146 and 147 are not saved. This causes lines to always be drawn from the original button press coordinate to the present mouse coordinate. This gives the starburst effect as the mouse is moved around.

As a bit of housekeeping, `MappingNotify` events are processed by a call to `XRefreshKeyboardMapping(3X11)`. The X Window system allows keyboard keys and mouse buttons to be remapped differently according to the user's preference. To support this flexibility, a client program can pass the `XMappingEvent` structure directly to `XRefreshKeyboardMapping(3X11)`. It will then handle any necessary mapping changes for you.

The `case` statement in line 155 intercepts the `KeyPress` event. The `XKeyEvent` member `xkey` holds an untranslated key symbol reference. The call to `XLookupString(3X11)` causes this key to be translated into ASCII form in the supplied buffer `kbuf[]`. The length of the translated key is returned.

When the key translates to an ASCII `q` in line 160, the variable `quit` is set to `True` to allow the program to exit the event-processing loop. Upon exiting the loop, the graphics context that was created earlier is freed in line 165 by calling `XFreeGC(3X11)`.

That concludes the code walk-through for this demonstration program. This simple drawing program has demonstrated event-driven programming and has also provided you with a taste of how X Window programming is performed.

As an exercise, you are encouraged to improve upon this program. Complete the program by adding code to keep track of all drawing commands performed within the window. Then, when the `Expose` events occur, it should be possible to re-create the lost artwork. Another method is to learn about the `XCreatePixmap(3X11)` function. The drawn image can be maintained in a pixmap, and then the window regions can be refreshed from it when `Expose` events occur.

Summary

Software development today remains a costly process. While UNIX has been around for a time, it continues to be a popular place to invest those software development resources. It continues to be a mature platform that is also fun and well understood. Your investment continues to be well protected when it runs under UNIX.

INDEX

Symbols

! meta-character (shell patterns), 407-408
$ anchor, 431-432
& feature (/etc/passwd file Comment field), 234
^ anchor, 431-432
| (pipe symbol), 435
* meta-character, 406, 434
+ meta-character, 434
. meta-character, 433
( ) (parenthesis characters), 434
[ ] meta-characters (shell patterns), 406-407, 433
[] (square brackets), command-line, 173
0 (zero) gid number, 228
0 (zero) uid number, 228
64-bit C data types, 201-202
64-bit integers, 201
? meta-character, 406, 434

A

access
    files, testing, 119-120
    semaphores, 492-494
access protections (memory-mapped regions), changing, 548-549
access time (files), 118
access(2) function, 119-120
adding signals to signal sets, 312-313
address argument, shl_load(3X) function, 270
advisory locking, 88, 94
    lockf(2) function, 98
AIX 4.3 feature tests, 28-29
alarm(3) function, 320-322
alphasort(3)function, scanning directories, 139-141
ampersand feature (/etc/passwd file Comment field), 234
anchors, 431-432
ANSI C compile options, 18

APIs (application program interfaces)
    interval timer API, 361-362
    reliable signal API, 308, 311-317
        applying reliable signals, 316-317
        setting signal actions, 314-315
        sigaction(2) function, 314-317
        sigaddset(3) function, 312-313
        sigdelset(3) function, 313
        sigemptyset(3) function, 312
        sigfillset(3) function, 312
        sigismember(3) function, 313
        signal action flags, 315-316
        signal sets, 311-313
    signal(3) API, 308-311
applications. *See* programs
applying
    I/O, 72-73
    lseek(2) function, 74-75
    old errno variable, 55-56
    strerror(3) function, 61
apropos(1) command, 10
ar(1) command, 253-254
archives (static libraries), 253-254
arguments
    base (radix conversions), 196-197
    buf (current directory null buffers), 130
    bufsiz (readlink(2) function), 121
    command-line, 174
    compar, 140
    dbm_fetch(3) function, 277-278
    dbm_open(3) function, 275
    dbm_store(3) function, 276
    depth (ftw(3C)/nftw(3C) functions), 144
    dir (tempnam(3) function), 159
    dirname (scandir(3) function), 140
    execve(2) function, 397-398
    flags (nftw(3C) function), 144
    fn function, 145
    fnmatch(3) function, 408-409
    glob(3) function, 416
    group (chown(2) function), 123
    identifying, 174

E

N

O

T

U

V